Signposts and Settlers

The history of place names west of the Rockies

Robert I. Alotta

Bonus Books, Inc., Chicago

98 97 96 95 94   5 4 3 2 1

Library of Congress Catalog Card Number 93-72146

International Standard Book Number: 1-56625-028-5

Bonus Books, Inc.
160 East Illinois Street
Chicago, Illinois 60611

Printed in the United States of America

To the little "lightbulbs" of Arthur Rimbaud.

Contents

v

Other books by the author:

Signposts & Settlers: The History of the Place Names in the Middle Atlantic States

Another Part of the Field: America's Revolution 1777–78

Mermaids, Monasteries, Cherokees and Custer: The Stories Behind Philadelphia Street Names

Civil War Justice: Union Army Executions Under Lincoln

#2: A Look at the Vice Presidency

Old Names and New Places

Stop the Evil: A Civil War History of Desertion and Murder

Street Names of Philadelphia

Senior Editor, Street Names of America Project:

Stories Behind New Orleans Street Names

Stories Behind the Street Names of Nashville and Memphis

George Washington Never Slept Here: Stories Behind the Street Names of Washington, D.C.

Preface

When I was born, my father decided to honor his father and name me Ignatius. It was a fine name, given to my grandfather so many years ago by his father to honor some other relative. And back through generations of Alottas the name went—all the way back to St. Ignatius of Loyola, founder of the religious order of the Society of Jesus, better known as the Jesuits.

My father did not ask my mother if she liked the name. In fact, he never even broached the subject. It is amazing how times have changed. Let a husband try that today! My mother held no animosity toward her father-in-law, but she almost passed out when she learned that "Baby Boy Alotta" had become "Ignatius Alotta"!

"I couldn't see my son going through life as 'Iggie'," she said at a much later date. "So, I scratched in 'Robert' before Ignatius. I'd fight with my husband later."

Being a con artist, as are most mothers, she was able to convince my father that "Robert" was really in his honor. I could never figure this out, because my dad's name was Peter! Later I learned that my father's nickname was Bob. Of course, that makes plenty of sense.

When I was old enough to be confirmed, I took my father's name and became Robert Ignatius Peter Alotta. I carried all four names proudly until one eventful day when I received cards to accompany my high school graduation announcement. The cards read: "Robert I. P. Alotta." After a single meaningful laugh, I dropped the Peter—not out of disrespect for my father, but for self-preservation. No one really cares about the state of my bladder.

Now, what does all this have to do with the cities, towns and villages of the West Coast?

Plenty.

Just as my father wanted to honor his father by naming his son Ignatius, town planners want to put the best possible spin on a name. A good, solid name helps sell real estate. It helps draw people to settle in a new community. Would someone be truly proud to tell the world they are from "The Pits"? I seriously doubt it. But there were people who were proud enough of their heritage to name their community for a favorite saint, a pet animal, a geographic feature. In each case, there is a reason behind the naming. Sometimes the source is so hidden that no one is certain how it came about.

When you read through this book, I am sure you will not agree with every statement I make about the source of a name. You may decide that you know the "true" story, and that your ever-so-great grand relative knew the story and passed it down from generation to generation. That relative, however, never wrote the story down and it reposes only in one family. As I have researched and written place-name books over the years, people have written and suggested other ideas. I encourage this, but caution you. Do not write and say you know the truth because you heard it one time. Try to give me a source, a newspaper article, a book, a magazine, anything concrete. By the way, I answer each and every letter with a personal note. That is the least I can do for the money you spent on the book.

Another note . . . People who read this book after reading the one on the Middle Atlantic States will notice one major difference: There is no index. This allows the maximum number of place-names to be put in the book. Another thing that is missing—and is from all my street- and place-name books—is the footnotes, endnotes or whatever you call them. I believe that these interfere with the flow of the reading and are only read by those who are conducting their own research. Those people are quite comfortable with interlibrary loan and can access the notes to this book at the Mullen Library at The Catholic University of America, Washington, DC 20064—or through their own library.

No research for a book is ever so easy that an author can do it alone. This book is not an exception to the rule. A large number of people have been quite helpful in my pursuit of answers. Some have been of more help than others, but all have been helpful. So as not to offend anyone, I have listed my "helpers" in alphabetic order. Thanks must be accorded:

George Applegate, director of sales & marketing, Big Island Chapter of the Hawaii Visitors Bureau—he located a copy of *Place Names of Hawaii* by Mary Kawena Pukui, and got it to me fast. He even trusted me to pay him back. He did get his money. I know; I have the cancelled check!

Manu Boyd, communications for the Hawaii Visitors Bureau in Honolulu. She helped shepherd me through the islands.

Adele Chwalek, the director of Catholic University's libraries. Without Adele's help and expertise in the librarying game, a great deal of data would never have reached my hand. At the same time,

God bless the WRL Consortium! Without access to the libraries at George Mason, George Washington, Howard, American, UDC, Gaulladet, and elsewhere, I doubt I would have been able to finish on time. For people who are unaware of how far libraries have come, they should talk to their neighborhood librarian. Adele introduced me to ALADIN, and I'm hooked!

Laura Downey, Geographic Names Information System, who tried to find things for me that did not exist . . . but should.

Brother Patrick Ellis, president of The Catholic University of America. Pat has been a friend since 1951, when we first met at West Catholic High School. Throughout my career—business, academic and writing—he has always been one of the loudest cheerleaders. I am forever in his debt; my donations to Catholic's libraries notwithstanding.

Anne Gearan, of Associated Press, and Laura Goldstein, of *The Washington Post*, who wrote quite favorable accounts of the first book in the series: *Signposts & Settlers: The History of Place Names in the Middle Atlantic States*. Their articles, particularly Anne's, which ran all over the East Coast, proved there is a strong desire on the part of the public to know about how their towns' names came into being.

Sue Holmes, auto travel supervisor, AAA of Virginia, Staunton, Virginia, for the maps and tour books which were invaluable at the earliest stages of research. I wonder how many people realize how current and correct Triple A's maps and tourbooks are and that they can be used as a research tool.

Tom Risko, marketing coordinator, Maui Visitors Bureau of the Hawaii Visitors Bureau, Kahului, Maui, for digging up some super photographs—and letting me keep them for a longer period than allowed.

I also have to thank Paul Silverman, father of one of my very best students, Michele Kamber, and a friend. He got tied up meeting me for lunch at Szechuan Gallery Restaurant in Chinatown. While I waited, I was able to outline my introduction. Later, we enjoyed a fantastic lunch. I have to thank him for introducing me to the restaurant besides.

Last, but far from least, is my wife Alice. What I said about her in the first volume goes double or triple here.

Introduction

Beats there a heart of a middle-aged male who has not fantasized about heading West and finding that gold mine that would put him on Easy Street for life?

Is there a middle-aged woman who has not, in the still of the night, dreamed about heading West and being whisked off her feet by a dashing cavalry officer?

Go on. Tell the truth. We've all dreamed, at one time or another, about the Golden West. The movies of my youth, "San Francisco" with Clark Gable, "Nob Hill," and the rest, presented a rough-and-ready view of the West Coast that was mesmerizing.

Where the movies left off, television took over. Series like "Here Come the Brides" showed us an old view of Seattle and the days when men were men and women were pursued. "Malibu" and "Santa Barbara" presented us with the beautiful people of California and their glistening suntanned skins. "Hawaii Five-O" and "Magnum P.I." gave us a panorama of Hawaii. The scenes they presented, however, were the subjective view of the director through the lens of the camera operator. But were they the real Washington State, the real Hawaii, the real California? I doubt it. Even the popular "Northern Exposure" television series that depicts everyday life in a small town in Alaska was actually filmed somewhere else.

I can recall my first visit to the West Coast. While there, I discovered one of the bordellos I had read about in some forgotten history book. I even purchased a keychain with a token that was "Good for All Night" at Madame Olga's Parlor in San Francisco.

It was exciting and, at the same time, depressing to visit California, Oregon, Washington, and the rest. The Gold Rush is over; the dance halls are gone. The cavalry outposts are skeletons or museums. Everything is different. Well, almost everything has changed; many of the names remain.

It was not until I had completed this book and looked over the names and the paragraphs I had written about them that I was able to see accurately what these places were before we became so into ourselves and so unaware of our culture, our heritage.

A former student of mine once complained about being forced to look through her family albums with her grandmother. She griped at how boring it was to look at the fading photographs of men and women she never knew. "It's child abuse!" she cried. She did not realize that those people were just like her. They were her flesh and blood. If she threw the photos away when she got them after her grandmother's death, she would be throwing away her heritage. Her family's legacy, its traditions, would be lost forever.

Another student, when we discussed the Holocaust, expressed that the study of the past was necessary so that we could see how bad people were. I had to correct him. History must be studied so we can see how great people were—or could be. We must look at the past to see how people did things. We do not have to reinvent the wheel. We must learn from their successes, their failures. We must be able to see what motivated them. The study of place names is a good place to begin.

Through my research I found, and you will soon learn, that the influence of industry and business was perhaps the single strongest factor in the determination of naming on the West Coast. The incursion of the Spanish into California was ostensibly for the spread of Christianity, or at least that is what Father Junipero Serra would have believed. In reality, the Spaniards with their string of missions were developing a Spanish presence in America, a presence that would loot the land of its riches for the royals in Spain. We cannot forget the influence of the Russians in Alaska, nor that of the Hudson Bay Company, John Jacob Astor and the others.

The railroad companies and the railroad tycoons that ran them forged through the canyons and mountains to establish a line of communication with the East. They left their mark on the towns with the names of stations and depots. The lumber barons and the mining operators left their legacy not only with the depletion of natural resources but also with the addition of their names on many town signposts. Even the retail merchants who provided the sustenance for the workers exacted their measure of immortality.

Another prime influence, and one that is often ignored, was that of the U. S. Post Office. Postal authorities, in an attempt to streamline the naming of America, did much to destroy the fabric of the country.

In 1891, the postmaster general alerted all postal clerks that they were to "use the spelling of post office names published in the bulletins of the United States Board on Geographic Names." Three years later, an order was issued from the postmaster general's office: "To remove a cause of annoyance to the Department and injury to the Postal Service in the selection of names for newly established post offices, it is hereby ordered that from this date only short names or names of one word will be accepted. (Names of post offices will only by changed for reasons satisfactory to the Department.)" This resulted in names that meant nothing, that had no relationship to the people or the place. They were just short names. Under that same directive, postal officials tried to remove the prefixes and suffixes that set off one place from another, such as "East," "New," "Corners," "Cross Roads," and the like. It was thought that these prefixes and add-ons were objectionable and would cause confusion and delay in the delivery of the mail.

That same year, 1894, the postmaster general ordered a standardization of postal records "in the orthography of the names of post offices to that used in the lists of post offices contained in the Official Postal Guide." In other words, the spelling of town names was to be established by postal authorities. In numerous cases, we find that the name submitted by the people of a town or village was misspelled by clerks in the post office and that erroneous name was carved in stone.

In 1906, the Board on Geographic Names was given the authority to "determine and change place-names," and they did. Twenty-seven years later, that board came up with a list of twelve principles that established postal policy regarding names.

The board's recommendations included the removal of apostrophes, the elimination of the "h" from "-burgh," and others. The rules were ironclad, except where the post office and the board decided they were not. While the board recommended that one should "rarely apply names of living persons; only those of great eminence should be so honored," on numerous occasions the board's own surveyors considered themselves to be of "great eminence" and, while still living, named places for themselves, their friends.

Certain localities did not take the rules sitting down. Concerned citizens joined the fracas. They fought against the government and were sometimes able to keep their names intact. Pittsburgh, Pennsylvania, is a good example of such a battle. When told to get the "h" out, Pittsburghers dug in their heels and retained the English flavor of their name, not the harsh German suffix.

In their attempts to expedite mail delivery, postal authorities destroyed much of our heritage. They did not speed up the delivery of mail either.

The Board on Geographic Names also concluded in 1933 that there were only three types of place names: "names transplanted from abroad and usually assigned through sentiment without reference to topographic similarity or to geographic relationship, names of Indian origin, and casual, whimsical, and freakish names." Again, government minions made decisions that were not based in reality.

Introduction

A look at the place names of America shows us there are other types of names, names that have been spawned by egotism, nepotism and patronage. There are names that are descriptive of the land, the waterways. There are directional place names. Again, government goofed.

The names of the places studied in this volume are different from those in the Middle Atlantic States, and from those found elsewhere in the United States. Hawaii is a good example.

Hawaii is virtually unspoiled by mainland names and, for the most part, retains the purity, the simplicity of its origins.

Alaska, the other newcomer, is a mishmash of native names, Russian interpretations of Indian names, and English interpretations of Russian interpretations of Indian names. Add to that the Chinook slang and you have an Alaskan smorgasbord.

Part of Alaska spills into Washington State, through its Canadian connection. But Vancouver's sibilance overpowers that association. Oregon is fed by the influences that affected Washington State, but remains itself. California, on the other hand, is in a class by itself with its Spanish and Mexican influences. Nevada, fitting in where it does on the map, is affected by the naming from California and elsewhere. The strong Mormon influence that once pioneered settlement in Nevada—and helped found Las Vegas—has little effect on the names we found.

Each place we studied is unique in itself. Each has something special about it. Perhaps that special quality is the affection early pioneers and settlers had for the land. They wanted to put the best face on their homes, just as my mother wanted to put the least offensive name on her only child.

It is sometimes amazing how little we know about our nation's history. Many think of the Evergreen State as beginning when Captain George Vancouver of the Royal Navy met up with Captain Robert Gray of the U. S. Navy at the entrance to the Strait of Juan de Fuca, in 1792. By the time these two seasoned sailors met, Spanish explorers had been here and had left their names on the land and on the arms of the sea. Bruno Hezeta had been here at least seventeen years earlier. The Spanish presence was one of the reasons Vancouver was in the area.

Vancouver was in the area to settle a few differences with the Spanish before the problems became insoluble. Gray was not here for blatant military purposes; he was merely obeying orders from Washington to locate the Northwest Passage. Few people outside of the Pacific Northwest remember Gray. They do remember Lewis and Clark.

This highly-publicized expedition had been sent from the federal capital by President Thomas Jefferson to locate the elusive, legendary Northwest Passage. They explored Washington State in 1805–06, when it was still part of the Oregon Territory.

When it did not seem that anyone was going to discover the Northwest Passage, the different nations decided to take advantage of the natural resources of the area, particularly the animals who were trapped, killed and divorced from their pelts. The first fur trading post established here was Spokane House, built in 1810 by the North West Company. That was the first structure to be built by non-Indians in what is now the State of Washington. With the outbreak of the War of 1812, American interests quickly left the territory. When that happened, the North West Company and its major rival and ultimate successor, the Hudson Bay Company, controlled the area.

With the establishment of fur trading posts came the missionaries to serve the trappers who were French-Canadian—and Catholic. As the industry grew into the heart of Indian territory, so too did the missionary effort.

In 1846, the boundaries between the United States and Canada were settled with Great Britain, and the territory began its major growth. Seven years later, settlers north of the Columbia River, in what was then the Territory of Oregon, petitioned Congress for a divorce. In that year, the Territory of Washington was established. In 1863, the eastern portion of this new territory became the panhandle of the new Territory of Idaho.

Despite the violent expression of Indian dissatisfaction with the incursion of white settlers, immigration was not deterred. The new arrivals did things "the American way" and exploited nature, reaping the rewards of the territory's trees and minerals. Though settlers continued to arrive at a steady rate, it was not until the arrival of the Northern Pacific Railroad in 1883 that development skyrocketed.

Because of the growth, members of Congress finally heeded the petitioning of the residents here and granted them statehood in 1889. Part of the willingness on the part of the federal bureaucracy to welcome Washington into the Union was the Klondike and Alaskan gold rushes.

Prosperity continued until the Great Depression. But the people of Washington were not daunted. With the harnessing of the powers of the Columbia River and the channeling of these powers into the Bonneville and Grand Coulee dams projects, a new life began. Federal irrigation projects opened up farming opportunities, and the electric power that flowed allowed new industry to prosper and grow.

The place names of the Evergreen State reflect the raw wilderness that was bested by Indian and white settler alike. They resound with the names of the settlers, the Indians, the companies, the corporate leaders, the self-important bureaucrats. The valleys, the forests, the mountains, the streams are all remembered. Through these names we are able to glimpse a picture of the Washington that was.

ABERDEEN

Aberdeen and Hoquiam are twin cities in the Grays Harbor area. They are the oldest logging, sawmilling and paper manufacturing towns in the Northwest. Because the harbor could accommodate ocean-going vessels, the twin cities became important shipping centers for the area.

There are several suggestions as to the source of Aberdeen's name. The first is that the name honored Lord Aberdeen—the British foreign secretary who proposed the solution to the Oregon problem in 1846. Aberdeen suggested the 49th parallel as the boundary to the sea, giving England all of Vancouver Island.

Another idea is that the name came from the Aberdeen Packing Company of Ilwaco. The company established a plant here "in the early days." A final suggestion is that the name came from Mrs. James Stewart who arrived here in 1874 and said: "Being the firm name [the Aberdeen Packing Company was located on the waterfront] of the cannery here and to our ears quite pleasing."

The former Joan B. Kellan, Mrs. Stewart was a native of Aberdeen, Scotland.

The harbor was named for Captain Robert Gray who explored the northwest coast and established the United States' claim to the Oregon country in 1792.

Samuel Benn, who came from New York—not Scotland—, platted the townsite on his homestead in 1884. In 1941, the Weyerhauser Corporation opened the first tree farm in the United States, right outside Aberdeen. It served as a model for tens of thousands of others across the nation.

ACME

Acme, of course, is derived from the Greek and means the highest point. In this town's case, the name came about through a joke.

In the late 1880s, Thomas Stephens and Samuel Parks sent East for a supply of Acme hymnals. People laughed about it, but when Parks went to Bellingham to plead for a new post office, he asked if Acme would do, and it did!

Another authority suggests the town was named by George Parls in 1887, after the newly-received Acme hymn book.

ADDY

Formerly a Swiss dairy community, Addy was named in the early 1890s for Addie Drudey, the wife of E. S. Drudie, storekeeper and postmaster.

ADNA

The original name for this Lewis County town was Willoway. An early settler named it that because of his wife's favorite saying: "Where there's a will, there's a way."

In 1892, the railroad changed the name to Pamona, to avoid confusion with Willapa. When the government discovered a Pamona post office east of the Cascades, the railroad superintendent changed the name to Adna, for Adna Marian, a member of his family.

AENEAS

Aeneas, located in Okanogan County, was named, we are told, for an Indian guide who died about 1913. He was supposed to have been more than a hundred years old.

AGATE BEACH

Agate Passage, which connects Port Orchard and Port Madison, was named for artist Alfred T. Agate, a member of the Wilkes Expedition.

AGNEW

Agnew Islet, the entrance to Thompson Bay, was named for R. I. Agnew, a captain in the Royal Canadian Navy. He was at Dockyard in 1931. Another source suggests the Clallam County town was named for Charles Agnew, an 1899 pioneer. The town is a consolidation of Reeveton and Lindsay.

AHTANUM

Ahtanum, Yakima County, takes its name from the Ahtanum Creek. The name comes from *ahatahnum*, "stream by long mountain." Catholic priests once operated the Ahtanum Mission where the village of Ahtanum now exists.

AIRWAY HEIGHTS

Airway Heights was named because of its location near two airfields on the west side of Spokane.

AJLUNE

Ajlune, Lewis County, was named by the first postmaster, Ghosn Ghasn, for his birthplace in Lebanon.

ALBION

Albion is the poetic term used to describe England. The word is descriptive of the white cliffs that are located along the southeastern shore of the British Isle.

The former name for this Whitman County community, Guy, was changed in 1901 at the insistence of an English miller who wanted to commemorate the contribution of the British to the exploration of the Northwest. The British, by the way, referred to the region as Nova Albion.

ALDER (—dale, —ton, —wood Manor)

The community of Alder was named in 1902 by Martin Hotes after a grove of alder trees where the town was situated. The other communities derive their names from the appearance of these trees. Alderdale, however, was named because of its location near the mouth of Alder Creek.

Alderton, on the other hand, was named by Orson Annis for the alder wood that was stacked along the Northern Pacific Railroad tracks to be used as fuel.

ALFALFA

Alfalfa was one of the most promising forage crops in Washington State. This town was so named because of the large quantities of alfalfa hay shipped from here.

ALGONA

When the townspeople of Valley City went to get a post office by that name, they were turned down.

At a mass meeting held in 1910, they selected Algoma as the name. That name means "valley of flowers." When the people in Washington got hold of it, the "m" became an "n" and the name became virtually untranslateable.

ALLEN

Allen, Skagit County, takes its name from one of Vancouver's friends, Sir Alan Gardner. As time went on, the name was misspelled into its current form.

Vancouver was a little quirky with this name. He named one waterway Port Gardner, after Sir Alan; the other, Port Susan, after Lady Susana Gardner. The point got the friend's first name, so that the Gardners were remembered individually and as a family.

Another source disagrees with this, and contends that the name came from the Allen, Roray & Sanburn shingle mill that operated here.

ALLYN

Allyn, Mason County, was named in about 1889 for Judge Frank Allyn from Tacoma who took interest in the land development here.

ALMIRA

Almira, Lincoln County, was founded in 1889 or 1890 and given the name of the town promoter's wife, Mrs. Charles C. (Almira) Davis.

ALMOTA

Almota's name comes from the Nez Perce Tribe's language, and means "torch-light fisher." At one time it was a principal port of entry. The name is an apparent corruption of the Indian term *alla motin.*

ALOHA

"Aloha" is the traditional Hawaiian greeting.

ALPHA

Alpha takes its name from the British trading school, Alpha, which was built at Nanaimo in 1859. The ship also gave its name to Alpha Bay on the Canadian coast.

ALSTOWN

Al Rogers was a local civic leader and a one-time regent of the University of Washington. He was a civil engineer from Waterville.

ALTO

Alto's name is descriptive. A railroad engineer gave it that name because the town was located at the summit of the divide between Whetstone Hollow and Tucanon.

ALTOONA

Altoona bears the name of the town in Pennsylvania founded by the Pennsylvania Railroad.

Another source disagrees and says the name came from Altona, Germany, the major fish processing city on the Elbe River. (See ALTOONA, Pennsylvania.)

AMANDA PARK

Amanda Park was named for the wife of Joseph J. Southard, who ran a store-motel/private-park operation here in 1926.

AMBER

Originally called Calvert for an early settler, this town was forced to change its name to Amber to conform to the post office designation of Amber which was already in existence.

AMBOY

Amos M. Ball, a mill operator, selected this Clark County town name in 1886 from a list provided by the postal officials.

AMERICAN RIVER

American River was so named at a time when British influence was strong in the area. Not everyone was enthusiastic.

ANACORTES

Amos Bowman, a civil engineer, planned this town and named it in 1876 for his wife, Anna Curtis. He modified her name to conform to the Spanish-sounding names in the area—the town is on Fidalgo Island.

Before Bowman's arrival in about 1860, the village was known as Ship Harbor.

ANATONE

One source suggests the name came from the personal name of a local Indian woman. Another indicates the name came from the Indian name for Ten Mile Creek, but also accepts the Indian woman legend.

APPLE (—dale, —ton)

In the earlier days of Washington's settlement, settlers—particularly members of the Wilkes Expedition—mistook the flowering dogwood for apple blossoms.

One source contends, however, that when the Great Northern Railway built a branch line from the Columbia River to Mansfield, they named the Douglas County place Appledale "on account of the many apple orchards there." Appleton, in Klickitat County, was also named because it was a railroad apple-shipping center.

ARDEN

See ARDEN, California.

ARDENVOIR
The "son" in the C. A. Harris & Son, Inc., sawmill operation located here was Ardenvoir Harris.

ARIEL
This locale is most commonly thought of in reference to the Ariel Dam, one of a string of power-generating plants on the Lewis River.

The first postmaster in this Cowlitz County town named it for his son, Ariel Chitty. The name means "lion of God" and comes from the Old Testament.

ARLETTA
Arletta was named in about 1893. The name was created by Mrs. G. W. Powell, who combined the name of her eldest daughter, Arla, with Valetta, a beautiful city on the Island of Malta.

Another source believes that Mr. Powell, the first postmaster, combined the names of two of his daughters: Arla and Letty Powell.

ARLINGTON
Arlington could possibly be named in honor of Robert E. Lee's home in Virginia. Lee's home later became a national cemetery.

At one time, this Snohomish County town was called The Forks, Alkali, and, in 1888, Haller City, for the father of town founder Morris G. Haller. When the railroad purchased the townsite, they changed the name to memorialize Lord Henry Arlington, one of the "Cabal" members of the cabinet of England's Charles II.

ARTIC
In the 1880s, when the name of Arta Saunders, a local woman, was sent to Washington as the name for this town, postal authorities goofed. Instead of naming the town Arta, as the citizens wanted, they established it as Artic.

ASHFORD
Ashford was named for Walter A. Ashford, who settled here in 1888.

ASOTIN
Asotin is not an Indian word as some contend. The current spelling of the town's name was decided by an act of the legislature in 1886.

The original name for this town, located on the Washington-Idaho border, was Has-hu-tin, or "eel creek." Numerous eels, we have heard, were caught at the point where the Asotin Creek meets the Snake River.

ATTALIA

The local legend has it that Attalia was named in 1906 for a town in Italy. Others think the name is a local pronounciation of Italia.

One authority indicates that Mrs. V. K. Loose of Seattle fell in love with the name of a small town in Italy when she visited there. She liked this name so much that her husband picked it when he began his irrigation and townsite projects in 1906.

AUBURN

When Dr. Levi W. Ballard laid out part of his claim as a townsite in 1886, he named the new town Slaughter for Lieutenant W. A. Slaughter, who died during the Indian Wars of 1855 and 1856.

Some were not enamored with that name and, after the railroad was completed, they demanded a change in name. One contended it did nothing for the town's image for the boy from the hotel to yell at arriving railroad passengers, "Right this way to the Slaughter House." In 1893, the name was changed to Auburn, after the town in New York. Auburn, New York, was named in 1805 for a line in an Oliver Goldsmith poem: "Sweet Auburn! loveliest village of the plain."

AVON

The first settler here was W. H. Miller in 1882. He called his town Avon, ostensibly to honor the Bard of the Avon.

When founded, Avon was declared a "no saloons" town.

AZWELL

Camels were brought into this area in the early 20th century to be used as pack animals. Unfortunately, these animals were more accustomed to desert sand than to the rocky or marshy ground hereabouts. Their use was quickly abandoned.

The original name for this Chelan County community was Wells. It was renamed in 1906 to honor A. Z. Wells, a prominent merchant.

BABCOCK

Dr. Ira L. Babcock was the judge of probate court when it was organized in 1841. He was also a lay member of the Lee Mission.

BACON

Railroad officials named this town as a joke. Somehow the joke is on them: The name has survived; they have not.

BAIRD

Baird takes the name of James Baird, upon whose homestead the post office was located. By the way, he was also the first postmaster.

BALCH

Balch takes its name from Balch Passage, which was named before 1846 for Lafayette Balch, a ship and business owner.

BARING

Baring, King County, was established as a lumber center on the Great Northern Railroad. Platted in 1901, the town was named for nearby Mount Baring.

BATTLE GROUND

The basis of the name of Battle Ground, Clark County, is a jibe against a military commander who promoted—before the fact—what he was going to do when he met up with a band of renegade Indians. His bark was worse than his bite.

During the fall of 1855, federal troops of the 21st Infantry began to relocate members of the Klickitat tribe from their homes along the Lewis River. The Indians were camped at Fort Vancouver when a rumor began that the troops were gathering the Indians for a mass slaughter. So, the more stalwart tribe members struck their tents and left the camp. Captain William Strong, the post commander, gathered a band of roughly 30 troopers and, with great fanfare, took off after the Indians.

When Strong and his men were about 16 miles north of the fort, they happened upon the Indians who had established fortified positions and were ready for a fight. Rather than engage in a battle he could not win, Strong called for a parlay with Chief Umtux, the Indians' leader. The two agreed that tribe members would return to the fort . . . peaceably. To make the trip back a little safer, Strong and

Umtux agreed to clear their weapons. The troops fired off about 50 shots; the Indians, about 70. But one of the Indian bullets killed the chief; allegedly, it belonged to a disgruntled young buck who thought Umtux sold them out.

The sound of gunfire sent terror to the hearts of the settlers back at the fort and, since the troops did not return back quickly—Strong was conducting an investigation—they thought the worst.

Strong and his men returned with the Indians, after determining that the chief was killed by "person or persons unknown" and permitting the tribesmen to bury the chief with proper ceremony. Strong's tact and good judgement was not looked upon with great respect by the townspeople. They considered his behavior reprehensible and gave him a lacy petticoat to use as his personal standard.

Augustus H. Richter opened his store here in 1886, and called it Battle Ground Store. Though no battle was ever fought here, the townspeople adopted that name for their own when the town was established in 1902.

BAY (— Center, — City, — View)

Bay City was so called because of its South Bay location.

Bay View was platted and named in 1884 by William J. McKenna. McKenna was working for D. A. Jennings, a wholesale grocer from Seattle who wanted to establish a branch store here.

Bay Center received its name simply because it was the midway point on the eastern shore of Willapa Bay.

BEAUX ARTS

When the Beaux Arts Society attempted to create a village patterned after the garden villages of England in 1908, it intended this King County community to become the arts and crafts center of the Pacific Northwest. It became, instead, a residential area on the lake.

BEAVER

Beaver was the name of the Hudson Bay Company's paddle steamer. She was the first steam vessel on this coast. Others wonder if the name came from the profusion of beavers in the area.

This particular Clallam County town was named for the nearby Beaver Creek and lake. These bodies of water, we are told, were overrun with beavers.

BELFAIR

This town was named Clifton until postal authorities in Washington requested a name change. In 1925, Mrs. Murray, the postmistress, submitted this name. It had been mentioned in *St. Almo*, a book that she was reading at the time.

BELLEVUE

Bellevue is what one author called a "station-wagon land." For years it was a bedroom community for Seattle, but in recent years it has attempted to develop its own image.

Bellevue is one of the former names of San Juan Island, and probably draws its roots from there. The name, of course, translates to "beautiful view" in French. According to one authority, the name was given by a committee in the early 1880s because of the community's "excellent view" of the Olympics Mountains.

BELLINGHAM

Bellingham overlooks Bellingham Bay, which was discovered by George Vancouver in 1792.

Vancouver named the bay for Sir William Bellingham, who helped in the preparations for the voyage. During the late 19th century, immigrants from Norway and Sweden found this area amenable.

The bay and the channel were first observed by Eliza who entered in 1791, and named it Seno de Gaston, "Gulf of Gaston." The same year Vancouver's new name appeared, the Spaniards renamed it Bahia de Gaston, "Gaston's Bay," though they did not immediately publish the name.

Over the years there have been several adjacent communities that have become Bellingham. These include Whatcom, an Indian name, Sehome, New Whatcom, Pattle's Point, Unionville, and Fairhaven.

BENGE

When the railroad cut through his property in 1907, Frank Benge donated the townsite which bears his name.

BENTON CITY

Benton City takes its name from its county—named for Thomas Hart Benton, the legendary senator from Missouri who was such a strong supporter of the West. This town was named in 1909 by representatives of the North Coast Railroad.

Another authority maintains that the name honors Benton C. Grosscup, who was active in the separation of Benton County from Yakima.

The town was platted by the postmaster from Kiona, who wanted to name it for himself: J. G. Giezentanner!

BEVERLY

H. R. Williams, a vice president of the Chicago, Milwaukee & St. Paul Railway Company, selected the name for this Grant County site which he drew from Beverly, Massachusetts.

Williams was responsible for the assignment of many Eastern names along his railroad's line.

BICKLETON

Bickleton, Klickitat County, was platted in the late 19th century. It was named for Charles N. Bickle, the first store keeper and postmaster. He settled here in 1879.

BIG LAKE

In 1859, the "big lake" in Skagit County was known as Delacy's Lake.

BINGEN

Bingen, Klickitat County, is sister-city to Bingen, Germany. It was so named by landowner P. J. Suksdoft because its location on the Columbia River reminded him of the German towns on the Rhine.

Bingen, Washington, was laid out as a town by Suksdoft in 1892.

BIRCH BAY

Birch Bay, Whatcom County, was named by Vancouver in 1792, ostensibly for the proliferation of black birch trees in the area. In his journal, the navigator wrote of the town, "... black birch ... grew in such abundance that it obtained the name of Birch Bay." The town assumed that name.

Earlier names for the bay include the Spanish Ensenda de Garzon and the Indian Tsan-wuch.

BIRDSVIEW

The name for Birdsview, in Skagit County, has nothing to do with avian observation. The first postmaster of this town in 1880 was Birdsey D. Minkler. Townspeople often called him "Bird" for short.

BISHOP

Railroad officials did not have any ecclesiastical office in mind when they named this town in the 1870s.

On the contrary, the town was named for the Bishop Brothers who settled on a bar here in 1877.

BLACK DIAMOND

The primary developer of a major coal vein located here in King County during the late 19th century was the Black Diamond Coal Company of California. The town that grew up around the mine became known as Black Diamond.

BLAINE

Blaine, Whatcom County, was first settled in 1856 as a port on Drayton Harbor, near the British Columbia border. It flared up during the Fraser River gold rush, then declined. Following the Homestead Act, farmers began to arrive in the area. About 1870, Blaine became a port city for dairy products and fish.

It is possible that this community was named for the Reverend David E. Blaine who, in 1854, organized a Methodist Church in the Seattle area.

Another view, and a much more popular one, is that the town's name honors William Gillespie Blaine, a candidate for president against Grover Cleveland in 1884. The town, we are told, was named a year after his defeat for the presidency.

BLANCHARD

When George B. Blanchard founded this town in about 1885, he named it for himself. Postal officials, to prevent duplication of names, changed Blanchard to Fravel. When the other Blanchard post office closed in 1913, the name was changed back to Blanchard.

BLUESLIDE

Blueslide, Pend Oreille County, obtained its name from the landsliding of part of a hill into the river, leaving a gap there. Facing the river, the "slide" is blue. The town, one source contends, "must have been named during rainy weather. The face is principally clay and when wet is blue, but when dry is more of a gray."

BLUESTEM

Bluestem is a kind of wheat, and it is the principal kind grown in this Lincoln County area.

BLYN

Located in Clallam County, this community was named—with a slight misspelling—for mill operator Marshall Blinn. Blinn also founded Seabeck.

BODIE

Bodie takes its name from either Bodie Creek or the Bodie Mine, both of which are located here.

BOGACHIEL

Bogachiel is a community in Clallam County. It takes its name from the Bogachiel River. That name translates from the Indian as "muddy waters."

BOISFORT

French-Canadian members of the Hudson Bay Company left their mark in the naming of the Boisfort Prairie. The name is a combination of two French words: *bois*, "woods" or "forest," and *fort*, "strong."

Pierre Charles, a Canadian half-breed, was the first settler in this Lewis County area, but the first white settler did not arrive until 1852. The mispronounciation of Pierre's name ended up as the source of the name for nearby Pe Ell. (See PE ELL, Washington.)

BONNEY LAKE

Bonney Lake, Pierce County, was platted alongside the lake of that name in 1947, by Kenneth Simmons. Simmons purchased the lake and the land for the development of this community.

The lake was named for an early pioneering family.

BOSSBURG

Platted in 1892, this Stevens County town's name is a combination of the town's owners: Chester S. Boss and John Berg. The original name of the town, Bossberg, as found on the 1891 post office, clearly reflected those names. Bossberg remained as late as 1929, when postal authorities modified the name and the meaning.

BOTHELL

George Bothell and his brother began a logging and shingle operation at this King County site in 1886. They named the town in honor of their father, David C. Bothell.

15

BOW

When William J. Brown obtained the land here for homesteading in 1869, the area became known as Brownsville. By the turn of the 20th century, the railroad had arrived, a post office had opened (1901), and the town was booming.

It was then that the postmaster, at the Browns' suggestion, petitioned that the name be changed to Bow for the Bow railroad station in London, England.

BOYDS

Boyds, Ferry County, bears the name of an early family.

BOYLSTON

Boylston was named by H. R. Williams, a vice president of the Chicago, Milwaukee & St. Paul Railway Company, after the town of the same name in Massachusetts.

BRADY

Brady, in Grays Harbor County, was named for John Brady. Brady settled on the Satsop River in the mid-19th century, and served as one of the first commissioners.

BREIDABLICK

Breidablick, Kitsap County, was settled by immigrants from Scandinavia. The name is drawn from Norse mythology, and translates to mean "broad view."

BREMERTON

Bremerton was named for William Bremer (1863–1910), a German immigrant who made his home in Kitsap County at Point Turner in 1891. Born in Seesen, Duchy of Brunswick, he is regarded as the founder of the city.

BREWSTER

Brewster, Okanogan County, was named for John Bruster after he sold his landing site at the confluence of the Okanogan and Columbia Rivers to a steam boat company in 1896.

The town was named Bruster by Bruster and his partner Captain Alexander Griggs, but in 1898, the town's postmaster, D. L. Gillespie, sent in the current name, which was accepted in Washington. The name might not be spelled correctly, but it sure does sound right!

BRIDGEPORT

The river service offered by the Columbia & Okanogan Steamboat Company that began at Brewster ended at Bridgeport, Douglas County.

Railroad surveyors changed the original name, Westfield, to Bridgeport in 1891—for their home in Connecticut.

BRINNON

Brinnon, Jefferson County, was once a thriving lumber center. The name honors Ewell P. Brinnon, an early settler.

BROOKLYN

Emma C. Roberts, the first postmistress in this Pacific County location, submitted the name Clifton to postal authorities in 1891 when the post office was established here. The name was a contraction of her son's name.

Postal authorities rejected her name because they thought it duplicated another. They granted her application—but named her town Brooklyn, for no known reason.

BROWNSTOWN

Brownstown, located on a two-mile wide plateau in Yakima County, was originally named Bench because of its location. The name was changed to Brownstown to honor a local business leader, Reece Brown.

BROWNSVILLE

This Kitsap County community bears the name of Solomon Brown, one of the first settlers.

BRUSH PRAIRIE

The name for Brush Prairie, Clark County, was given by Elmorine Bowman for a large, bushy swamp on her father's property.

BRYANT

This town was named about 1892 for its major industry: the Bryant Lumber & Shingle Company.

BRYN MAWR

William E. Parker and his family named this town after the Philadelphia suburb of Bryn Mawr, the town from which they migrated. The name is Scotch for "big hill."

Bryn Mawr, King County, was platted in 1890 by Parker. (See BRYN MAWR, Pennsylvania.)

BUCKLEY

Previous names for this community include Perkin's Prairie and White River Siding. In 1888, the name became Buckley to honor the superintendent of the Ellensburg Division of the Northern Pacific Railroad that ran between Ellensburg and Tacoma.

BUCODA

This Thurston County town's name is formed from the first part of the names of three of the town's founders: J. M. Buckley, Samuel Coulter and John B. David.

An earlier settlement here was started in 1854 by Aaron Webster who opened a small sawmill. He sold his land and business to Oliver Shead, who called the settlement Seatco, an Indian word that is supposed to mean "ghost" or "devil." Seatco was home to the first territorial prison, in operation from 1874 to 1888.

When coal was discovered across the river, the land became part of Samuel Coulter's holdings. Later he joined up with Buckley and David. By 1890, the name became theirs, though they had proposed it a good seventeen years before it was accepted. Shead was the biggest opponent to the name change.

BUENA

Buena, Yakima County, takes its name from the Spanish for "good," but pronounces it Byu-eh-na.

BURBANK

Will H. Parry, while a member of the Federal Trade Commission, became interested in an irrigation project which he called the Burbank Power & Water Company.

The name for this Walla Walla County location was derived from the power company's name. That name honored Luther Burbank, the horticulturist. (See BURBANK, California.)

BURIEN

Gottlieb Burian settled on the shores of what is now called Lake Burien in 1884. His family name, slightly modified, is commemorated today in this King County community.

BURLINGTON

John P. Millett and William McKay opened a logging camp here in 1882, and platted the town nine years later. The post office was opened that same year as Burlington, possibly for Burlington, Vermont.

BURTON

Mrs. M. F. Hatch named this town in 1892. She selected it because it was the name of her hometown in McHenry County, Illinois.

BYRON

Legend has it that when the first settlers arrived here they found a railroad post marked "Byron," and took that name for their own.

CAMANO

The name of this community is a relic of the Spanish explorations.

Eliza originally named Camano Island Boco de Caamano in 1790. In 1841, Wilkes named it McDonough's Island to honor Master Commandant Thomas McDonough, whose flagship *Saratoga* achieved fame on Lake Champlain during the War of 1812.

Six years later, when Kellet was attempting to restore some of the Spanish names, he reverted to Caamano, for Jacinton Caamano. The current spelling is really a misspelling.

The ship's name is still remembered here in Saratoga Passage, which separates Camano and Whidbey islands.

CAMAS

Camas takes its name from the Camas Prairie. The town's name originally was Las Camas, and the name was taken from a delicacy of the western Indians, *Camassia esculenta*, a relation to the hyacinth. The word is derived from the Nootka Indian *chamass*, "fruit" or "sweet." This locality was where the Indians went to gather up the sweetish bulbs. The same is true of Camas Valley, Oregon, and Kamas, Utah.

CAMDEN

Camden, Pend Oreille, was named for Senator J. N. Camden from West Virginia. Camden was a strong supporter of the expansion of the Great Northern Railroad.

CANBY

Like Fort Canby, this community bears the name of U.S. Army Major General Edward Richard Sprigg Canby. Canby served with distinction in the Mexican and Civil wars, but was killed in 1874 during the Modoc Indian War in California.

CARBONADO

This Pierce County town was named after the Carbonado River which got its name after coal was discovered on its banks. In 1883, the mines here were the second largest in Washington Territory.

The community was owned, planned, and operated by the Pacific Coast Coal Company. The company provided paved streets and sewers. They even repainted the homes. The average monthly rent? Fourteen dollars. Who said there were no "good old days"?

CARLSBORG

Charles (Carl) J. Erickson named this Clallam County community for himself while he was constructing a branch line of the Chicago, Milwaukee & St. Paul Railroad in 1916. The Carlsborg post office was established in 1917.

CARLSON

John E. Carlson, an immigrant from Sweden, was the first settler in this Lewis County area. He also operated the local saw mill. Carlson was born Johan Edvard Lindgren. No one is certain when or why he changed his name.

CARLTON

The name for this Okanogan County community honors an early settler: Carl Dillard.

CARNATION

Carnation, settled by Scandinavian dairy farmers in 1865, received its name from a local dairy farm that was famous for its quality herds. Carnation Farms is open to the public for tours. The product, Carnation Milk, can be purchased at your local supermarket. An earlier name for the town was Tolt—because of its location on the Tolt River. That name succumbed to Carnation by act of the Washington legislature in 1917.

CARROLLS

Located on the Columbia River in Cowlitz County, Carrolls was formerly Carrollton. The name was changed in 1915, but it still honored Major Carroll, one of the town's first settlers.

CARSON

Carson takes its name from the creek of the same name. Some feel the name is a corruption of the family name, Katsner.

When Lewis and Clark stumbled upon this Skamania County area, they discovered the first ash timber in the West, so an earlier name for the town was Ash. That name was changed to Carson in 1895, at the request of A. C. Tucker. According to one source, Tucker submitted Casner, and postal authorities goofed.

CASHMERE

Settlers here, we are told, compared the area with the Vale of Kasmir in India. Originally this Chelan County town was called Mission, because of the Indian mission that was in operation here under the guidance of the Oblate Fathers (mid-19th century) and later the Jesuits (1873).

The name was changed in 1903.

CASTLE ROCK

Castle Rock, Cowlitz County, was named for a 150-foot-high rock—more than an acre in area, used as a landmark by local Indian tribes and traders of the Hudson Bay Company as early as 1832. It was not, however, until 1853 that William Huntington gave the name to the rock mass. When the town grew up around the rock, it assumed that name.

A sawmill at Castle Rock was the first to produce cedar shingles, using the California red cedar which proliferates this area.

CATHLAMET

The name of this Wahkiakum County town is derived from that of an Indian tribe. The tribe's name is spelled, however, with a "k." Lewis and Clark wrote the name as Cathlamah in 1805–06.

Some authorities feel the name is derived in some way from the Indian *calamet*, "stone," and was first given to the river because it had a stony bed throughout its course.

Cathlamet is sometimes called "Little Norway" because of its large Scandinavian population.

CEDAR (— Falls, — Grove, —hurst, —ville)

The name of Cedar Falls is descriptive of this King County town's location near the falls of the Cedar River. In a similar way, Cedar Grove, King County, took its name from a stand of cedar trees near Cedar Mountain.

Cedarville took its name from its major industry: the Cedarville Shingle Company.

CEDONIA

When the settlers originally moved here, they called this Stevens County site Cadonia. When the post office was established here in 1898, the name was modified to Cedonia.

The name is an adaptation of the name ascribed to Persian tribes in the Old Testament.

CENTER (—ville)

Center received its name because it was supposed to be located at the center of Jefferson County. The same reason is given for Centerville, Klickitat County; it is located near the center of the lower part of the valley.

CENTRALIA

Centralia is located in, of all places, the commercial center of the Chehalis Valley.

The town was founded in 1875 by George Washington, a pioneer and son of a Virginia slave and a white servant. Washington had recently been freed and adopted by his Missouri master. His settlement—he called it Centerville—grew around the Borst Family Homestead or Fort Borst, which was in existence during the 1860s. Confusion arose over the name because of another Centerville in eastern Washington.

When the problem reached its peak, David Fouts suggested the name be changed to Centralia, as in Illinois. As luck had it, that is from where Fouts hailed.

CENTRALIA. George Washington founded this town, but it was not "The Father of His Country." It was another George Washington from Virginia. This one was the son of a slave and a white servant. (St. Peter's Episcopal Church, Philadelphia)

On Armistice Day, 1919, during an American Legion parade, gunfire broke out between the legionnaires and members of the Industrial Workers of the World, the "Wobblies," with several deaths resulting. The reason for the battle was the Legion's desire to rid the area of the IWW which was still associated with pacifism during World War I.

CENTRAL PARK

Central Park, Grays Harbor County, received this name because of its location between Aberdeen and Montesano.

CHATTAROY

The town name of Kidd, Spokane County, was deemed unacceptable for a community name by Mrs. D. C. Cowgill, wife of the first postmaster. At her insistence, the name was changed to Chattaroy in the 1890s. No one is certain where she got this name, but there are suspicions.

She may have gotten the name from a poem she read, or from an original Indian name, or—more likely—from the French *chateau roi*, "royal house."

CHEHALIS

Chehalis, Lewis County, was established when the county seat was moved here from Claquato. It was first named Saundersville, but that name was changed in 1879 to reflect the name of the river.

The town was built on land from S. S. Saunders in 1851, and named Saunders Bottom. Seven years later, with the establishment of the first post office, the name became Saundersville. The post office name was changed to Chehalis in 1870; nine years later, the town name conformed to that of the post office.

The name of the river came from the local Indian language and means "sand," a reference to the sand bar at the mouth of the river. The name is also that of an Indian tribe.

CHELAN (— Falls)

Both Chelan and Chelan Falls take their names from Lake Chelan, whose name means "deep water" or "bubbling water." The stream's name was first recorded in about 1810.

Lake Chelan, one of the most scenic lakes in the Pacific Northwest, is more than 1,500 feet deep. At its deepest point, the lake drops to 400 feet below sea level.

The city of Chelan was established by the U.S. Army as Fort Chelan in 1870. Chelan Falls was originally a steamboat landing.

CHENEY

This Spokane County town was named for Benjamin P. Cheney, one of the founders of the Northern Pacific Railroad. Earlier the town was known as Depot Springs. There was more to the name change than just an honor to the railroader.

The town fathers had wanted to establish a school or academy, so when they notified Cheney they pulled no punches. He donated $10,000 to their project and they named the town for him. Since 1890, Cheney has been home to Eastern Washington University.

Over the years, Cheney has fought bitterly for power with Spokane Falls. Spokane Falls was selected over Cheney for county seat. Cheney did become the location for railroad shops over its competition.

CHENOIS CREEK

Though the meaning of the name is unknown, Chenois Creek, Grays Harbor County, is located on the site of an early Indian village—and has kept the same name.

CHESAW

Chesaw, it is said, was named for Chee Saw, a Chinese miner who married an Indian woman and worked as a farmer in this Okanogan County area after the placer mines played out.

CHESTER

This town was named by the Oregon Railway & Navigation Company. Why Chester? No one knows.

CHEWELAH

Chewelah's name comes from the Indian *cha-we-lah* and refers to a small striped snake. The reason for the naming is clouded. Some feel the name refers to an abundance of snakes; others believe it is because of the serpentine shape of the Chewelah Creek, which runs through the town.

CHICO

Chico was named in 1889 by B. S. Sparks. He named the community for an Indian chief who owned land nearby. Chief Chico died in 1909 at the modest age of 105!

CHIMACUM

Chimacum is an Indian tribal name that first appeared on the maps as the name for a stream. The town that grew on the stream's banks assumed its name. The tribe was small, but quite warlike, and lived between Port Townsend and Hood Canal.

CHINOOK

Located in Pacific County, Chinook takes its name from an Indian tribe that was noted for making baskets from cattails and cedar bark. The Chehalis Indians called the tribe Tsinuk.

Captain Robert Gray arrived at the mouth of the Columbia River at this point in 1792. Meriwether Lewis and William Clark camped here in 1805 just before they completed their journey across the American continent.

The language of this tribe, with a certain touch of French and English, became the jargon used by traders, trappers and explorers.

CHUCKANUT

Chuckanut is not the Pacific Northwest's version of George Washington tossing a sovereign across the Rappahannock—Parson Weems had it a silver dollar across the Potomac!

The Whatcom County town takes its name from Chuckanut Point, which was named in 1852 by Henry Roeder. The name is supposed to be Indian. Although no one knows what it means, we do know that an earlier name was Puerto del Socorro, "Port of Help," given by Eliza.

CINEBAR

The name of Cinebar, Lewis County, is a reference to the presence of the red ore of mercury. The name of the ore is more properly *cinnabar*.

CLALLAM BAY

Clallam Bay is located on the tip of northwest Washington. Clallam is derived from the Indian *Do-skal-ob*, or "brave people," and was the name of a tribe.

The bay was referred to as S'Klallam in the Point-no-Point Treaty of 1855. A year earlier, a county was established by the name of Clallam. Other spellings include Challam and Callam.

CLARKSTON

The name for this Asotin county site came from Captain William Clark of the Lewis and Clark expedition.

The town was first begun in 1896, heavily promoted by the president of the Union Pacific as Concord. After several name changes, the townspeople decided in 1902 to honor Clark. At the same time, their neighbors across the state line in Idaho named their community Lewiston, for Meriwether Lewis. The explorers had ties to these communities. They camped here at the confluence of the Snake and Clearwater Rivers.

The original name for the town was Concord; many of the town's investors came from the town of the same name in Massachusetts.

CLAYTON

This Stevens County site was established in 1889, and named for the great amount of commercial quality clay found here.

CLEAR LAKE

Clear Lake, the body of water, was named by W. F. Bassett because of the clearness of the water. The Skagit County town that grew up around its banks assumed that name. Platted in 1890, the original town name was Mountain View.

CLEARVIEW

The name of this Snohomish County site is descriptive.

CLE ELUM

Cle Elum is the English equivalent of the Indian *tle-el-lum*, "swift water," a reference to the Yakima River. The name has appeared variously as Clealum, Kleallum and Samahma.

The first white settlers arrived at this Kittitas County location in 1883 to look for gold, but it was not until the arrival of the Northern Pacific Railroad three years later and the discovery of coal that an actual town was established.

The wideness of Cle Elum's streets was brought about by the insistence of Barbara Steiner Reed, wife of the town's founder. She wanted this town to become the Pittsburgh of the West.

CLEVELAND

Cleveland was platted in the late 19th century, almost simultaneously with Bickleton. It takes its name from President Grover Cleveland who, before he left office in 1897, established 13 forest reserves—more than 21 million acres—to keep the land from falling into private hands. By 1907, the lumber barons were able to lobby

Congress to prevent the establishment of any more reserves from federal land.

CLINTON

An earlier name for the post office at Clinton was Phinney, for postmaster John G. Phinney.

The name was changed to Clinton, for the city of that name in Michigan.

CLIPPER

Clipper was named in 1900 for the Clipper Shingle Company. (See CLIPPER MILLS, California.)

COLBERT

When established as a sawmill town in 1890, this Spokane County site was known as Drygoon. Harry Colbert renamed it in 1902. Colbert was the town's storekeeper—and postmaster.

COLBY

Originally named Coal Bay because of the coal found here in the 1880s, the name was modified by common usage to Colby.

COLCHESTER

Located between Colby and Manchester in Kitsap County, this community has a composite name.

COLFAX

Colfax was the first town in Whitman County and the county seat. In August 1876, a federal land office was opened at Colfax. It relieved homesteaders of the task of only going to Walla Walla for claims.

By the late 19th century, Colfax was a haven for Russian and Dutch immigrants. It was named, according to the legislature, "in honor of the vice-president of the United States," Schuyler Colfax. "Smiling Schuyler" served under U. S. Grant.

COLLEGE PLACE

College Place, Walla Walla County, was just a place that grew up around a college. The name was given in about 1892 because of the Seventh Day Adventist college that opened here.

COLFAX. Schuyler Colfax, vice president under Ulysses S. Grant, was known as "Smilin' Schuyler." He lost that grin when his involvement in the Credit Mobilier scandal became known. Colfax had accepted stock and cash as payoffs for helping getting legislation through Congress. (National Archives)

COLTON

The earliest settlers to this Whitman County site were named *Cole* and Worthing*ton*. Letters from their names make up the corporate name for the community.

COLVILLE (— Indian Agency)

The name for the community of Colville in Stevens County comes from the old Hudson Bay Company fort located near the Columbia River.

Originally called Kettle Falls, Fort Colville was the company's chief inland port . . . until the 1855 gold rush. Old Fort Colville is commemorated in a historical marker on a state road. The name was given in 1847 by Captain Henry Kellett. The name was selected to honor Andrew Colville, the governor of the Hudson Bay Company from 1852 to 1856. A few miles east of Fort Colville was another fort, Fort Pinkney, commanded by Major Pinkney Loughenbeel and known as Pinkney City. When the county was formed, Pinkney City and Colville became one.

In 1852, Angus McDonald, the agent for the Hudson Bay Company, showed his workers a sack of gold-bearing sand which he obtained in California. Later, one of the men scooped up a drink of water from the Columbia River and spied what looked like black California dirt. He filled his hat with the sand and gently swirled it around. When he poured off the water and sand, he saw tiny flakes of gold in his hat. In order to keep others from finding out about his discovery, he did not publicize the find. Three years later, enough people knew about the gold anyway.

The most famous Catholic missionary in the Oregon area, Father John DeSmet, established a mission, St. Paul's, near here.

COLVOS

Colvos takes its name from the same source as Colvos Rocks and Colvos Point: George W. Colvocoressis. Colvocoressis was a midshipman on a ship during the 1841 Wilkes Expedition. Because his name was too long, the captain shortened it.

CONCONULLY

Conconully takes its name from the creek, whose name comes from a corruption of an Indian word meaning "cloudy." Other sources feel the name really means "money hole," because it was said that a hunter could shag a beaver a day and sell it to the Hudson Bay people at Fort Okanogan for cash.

Two prospectors who had previously discovered gold along Salmon Creek began to work the Homestake and Toughnut mines above the town of Ruby in 1886. Within a few months, their activity drew a large number of other prospectors and brought about the creation of Salmon City. In 1888, the town was renamed Conconully.

CONCRETE

Concrete got its name in 1905 from the creation of a local cement industry.

Prior to being named Concrete, the town was known as Baker because of its location at the junction of the Baker and Skagit rivers. The town was founded by Magnus Miller in 1890, though an early settler named Richard Challanger arrived there in 1888. A post office opened under the Baker name five years later.

CONNELL

A previous name for Connell, Franklin County, was Palouse Junction. In 1883, the Northern Pacific Railroad opened a line from here to Colfax. The town, however, was not platted until 1901 or 1902.

The Connell name, we are told, came from an employee of the Northern Pacific.

CONWAY

Conway, Skagit County, was settled in 1873 by Thomas P. Jones and Charles Villeneuve. The Great Northern Railway opened its line through here in 1891, the same year that Jones platted the townsite and named it after his hometown in Wales.

COOK

A number of places in the Northwest honor the memory of Captain James Cook, the British navigator who made a determined effort to discover the Strait of Anian and the Northwest Passage. By the time he arrived in this area, he had explored and charted the Society Islands, New Zealand, a large part of the South Pacific, and the Hawaiian Islands (he named them the Sandwich Islands).

He traveled north and went past Alaska and through the Bering Strait, until he could sail no more because of the thickness of the ice.

That is not the case with this Skamania County community. It was named in 1908 by the first postmaster, S. R. Harris, in order to honor Charles A. Cook, who was one of the first homesteaders.

COPALIS (— Beach, — Crossing)

Located at the mouth of the Copalis River, these communities take their names from that body of water. The river's name comes from a Salish Indian tribe that once lived on its banks.

CORFU

The name for this Grant County community, we are told, was imported from Greece by the Chicago, Milwaukee & St. Paul Railway Company. Corfu is one of the Ionian Islands, west of Greece.

COSMOPOLIS

Cosmopolis is a made-up word, drawn from Cosmopolitan and Metropolis. While some think the roots are Greek, an attempt to sound important, others suggest the name was derived from that of an Indian chief. Chances are that when R. Brunn, a homesteader from France, decided on the name in 1853, he was trying to create a "city of the whole world," using the Greek words.

COTTONWOOD BEACH

This community was given its name because it was located amid a profusion of cottonwood trees.

COUGAR

When the townspeople of this Cowlitz County community petitioned for a post office in 1906, the name of Cougar was selected. No reason was given, except that it was a short and different name.

COULEE CITY

Coulee City, once nicknamed "Engineers' Town," was at the junction of the railroad and stage coach lines that ran along the Columbia River. According to a 19th century author, it was pre-arranged that the railroad and the stage would not have connecting schedules, so travelers would be required to spend a night in town! The name, of course, comes from Grand Coulee.

The word "coulee" refers to a stream course. In this case, it was the dry bed of a prehistoric Columbia River.

COULEE DAM

See Coulee City.

COUPEVILLE

Coupeville, Island County, owes its name to a navigator, Captain Thomas Coupe, who founded the place. Established in 1853, it is one of the oldest cities in the state of Washington.

Today, Coupeville is a restored 1875 town, and the site of Alexander's Blockhouse, an Indian defense.

COVE

The name for this town is descriptive of its location on Vashon Island Bay.

COWICHE

Cowiche took its name from the nearby river. An Indian name of uncertain origin, it was spelled *Kwiwichess* and *Kwai-wy-chess* by railroad surveyors in 1853.

It has been suggested that the name means "capturing the medicine spirit," a reference to the fact that young braves were sent to a small nearby prairie to commune with the great spirits and gain "medicine" or "power." Another thought is that the waters of the river were considered "good medicine." Yet another suggestion is that the name came from the Indian *kwiwichess*, "foot log," a reference to a foot bridge over a nearby stream.

CREOSOTE

Creosote, Kitsap County, began its life in 1884 as Eagle Harbor. With the establishment of a post office in 1908, the name was changed to reflect the community's main industry: a creosoting plant.

CRESCENT BEACH

The name for this site was suggested by the Crescent Bay.

CRESTON

Named about 1889, this Lincoln County town's name was given by the Northern Pacific Railway because Brown's Butte, which overlooks the town on the south, is the crest of land in the Big Bend Country.

A more logical reason would be that the railroad station here was located at the highest point, or crest, along the tracks in the county.

CUMBERLAND
The name for Cumberland, King County, was suggested by F. X. Schriner in 1893. When a coal mine opened that year, Schriner thought he would apply some good luck to the dig by naming it for the Pennsylvania coal region.

CUNNINGHAM
Cunningham, Adams County, was platted as a town in 1901 or 1902 by W. R. Cunningham, a land promoter—and preacher.

The community got its first start as Scott when the railroad opened a station here.

CURLEW
Curlew, Ferry County, was named in 1896 by Guy S. Helphrey. The name came from the Curlew Creek and Curlew Lake. Both were derived from the Indian *Karanips*, which means "curlew." The Curlew is a snipe-like bird indigenous to the area.

CURTIS
The first postmaster of this Lewis County village was Ben Curtis.

CUSICK
An early settler to this Pend Oreille County area was Joe Cusick.

CUSTER
Many towns in the United States were named for George Armstrong Custer. This Whatcom County village is not one of them. It was named in 1886 for Albert W. Custer, an early settler—and postmaster.

DABOB
Though this Jefferson County site is Dabob on every map, the real name was Dabop, an Indian word of unknown meaning.

DAISY
Daisy, Wahkiakum County, was named for a nearby silver mine, the Daisy. The other mine close at hand was the Tempest.

DALKENA

Dalkena's name is a merger of the family names of two lumber operators: Dalton and Kennedy. Dalkena is located in Pend Oreille County.

DALLESPORT

Over the years, this Klickitat County community has been known as Rockport, Grand Dalles, and North Dalles. The current name was agreed to in 1937. Each name was an attempt to identify the community as the Washington shore equivalent of The Dalles, Oregon.

DANVILLE

Danville, Ferry County, was named for an enterprising man who opened a business that straddled the United States-Canada border. He would buy from one country and sell to the other without paying duty. He was finally caught by customs officials and moved his operation a little further south.

DARRINGTON

According to local lore, this Snohomish County town was to be named in honor of a man named Barrington, but postal authorities goofed.

DAVENPORT

This location in Lincoln County was named for the town's first storekeeper, J. C. Davenport.

DAYTON

The majority of Daytons in the United States were named for Jonathan Dayton, founder of the Ohio town that bears his name. However, this particular city in Columbia County, the county seat, to be precise, was named for Jesse N. Day (1828–92), owner of the townsite. Day and his wife Elizabeth filed a plat for the town in 1871.

Dayton claims the oldest courthouse and railroad station in the state. The station, built in 1881 by the Oregon Railroad & Navigation Company, was in operation for 93 years.

DEEP CREEK

First settled by Daniel and Alfred Stroup, the town takes its name from the body of water. The town, located in Spokane County, was originally called Deep Creek Falls, a descriptive name, but the name was shortened in 1894.

DEEP RIVER

The source of Deep River's name is gone. Deep River was the former name for the Alamicut River. This particular town, located in Wahkiakum County, is situated on a slough that the Indians called *alimicut*, "deep river."

DEER HARBOR

Captain Richards named Deer Harbor because of the abundance of deer. He also named Fawn Island at the same time, about 1858 or 1859. The town takes its name from the harbor.

DEER PARK

In the early days of settlement, this Spokane County location was a good hunting place.

DEL RIO

The granddaughter of Mrs. A. C. Earl, the first postmistress of this Douglas County village, named this town in the Spanish for "of the river." Violet Bailey gave the name in 1904. A later postmaster tried to change the name to Lella to honor his wife, but it did not stick.

DEMING

This Whatcom County community took its name from the Deming Land Company, owned by Frank and George Deming. It really had nothing to do with the fact that the first postmistress, in 1888, was Mrs. S. J. Deming, though some historians think it was George Deming.

DENISON

Denison, Spokane County, was first called Buckeye for the Buckeye Lumber Company. When the company moved to another place on the Spokane Falls & Northern Railroad and called the place Hock-spur, confusion reigned. So this Spokane County spot was renamed Pratt.

Later, when F.H. Buell revived the town, he selected the name Denison, his wife's maiden name.

DES MOINES

Des Moines was settled between 1867 and 1870, and named for the Des Moines Improvement Company in 1889. The company's name came from the hometown of one of the owners . . . in Iowa. Des Moines, King County, is located on the eastern shore of Puget Sound.

DEWATTO

Dewatto was the name the local Indians gave to a mythical underground region. They called it *du-a-ta*, and the exit was supposed to be at this place.

More likely the name for this Mason County town came from the creek which flows into Hood Canal—supposedly the spot where spirits rose from the netherworld and entered human beings, driving them crazy.

DIABLO

Diablo is the Spanish word for "devil." The name was given to this Whatcom County site by a prospector in the 1880s. This area also has a Big Devil Mountain, a Little Devil Mountain, and a Devil's Elbow in the Skagit River.

DIAMOND (— Lake)

This Pend Oreille County site got its name from the nearby Diamond Lake. The body of water, it is told, was named by hunters in 1888, who came upon the lake and found a single playing card, the ace of diamonds, on the shore.

DIERINGER

Dieringer, Pierce County, is named for a Tacoma restauranteur, Joseph C. Dieringer, who was a land speculator.

DISCOVERY BAY

This community, located in Jefferson County, ties its name to Vancouver's ship and Port Discovery Bay.

DISHMAN

This town, located in Spokane County, was founded in 1889 by A. T. Dishman, who also founded the town's first industry: a granite quarry.

DIXIE

According to local legend, the three Kershaw brothers who lived in these parts were musicians and they loved playing "Dixie." In fact, they were known as the Dixie Brothers and their homestead was called Dixie Crossing.

Herman C. Actor was the first settler, but no one knows about his interest in music. (See DIXIE VALLEY, Nevada.)

DOCKTON

Docton's name came from the simple fact that the town had a dock.

This King County community was named by the Puget Sound Dry Dock Company in about 1891, when they operated a dock here.

DOE BAY

The abundance of deer on Orcas Island gave rise to the name of this San Juan County site. The animals are also remembered with Buck Bay, Doe Bay, Doe Island, and Deer Point.

DOTY

C. A. Doty established a sawmill here about the turn of the 20th century. This Lewis County town was named in his honor.

DOUGLAS

Douglas was a community created by the Great Northern Railroad in the early 20th century. The town may have been named for David Douglas, an important British botanist who accompanied the Hudson Bay Company in its explorations. Others think the name came from Stephen Douglas, Lincoln's debate partner. The latter historians are probably right.

Douglas, located in Douglas County, most likely took its name from the county in 1884 when the town was settled by Ole Rudd. The county, established the year before, was named in honor of Stephen Douglas.

Douglas Mountain, in nearby Okanogan County, however, was named after an early prospector, Douglas Joe.

DRUMHELLER

This Franklin County location has nothing to with a crazy drummer. The name commemorates the family of the more sedate Sam Drumheller, an early farmer in the area.

DRYAD

Dryad is the Greek name for the tree nymph. The railroad name for this community might have been given because of its location in a forest. More likely the name came from the ship owned by the Hudson Bay Company, the *Dryad*. The town was named in about 1890 by members of the Northern Pacific Railroad Company.

DRYDEN

This Chelan County community was named by the Great Northern Railway Company in 1907. At that time, the famous Canadian horticulturist was visiting the area as a guest of Great Northern's president, James A. Hill.

DUCKABUSH

This town's name has no reference to a modification of the old saw about a "bird in the hand is worth two. . . ."

Duckabush takes its name from the nearby river, whose name comes from the Indian descriptive, *do-hi-a-boos*, referring to the "reddish-face" mountainside.

DUNGENESS

The name for this Clallam County town was given by Vancouver to a low piece of land in the county. In 1792, he wrote: "The low sandy point of land, which from its great resemblance to Dungeness in the British Channel, I called New Dungeness." The new name was later dropped and given to the town.

It is also the name of the delicious North Pacific crab.

DuPONT

The name of this Pierce County community, like others across the nation, comes from the establishment of an E. I. du Pont de Nemours Powder Company plant at this location.

DuPont stands on the site of Fort Nisqually, established by the Hudson Bay Company in 1833.

DUSTY

Early settlers named this town in Whitman County, Dusty, because it was.

DUVALL

Duvall, King County, was named in honor of James Duvall, the pioneer who held the land from 1875 until settlement began in 1910, when John D. Bird platted the site.

EASTON

Easton is located near the entrance to the Northern Pacific Railway tunnel through the Cascade Mountains in the western section of Kittitas County. Near the other entrance to the tunnel is a town named Weston.

EASTSOUND

Eastsound, or East Sound, was named in relation to West Sound. Wilkes had named it Ironsides Inlet in 1841, after the popular nickname for the U.S.S. *Constitution*. Orcas Island was named Hull Island, after the commander of "Old Ironsides."

EATONVILLE

T. C. Van Eaton platted this Pierce County townsite in 1880.

EDEN

The only likely argument for this name is that early settlers were so enamored with their location that they likened it to the Garden of Eden.

EDGECOMB

Carl Ostrand settled a homestead here in 1888. The next year, the Northern Pacific Railroad arrived, and John Edgecomb opened his logging operation. The railroad spur was named for him, as was the resulting town.

EDISON

Edison, Skagit County, like places in New Jersey and elsewhere, was named for Thomas Alva Edison.

The town began in the late 19th century as a socialist colony called Equality. The object of the community was that each individual would do the type of work at which he was skilled. Everyone was to have full freedom over thought and action. Before long, this emphasis on complete freedom gave rise to an inability to agree on anything. After a while, the whole project collapsed.

Ben Sampson was the first settler, locating here in 1869. By 1876, there were 46 settlers and they petitioned for a post office. Edward McTaggart was the first postmaster and a fan of the great inventor.

EDMONDS

Local legend has it that when George Brackett (or Bracken) petitioned to establish the town of Edmonds in 1890, he did not have enough signatures, so he added the names of his oxen team! He had started the town in 1876 when he built his store here, began logging operations and became the town's postmaster.

Brackett also named the town for a Vermont senator, George Franklin Edmunds. As one may notice, Brackett had a problem with his spelling.

The first settlement at this Snohomish County site was made by Pleasant H. Ewell in 1866. Four years later, Brackett arrived.

EDWALL

This Lincoln County community name honors Peter and Eric Edwall who platted the town. The Edwalls changed their name from Andersson sometime after they arrived in this country in the mid-19th century. The town was formally organized in 1892.

ELBE

Elbe was not, like so many other places in the United States, named for Napoleon's place of confinement.

Originally named Brown's Junction when the Tacoma & Eastern Railway was built here, the townspeople changed the name to recognize the birthplace of pioneer settler Henry C. Lutkens. Lutkens was born in Germany's Elbe Valley. The main reason for the change, however, was that postal authorities wanted a shorter name.

ELBERTON

Like Mount Elbert, this town was named for S. H. Elbert (1833–99), a government official who held office while Colorado was a territory and then as a state. At least that is what one source contends.

A more logical possibility is that a landowner, whose son, Elbert Wait, died just as the town was being platted, asked that the Whitman County town be named in his son's honor.

ELECTRIC CITY

Electric City, Grant County, began with the construction of Grand Coulee Dam. The name was given in 1934 because the site was close to a major source of electric power.

Town planners also hoped that the place would become all electric—electric heat, cooking, heating: the works. The name stuck; the all-electric idea did not.

ELECTRON

Electron, Pierce County, was named in the early 20th century because of its location near an electric power plant on the Puyallup River.

ELGIN

Elgin was named by the second postmaster, a Mr. Kernodle, for his hometown of Elgin, Illinois. The original name for this Pierce County location was Minter. That was the first postmaster's family name.

An Elgin of the same derivation also exists in Colorado.

ELK

Elk, then known as Elk City, was founded in late 1861 when ore was discovered on the South Fork.

The name was selected by Mrs. David R. Mace, an early settler, because of the many elk herds that grazed through this Spokane County area.

ELLENSBURG

The first name of this Kittitas County community was Robber's Roost, the name of the local store. The name was tamed down a bit, and the town was renamed Ellensburg.

The name honors Mary Ellen Stewart Shoudy, wife of the town's founder, John A. Shoudy. The Kittitas County town was platted in 1875.

ELLISFORDE

This Okanogan County site bears the merged name of two pioneer merchant-partners: G. H. Ellis and J. E. Forde. Together they ran Washington Commercial Company stores.

ELLISPORT

One of the first homesteaders in this King County area was the Rev. Mr. Ellis. The town was named in his honor in 1912.

ELMA

Elma, Grays Harbor County, was named for Elma Austin, an early settler. A disproved legend that still crops up from time to time has it that the name belonged to a soldier who was killed in Baltimore, thought to be the first casualty of the Civil War.

ELMER CITY

Located in Okanogan County, Elmer City was platted in 1937 and named after Elmer Seaton, the operator of a Columbia River ferry that ran prior to the construction of the Coulee Dam.

ELTOPIA

Eltopia, Franklin County, has a name that is allegedly a contraction of "hell to pay." That was what railroaders called it after heavy rains washed out the grade and delayed construction.

ELWHA

Elwha, Clallam County, takes its name from the Elwha River. Most authorities believe the word is Indian for "elk." The town was originally named McDonald.

ENDICOTT

Endicott, Whitman County, bears the name of a survey engineer of the Oregon-Washington Railroad & Navigation Company.

The town was platted in 1882 by John O. Courtright. He named his son, Endicott T. Courtright, for the same individual.

ENTIAT

In 1896, the town of Entiat, Chelan County, assumed the name of the Entiat River. The word is Indian, and translates to "rapid water." Another source believes the name is Chinook jargon for "crossing" or "across."

Once called Port Orchard, the town was a thriving lumber town run by Captain William Renton and Daniel Howard.

ENUMCLAW

Local Indians called a nearby mountain Enumclaw, "place of the evil spirits," when they were frightened by terrible thunderstorms. When a town was established here in King County in 1885, Frank Stevenson, the original settler, assigned it the mountain's name.

EPHRATA

Ephrata, Grant County, was not named for the Ephrata Cloisters in Pennsylvania. When surveyors for the Great Northern Railway were measuring hereabouts, they found the only orchard in the area and, using their knowledge of the Bible, called the town site Ephrata.

Ephrata is mentioned three times in the Bible. It is also the name of a Pennsylvania town. Biblical dictionaries translate the word to mean "fertility," and indicate it as the ancient name for Bethlehem, the birthplace of Christ.

The town was platted in 1901 at Beasley Springs, which had been a roundup campsite.

ETHEL

Postmaster-General William F. Vilas named this Lewis County community Ethel in 1886. No one has any idea why.

EUREKA

Eureka, located in Walla Walla County, was platted by Mrs. A. B. Blanchard in 1904. She called her settlement Eureka Flat. *Eureka* comes from the Greek, "I have found it!"

EVANS

The name of this Stevens County town was granted in 1901 to honor J. H. Evans, president of the Idaho Lime Company. The company operated lime works here.

EVERETT

Everett, Snohomish County, was settled largely by Norwegians and Swedes in the 1880s. Originally called Port Gardner by W. J. and B. J. Rucker, the town was renamed by a group of entrepreneurs. Led by Henry Hewitt, Jr., John D. Rockefeller and Charles Colby, the group named the town after Colby's son Everett.

EVERSON

Everson, Whatcom County, carries the name of Ever Everson, the first white settler north of the Nooksack River.

EWAN

Though no one is sure what the name of this Yakima County village means, people are confident that Chief Kamiakin farmed in this area. The chief was the leader of the resistance against white settlers in the mid-19th century.

FAIRFIELD

This Spokane County community was named by E. H. Morrison in 1888. He selected the name because there were extensive fields of grain around the town. Another reason, perhaps a more important one, was that Mrs. Morrison once lived in Fairfield, Connecticut.

F

FAIRHOLM

Fairholm was the name of this Clallam County community when the post office was opened here in 1893; Mrs. George E. Machelle was the person who came up with the name.

FALL CITY

Located in King County, Fall City began its life as The Landing or The Falls. The site is located below the falls of the Snoqualmie River. The Bohen brothers operated an Indian trading post at the site. In about 1870, the Bohens and James Taylor petitioned for a post office, and the name Fall City became official.

The land on which the town was built was owned by Jeremiah W. Borst. He settled here in 1858, and became a farmer and hop grower.

FARMINGTON

Farmington was one of the earliest communities in Whitman County. The town was named in 1878 by G. W. Truax, who borrowed it from a town of the same name in his home state of Minnesota.

FARRINGTON

This Franklin County community was originally known as Windust. That name came from a ferry and its owner. The name was changed to remember R. I. Farrington, the comptroller of the Great Northern Railway Company.

FEDERAL WAY

Federal Way is a large suburban community, part of the Seattle-Tacoma metropolitan trading area.

The Pacific Highway South (Route 99) was financed by federal funds, and was known as the "federal highway." When a new school opened along the route, it was called Federal Way High School. The community that grew up around the school became known as Federal Way.

FERNDALE

Ferndale was named in 1872 for the clumps of ferns the area's first school teacher, a Miss Eldridge from Bellington Bay, noticed around the schoolhouse.

FERRY

Elisha P. Ferry was the first governor of Oregon. In 1899, Ferry County was created and named for him. This particular community takes its name from the county.

FIFE

The "fife" in this Pierce County name is not of musical origin. It was the name of the millionaire from Tacoma, William Fife, who was active in the community's development.

FINLEY

Finley, Benton County, took the name of George E. Finley, one of the first settlers under the Northern Pacific Irrigation Canal. His home was adjacent to the town.

FIRCREST

Edward J. Bowes, known to an earlier generation as "Major Bowes" of the Amateur Hour, platted the townsite here in Pierce County in 1907 and called it Regents Park.

Bowes' project was a failure and, in 1925, the development was incorporated . . . under the name of the nearby golf club.

FISHTRAP

Fishtrap takes its name from the nearby lake. The lake was named for the Indians' practice of using natural traps to catch fish. Fishtrap Creek's name was derived in the same manner.

The original name of this Lincoln County town was Vista. The name was changed in 1906 when the post office was opened on the land of John W. Lawton.

FLORENCE

Florence, Snohomish County, grew from the diggings opened up on the lower Salmon River in 1862. Two years later, a town was settled by Harry Marshall.

In 1884, F. E. Norton opened the first post office and named it after his old sweetheart.

FORD

The name of this Stevens County community was derived from the "ford" across Tshimakain Creek in Walkers Prairie.

It was the site of a famous mission, founded by Elkanah and Mary Walker, under the Indian name of Tshima-kain, "plain of many springs."

FOREST

Forest, Lewis County, was named by W. R. Monroe in 1897. At one time, the community was called Newaukum Prairie.

FORKS

Forks came into existence at the forks of three rivers: the Bogachiel, Calawah and Soleduck. The town began as a farming community in the late 1870s, but commercial logging took over a decade later.

Forks is the westernmost incorporated city in the contiguous United States.

FORTSON

Located in Snohomish County, Fortson was named to honor Captain George H. Fortson, a member of the 1st Washington Infantry. Fortson was killed in the 1899 Philippine War.

FOUR CORNERS

The name was given because the town is located at the junction of four states.

FOUR LAKES

U. S. Cavalry clashed with Indians here on 1 September 1858, beginning a running battle that ended four days later in the battle of Spokane Plain.

At that battle, Colonel George Wright avenged the loss suffered by Major Edward J. Steptoe at the hands of the Spokanes, Palouses, and Coeur d'Alenes. An arrow-shaped stone in Four Lakes commemorates Wright's victory.

This Spokane County town name was derived simply from the presence of four small lakes in the area.

FOX ISLAND

Fox Island, Pierce County, was named by the 1841 Wilkes Expedition. The name honored J. L. Fox, an assistant surgeon on that expedition.

FRAGARIA

Fragaria was named for the botanical genus to which the strawberry belongs. It seems that settlers in 1912 located early ripened berries here. The Latin name was given by Ferdinand Schmitz.

FRANCES

A Northern Pacific Railroad survey engineer named this Pacific County town in honor of his wife.

FREELAND

Founded by a group of Socialists who began a cooperative sawmill, this Island County community was first known as Equality.

The group, known as the Freeland Colony, disbanded in 1904; their property was sold to satisfy their creditors.

FRIDAY HARBOR

Local legend tells us that this community was named for a Kanaka sheepherder from the Hawaiian Islands who knew very little English and told people his name was Friday. Others think the name is reminiscent of *Robinson Crusoe*. Still others think the name came from someone aboard ship asking what the name of the bay was, and being told instead what day it was.

Another choice is that the harbor was discovered on a Friday. The name first appeared on British Admiralty maps in 1858 or 1859.

Over the years, attempts have been made to change the name of this San Juan County town to Bellevue.

FRUITLAND

Located on the Columbia River in Stevens County, Fruitland takes its name from apple orchards that thrive in the area.

Originally known as Price's Valley (one of the early land claimants was a Mr. Price), the town was named by Mrs. J. N. Allison, who placed an apple on the table and stated that the entire region should be called Fruitland Valley. Everyone agreed, and, when the post office was established in 1887, Fruitland was accepted.

GALVIN

When originally platted in 1910 by the Galvin Teal Company, this Lewis County community was named Lincoln, for the president. Later, the name was changed to honor the company's cofounder, John Galvin, who also was mayor of Centralia.

GARDENA

This town, located in Walla Walla County, was platted by the Walla Walla Irrigation Company.

GARDINER

The name of this Jefferson County village appeared as early as 1857. In its earliest form, the town's name was Gardner, for Herbert Gardner. The name was subsequently misspelled to avoid confusion with another post office of the same name in the state.

GARFIELD

Garfield takes the name of the county which came into being in 1881. It was named in 1882 by S. J. Tant in honor of President James A. Garfield, who had died the previous fall. Tant was the town-platter and first postmaster.

GATE

Originally known as Gate City, this Thurston County town received its name because of its location.

Gate is located where the Black Hills come close to the Black River, and the Chehalis River on the south draws that valley into its narrowest portion.

G

GENEVA

In 1882, David Jenkins was responsible for naming this Whatcom County community, located on the shore of Lake Whatcom. Jenkins decided on Geneva because he saw a resemblance to the location in Switzerland.

GEORGE

Charles Brown, the first mayor of this Grant County community, bought the townsite from the U.S. Reclamation Bureau. He dedicated the town on 4 July 1957. The streets of his city are lined with cherry trees, and are named for different varieties of cherry trees. Three guesses who George was?

GIBSON

The name of James H. Gibson, a coxswain on a ship in the 1841 Wilkes Expedition, also appears on Gibson Point.

GIFFORD

James O. Gifford was a pioneer in this Stevens County area in 1890. It was in his honor that the town was named.

GIG HARBOR

The name for this Pierce County town comes from the harbor. Members of the Wilkes expedition in 1841 named the harbor because it "has a sufficient depth of water for small vessels," or gigs.

GILMER

Gilmer takes its name from the Gilmer Creek, a tributary of the White Salmon River. The name honors George W. Gilmer, postmaster at Gilmer for 37 years.

GLACIER

Glacier, located on Glacier Lake in Whatcom County, drew its name from the lake which was named for a large glacier on nearby Mount Baker.

GLEED

When initially established, this Yakima County site was a railroad shipping point called Gleed Siding. The siding and later the railroad station were built on land owned by James Gleed, a hay farmer.

GLENOMA

The name of this Lewis County town, we are told, is a combination of Gaelic and Hebrew. *Oma* is Hebrew for "a measure of grain." The whole name is meant to connote a "fruitful valley." The name was coined by Mrs. Beverly W. Coiner.

GLENWOOD

Glenwood, Klickitat County, is located in a valley surrounded by forests: ergo, Glenwood!

GOLD BAR

Gold Bar, Snohomish County, was formerly a prospector's camp. During construction of the Great Northern Railroad, sentiment against the Chinese laborers ran so deep that the laborers were forced to flee the camp—in coffins!

The name was given in 1869 by prospectors. Using that name, the town was platted in 1900 by the Gold Bar Improvement Company.

GOLDENDALE

Goldendale was named for John J. Golden, the man on whose land the town was located in 1872. Golden had homesteaded the site nine years earlier.

GOODNOE HILLS

In the early 20th century, a rural post office and a railroad station at this Klickitat County site were named for Chauncey Goodnoe. Goodnoe operated a ranch along the Columbia River in 1865.

GOOSE PRAIRIE

This community takes its name from the natural meadow on the Bumping River. The prairie was named in the 1860s by John and Tom Fife. The Fifes, Scottish immigrants, decided on the name for the lone goose that homesteaded on their homestead.

GORST

Samuel Gorst was an early settler to this Kitsap County area.

GOULD CITY

Gould City, Garfield County, was platted by George R. McPherson and T. E. Griffith in 1891.

GOVAN

Govan bears the name of one of the engineers from the Washington Central Railroad. That line became the Northern Pacific.

GRAND COULEE

The community of Grand Coulee, of course, bears the name of the Grand Coulee. Some suggest that it was the former bed of the Columbia River. The name first appeared in 1825 when Hudson Bay's John Work referred to it as "Grand Coolley."

The idea for the Grand Coulee Dam was suggested by William Clapp who proposed damming the Columbia River and pumping the water into the Grand Coulee in order to create a reservoir. The project was authorized by the Roosevelt Administration's Public Works Administration. The Bureau of Reclamation's work began in 1933, with electricity being transmitted in 1941. Ten years later, the first irrigation water flowed from the dam.

The present Grand Coulee depicts the route that the Columbia took before the glaciers melted.

GRAND MOUND

Grand Mound took its name from the peculiar mounds that have confounded geologists and that gave rise to Mound Prairie.

This Thurston County site is located near the largest of those mounds.

GRANDVIEW

The name for this Yakima County community is apparent to anyone who has ever visited the lower Yakima Valley and seen the view from this town of Mount Rainier and Mount Adams.

When, in 1906, two members of the town-site committee were searching for a name for the town, F. L. Pittman said, "What a grand view!" His partner, Elza Dean, replied, "That's the name."

GRANGER

Located in Yakima County, this community, established in 1902, bears the name of Walter N. Granger. Granger was president of the Sunnyside Canal Company, one of the first irrigation projects in Washington State. He was also active in the development of the towns of Sunnyside and Zillah.

GRANITE FALLS

This Snohomish County community is located at the falls of the Granite River. The river's name came from the presence of granite in both the bed of the river and the walls of the canyon through which the river flows.

GRANT ORCHARD

Grant Orchard was so named because it was the principal fruit district in Grant County.

GRAPEVIEW

Originally platted as Detroit in 1891, this Mason County community was renamed because it faces the vineyards on the Isle of Grapes.

GRAYLAND

Grayland was so named because of its location at the southeastern end of Grays Harbor County. The town was established by cranberry growers from Finland.

GRAYS RIVER

Grays River, the waterway, bears the name of Robert Gray, who "discovered" the Columbia River. He named the Columbia after his ship. Earlier names for the river include the Indian Ebokwol (1841) and Moolhool (1853).

The town, located in Wahkiakum County, was named for the river.

GREENACRES

The name of Greenacres is purely descriptive of the Spokane County area. Originally the town was a community of truck garden tracts.

GREENWATER

Greenwater River is a tributary of the White River. The town was named for the waterway.

The river was noted as Smalocho by Lieutenant Robert E. Johnson, a member of the 1841 Wilkes Expedition.

GROTTO

From a distance, many of the deep gorges resemble caves—the reason for the name of this King County town.

GUEMES

Appearing on the island and the channel, the name of Guemes was given in 1791 by the Spanish explorer Eliza. He used the name to honor one of the many names of the viceroy of Mexico, the Conde de Revillagigedo. Officially, he was known as Don Juan Vincente de Guemes Pacheco y Padilla Orcasitees y Aguayo, Conde de Revilla Gigedo.

HADLOCK

Originally known as Port Hadlock, this town on Port Townsend Bay, Jefferson County, honors Samuel Hadlock (1829–1912).

Hadlock built the first steam sawmill at Tacoma in the late 1860s. A decade later, he purchased 400 acres on the bay and, beginning the Washington Mill Company, built a large sawmill here.

In 1886, he laid out the townsite and called it Port Hadlock.

HAMILTON

William Hamilton settled in this Skagit County area in 1877. When the town was incorporated in 1891, it was named for its founder.

HANSON

John Hansen, his wife and his two sons settled here in 1882, and started a ferry.

In 1890, Hansen's son Henry, the first postmaster, named the town Hanson Ferry. The change in spelling took place at the time of the post office establishment. One would hope that Henry Hansen knew how to spell his own name.

HANSVILLE

Hansville is a resort community on Kitsap Peninsula in Kitsap County. Its name came from an early settler, Hans Zachariason.

HARPER

F. C. Harper, then a state senator, helped establish a post office at this Kitsap County location in 1902. The town was named after him, though a number of townspeople preferred the local name: Terra Vaughn.

HARRAH

A reservation town in Yakima County, Harrah was established in 1913 as Saluskin, for Chief Saluskin of the Yakimas.

Two years later, the name was changed to Harrah for J. T. Harrah, who operated the area's largest ranch and was the community's main source of revenue. Until he died in 1917, Chief Saluskin angrily opposed the business pressure that changed the name. He referred to the town as "Thief Town."

HARRINGTON

"Corporation farming" was started on a small scale at Harrington, Lincoln County, in 1882. After the railroad came in, the California Land Company greatly enlarged its holdings. By 1904, it had nearly 25 sections of wheatland in cultivation.

The original townsite was owned by a combine led by Horace Cutter. Cutter's wife was a close friend of the Harrington family, of which W. P. Harrington, a banker from Colusa, California, was the leading member.

Harrington made some critical investments in this Lincoln County area and, when it came time for Mrs. Cutter to select a name, she decided to honor Harrington.

HARTLINE

Hartline bears the surname of the town's promoter, John Hartline. An earlier settlement here was called Parnell after an old settler.

HATTON

The original name for Hatton, Adams County, was Two (or Twin) Wells. When the post office was established in 1888, postal authorities asked for a new name.

At the request of the railroad superintendent, J. D. Hackett asked town leaders for suggestions. One was Sutton. According to local legend, the superintendent took the first two letters of Hackett's name and the last four letters of Sutton and conjured up Hatton. Another source mentions that Hackett's wife, Belle, was born Sutton and was the town's first postmistress. That seems like a more logical scenario.

HAVILAH

Postmaster Martin H. Schweikert selected this name for his Okanogan County community in 1905. Schweikert, who also ran the store and a gristmill, picked the name from the Bible, Gen. 2:5–11.

HAY

During the blizzard of 1892 and 1893, the railroad siding at this Whitman County site was listed as "hay station." A large quantity of hay had been shipped here to feed the cattle. As a community developed, the reference became the town's name.

HAZEL

Because of the abundance of hazel trees, this town received its name. Another source suggests the name was given by P. D. McMartin, a pioneer, on whose land the town was situated. He was supposed to have named the town in honor of his first-born.

HEISSON

Alexander and Marie Heisson were German immigrants who settled here in Clark County in 1867.

HIGH POINT

High Point, King County, was founded by John Lovegreen in 1905. He named it because it was located at a particularly steep grade on the railroad.

HOBART

When the post office was opened at this King County location in 1888, it was named Hobart for some important person—whose fame quickly became forgotten.

HOCKINSON

The people of this Clark County community used the name of an early Swedish settler, Ambrosius Hokanson, for their own. Unfortunately, they anglicized his name. Hockanson was the first postmaster when the office was established in 1884.

HOLDEN

Holden takes its name from the Holden mines, staked out in 1892 by James Henry Holden. Holden struck it rich in copper, gold and zinc four years later, and established the Howe Sound Mining Company. After the mine closed, the Lutheran Church purchased the property and turned it into a religious retreat village.

HOLLY

Robert Wyatt named this community in 1895 for a large holly tree that stood near the town's new post office.

HOODSPORT

Hoodsport, Mason County, takes its name from its location on the Hood Canal.

Hood Canal, originally Hood's Canal—the apostrophe and "s" were removed by the U. S. Geographic Board—was named by Vancouver in 1792 for Samuel, Lord Hood. Vancouver also honored that British naval officer in naming the beautiful mountain in Oregon, Mount Hood.

The Twana Indians originally called the townsite Slat-atl-atl-tul-hu.

HOOGDAL

Early Swedish settlers named this Skagit County site for their home district, Ytter-Hogdahl.

HOOPER

One of the earliest settlers to this Whitman County site was Albert J. Hooper. The Oregon Railway & Navigation Company named the town in his honor in about 1883.

HOQUIAM

Hoquiam takes its name from the river. The name, it has been suggested, comes from the Indian *Ho-qui-umpts,* "hungry for wood." The reference is that great amounts of driftwood could be gleaned at the river's mouth.

The city was settled in 1859 by James Karr and his family. (See ABERDEEN, Washington.)

HUMPTULIPS

Humptulips, Grays Harbor County, takes its name from its river. The name is drawn from the Indian and means either "hard to pole" or "chilly region." Both names are apt for the river.

HUNTERS

Both this town in Stevens County and a creek which flows into the Columbia River bear the name of James Hunter, the first white settler in the area.

HUNTSVILLE

Huntsville, Columbia County, was founded as a site for an academy by the members of the United Brethren Church.

With John Fudge, B. J. Hunt donated 90 acres to the school, which opened in 1879.

HUSUM

When this Kittitas County village was established in 1880, the majority of the settlers had migrated here from Husum, Germany.

HYAK

This name is Chinook slang for "hurry," and appears on a town, a lake and a creek.

ILIA

Ilia, Garfield County, began in 1879, when E. L. Hemingway obtained 50 acres and built a warehouse.

ILWACO

Ilwaco, Pacific County, was named for El-wah-ko Jim, a local Indian. The Indian was quite intelligent, the story goes, and quite proud of his wife who, he said, was the daughter of a chief.

Before it became Ilwaco, the town was known as Unity.

INCHELIUM

The name for this Ferry County site was adapted from the Indian word for "surrounded by water."

INDEX

This Snohomish County town took its name from Index Rock, a rock formation that resembled a pointing index finger.

INDIANOLA

The name is a combination of "Indian" and a Latin-like ending of "ola." This was a popular practice when people thought all place names should end in "a."

When originally established by a real estate developer in 1916, this Kitsap County community was called Indianola Beach. The name was given, we are told, because the land was originally part of an allotment granted to a member of the Port Madison tribe. When Indianola Beach was submitted to them, postal authorities rejected the name and called the post office Kitsap, after the chief. In the late 1950s, the name was changed to conform to local usage: Townspeople had always called the community Indianola.

IONE

Ione, Pend Oreille County, was named in 1896, for Ione Morrison. She was the niece of the town's first postmaster and the daughter of the second.

IRBY

Irby, Lincoln County, was named for an old settler, John Irby. Irby later moved away to Wenatchee.

IRONDALE

When the Western Steel Company decided to build an iron works on Port Townsend Bay here, the townspeople decided to name the town in honor of the iron bogs in the area. When the blast furnace went into operation, it produced pig iron . . . from Chinese ore! The company did not last long at this site.

ISSAQUAH

When the Seattle Pacific & Lakeshore Railroad extended its line to Squah Mountain in the late 19th century, this caused a coal-mining boom and the settlement of the King County town of Squak, then Gilman, Olney and Englewood. In 1899, the town's name was changed to Issaquah.

The word, *isquowh,* is Indian, but . . .

JARED

Robert P. Jared opened a store in about 1908 at this Pend Oreille County location.

J

JOHNSON

The site for this Whitman County town was purchased in 1877 by Jonathan Johnson. A post office opened under that name 11 years later.

JOYCE

The first postmaster of this Clallam County site in 1913 was J. M. Joyce. In addition to assuring the prompt delivery of mail, Joyce also ran a store, a shingle mill and a farm.

JUANITA

When the first post office opened at this King County site, the postmaster was Martin W. Hubbard. He named the town after himself. But that was not to last. The Hubbard post office closed in 1905, and the place became a summer resort area called Juanita. No one knows where that name was drawn from, but it was in place in 1921 when the townsite was platted.

KAHLOTUS

Kahlotus is an Indian word which, according to local tradition, means "hole in the ground."

The original name for this Franklin County town was Hardersburg, but postal authorities complained about the length of the word, so Mr. Harder was forgotten.

KALAMA

After marrying the daughter of a Nisqually chief, John Kalama, a native of Hawaii, settled in this Cowlitz County area. Kalama was founded in the 1840s and named for him. One authority contends that a land claim was made in 1847 by a Mr. Burbee.

Other sources think the word is Calumet Indian and means either "stone" or "pretty maiden." Still another suggests the name was given in 1871 by General J. W. Sprague of the Northern Pacific Railroad.

KANASKAT

This King County community carries the name of the Indian chief who was killed by federal troops, commanded by Lieutenant William A. Slaughter, during the 1855–56 Indian Wars.

KAPOWSIN

The name of the lake and the town in Pierce County is definitely of Indian origin, and has appeared on maps as Kipowsin and Kapousen.

The first name of the town was Hall, but that was changed in 1903.

KELLER

In 1898, J. C. Keller took advantage of a placer mining boom in Ferry County. He opened a store in a tent!

Keller also opened the first store in Republic. While in Republic, he referred to the other place as "Keller" and the name stuck. Then some miners platted a town a mile or so up the Sanpoil River and called that Keller. On the old site, R. L. Boyle incorporated the town and called it Harlinda, but postal authorities would not recognize that name and Keller remained.

KELSO

Kelso, Cowlitz County, is known as the "Smelt Capital of the World."

The town was named by Peter W. Crawford, who came from Kelso, Scotland. Crawford platted the town in 1884.

KENMORE

This King County town was named in 1901 by John McMaster, a leader in the shingle industry, for his hometown in Kenmore, Ontario, Canada. The Canadian town, by the way, adopted the name of the village on the River Tay in Scotland.

KENNWICK

Kennwick, Benton County, was a wasteland of bunchgrass until the late 19th century when a series of irrigation projects transformed it into fruitful farmland. The arrival of the Northern Pacific Railroad did not hurt either.

Because of the short winter here, the town was named after the Indian for "winter paradise." Another source contends that the name came from *kin-i-wack*, "grassy place." The name was given in 1883 by H. S. Huson of the Northern Pacific Irrigation Company.

A bridge across the Columbia River was opened here in 1887.

KENT

Unlike Oregon's Kent, where the name was drawn from a hat, this town took the name of the county in England. In both areas, hops were being produced. Another source contends that the name came from Ezra Meeker, a pioneer writer-promoter and the area's largest hops grower.

Located in King County, Kent was originally two separate communities. One, platted in 1884, was known as Yessler, for Henry

L. Yesler, Seattle's first sawmill operator. The other was called Titusville because the land was owned by James H. Titus, but was platted in 1888 by John Alexander and Ida L. Guiberson.

KETTLE FALLS

The name of this town, taken from the falls and river, has nothing to do with a cooking utensil. The word "kettle" is a mistaken translation of the Salish Indian words, *Ilth-kape*, "basket tightly woven," and *Hoy-ape*, "net." This was a reference to the way tribal members used to catch fish. Kettle Falls was on the maps as early as 1825.

Fort Colville was located here.

KEYPORT

O. A. Kuppler, H. B. Kuppler and Pete Hagen constructed the first wharf at this Kitsap County locale. When it was completed in 1896, the trio took an atlas and looked for a name for their new settlement. They finally decided on the name of a town on the coast of New Jersey.

KEYSTONE

Keystone, located in Adams County, was named in 1900 or 1901 by the town's first postmaster, John W. Smith. Smith was a native of Pennsylvania, the "Keystone State."

KINGSTON

The town planners, Mr. & Mrs. C. C. Calkins, were the principals of the Kingston Land Development Company. The name was adopted in 1890.

KIONA

Local tradition has it this Benton County town's name is Indian for "brown hills."

The original name for the town was Horseshoe Bend, because of the resemblance to the bend in the Yakima River.

KIRKLAND

Kirkland, King County, was named for Peter Kirk. Kirk was a millionaire iron maker from England. He founded this town in 1886 with hopes of establishing vast ironworks here.

Disappointed in his attempts, he retired to San Juan Island, where he died in 1916.

KITTITAS

Located in Kittitas County, this town takes its name from the county, which borrowed that of the valley, which came from the river. The town was named by H. R. Williams.

The name translates from the Indian to mean "grey gravel bank," "clay gravel valley" or "shoal people." Others think it is an Indian tribal name, *K'tatas*.

Kittitas County was established in 1883, and named for the tribe.

KLICKTAT

Klicktat is located on the Klicktat River near the Oregon state line. The river takes its name from the Indian tribe; the town was named for its location on the river. The mountain in Oregon that bears this name was the point where the tribe sometimes traveled.

The name has been variously translated to mean "robber" or "beyond." It appears on the town, a river, a county, a creek, a glacier, a pass, and a prairie.

Prior to its renaming in 1910, Klicktat was known as Wrights, for L. C. Wrights who settled here in 1890.

KLIPSAN BEACH

Town historians indicate this Pacific County town's name comes from the Indian and means "sunset" beach. It was named in 1912 by Captain Theodore Conick and Captain A. T. Stream, who were posted at the Coast Guard Station located here.

KNAPPTON

Knappton, Pacific County, was named for J. B. Knapp. He operated a sawmill here.

LA CENTER

When this Clark County village was laid out as a river port in 1875, it was on John H. Timmen's land and, of course, good old John called it Timmen's Landing.

As time went on, townsfolk considered the port as a "center" of commerce, and changed the name to signify this.

L

LACEY

Isaac Wood settled this Thurston County area in 1852, and it was known as Woodland. When Wood decided that a post office would enhance the prestige of his community, he entertained the services of his attorney, O. C. Lacey, of Olympia.

Postal officials turned down the Woodland name, indicating that it would duplicate one already in use. The ever resourceful lawyer substituted his own name on the form, and Woodland became Lacey. Records do not indicate that the lawyer charged his client for this service.

LA CONNER

La Conner, Skagitt County, was named in 1869 by the owner of the local trading post after his wife, Louisa Ann Siegfried Conner.

The site was first settled by Alonzo Low in 1867; the post office was then known as Swinomish. Two years later, J. S. Conner bought the trading post and, in 1870, changed the name.

LA CROSSE

This Whitman County community was not named for the game. It was named by two railroad construction engineers who surveyed the first line through the area.

One of the men came from LaCrosse, Wisconsin; the other, from Winona, Minnesota. Two consecutive stations on the Union Pacific are named for their respective home towns.

LA GRANDE

French-Canadians working for the Hudson Bay Company named the 700-foot-deep canyon of the Nisqually River as La Grande, "the big one."

As part of a later land promotion, Judge John McMurray, who owned a large parcel of land here in Pierce County, placed a sign along a roadway in 1904, announcing "Watch The Grand Canyon Grow." The town became known as La Grande, but it was not until a hydroelectric plant opened here in 1912 that the name became official.

LAKE BAY

Lake Bay is the name of a town in Pierce County and a bay on the western shore of Carr Inlet. It was named after Bay Lake, through which a mill race emptied into the bay.

LAKE STEVENS

The lake was called Stevens Lake for Isaac I. Stevens, the first governor of the Washington Territory. When the town was laid out, the names were reversed.

LAMONA

During the winter of 1892–93, J. H. Lamona opened a store in this Lincoln County area. The town later assumed his name.

LAMONT

Located in Whitman County, Lamont carries the name of Daniel Lamont, a vice president of the Northern Pacific Railway Company.

LANGLEY

Langley was founded in 1890. The name could come, as some have said, from that of S. P. Langley, an astronomer and physicist who conducted experiments in the Northwest in 1881. A mountain in California also bears his name.

A more likely choice, however, is Judge J. W. Langley from Seattle. Together with a number of his associates, he helped purchase acreage and organize the town. The townsite was platted by Jacob Anthes in 1890.

LA PUSH

The name for La Push is Chinook slang for "mouth," a reference to a stream. It appears to be a corruption of the French *la bouche*.

LATAH

In retaliation for the defeat of Colonel Steptoe, Colonel George Wright killed about 800 Indian horse soldiers and hanged another large number. The hangings took place in 1858 near a creek which became known as Hangman Creek.

Upset with that name, state legislators changed the name to Latah, "a clumsy corruption of the more euphonious Indian word *Lahtoo*." That word translates to "stream where little fish are caught."

The town of Latah, Spokane County, was settled in the early 1870s by Major R. H. Wimpy. In 1875, the post office established here was called Alpha. That name did not last long, and the name of the creek became that of the town. Latah was platted in 1886.

LAUREL

Laurel, Klickitat County, took its name from the profusion of laurel bushes on the Camas Prairie.

LAURIER

Representatives of the Great Northern Railroad Company named this Ferry County community in 1902 for Sir Wilfred Laurier, premier of Canada.

LAWRENCE

Lawrence, Whatcom County, was named—we are told—for Laura Blankenship, the daughter of the town's sawmill owner. We can only guess that he wanted a boy!

LEADPOINT

This Stevens County site was named for the nearby Electric Point Lead Mine.

LEAVENWORTH

Leavenworth, Chelan County, began as a construction camp for the Great Northern Railroad. It was platted in 1893 by "Captain" Charles F. Leavenworth, nephew of the founder of Leavenworth, Kansas. The town was designed as a Bavarian village.

LEBAM

The founder of Lebam, Pacific County, J. W. Goodell, took his daughter Mabel's name and spelled it backwards.

LELAND

The first woman to settle in this part of Jefferson County was Mrs. Laura E. Andrews. She arrived in 1874. When it came time for a post office to be named, the townspeople sought to honor her. Unfortunately, postal officials could not spell Lealand!

LESTER

This King County community was established in the 1880s by the Dean Sawmill Company, and was called Deans.

About 1891, the name was changed to Lester, in honor of Lester Hansacker. Hansacker was a telegrapher here during the construction of the Northern Pacific Railroad.

LEVEY

Levey, Franklin County, bears the name of C. M. Levey, a vice president of the Northern Pacific Railway Company.

LIBERTY

Liberty was established as Williams Creek in 1880. It is one of the oldest mining towns in the state of Washington. Gus Nelson dubbed it Liberty in 1892.

LILLIWAUP

Lilliwaup is Sokomish or Twana Indian for "inlet." A small bay exists here in Mason County by that name, which makes it redundant like the Rio Grande River.

LINCOLN

Lincoln takes its name indirectly from Abraham Lincoln. The town's name came from the county, established in 1883.

LIND

In 1890, Lind was staked out—four blocks of 16 lots each. The Adams County town was named by the Northern Pacific Railroad Company. No one is sure of the source of the name, but there are three possibilities. The name came from (1) a woman who cooked for the railroaders, (2) an early settler's name, or (3) a reference to Jenny Lind, the Swedish Nightingale.

There was, indeed, a strong Scandinavian influence in the community. When the Nielson brothers platted the town, they arranged that the first letter of each street name would spell out their family name.

LISABEULA

The first postmaster, a man named Butts, was not going to take chances offending his daughters. He named this post office in King County in honor of both of them: Elisa and Beulah. To satisfy his superiors, he shortened the name by dropping the first letter of one and the last letter of the other girl's name.

LITTLEROCK

Littlerock, Thurston County, was named by a Mr. Shumach for a rock "which is shaped by nature for a perfect mounting stone."

LOCKE

Locke, Pend Oreille County, carries the name of the man who founded it.

LOFALL

When the post office was established at this Kitsap County site, the largest landowner was H. Lofall.

LONG (— Beach, —branch, — Lake, —mire, —view)

Long Beach is located at the southern end of Long Beach Peninsula in Pacific County. The peninsula is 28 miles of hard sand beach.

Longbranch, Pierce County, was named for the New Jersey town.

Long Lake, Kitsap County, carries a name that describes the shape of the body of water. The nearby town took that name for its own.

Longview was established as a planned community in 1923. It was first called Gravel because of the abundance of that material. The name later became Francis, then Tuton. Tuton was not acceptable to postal officials who thought people would confuse the name with Luzon, so the name became Longview—a description of "the long view" the townspeople had of the Columbia River.

LOOMIS

The first merchant in this Okanogan County locale was J. A. Loomis.

LOON LAKE

This Stevens County town takes its name from Loon Lake. The lake was named "on account of the large number of loons."

LOPEZ

Lopez shares its name-source with Lopez Island, Lopez Pass and Lopez Sound. All were named in honor of Lopez Gonzales de Haro.

He was the first mate on Eliza's ship. His name is also recalled on Haro Strait, east of the south end of Vancouver Island.

The Wilkes Expedition of 1841 called the island, Chauncy's Island, in honor of Captain Isaac Chauncy, an American naval hero. British Navy Captain Henry Kellet restored the Spanish name in 1847.

LOST CREEK

Lost Creek, Pend Oreille County, takes its name from that waterway.

The creek was named because it seems to get lost in part of its course. Another suggestion is that a trapper from the Hudson Bay Company got lost on the creek and was never found.

LOWDEN

Lowden, Walla Walla County, bears the name of a pioneering settler, Francis M. Lowden, Sr. The town was named in his honor in 1899.

LOW GAP

Low Gap, Grant County, was named in 1905 for a gap in Frenchman Hill.

LUCERNE

Lucerne, Chelan County, was named in 1903 by a woman from Switzerland. The Lake Chelan area reminded her of home.

LUMMI

Lummi, Whatcom County, bears an Indian tribal name which it shares with a bay, an island, a point, a river, and rocks.

The Spanish called Lummi Bay Ensenada de Locra in 1792; the island, Isla de Pacheco. The 1841 Wilkes Expedition changed the name to McLaughlin's Island, for Dr. John McLaughlin, chief factor of the Hudson Bay Company at Fort Vancouver. That name was changed to Lummi Island in 1853 "because inhabited by that tribe."

LYLE

Lyle, Klickitat County, bears the name of John O. Lyle, the original owner of the townsite. The town began as a steamboat landing on the Columbia River.

LYMAN

The first postmaster in this Skagit County location was B. L. Lyman. He was appointed in 1880. Four years later, Otto Klement platted the site.

LYNDEN

First settled in the 1860s by miners returning from the 1858 gold rush, Lynden, Whatcom County, became a farming community.

The town was named by Mrs. Phoebe N. Judson in 1870. Mrs. Judson took the name from Thomas Campbell's *Hohenlinden*, the first line of which reads, "Oh Linden, when the sun was low." She changed the spelling because she thought the substitution of the "y" for the "i" made for a prettier word.

In the late 19th- and early 20th-century immigration period, Lynden had the largest Dutch settlement in the state of Washington.

LYNNWOOD

The name for this Snohomish County site was created by combining the first name of Lynn Oburn, wife of one of the town's promoters, and "wood" to connote a sylvan setting.

MABANA

The way J. A. Woodard named this Island County town in 1912 was by taking the first letters of Mabel Anderson's first and last names and adding an "a." The name first appeared on the post office.

Anderson was the daughter of old-time settler Nils Anderson who arrived here in 1881.

MABTON

Like Mabana, Mabton, Yakima County, was named for another Mabel, Mabel Baker Anderson. She was the daughter of railroad builder, Dr. Dorsey S. Baker, of Walla Walla.

MAE

The first postmistress of this Grant County community was Mrs. Mae Shoemaker. J. B. Lee named it in 1907.

MALAGA

Malaga, Chelan County, was named by a farmer and early irrigation system promoter for the Malaga grapes he grew here.

MALDEN

Malden, Whitman County, was established as a division point on the Chicago, Milwaukee & St. Paul Railroad. H. R. Williams, a vice president of the line, named the town after a town by the same name in Massachusetts.

MALONE

Malone, Grays Harbor County, was once a company town of the Vance Lumber Company. Joseph A. Vance named it for a New York community.

MALOTT

This Okanogan County name honors early settler W. G. Malott.

MALTBY

This Snohomish County site was initially homesteaded by a Mr. Dunlap in 1887. The next year a post office was opened under the name of Yew. That was changed a short while later to Maltby in honor of Robert Maltby, a real estate operator.

MANCHESTER

When first established as a lumber- and shingle-mill town in 1883, this Kitsap County location was called Brooklyn. Later, when the town fathers thought it would become a major seaport, they re-named it after the English city.

MANITOU BEACH

For the Algonquins, a *manitou* was a "spirit." The name for this Kitsap County village (with different spellings) has moved away from its Great Lakes origin to several places across the nation.

MANSFIELD

Mansfield, Douglas County, was established as a terminus for the Great Northern Railway. The town was named about 1905 by R. E. Darling. He was honoring his hometown, Mansfield, Ohio.

The Ohio town was named for Colonel Jared Mansfield, surveyor-general of the United States.

MANSON

Manson, located on Lake Chelan, was named in 1912 for Manson F. Backus, of Seattle. Backus was president of the Lake Chelan Land Company.

MANZANITA

This village, located on Bainbridge Island, gets its name from the manzanita shrub, a member of the family that includes arbutus, azalea and rhododendron.

MAPLE FALLS

George A. King, a mill owner in Whatcom County, named his community for the falls of the Maple Creek, where he platted his townsite.

MAPLE VALLEY

The first name that the first settlers, G. W. Ames, C. O. Russell and Henry Sidebotham, selected for this King County community was Vice Maple Valley. A year later, in 1888, when Russell secured a post office for the town, the name was shortened to Maplevalley. The name later reverted to two words.

   The name itself is descriptive of the forest land here.

MARBLE (—mount)

The town of Marble, Stevens County, took its name from the extensive marble deposits found here. Marblemount, Skagit County, received its name in a similar manner; there is marble in the mountains surrounding the town.

MARCELLUS

This Adams County town was named by H. R. Williams, who named a total of 32 places in the state. An executive of the Chicago, Milwaukee & St. Paul Railway, he said some years later that he named it "after some person in the East. I cannot now recall who it was."

MARCUS

The founder of the town of Marcus, Stevens County, was none other than Marcus Oppenheimer.

Oppenheimer and W. V. Brown took possession of several buildings abandoned by the British Boundary Commission in 1863. After Brown's death, Oppenheimer filed a homestead and named the community after himself.

Marcus, though the oldest town in the county, was relocated north of its original site because of backwater from the Coulee Dam.

MARENGO

Marengo, Columbia County, was laid out as a town in 1877. It took its name from Louis Raboin, who was known locally as "Marengo." That is one story.

Another has it that the town was named by H. R. Williams for the battle of Marengo in Italy. In that 1800 battle, Napoleon's forces defeated the Austrians.

MARIETTA

Solomon Allen platted this Whatcom County town in 1883, and adapted the names of his wife and daughter into the town's corporate name. Both women were named Mary. (See MARYHILL, Washington.)

MARSHALL

Located in Spokane County, Marshall bears the name of William H. Marshall who arrived in the Washington Territory from California in 1878. He must have been quite influential: The town was named for him in 1880.

MARYHILL

Maryhill, Klickitat County, was selected by Samuel Hill in 1907 as the site of his estate. Hill, an eccentric lawyer and Quaker pacifist, was the builder of both the International Peace Arch at Blaine and the Columbia Scenic Highway on the Oregon side of the Columbia River Gorge.

Hill also built a concrete replica of Stonehenge, Wiltshire, England, as a memorial to the men of Klickitat who died in World War I. The town's founder is buried beneath the stone.

Originally known as Columbus, the town's name was changed at the suggestion of one of Hill's guests, the French ambassador to the United States. The ambassador noticed that Hill's mother, wife and daughter were named Mary. (See MARIETTA, Washington.)

MARYSVILLE

J. P. Comeford, the Indian agent at the Tulalip Reservation, bought land here in Snohomish County in 1872. Five years later, he built a store and wharf on Ebey Slough.

Among the first settlers were James Johnson and Thomas Lloyd. The two suggested the new community be named Marysville for their old hometown of Marysville, California.

MATLOCK

The original name for this Mason County community was Mason. It was renamed in the late 19th century by James Hodkinson for his home in England.

MATTAWA

Mattawa bears a name that translates from the Indian to mean "Where is it?" Of couse, we know it is in Grant County. The town is built on the site of the old Priest Rapids, which was platted in 1909.

MAY CREEK

May Creek, a village in King County, was named for a Mr. May, who was the first to begin homesteading on the land here.

MAZAMA

The name of this town is Spanish for "mountain goat." The name, one authority maintains, was supplied by a mountaineering club in 1899.

Another source, which we think is more on target, states that the community was originally known as Goat Creek. When the post office was established at this Okanogan County location in 1899, the townspeople thought they had selected the Greek word for "mountain goat." Sadly, their geography was a little off. The word does mean "mountain goat," but it is Spanish.

McCLEARY

Henry McCleary was president of the Henry McCleary Timber Company in 1910. The next year, when the post office was moved here from Summit, the name was changed to McCleary.

McGOWEN

This Pacific County community bears the name of Patrick J. McGowen, an early settler. In 1853, McGowen purchased 320 acres of an old Catholic mission land grant and created a salmon-packing plant. This area was once the principal village on the Columbia River of the Chinook Indians.

McKENNA

McKenna, Pierce County, took the name of a resident who built a sawmill here in 1906.

McMILLAN

The first name for McMillan, Pierce County, was Lime Kiln. The name was officially changed in 1891 by John S. McMillan when he platted the townsite around his lime company's office.

McMURRAY

Dr. Marcus Kenyon platted this Skagit County town in 1890 when the railroad arrived. He named it to honor an early settler.

MEAD

James Berridge named this Spokane County community in honor of Civil War General George Gordon Meade. Somewhere along the way, postal authorities dropped the "e".

MEDICAL LAKE

The town of Medical Lake, Spokane County, takes its name from the body of water of the same name. Andrew Lefevre was the first settler in the mid-19th century.

The Indians believed the water from the lake contained the cure for rheumatism.

MEDINA

Mrs. S. A. Belote named this place in 1892 after the holy place by the same name in Saudi Arabia, where the prophet Mohammed is buried.

This town, located on the eastern shore of Lake Washington, was named by Mrs. Belote in 1892.

MEGLER

Joseph Megler operated a fish cannery on the Columbia River. He was a frequent member of the state legislature . . . and the donor of the name for this Pacific County location.

MENLO

Menlo, Pacific County, was originally a flag station on the Northern Pacific Railway named Preston. The station was built on land owned by Lindley Preston.

About a mile south of the station, John Brophy held an option on some land he wanted to develop. Assuming the name of Menlo Park, California, he erected a big sign calling attention to the sale of homesites.

The construction crew for the railroad, learning that Preston had already been used for a stop, purloined Brothy's sign, and chopped off the "Park." (See MENLO PARK, California.)

MERCER ISLAND

The first president of the Territorial University (University of Washington) at Seattle in 1861 was Asa Mercer. Mercer once owned land in this King County area. He was also the man who brought the Mercer Girls, the contingent of husband-seekers, to Seattle from the East Coast.

Another source disagrees with that logic. The name came, it is contended, from Judge Thomas Mercer, who led a wagon train into Seattle in 1853. He also named Lake Washington and Lake Union.

The Indians called the place Klut-use.

MESA

The name for Mesa, Franklin County, was the creation of the Northern Pacific Railway. It is Spanish for "table-land," even though this town is located on flat land surrounded by hills.

MESKILL

Another railroad stop, Meskill, Lewis County, was once called Donahue or Donahue Spur, for Francis Donahue, who owned the land.

METALINE (— Falls)

Metaline Falls was founded in 1849 by prospectors on the Pend Oreille River who thought the entire district was covered with minerals. The original town was across the river from the present-day town, which was established in 1909.

METHOW

Methow took its name from that of an Indian tribe. It is also the name of a river, rapids, and this town. The spelling of the name has gone through many forms over the years. The Indians called the river Buttlemulee-mauch, "salmon falls river."

MICA

Mica, Spokane County, and Mica Peak derived their names in the same manner. Both were named for the mica deposits located here by early miners.

MIDLAND

The naming of this Pierce County community is logical: Midland was the middle station on the Tacoma-Puyallup electric rail line in the late 19th century.

MILAN

One of the construction workers on the Great Northern Railroad crew who built the station at this Spokane County site in 1890 came from Milan, Italy.

MILES

Miles, Lincoln County, was named for General Nelson A. Miles. The general was responsible for locating Fort Spokane at the mouth of the Spokane and Columbia rivers.

MILL CREEK

There are 11 counties in the state that have streams with this name. The waterways' names came from the presence of a mill, usually a sawmill, along the way.

MILLWOOD

When an electric railway station was located here, the Spokane County site was known as Woodward, for Seth Woodward who settled in the valley in 1883. The name was changed in 1910 when a saw mill was established.

MILTON

This Pierce County community name is a contraction of what it was, a "mill town."

MINERAL

In Lewis County, a town, a creek and a lake are all called Mineral. The town is located on Mineral Lake from which it took its name. In 1857, the body of water was called Goldsboro Lake.

The area was rich in ore deposits, specifically red realgar, from which arsenic is drawn.

MOCLIPS

The name for Moclips came from the Quinault Indian place where young girls were sent at the time of the puberty rite. In New Jersey, the rite is commemorated in the name of Crosswicks.

MOHLER

The Great Northern developed this Lincoln County area as a siding in 1892, but the town did not see much development until after the turn of the 20th century.

The name comes from Morgan Mohler. He drove a mail-stage coach.

MOLD

The name of Mold, Douglas County, was given because the soil was rich. In 1899, postmaster Marshall McLean selected the name for that reason—and also because it was different from any other in the state. Since we have been unable to find another town by this name, perhaps they broke the . . .

MOLSON

Molson, Okanogan County, took the name of John W. Molson, a Canadian businessman. Molson had mining interests in the area, but never visited them.

MONITOR

Reuben A. Brown settled here in 1884, and named this Chelan County locale after himself. By the time the town grew, and established a post office in 1902, the consensus of a name shifted.

George T. Richardson, a town leader, suggested the name of the Union's iron-clad *Monitor* over the Confederacy *Merrimac*.

MONROE

Salem Wood (or Woods) attempted to establish the town of Park Place at this Snohomish County location in 1878. He liked that name because it was descriptive of the area.

In 1889, John A. Vanasdlen arrived and opened a store. When he established the post office, he was told he could not call it Park Place. He quickly decided on Monroe. No one knows why he made that selection.

When the Great Northern Railway came through the valley, Vanasdlen platted another town about a mile east of the old Park Place and called it Tye, for a railroad engineer. When a station was built, railroad officials called it Tye-Wales. Vanasdlen moved his post office there and got the railroad to change the name of the station to Monroe to agree with the post office.

MONSE

The little community of Swansea, Okanogan County, decided to change its name in 1914. The name they selected commemorated Mons, Belgium, where the British had fought the first battle of World War I two years earlier.

MONTBORNE

Montborne, Skagit County, bears the name of one of the original settlers, Dr. H. P. Montborne of Mount Vernon. He arrived in 1884. At one point, the place's name was spelled Mt. Bourne.

MONTE CRISTO

Monte Cristo, named in 1889, took its title from a local mine. The mine was named for the popular novel by Alexandre Dumas, *The Count of Monte Cristo*. Because of the book, the name was associated with great riches.

The naming of this Snohomish County locale took place in 1889, when Joseph Pearsall and Frank W. Peabody climbed over the hills and saw evidence of large mineral deposits. One of them threw his hands in the air and cried: "It is as rich as Monte Cristo!" Authorities vary on who did the shouting.

Monte Cristo's main street was named Dumas after the author.

MONTESANO

Montesano, Grays Harbor County, was founded in the mid-19th century near the confluence of the Chehalis and Wynoochee Rivers.

The first settler was Isaiah L. Scammon who arrived from Maine in 1852. When it came time for naming, Mrs. Lorinda Scammon, who was something of a religious zealot, suggested Mount Zion. The name was not accepted, but Samuel James came up with a similar-sounding name, Montesano, which is Italian for "healthful mountain."

A few years later, a number of investors bought some acreage on Medcalf Prairie and recorded their new town as Montesano. The old Scammon site became known as South Montesano.

MOORE

Located on the eastern shore of Lake Chelan, Morre was named for J. Robert Moore, who operated a summer hotel at Moore's Point for many years. He was also the town's first postmaster.

MORTON

When this Lewis County community established its first post office, they named it for Vice President Levi P. Morton. Morton, from Vermont, was in office the year Washington was granted its statehood.

MOSES LAKE

The community of Moses Lake took its name from the body of water. Chief Moses and his tribe used the banks of the lake for camping grounds. A post office was opened under that name in 1906.

MOSSYROCK

Mossyrock, located in Lewis County, was named in 1852 by a Mr. Halland for a point of moss-covered rock that jutted about 200 feet into the sky at the east end of Klickitat Prairie.

MOUNT BAKER

Mount Baker, Whatcom County, took its name from the 10,778-foot mountain of the same name. The mountain was named by Vancouver in 1792 for a lieutenant on his staff who first sighted the peak. Lieutenant Joseph Baker married a niece of Admiral Vashon (for whom Vashon Island was named) and fathered three sons, an admiral, a captain and a general!

The mountain's original name, by the way, was La Grande Montana del Carmelo. The Indians called it Kulshan.

MOUNT VERNON

Mount Vernon, Skagit County, was named in 1877 by Harrison Clothier and E. C. English in memory of George Washington's home in Virginia.

MOXEE CITY

In the early 20th century there was a Dutch community here. Pioneers accepted the Indian name. It means "whirlwinds" and refers to the dust spirals that appear frequently in the area.

MUKILTEO

Mukilteo, Indian for "good camping ground," was the 1855 site of the Point Elliott Treaty. By signing the document, leaders of 22 Indian nations gave up their land rights to white settlers.

   The first settlers at what was then called Point Elliott were J. D. Fowler and Morris H. Frost—partners in a store. Fowler became postmaster in 1862 and renamed the town to its Indian name.

NACHES

Naches is a name that appears on a town in Yakima County, a pass, a river, a canyon, and a valley.

   The word has gone through various spellings, such as Nachchese (1853), Wachess (1857), Nahcheess (1859), and its current form. The only translation for it, we have found, is the Indian *nahchess*, "plenty of water."

NAHCOTTA

Nahcotta, Pacific County, was named in the 1880s by John P. Paul for a local Indian chief who camped in front of his home.

NAPAVINE

When Napavine was named by James Urquhart in 1883, the name was taken from a local Indian word, *napavoon*, meaning "small prairie." Urquhart settled here in 1855.

NASELLE

This town, located in Pacific County, takes its name from the river. The original name for both was Nasel, after the Nasal Indians, a branch of the Chinook tribe.

NEAH BAY

Spanish settlers, the first non-Indians to visit Washington, landed in Neah Bay in 1791. They established a fort here that lasted about five months. A Japanese ship, wrecked off the coast of Cape Flattery, brought the first Orientals to the area in 1834.

The name came from that of a Makan Chief Dee-ah.

NEILTON

When first founded by Neil A. Jones, this Grays Harbor County community was known as Jonesville. In the 1920s, the name was changed to Neilton—for the same individual. Postal officials were worried there were too many towns across the nation with his surname.

NEMAH

Nemah is located on the site of an old Indian village of the same name. There have been several different spellings of the name over the years, but no definition can be found.

NESPELEM

Nespelem is the name of an Indian tribe, a river, a canyon, a bar, rapids, and a town. It was near here—Colville Indian Reservation— that Chief Joseph lived until his death in 1904.

The name is translated as either "a large, open meadow beside a stream" or "it, the flat land."

NEWAUKUM

Newaukum is a tributary of the Chehalis River, as well as a prairie and this town in Lewis County.

Before the territory changed hands, the Puget Sound Agricultural Company farmed this area and called it Nawakum as early as 1849. The present river name was charted in 1856.

The name, we are told, comes from the Indian vernacular and means "gently flowing waters."

NEWCASTLE

Newcastle, King County, received its name from a careless remark made by a miner. The miners felt that the coal vein extended to near Lake Washington, though they were digging a mile and a half further west. In 1869, the Reverend George F. Whitworth, J. E. Whitworth and F. H. Whitworth attempted to prove their contention.

After tracing the vein, they found they were right. If we dig here, they said, we won't be carrying coals to New Castle. That became the name of the mine . . . and the subsequent town.

NEWHALEM

Newhalem, Whatcom County, was named for the Newhalem Creek. The creek meets the Skagit River at this point. The name is a corrupted form of *ne-whalem*, "goat snare."

NEWMAN LAKE

Newman Lake, Spokane County, takes its name from, of all things, a body of water of the same name. Newman Lake was named for a French-Canadian farmer who lived near here. The town's original name was Moab, but postal authorities requested a name change to avoid confusion with a place by that name in Utah.

NEWPORT

Newport is the county seat of Pend Oreille County. When the first steamboat was put into river service, a new landing site was selected, and M. C. Kelly suggested that it be the "new port."

NIGHTHAWK

Nighthawk, Okanogan County, took its name from a nearby mine, which was named for a relative of the whippoorwill.

NINE MILE FALLS

In 1904, this town was called Helen for the female member of a pioneer family. Eight years later the name was changed to Nine Mile Falls for one of several power dams on the Spokane River. The town is located roughly nine miles from the falls or spillway on the river.

NOOKSACK

Nooksack takes its name from the Indian tribe. It also appears as the name of a river.

Nook or *Nooh* means "people," and *sa-ak*, "edible root of bracken or fern." The name refers to what this particular tribe of Indians ate. Another source refers to the tribe as the "mountain men."

NORDLAND

When, in about 1890, they were getting around to naming this town in Jefferson County, they commemorated Peter Nordby, a local land-owner.

NORMANDY PARK

Normandy Park, King County, was developed in the 1920s by the Seattle-Tacoma Land Company. The name was in keeping with the planned architecture, French Normandy.

This was not the case with a planned development in Northeast Philadelphia. That development, called Normandy, was a play on the developer's name: Norman Denny.

NORTH BEND

North Bend was a lumbering community in King County when originally settled. Its name is drawn from its location, where the South Fork of the Snoqualmie River bends to the north.

When William H. Taylor platted the site in 1889, he called it Snoqualmie, but he could not use that name for long. There was another town of that name closer to the river falls. Other names it bore include Mountain View and South Fork.

NORTH BONNEVILLE

North Bonneville—there is no "Bonneville" in Washington State, but there is one in Oregon—was named for Captain Benjamin Louis Eulalie Bonneville, a French-born American officer who explored vast portions of the Northwest in the early 1830s.

His exploits are recalled in Washington Irving's 1837 *The Adventures of Captain Bonneville, U.S.A., in the Rocky Mountains and the Far West.*

Other names for this Skamania County site include Hamilton, Moffett Springs, Table Rock, Wacomac, and Moffetts. With the construction of the Bonneville Dam, the town's luck improved and its name was changed to capitalize on its location on the north side of the dam. (See BONNEVILLE, Oregon.)

NORTHPORT

Northport, Stevens County, was named because it was the most northern United States town on the Columbia River. The town was platted in 1892 as a smelter site.

OAKESDALE

The town of Oakesdale, Whitman County, has nothing to do with the product of tiny acorns.

Oakesdale was named in 1886 for Thomas F. Oakes who was a vice president of the Northern Pacific Railroad Company and a member of the board of directors of the Oregon-Washington Railroad & Navigation Company.

OAK HARBOR

Oak Harbor, Island County, is the largest town—and second oldest settlement—on Whidbey Island. It takes its name from the white oak trees found here. Many of the first settlers here were Dutch.

OAKVILLE

Oakville, Grays Harbor County, was named—like Oak Harbor—for the oak trees hereabouts. In this case, the oaks were scrubs.

OCEAN CITY

Ocean City, Pacific County, is basically that: a town on the Pacific Ocean!

OCEAN PARK

When Isaac Alonzo Clark, the founder of Oysterville, bought land on the ocean shore in Pacific County, he asked the Reverend A. Atwood, presiding elder of the Methodist Episcopal Church, to help him organize a camp-meeting and resort. Atwood sought the help of the Reverend William R. Osborne, who founded Ocean Grove in New Jersey. The group then brought their dreams to reality.

OCEAN SHORES

Ocean Shores, Grays Harbor County, is a real estate development of the mid-20th century. It was promoted as a year-round resort and tourist center.

OCOSTA

The name for this Grays Harbor County town was coined in 1891. The namers, Mrs. George E. Filley and the Honorable William H. Calkins, took the Spanish *costa*, "coast," and added an "o" for euphony.

Before that, the Indians called it Nushiatska.

ODESSA

The Great Northern Railway built Odessa as a siding in 1892, but the Lincoln County town did not see any growth until the turn of the 20th century.

The first group of settlers were wheat growers who came from Russia, which explains the source of the name. The name was given by officials of the Great Northern Railway.

OHOP

The name Ohop appears on a town, a lake and a creek in Pierce County. The creek and lake were marked Ow-hap River and Ow-hap Lake in 1857. The name, we are told, is from the Indian *owhap*, "water rushing out."

OKANOGAN

The Okanogan River is located near the Canadian border, and its name translates to "meeting place" or "rendezvous."

The site was first visited by General G. W. Goethals, chief engineer of the Panama Canal. He camped here in 1883 while exploring the Pacific Northwest.

In 1888, a town was established as Alma. It became Pogue in 1905, and finally Okanogan, after its county, in 1907. Okanogan County was named for the river, which was borrowed from the name of an Indian tribe.

OLALLA

Olallie is Chinook slang for "berry," a reference here to huckleberries. Apparently the Olallie Creek and this town in Kitsap County share the same name origin. The area was settled by Scandinavian strawberry growers.

OLGA

The first postmaster of this San Juan County town named it after his mother.

OLYMPIA

Olympia, Thurston County, is the state capital. Settlers arrived at Budd Inlet in the 1840s and started a community called Smithfield. Michael T. Simmons, who served as an official for Clark and Lewis counties under the provisional government, was a part of that first settling group, arriving in 1844. He and his family settled at the edge of what is now Olympia and called their village New Market, later Tumwater. The Indians who were here first called it Stichas, "bear's place."

Located at the southern tip of Puget Sound, Olympia is one of the oldest communities in the Pacific Northwest.

The city's name is drawn from the Olympic Mountains whose highest peak is Mount Olympus, a name obviously drawn from the mythical home of the Greek gods. The Spanish, who first saw the mountain, did not think in those terms.

In 1774, Captain Juan Perez named the mountain El Cero de la Santa Rosalia. That name lasted until four years later when Captain John Meares, sailing with Vancouver, came up with the mythologic name.

An interesting sidelight to Olympia's history is that the original wagon train was turned away from Fort Vancouver because it contained one free-born Negro, George Bush.

OMAK

The Indian *omak* means "good medicine." Does that have anything to do with the fact that apple growing is this area's prime industry?

Omak, the largest city in Okanogan County, was platted in an alfalfa field in 1907.

ONALASKA

The first time this name appeared as a place name was in 1851, when T. G. Rowe, founder of a town in Wisconsin, decided on the name. He took it from Thomas Campbell's *Pleasures of Hope*, in which was written, "The wolf's long howl from Oonalaska's shore." The reference was not to Washington State, but to an Alaskan village. He liked the name and modified the spelling, of course.

Later, when Rowe became heavily involved in lumbering, he founded the Carlisle Lumber Company. Wherever he extended his operations, he named the towns Onalaska!

OPPORTUNITY

The Modern Irrigation & Land Company held a contest in 1905 for the name of a new town created by an irrigation project. The winner was Opportunity, and its winner, Miss Laura Kelsey, received a ten-dollar bill!

ORCAS

The name for this town was much abbreviated before it could be placed on an envelope. The name is taken from one of the names of

Viceroy Don Juan Vincente de Guemes Pacheco y Padilla Orcasitees y Aguayo Conde de Revilla Gigedo. In another way, the word *orcas* is Spanish for "grampus."

ORCHARDS

Orchards, Clark County, bears the name of H. M. Orchard, clerk on Vancouver's *Discovery*. Another source disagrees and suggests the village was named because of the vast prune orchards planted here in 1909. The former name was Fourth Plain.

ORIENT

This Ferry County town was named for a local mine. The Orient Gold Mine was so named because the Orient—in fact, anything Eastern—was considered rich. Alexander Ireland did the honor in 1901.

The original town name was Morgan.

ORIN

Orin is named in honor of Orin S. Winslow.

ORONDO

A store and post office was opened here in 1888. Two years later, the town had its own newspaper, the *Orondo News*.

This Douglas County community was named in about 1886 by Dr. J. B. Smith. He was reacting to a postal ruling that the new post office here had to have an unduplicated name.

Smith named it for the "supposed superintendent" of the ancient Lake Superior copper mine. The people of Orondo were thought to be the ancestors of the mound builders "from Lake Superior to the Isthmus where their Atlantis joined America."

OROVILLE

Oroville, Okanogan County, takes its name from the gold that once was discovered here. *Oro* is Spanish for gold.

When the post office was established here in 1892, postal authorities made the town add "-ville" to the name the next year, to keep postal patrons from confusing it with Oso, Snohomish County.

ORTING

Orting was originally called Carbon, but, because of some confusion over nearby Carbonado, its name was changed.

The Indian *orting* means "prairie village." At least that is what the railroad thought in 1878, when they put that name up on their sign.

OSO

When a post office was opened at this Snohomish County site in 1889, it was called Allen, in honor of congressman, later senator, John B. Allen.

When a town in Mason County called itself Allyn, the people changed Allen to Oso, Spanish for "bear." The name was suggested by J. B. Britizius, for a town he knew in Texas.

OSTRANDER

Ostrander, the name for both a creek and a community in Cowlitz County, honors Dr. Nathaniel Ostrander, a local homesteader, who died in 1901.

OTHELLO

This Adams County town was established and named by H. R. Williams, a vice president of the Chicago, Milwaukee & St. Paul Railway Company. The name was derived from the name of Shakespeare's play.

Williams was responsible for other nearby names, such as Corfu, for an island off the Greek coast; Jericho, Joshua's city in biblical Palestine; and Smyrna, a gulf in the Aegean Sea.

OUTLOOK

When a telephone station connected E. W. Dooley's ranch with his home in Yakima, he rejected the idea of using his name for a calling code. Since his ranch "looked out" over a wide expanse of sagebrush, Outlook became the name. The railroad took that name when it built a siding in this Yakima County area.

OYSTERVILLE

The discovery of oyster beds in this Pacific County community by town founders, Isaac Alonzo Clark and R. H. Espy, assisted by Chief Nahcata at Willapa Bay in 1854, led to the growth of Oysterville.

At one point, a plateful of Shoalwater Bay oysters cost $50 in San Francisco! Clark did the honor of naming the town.

OZETTE

Ozette is the name of an Indian reservation, a lake, a town, a creek, and an island. Though we have no idea what the name means, we do find that in 1887 Judge James G. Swan referred to it as the "Lake of the Sun."

The word, we are told, is derived from the southernmost Makah Indian settlement, Ho-selth.

PACIFIC (— Beach)

Pacific, King County, was platted in 1906 as a "real estate addition" to Seattle. The name was meant to connote peace and tranquility.

Pacific Beach, Grays Harbor County, is located on the Pacific Ocean.

PACKWOOD

Packwood Lake and this Lewis County town bear the name of William Packwood, a Virginia pioneer who explored Oregon and Washington in the 1840s. He settled on the Nisqually Flats in 1887.

PAGE

Page, Franklin County, honors an old resident: Dan Page.

PAHA

Local tradition has it that Paha's name is Indian and means "big water," for a natural spring.

The Adams County town originally began as a private project, but failed. The Northern Pacific Railway replatted the town in 1889.

PALISADES

George A. Virtue named this Douglas County town in 1906. He selected it because of the "sharp pointed basaltic rocks" characteristic of the walls of Moses Coulee.

PALMER

Palmer, King County, carries the surname of the first agent in charge of the railway station here.

PALOUSE

The first rendition of this Whitman County name, Palloatpallah, was recorded in the Lewis and Clark records. The name, an Indian tribal one—variously spelled as Pallata-palla, Palus, Palloatpallah, or Pelusha, was apparently altered by French-Canadian trappers. One source thinks the French *pelouse*, meaning grassy expanse, is the real definition.

In Washington, the name appears on the city, a river, a falls, a rapids, and an Indian tribe. The name also appears in Idaho.

PARADISE

Paradise is a much-used name in Mount Rainer Park. It appears on a glacier, a river, a park, a valley, and a town.

PARK

This Whatcom County town was not named for an expanse of lawn. The name honored Charles Park, an early pioneer.

PARKLAND

This Pierce County suburb of Tacoma began in 1890 with the establishment of the Pacific Lutheran Academy. Four years later, a townsite was platted around the school's campus.

PASCO

Pasco, Franklin County's seat, was founded in the late 19th century. Growth came after 1889 when the Northern Pacific Railway moved its round house, car repair shop and coal bunkers to Pasco. When location engineer Virgil Gay Bogue thought of a name, he looked around him and saw a dusty, hot and disagreeable town. He had read of a mean place in Mexico called Pasco, and decided that the two fit together perfectly. Little did he know the town would prosper and grow, and cease to be disagreeable.

Another authority suggests the name was given in contrast to Cerro de Pasco, a cool Peruvian mining community atop a 15,000-foot-high mountain.

Pasco is considered part of the Tri-City Columbia Basin area. The other two towns are Kennewick and Richland.

PATAHA

Pataha comes from the Nez Percé language for "brush creek." The town takes the name of the stream.

Pataha was settled in 1861 by James Bowers, who sold it to his brother-in-law, J. Benjamin Norton. Norton sold it six years later to Angevine June Favor, who platted the town in 1882. The town was also known as Favorsburg and Watertown, but Pataha won over all the others.

Favor was nicknamed Vine and came from Maine. His parents lived in a small town. When the circus came to town for the first time in that town's history, the family was impressed—so impressed that the next day when their baby boy arrived, they named him after the circus company: Angevine, June, Titus & Company!

PATEROS

When this Okanogan County site was first settled, it was called Nosler's Hotel. When the town was established in 1896, the name changed to Nera. Four months later, it was Ive's Landing.

In 1900, Charles E. Nosler, a former Army lieutenant, renamed it Pateros, for a town in the Philippines where he had fought during the Spanish-American War.

PATERSON

Henry Paterson, an early settler, named this Benton County community, established in 1907, for himself.

PE ELL

The name of an early resident was a one-eyed, French half-breed by the name of Pierre who pastured his horses in this Lewis County area. Apparently, Pe Ell is how the local Indians pronounced his name.

The town was platted by Omar Mavermann on his land in the 1880s. He took the name of the Pe Ell Prairie, thinking it was of Indian origin.

PEONE

The name of Peone, a creek, a prairie and a town, came from Chief Peone, leader of the Peone tribe.

PESHATIN

Peshatin, Chelan County, has a name that translates from the Indian to mean "wide bottomed canyon."

PIEDMONT

Piedmont is French for "foot of mountain," and that is how William Dawson named this Clallam County town in 1893.

PILLAR ROCK

The name for this Wahkiakum County village was taken from a rock of that name. In 1805, Lewis and Clark described the rock, but did not give it a name. The 1841 Wilkes Expedition noted it also, but indicated that the name was well established by the time they arrived.

The Indians called it Taluap-tea, for a chief who lived at the falls of the Columbia and who was supposedly turned into a rock.

PINE CITY

The name of Pine City, Whitman County, was in local use when the Chicago, Milwaukee & St. Paul Railway Company came through.

The name came from the proliferation of pine trees in the area.

PLAIN

Postmaster C. F. Rupel suggested this name when the post office was established here in 1913.

The Chelan County town is located on a flat expanse of land, surrounded by mountains.

PLAZA

Plaza is the Spanish word used to indicate a public square or market place. No one knows why this name was given to this Spokane County location. The most logical explanation is that the post office wanted a short name that was not duplicated elsewhere in the state.

PLEASANT VIEW

The town of Pleasant View, bearing a descriptive name, was platted by W. C. Painter in 1894.

PLYMOUTH

Settlers in this Benton County area hoped for a city when the Spokane, Portland & Seattle Railway dug a tunnel through 800 feet of rugged basalt rock here.

The first name, and quite a logical one, was Gibraltar, but that was considered foreign and inhospitable. The more American name, reminder of the Plymouth Rock, was finally the one. The Indians referred to the area as Soloosa.

POINT ROBERTS

Point Roberts received its name from Vancouver, who—once again—honored one of his friends. This time the honoree was Royal

Navy Captain Henry Roberts, "my esteemed friend," as Vancouver wrote, "and predecessor in the *Discovery*."

Vancouver and Roberts had been shipmates on Cook's voyage to the South Pole and on Cook's last voyage. In fact, Roberts attempted valiantly to save Cook's life at Karakakooa Bay in 1779.

POMEROY

Walter Sunderland sold his Garfield County ranch to Joseph M. Pomeroy in 1863, and proceeded to plat out his town in 1878.

Pomeroy, a native of Ashtabula, Ohio, ran a stage coach station and ranch at what is now Dayton.

PORTAGE

Portage, King County, took its name from white settlers' practice of transporting their small boats over the narrow strip of land to reach the other body of water.

PORT ANGELES

Port Angeles was named by Mexican Captain Francisco Eliza in 1791 as Puerto de Neustra Señora de Los Angeles, the "Port of Our Lady of the Angels." The name was later shortened. Eliza was the first non-Indian to see this area.

An interesting sidelight to the history of this town is that it was originally a federal land preserve, set aside by Lincoln in 1862 for lighthouse and military use. A year later, when funds were needed to finance the Union war effort, the government tried to sell off the land—except for a lighthouse site. The sale was not as successful as the government expected, and, in 1894, the U.S. Land Office in Seattle was authorized to sell off the land to the highest bidders.

The first of the "utopian" groups to establish itself in Washington was located here. It had been started by George Venable Smith in 1877. Everything in this Clallam County town was held in common, with no taxes or rents and "free lands, free water, free lights, free libraries." The community prospered for two years, then broke up when its leaders accused each other of fraud.

PORT BLAKELY

This Kitsap County town borrowed its name from Blakely Harbor.

Wilkes named the harbor for Johnston Blakely, a War of 1812 hero.

PORTER

This Grays Harbor community was named in honor of Fairchild Porter, who settled here in 1860.

PORT GAMBLE

Port Gamble, Kitsap County, was established in 1853 as part of the prosperous lumber operation of Pope & Talbot Lumber Company. One of the oldest sawmills in the nation is still in operation at Port Gamble.

The community's name was given in 1841 by the Wilkes Expedition. The name honored Lieutenant Robert Gamble, who was wounded aboard the frigate *President* in a battle with the *Belvidere* during the War of 1812. For a time, the name was Teekalet, Indian for "brightness of the noonday sun."

PORT LUDLOW

Members of the Wilkes Expedition named Port Ludlow in 1841. The name was drawn from that of U. S. Navy Lieutenant Augustus C. Ludlow, who had been killed on the *Chesapeake* while battling with the *Shannon* during the War of 1812.

Prior to becoming Port Ludlow, this Jefferson County community was known as Sna-nul-kwo by the Chimacums and Dos-la-latl by the Skokomish or Twana Indians.

PORT MADISON

Port Madison was named for James Madison, fourth president of the United States and the "Father of the Constitution." The port was named by the Wilkes Expedition in 1841 in association with Point Jefferson and Point Monroe.

The Indians called it Soquamis Bay (1824) and Noo-sohk-um (1855). Old Chief Seattle had his principal place of residence here. His large community home gave rise to the name, Oleman House.

PORT ORCHARD

The seat of Kitsap County, Port Orchard began its life when pioneers built homes on the shoreline of Sinclair Inlet in 1854. They called their settlement Sydney. Port Orchard's name was for George Vancouver's clerk, H. M. Orchard.

Sydney, which honored developer Sydney Stevens, was renamed in 1903 for the harbor, which was named for its discoverer.

PORT TOWNSEND

Port Townsend occupies a strategic location at the entrance of Puget Sound. The name came from Fort Townsend, an Army post that was built in 1856 to protect settlers. The military installation was destroyed by fire in 1895 and abandoned.

There were settlers here before the military arrived, notably Charles Bachelder and Alfred A. Plummer, who arrived in 1851.

The port was named by Vancouver in 1792 "after the noble Marquis of that name." The correct spelling of that chap's name, however, is Townshend.

POULSBO

Poulsbo, Kitsap County, is not one of those place names that resulted from a typographical error or a particular pronunciation. The name is derived from the Norwegian and means "Paul's Place." Another source contends that the name came from a place in Norway. In fact, it is suggested that the name was given in 1883 by I. B. Moe, a Norwegian settler.

Norwegians settled at the head of Liberty Bay in 1882 and 1883 and developed fishing and farming interests. When they first arrived, they thought the area resembled a fjord.

PRAIRIE

Prairie, Skagit County, was named for its location.

PRESCOTT

Prescott's name came from that of the general superintendent of the Oregon-Washington Railroad & Navigation Company, C. W. Prescott. Prescott picked this community as the site for the railroad's division yards.

This Walla Walla County town was named in 1881, and platted a year later.

PRESTON

Along with D. H. Gilman and others, William T. Preston helped build the Seattle Lake Shore & Eastern Railway. This King County site later became a branch of the Northern Pacific. The name was given in 1888 in Preston's honor.

PRIEST RAPIDS

Priest Rapids is the head of navigation for this area of the Columbia River. This Grant County town took its name from the rapids of the river. Alexander Ross gave the name in 1811 when he was part of the Astoria party. He honored a local Wanapum medicine man, or priest, who greeted the explorers with religious rites that included smoking a peace pipe.

PROEBSTEL

Proebstel, Clark County, took its name from an early pioneer, John Proebstel.

PROSSER (North —)

The promoters of the Benton County community pushed for growth in the late 19th century with the formation of a power and irrigation company and plans for such developments as a dam, a canal system and electric lights. Little was accomplished at first.

In 1882, Colonel William Prosser opened a trading post and called the settlement Yakima Flats. A year later, the town was renamed Prosser Falls. Later, it was shortened to Prosser. In the early 20th century, a strong Dutch community appeared here.

PULLMAN

Pullman is home to Washington State University, founded in 1890.

The Whitman County town takes its name from George Mortimer Pullman (1831–97), the inventor and manufacturer of the railroad sleeping car. He opened the Pullman Palace Car Company in 1867. The next year, he introduced dining cars. By 1880, he founded "Pullman City" where his workers lived. The area has since been incorporated into the city of Chicago.

Prior to the Civil War he could not sell his idea, even though he had successfully tested two converted railway coaches. In 1863, Pullman and his friend, Ben Field, built a luxurious sleeping car, the Pioneer. But the car was too wide to pass through conventional stations and there the Pioneer sat at the site of Chicago's Union Station. Then, in 1865, Lincoln was assassinated. Every town brought out its finest rail equipment, and Lincoln's home state of Illinois was no exception. Station platforms were cut down and bridges were raised between Chicago and Springfield to accommodate Pullman's Pioneer. The Michigan Central was impressed and cleared the way for the big car. Other railroads followed suit, and Pullman's fame—and fortune—was made. For a time, Pullman lived in Colorado and operated a store.

The city began meteoric growth when it boasted two railroads and became a center for shipping wheat. The town was platted in 1882 as Three Forks, descriptive of its setting. The current name was given in 1884, in hopes that Pullman would donate money to the college.

PURDY

The Tacoma grocer who donated lumber for the first schoolhouse in this Pierce County area loaned his name to the community.

PUYALLUP

The town of Puyallup was founded in 1877 by Ezra Meeker, a famous Oregon Trail pioneer, entrepreneur and the town's first mayor. He named the town for the Puyallup River, which was named for the Indian tribe, "the generous people."

Meeker's 1890 home is open to the public.

PYSHT

Pysht—both the town in Clallam County and the river—is a name derived from Chinook slang. *Pish* or *Pysht* means "fish."

QUEETS

The name for this Jefferson County village was taken from that of the river, which bears an Indian tribal name. The Quai'tso was the tribe "next north of the Queniult tribe."

QUILCENE

Located at the head of Quilcene Bay, this Jefferson County town was named for that arm of the Hood Canal. Quilcene is a Twana Indian tribal name. The tribe's name, *Quil-ceed-o-bish*, translates to mean "salt water people," to distinguish its members from the *S-kaw-kaw-bish*, the "fresh water people."

QUINAULT

Quinault took its name from that of an Indian tribe. The name appears on this Grays Harbor community, a lake, a river, and an Indian reservation. The name is derived from Kwinaithl, the name of the largest village inhabited by the tribe.

QUINCY

Quincy took its name from Quincy, Illinois. The name commemorates President John Quincy Adams. It is popularly believed that the name was selected by the daughter of railroader James J. Hill. She chose the name but, as the lore goes, never said which town. It was only assumed to be a town in Illinois. Towns could not be named Adams because honors to John Quincy's father took care of that.

This particular town was laid out in 1902.

RAINIER

Rainier took its name from Mount Rainier, named in 1792 by Vancouver for his friend, British Admiral Peter Rainier. There has always been a bit of controversy over the name, since the admiral made his reputation by defeating American colonists during the War for Independence.

RALSTON

The railroad named this Adams County town after a brand of packaged wheat cereal, now sold under the imprint of Ralston-Purina.

RANDLE

Randle, Lewis County, bears the name of the Randle family, early settlers to the Rainey Valley.

RAVENSDALE

This King County community drew its name both from the Dale Coal Company—the town is in the center of the Black Diamond-Franklin-Ravensdale coal fields—and from the fact that ravens fed on grain spilled from Northern Pacific boxcars.

Before it became Ravensdale, the town was known as Leary, for the Leary Coal Company.

RAYMOND

The first postmaster of this Pacific County town was L. V. Raymond.

REARDEN

Originally called Capp's Place, this Lincoln County village was renamed in honor of a civil engineer for the Central Washington Railway. He arranged for a station after the townspeople dug a well to prove that water was accessible.

REDMOND

Because there were a large number of spawning salmon on the Sammamish Slough, William W. Perrigo and Luke McRedmond first called this King County place, Salmonberg. They settled here in 1871. After a while, they renamed the town Melrose, for Perrigo's hometown in Massachusetts. Finally, after McRedmond became postmaster in 1891, he renamed it Redmond.

REDONDO

This King County town was originally called Stone's Landing and then Stones, for S. P. Stone who settled here in 1872. When, in 1904, the town changed itself into an amusement center, the townspeople changed the name and tried to capitalize on the attraction of Redondo Beach, California.

RELIEF

The first railroad engines, we are told, "pulled two cars each up to the point where each dropped a car and went on." The result was that "it was such a relief to the engine crews that the place has been known as Relief ever since."

RENTON

Renton was originally an encampment of the Duwamish Indians. The King County town grew in the late 19th century with coal mining and lumbering. Dr. M. Bigelow discovered coal in the hills nearby in 1853. The town was platted in 1876.

Renton takes its name from Captain William Renton, of the Port Blakely Mill Company.

REPUBLIC

Republic was incorporated in 1900, and named for the Republic Mine, the major gold claim in this Ferry County area.

Gold was discovered on Granite Creek near the site of this town in 1896 by Philip Creaser and Thomas Ryan, and a rush followed. A tent camp sprang up that was first called Eureka, and then Republic. The name Republic was borrowed from the Republic Gold Mine. The Indians called the site Kleopus, "valley of the cliffs."

At the turn of the century, Republic was one of Washington's largest towns, with a total of 28 saloons!

RETSIL

This Kitsap County community name honors Governor Ernest Lister, only in reverse.

It seems the town had a rough time finding a name that was acceptable until W. H. Cochran jumbled the name.

REVERE

Paul Revere did not ride this far to spread his warning, but he so impressed H. R. Williams, a vice president of the Chicago, Milwaukee & St. Paul Railway, that this Whitman County site was named in his honor.

RICE

William B. Rice, the first postmaster of this Stevens County location, named the town after himself.

RICHLAND

Along with Oak Ridge, Tennessee, Los Alamos, New Mexico, and the Argonne Laboratory in Chicago, Richland, Benton County, was designated as a site for the development of the atomic bomb in 1943 by the U. S. Atomic Energy Commission.

In 1905, the name was given for Nelson Rich, a state legislator who helped pick the site. Rich was also a land developer who was involved in irrigation projects in this area.

RICHMOND BEACH

The Reverend Dr. and Mrs. John P. Richmond, Methodist missionaries, were the only Americans who lived in the Puget Sound area up until 1843.

Another source, however, thinks the name was given in 1889 by E. W. Mills and John Pappendick in order to please John Spencer, a former resident of Richmond, England. Whichever the case, the King County town was named in 1899.

RIDGEFIELD

Because this Clark County town is located on a flat field on a ridge, the townspeople decided in 1890 to change the name from Union Ridge to Ridgefield.

RIPARIA

Taken from the Latin *riparius*, "of the bank," this Whitman County community's name is similar to Riverside. Riparia is located on the banks of the Snake River.

RITZVILLE

Philip Ritz, a cattleman, settled in this Adams County area just west of upper Cow Creek in 1878. He then met up with a group of immigrants in Walla Walla and encouraged them to settle in his area.

RIVERSIDE

Riverside, Okanogan County, was named because it was settled on the side of the Okanogan River.

ROBE

The name of this Snohomish County village has nothing to do with wearing apparel. It came from the surname of an early settler.

ROCHE HARBOR

Roche Harbor, San Juan County, is a resort community located on the harbor of the same name. The harbor was named in 1858, in honor of Richard Roche, who sailed in San Juan waters under British Captain Henry Kellett in 1846 and under Captain James C. Prevost from 1857 to 1860.

A Hudson Bay Company trading post opened here in 1850.

ROCHESTER

When originally settled, this Thurston County site was called Moscow by a Russian pioneer. When the post office was established here in 1890, the name was changed to reflect the New York hometown of another settler.

ROCK ISLAND

Rock Island is a descriptive name.

ROCKPORT

Established in the late 19th century, Rockport, Skagit County, like Rock Island bears a descriptive name.

ROCKY POINT

Though there are many "rocky points" throughout the State of Washington, this particular one, located in Island County, was named by the 1841 Wilkes Expedition.

RODNA

The original name for Rodna was Ray, for E. W. Ray, an official of the Spokane, Portland & Seattle Railway. When confusion arose with another Ray on the Northern Pacific, old E. W. lost out!

ROGERSBURG

This Asotin County location was named in 1904 for G. A. Rogers, who owned the townsite.

ROLLINGBAY

First named Murden's Cover in 1856 by the U.S. Coast Survey, this Kitsap County spot was locally known as Rowle's Bay, for an early settler. The town's name was changed in 1892 with the establishment of a post office.

RONALD

Alexander Ronald was superintendent of the Northwestern Improvement Company's coal mines here in Kittitas County when the town was named.

ROOSEVELT. Theodore Roosevelt ran as vice president with William McKinley. When McKinley was killed, Roosevelt assumed the office. This prompted Marcus Alonzo Hanna, boss of the Republican Party, to cry: "I told William McKinley it was a mistake to nominate that wild man at Philadelphia. Now look. That damned cowboy is President of the United States." (Print and Picture Department, Free Library of Philadelphia, photograph by George S. Bain, 1885)

ROOSEVELT

Located in Klickitat County, Roosevelt was named by T. B. Montgomery, in honor of Theodore Roosevelt.

ROSALIA

For many years, military officers stationed in the interior did not think it was necessary to have a decisive battle with the Indians. That concept changed in May of 1858, when Colonel Edward J. Steptoe neared the present-day town of Rosalia.

Searching for some Indian cattle thieves with a detachment of 158 men, the colonel went out to meet with members of the Spokane tribe and determine whether rumors that the Indians were growing hostile were true. Steptoe met up with more than six hundred mounted Spokanes. The Indians, fearing an attack, did not want the troops to cross the Spokane River. The next morning, the Indians began firing at the federal troops. Lacking a normal supply of ammunition, the troops suffered casualties and were cut off from the water supply.

Under cover of night, the troops buried their dead and, strapping their wounded to their horses, quietly rode away. Questions about why Steptoe and his men were allowed to escape has haunted historians. Some feel that the troops were allowed to leave in return for the horses and materials they left behind. A marker near Rosalia commemorates the engagement.

The name was given in 1872 by the postmaster, for his wife: Rosalia Favorite.

ROSBURG

The name of this Wahkiakum County site honored Christian Rosberg, the first postmaster. The name was adapted to the present form.

ROSEDALE

W. E. White named this Pierce County community in about 1888 because of the abundance of wild roses bordering Henderson Bay.

ROSLYN

Founded in 1886, Roslyn had its heyday in the 1920s with the booming coal industry's exploitation of the local coalfields.

The name was suggested in 1886 by Logan M. Bullock, general manager of the North Pacific's coal mine here. Bullock was currying favor with his sweetheart, who lived in Roslyn, New York.

ROXBORO

Representatives of the Chicago, Milwaukee & St. Paul Railway named this Adams County community for a town in Massachusetts.

ROY

The first name of this Pierce County town was Muck. The settlement was renamed in about 1884 for the son of James McNaught, who platted the site.

ROYAL CITY

At an earlier time in its existence, this Grant County town was called by the descriptive name of Red Rock. The new town, located on

Royal Flat, took on its current name in 1957 when a federal reclamation project made it the center of a flourishing agricultural district.

RUBY (— Beach)

When Thomas Fuller built his cabin in Okanogan County in 1885, the town of Ruby began. Fuller was part-owner of the Ruby Mine and called his settlement after the mine. Unfortunately, that town disappeared after silver dropped in the 1890s, a flood happened in 1894, and a fire occured in 1900.

The current Ruby, located in Pend Oreille County, was named in 1905 for the nearby Ruby Creek. That waterway was christened by prospectors who found red garnets in their pans.

RUFF

Gotfred Ruff takes the honor for Ruff, Grant County. It was on his property that the town was established.

RUSTON

Folklore has it that Ruston was named for W. R. Rust, a founder of the smelting operation here. Rust was also president of the Tacoma Smelting Company.

RYDERWOOD

This Cowlitz County spot was established as Ryder Wood in 1923. It was a logging town, named for William Ryder, a superintendent with the Longbell Lumber Company.

SAINT ANDREWS

The town of Saint Andrews, Douglas County, has no religious significance. It was named in 1890 for the first postmaster, Captain James Saint Andrews. Andrews was a Civil War veteran who settled here.

SAINT JOHN

Like Saint Andrews, Saint John was named for a lesser luminary. Representatives of the Oregon Railway and Navigation Company named it in 1888 for E. T. St. John, who owned the land when the railroad came through this Whitman County area.

SALKUM

Salkum, Lewis County, takes its name from Mill Creek, which once was called Salkum. The name is derived from an Indian word which means "boiling up," a reference to a series of waterfalls in the stream.

SAN DE FUCA

Some authorities believe the town namers of this Island County village confused the Strait of Juan de Fuca with San Juan Island. They add very rapidly that the mythical Juan was no saint!

The townsite here in Island County was platted in 1889 by L. H. Griffiths, H. C. Power and J. W. Gillespie.

SAPPHO

For some unknown reason, this Clallam County town was named for the Greek poetess who lived on the Isle of Lesbos in 600 B.C. Sappho was noted for her particularly erotic writings.

SATSOP

Satsop takes its name from a tributary of the Chehalis River and, ultimately, from the name of an Salish Indian tribe that once lived along the river. The name comes from *sachap* or *sats-a-pish*, "on a creek."

SATUS

Like Satsop, Satus takes its name from a waterway, a tributary of the Yakima River. In this case, it is Satus Pass.

The name is derived from a tribe of Yakima Indians known as the *Setaslema*, or the "people of the rye prairie."

SAXON

Saxon was named in about 1888 to honor a widow by the name of Saxon.

SCANDIA

Following the arrival of the railroads in the late 19th century, companies began to advertise all over the United States and Europe, promoting the "free" land in the West. By 1883, more than a hundred newcomers reached Seattle daily for several months. Most of these immigrants were from Norway and Sweden.

The original name for this Kitsap County site was Frykholm, for John Frykholm, a retired Lutheran minister who built the town's first dock and store. The name was changed to reflect the composition of the village.

SEABECK

The 1841 Wilkes Expedition recorded the bay at this Kitsap County location as Scabock, an English rendition of an Indian word whose meaning is unknown. Rather than translate it, they made it sound more English. The name was changed to Seabeck in 1847 by Kellett.

Another source contends that the name came from Seabeck, Maine, home of Marshall Blinn. Blinn started a sawmill here in Kitsap County in 1857.

The Skomish Indian name for it was L-ka-bak-hu.

SEABOLD

Because this Kitsap County village was located near a tidal shore, William Bull gave it this name in 1894, suggesting that "the sea is bold."

SEA TAC

Sea Tac is a combination of Seattle and Tacoma.

SEATTLE

Seattle, King County, is the largest city in the Pacific Northwest. It was named by Dr. D. S. Maynard for his friend, the chief of the Duwamish tribe: See-aa-thl, also spelled Sealth. In fact, his baptismal name was Noah Sealth. He was known to the Indians, however, as Tsu-Suc-Cub.

Though sighted by explorers before the end of the 18th century, pioneers did not arrive here until 1851, when they settled at Alki Point. At that time, the Indian name was Tzee-Tzee-lal-itch, "little portage." The town was so beset by heavy winds that it was moved to the protected waters of Elliott Bay.

Chief Sealth was still alive at the time of naming, and settlers paid him $16,000 for the use of his name. He conned them into believing that he would spin in his grave if his name was mentioned after his death!

Seattle was destroyed in 1889, when a painter's glue pot boiled over and started the "Great Fire." Before the fire, most of the buildings were constructed of wood. Following it, however, the residents made use of stone, iron and concrete.

An interesting sidelight to the history of Seattle: The first industry was lumbering, and the first sawmill was that of Henry Yesler. The road down which the logs were rolled was known as the "skid road." This road was not conducive to any business dealing with the elite, so establishments catering to the lower elements of society cropped up here. The phrase that described the logs careening down the street later developed into "Skid Row."

Seattle's history is also one of strong citizen support. Townspeople donated land and buildings for a university in 1862, before the territorial government could change its mind about the location. Later, they raised money for a terminal on the Northern Pacific Railroad. When that company decided to develop at Tacoma, Seattle people organized two railroads of their own!

SEAVIEW

Seaview was the original name of a summer hotel, opened here in Pacific County in 1871 by J. L. Stout. The lodging name became that of the town.

SEDRO WOOLLEY

At one time, there were two towns: Sedro and Woolley. The area around Sedro was a proliferation of red cedar trees; the name Sedro, given in 1884, is a modification of the Spanish *cedro*, for "cedar."

Logging interests arrived in the late 19th century. Prospectors followed soon after. When Sedro became the head of navigation on the Skagit River, the town merged in 1898 with Woolley, which was a junction of the Great Northern and Northern Pacific Railroads. Woolley was founded in 1890 and named for the town's founder, Philip A. Woolley.

Originally settled in 1878 by David Batey and Joseph Hart, Mortimer Cook bought the land six years later and decided to name it Bug. His fellow settlers did not like that, and threatened to prefix the name with "Hum." David Batey's wife came up with Sedro in a Spanish dictionary, even though her spelling was off.

In 1890, Norman R. Kelly platted a separate townsite and called it Kellyville. The same year, Woolley started his rival town, and called it Woolley. For nine years, the separate—but expensive— governments existed, only to merge in 1898 as Sedro-Woolley. Woolley has since been dropped.

SEKIU

This Clallam County town's name came from an Indian word that means "calm water."

SELAH

The name of Selah came from a local Indian word for "still water" or "smooth water." The name was first used to describe a part of the river. The name appears on not only the Selah Creek but also the Yakima County town and the valley.

Some confuse this name with the Hebrew musical term, but there is no connection.

SELLECK

When this King County community was named, F. L. Selleck was the superintendent of the Pacific States Lumber Company—the principal industry here.

SEQUIM

A popular retirement spot, Sequim took its name from the Indian word which means "bountiful creature comforts" or, as one authority writes, "quiet water." The Indian village that preceded this spot was known in the Challam language as Such-e-kwai-ing.

An early settler, Matthew Fleming, felt that the spelling was the closest they could get to the Indian word.

SHAW

Shaw, San Juan County, took its name from Shaw Island, which was named by the 1841 Wilkes Expedition. The name honored Navy Captain John D. Shaw, a hero in the war against the Barbary pirates in 1815. Shaw served under the legendary Stephen Decatur.

SHELTON

Shelton, Mason County, is located on an inlet of South Puget Sound. It was named for an early settler, David Shelton (1812–97). He owned land here and lived on it until his death.

Shelton was a colorful character, being a trapper, an Indian fighter, a prospector, and an elected official to many important political offices. He was also responsible for changing the name of Sawamish County to Mason County in order to honor Charles H. Mason, territorial secretary to Governor Isaac I. Stevens.

SHINE

When the people from this Jefferson County village established their post office, postal authorities shortened the name they sent in: Sunshine.

SILVANA

When this Snohomish County site was first settled, it was called Stillaguamish. By 1892, with the arrival of the railroad, the name did not seem appropriate for a growing community. The townspeople took the Latin *sylvan*, "wooded," and made a slight modification to honor old-time settler Michael Sill.

SILVERDALE

Silverdale is located at the head of Dyes Inlet in Kitsap County. In 1889, when townspeople met to name their town Goldendale, they learned there already was a Goldendale in eastern Washington, so, as one sage put it, they dropped down a notch on the precious-metal scale.

SILVER LAKE

There are five lakes and one town in Washington that bear this name. This town in Cowlitz County took its name from one of those lakes with the silvery color.

SILVERTON

The name for Silverton, Snohomish County, was decided by a mass meeting of miners in 1891.

SKAMANIA

Skamania took its name from the county that was established in 1854. The name comes from an Indian word that means "swift river." Some believe it describes the "troubled waters of the Columbia River." This town was originally known as Butler, until townspeople requested a closer relationship with the county.

SKAMOKAWA

Skamokawa, Wahkiakum County, bears the name of the Skamokawa Creek. The waterway was named for a local Indian chief. It is often misspelled as Skamokaway, which was the chief's real name.

The name, we are told, means "smoke on the river," a reference to the morning fog that sits above the creek.

Because the creek was the main drag in town, the community was nicknamed "Little Venice."

SKYKOMISH

Skykomish took its name from the river, which bears an Indian tribal name: *skaikh*, "island" and *mish*, "people." Again, there are several spellings for the name, including George B. McClellan's Skywhamish.

SMYRNA

Smyrna was a popular place name based on both its appearance in Revelation and on an ancient city of importance in Asia Minor. No one is sure why the name was so popular. In this Grant County community, the name was selected by H. R. Williams.

SNAKE RIVER

The Snake River is the largest tributary of the Columbia River. The original English name for the waterway was the Lewis River, named in 1805 by Captain William Clark for his close associate, Captain Meriwether Lewis. The Snake Indians, however, had prior ownership.

SNOHOMISH

Snohomish took its name from its county. It was named for an Indian tribe. The name also appears on a river and an Indian tribe.

The town was founded about 1859 by E. C. Ferguson and E. F. Cady as a trading post at the confluence of the Pilchuck and Snohomish Rivers. Initially, they called their settlement Cadyville. Later, it became Snohomish City.

The source word, first applied to the Indians, translated to "a style of union among them." This particular tribe did, in fact, dominate their confederation. The corporate title of Snohomish City was abbreviated to conserve space.

SNOQUALMIE

The town was named for the nearby river, which was named for an Indian tribe. In 1849, this tribe attacked Fort Nisqually and killed Leander Wallace. Governor Lane ordered troops into the area, camping at the site where Fort Steilacoom was built a short time later. This stopped the uprising.

The early white settlers softened the Indian *Sdoh-kwahlb-bhuh* to Snoqualmie. The name supposedly refers to the Indians' legend that they came from the moon.

SOAP LAKE

Soap Lake was originally known as Smokiam, Indian for "healing waters." The town was named for the body of water.

The lake, of volcanic origin, has a strong concentration of minerals and salts that are reputed to be of therapeutic value. The name was changed to Soap Lake to reflect the soapy texture of the water.

SOL DUC HOT SPRINGS

Indians were first to discover the springs here, and named them—in their language—"magic waters" or "sparking waters."

SOUTH BEND

South Bend, Pacific County, was a principal spot in the water and stage coach transportation system of Washington territory in the late 19th century.

When threatened with losing its county seat to Oysterville in 1892, law-abiding citizens of South Bend confiscated all county books and records from Oysterville.

The name came from the fact that the Willapa River bends to the south where the city is now located.

SOUTH PRAIRIE

This Pierce County site was established in 1884 as Melrose. The name was changed five years later to describe geographically its location on the South Prairie Creek.

SOUTHWORTH

Southworth got its name by just sitting there. Located on Point Southworth in Kitsap County, the community carries that name. The point's name source was Edward Southworth, a quartermaster on one of the Wilkes' expeditions.

SPANAWAY

First recorded as Spanuch, an undefined Indian word, the word was transmogrified into an English-sounding one. The name appears on this Pierce County community and also on the lake.

More recent historians believe the name is a reversal of the Indian name for the lake, Yawanaps, "beautiful water."

SPANGLE

Both the creek and the town in Spokane County were named for William Spangle, a Civil War veteran who squatted on the land in 1872. When he was given a soldier's claim, he platted the townsite in 1886.

SPIRIT

Spirit took its name from Spirit Lake, so named because the Indians thought it was haunted by spirits. In fact, the Cowlitz Indians called it Nyas Cultus, "very bad" lake. Early volcanic eruptions caused steam spouts and unpredictable currents on the water surface that frightened the natives.

The post office was established as Spirit Lake in 1903; the name was later shortened to its present size.

SPOKANE

Spokane, Spokane County, was named for its county, whch was named for either the Indian tribe or the tribe's chief. *Spo-can-ee* translates in Siwash Indian to mean "sun" or "child of the sun." The chief's name was recorded as Illim-spokanee in 1812. The tribe might just have borne the chief's name. This was not uncommon.

The trading post established by the Northwest Fur Company in 1810, soon after the Lewis and Clark Expedition, was the embryo of Spokane, even though it was started along Little Spokane Creek, about 10 miles from today's city.

In 1872, a concerted effort to build a city began at Spokane Falls. Fire destroyed more than 30 city blocks in 1889, but Spokane fought back and grew until it became Washington's second largest city.

SPRAGUE

Named for General John W. Sprague, who held interests in the Northern Pacific Railroad, this Lincoln County community was the major shearing center in the mid-1880s.

SPRINGDALE

Springdale took its name from the Spring Creek. The waterway was originally called Sheep Creek. The Stevens County town was called Squiretown, in honor of homesteader Charles O. Squire. Daniel C. Corbin changed the town's name after the creek's name was changed.

STANWOOD

Robert Fulton first settled this Snohomish County site as a trading post in 1866. The land passed on to George Kyle, who established a post office and called it Centerville.

In 1877, D. O. Pearson arrived. He built a store, wharf and warehouse. When he became postmaster, he changed the name to Stanwood, his wife Clara's maiden name.

STARBUCK

Starbuck took its name from that of a member of the board of directors of the Oregon-Washington Railroad & Navigation Company.

When General Starbuck visitied this Columbia County area, he promised the people a bell once the first church was built, and he delivered on his promise!

STARTUP

The manager of the local lumber company, G. G. Startup, gave his name to this town in 1911. Before his arrival, the land had been homesteaded by F. M. Sparlin in the 1880s. In 1890, William Wait laid out the town, and called it Wallace. When mail was constantly being missent to Wallace, Idaho, the townspeople selected Startup's name for their own.

STEHEKIN

This Chelan County town took its name from the river of the same name. The word translates from the Skagit Indian to mean "the way, the pass."

STEILACOOM

The first library, jail and court house in Washington State were built here. Steilacoom, Pierce County, was founded in 1854, and named for either an Indian chief or tribe. The chief's name was Tail-a-koom.

Fort Steilacoom, located about three miles east of town, was activated in 1849. The fort was almost captured by Indians in the 1855–56 campaign that ended with the assault on Seattle. The Army abandoned the fort in 1868.

STELLA

Stella Packard was the daughter of this Cowlitz County town's first postmaster who opened a store and a post office here in the 1880s.

STEPTOE

Steptoe, Whitman County, received its name from Steptoe Butte, a 2,700-foot mountain that stands alone. The butte was once called Pyramid Peak. The closest mountains are 18 miles away. The butte was named for U.S. Army Lieutenant Colonel Edward J. Steptoe.

In 1858, Steptoe and a contingent of dragoons were beaten by a combined force of Spokane, Coeur d'Alene and Palouse Indians at what is now called Steptoe Butte. The troops retreated under cover of night to the safer Snake River Canyon. Steptoe's defeat, the battle of Rosalia, has been considered one of the worst defeats of the regular Army by the Indians.

In earlier days, the town was known as Steptoe City and Steptoeville. (See ROSALIA, Washington.)

STEVENSON

Stevenson, Skamania County, was platted by and named for George H. Stevenson. Stevenson was a pioneer fisherman and early legislator who arrived here from Missouri in 1880.

STRATFORD

Stratford, Grant County, was named about 1890 by representatives of the Great Northern Railroad. The source, most suspect, was Stratford-on-Avon. In fact, the hotel there was called the Shakespeare.

SULTAN

Local tradition has it that the name of the river and the town in Snohomish County came from the mispronounciation of the name of an Indian chief, Tseul-tud.

The first settler here was John Nailor in 1880. With the start of placer mining in the area, Nailor became postmaster and named the town after the river.

SUMAS

The name for this Whatcom County town, the stream and the mountains came from that of a Cowichan tribe of Indians who lived in this vicinity. The word, from the Indian, means "big level opening."

SUMMIT

Summit, Pierce County, was named because that is just what it was: the high point on the tracks of the Tacoma-Puyallup electric railway of the late 19th century.

SUMNER

John Francis Kincaid was the original platter of his father's land here in Pierce County. He named his community for Charles S. Sumner, the American statesman and ardent abolitionist.

SUNNYSIDE

Sunnyside, Yakima County, is known as the asparagus capital of the Northwest.

The town dates back to the mid-19th century. The cabin of one of its first settlers, Ben Snipes, was built in 1859 and is still standing. It is considered one of the oldest homesteads in the Yakima Valley. The town, however, was platted by Walter N. Granger in 1893.

Sunnyside has sometimes been called the "Holy City," because its founder imprinted Protestant morality on it, including no drinking, gambling, prostitution or any other form of fun!

Before there was a town here, there was the Sunnyside Canal and, some think, that was the source of the name. Others lean toward a story told by a group of local residents who said they named it while hunting bunch-grass.

SUNSET

Sunset, located in King County, was named in 1897 by officials of the Sunset Cooperative Company.

SUQUAMISH

The Suquamish Cemetery, located here, contains the remains of Chief Sealth, one of the most important Indian leaders of the Pacific Northwest. He died in 1866, at the age of 80.

The town bears the Indian tribal name. In fact, Sealth was chief of the Suquamish, a Salish sub-tribe, and the Dwamish.

SUTICO

Sutico, Pacific County, bears a made-up name. The name came from the first two letters of each of the words, *Su*nset *Ti*mber *Co*mpany. The company was the chief logging operation here.

T TACOMA

Tacoma, Pierce County, took its name from the Indian *tah-koma*, "the mother of us all," or "mountain." The Indians called Mount Rainier by that name. In fact, the word was used to describe all mountains.

The name appeared in Theodore Winthrop's 1863 *The Canoe and the Saddle*. The Indians called this settlement Chebaulip.

Though discovered by George Vancouver in 1792, it was not until 1852 that the first business arrived. In that year, Swedish settler Nicholas de Lin opened his sawmill. The name was given not by de Lin but by General Morton Matthew McCarver, who bought a large amount of acreage here in an attempt to encourage the Northern Pacific Railway to make this the road's terminus. During the 1880s, in fact, Tacoma was virtually a company town of the railroad. McCarver platted the townsite and called it Commencement City. He was talked out of it, and Tacoma came into being as a community.

The suspension bridge across the Narrows of Puget Sound is nicknamed Galloping Gertie. During a 1940 storm, the bridge twisted and turned and pitched automobiles into the water below.

TAHOLAH

The town of Taholah, Grays Harbor County, is inside the Quinault Indian Reservation. The town was named for the chief of the Quinaults, Taholah.

TAHUYA

Tahuya, Mason County, took its name from the creek, which is the Twana Indian *ta*, for "that," and *ho-i*, "done." In other words, it means "that done," signifying some incident at the waterway.

TAMPICO

Tampico, we are told, was named by A. D. Elgin for a town where he once lived in Oregon.

TEANAWAY

The Teanaway is a tributary of the Yakima River. The name was first mentioned in 1853 as Yannoinse River. The town takes its name from the waterway.

TEKOA

Tekoa, Whitman County, has a name with Biblical roots.

In the early 20th century, people thought the name was of Palouse Indian origin. In 1913, the Reverend Frederick Tonge published his comments that the name was given by a woman settler who took it from the Bible. The settler was, in reality, the first postmaster Dan Truax, and his wife made the selection.

In the Bible, the name is that of a town a few miles from Bethlehem. It was in Tekoa that the prophet Amos lived. The word translates to mean "settlement of tents."

TENINO

Tenino, Thurston County, was named for an Indian tribe that inhabited the interior. Another source, however, believes the name was coined by railroaders who saw that this spot was number 1090—pronounced by them as "ten-nine-o." Others contend that the word comes from the Indian and means "junction." Still others argue that Northern Pacific engine Number 1090 made regular stops at this station. We lean to the Indian root, because the name appeared before the railroad arrived. *Tenino*, in Chinook jargon, means "fork" or "junction."

The town made news in the 1930s when it issued wooden coins after the local bank failed.

THOMAS

Thomas, King County, was named for John M. Thomas, a Kentuckian who came to this White River Valley in 1853. He served as a county commissioner from 1857 to 1859.

THORNTON

J. Quinn Thornton was quite influential in persuading Congress in the mid-19th century to organize the Oregon Territory. Another source believes the name came from the Whitman County town's location on the Thorn Creek.

THORNWOOD

Thornwood is not related to some form of flora. Rather the name honors W. J. Thorne, a settler in this Kittitas County area.

THORP

Milford A. Thorp purchased land here in this Kittitas County location in 1885. Thorp Creek, a tributary of the Che Elum River, also bears his name.

THRALL

Thrall, Kittitas County, bears the name of an official of the Northern Pacific Railroad. The town was named in 1889.

TIETON

Tieton took its name from the Tieton River, a tributary of the Naches. The stream was named in the 1880s, with an adaptation of an Indian word meaning "roaring water."

TIGER

Just as Thornwood has nothing to do with flora, Tiger has nothing to do with fauna. The town, located in Pend Oreille County, was named for George Tiger, one of the earliest settlers. He operated a steamboat stop, Tiger's Landing.

TILLICUM

This Pierce County community bears a name that comes from *tilakum*, Chinook jargon for "friend."

TOKELAND

Tokeland, Pacific County, and Toke Point were both named after an Indian chief who was described as "a man of a great deal of importance among the Indians, but advancing years and an inordinate love of whiskey had reduced him to being regarded as an object of contempt and aversion by the whites, and a butt for the jests and ridicule of the Indians."

Chief Toke's wife, Suis, was quite remarkable, we are told. She possessed "a fund of information in all matters, . . . with a shrewdness and tact in managing her own affairs uncommon among the Indian women."

TOLEDO

Located at Toledo is St. Francis Xavier Mission. The mission, founded by 1838 by Fathers Blanchet and Demers, is the site of the first Catholic church in the state and one of the oldest missions in the Pacific Northwest.

The town was named for a steamboat, operated by the Kellogg Transportation Company. In 1879, Orrin Kellogg arrived in the area and purchased one acre of land on which to build a warehouse and docks. While there, he asked Celeste Ronchon, wife of the landowner, to name the town. She selected the steamboat's name. (See TOLEDO, Oregon.)

TONASKET

Both the Tonasket Creek and this town received the name of Chief Tonasket, also spelled Tonascutt, of the Colville Indian tribe.

TOPPENISH

Toppenish, Yakima County, is the headquarters of the Yakima tribe. It began as a town in the early 20th century with the establishment of a Northern Pacific Railway siding here.

The town took the name of the creek, whose name is an adaptation of the Indian *Qapuishlema*, "people of the trail coming from the foot of the hill." In 1853, Captain George B. McClellan spelled it Sahpenis.

TOUCHET

The first appearance of a name at this Walla Walla County site was in 1843, when the Reverend Gustavus Hines, a Methodist missionary, wrote it as Toosha. It appears to be an Indian word, *tousa*, "curing salmon before a fire," that was reshaped into a French-sounding word. It is the name of the local river.

The town was platted in 1884 by John M. Hill.

TOUTLE

The Toutle River, a tributary of the Cowlitz River, takes its name from an Indian tribal name. The Cowlitz County town takes its name from that waterway.

TRACYTON

This Kitsap County community, located on Dyes Inlet, was named in honor of Benjamin Franklin Tracey, secretary of the Navy from 1889 to 1893 under President Benjamin Harrison.

TRINIDAD

Surprise! This Grant County village was actually named for a town in Colorado that shared the same geographic features.

TROUT LAKE

Located in Klickitat County, this town took its name from a nearby lake and stream.

TUKWILA

Tukwila, King County, was named in 1905 when the post office was established.

The name submitted by Joel Shomaker to replace the former name of Garden Station was the Indian *Tuck-wil-la*, "land of the hazelnuts." Postal authorities modified the name to its current configuration.

TUMTUM

Tumtum, it is said, is a Chinook Indian word for something that is good or unusual. Another source suggests the name comes from Chinook slang for "heart" or "thump-thump," and refers to the sound of falling water.

This locale was also the campground, we are told, of an Indian chief by that name.

TUMWATER

Tumwater, founded in 1845 by Michale T. Simmons, was the first American settlement north of Fort Vancouver and the Columbia River. It is also the home of Olympia Brewing Company. Some feel that this is more important than the age of the town.

One source believes the Thurston County name is drawn from Tumtum, with an American suffix. An earlier name for the town was New Market. The Indian name for the site was Spa-kwatl, "waterfalls."

TURNER (— Corner)

Turner, Columbia County, was named in honor of B. M. Turner, the owner of the land on which the town was built. Turner platted the site in 1902, when the Oregon-Washington Railroad & Navigation Company extended its line here from Dayton.

TWISP

Twisp took its name from the Twisp River, and is located at the junction of that river with the Methow River. Settlement took place in the late 19th century. The name, most authorities agree, comes from an Indian word that was garbled by railroad workers.

An earlier name for the Okanogan County community was Gloversville in 1898, for the first postmaster. The name had to be changed to avoid confusion with Clover in the same county.

TYLER

Tyler, Spokane County, was once known as Stephens. The Tyler name came from the Northern Pacific Railway when they named the station here by that name. When the post office was established, it also carried the Tyler name. Local tradition has it the name came from the successful claimant to a suit against the railroad.

UNDERWOOD

Underwood, Skamania County, was named for Amos Underwood. Underwood crossed the plains in the mid-19th century and spent the rest of his life along the Columbia. He settled the town that bears his name in 1875.

UNION (— Gap; —town)

When Union, in Mason County, began as a logging center in 1858, its name was Union City. When the post office was established in 1904, it dropped the "city" from its name.

Union Gap, Yakima County, was earlier known as Yakima City. The name was changed to represent the location of the community: It connects the central and lower sections of the Yakima Valley.

Whitman County's Uniontown received its name as a compromise. Townspeople were divided over a name, and the Reverend Joseph Cataldo, S.J., suggested this name. It was accepted because the people could see their town was a junction, or "union," of creeks and roads.

UNIVERSITY PLACE

This Pierce County town was laid out as the future home of the University of Puget Sound, an idea that was never realized.

URBAN

Urban has nothing to do with the appearance of a city. Urban was named by L. U. Stenger for his son, Urban.

USK

Usk was named in about 1890 by George H. Jones, for the Usk River in Wales.

UTSALADDY

Located on the north shore of Camano Island, this Island County village derives its name from the Indian word for "land of berries."

VADER

Vader, we are told, received its name from an "old German" resident.

The original name for the Lewis County town was Little Falls, but when the Northern Pacific Railway came to town they did not use that name because the company had another station by that name—in Minnesota. The railroaders decided to call it Sopenah, but the townspeople were not satisfied with that name.

The railroad agreed to change the name of the station, if the people were willing to change the name of the town. In fact, the railroad was willing to accept any name—except one in use along their line. No agreement could be reached until, finally, someone mentioned an old resident by the name of Vader, an early settler.

Everyone thought the old man would be highly honored by the name change, but he was not. He left Vader and moved to Florida!

VAIL

This Thurston County location was named for the family that donated the land for the townsite to the Weyerhauser Company.

VALLEY (—ford; — Grove)

The name for Valley Grove, Walla Walla County, was given by Charles McInroe and his wife. The family settled here in 1879. The name was first used as the name for a station of the Oregon Railroad & Navigation Company. Mrs. McInroe was also postmistress of the town.

Valley, Stevens County, has a descriptive name.

VANCOUVER

Founded as Fort Vancouver in 1824 by the Hudson Bay Company, Vancouver is the oldest city in Washington State. For more than two decades after its establishment, the fort was one of the most important settlements in the Pacific Northwest. Under the direction of John McLouglin, the company monopolized the fur trade in the Oregon country. A town grew around the fort and became Vancouver.

Located in Clarke County, Vancouver was named for Captain George Vancouver (1757–98), the British naval officer, who explored this area aboard the *Discovery* in 1791. In retrospect, it is difficult to imagine this man, who died at age 41, accomplishing so much in so few years. The only answer is the fact that he joined His Majesty's Navy at age 13!

VAN HORN
This town, located in Skagit County, was named for its founder: James V. Van Horn.

VANTAGE
Local tradition has it that this Kittitas County site was named for a Mr. Van Slack, who operated a ferry from this site until the early 1930s.

VAN ZANDT
Situated in Whatcom County, Van Zandt was named in 1892 for J. M. Van Zandt, the town's first postmaster.

VASHON (— Center; — Heights)
Vashon Island was named by Vancouver in 1792 to honor yet another friend, Captain James Vashon. Vashon later became an admiral in His Majesty's Navy, partially for his heroic activities against rebel ships during, of all things, the American Revolution.

VASSAR
The name of this Adams County community came from that of the women's college in Poughkeepsie, New York. It was named by H. R. Williams of the Chicago, Milwaukee & St. Paul Railway Company.

VAUGHN
Both the bay and the Pierce County town of Vaughn bear the name of W. D. Vaughn. He first homesteaded the area in 1851, but later lost the rights to the land because of illness.

Nonetheless, his name was carried on. His nickname was Nimrod, so the townspeople should be happy they took his family name for theirs instead.

VESTA
The Vesta Creek and this town in Grays Harbor County both carry the name of Mrs. Vesta Dwinell. They were named in 1882, the year the creek was explored by M. J. Luark and Mrs. Dwinell's husband, Milton.

VIRDEN
This town, located in Kittitas County, was named for G. D. Virden.

WAHKIACUS

This town was named for Sally Wahkiacus, a well-known local Indian. Sally owned land here and, according to tradition, was quite a local character.

WAITSBURG

In 1864, Sylvester M. Wait built a mill here, and called the place Wait's Mill. When the post office opened two years later, the local school teacher arranged to call it Delta.

In 1868, the townspeople voted to change the name to Waitsburg, and the postal authorities followed their lead.

WALLA WALLA

Originally called Steptoeville and Waiilatpu, this Walla Walla County city became Walla Walla in 1859. In that same year, it became the county seat, taking its name from the county. It served the Idaho mines at Orofino.

The county's name is derived from the Nez Percé word used to describe a "rapid stream" or "running water." It has also been translated to mean "many waters." With the duplicated word, it seems more likely that the latter definition is most appropriate, such as "water, water." Another source contends that the name is made diminutive by repetition and believes the name translates to "little swift river." Yet another indicates that the Cayuses called the spot Waiilatpu, "Place of the Rye Grass." The tribe gave its name to a breed of pony which was rarely properly broken by the white man.

In 1836, Dr. Marcus Whitman and Narcissa, his wife, established the first permanent white settlement in the Pacific Northwest at this site. Their mission was the second Protestant mission in the Oregon country. The influx of settlers and misunderstandings between the missionaries and the Cayuse Indians brought about the Whitmans' deaths eleven years after their mission was founded.

WALLULA

(See WALLA WALLA, Washington.)

WAPATO

A crew from the H.M.S. *Chatham,* led by Lieutenant William R. Broughton, claimed the Columbia River for Great Britain in 1792. They landed at Reed Island, a few miles from Wapato. The dispute was not settled until 1846, with the signing of the United States-Canada boundary treaty.

The town, however, began as a siding for the Northern Pacific Railway. The name was given in 1902, and comes from the Chinook jargon word, *wap-patoo*, "potato."

WARDEN

The creation of dams, especially the Grand Coulee Dam, changed Warden into a thriving community. The town was established in 1909, at the junction of the Northern Pacific with the Milwaukee Road. The name came from a major stockholder in the Chicago, Milwaukee & St. Paul Railway Company, and was conferred by H. R. Williams.

Archeology work near here, at Lind Coulee, unearthed burned bison bones that have been estimated to be between 8,300 to 9,100 years old.

WARNICK

Warnick, Klickitat County, received the name of the engineer who surveyed the Sumas extension of the Bellingham Bay & British Columbia Railroad in about 1903.

WASHOUGAL

Originally known as Parker's Landing, Washougal takes its name from the Indian, and means "rushing water."

WASHTUCNA

Washtucna, Adams County, took its name from the lake in Franklin County. The lake was named for a Palouse Indian chief.

WATERMAN

Delos Waterman's name is carried on this Kitsap County community. The name was given in honor of the early homesteader in 1904, when the post office was established.

WATERVILLE

At one time, Waterville was promoted as "the great railroad center of the Big Bend."

In 1884, this Douglas County site was known as Okanogan City. Then it became Jumper's Flats because of the prevalent claim-jumping in the area, and was finally platted as Waterville—after a 30-foot well produced water.

WAUCONDA

This Okanogan County community borrowed its name from a town in Oregon, Waconda. Though that town no longer exists, the name remains. It is Indian for "up valley."

WAUKON

Some authorities believe that Waukon borrowed its name from Iowa. There, the name came from Waukon-Decorah, a prominent Winnebago chief in the 19th century. This town was named by rail-roaders when the Spokane, Portland & Seattle Railroad was built.

WAUNA

Wauna was the name given to a particular spirit that the Klickitat Indians believed represented the Columbia River.

The Pierce County village was named in 1906 by Mary F. White, who had served as postmistress. Wauna is supposed to mean "mighty" or "strong."

WAVERLY

In most cases, this name came from the ever-popular *Waverley Novels* by Sir Walter Scott. Not the case here.

Saville Farnsworth and Fred Buckmaster named the Spokane County site in 1879, after their former home in Iowa.

WAWAWAI

White settlers supplanted the Nez Percé and Palouse Indians around 1870. Prior to that invasion, the Indians used the area along the Snake River as their campgrounds. A landing was established here in the late 1870s.

The word is Nez Percé and means "council grounds," an indication of what the Indians did at their camps.

WELLPINT

Wellpint, Steven County, was originally the site of a Presbyterian mission on the Spokane Indian Reservation. Local tradition has it the name is adapted from the Indian and means "two small creeks in the valley."

WENATCHEE

Wenatchee, Chelan County, took its name from a Yakima Indian name, *wenatchi*, "river coming from canyon."

Lewis and Clark heard of the Wenatchee River when they were exploring and naming the Columbia Valley in 1805–06. They spelled it Wahnaachee, however.

WESTPORT

Westport likes to proclaim itself the salmon sport-fishing capital of the world. They might just be right!

The Grays Harbor County town was settled as Peterson's Point in 1858. Glenn Peterson was honored by the naming. It was the site of Old Fort Chehalis and the county's first school house.

WEST SOUND

West Sound was named because of its location. The namer was Captain Richards, who did the deed in 1858 or 1859. It had formerly been called Guerrier's Bay by Wilkes, after the captured British ship.

WHEELER

Wheeler was created in 1910, before the railroad arrived, and it assumed the name of an older settlement.

WHITCOMB

Formerly known as Luzon when it was established in 1909, Whitcomb's name was changed the next year to please the town's landowners, James A. Moore and G. Henry Whitcomb.

WHITES

This Grays Harbor County locale was named by officials of the Northern Pacific Railway in honor of Allen White. White started a sawmill here in the 1890s.

WHITE SALMON

White Salmon takes the name of the river. In 1805, Lewis and Clark called the waterway Canoe Creek because of the appearance of Indians in canoes. Their journals also speak of the delicacy they tried, white salmon.

On the other hand, a long-time resident once related a story about salmon infected with a strange fungus that turned their bodies white, and killed them off by the hundreds. Last we heard, white salmon is still a delicacy. The fish turn white during spawning season.

The post office here in Klickitat County was established as White Salmon, regardless of the folklore, in about 1886.

WHITE SWAN

White Swan, we are told, was a famous chief of the Yakima tribe. This town, located in Yakima County, was his home. The town was laid out in 1910.

WICKERSHAM

Noah and William Wickersham settled in this Whatcom County area in the late 1880s. They donated land for the railroad right-of-way, and—for a bonus—got their name on the town signs.

WILBUR

Wilbur was platted in 1889. The Reverend J. H. Wilbur was the first presiding elder of the Walla Walla Circuit of the Methodist Conference for Oregon. He was named in 1859. As important as he was, he was not the source for the name of this Lincoln County town.

Wilbur, Lincoln County, was named for its founder, Samuel Wilbur Condit, in 1887. His town was incorporated two years later.

Once, while out hunting, Condit mistook a neighbor's tame fowl for game and shot it. Ever after, he was known as Wild Goose Bill. He took it all in good nature. Before Wilbur was formally incorporated, Condit called his trading post Goosetown.

WILEY CITY

This town in Yakima County honors Hugh Wiley. The name was given by his son in 1910 to honor the old pioneer.

WILKENSON

Wilkenson, Pierce County, took the name of Samuel Wilkenson, secretary to the board of the Northern Pacific Railroad. The railroad laid track to this town in 1876, and started coal-mining operations three years later.

WILLAPA

This Pacific County community takes its name from the name of the Indian tribe that lived here, the Ah-whil-lapah. The same name was applied to the Willapa River.

WILLARD

Emil Willard, a pioneer rancher, left his name to this Skamania County location.

WILSON CREEK

Wilson Creek, Grant County, was named after the waterway.

WINESAP

When W. J. Taylor and the Wenatchee Commercial Club got the go-ahead to establish a post office at this Chelan County location in 1909, they requested that the name be Cole's View; Mrs. Elizabeth Cole was postmistress.

Authorities in Washington would not consider a two-word name, so the townspeople submitted a list. One of the names on the list was Winesap.

WINLOCK

General Winlock W. Miller (1822–76) owned the land on which this Lewis County town stands.

Miller was one of the first federal officers in the Washington Territory, an officer during the Indian Wars of 1855–56, and a close personal friend of Territorial Governor Isaac I. Stevens.

WINONA

Winona is a Santee Indian word, meaning "first-born daughter." The name for this Whitman County location was put there by a railroad survey engineer. He just happened to come from Winona, Minnesota.

WINSLOW

Winslow, Kitsap County, is located on Bainbridge Island, and began in the late 19th century as a shipbuilding center for tall-master schooners.

Winslow was named by H. K. Hall for his brother, a partner in the Hall Brothers Marine Railway & Shipbuilding Company.

Bainbridge Island, discovered by the Wilkes Expedition in 1841, was named for Captain William Bainbridge, a legend in American naval history.

WINTHROP

Winthrop goes back to the late 19th century. In the early 20th century, Owen Wister made his home here. Some of Winthrop's sites and people are commemorated in Wister's *The Virginian*.

The town was named by Senator John H. Wilson in 1890. Wilson could not remember for whom he named it, but he thought it was in honor of Theodore Winthrop.

WINTON

This town in Chelan County was platted in 1914 by the Winton Lumber Company. At first they called it Winton Place, but they finally dropped "place" from the name.

WISHKAH

Wishkah takes its name from the river of the same name. *Hwish-kahl* is Chehalis Indian for "stinking water."

WISHRAM

Wishram, Klickitat County, was, for centuries, an Indian food-trading spot, before Lewis and Clark arrived in 1805. The name is drawn from that of an Indian chief. Another source attributes the name to an Indian tribe, native to the coast. The name translates as a particular species of louse or flea that abounds in the area.

WITHROW

Withrow, Douglas County, was named for J. J. Withrow, a prominent rancher who grew wheat there before the town was conceived.

WOODINVILLE

Early settlers named this King County area in about 1868 for Ira Woodin, a pioneer.

WOODLAND

Woodland, Cowlitz County, was settled in the mid-19th century by immigrants from Finland who turned it into a dairy, poultry and farming community.

Christopher Columbus Bozagth, the first postmaster, named the town at the suggestion of his wife.

WOODWAY

This Snohomish County location, a suburb of Seattle, bears a descriptive name.

YACOLT

This Clark County community took its name from a prairie which Indians called the "haunted place." It seems that at one time several children were lost in what appeared to be a mysterious way. The Indians blamed it on evil spirits.

YAKIMA

Located in Yakima County, this city takes its name from the county which was named for the river. The Yakima River was named for a tribe of Indians.

The tribal name means "black bear" or "coward." The Indians were involved in a long-running battle with federal troops, the Yakima War. The strategy for this "war" ended with Steptoe's debacle at Rosalia. The war ended in 1857, with the hanging of several of the Indian leaders.

In the 1880s, the Northern Pacific Railroad forced the relocation of a great deal of Yakima to the railroad's site at North Yakima.

YALE

Yale was named for the university in New Haven, Connecticut. Yale University was named for Elihu Yale, of London, England. The town was named by postal authorities. Previously, it bore the Indian name Spillei.

YELM

Yelm is an Indian word of unknown definition that appears on a town and prairie in Thurston County. The name might be that of a person, since an 1849 reference indicates that someone went to "Yelm Ferry," which is usually a reference to an individual.

Some prefer to think the name came from *chelm*, "heat waves rising from the earth."

ZENITH

Zenith, in King County, was named because of its location at the top of a hill. This name was selected over South Des Moines when this community got its own post office—separate and apart from Des Moines in the late 19th century.

ZILLAH

Zillah was incorporated in 1911, named by railroad officials. Early settlers were strongly represented by immigrants from Holland.

The Yakima County town was named by Walter N. Granger, for Miss Zillah Oakes, daughter of T. F. Oakes, president of the Northern Pacific Railroad.

T

he land that was once the Oregon Territory was claimed by three different nations, and those national names add to the romance of the Beaver State.

Lewis and Clark are given credit for exploring much of this area, especially after they met up with Indians on the lower Columbia River in 1805. But Lewis and Clark were newcomers to the area.

The white men who arrived with these explorers did not surprise the residents of the area. After all, the Indians had been trading furs to the British for more than 20 years. Besides, their land had been claimed by Spain in 1775, then by England, and, finally, after Captain Robert Gray discovered the Columbia River in 1792, by the United States.

Five years after the arrival of the Lewis and Clark expedition, John Jacob Astor's Pacific Fur Company set out for the West. Astor led one party overland, establishing the Oregon Trail. The second group sailed around Cape Horn to meet up at the mouth of the Columbia River. The combined group built a trading post at the site, and called it Fort Astor, later to be known as Astoria.

Astor's operation here was short-lived. The War of 1812 forced the company to sell its holdings to the Canadian North West Company and get back to safer surroundings. American absence from the area did not last that long.

In 1818, Astoria was returned to the United States as part of an agreement with the British to occupy the Oregon country jointly for 10 years. In reality, neither country took advantage and "ruled" this vast country which stretched from California to Alaska, from the Rockies to the Pacific. Jurisdiction fell to the Hudson Bay Company, which acquired its rival, Astor's operation, in 1821.

The company continued its "governing" of the territory until the 1840s, despite many attempts by settlers to establish their own government. By 1843, the first gigantic wave of settlers arrived via the Oregon Trail and made this place their home. When the flow of immigration increased to such a level that the bureaucrats in Washington could no longer ignore the area, action had to be taken.

After a great deal of diplomatic maneuvering between the United States and Great Britain, a boundary between the United States and Canada was established by treaty in 1846 at the 49th parallel.

Three years later, the Territory of Oregon was recognized by the federal government. The area north of the Columbia River was set off from it in 1853, and became the Territory of Washington. With the announcement of a gold rush in the area in 1859, Oregon became a state. The officials in the federal city were not dumb.

From the time Oregon joined the Union until the late 19th century, the area was cut off from the rest of the country. In 1883, the Northern Pacific Railroad connected the state by rail with the rest of the Union. As the railroads grew, immigrants flooded the area. By the end of the 19th century, Oregon's population had doubled, and the state began to exploit its vast natural resources.

Through the place names of Oregon, we find relics of the past. We learn, to some degree, how relations between the native residents and the settlers were tense at best. We find in the names the resonant sound of the great Columbia River and its tributaries. We meet the explorers, the settlers, the miners, and their families. And we can experience, ever so vicariously, the exhilaration and depression that the search for gold and silver inspired: the sheer pleasure of discovery.

ADAIR VILLAGE

Adair Village, Benton County, has a name of recent origin. The post office opened here in 1947; Mrs. Barbara G. Strickland was postmistress.

The name came from General John Adair. Adair, a native of Kentucky, was the first Collector of Customs in Oregon. He settled on a claim that ultimately became Adairville.

ADAMS

According to one authority, Adams, Umatilla County, was named for an early wheat rancher.

AIRLIE

Airlie was named in honor of the Earl of Airlie. The earl headed a syndicate of Scotch businessmen who bought a narrow gauge railroad and brought it to the town site in 1881.

ALBANY

Before Walter and Thomas Monteith, two brothers from Albany, New York, settled here in 1848, this area was inhabited by the Calapooia Indians. In 1853, the name was changed back to its original name: Takenah.

Takenah is an Indian word that describes the "depression" or "deep and placid pool" that is formed where the Calapooia River enters the Willamette. Two years later, the town was again called Albany. Townspeople were disgusted because too many people translated the Indian name as "hole in the ground."

Albany was a political hot spot for many years, beginning in 1856 when the Oregon Republican Party was started here.

ALGOMA

Algoma's name comes from that of a local lumber company. The company's name is derived from an Indian word meaning "Algonquin waters."

ALICEL

Alicel's name comes from a combination of the first name and the initial of the last name of Alice Ladd.

ALLEGANY

The name of Allegany, Coos County, is said to have migrated from Pennsylvania. The first post office opened here in 1893.

ALOHA

Aloha is a bedroom community for Portland. The name itself is the traditional Hawaiian greeting.

ALSEA

Alsea was named for the valley in which it finds itself, at the confluence of the North and South Forks of the Alsea River.

Located in Benton County, Alsea's first post office opened in 1871; Thomas Russell was the postmaster.

ALVADORE

The name of this town honors Alvadore Welch, the promoter of a local railroad.

AMITY

Amity, Yamhill County, was the location of one of the first woolen mills in Oregon.

The town was founded in 1848 or 1849 when Ahio and Joseph Watt, Oregon Trail immigrants, settled here. The town's name came from a dispute over the location of a local schoolhouse in 1849. Once an agreement was reached, it was decided to call the school "Amity." The name was suggested by Ahio S. Watt, the first teacher. The town that grew up around the school took on that name.

Joseph Watt brought with him to this area 400 sheep, cards, reeds, and castings for a loom and spinning wheel. This was the start of the first woolen mill in Oregon. In addition to developing that industry, Joseph Watt was also responsible for the first shipment of grain from Oregon to England in 1868. That was the state's first effort at international marketing.

ANDREWS

Andrews was named for an early cattle rancher.

ANTELOPE

The origin of this town's name should be quite obvious. It was named for that "home on the range, where the deer and the antelope play. . . ."

APPLEGATE

Applegate, Jackson County, was named for Jesse and Lindsay Applegate, early settlers. Jesse Applegate's name runs throughout the early history of Oregon. When he arrived in the territory, he was a livestock guard on the wagon train west. He was a 32-year old ex-school teacher who had worked as a surveyor in Missouri. Through his dilligence and hard work, Applegate became the expedition's leader, becoming involved in the newly-formed government. Later in life, he was able to use his tact and diplomacy to quell warring factions in the provincial government in the 1840s by modifying the oath of office.

Applegate was the model for the hero in Theodore Winthrop's *John Brent*, a novel popular during and after the Civil War.

Legend has it that Chiny Linn, a Chinese laborer, removed more that $2 million in gold from a claim. More sober minds indicate that the whole district did not produce that amount.

ARLINGTON

Arlington was first known as Alkali. The name was changed by N. A. Cornish, who wanted to honor the home of Robert E. Lee.

Elijah Ray built the first dwelling here in 1880. Two years later, J. W. Smith laid out the town of Alkali. Arlington became incorporated in 1887.

AROCK

Arock was named for just that—"a rock": A very large rock was located near the town.

ASHLAND

Ashland, Jackson County, was named by Abel D. Hillman in 1852. Sources suggest that the name came either from Ashland, Ohio, or Henry Clay's birthplace at Ashland, Virginia.

The town was founded when R. B. Hargadine and a fellow by the name of Pease settled here in 1852. After providing themselves with shelter, they began building the Ashland Sawmill.

When a post office was opened, the town called itself Ashland Mills, for a grist mill located here. The town was incorporated in 1874 and, at that time, dropped the Mills from its corporate title.

ASTORIA

Astoria, Clatsop County, was first sighted by white men in 1792, when Captain Robert Gray sailed into "Columbia's River." Gray, a British explorer, discovered Tongue Point and named it that year. Thirteen years later, when Lewis and Clark arrived, they landed "on a beautiful shore of pebbles of various colors" and named the spot "Fort William," for Clark. The British name, however, prevailed.

The settlement, on the other hand, dates back to the winter of 1805–06, when the Lewis and Clark expedition camped here and called their camp Fort Clatsop.

By 1811, the settlement was named for John Jacob Astor, founder of the major fur-trading company. His company, under the leadership of Alexander McKay, established a fur-trading post here, and called it Fort Astoria. The site was not ideal, but the company wanted to begin trading immediately. The fort was "sold out" in 1813 to the British, who commanded it as Fort George—until 1818, when it was returned to the United States.

As time passed, Fort Astoria's importance declined. By 1841, there was little trace of the old fort. Six years later, a post office was opened as Astoria; John M. Shively was postmaster. It was the first post office west of the Rockies.

Astoria is the county seat.

ATHENA

Athena, located by Wild Horse Creek, was once the regular site for camp meetings, complete with horse races.

The town was named in 1889 for the Greek goddess by a man with "a romantic and classical turn of the mind."

AUMSVILLE

Aumsville was named in the late 1860s for Amos Davis. Davis was son-in-law to Henry L. Turner, who owned the land on which the town was built. Local townspeople called Davis "Aumus."

AURORA

Aurora was founded in 1856 by what has been called a "colony of old-country German and 'Pennsylvania Dutch,' " led by Dr. William Keil (1812–77). The credo of the group, as articulated by Keil, was "Every man and woman must be a brother or sister to every other man and woman in our family under the fatherhood of God. No man," he continued, "owns anything individually but every man owns everything as a full partner and with an equal voice in its use and its increase and the profits accruing from it."

The group had settled for more than a dozen years at a six-thousand-acre site in Bethel, Missouri. Keil felt the need for a fuller community life, and moved the group to Oregon. The original name for this town was Aurora Mills, which Keil chose for his favorite daughter.

At one time, while there was no railroad station at Aurora, the trains would stop here to eat because, as one railroad passenger wrote, "the trainmen wanted the better meals they could get at Aurora—better meats, better vegetables, better pies and puddings."

Keil's experiment lasted 25 years, and then the people tired of his tyrannical rule. The group broke up following Keil's death in 1877 and divided up the property.

AUSTIN

The town was first called Newton Station because a Mrs. Newton ran a hotel and stage station here, but Austin became the official name when Minot Austin purchased the hotel and station. Mrs. Austin had a widely-known reputation as a superior cook.

BAKER CITY

Baker was named for the county, which got its name from Edward Dickinson Baker, a Union Army officer and senator from Oregon.

Baker was serving as colonel of a regiment of volunteers when he was killed in the battle of Ball's Bluff. Some consider him the first Union officer to die in the Civil War.

The first post office under the name of Baker City was opened in 1866; William F. McCary was postmaster.

Gold was discovered in the county in 1861, and the famous Armstrong gold nugget was found here. It is on display, all 80.4-ounces of it, in the U. S. National Bank in Baker City.

In 1864, Colonel J. S. Ruckel built a quartz mill. Four years later the town was laid out.

BANDON

First called The Ferry and then Averill, Bandon, Coos County, was destroyed by fire; only 20 houses, three sawmills, a bakery, and the high school survived. The town was reconstructed by the federal government in 1938.

Lord George Bennet, an Irish peer, gave the town the name of his hometown. He imported the Irish furze, a thorny shrub that produces yellow pea-like flowers in the early spring.

Bandon, with a beach on the Conquille River, is known as the "cranberry capital of Oregon."

Jonathan Lewis was the first postmaster in 1877.

BARLOW

Located in Clackamas County, Barlow was supposedly named for Samuel K. Barlow, a leader of the 1845 emigration who built the Barlow Trail, a pioneer road across the Cascade Mountains. One of his favorite sayings was, "God never made a mountain that He didn't make a way to get over it."

Barlow's son, William, made a small fortune from the sale of black walnut trees. He was also the first postmaster when the office opened here in 1871. In fact, he and his son, Cassius, platted the townsite in 1891. He is the more likely choice for the name source.

William Barlow ordered a bushel of black walnuts from a dealer in the East. The shipping cost was $65, and Barlow sold young trees grown from these nuts for a profit of almost $500! A different authority suggests the name giver was another early settler, John L. Barlow.

BARVIEW

Barview, located at the entrance to Tillamook Bay, is named for the sand bar that narrows the entrance to the bay.

Captain Robert Gray crossed the bar in 1788. His mate on the *Lady Washington*, Robert Haswell, named the place Murderer's

Harbor because Marcos Lopius, a young black member of the crew, had been murdered by Indians when he went after them to retrieve a cutlass they had stolen.

Haswell wrote of the murder: "We were observed by the main boddy of the Natives to haistily approach them they instantly drenched their knives and spears with savage fuery in the boddy of the unfortunate youth. He quieted his hold and stumbled but rose again and stagered towards us but having a flight of arrows thrown into his back and he fell within fifteen yards of me and instantly expired while they mangled his lifeless course."

BASQUE STATION

This community takes its name from the ancient European people who emigrated to Oregon in the 1870s. Their chief occupation here was sheep-herding, a craft they practiced for centuries in the Pyrenees.

BAY CITY

Bay City was named for Bay City, Michigan. Both are fishing towns.

BEAVER (—creek; —ton)

Beaver was the name of Astor's ship. It was also the name of the first steamer to sail the Pacific. It was built in England in 1835, and sailed around the Horn in 163 days, arriving at Fort George in 1836.

Beavercreek, Clackamax County, takes its name from, of all things, the Beaver Creek.

Called Hoff in 1916, the town became Beavercreek in 1922, when Joseph R. Hoff opened the first post office.

Beaverton was established in 1868 as a shipping point for the Oregon Central Railroad. It obtained its name from the abundance of beaver dams in the area.

BEECH CREEK

Beech Creek took its name from the nearby waterway. One source suggests that the name of the creek came from the family name of a pioneer who once lived near the mouth of the creek.

BELLFOUNTAIN

When Helen Elgin opened the first post office in this Benton County community in 1895, the town's name was Dusty. Dusty became Bellfountain in 1902.

Bellfountain was the center of Methodism and camp meetings in pioneer days. Settlers arrived in 1848, and over the years circuit riders of all denominations came here to try to convert people.

BEND

Bend, Deschutes County, takes its name from a practice of early settlers. It seems pioneers would stop here and rest after they had traveled through the wastelands, and before they entered the inter-mountain deserts. It was the only place for miles that the river could be forded. Another source suggests that the name came from a "bend" in either a road or the river.

At first it was called Farewell Bend, but the first half was dropped as time passed. After a while, better routes were found, and Farewell Bend lost its popularity. In 1900 or 1901, A. M. Drake came from the east in search of a place where he could improve his health. Four years later, the Pilot Butte Development Company platted the town. After 1909, the town prospered and grew. In 1916, Bend saw the opening of sawmills, generated by the need for timber that World War I had precipitated. Many settlers, tired of their hand-to-mouth existence, converged on the town and caused it to expand.

Originally located in Crook County, the first post office was opened here in 1904 by Alfred H. Grant. Earlier, the area had been known as Arrow because it was served by the Arrow post office.

BIRKENFELD

Birkenfield, Columbia County, was named for its first postmaster, Anton Birkenfield. He opened shop here in 1916.

BLALOCK

This Gilliam County name honors a Dr. Blalock—an early settler.

BLODGETT

Blodgett, located on the banks of the Marys River in Benton County, was originally called Emerick when it was established in 1888. James A. Wood was the original postmaster.

The name was changed to Blodgett to honor William Blodgett, an early settler.

BLY

Bly has no relationship whatsoever to the commanding officer of H.M.S. *Bounty.*

The town takes its name from the river that flows about two miles north. The stream is now called the Sprague River, for Captain F. B. Sprague, who fought Indians and commanded Fort Lamath in 1866.

Bly comes from the Indian word *P'lai*. The P'laikini were Indians who lived high above the plain. The word translates to "high" or "heavenly."

BOARDMAN

Oregon's first State Parks superintendent was Samuel Herbert Boardman (1874–1953). A native of Massachusetts, Boardman came to Oregon in 1901 and settled near the present-day town of Boardman.

BONANZA

Bonanza was named because the natural springs in the area were expected to produce a continuous flow of water for irrigation, and, hence, prosperity for its residents.

BONNEVILLE

The life of a trader in the Rocky Mountain country, as recorded by Washington Irving, became the source of the name for this town.

Captain Benjamin Louis Eulalie de Bonneville (1796–1878) was the principal character of *The Adventures of Captain Bonneville*. Little would have been heard of him if he had not turned his journals over to the author. Some, however, suspect he was a "history-made man," a creation of publicity.

Captain Bonneville, a native of France, left his country when his family fell into disfavor. Through political influence, the young man received an appointment to West Point. He served in both the Seminole and Mexican wars, and assumed command of Vancouver Barracks in 1853. Though he sympathized with the South at the outbreak of the Civil War, he remained loyal to the Union. He received a brevet as brigadier general. He died at Fort Smith in 1878.

Bonneville is located at the Bonneville Dam. The dam, completed in 1938 on plans made by the Corps of Engineers, destroyed many of the Columbia River's historical and scenic spots.

BORING

Tony O. Foster was the first postmaster in this Clackamas County locale when it opened in 1903. The name is not intended to indicate any lack of action in town; it is a family name.

BREITENBUSH SPRINGS

Breitenbush Springs takes its name from the nearby Breitenbush Mountain and the location of more than 50 mineral hot springs.

BRIDAL VEIL

Located in Multnomah County, Bridal Veil received its name from an off-handed comment.

A woman passenger on a river boat was astounded by the beauty of the cascading falls near today's town. She remarked how much like a bride's veil they looked. That section became known as Bride's Veil, later changed to Bridal Veil. When a community grew up in this location, it assumed the same name.

BRIDGE

The source of the name for Bridge, Coos County, is quite simple: It was named for the bridge that crossed the Coquille River, built in 1881. The name was made official with the opening of a post office in 1894. Thomas E. Manly was the first postmaster.

BRIGHTON

Brighton was named for Brighton Beach, England. In fact, the original name for the locality was Brighton Beach.

BRIGHTWOOD

When Winnie McIntyre opened the first post office in 1891 at this Clackamas County location, the town was called Salmon. The name was changed to the more descriptive Brightwood in 1910.

BROOKINGS

The only Japanese aerial attack on the United States mainland took place just east of town in the Mount Emily area.

Brookings, Curry County, is located near Chetco Cove, and grew up around a sawmill. The first post office here was opened in 1913 by John S. Thornton, and took on a local family name.

BROTHERS

Brothers, Deschutes County, was a supply station that was named in opposition to Sisters, which took its name from the Three Sisters mountains.

Originally located in Crook County, Brothers had its first post office opened by Patrick H. Coffey in 1913.

BROWNSVILLE

Brownsville is located at the entrance to the Calapooya Valley. It was originally named Kirk's Ferry, but the name was changed to Brownsville to honor Hugh Leeper Brown (ca. 1812–88) who settled here in 1846.

Together with his nephew, Captain James Blakely, Brown laid out the town in 1853. The town grew around community-run woolen mills. Famous residents include George A. Waggoner, Z. F. Moody and the Reverend H. H. Spalding.

Waggoner arrived in 1852 and became one of the first railroad commissioners of Oregon. He was also the author of *Stories of Old Oregon*. Moody was Oregon's governor from 1882 to 1887. Spalding crossed the Rockies with Marcus Whitman and the two men's wives.

BUCHANAN

The composer of the official state song, "Oregon, My Oregon," was John A. Buchanan (1863–1916). Buchanan was an officer in the Oregon Coast Artillery during World War I, then a lawyer and, finally, a judge.

BUENA VISTA

The name comes from the Spanish for "good view."

The town of Buena Vista is famous for Smith & Company pottery. Starting out in 1865, Freeman Smith began the whole operation, but he limited himself to domestic pottery which was shipped far and wide.

Later, the company got involved in the manufacture of drain- and sewer pipes.

BURNS (— Junction)

Burns, seat of Harney County, was once the capital of the old cattle empire. Located on the cattle ranch of Pete Stinger, the town was named by Scotsman George McGowan after Robert Burns, the Scottish poet, and was established before 1889.

Burns struggled through its existence, hoping for the arrival of the railroad—for almost 50 years. The railroad arrived in 1924!

BUXTON

This Washington County town was named for Henry Buxton, an early settler.

CAMAS VALLEY

The first permanent settlement here was made in 1853. The pioneer residents were William Day, Abraham Patterson and Alston Martindale. The settlement was then called Eighteen-Mile Valley, the approximate distance from the settlement at Flournoy.

Camas is the name of the sweet onion found on moist prairies from British Columbia to California. It was a food staple for Pacific Northwest Indians in the early days.

CANBY

Most sources contend that Canby, Clackamas County, was named for General Edward Richard Sprigg Canby (1817–73), commanding general of the Department of the Columbia. Canby, a veteran of the Seminole, Mexican and Civil wars, was killed during the Modoc war of 1873 at the peace council in the Lava Beds.

One point of disagreement comes from the establishment of the post office here. Charles Knight opened it as Canby in 1871, two years before the general's death. (See CANBY, California.)

CANNON BEACH

When a cannon washed ashore from the shipwrecked sloop *Shark* in 1846 at the mouth of the Columbia River, the event seemed momentous and worthy of remembering in the name of this town.

Offshore of Cannon Beach is the famous Haystack Rock, one of the most photographed spots in Oregon.

According to postal records, Cannon Beach, Clatsop County, was once called Ercola, as early as 1891. The name was changed to Cannon Beach in 1922.

CANYON CITY

When gold was discovered in Canyon Creek in 1862, this mining community grew overnight.

Canyon City is the seat of Grant County. During the Civil War, heated clashes took place between loyal-to-the-Union Oregon miners and the Confederate-leaning Californians.

CANYONVILLE

Canyonville is located at the northern end of Canyon Creek Gorge. It takes its name from the waterway. Or does it?

In 1851, the original name for this community was Kenyonville. Is it possible that postal authorities misspelled the name? At the time, there were only two cabins, occupied by Joseph Knott and Joel Perkins. Perkins operated the ferry across the South Umpqua.

CARLTON

Carlton was the home of William Anderson Howe. Howe invented the baseball catcher's mask.

The town's name came from the family name, Carl, with the addition of "-ton."

CARPENTERVILLE

Carpenterville, Curry County, took its name from its first postmistress: Mrs. Lida E. Carpenter. She opened the office in 1932.

CASCADE LOCKS

Cascade Locks, Wasco County, is located at the locks built at the Cascades Rapids in the Columbia River. Built in 1896, the locks allowed faster, more convenient travel and transportation on the river.

CASCADIA

Located in the Willamette Valley, Cascadia took its name primarily from the fact that it is located in the Cascade Range.

CAVES JUNCTION

Caves Junction was once known for its rich goldfields. In the late 1850s, one prospector discovered a nugget worth $1,200! The name came from the Oregon Caves National Monument.

The Oregon Caves are a series of caverns in Elijah Mountain. The mountain was named for Elijah Bristow who discovered the caves in 1874 while chasing a bear. The Caves are also known as "The Marble Halls of Oregon."

CAYUSE

Cayuse, Umatilla County, was named for the local Indian tribe. This tribe was considered to be warlike, according to pioneer lore. A *cayuse* was also an Indian pony. The Waiilatpuan tribe bred these small fast horses.

CEDAR MILL

Cedar Mill takes its name from a combination of things. It was established on the banks of Cedar Creek which was so named because of the large number of cedar trees in the vicinity. Elam Young opened a sawmill here in 1848 to mill the cedar wood.

CENTRAL POINT
Central Point, Jackson County, was named for its location: It was situated at the center of Sams Valley where two stagecoach routes intersected.

CHEMULT
Chemult was named for the Indian chief who was one of the signers of the treaty of 1864.

CHENOWETH
Chenoweth bears the name of Francis A. Chenoweth (1819–99), speaker of the lower house in the state legislature in 1854 when territorial government was established. He was also quite active in the organization of the Corvallis & Yaquina Bay Railroad. He later became its president.

CHERRY (— Grove; —ville)
The State of Oregon pioneered in the development of new fruit varieties, many of which were varieties of cherries. A number of streams and towns bear the name of this fruit, such as Cherry Grove and Cherryville.

William L. Long opened the first post office at Cherryville, Clackamas County, in 1884.

CHESHIRE
Cheshire was established as a shipping point on a spur of the Southern Pacific Railroad.

CHILOQUIN
According to one source, Chiloquin takes its name from an English adaptation of an Indian family name. Another source believes it was the name of a local Indian chief. Both may be correct.

CHITWOOD
Chitwood, Benton County, took the name of its first postmaster, James B. Chitwood. He opened shop in 1887.

CHRISTMAS VALLEY

The town of Christmas Valley is located in Christmas Lake Valley, which was discovered on Christmas Day.

CLACKAMAS

Originally located in Marion County, Clackamas is now in Clackamas County. The first post office opened in 1852, with John Foster as postmaster.

The town takes its name from the river; the river, from the Indian tribe. The tribe was Chinookan and their villages lined the shore of the lower Clackamas River.

CLARNO

Located on the John Day River, Clarno was named for Andrew Clarno. Clarno was an Indian fighter and one of the river's earliest settlers. He settled on Pine Creek in 1866.

CLATSKANIE

Clatskanie, Columbia County, was once the home of the Tlatskanai—a fierce, though small, Indian tribe. They were so formidable that in the mid-19th century the Hudson Bay Company would not send men near here in numbers less than an armed platoon. By 1851, the warring tribe was decimated by a smallpox epidemic that moved the group into extinction.

Located at the confluence of the Columbia and Clatskanie Rivers, the town was named for the river. Originally, the town was named Bryantsville, for E. G. Bryant who settled the land in 1852. The name was changed to Clatskanie in 1870.

A post office was opened here in 1871, with E. W. Conyers as the first postmaster. Conyers built a small steamboat eight years later that he used to go to the Columbia River to meet with other boats. This was the only means by which people here could receive goods and materials. By the end of the 19th century, the railroad arrived and brought civilization with it.

COALEDO

The first post office at Coaledo, Coos County, was opened in 1875 by James C. Kelly. The name came from a combination of "coal" and a reference to Toledo.

COBURG

Coburg was, we are told, the name given to a local stallion that was brought to the blacksmith for shoeing.

COLUMBIA CITY

The post office at this Columbia County village opened in 1871. Devereaux J. Yeargain was postmaster.

The village took the name of the county which was formed in 1871 and named for the Columbia River. Captain Robert Gray named the river in 1792 for his merchant ship, the *Columbia Rediviva*.

CONDON

Condon, seat of Gilliam County, was originally called Summit City, then Summit Springs. The current name honors Harvey C. Condon, nephew of Dr. Thomas Condon (1822–1907). Dr. Condon was the geologist who brought the nearby fossil region to the attention of the world.

COOS BAY

When J. C. Tolman of the Coos Bay Company founded this port city in 1854, he called it Marshfield, for his hometown in Massachusetts. A referendum in 1944 changed the name to Coos Bay, for the bay itself. Marshfield's post office opened in 1871, and postal authorities waited until 1945 to alter the name to Coos Bay.

COQUILLE

Coquille, seat of Coos County, takes its name from the river. The Coquille River's name is French for "shell."

Titus B. Willard was the first postmaster when the office opened in 1870.

CORBETT

Corbett, Multnomah County, was named in honor of Henry Winslow Corbett (1827–1903), the U.S. Senator from Oregon.

In addition to having legislative duties, Corbett was quite active in the world of business and finance. At different times, he was an officer of the First National Bank of Portland, the Oregon Steam Navigation Company, the California Stage Line, and others.

CORNELIUS

Cornelius, Washington County, was named for Colonel Thomas R. Cornelius (1827–99), a volunteer in the Cayuse war. Cornelius was not successful in his Indian fighting in 1856. His regiment was disbanded by the governor. When he discussed with Lieutenant Colonel Edward J. Steptoe the problems of dealing with Indians, the junior officer said, "With raw volunteers like yours, it may seem difficult, but with trained soldiers like mine it is different." Two years later Steptoe and his men suffered similar disaster.

Colonel Cornelius also operated a store, a grist-mill and a saw-mill here.

CORVALLIS

Corvallis, Benton County, has a name that is a combination of two Spanish words translating to "heart of valley," a reference to the town's location in the Willamette Valley.

The town was established in 1845 by James L. and Johnson Mulkey and by William F. Dixon. The name was Marysville when the town was platted. Other sources believe the founder was Joseph C. Avery, and the year, 1849. Avery was the postmaster in town when the first office opened in 1850. At that time, the place was called Avery's. It officially became the county seat in 1851. Two years later, the name was changed to Corvallis to differentiate it from Marysville, California.

Corvallis is the home of Oregon State University. Edward Finck, a composer of the Northwest, tried to create music with a native flavor. He wrote "Corvallis Polonaise" in honor of this town. Earlier, he tried the "Salem Mazurka." Neither is well-remembered today.

COTTAGE GROVE

Cottage Grove has one of those histories that gets to the heart of the rugged individualists who forged the American frontier.

The Coast Fork of the Willamette River cuts this town in half. In 1894, the residents of the west side petitioned the state legislation to name their section Cottage Grove, and the east side East Cottage Grove. The people in the east did not like the idea and incorporated themselves as Lemati. This change left Cottage Grove off the railroad.

Cottage Grove had the post office, but Lemati had the train station. The situation required the Cottage Grove marshall to cross over to Lemati to meet the mail train. Whenever he wore his badge in the other town, they would arrest him. He'd be kept in confinement until the town of Cottage Grove paid his bail. Two years later, they cut out all their nonsense and united under a common name!

During the 1920s, Cottage Grove created quite a stir after the *Atlantic Monthly* published the alleged diary of a local six-year-old girl, under the title of "The Story of Opal: The Journal of an Understanding Heart." The only problem was that the six-year-old, Opal Whitney, had to have been conversant in Greek mythology and Roman history in order to have written the document.

COVE

Cove is located on the eastern side of a valley. It is a pocket made by Mill Creek near the Mount Fanny foothills.

CRABTREE

Crabtree, Linn County, was named for John J. Crabtree, an early settler.

CRANE

Crane takes its name from the nearby Crane Creek. Sandhill cranes nest in the creek area, which is the source of the name.

CRATER LAKE

During the Glacial Age, Mount Mazama, a volcano in southern Oregon, fell into itself. All but three of its cones were choked out and the resulting 2,000-foot hole was filled by spring water. The community that grew up around Crater Lake assumed that name.

CRAWFORDSVILLE

This Linn County town was named for George F. Crawford, an early settler. His father was the first child born of white parents west of the Williamette River.

CRESCENT

Crescent, Crook County, was the site of an early station on the stage coach route. In 1855, Lieutenants R. L. Williamson and Philip Sheridan (later known for his exploits in the Indian and Civil wars) led a group of one hundred men to explore the area and determine if it could be used for a rail route from California to the Columbia River.

The first post office here was opened in 1891 by Henry D. Jery.

CRESCENT LAKE

Crescent Lake takes its name from the nearby lake of the same name.

CRESWELL

Creswell was founded in 1872 by Ben Holladay. He named his town for the incumbent postmaster-general.

DAIRY

Dairy was once an arid area, part of the Alkali Valley. With the introduction of irrigation techniques, it became a center for dairy ranches.

DALLAS

Dallas was settled in the 1840s, and incorporated in 1874. The town was named for George Mifflin Dallas, James K. Polk's vice president. His name also appears on townsites in Pennsylvania and Texas.

Located on the banks of La Creole Creek, Dallas was originally named Cynthia Anne, in honor of the wife of Jesse Applegate, the trail-maker. It was later shortened to Cynthian.

DALLAS. George Mifflin Dallas was one of the most capable, highly principled men ever to be vice president of the United States. As a result, he only served one term—under James K. Polk, the nation's first "dark horse" candidate. (National Archives)

DANNER

Danner was originally called Ruby, for the old Ruby Cattle Ranch.

DAYS CREEK

Days Creek takes its name from the unfortunate John Day (1771–1820). Day, a member of the Astoria Overland Expedition, died after enduring starvation, robbery and physical assault.

DAYTON

Dayton was founded in 1848 by Joel Palmer, the first superintendent of Indian Affairs in Oregon. In his home, built in 1852, he entertained luminaries including Ulysses S. Grant and Philip H. Sheridan.

DEER ISLAND

Deer Island is a strip of land formed by two branches of the Columbia River. It was named by Lewis and Clark during their 1805 expedition.

Captain Clark recorded that his hunters had gone out early in the morning to hunt for food. "At 10 a.m. they all returned to camp," he wrote, "having killed seven deer. The Indians call this large island *E-lal-lar,* or Deer Island." The Columbia County community that is opposite the island takes its name from the body of land.

The first post office for Deer Island was opened by Nelson Pinckney in 1887.

DENMARK

Denmark was settled by dairy farmers who came from, where else? Denmark! The original name for this Curry County community was

Langlois—the name of the first postmaster in 1881, Frank M. Langlois. The name was changed to Denmark the next year.

DEPOE BAY

The most probable source for this name was Depot, because it originally was a supply depot for the mining industry. Residents like to refer to the town as the "Smallest Harbor in the World."

DESCHUTES

Deschutes, Crook County, takes its name from the river. The name of the Deschutes River comes from the French *riviere des chutes*, "river of the falls."

Deschutes was formerly known as Bend. Deschutes, Deschutes County, had its first post office opened in 1916 by William E. Van Allen.

DETROIT

Detroit, like Denmark, took its name from the original location of the early settlers. In this case, Detroit was named by settlers from Michigan.

DEXTER

The original name for Dexter was Butte Disappointment. The old name was given because of the disappointment experienced by Elijah Bristow and five others. The band of men were pursuing a band of marauding Indians in 1848. They didn't capture them because the Willamette River was swollen and they were prevented from reaching the butte and picking up the trail.

DIAMOND

Diamond's name came from the Diamond Ranch. The ranch's brand was in the shape of a diamond.

DILLARD

Dillard was named for the family that donated land on which the town was built.

DISSTON

Disston was not named, like Dillard, for the family that gave lands on which the town was built. The early town's fathers named it after a popular brand of saw.

DOLPH

This Tillamook County community was named for J. N. Dolph, a one-time U. S. Senator.

DORENA

This town's name was given in 1901. It was made up of a combination of the names of two women: Dora Burnette and Rena Martin.

DRAIN

Drain was named for Charles J. Drain (1816–94). Drain was the last president of the Oregon Territorial Council. When this town was laid out in 1871, he donated 60 acres to the railroad.

One of the first normal (teacher's) schools in Oregon was located here.

DREWSY

Drewsy was originally named for the frontier's way of settling arguments: Gouge Eye. The name was given by Abner Robbins who opened a store here in 1883. When the town applied for a post office under that name, postal authorities rejected the name and selected Drewsey for Drewsey Miller, daughter of a local rancher.

DUFUR

Located in Wasco County, Durfur was named for an old settler, Andrew J. Dufur, Jr. He and his brother, Enoch, purchased a great deal of acreage here in 1872. The town grew on the Dufur's land.

DURHAM

Albert Alonzo Durham (1814–98) was a transplanted New Yorker who operated sawmills until he chased after gold. Unlike the rest, he found it. First calling his town Oswego, he platted it for his home in New York State.

DURKEE

The original name for this Baker County community was Express. The name was changed to the family name of Durkee in 1902. The town had carried the name of Express since 1884.

EAGLE CREEK

Eagle Creek was named for a nearby stream. A post office was opened under that name in 1867. Philip Foster was the first postmaster.

Eagle Creek was also the site of a battle between Colonel Nelson A. Miles and Chief Joseph. General Howard had created a ruse to divert the Indians by suggesting that they were no longer being pursued. When the Nez Percé went into winter camp, Miles attacked. Though the Indians were unhappy with the terms of surrender, they did. Chief Joseph said: "I am tired of fighting . . . Hear me, my chiefs. I am tired. My heart is sick and sad. From where the sun now stands I will fight no more forever."

Miles accepted the surrender, but it was not until seven years later that the terms of the surrender were lived up to by the federal government. By then the number of Indians had been reduced almost by half because of accident and disease.

ELGIN

After the Oregon Railway & Navigation Company's branch was completed in 1890, Elgin became a central point for shipping and distribution for the area.

The name of the town, given in 1860, was derived from a popular song, "Lady Elgin." The song was about the wreck of a lake steamer.

ELK CITY

Elk City was platted in 1868 by A. Newton. The town, first in Lincoln County, was named for the herds of elk that once drifted through the area.

ELKTON

The Hudson Bay Company opened a post at this site in 1832. The company's interest here was primarily in furs, and the company members did little else to cultivate fields and farm than to supply enough for the post. Hudson Bay abandoned the post after 1850, the year the federal government took control of the territory.

In that year, Winchester & Payne Company sent a boat from San Francisco to the Umpqua to locate a site for a town. They settled on this location and, in 1854, Elkton was surveyed and named the seat of Umpqua County. Since then, the town's importance has diminished. It is no longer even frequented by the herds of elk that once visited the area.

ELMIRA

Elmira takes its name from the city in New York.

ELSIE

When a post office first opened in 1876, the name of this Clatsop County town was Mishawaka. By 1892, the name became that of a woman: Elsie.

ENTERPRISE

Enterprise was once what its name implied: a hustling, bustling trade center in the Wallowa Valley.

Located in Benton County, Enterprise opened its first post office in 1878, with Justus Brooks as postmaster.

ESTACADA

Estacada, Clackamas County, takes its name from the Texas town of Estacado. The town namers felt the "a" was better sounding for a village. Another source feels the name is descriptive, drawn from the Spanish for "the bag." The town is located in a valley at the foot of the Cascade Mountains.

The first post office was opened here in 1904 with William K. Haviland as postmaster.

EUGENE

Eugene was settled in 1846 by Eugene F. Skinner. Skinner built a log cabin here in Lane County at the foot of a small peak. The Cala-pooya Indians called the peak Ya-po-ah, but white settlers called it Skinner's Butte. The small settlement that grew around the Skinner family's cabin was known as Skinner's, and was located in Lane County.

When the post office opened here in 1853, it also honored the first settler. In fact, the first postmaster was, of all people, Eugene F. Skinner! In the same year, Skinner was named the seat of Benton County, but when the town was incorporated 11 years later, the name was changed to Eugene City.

FIELDS

Fields was not named for some expanse of farm or cattle land. It was named in honor of Charles Fields. Fields arrived here in the early 1860s and established an overland stage and freight station. In those days, the site was Fields Station.

FLORENCE

Florence is located by the Siuslaw River. Melvin Miller, brother of poet Joaquin Miller, helped establish the town. It is said the town was named for A. B. Florence, a state senator. Others say it was named for a ship that was wrecked here.

FOREST GROVE

This town was appropriately named: It is surrounded by forests of white oak and fir. Also located here is Pacific University, established in 1849 as Tualatin Academy, one of the oldest academic institutions in the Northwest.

The university began as a log cabin school, established by the Reverend Harvey Clark and Alvin T. Smith in 1845. Clark and Smith were joined the next year by sixty-six-year-old Mrs. Tabitha Moffett Brown. While Mrs. Brown was visiting at Tualatin Plains, the idea of a boarding school came to mind. That dream became reality at Tualatin Academy.

FORT KLAMATH

The first Fort Klamath was established here in 1863 as headquarters for the cavalry during the Modoc Indian Wars. The main purpose of the military installation was the protection of settlers from the Modoc, Klamath and Shasta Indians.

The troops that sparked the war came from this fort. They attempted to force Captain Jack, the Modoc leader, and his men back to the Klamath Indian Reservation. After he surrendered in June 1873, Captain Jack was confined in a special stockade at the fort. He and three of his lieutenants were hanged there in October of that year.

Fort Klamath was abandoned as a military installation in 1890. The current town was built upon the horse pasture of the fort.

During its twenty-seven-year active duty, the fort was located in four different counties—but it never moved. It currently resides in Klamath County. The town, established in about 1885, was named for the fort, and the fort took its name from the Indian tribe.

FORT ROCK

Fort Rock, founded in 1908 as an attempt to farm the arid Fort Rock Valley, takes its name from the valley. The name was given because of the unique shape of the rocks and their resemblance to the walls of a fort. The first office here was opened in 1908.

FOSSIL

Before Thomas B. Hoover assumed the duties of postmaster in this Wheeler County community, he discovered fossil remains on his ranch. So, when he opened the doors to the post office on 28 February 1876, he named it Fossil.

FOSTER

Foster is located in the foothills of the Willamette Valley and takes its name from the Foster Creek.

FOX

Fox, once the 1880s center of gold-mining, was named for Fox Creek, an arm of the North Fork of the John Day River.

FRENCHGLEN

Frenchglen was named for Peter French, a prominent cattle baron, and his wife's family, the Glens. The town was once the center for the P Ranch, a legendary Oregon cow ranch.

Peter French came into the Blitzen Valley in the 1870s, hoping to establish a cattle realm like those developed by the Spaniards. French was at once the most-loved and the most-hated cattle baron in Oregon. His men never traveled unarmed, and some were killed by snipers. French himself was eliminated by an irate settler in 1897. The settler's trial marked the end of the old cattle regime.

GALES CREEK

Gales Creek, originally called Gales City, was named for the nearby stream. The waterway, the town and Gales Peak, the highest point in Washington County, were named for Joseph Gale (1800–81).

Joseph Gale was the captain of *The Star of Oregon,* the first sailing vessel built in Oregon. An inexperienced Gale sailed his ship to San Francisco and swapped it for cattle and sheep in 1842. He and his friends drove the herd to Oregon, then built the first saw- and grist mill in the county. Two years later, he was a commissioner of the provisional government and a member of its executive committee.

GALICE

Galice takes its name from the nearby Galice Creek. The name of the stream has a humorous origin.

At one time, there was an Indian, Old John, who would sponge off the pack trains. He would bundle himself up in a blanket, with only his eyebrows and forehead exposed, and say: "Nika Tika Mucka Mucke," which translated as a request for food. He was never refused a free meal.

The next morning he would return and go through the same ritual, except he would demand *gleece*, "bacon." His appetite was insatiable. Finally, one frustrated man cocked his revolver and ordered the Indian to eat "gleece" until he could eat no more. Old John finally lost his appetite for bacon, but the stream—and later the town—recalled the incident.

Another source suggests the name came from an early miner, Louis Galice.

GARDINER

Gardiner was established in 1850. The first settlers were ship-wrecked sailors from the *Bostonian*.

Dr. Allan Hart's *Doctor Mallory*, published in 1935, was set in Gardiner. The good doctor practiced here briefly in 1918.

GARIBALDI

Garibaldi faces Tillamook Bay, and it was once an important mill town. It was named for Guiseppe Garibaldi (1807–82), the Italian patriot.

GASTON

Joseph Gaston (1833–1913) laid out the town in 1862 as a station on Oregon Central Railroad. He was the line's president, and had his farm home here. In addition to running the railroad, Gaston was a journalist and historian.

GATEWAY

Gateway was so named because it was the "gateway" to the mountain regions.

GEARHART

John Waterhouse opened the first post office at this Clatsop County site in 1897.

The community took the lead from Pacific Grove, California, and began to cater to the religious movement at the turn of the 20th century by selling lots for summer homes and camps.

The town was named for Philip Gearhart (1810–81) who operated his fish cannery and sawmill not far from this town.

GERVAIS

Gervais was named for Joseph Gervais (1777–1861). A French-Canadian, Gervais was a member of John Jacob Astor's party, which reached Oregon in 1811. He remained at his post after the Pacific Fur Company sold the trading post to the North West Company, which later became part of the Hudson Bay Company.

The town bearing his name was founded in 1871.

GIBBON

Gibbon, Umatilla County, was named for General John Gibbon, an Indian fighter during the Nez Percé Wars.

GLENBROOK

Ella Atkins opened the first post office at this Benton County village in 1898. The name is descriptive.

GLENDALE

According to one authority, Glendale was named for Glendale, Scotland.

GLIDE

When Mrs. Carrie Laird was trying to think up a name for the new post office here in 1890, she overheard her young son singing something about a river gliding by . . . and came up with the name.

GOBLE

Goble, Columbia County, was once the river landing for the Northern Pacific Railway Ferry at Kalama, Washington. That ended when the railroad built a bridge between Vancouver and Portland. The name was given by the railroad, without explanation.

Flora A. Fowler opened the first post office here in 1894.

GOLD BEACH

This town was named for the placer mining that was done here in the 1850s at the mouth of the Rogue River. That practice ended in 1861, when a flood swept the gold deposits out to sea. Previously known as Ellensburg and Ellensburgh, then Sebastapol, Gold Beach is the seat of Curry County.

Gold Beach was also the site of an 1856 massacre. After murdering Indian Agent Ben Wright here, the renegade Enos and his

Rogue followers massacred 22 white people in the village. The remaining few fled to a fort, where they were under seige for 35 days. They were finally saved by a detachment of troops from Humboldt, California.

John Dewey opened the Ellensburg post office in 1863. Gold Beach became the official name in 1890.

GOLD HILL

Gold Hill, Jackson County, took its name from the Gold Hill Lode, a mine that produced enormous riches for its owners. The mine was located just north of the current town site.

The first quartz mill in the county was opened here in 1860.

GOSHEN

Goshen was named by Elijah Bristow who, when he saw the area, decided it was the Promised Land.

GOVERNMENT CAMP

This particular area was a camp in Clackamas County on the stagecoach road from The Dalles to Oregon City, across the Cascade Mountains. In 1849, a detachment of U. S. Cavalry was forced, because of heavy snows, to leave their wagons and supplies here and proceed to Oregon City on horseback. They left a warning that read: "Government Property—Do Not Touch." From that time to the present, the town was known as Government Camp.

A post office was established under that name by Mrs. Margaret E. Villiger in 1931.

GRAND RONDE

Grand Ronde was originally the headquarters of a reservation for all tribes of Indians from western Oregon. The reservation ceased in 1908, when the lands were divided up among the remaining tribal members.

The name is descriptive: "circular valley."

GRANTS PASS

Grants Pass was originally a stopping spot on the California stage route. The name was given by enthusiastic members of the road crew when they received the news in 1863 that General Ulysses S. Grant had captured Vicksburg.

The name was given to the town two years later. Townsfolk really wanted the town to be called Grant, but there was already one in the state.

GRASS VALLEY

Before the town was built here, the area was filled with bunch grass.

GRESHAM

Gresham was founded in 1852 by settlers who carved the trail through the wilderness over Mount Hood to the Willamette Valley. Gresham is also the source of the largest strawberry crops in Oregon.

HALFWAY

Edwin T. Munsey opened the first post office at Halfway, Baker County, in 1930. The town was named because it was "halfway" between two points. However, the town moved closer to one point than the other, and is no longer halfway.

HALSEY

At the time the Willamette Valley Railroad came into this area and constructed a station, company officials named it Halsey, for company vice president William L. Halsey.

HAMILTON

Hamilton was named for John H. Hamilton, a rancher who settled here in 1872. The first settler, Hamilton was an ambitious man, and he continually added to his homestead holdings until he amassed a ranch with an area of one thousand acres. Sadly, misfortune overtook him and he lost most of his property in later life.

HAMMOND

Hammond, Clatsop County, was originally named Flavel when Ellen M. Sally opened the first post office here in 1895. The name was changed to the family name in 1897.

HAMPTON

Though Hampton, Deschutes County, is located at the foot of Cougar Butte, it is named for Hampton Butte which is situated some distance from the town.

Once located in Crook County, Hampton had its first post office established in 1911 by Adna S. Fogg.

HARRISBURG

Harrisburg was a river town, with an archaic ferry in operation by 1848. The ferry was nothing more than two boats lashed together, with a platform joining them. The wagon was placed on the planking. The horses were made to swim behind.

The ferry was replaced by a bridge in 1925.

HEBO

The village of Hebo was named for Mount Hebo.

HECETA (— Beach)

Heceta, Lane County, takes its name from Heceta Head, which was named for Bruno de Heceta, the Spanish explorer who spotted it in 1775. He suspected that this place was "the mouth of some great river, or of some passage to another sea." He was referring to the Columbia River.

HELIX

According to local lore, the townspeople had great trouble finding an agreeable name. One fellow with an earache mentioned he heard his doctor use the word "helix." Since no one could come up with a better name, Helix stuck.

HEPPNER (— Junction)

Heppner was established as a junction of the Union Pacific Railroad. It was named for Henry Heppner (1829–1905).

Active in a number of business enterprises, Heppner finally joined forces with Jackson L. Morrow. Together they opened a store at this town.

HEREFORD

Hereford, Baker County, was not named for some English shire. Instead the town was named to recall a Hereford bull with a reputation throughout the territory.

Charles E. Seton was the first postmaster in 1887.

HERMISTON

Townspeople in this reclaimed land named their village for the *Weir of Hermiston* by Robert Louis Stevenson.

HILLSBORO

Founded in 1842, Hillsboro, seat of Washington County, was home to several of the men who helped establish civil government for the Oregon Territory. Originally called East Tualaty Plains, the town's name was changed in 1842 to Columbia by David Hill (1809–50). Later, the county court changed the name to Hillsboro.

Hill was a member of the territorial government and a member of its executive council.

Hillsboro also has the distinction of being the place where the oldest inhabitant of Oregon once lived. Grandma Mary Ramsey Lemon Wood died in 1908. She was 120 years old!

HINES

Hines was the $4 million development of the Edward Hines Lumber Company. The town grew around a gigantic—for the times—electric plant built in 1930.

HOLDMAN

Holdman was named for a pioneering family.

HOMESTEAD

Homestead is located beside the Snake River. It was a copper mining center during World War I. Operations, however, ended in 1922.

HOOD RIVER

When Lewis and Clark arrived at the confluence of the Columbia and Hood Rivers in 1805, Hood River, seat of Hood River County, was known as the village of Waucoma (Place of the Cottonwoods). It was not until almost 50 years had passed that W. C. Laughlin and Dr. Farnsworth discovered the extensive grazing lands here and moved in.

Nathan Coe, the first permanent settler, moved here with his wife in 1854. The site was then known as Dog River because a wagon train had to exist on dog meat during an unplanned visit. Mrs. Coe would not accept mail to such an odious name, so the name was changed to Hood River.

HOSKINS

This village took its name from Fort Hoskins, which was built in 1856 under the supervision of Lieutenant Philip H. Sheridan. The fort was named for a Lieutenant Hoskins who was killed during the Mexican War at the battle of Monterey.

The fort's responsibility was to protect the settlers and to deter the Rogue River Indians in the Siletz Indian Reservation from foraying into the valley. The fort ceased to be an active military installation in 1865.

The first post office at this Benton County location was opened in 1891 by Jonathan Hoffman.

HOT LAKE

Hot Lake is located near the body of water of the same name. The lake was named because its waters are warmed by a local hot spring.

HUBBARD

Charles Hubbard built a cabin here in 1849. Later, when the Southern Pacific came into town, he gave land for a townsite.

HUNTINGTON

One source suggests that Huntington, Baker County, was named for J. B. Huntington, upon whose ranch the town was built. Others indicate the name was borrowed from two brothers who platted the townsite.

The original land claim was to Henry Miller, who settled the land in 1862. Miller built a stage tavern and, for many years, the tavern and the site were known as Miller's Station. Twenty-two years later, the town became a division point for the Oregon Short Line, and the Oregon Railway & Navigation Company joined their rails here.

IDLEYLD PARK

Earl Vosburgh built a small grocery and a few log cabins on the banks of North Umpqua River in the early 1920s. He thought the fishing was good; the scenery, great. Just the place for a body to "idle-a-while," so he named his settlement Idelyld Park (pronounced Idle Wild).

ILLAHEE

A story told about this Curry County town centers around miner John Fitzhugh. Fitzhugh found himself out of food, and went in search of game. Barefoot because his shoes had worn out, the miner noticed bear tracks and began to follow them. He spent a whole day searching for this bear, only to realize that the tracks were, in fact, his own footprints. He had been tracking himself!

When telling the story, Fitzhugh would remark: "I don't know what would have happened if I had caught up with myself, as I am a pretty good shot."

Elijah H. Price opened the first post office here in 1895. The town's name seems to be a local pronunciation of the postmaster's name. One authority contends that the word is Chinook slang for "earth, country."

IMNAHA

Imnaha, Wallowa County, takes its name from the Imnaha Canyon. The canyon was named in 1865 by a group of government surveyors who met a group of Nez Percé Indians led by Chief Imna. As was the practice in those days, they took his name, added "ha" and created the canyon's name. When a settlement developed, it assumed the name of the canyon.

IONE

When Ione Arthur was visiting this area, the gentleman responsible for the town's name became infatuated with her. He named the town in her honor, but it did not get him anywhere.

IRONSIDE

Ironside takes its name from Ironside Mountain, nine miles southwest of town. The mountain was named for the metallic look of its rocks.

IRRIGON

Irrigon is located in a very dry part of Oregon. As a result, irrigation is a major issue, and the town's name is a combination of irrigation and Oregon.

The original name for this Morrow County town was Stokes, a name given it when it was a railroad siding in the late 19th century. In 1905, the name was changed because of an extensive irrigation project that was taking place. The town was incorporated 51 years later.

ISLAND CITY

Island City is just that: an island in the Grande Ronde River. The town grew up around a store, opened in 1874 by Charles Goodenough.

IZEE

Izee is really the spelled-out initials from the cattle brand: "IZ."

JACKSONVILLE

J

Founded in 1852 when James Cluggage and John R. Poole discovered gold, Jacksonville's population held hope for the future. In fact, in 1853, it was named the seat of Jackson County. It was known as the kind of town where a man could bring his wife and family, and build a home and churches. But with the decline in mining in the '60s, development slowed. The town rebounded as a trade center for agriculture, only to find itself bypassed by the Oregon & California Railroad in 1884 for Medford. The final blow came in 1927 when Medford was named county seat.

Jacksonville is located on Jackson Creek—the source of its name.

JEFFERSON

Jefferson was home to an early pioneer school, the Jefferson Institute. The institute was organized in 1856, incorporated the next year, and opened for business in 1858. In reality, it was a collection of half-a-dozen neighborhood schools. The Jefferson Institute went out of business in 1899 when its property was transferred to the school district.

JENNINGS LODGE

Jennings Lodge, Clackamas County, takes its name from Berryman Jennings (1807–88), an 1847 pioneer. Jennings was Receiver of the Oregon City Land Office under President Buchanan.

The first post office here was opened in 1910 by Lenora D. Miller. At that time, the town's name was Jennings. It was lengthened in 1911.

JEWELL

William H. Kirkpatrick opened the first post office at this Clatsop County location in 1874.

JEFFERSON. Old Tom Jefferson would have appreciated his name on this town, because of the pioneer school founded here. Sadly, the school did not last as long as Jefferson's University of Virginia. The Jefferson Institute closed its doors in 1899. (Print and Picture Department, Free Library of Philadelphia)

JOHN DAY

John Day, Grant County, took its name from the river, which was named for John Day, a young Virginian and scout for Hunt's Astoria overland expedition in 1811. While his party was fighting its way through the Snake River area, Day took sick. Two of his friends stayed with him, but one died that winter because of exposure and malnutrition.

Day and the other man, Ramsay Crooks, made it to the Columbia River by the spring of 1812 and were found there by a party from their company. They were in such dire straits that their rescuers could not be sure they were white men. Day became insane and died at Astoria.

The town is located at the confluence of the river and Canyon Creek.

JORDAN (— Valley)

Jordan Valley was settled by the Basque in the early 20th century.

Depending on which story one believes, the valley might have been discovered by a Basque sea captain from San Francisco who found his way in the 1870s to Winnemucca. He stayed there, taking advantage of the grazing land to establish his own fortune. He returned to Spain and promoted the area as sheep country to his countrymen.

Another story has it that a number of young Basque came to the area via Ellis Island. One of the earliest recorded Basque settlers was Augustine B. Azcuenaga. Azcuenaga arrived in 1880 and began a sheepherding operation.

The towns of Jordan and Jordan Valley take their names from the Jordan (Creek) River.

JOSEPH

The town of Joseph honors two men: the Chiefs Joseph—father (1790–1870) and son (ca. 1840–1904)—of the Nez Percé tribe. The chiefs ruled the Valley-of-the-Winding Waters, the home of the tribe until 1872 when the white incursion reached its greatest point and the Indians were expelled.

Chief Joseph the Elder refused to sign the treaty of 1855 because the document did not include his beloved Wallowas. When the treaty was changed, he signed his name. He brought his people together and moved to the designated area—in peace.

Chief Joseph the Younger refused to agree to the treaty of 1863. He has been rated as one of the most remarkable men of his race. Military historians recognize him as a great general. In addition, he had fine skills as an orator. A speech he gave in Washington in 1897, in behalf of his starving people, is considered by many as one of the finest speeches in world literature.

JUNCTION CITY

Junction City was named in 1871. Townspeople selected the name in anticipation of the town becoming the meeting place for two railroads.

JUNTURA

The name of this town means "junction." It is located at the point where the North and South forks of the Malheur River join. Henry Miller, a legendary cattle baron of eastern Oregon, once controlled the area with his Juntura Ranch.

KAMELA

Kamela is located at the highest railroad pass in the Blue Mountains.

One authority contends the word is Nez Percé and means "tamarack."

K

KEATING

Keating is located where the Ruckles Creek meets with the Powder River in Baker County.

Originally a part of Union County, Keating received its first post office there, with Herbert B. Cranston as postmaster.

KELLOGG

Kellogg was named for Noah S. Kellogg, discoverer of the Bunker Hill and Sullivan mine, the richest in the Coeur d'Alenes. Kellogg was involved in a great deal of legal maneuvering to gain control of his discovery.

It seems that his donkey uncovered the ore by scuffing the earth with its paw. Since the animal was part of Kellogg's grubstake, Kellogg should have shared the find with his investors.

KENO

Situated on the banks of the Klamath River, Keno owes its name to a bird dog. The dog, however, was named after a popular card game.

KENT

Kent's location, it is said, was the setting for Zane Gray's *The Desert of Wheat*.

This name was drawn from a hat when they were trying to decide on the town's identification. The man who suggested it thought it "nice and short."

KINGS VALLEY

Nahum King (1783–1856) settled this area in 1847. The town, located in Benton County, grew up around a flour mill that was built in 1853.

The town's first post office opened in 1855; Rowland Chambers was postmaster.

KLAMATH AGENCY (— Junction)

Klamath Agency was once the headquarters for the Klamath Indian Reservation. Earlier, the tribe's name was spelled Tlamath.

KLAMATH FALLS

The Klamath Lake area was not settled to any degree until 1867 due to the hostile Klamath tribe. The history of the region is plagued with Indian attacks on wagon trains and bloody massacres.

By 1864, federal troops had subdued the tribe so that settlers could establish themselves along Link River. Wendolen Nus was the first permanent settler in Klamath County. He built a cabin on the west shore of the lake in 1858. Others followed suit in the 1860s.

In 1863, the Army had a post near here, called Fort Klamath. Three years later, George Nurse, who had been a sutler at the fort, built a cabin on the east bank of Link River, and called his settlement Linkville. Linkville became a thriving community after Nurse opened a trading post, and the Indians were confined to the Klamath reservation.

Peace and prosperity were fleeting. In 1872, the Modoc Indians decided they no longer wanted to remain on the reservation, and they made strong efforts to return to their former homes. This attempt erupted into the Modoc Wars. Federal troops finally subdued the Indians and executed their leaders.

Klamath County was created in 1882, and the city grew. Though platted as the town of Linkville in 1878, it was not incorporated until 1889. The name became Klamath Falls in 1893.

Upper Klamath Lake is one of the largest bodies of fresh water in the state.

KNAPPA

Knappa, Clatsop County, had its first post office opened in 1872. The first postmaster, Auren Knappa, gave it his name.

LACOMB

When the townspeople were discussing a possible name for the post office, they came up with Tacoma. Postal authorities rejected that name, so the people played around with the name and came up with something similar: Lacomb.

LAFAYETTE

Lafayette, once the seat of Yamhill County, was founded by Joel Perkins in 1847. He named it after Lafayette, Indiana.

When Lafayette became the county seat, it lacked a court house. That did not stop county lawyers, judges and citizens. Court was held under a large oak tree, later known as the "Council Oak." The seat was moved to McMinnville in 1889.

Lafayette was home to Abigal Scott Duniway, writer, editor and associate of suffragette Susan B. Anthony.

LA GRANDE

La Grande is located at the western edge of the Grande Ronde Valley at the foot of the Blue Mountain. It is the seat of Union County.

In 1861, settlers began to make claims in the vicinity. A year later, Ben Brown moved his family south to the banks of the river and built a house. He later converted the house into a tavern, around which a community developed. At first it was called Brown Town and Brownsville.

When a post office was opened in 1863, the name was changed to La Grande, in recognition of the lush scenery. Another possibility is that it relates to the name that French Canadian explorers gave to the river, Riviere de Grand Ronde. La Grande was incorporated in 1864.

LAKE OSWEGO

When the first post office was opened in this Clackamas County area in 1885, the town was called Oswego and was located in Washington County. The name was changed to Lake Oswego in 1961.

LAKEVIEW

During prehistoric times, this area was dotted with many lakes. Most of them evaporated or were filled with volcanic ash. One exception is Lake Albert, located near Lakeview, the seat of Lake County.

Lakeview, founded in 1876 on the site of the Bullard Cattle Ranch, is one of the highest towns in Oregon. When the federal land office was located here in the late 19th century, Lakeview was the scene of some legendary tales, such as that of T. M. Overfelt.

Overfelt, a partner to Henry Miller, had only learned at the last minute of the impending sale of the famous Agency Ranch. He rode the 200-mile distance from the Silvies River to Lakeview—changing horses from ranch to ranch—in less than 24 hours. He arrived in time to beat out his two competitors. Though his check was refused at the sale, the government later accepted it.

Lakeview was devastated by fire in 1900, but was substantially rebuilt.

LANGLOIS

In its earliest days, Langlois' two cooperage operations supplied the area with tubs for preserving fish. The name apparently comes from that of a French priest who acted as intermediary following the emigration of 1843 and the development of the provisional government.

Alexander H. Thrift opened the first post office at this Curry County location in 1887.

LaPINE

LaPine was named for the abundance of pine trees in the area.

The original name for this Deschutes County town was Rosland. The first post office under that name was opened by Byron J. Penagra in 1897 when the town was located in Crook County. The name was changed to Lapine in 1908. The change to LaPine took place in 1951.

LAWEN

Located on the Malheur Lake before the lake receded, Lawen was named for Henry Lauen, who settled here in 1869. Why the "u" became a "double u" is anyone's guess.

LEBANON

Lebanon, located on the South Santiam River, was a stopping-off spot on the Cascade Wagon Road in the 19th century.

The town was surveyed and platted by Jeremiah Ralston in 1851, though settlement began four years earlier. It was named for a town in Tennessee, where Ralston was born.

LEWISBURG

Lewisburg honors the memory of famed explorer Meriwether Lewis (1774–1809). Lewis explored the Northwest with his partner, William Clark.

LEXINGTON

Beginning its existence as a "wide place in the road," Lexington, Clatsop County, was named for the Massachusetts town. In 1885, Lexington competed with Heppner for the seat of Morrow County.

The town was built on the homestead of William Penland, for whom Penland Buttes were named.

The first post office opened here in 1850. David Pease was postmaster.

LIME

Lime was named because of its chief business: the production of cement.

James Thomlinson was postmaster when the first post office opened at this Baker County site in 1899.

LINCOLN (— Beach; — City)

Lincoln was originally called Doak's Ferry. The town grew as a steamboat shipping center for wheat. At Lincoln City, about a mile from the town's information center, is a statue of guess-who?

All three Lincolns was named for Abraham Lincoln.

LONDON

London took the name of London Peak, named for writer Jack London.

LOOKINGGLASS

Lookingglass took its name from the creek. The creek was named for an Indian who carried a mirror with him. Looking Glass was war chief of the Nez Percé.

LOSTINE

Lostine is named for a river of the same name. It was once called the "lost city of Lostine" because it is located in a valley about 30 miles from the nearest surveyed land, which is on top of a mountain. A surveyor's goof accounts for the error.

LINCOLN. There are three towns in Oregon that honor the memory of Abraham Lincoln, but not one town remembers his first vice president, Hannibal Hamlin. But who remembers vice presidents anyway? (Lithograph by William H. Pease, 1860; Print and Picture Department, Free Library of Philadelphia)

LYONS

Lyons commemorates Caleb Lyon, one-time governor of the Idaho Territory. Though justifiably accused of acting dishonestly and misusing public funds, Lyon was reappointed governor in 1865. He continued to abuse his power for another six months before leaving office.

MADRAS

The seat of Jefferson County, Madras is rich in semi-precious stones and "thunder eggs," agate and opal-filled nodules. Warm Springs Indians thought these rocks were hurled out of the craters of Mounts Jefferson and Hood by the Spirits of Thunder.

The derivation of the town's name is not so sinister. The town was named for a bolt of madras fabric!

MANNING

William Manning was a dime-novel author of the Northwest who came from Salem, Massachusetts. He and Nathaniel Hawthorne's mother, Betsy Manning, shared a common lineage. Manning used the money he earned from such novels as *Hotspur Hugh* and *The Banded Brothers of Giant's Army* to finance his life-long project: *The Genealogical and Biographical History of the Manning Families of New England*.

MARCOLA

Marcola was named for Mary Cole. The "a" was added for euphony.

MARION (— Forks)

On the outskirts of Marion is a monument to Viva la France, a Jersey cow that once held three world championships for milk and butter-fat production.

Marion County was originally Champooick County. The name was changed in 1849 to honor General Francis Marion, the "Swamp Fox" of Revolutionary War fame.

MARQUAM

Marquam, Clackamas County, was named for Philip Augustus Marquam (1828–1912), an old resident of Portland. In fact, Marquam Hill in Portland was named for him. It was said that "nearly all the public roads outside of the city (of Portland) were laid out during his administration."

Another source, however, gives the honor to Alfred Marquam, an early settler of the town. Alfred was the postmaster in 1889, when the town's name was changed from Butte Creek, a name under which it had been known since 1867, to Marquam.

MAUPIN

Maupin was named for Howard Maupin (1815–87). Maupin is alleged to be the killer of Paulina, chief of a band of Snakes, in 1867. He was also the owner of a ferry that traveled to Portland.

MAYGER

Mayger, Columbia County, was named for its first postmaster, Charles Mayger. He opened the office here in 1889.

McCREDIE SPRINGS

McCredie Springs is located on Salt Creek, and is one of Oregon's original health resorts. The name came from that of an early owner.

McEWEN

Charles E. Duckworth was the first postmaster at this Baker County site in 1893. The name, of course, is that of a local family.

McKENZIE BRIDGE

McKenzie Bridge has a purely descriptive name: For many years it was the crossing over the McKenzie River.

The river bears the name of Donald McKenzie (1783–1851). McKenzie explored the area in 1812 for John Jacob Astor's Pacific Fur Company. No little man, McKenzie weighed over 300 pounds, but was nicknamed "Perpetual Motion."

McMINNVILLE

McMinnville, seat of Yamhill County, has a name imported from the town of the same name in Tennessee, the former home of early settler, William T. Newby.

Newby arrived in Oregon in 1844, built a grist mill and created the town. McMinnville, Tennessee was named for Gen. Joseph McMinn, an early governor.

In 1849, the Oregon Baptist Educational Society was formed at Oregon City to create "a school of high moral and religious character." In 1858, the McMinnville School was chartered. In 1922, because of a grant of more than a quarter of a million dollars, the school changed its name to Linfield College in honor of the donor—Frances E. Ross Linfield—for her deceased husband, George Fisher Linfield.

McNARY

Charles Linza McNary (1874–1944) was a prominent politician from Oregon. He served several terms as a U. S. senator, and he ran unsuccessfully as Wendell Willkie's vice president in 1940.

MEACHAM

Meacham was platted in the late 19th century as Jerusalem. The plaza in the town's center was called Solomon Square. The town never realized its dream of becoming the new Jerusalem.

Meacham was named for Colonel Alfred B. Meacham (1806–82), a member of the Modoc Peace Commission, and former superintendent of Indian Affairs in Oregon. When the Indians at the conference killed General R. S. Canby and the Reverend Eleazer Thomas, Meacham fell to the ground with five bullets in him. Supposed dead, his body was stripped, and an Indian partially scalped him. T. F. Riddle's wife, a Modoc herself, shouted "Troops," and the Indian stopped. Meacham recovered from his wounds.

He opened the Blue Mountain Tavern here in 1863, on the outskirts of the Umatilla Indian Reservation. The town had been known as Meacham for almost 30 years when the town promoters tried Jerusalem. When the townspeople regained their senses, the old name of Meacham was returned.

MEDFORD

Medford was established in 1883 as an "opposition" town. Central Point, a few miles north, refused to contribute to the expansion of the Oregon & California Railroad, later the Southern Pacific. "Though poor in purse," one contemporary wrote, "the people of Jackson County contributed wheat, grain, beaver skins, and cash."

When the town was completed, it was called Middleford, because it was located at the middle of three fords on Bear Creek. David Loring, a railroad engineer, had lived in Medford, Massachusetts and suggested that name.

The railroad did not let Central Point forget its stinginess. There was no way that the company could take the town off the main line, but for years it refused to stop or sell tickets there. Medford was incorporated as a town in 1884 and reincorporated as a city in 1905.

MEDICAL SPRINGS

At one time, it was thought that the waters from the nearby spring had health-producing qualities.

METOLIUS

Metolius takes its name from the Metolius River. The name is a smorgasbord! The original Indian name for the waterway was Mpto-ly-as, and meant "light-colored fish." The name was then blended through a Latin primer to become Metolius.

MIDLAND

Some suggest that Midland received its name from its location. It is partially surrounded by marshes.

MIKKALO

The name of this town remembers John Mikkalo, an early settler.

MILL CITY

Mill City was named for the fact that it grew around a large sawmill.

MILLER

Miller was originally a shipping center for grain.

MILLICAN

At an earlier time, Millican, Deschutes County, was called a "one-man town." George Millican was the sole resident and mayor of the town. He was one of the first pioneers to raise cattle in the region.

Once located in Crook County, Millican opened its first post office in 1911, with Mabel C. Tozier as postmistress.

MILTON-FREEWATER

When first settled, Milton was a dry town. The early settlers banned the sale of all alcoholic beverages, but this did not sit well with latecomers.

In the late 19th century, the "wets," who owned water rights on a nearby stream, moved beyond the town's limits. People who bought lots in this new town received rights to the water as a bonus. That is the reason behind the name of Freewater. In Freewater, liquor was sold by the gallon at "gallon houses." Federal rules allowed them to sell liquor only by the gallon!

The towns, which really overlap, usually go by the name of Milton-Freewater.

MILWAUKIE

Milwaukie, Clackamas County, was founded in 1848 by Lot Whitcomb (1806/7–1857). The town soon became a rival to Portland. Here on the banks of the Willamette, Whitcomb and other investors built the *Lot Whitcomb*, a famous steamboat of the time. In spite of its ambitions, intentions and steamboat, Milwaukie never won out over Portland.

When the first post office opened here in 1850, with Whitcomb as the postmaster, the town's name was spelled Milwaukee.

MINAM

Minam takes its name from the Minam River.

MISSION

When first established, Mission was headquarters for the Umatilla Indian Agency.

MIST

Joseph Ranger opened the first post office at this Columbia County location in 1874. At that time, the town's name was Riverside. It became Mist, a more descriptive name, six years later.

MITCHELL

Mitchell, Wheeler County, was named for Senator John Hippie Mitchell (1835–1905). Mitchell was quite a colorful individual. While in the Senate he was accused of financial dishonesty and bigamy. At the time, he was living in Pennsylvania under an assumed name— really his middle name. He quickly got a divorce and stemmed the controversy. He died during an appeal over a conviction for bribery.

Established in 1867 as a station on The Dalles-Canyon City stage route, Mitchell had its problems. In 1884, the town was hit by a nine-foot wave that rushed over the bluff above the town. Raining boulders, the wave washed away houses, wagons and anything else in its way. Twenty-two years later, the town was struck by fire and nine buildings were destroyed. Another fire in 1899 destroyed 10 buildings.

In 1904, a cloudburst caused a 30-foot high wall of water to plummet over the town, demolishing everything in its path save those buildings taller than the water wall. Two months later, a smaller flood hit the town, but there was little left to destroy. Mitchell still survives.

MODOC POINT

Modoc Point was home to the Modoc Indians, under Captain Jack, before their return to Lost River. This move caused the Modoc War, and the resultant treacherous murder of General Canby.

The Modocs were native to California and Oregon.

MOHAWK

Mowhawk was named for the Mohawk River. The stream's name was given by settlers from New York who never gave consideration to remembering the Iroquois tribe. More likely they wanted to commemorate either the Mohawk river or a valley in their home state.

MOLALLA

The first white man to settle at this Clackamas County site was William Russel in 1840. The town's name comes from that of a river, derived from the name of an Indian tribe.

The tribe occupied the Molalla River Valley and roamed along the Cascades from Mount Hood to Mount Jefferson.

The first post office under this name was opened here in 1850, with Harrison Wright as postmaster.

MONITOR

In this lumbering region, a "monitor" was the type of raft that men used to grapple for sunken logs. Another source thinks that the name, given to the post office in 1869, really commemorates the exploits of the Civil War *Monitor*.

MONMOUTH

Monmouth, Polk County, was settled in 1852 by pioneers from Monmouth, Illinois. The next year, they donated 640 acres to the establishment of the town and the creation of a college under the auspices of the Christian Church (Disciples of Christ).

MONROE

When Samuel F. Starr opened the first post office in this Benton County community, he called it Starr's Point.

The name was changed to Monroe in the 1860s. The town is situated on the donation land claim of Joseph White. White received his claim in 1846, and built a sawmill here four years later.

MONUMENT

The Painted Hills, adjacent to town, contain fantastic shapes and colors that suggest monuments.

MORGAN

In its earliest days, this town was known as Saddle because of its location near Saddle Butte. The name was latter changed to reflect a more human appellation.

MOUNT ANGEL

Mount Angel was founded in 1880 as a German community. Monks of the Benedictine Order from Switzerland were attracted to the location, and, in 1904, built Mount Angel Abbey which overlooks the town. Earlier, in 1877, Father Adelhelm Odermatt, O.S.B., had established a monastery here.

The town actually took its name from Mount Angel Butte.

MOUNT HOOD

This community took its name from the majestic Mount Hood, which rises 11,239 feet into the sky. It is the highest point in the state of Oregon.

The mountain was named by Lieutenant William Broughton, who explored the Columbia River in 1792. The name was given in honor of Rear-Admiral Samuel Hood of the British Navy.

MOUNT VERNON

Mount Vernon took its name from a nearby mountain.

MULINO

In 1882, the original name selected for Mulino, Clackamas County, was Molino, the Spanish word for "mill." The post office felt the name was too close to Molalla, so they made a slight modification.

The community was first called Howard's Mill, when a grist mill was built here in 1851.

The first post office, whose postmaster was James G. Foster, did not open here until 1883.

MYRTLE CREEK

Myrtle Creek took its name from a nearby waterway. At one time, this area was the stomping ground for prehistoric animals. In 1927, a fossil tusk was uncovered. The tusk measured six feet in length and 10 inches in diameter.

The creek's name was given because of the abundance of Oregon myrtle growing there.

MYRTLE POINT

Myrtle Point was named for the abundance of the myrtle shrub in the area.

The first post office to open at this Coos County site in 1872 was named Ott, and operated by Christian Lehnherr. The name was changed from Ott to Myrtle Point in 1876.

NARROWS

Narrows is a slender connection of land between Harney and Malheur Lakes, which explains its name.

NASHVILLE

There is no Tennessee connection here. Nashville, Lincoln County, was named for Wallis Nash (1837–1926), an Englishman who helped build the Oregon Pacific Railroad. Nash was also one of the drafters of the framework for Oregon State University.

NECANICUM

When the first post office was opened at this Clatsop County location in 1896, the postmaster was Herman Ahlers and the town bore his name. Three years later, Ahlers became Push. Finally in 1907, Push did not become shove; it became Necanicum.

The town's name, we are told, is that of an Indian village.

NEHALEM

Nehalem's name was taken from the nearby Nehalem River. The river name comes from the Indian *ne*, "place," and *halem*, "a peaceful place." The name was an Indian tribal one.

A great—and mysterious—quantity of beeswax was discovered at Nehalem in the 18th century. Alexander Henry mentioned the deposit in his journal in 1815, explaining that the wax had arrived aboard a Spanish ship. It was reported that the Hudson Bay Company purchased quantities of it from the Killamooks. Much of the wax was in 20-pound blocks and marked with "I.H.S." and "I.H.N.," both Latin initials for phrases used by Roman Catholics. It is now believed that the wax was brought here by the Spanish ship,

San José, in 1769. The ship was carrying supplies to the mission at San Diego. It was lost at sea.

David E. Pease opened the first post office at this Clatsop location in 1870.

NEOTAU

When the post office was opened in this Lincoln County area, the people wanted to name it Devil's Lake because the town is located near the northern end of the body of water. But postal authorities feared confusion with Devils Lake, North Dakota, and Delake, Oregon (now a part of Lincoln City).

Searching for an unusual name, someone came up with the Indian name, Neotau. Though local tradition has it that the word translates to "devil's lake," no one can prove it.

NETARTS

Taking its name from the nearby Netarts Bay, Netarts is a beach resort.

NEWBERG. As a boy, President Herbert Hoover lived here with his uncle, and attended nearby Pacific Academy. (The Hoover-Minturn House Museum Committee, Susan B. Campbell, co-chair. Photograph by John C. Beckman)

NEWBERG

Newberg was the first Oregon community permitted to hold formal Quaker meetings.

As a child, Herbert Hoover lived here with his uncle. The former president was in the first graduating class at Pacific Academy, a school established by the Quakers and later renamed George Fox College. Fox was the founder of The Society of Friends.

The town was named in 1869 by Sebastian Brutscher. He gave the town the English spelling of his own hometown, Nauberg, Germany.

NEWBERG. As a young man, Herbert C. Hoover earned his living as a mining engineer. He is pictured here in 1904. (The Hoover-Minturn House Museum Committee and Oregon Historical Society; photograph by Associated Press)

NEW BRIDGE

New Bridge was named by the town's first postmaster, Joseph Gale.

Originally located in Union County, New Bridge became part of Baker when that county was established.

NEWPORT

Newport, Lincoln County, was once a "new" port at the entrance to Yaquina Bay. At the southern tip of town is Yaquina Bay State Park, home of the Old Yaquina Bay Lighthouse, established in 1871.

The first settler arrived in 1855, but several years passed before a village grew. Newport was incorporated in 1882 and called the "San Francisco of the North."

Newport is one of only a few cities in Oregon which was established as a government site. Property previously contained in Alsea and Siletz Indian reservations was thrown open to white settlers in 1866. This spurred population growth in the area.

NORTH BEND

Protruding into Coos Bay, North Bend, Coos County, was called Yarrow when first settled in 1853. Growth did not begin until 1856–58 when Captain Asa M. Simpson built a sawmill and a shipyard here.

The captain took credit for naming the town, but it might have been F. G. Lockhart, a member of the Coos Bay Company, who named it in 1853.

NORTH POWDER

North Powder was founded in the 1870s by James DeMoss. The town was named for a branch of the Powder River that meets the main river at this point.

NORWAY

The first post office at this Coos County site was opened in 1876 by Jonathan Henry Schweder. The town's name came from the fact that it was settled by Norwegians.

NOTI

Depending on which authority you believe, Noti could have been named:

(1) after a trapper who lived in the area;

(2) for a pair of pioneers with only one horse, who practiced "ride and tie" (one would ride a specified distance, then tie the horse for the other man who walked); or,

(3) by an Indian witnessing such an operation, who noticed that the rider did not tie up the horse.

The decision is up to the reader, but those of us who have children will always remember the universal disclaimer: "Not I!"

NYSSA

The railroad named the station here with a short, unique name. No reason was given. The fact that the name appears in Greek mythology has no connection. Neither does the fact that Nyssa is the generic name for the tupelo or gum tree.

OAKLAND

Oakland, located on Calapoya Creek, was named for the abundance of Oregon white, or Garry oak, in the valley. The first Oakland, located about three miles north of the present site, was a stop on the California State Company's route.

OAKRIDGE

Oakridge is named for the oak trees located here.

ODELL

William Odell, who settled here in 1861, donated his name to the community.

OLEX

The printer's imp was at it again! When they decided to honor Alex Smith, a local resident, with the name of this town, someone changed the "a" to an "o."

OLNEY

Olney, Clatsop County, had its first post office opened in 1875 by Mrs. Mary A. Gray. In 1855, Nathan Olney (ca. 1829–89) was the Sub-Indian Agent at The Dalles.

Olney was a colorful character who worked at just about everything available during the pioneering days. He was a prospector, ran a stock ranch, raised a company of volunteers for service in the Civil War, was sheriff of Wasco County, and was even adopted by the Yakima tribe. Besides, he was married three times—twice to Annette, a Yakima squaw. She was his first and third!

ONTARIO

Ontario was settled in the 1880s and took its name from the Canadian province.

OPHIR

Elizabeth J. Burrow opened the first post office in this Curry County community in 1891.

Ophir is mentioned in the Bible as being rich in gold. The name was given here with the hope that the Biblical promise would come true.

OREGON CITY

Originally in Clapsop County, Oregon City was the state's first capital and the end of the Oregon Trail. It is the seat of Clackamas County.

The Hudson Bay Company did not want to settle this area, but was obliged to do so because of an impending settlement of the boundary dispute between the United States and England. "It becomes an important object to acquire as ample an occupation of the Country and Trade as possible," company officials wrote in 1828, "on the South as well as on the North side of the Columbia River, looking always to the Northern side falling to our Share on a division, and to secure this, it may be as well to have something to give up on the South when the final arrangement comes to be made."

The company ordered Dr. John McLoughlin, of Vancouver, to establish a sawmill at "the falls of the Wilhamet where the same Establishment of people can attend to the Mill, watch the Fur & Salmon Trade, and take care of a Stock of Cattle."

In 1842, Dr. McLoughlin named the town and had it platted by Sidney Walter Moss, who just happened to have a pocket compass.

The first post office under the name of Oregon City opened in 1850, with John D. Holeman as postmaster.

The name for the city obviously came from that of the state. The state's name, on the other hand, came about from a typographical error. When Major Robert Rogers, an English army officer, requested to explore the American country west of the Great Lakes in 1765, he referred to the area as Ouragon. He did not get the grant he requested. Later, Captain Jonathan Carver wrote up the account of his explorations in 1766–67. His account, published more than a decade later, spelled the name Oregon, but on his charts he continued to use Ouragon.

Thomas Jefferson used the accepted form in 1803 when he issued instructions to Meriwether Lewis. William Cullen Bryant, in his 1817 poem, "Thanatopsis," immortalized the current spelling. Since then there has been no argument.

ORETOWN

The name of this town has nothing to do with mining. The name is an abbreviation of Oregontown, an earlier name!

ORIENT

(See ORIENT, Washington.)

OTTER ROCK

This name was given because the place was once the stomping ground of the sea otter.

OWYHEE

Owyhee takes its name from the lake of the same name. The lake was named by Hawaiians (then known as Sandwich Islanders) who worked for the Hudson Bay Company. Owyhee was the 19th century spelling of Hawaii. Apparently, two Sandwich Islanders were killed in 1819 at this waterway. The stream was then called Sandwich Island River. The name was changed in 1826 to Owyhee.

Owyhee was also the name of John Dominis' 1829 brig that allegedly was the first sea-going craft to navigate the Willamette River.

The Vale-Owyhee Irrigation Project was the largest irrigation project in Oregon.

OXBOW

The name for this Baker County community is of fairly recent origin. Originally named Homestead, the town changed its name to Oxbow in 1965. The name is descriptive of something that is curved back on itself.

PACIFIC CITY

Pacific City was the site of one of the earliest Pacific Coast town-site frauds! In the mid-19th century, Dr. Elijah White, "the original town-site boomer in the Northwest," sold a large number of lots in his model town to people who had never seen the town. In fact, the town only existed on paper. One of the people duped by White was the famous artist Charles Russell. He left the site and moved to Willapa Harbor where he made a fortune shipping oysters to California.

Dr. John McNulty, the Pacific Mail Steamship Company's physician, was also involved in the promotion of this town, offering "the most desirable lots in Pacific City, at the mouth of the Columbia River, Oregon."

PAISLEY

Paisley, it is said, was named in 1873 by Charles Ennis. He named it after his hometown in Scotland.

PARKDALE

Located on the northeast edge of Mount Hood National Forest, Parkdale was established in 1910. It is the southern terminus of the Mount Hood Railroad, one of the nation's few remaining railroads operating on a switchback. This allows trains to climb from the Mount Hood canyon to the valley.

PAULINA

Paulina does not recall the memory of a wife or lover. Rather, the name came from a very warlike Indian chief (?–1867). He was considered by his federal counterparts to be the "most intelligent and crafty" of the Indian chiefs.

Chief Paulina was accused of countless atrocities, and was finally murdered while he was eating roasted ox. Howard Maupin took the credit for killing him. The chief's name also appears elsewhere as Paunina.

PEEDEE

Peedee takes its name from a South Carolina town by the name of Pee Dee. That town took its name from the river, which bore an Indian tribal name.

PEEL

The name for this community goes back to England. Sir Robert Peel was the British prime minister in the 1840s. Along with Lord Aberdeen, Peel was willing to negotiate with the Americans over land north of the 49th parallel. The English, however, made defensive by Polk's inaugural address, sent a group from Canada to the Columbia to determine how to protect their interests. Two members of that group were Lieutenant William Peel, a son of the prime minister, and Sir John Gordon, Lord Aberdeen's brother.

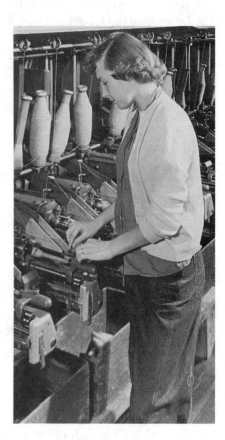

PENDLETON. The name Pendleton is the hallmark of fine woolen goods. These archival photographs show the process of taking the wool and making it into blankets and shirts. (Pendleton Woolen Mills)

PENDLETON

Pendleton, Umatilla County, was named for George Hunt Pendleton, the Democratic candidate for president in 1868. Pendleton shared the unsuccessful McClellan-Pendleton ticket of four years earlier. The Pendleton Woolen Mills still operates here.

Land was cheap in this area, and Moses E. Goodwin traded a team of horses to a squatter for 160 acres near the mouth of Wild Horse Creek on the Umatilla River. The only other person to occupy land on Goodwin's tract was G. W. Bailey.

When the county was organized in 1862, Goodwin and Bailey fought for the county seat. Bailey was selected as county judge, and when it seemed the tide was going against his town, county records were moved to his house. After surveying the records, he decided that the county seat would be here. The people from Umatilla City, the main opponents, sued—and lost. Pendleton was surveyed and platted in 1870.

An interesting feature of Pendleton is the underground system of tunnels built by Chinese workers in the late 19th century. Tours are conducted of these tunnels, featuring the Shamrock cardroom, the laundry, meat market, the jail and a bordello.

PHILOMATH

The town of Philomath, Benton County, takes its name from Philomath College, chartered in 1865 by the United Brethren Church. The name itself comes from the Greek and means "lover of learning."

Philomath College was located here until 1929. Organized by the Church of the Brethren in 1865, the school was chartered as a Christian co-educational institution that specialized in the liberal arts.

George W. Henkle was the first postmaster in 1868.

PHOENIX

Phoenix was settled by Samuel Cover in 1850. The name, we are told, was the result of a catastrophic fire.

A blockhouse was built here in 1855, and called Camp Baker. At that time, a year after it was platted, the town was known as Gastown. Though Camp Baker was only manned by 15 men, it withheld a siege by the Rogue River Indians.

Though perhaps having nothing to do with this town, the famous "Phoenix Buttons" are located at several Columbia River sites. These brass buttons, whose origin is unknown, were used by traders in their dealings with the Indians. Each button was numbered and emblazoned with the legendary bird rising from the ashes.

PIKE

Pike takes its name from Zebulon M. Pike, the famous explorer and hero of the War of 1812. Pikes Peak bears his name, though he did not name it after himself.

PILOT ROCK

The town was named for a "large basaltic bluff" in the area.

PINE (— Grove; —hurst)

Pinehurst was once known as Shake because of the hand-hewn "shakes" or shingles that the early settlers used to frame their homes.

PISTOL RIVER

The name of the river, from which the town drew its name, was given because of a pistol lost in the stream in 1853.

Richard E. Guthridge opened the first post office at this Curry County locale in 1927.

PITTSBURG

When Peter Brous opened the first post office here in Columbia County in 1879, he named it Pittsburgh, like the Pennsylvania town. Postal officials got the "h" out of there in 1892.

PLEASANT HILL

Pleasant Hill, originally located in Lane County but now a part of Benton, opened its first post office in 1850. Elijah Bristow was the first postmaster. Bristow was also one of the first settlers to arrive here in 1846.

The word "pleasant" was used to give some descriptive sense of the area. In fact, Bristow was supposed to have looked around him and cried: "What a pleasant hill. This is my claim."

PLEASANT HOME

Once located in Clackamas County, Pleasant Home is now situated in Mutnomah County. The first post office at the site was opened in 1876; Orlando S. Murray was postmaster. (See PLEASANT HILL, Oregon.)

PLEASANT VALLEY

Pleasant Valley, Baker County, opened its first post office in 1868, with Jared Lockwood as postmaster. (See PLEASANT HILL, Oregon.)

PLUSH

The story told about the naming of this town is that, in the early days, a local Piute chief liked to gamble in a saloon in the yet-unnamed town.

The chief, they say, liked poker and would gamble horses and wives—which is about all the Indians had to trade. One night he was engaged in a fixed game, when he was dealt a flush. The chief was ecstatic! Unfortunately, the next player was dealt a higher flush. Perhaps realizing that he was set up, the Indian talked about that hand a great deal. His English, we are told, was not the best, and "flush came out "plush." That's how the name came into being.

The village actually began in about 1904 with the building of a store by Daniel Boone (no relation).

PORTLAND

The name of this Multnomah County city was decided by the toss of a coin.

Amos Lovejoy and Francis Pettygrove started to build a city on this site in 1844. They called it Stumptown because all they could see were the remains of large trees. A year later, they decided to rename the city, but could not agree. Pettygrove came from Portland, Maine; Lovejoy, from Boston, Massachusetts. The name came from the coin toss.

Although far enough away to avoid the problems experienced in San Francisco during the gold rush, Portland was close enough to take advantage of the need for provisions and supplies. Today, it is the largest city in Oregon.

PORT ORFORD

Port Orford, Curry County, was named for George, Earl of Orford, by Captain George Vancouver when he spotted the area in 1752. Settled in the mid-19th century, Port Orford became the center for the shipping of cedar.

A key attraction at Port Orford is Battle Rock. In 1851, nine white settlers held off an undetermined number of angry Indians here.

The town, previously located in Jackson and Coos counties, had its first post office opened in 1855 by Reginald H. Smith.

POST

Post, Crook County, is the approximate center of the state of Oregon. The town takes its name from its first postmaster, Walter H. Post, who opened the office here in 1889.

POWELL BUTTE

This site takes its name from the nearby Powell Buttes. The buttes were named in honor of the Joab Powell family. The Reverend

Powell (1799–1873) was a circuit rider in Linn County. Once, while offering up a prayer as chaplain to the Oregon legislature, Powell prayed: "Lord, forgive them, for they know not what they do."

Moses Niswonger opened the first post office at this Crook County site in 1909.

POWERS

Powers was the end of the Coos Bay branch of the Southern Pacific Railroad. Gustaveous A. Brown opened the first post office at this Coos County site in 1915.

PRAIRIE CITY

Prairie City was named for the "prairie" of its original location, about three miles up the Dixie Creek.

Dixie Camp was an 1860s gold mining center. Ten years later, when the gold was placered out, miners left and other residents moved to establish Prairie City, founded in 1871.

PRINEVILLE

Barney Prine was the first settler to this area. Prine arrived in 1868, and eight years later Monroe Hedges laid out the town. Things did not move that slowly, if we can rely on a contemporary account: "During the summer of 1868 Barney Prine started Pineville," the account reads, "by building a dwelling house, store, blacksmith shop, hotel and saloon. He was all of one day building them."

Other sources believe the town was founded in 1870 by Monroe Hodges, but named for Prine, the first settler in the Ochoco region.

A post office was opened in 1873, with Daniel E. Thomas as postmaster. Many of the bloodiest "sheep and cattle wars" took place in this vicinity. During those wars, the town was a city of refuge.

Prineville is the seat of Crook County.

PROMISE

The founders of this town used its name to signify "a land of promise."

PROSPECT

The town was originally named Deskins, for the operator of a late 19th century sawmill. The name was changed to indicate that they hoped for a better future.

RAINBOW

This town was named Rainbow because it was a good place to find rainbow trout.

RAINIER

Founded in 1851, this Columbia County mill town took its name from Mount Rainier, which can be seen to the northeast. The mountain was named for Rear-Admiral Peter Rainier of the British Navy, an old friend of Vancouver.

When it was founded by Charles E. Cox, the town's original name was Eminence. The name was later changed to Fox's Landing and then to Rainier. Rainier was incorporated in 1885.

Formerly situated in Washington County, Ranier had its first post office opened under the Ranier name in 1854. Marshall B. Millard was postmaster.

RALEIGH HILLS

Henry Raleigh was a famous magazine illustrator, born in Oregon in 1800.

REEDSPORT

Reedsport is named for its most famous citizen: Robin Reed. Reed was editor of the *Port Umpqua Courier*, and a former amateur wrestler and Olympic champion.

Flooding was so prevalent in this town's early history that early buildings and sidewalks were sometimes elevated three to eight feet above the ground!

REMOTE

The name of this Coos County town was suggested because of its distance from other settlements. Herman S. Davis opened the first post office here in 1887.

RESTON

Unlike the Virginia community that was Robert E. Simon's town, this community received its name because it was a rest stop on the stage. To avoid duplication elsewhere, the namers tacked on the "-on."

RHODODENDRON

One can find Rhododendron and rhododenrons at the foot of Mount Hood in Clackamas County. In fact, in an effort to reduce confusion with the town of Rome, the town of Rowe changed its name to that of the flowers that grew in abundance in the area.

Rowe's post office opened in 1909. The name was changed from Rowe to Zig Zag in 1917. The next year it became Rhododendron.

RICHLAND

Richland, Baker County, was named because early settlers saw just that: fertile soil in the Eagle Valley. Originally located in Union County, Richland opened its first post office in 1899. Eli Chandler was postmaster.

RICKREALL

Rickreall, Polk County, has a name that is a corruption of the French *la creole,* "the Creole." But is that how it got its name?

John E. Lyle arrived in this area in 1845, and opened a school in Nathaniel Ford's house. The next year, Lyle and his friends established the Jefferson Institute on the farm of Carey Embree.

RIDDLE

Riddle obtained its original water supply from Cow Creek. The creek was so named because a settler recovered his cattle in the canyon. Another source believes the name was that of a family.

T. Frank Riddle (1832–1906) and his Modoc wife, Toby, acted as interpretors in the tragic Medoc "peace conference."

ROARING SPRINGS RANCH

The name of this community came from the ranch of the same name. The ranch took its name from a stream that broke noisily.

ROCKVILLE

Rockville obtained its name from fossil-bearing rocks discovered in the area.

ROGUE RIVER

The community of Rogue River takes its name from the waterway. French-Canadian trappers had low opinions of the Indians living on this waterway and called them *coquins,* "rogues." The river later became known as *aux Coquins.* By the 1840s, the name had been translated to English.

ROGUE RIVER. The trappers who worked this area didn't like the Indians who lived along this waterway, and they called them *coquins*, "rogues." The river became known as *aux Coquins*. (U.S. Department of Agriculture, Forest Service, Rogue River National Forest Historic Photograph Collection)

ROME

Rome was named for its imposing formations of fossil-bearing clay. The rock formations are called "the Walls of Rome."

ROSEBURG

Roseburg was named for Aaron Rose (1813–89), who settled here in 1851. An astute businessman, Rose traded a horse for the land claim. When the people were voting on the site for a county seat, Rose lavishly entertained them all and, guess what? Roseburg became seat of Douglas County.

The original name for the community was Deer Creek. Roseburg was home to Oregon's first territorial governor, Joseph Lane. Lane, a vice-presidential candidate in 1860, is buried in the local Masonic Cemetery.

ROSE LODGE

Rose Lodge was named by the first postmistress—for her garden.

ROWENA

Rowena was named, in part, to honor a railroad official, H. S. Rowe.

RYE VALLEY

The post office at Rye Valley, Baker County, goes back to 1878 when first postmaster William Blain opened its doors.

S

SAGINAW

The original place to bear this name was in Michigan. The name is Ojibway Indian, a place "where the Sauks live."

ST. HELENS

MOUNT ST. HELENS.
(Forest Service)

From the town of St. Helens, Columbia County, one can see its namesake to the northeast: Mount St. Helens.

First known as Wyeth's Rock for Nathaniel Wyeth, an early trader, the town was settled in 1834. Captain H. M. Knighton laid it out in 1847 as a donation land claim. St. Helens was created to compete with Portland which had newly been established. Knighton referred to Portland as "Little Stump Town." Some say Knighton named the town St. Helens for his native home in England. It is more likely he named it for the mountain.

Some records suggest that St. Helens carried other names, such as Plymouth and Plymouth Rock. According to postal records, St. Helens was once part of Washington County. Its first post office opened in 1853, with Benjamin M. Dickell as postmaster.

SAINT PAUL

Retired Hudson Bay trappers and their Indian wives settled here in the late 1830s.

The Reverend Francis Norbett Blanchet established a Roman Catholic parish here in 1839: St. Paul Roman Catholic Church. The church was built in 1846, a year after Father Blanchet left to become bishop of the archdiocese based in Oregon City. The church expanded on the chapel built by the traders in 1836.

SALEM

Jason Lee, a Methodist missionary, founded Salem, Marion County, out of frustration.

Lee and his nephew, Daniel, had come to Oregon in 1834 "to teach (Indians) to cultivate the ground and live more comfortably than they could by hunting, and as they do this, teach them religion." Their mission, located on the east bank of the Willamette River near French Prairie, was the first established by any denomination in Oregon. They were not very successful, so Lee tried his hand at real estate development.

In 1840, Lee moved his Willamette mission to a more favorable location, the present-day site of Salem. The missionary laid out a town and sold lots to finance his next dream: the Oregon Institute. He was more successful at this venture. The Institute is now Willamette University, the oldest institution of higher learning west of the Mississippi. Despite Lee's progress, his failure among the Indians got back to the Methodist Missionary Society. That group suspended him in 1843. He returned to the East.

When the settlers sought a name for the future capital of the state, they chose the Calapooya Indian word *chemeketa*, "place of rest." The missionaries, however, preferred the Biblical word *salem*, which means the same thing. Another source thinks the name was transported from Massachusetts.

J. B. McLane opened the post office here, while the town was still part of Clatsop County, in 1849.

SALISBURY

Charles R. Foster was the first postmaster in this Baker County community. He opened the office in 1906, in a town whose name migrated here from the East.

SAMS VALLEY

Sams Valley was once the home of Chief Sam of the Rogue River Indians.

The chief waged war against the white settlers early in 1852. He was in constant conflict with federal troops and volunteers. That all ended when he, along with several other chiefs, signed the Table Rock Treaty of 1853. The treaty established temporary reservations for the several tribes until more permanent arrangements could be made. After the treaty was signed, Chief Sam remained neutral.

SANTA CLAUS

Santa Claus was named for publicity purposes, especially for the sale of postmarks at Christmas time.

SCAPPOOSE

The name of Scappoose, a one-of-a-kind name, is Indian (no one is quite sure which Indian) and means "gravelly ground."

The first white settler here was James Bates, an American sailor who apparently jumped ship from the *Owyhee* in 1829. Scappoose was not incorporated until 1921.

When Samuel T. Gosa opened the first post office at this Columbia county location, the town's name was Columbia. Columbia became Scappoose in 1872.

SCIO

Scio was named for a town in Ohio. The Ohio town took its name from the Mediterranean island of Chios.

SCOTTSBURG

Scottsburg, originally a part of Umpqua County but now in Benton County, was founded in 1850 by Levi Scott (1797–1890), one of Jesse Applegate's companions. Scott had helped open the South Road across the Cascades in 1846.

Stephen F. Chadwick opened the first post office here in 1851. Scottsburg also was the spot where the first newspaper was published in southern Oregon.

SEAL ROCK

Seal Rock takes its name from the fact that sea lions bask in the sun on the rocks in Yaquina Bay.

SEASIDE

Seaside, Clatsop County, is located just where its name implies. It is the state's oldest and largest ocean resort. It is also the end of the Lewis and Clark Trail. A monument at the foot of Broadway commemorates their journey.

When Anthony J. Cloutue opened the first office here, the town's name was Summer House. The name was changed to Seaside House in 1873, and then shortened to Seaside five years later.

Not far from Seaside, at Klootchy Creek Park, is the world's tallest Sitka spruce, almost 200 feet high. This particular tree was 300 years old when Columbus arrived!

SERVICE CREEK

Service Creek, once a single word, was established in about 1885, and named for the abundance of service-berry bushes found in the vicinity.

SHEDD

The land of Captain Frank Shedd was the site of this town, which grew up after the arrival of the railroad in 1871.

SHERIDAN

Philip Henry Sheridan (1831–88) came to Oregon in 1855 as a recently-commissioned second lieutenant of the 4th U.S. Infantry. A kind and compassionate individual in his affairs with the Indians, Sheridan served here until 1861, and the outbreak of the Civil War. He went on to rise to general during that conflict.

Sheridan, Yamhill County, was named in his honor.

SILETZ

Siletz took its name from the river, which bears the name of an Indian tribe, part of the Salish family. Another possibility is the name of the chief of the Des Chutes.

SILVER LAKE

Silver Lake was established by 20 settlers in 1873. Two years later it had its own post office. H. F. West platted the town in 1885 and allowed 15 acres for further development.

On Christmas Day, 1894, Silver Lake was almost decimated by fire. During a community celebration, an oil lamp was overturned and 43 of the 200 residents were killed; 31, seriously burned. An Oregon state law that requires public building doors to open outward, it is said, came about because of the Silver Lake catastrophe.

SILVERTON

Silverton is just that: a "town" on Silver Creek. The earliest settlement here, centering around a sawmill built in 1846, was called Milford.

Silverton Bobbie, a dog from this town, was taken east in 1926. He disappeared from the car somewhere in Indiana. Finding his way back to Silverton, he became the hero of Charles Alexander's *Bobbie, a Great Collie.*

SILVIES

Silvies bears the name of its river. The stream was named for Antoine Sylvaille. He explored the area in 1826.

SIMNASHO

The name for Simnasho is an anglicization of the Indian *simnassa,* "thorn bush."

SISTERS

Sisters, Deschutes County, took its name from the three peaks of the Cascade Mountains. The peaks were originally known as Faith, Hope and Charity, but changed to North Sister, South Sister and Middle Sister.

When the townspeople of Camp Polk petitioned for a post office in 1885, they suggested that The Sisters be the name. Postal authorities approved only half the name. Originally in Wasco County, Camp Polk was officially changed to Sisters in 1888.

The town sports wooden sidewalks, and the Hotel Sisters, one of the few remaining original buildings in town, has been restored to a period saloon and restaurant.

SITKUM

In the slang of the Chinook Indians, *sitkum* means "half." The first use of the name was for the creek, which is small. Some feel the name was derogatory when given.

SIXES

The name of Sixes, Curry County, has no demonic reference. The town took its name from a nearby stream. The name of the waterway, most likely, came from the Chinook Indian's greeting: *Klahowya Sikhs.* Another source feels the word came from a tribal name, Sik-ses-tene, shortened and respelled.

Newton Divelbiss opened the first post office here in 1888.

SODAVILLE

Sodaville was named for the cold-water spring in the Sodaville Springs State Park. The spring had carbon dioxide which made it bubble, like soda water.

SPARTA

Sparta was a mining town founded in the 1860s. The name was taken from that of an ancient Greek city, where the ideal was strength and courage.

When the ore petered out, the miners moved on. They were replaced by hordes of Chinese who had been released from work on the first transcontinental railroad.

The Chinese were constantly harrassed, robbed and murdered by white miners who disliked having them around. Some who thought the provisions of the Chinese Exclusion Act were not enough threw them out of town.

Originally located in Union County, Sparta is part of Baker County. Its first post office opened in Union in 1889; Joseph A. Wright was postmaster.

SPRAGUE RIVER

Sprague River took its name from the waterway. The river acknowledges the contributions made by Franklin G. Sprague (1825–95).

Sprague, a soldier and industrialist, rediscovered Crater Lake in 1865, renaming it Lake Majesty. A year later, he acted as interpreter for General Crook.

SPRAY

Spray was settled in the 1860s and named for an early settler, J. F. Spray.

SPRINGFIELD

Springfield is located on the east bank of the Willamette River.

STAFFORD

Mrs. Sallie S. Henry opened the first post office at this Clackamas County location in 1878.

STANFIELD

Stanfield was named for the Stanfield family that owned a nearby ranch. Senator Robert Nelson Stanfield (1877–1945) was its most famous member.

STAYTON

The town of Stayton was named for Drury S. Stayton. Stayton's land claim was north of the town. Before the town was platted in 1872, a store was in operation here. The storekeeper and his family built a grist mill here in 1876.

STEAMBOAT

"Steamboat Code" was a term of derision used to describe the voluminous code of laws adopted by the first Territorial legislature in 1849. Amory Holbrook coined the phrase because he felt the code contained a "miscellaneous cargo."

SUBLIMITY

Sublimity College was established in this town. One of the first teachers at the college, chartered in 1858, was Milton Wright. Wright was the father of Orville and Wilbur Wright, thinkers who successfully launched the first airplane at Kitty Hawk.

The town was named because the original namer thought the scenery was totally sublime.

SUMMER LAKE

Summer Lake was discovered by Frémont in 1843. He wrote about discovering this beautiful lake in December, "not a particle of ice was to be seen on the lake, or snow on its borders, and all was like summer or spring . . . Shivering on snow three feet deep, and stiffening in a cold north wind, we exclaimed at once that the names of Summer Lake and Winter Ridge should be applied to those two proximate places of such sudden and violent contrast. . . ."

The town takes its name from that body of water.

SUMMIT

Summit, Benton County, opened its first post office in 1868; James P. Chilburg was postmaster. The town's name is descriptive.

SUTHERLIN

The first turkey farm in Oregon was established by a Mr. Sutherlin in 1851.

The valley in which Sutherlin lies, Sutherlin Valley, was originally called Camas Swale. In the spring, the valley floor was covered with the blue camus flowers, giving the impression of a blue lake.

This town was founded by the family of Fendal Sutherlin (1824–1901). Sutherlin was credited with developing the early fruit industry in Oregon.

SWEET HOME

Sweet Home is the sentimental name given to this community in the 1840s by pioneer Lowell Ames.

SWISSHOME

Early settlers to this community at the confluence of Lake Creek and the Siuslaw River came from Switzerland.

TALBOT

Major Theodore Talbot (?–1862) was a Kentuckian assigned to the second Frémont expedition from 1843 to 1844. When the area was opened as Oregon Territory in 1849, Talbot returned. He spent much of that year searching for coal.

TALENT

The first name for this community was Wagner. The name was changed in the late 19th century to Talent, in honor of A. P. Talent, who platted the townsite.

TANGENT

When the railroad came through this Linn County portion of the Willamette Valley in 1877, it encountered the longest stretch of land where it could use straight track. People called the town that grew around the railroad Tangent.

TENMILE

Tenmile, located in the Lookingglass Valley, was first settled about 1852 by John Byron. The most popular source for the name choice is that it was 10 miles from Folurnoy.

TERREBONNE

Terrebonne, Deschutes County, was platted in 1909, and named Hillman for a railroad official. Three years later, when the post office was established, the name was changed to Terre Bonne, French for "good earth." One source suggests the name was used "possibly to avoid confusion with Hillsboro, Oregon."

When the first post office was established at this site in 1910, the town was located in Crook County. Ervin A. Cleland was postmaster. The name was changed from Hillman in 1911.

THE DALLES

The Dalles, Wasco County, takes its name from the French *dalle*. It was the name French Canadian settlers used to describe the point where the Columbia River narrowed and then spilled over a number of falls. Another translation of the word suggests a stone used to flag gutters or troughs, and the basalt formations along the rapids resemble these gutters.

Until 1845, when a wagon road was built, the only means of continuing a journey on the Oregon Trail through this area was by floating wagons down the Columbia. The "dalles" have since disappeared, submerged by the backwater of The Dalles Dam.

Troops from Columbia Barracks, Fort Vancouver, founded an installation here called Fort Dalles in 1850. Within two years, a town had grown around the fortification.

The post office was opened here in 1851, as Dalles. Two years later, the name was changed to Wascopum. Finally, in 1860, it was renamed The Dalles.

TIDEWATER

Tidewater's name signifies its location: The Alsea River widens into an estuary here, with salt and fresh water merging together. The first white settler to the area was G. W. Collins who, in 1860, was the Indian agent for the Alsea Tribe Reservation.

TIGARD

Tigard was named for Wilson M. Tigard, a local land owner.

TILLAMOOK

Tillamook, the first town to be settled in Clatsop County, was indirectly named for the Tillamook Indian tribe that once lived here.

The first settler was Joseph Champion. He arrived in 1851, and took up residence in a hollow spruce tree which he called his "castle." Ten years later, a 70-year-old Thomas Stillwell and his family purchased land, and a year later they opened the first store.

The first name for the site was Hoquarten, Indian for "the landing"—the town is located on the eastern shore of Tillamook Bay. The name was later changed to its current one, which translates as "land of many waters."

Tillamook is the center of Oregon's dairy industry, and seat of Tillamook County.

TIMBER

Timber is a generally descriptive name. In the early days of Oregon settlement, pioneers were encouraged to cut trees for personal use. Selling timber to giant logging companies rapidly became a get-rich scheme for some. In the end, more than a million acres of the best timberland in the state fell into the hands of unethical businessmen.

TIMBERLINE LODGE

Timberline Lodge takes its name from the Timerline Lodge, a hotel built during the Depression by the Works Progress Administration.

The hotel, styled after a European mountain retreat, opened in 1937 and stands on the upper southern slope of Mount Hood. The first post office opened here two years later.

TOLEDO

Toledo, as one might suspect, was named for the Ohio town. The namer was Joseph D. Graham, son of an early settler who had come from Toledo, Ohio. Homesick, he asked that the name become that of his former hometown.

The post office was opened here in 1868, and the town experienced great growth during World War I by supplying spruce lumber for the building of airplanes.

TRAIL

Trail took its name from a twisting Indian trail that wandered around Trail Creek from the Rogue to the Umpqua River.

TRASK

Trask took its name from the Trask River which, in turn, was named for Elbridge Trask (1815–63), an early settler. Trask worked as a blacksmith during the day, and taught school at night.

TROUTDALE

The logical name for this community was drawn from a pond in the small valley that had been stocked with trout.

TUALATIN

Located in the Tualatin Valley, this town took its name from the river that runs through the valley. The name, of Indian origin, translates to mean "slow river." The Tualatin Tribe, also known as the Trality or Atfalati Indians, gave up their lands and settled on the Grande Ronde Reservation in 1854.

TUMALO

The name, Tumalo, comes from the Indian *tumallowa*, "icy water." This Deschutes County town was created during the construction of the Tumalo Irrigation Project in the early 20th century. When the post office was established here in 1904, with William G. Stiles as postmaster, the town's name was Laidlaw and it was located in Crook County. The name was changed from Laidlaw in 1915.

Another post office, called Tumalo, was listed in Crook County, with George W. Wimer opening the first post office there in 1904.

TWIN ROCKS

Twin Rocks was named for the arched Twin Rocks.

TYEE

The name, Tyee, comes from the Chinook slang for "chief." (See TYGH VALLEY, Oregon.)

TYGH VALLEY

The first store in Tygh Valley was built in 1856, and had a profitable career trading with the local Indians and settlers.

The town, Tygh Valley, is located in the valley of the Tygh Creek. The waterway's name comes from a local Indian word, *tyee*, "chief." The name translates as "Chief's Valley."

Another source suggests that the name came from the Tyigh Tribe. Frémont referred to the area as the Taih Prairie.

U

UMAPINE

When originally settled, this town was called Vincent. When a post office was established, authorities felt there might be some confusion with another Vincent, and asked that the name be changed. Vincent became Umapine, a name that would not confuse anyone.

The name, we are told, honors Chief Umapine of the Cayuse Indian tribe. *Umapine* means "friends" in the Cayuse tongue.

UMATILLA

Umatilla took its name from its county, and is one of the oldest settlements in the state of Oregon. The county was created in 1862 out of Wasco County, and took its name from the river, which was called the "water of the shifting sand." Another source suggests the word has another meaning: "water rippling over stones."

The town was founded in 1864 as Umatilla Landing because that is what it was: a landing spot at the confluence of the Umatilla and Columbia Rivers.

At one time, there was a town named Umatilla in Coos County.

UMPQUA

Umpqua takes its name from the Umpqua River. The river has many fascinating stories told about it. Some, one can believe; others . . .

Spanish explorer Bartolome Ferrelo is alleged to have reached the mouth of the river in 1543. Others suggest that Sir Francis Drake sailed his *Golden Hynde,* but most authorities believe that happened further south. Spanish records do indicate, however, that a disabled ship entered the Umpqua in 1732, and traveled as far as the site of today's Scottsburg. When white settlers arrived, they found the decaying stumps of the trees used by the Spaniards to repair their ship.

The forest area along the river was not hunted by the Indians because they feared the area was haunted. This superstition allowed the white pioneers access to plentiful game.

In 1828, Jedediah Strong Smith and a party of trappers and hunters followed the river and were nearly exterminated by the Indians; only three survived the attacks.

A townsite for the seat of Umpqua County was surveyed in 1854. The first court session was conducted in a woodshed. After several legislative surgeries, Umpqua County ceased to exist in 1852.

UNION (— Creek)

Union was once the seat of Union County. The town was settled in 1862 by loyal Unionists. Two years later, the county was created.

The town's name—and that of the county—conveyed the citizens' patriotic feelings.

UNITY

George M. Getreau opened the doors to the first post office at this Baker County locale in 1891. The name was given to convey the feeling of "oneness" in the community.

VALE

Vale is the seat of Malheur County, and was headquarters to the Vale Irrigation Project. The project, combined with the Owyhee Project, made up the largest irrigation development in Oregon.

Jonathan Keeney built a small house on the banks of the Malheur in 1864. His house became the center of the growth of this town.

The county's name came from an incident experienced by Peter Skene Ogden. Ogden left his furs and supplies hidden by the stream. When he returned from hunting, he found that his cache had been looted by Indians. He named the waterway the River au Malheur, the "river of the evil hour."

VALLEY FALLS

Valley Falls took its name from the falls of the Chewaucan River.

VERNONIA

Vernonia, Columbia County, was founded on the banks of the Nehalem River in 1891. Lake Vernonia was once the mill pond for the lumber mill. It is now stocked with bass, crappie and trout.

The first post office here was opened in 1878 by David F. Baker.

VIDA

Vida's name came from Vida Pepiot, the first postmaster's daughter.

WAGONTIRE

Wagontire was named for Wagontire Mountain. The mountain received its name because a wagon wheel remained beside the road on the slope of the mountain for years, and was looked at as a road marker.

WALDPORT

Waldport is located on the south side of the Alsea Bay, at the mouth of the Alsea River. The town, a port in a heavily forested area, was settled in 1880. Its name is a smorgasbord: It incorporates *wald*, German for "forest," and the English "port."

WALKER

Joseph Walker was one of the celebrated mountain men of the territory. He was, however, a mystery. He was the first to cross the Sierras and to explore the Yosemite area. At the same time, it was alleged by Washington Irving that he had been in secret alliance with the Mexicans.

WALLOWA

Wallowa takes its name from the Wallowa Lake. At the north end of the lake is the grave of Chief Joseph, leader of the Nez Percé tribe.

The name came from the Nez Percé for a kind of fish trap.

WAMIC

Wamic is how they pronounced the Womack family name. The Womacks were early settlers.

WAPINITIA

"Something on the edge" is how they translate this town's name from the Warm Spring Indian word.

WARM SPRINGS

Warm Springs, Crook County, is located in the 640,000-acre Warm Springs Indian Reservation. Residents of the reservation include members of the Warm Springs, Paiute and Wasco tribes.

Originally located in Wasco County, Warm Springs had its first post office opened in 1879 by Mrs. Sarah M. Farley.

WARREN

When Warren, Columbia County, first began, it was called Gilltown. William J. Fullerton was the postmaster in 1890. The name was changed to Warren in 1895. Other postal records, however, indicate that there was a Warren here in 1885, with James Gill as the postmaster. Gilltown may have merged with the old post office of Warren.

WASCO

Wasco is the largest town in Sherman County. By all rights, it should be called Sherman, but it was named when it was part of Wasco County, which was created in 1855. That county name came from the Indian tribe, the Wasco or Wascopam Indians.

WATERLOO

Waterloo was named after a particular severe court decision. (See WATERLOO, California.)

WEATHERBY

When C. W. Durke opened the first post office at this Baker County location, the town's name was Express Ranch. The name was changed to Weatherby in 1879, when Andrew J. Weatherby assumed the job as postmaster.

WEDDERBURN

R. D. Hume came into this Curry County area in 1894 and opened a cannery on the north bank of the Ronity. He called the area Wedderburn for his family's home in Scotland. The Gaelic name translates to "Sheep Creek."

Edwin M. M. Bogardus opened the first post office here in 1895.

WELCHES

Though Clinton W. Kern was the first postmaster at this Clackamas County village in 1905, the town's name came from the Welch family. In fact, the second postmaster was William E. Welch.

WEMME

Wemme, Clackamas County, took the name of E. Henry Wemme (ca. 1850–1914), a manufacturer and philanthropist from Portland. A colorful character, Wemme owned the first automobile in Portland, and he bought new models and makes as they were released.

He made a habit of driving up the road to Welches and, using his car as a barricade, "held up" tourists, making them contribute money to buy the old Barlow Road. He saw that as a route for motorists to view Mount Hood. The road was finally purchased in 1912, and Wemme's will donated his share of the Barlow Road to the state of Oregon.

The Wemme post office opened here in 1916; Leonard A. Wrenn was postmaster.

WEST LINN

The town of West Linn, Clackamas County, took the name of Linn City, a waterfront community on the Willamette that no longer exists.

Linn City was begun as Robin's Nest in 1840 by Robert Moore. Four years later, Moore was running the ferry between Oregon City and Robin's Nest. The name was later changed to Linn City in honor of a senator from Missouri. Linn City was washed away by the great flood of 1861, and was never rebuilt.

The doors to the West Linn post office first opened in 1914; George F. Horton was postmaster.

WESTPORT

Westport, Clatsop County, is located on the Columbia River. It was named for John West.

The first post office was opened here in 1863 by S. B. Plimpton.

WHEELER

Wheeler took its name from the county, which was named for Henry H. Wheeler, the first mail carrier between The Dalles and Canyon City. Wheeler arrived in Oregon in 1862. The county was created in 1899.

Another source thinks the name came from the peak which was named for Captain G. M. Wheeler, who led a group of surveyors through the area in 1869–70. The legislation setting up the county belies that fact.

WILBUR

The Umpqua Academy was opened here in 1864 by the Reverend James Harvey Wilbur (1811–87), a Methodist minister. The academy's name was changed to the Wilbur Academy, but was closed in 1900. The town commemorates the minister. "Father Wilbur," as he was called, later became the Superintendent of Education on the Yakima Indian Reservation.

WILDERVILLE
First called Slate Creek, for obvious reasons, the name was changed to Wilderville in 1878, when Joseph L. Wilder became postmaster.

WILLAMINA
Willamina takes its name from Willamina Williams, the first white woman in the area. The town is located where the Willamina Creek enters the Yamhill.

WILLIAMS
When gold was discovered on Williams Creek in 1857, the town that sprouted was called Williamsburg. The name was later shortened.

WINCHESTER (— Bay)
Winchester was founded by the Umpqua Exploring Expedition of 1850, run by the Winchester Payne & Company party. The town was named for Herman Winchester, the captain of the expedition.

Winchester was laid out by Addison R. Flint. It was the seat of Douglas County from 1851 to 1854, when the honor transferred to Roseburg. Not only did the residents of Winchester concede the election, many of them moved to Roseburg.

WOLF CREEK
The Wolf Creek Tavern, located in the center of town, has been in almost continuous operation since it opened in 1857 as a stagecoach inn on the Oregon Territorial Road.

WONDER
This village was named by townspeople who "wondered" if the local storekeeper could make a living in this rugged area.

WORDEN
Worden was named for William S. Worden, an early settler.

YACHATS

Yachats occupies the land once used as a reservation for the Coos, Umpqua, Calapoya, Siuslaw, and Alsea tribes from 1856 until 1875, when the Indians were moved to the Siletz Reservation.

That year, the land was opened to settlement. Since the town grew near the confluence of the Yachats River and the Pacific Ocean, its first name was Oceanview. That was considered a quite common name and, in 1917, the townsfolk changed the name to Yachats, for the river.

The river, it is said, was named for an Indian sub-tribe by that name. The name translates to "dark waters under the mountain." Another source indicates the name means "at the foot of the mountain."

YAMHILL

Yamhill, settled in the mid-19th century, was once one of the most important trading centers in Oregon.

The town was settled by William Bell, who called it North Yamhill. A post office was established at the site in 1851 as Yam Hill, its name until 1908.

The town's name is from that of an Indian tribe, first spelled Yamhela.

YONCALLA

Jesse Applegate, explorer, Indian fighter and road builder, lived here and applied the Indian name for a tall hill near his home. The hill was named for a powerful Indian chief. The name, however, translates to "haunt of eagles" in a local Indian dialect. The first settlers were Robert Cowan and his family. They arrived in 1848, followed a year later by the three Applegate brothers.

A post office under this name opened in 1851, with James B. Riggs as postmaster. Originally located in Umpqua County, Yoncalla is now part of Benton County.

ZIGZAG

Zigzag, Clackamas County, was so named because the Salmon River passes it by in a zigzag fashion.

The post office opened under that name in 1933, with Mrs. Gladys V. Perkins as postmistress.

The Golden State is not just one place. It is several different countries.

Juan Rodriguez Cabrillo, a Portuguese explorer, was the first European to discover what is now California in 1542. Thirty-seven years later, Sir Francis Drake anchored near Point Reyes and claimed the land for Elizabeth I. By 1602, Sebastian Vizcaino had explored throughout the area and named much of the coast. Most important, however, he reaffirmed Spain's claim to California. But Spain did nothing with the territory until 1768, when King Charles ordered colonization of the region. The king only took this action to prevent other nations from taking control. At the king's order, Gaspar de Portola led an expedition in 1769 from Mexico to what is now San Diego. There, California's first permanent settlement was established. The town was called Alta, or "upper" (as opposed to Baja, "lower").

More important, perhaps, than Portola—since many outside California do not even recognize his name—were two members of his party: Father Junipero Serra and Father Fermin Lasuen. The two priests led a movement to establish lines of communication throughout California. By 1823, the Franciscan friars had founded 21 missions and one *asistencia* from San Diego to Sonoma. The missions established a 600-mile route that became El Camino Real, "The King's Highway."

In addition to the religious establishments, the Spaniards built military fortresses, called *presidios*, at San Diego, Santa Barbara, San Francisco, and Monterey—the headquarters for the military government.

The first real town, or pueblo, was San Jose, established in 1777. Los Angeles was founded four years later. In 1822, Mexico secured its independence from Spain, and California swore allegiance to Mexico but considered itself self-governing. Traders and settlers from the United States began to converge on California during this period, intensifying after the minor 1842 gold rush north of Los Angeles.

Four years later, expatriate Americans staged the abortive Bear Flag Revolt that attempted to make California a separate nation. The revolt had lasted only 23 days when U.S. Navy Commodore John Sloat raised the American flag at Monterey upon learning that the United States was at war with Mexico. The Mexican War was short-lived, but had one major benefit for the United States. Under the terms of the Treaty of Guadalupe Hidalgo, 2 February 1848, California became part of the United States.

Just a few days before the treaty was signed, James Marshall, a foreman on Captain John Sutter's property, was inspecting a mill-race on the South Fork of the American River. In the water, he noticed shiny yellow flecks among the stones. Marshall had discovered gold! The rest is history.

Gold fever spread like the plague. People from all over the world converged on this area to make their fortune. Some did; many did not. Life was cheap and violence was taken for granted. Justice was meted out at the end of a rope or down the barrel of a six-shooter. And men like Mark Twain and Bret Harte used the power of their pens to bring those people and those times to life.

California became a state in 1850, the year after the Gold Rush began. When the gold deposits petered out, Californians looked to other activities. The mild climate of Southern California drew vacationers and the film industry, farmers and fruit growers, dreamers and wannabes.

As we look at the place names on the California land, we relive those glory days. We can see the hard-scrabble prospectors and the placer miners at work. We can see the strength and power of the railroad industry as it forged its way across the nation.

The names keep us from forgetting the influences of the Spaniards, the Mexicans, the English, and others. In California, more than in any other state in the entire United States, we find the saints preserved—in countless places, even in some where the saints' names were conjured up from nothing. The signposts on these towns, villages and cities force us to realize how timeless even the most insignificant name can be . . . and how being a good speller is not everything.

ABERDEEN

Inyo County. (See ABERDEEN, Washington.)

ACADEMY

Academy, Fresno County, was so named because, in 1874, the Methodist Episcopal Church South built a secondary school, or "academy." The school was razed a number of years ago.

ACERICO

This Sonoma County community bears the Spanish word meaning "pin cushion" or "small pillow."

ACOLITA

Located in Imperial County, Acolita's name is Spanish for "acolyte."

ACTON

Acton, Los Angeles County, was named for the town in Massachusetts . . . or some place back East.

The Southern Pacific named this station on the Saugus-Mojave section of the road in the 1870s.

ADAMS

President John Quincy Adams thought about acquiring the territory containing California, Texas and New Mexico as early as 1825. In 1835, Andrew Jackson authorized his chargé in Mexico to purchase "the whole bay of San Francisco." This Lake County community, some think, was named for him.

ADELANTO

Adelanto, San Bernardino County, carries the Spanish name for "forward," "onward." The name was given when the first post office opened here in 1917.

ADIN

Adin, Modoc County, was named in 1870 for Adin McDowell, an early settler. McDowell settled in the Big Valley the year before.

AETNA SPRINGS

Aetna Springs, Napa County, was supposedly named for Mount Aetna, in Sicily. A more likely story is that John Lawley, owner of the nearby Aetna Mine, discovered the hot mineral springs while mining quicksilver. The mine, we are sure, came from the Sicilian name.

AFTON

Located in San Bernardino County, Afton was named when the Union Pacific Railroad station was established here in 1904 or 1905.

Railroad officials had a habit of naming their stations after Eastern places. Afton is no exception.

AGOURA HILLS

This Los Angeles County name apparently came from the misspelling of the name of a local rancher family, Agoure.

AGUA CALIENTE

The name of this Sonoma County community first appeared in an 1836 land grant. The name is Spanish for "hot water," and refers to the hot springs located here.

AGUANGA

Aguanga is a town in Riverside County. The place was originally called Picha Awanga by a Temecula Indian. The name translates to "place at the water." The use of "-nga" usually indicates a place.

AHWAHNEE

Located in Madera County, this Yosemite Valley area was known by the Indians as Ahwahnee (they called themselves Ahwahneechees) before the white settlers arrived. The first ones to settle were members of the Sells family, who opened an inn here in 1889 or 1890.

Ahwahnee translates to "beautiful valley, home of the deer," or "the deep grassy plain." In an interesting aside . . . The Geographic Board changed the name of this place to Wassamma, for the original Indian name, Was-sa'-ma. No one paid any attention, and Ahwahnee remains Ahwahnee.

ALAMEDA

Almeda is Spanish for a "mall, public walk (lined with poplars or cottonwoods)." Others think the name means "grove of poplar trees."

Describing any shade-producing growth, the name was given in this case because of the great growth of oak trees in the area.

Alameda, Alameda County, was laid out in 1852, and named— by popular vote—the next year. That same year, the county was formed. The name first appeared in the area as a description of the southern part of the present county of la Alameda.

When it was a Spanish village, it was known as Encinal de San Antonio.

ALHAMBRA

Alhambra, Los Angeles County, takes its name directly or indirectly from a Moorish palace in Granda, Spain. The name, we are told, means "red" in Arabic, because the palace was constructed of red brick. The Alhambra tract was laid out by George Hansen in 1874, for the owners, "Don Benito" Wilson and J. D. Shorb, Wilson's son-in-law.

Alhambra, the palace, excited the imagination of author Washington Irving who wrote *The Alhambra*, a collection of medieval Moorish tales.

Originally, the Alhambra Valley was known as Canada del Hambre, "valley of the hunger (starvation)," based on some early incident. In the 1880s, a woman of gentle feelings asked for the name change because of the harshness of "hambre."

ALISO VIEJO

Aliso Viejo, located in Orange and San Bernardino counties, bears the Spanish name for "way of alder trees." Since these trees are found only where there is a permanent source of water, this name would indicate that the "way of the alders" was a stream.

ALLEGHANY

Alleghany, Sierra County, was a mining camp begun in 1853, and named by early settlers from Pennsylvania. A post office was established under that name in 1895.

ALLENSWORTH

Allensworth, located in Tulare County, was founded in about 1909 by Lieutenant Colonel Allen Allensworth, as part of a colonization scheme for African-Americans. Allensworth never got a chance to see if his idea worked. He was killed in an auto accident in 1914.

ALMANOR

Almanor, Plumas County, takes its name from Lake Almanor. The body of water, created by the Great Western Power Company, was named for the daughters (Alice, Martha and Elinor) of Guy C. Earl, the company's president.

ALPAUGH

This Tulare County site was named for John Alpaugh in 1905. Alpaugh was one of the officers of the Home Extension Colony. That group reclaimed the Tulare Lake "island."

ALPINE

B. R. Arnold established this San Diego County community in 1883. The name was suggested by an early resident who thought the area resembled her native Switzerland.

"To her," the *San Diego Union* wrote in 1894, "the changing lights on mountainside and valley, and the exquisitely tinted shadows on distant peaks recalled the similar glories of that other Alpine."

ALTADENA

Altadena, Los Angeles County, is located at the foot of the San Gabriel Mountains. The town is famous for the gigantic Himalayan deodars that flank Santa Rosa Avenue, causing it to be known as Christmas Tree Lane. The seeds for these deodars, uncommon cedar trees, were brought here from India and planted in 1885.

The name was derived from the Latin, *alta*, ("high" or "upper") and the root from Pasadena. The name was manufactured in 1887 because of this community's position above Pasadena.

ALTAVILLE

Altaville, Calaveras County, was established as Cherokee Flat in 1852. About five miles from town is Fourth Crossing, where a young Bret Harte did a little panning for gold.

The town, also known at various times as Fork-in-the-Roads and Low Divide, took on this name at a town meeting in 1857.

ALTON

R. S. Perry named his Humboldt County settlement in 1862 for his hometown in Illinois. The Illinois city was named for the son of the founder, Rufus Eaton.

In the 1880s, the Alton name was applied to both the post office and the station of the Eel River & Eureka Railroad.

ALTURAS

The name of the seat of Modoc County comes from the mountains, and translates from the Spanish to mean "summits of mountains" or "heights."

Until 1874, the town was known as Dorris' Bridge, named for Presley Dorris, scion of the town's first white settlers. He built a wooden bridge across the Pit River at the south end of town, and then built a house that became a stop-over for travelers. In 1874, the name appeared as Dorrisville. Two years later, the name was changed by the state legislature.

AMADOR CITY

Amador City, Amador County, takes its name from the county, which was named for Jose Maria Amador. He was the property manager of the Mission of San Jose. Another source suggests he was an Indian fighter.

In 1848, Amador and several Indians built a mining camp near the site of the current town. When gold fever hit this area in 1849, the four ministers who lived here found that gold mining was more rewarding than preaching. During the day, they would dig for gold; at night, they would preach. In 1869, the key mine, the Keystone, reached its peak but continued producing well into the 1880s.

Amador is Spanish for "love of gold." Amador County was formed in 1854. The Amador City post office was established in 1863.

AMBOY

This San Bernardino County location was named by representatives of the Atlantic & Pacific Railroad (later the Sante Fe) in 1883.

Lewis Klingman, it is suspected, did the naming. He named the stations on the new line that extended from here to Arizona in alphabetical order: Amboy, Bristol, Cadiz, Danby, Edson, Fenner, and Goff. All of those names have ancestors in other American locations.

ANAHEIM

According to one source, this Orange County city was named for the first child born in the area, Anna Fisher. The word ending, *heim*, is German for "home." Another source, however, suggests the entire name means "home by the river" in German. A third source suggests the name was taken from the nearby Santa Ana River and the German *heim*.

The town was settled in 1857 by the Los Angeles Vineyard Association, a group of German immigrants on twelve hundred acres of Rancho San Juan Cajon de Santa Ana. The name was given at the suggestion of T. E. Schmidt, and voted on by the stockholders. An earlier name was Campo Aleman, "the German field."

Much of Anaheim's history is forgotten in light of its major attraction: Disneyland.

ANDERSON

The California & Oregon Railroad (later the Southern Pacific) arrived here in 1872. They named their station for Elias Anderson, owner of the American Ranch. He granted the railroad the right of way. Another source feels the name came from the fact that this town was settled by pioneers from Anderson County, Kentucky.

ANGELS (Angels Camp)

The name of this Calaveras County town honors George (or Henry) Angel. Along with James H. Carson, he discovered gold in this area in 1848. The original name was Angel's Camp, for the trading post Angel established that year.

It was at this camp that Mark Twain (Samuel Langhorne Clemens) (1835–1910) received inspiration for his classic tale, "The Celebrated Jumping Frog of Calaveras County," published in 1865, which had been told for many years in the county's mining camps. The actual frog-jumping contest was originally planned as a celebration for the paving of the downtown Angel Street. It was Twain's first published success. A statue of Twain stands in a small city park as a reminder, even though Twain was not too impressed with the town. He described the coffee served here as "day-before-yesterday dishwater."

Bret Harte, no friend of Twain, also made this place famous with his *Brown of Calaveras* and "Thompson, the Hero of Angels."

The post office was established in 1853. Though the town was incorporated as Angels in 1912, there is still a tendency to refer to it as Angels Camp.

ANGWIN

Angwin, Napa County, was named for Edwin Angwin in 1874. He operated a summer resort on his property. Angwin's land was part of Rancho La Jota.

ANNAPOLIS

This Sonoma County site was not named directly for the home of the U. S. Naval Academy. The name came from the Annapolis Orchards. The orchards were founded by the Wetmore brothers in the 1880s. A post office bearing this name first appeared in the early 20th century.

ANTIOCH

Antioch, Contra Costa County, takes its name from the ancient city in Syria. The name was selected by the town's residents at their Independence Day picnic in 1851.

In 1849, the town was called Smith's Landing, for the first settlers: twin brothers, J. H. and W. W. Smith. A year later, W. W., who was a minister, invited a group of New Englanders to settle on the land. When the people voted on the name, they selected one with biblical overtones, as opposed to two others offered: Minton and Paradise!

ANZA

Juan Bautista de Anza, a man "of heroic qualities, tough as oak, and silent as the desert from which he sprang," made the first land journey to the Pacific in 1774. He established the famous Presidio of San Francisco in 1776. His expedition also resulted in the mission at San Francisco.

This Riverside County community was originally called Cahuilla, but that was changed to Anza in 1926.

APPLEGATE

This Placer County place was settled by Lisbon Applegate, and was originally known as Bear River House.

The post office was established here in the 1870s, with George Applegate as postmaster.

APPLE VALLEY

Apple Valley, San Bernardino County, is a resort town developed by Newt Bass. The name was given at the turn of the 20th century by Mrs. Ursala M. Poates. Mrs. Poates, a long-time resident of the Mojave Desert, convinced buyers that fruit could be grown in the desert. She planted three apple trees in her yard!

The post office, bearing the Apple Valley name, did not open until 1949.

APTOS

Aptos, Santa Cruz County, has a name that was first mentioned in 1807 as Rancho de Aptos, a sheep ranch at Mission Santa Cruz.

One source believes the name comes from the Spanish adaptation of "a Costanoan village or its chief."

ARBUCKLE

Arbuckle, located in Colusa County, was named by surveyors for the Central Pacific Railroad when they opened a station at this Colusa County site in 1875. The station and town were located on the ranch of T. R. Arbuckle. He took title to the land in 1866.

ARCADIA

The name for Arcadia, Los Angeles County, came from an area in southern Greece, a department in the central Peloponnese, that was famous as a paradise of peace and revelry. Theocritus, the Greek poet, created the image that was bolstered during the Renaissance of nubile nymphs and romantic shepherds. The name was further reinforced by Sir Philip Sidney's romantic *Arcadia*.

Arcadia was founded by E. J. "Lucky" Baldwin, a bombastic mining investor. He purchased Santa Anita Ranch in 1875. Arcadia was laid out as a town, and named by Herman A. Unruh, a surveyor for the Gabriel Valley Railroad.

During World War I, the Army operated a balloon school near here.

ARCATA

Arcata's name is descriptive, and comes from an Indian word meaning "sunny spot."

This Humboldt County community was founded in the mid-19th century as a mining supply center. Bret Harte (1836–1902) once worked here as a journalist and a miner, and used Arcata as the scene for some of his mining camp stories.

Another source contends that the name comes from some Indian tongue and means "union." Arcata's original name, by the way, was Union or Union Town, when it was founded in 1850. The name was changed to Arcata a decade later.

ARMONA

Leave it to the railroads! This Kings County community's name was coined by a railroad construction engineer from Ramona. The name was applied elsewhere, but moved here in 1891, when the Southern Pacific opened a new junction here.

ARNOLD

Arnold, Calaveras County, took the name of its first postmistress when the office was established in 1934. In addition to running the post office, Bernice Arnold McCallum owned the local resort.

AROMAS

An early Spanish settler thought that "this rich air (was) like wine." At least that is the romantic tale told.

The original name for this Monterey County town was Los Aromas. It was taken from an 1835 land grant, Aromitas y Agua Caliente, "little odors and warm waters," a reference to the odors from sulphur springs.

Later, when the Southern Pacific Railroad built a tunnel here in the 1870s, it was known as Sand Cut. The present name appeared on the town's first post office in 1895.

ARROYO GRANDE

Arroyo Grande, San Luis Obispo County, took its name from Arroyo Grande Creek. The name seems to be a contradiction in terms, since the Spanish *arroyo* means a "creek" or "rivulet," (the word sometimes translates to "canyon" or "gulch") and *grande* means "large." So we end up with a big creek.

ARTESIA

Artesia, Los Angeles County, was named by the Artesia Company that drilled artesian wells here in the 1870s.

ARTOIS

Artois was a name brought back from World War I. The town of Germantown—a popular name when the town voted on it in 1876, but unpopular in 1918—changed its name to that of the French-sounding Artois.

Located originally in Colusa and later in Glenn County, Artois received its first post office as Germantown in 1877 and then as Artois in 1918.

ARVIN

This Kern County spot took the name of the first storekeeper in town, Arvin Richardson. The town was established in 1910.

ASPEN VALLEY

This community's name came from the appearance of quaking aspen trees in the area.

ASTI

Asti, Sonoma County, took its name from the Italian vineyard town, which was founded by Italian immigrants in the late 19th century. The Asti post office was established here in 1892.

ATASCADERO

Atascadero, San Luis Obispo County, bears a fairly unpleasant name. The word is Spanish and means "quagmire," "obstruction," or "a deep, miry place." Its founder, a man by the name of Lewis, had grandiose plans for this community. Unfortunately, he spent his last days in prison.

Atascadero first appeared as the name of a land grant on an 1847 map, and it was the name given by the Southern Pacific when it opened its station here in 1886. The modern community only dates back to 1913, developed as Atascadero Estates.

ATHERTON

Located in San Mateo County, Atherton was named for Faxon D. Atherton. He first visited California in the 1830s, but he returned in 1860 to acquire five-hundred acres of Rancho Las Pulgas, on which the town of Atherton was established.

Atherton was also father-in-law to novelist Gertrude Atherton.

ATOLIA

Atol is a hot, non-alcoholic drink widely imbibed in Mexico and Central America. Another source contends that the name is an amalgam of the names of two mining company officials: Atkins and DeGolia. The town was named by the Tungsten Mining Company in the early 20th century, and both Atkins and DeGolia were officers of the firm.

ATWATER

Atwater, Merced County, is home to the delicious Merced sweet potatoes. It was also home to Marshall D. Atwater, a noted wheat farmer, on whose land the railroad station was built in the 1870s.

The town was developed in 1888 by the Merced Land & Fruit Company.

AUBERRY

The people in this Fresno County town called Al Yarborough "Al Auberry." The name of this early settler is remembered in the town's name. Yarborough was one of four hunters who named Dinkey Creek in 1863.

The post office was established here in the 1880s, and the mispronounced name became fact.

AUBURN

This Placer County town was founded in the mid-19th century by settlers from New York. The town was named by Samuel W. Holladay, who named the digs after the town of that name in New York State. The name is a reference to Auburn in Oliver Goldsmith's 1770 poem, "The Deserted Village."

Auburn, located only 20 miles from Coloma, the scene of the first gold strike in California, was one of the state's earliest gold mining camps. A Frenchman, Claude Chana, made the discovery in 1848. For a few months in that year, the town was known as Rich Dry Diggings, North Fork Dry Diggings and Wood's Dry Diggings. The town continued to grow as a center for the stages and freight trains until 1865 when the Central Pacific Railroad reached here. The railroad terminus was denounced at the time as the "Dutch Flat Swindle."

"Rattlesnake Dick," who called himself the "Pirate of the Placers," was shot down near Auburn in 1859 by a posse. He had terrorized the area for years.

The Auburn post office was established here in 1853.

AVALON

Avalon, located on Santa Catalina island in the Pacific off the coast of California, is in a position similar to that of the legendary Avalon. The name was made popular by Alfred Lord Tennyson in his *Idylls of the King*. The town was founded by George Shatto and named in 1888. Shatto had purchased the land a year earlier from the Lick Estate.

AVENAL

Avenal carries a Spanish word that means "a field sown with oats." The name seems to have been borrowed from the Avenal Creek.

The name for the waterway first appeared on an 1891 Mining Bureau map, but by 1901, the name was altered to Avendale. In 1908, the decision was made to stick with Avenal. The community was named by the Standard Oil Company in 1929.

AVILA BEACH

Avila, San Luis Obispo County, was the name of the *exalcalde* of Los Angeles, José Maria Avila. He led the 1831 attack against Mexico's first president, Guadalupe Victoria, after the rest of the troops under Pablo de Portilla fled. Avila was daring and courageous in battle, but fell to the sword wielded by the president.

This town, however, was laid out in 1867, and named for Miguel Avila who was a corporal at Mission San Luis Obispo and the grantee of Rancho San Miguelito in 1839. The name, containing the "beach," was assigned in 1966.

AVON

Avon, Contra Costa County, was named by the Southern Pacific Railroad when a station was established here in 1877 or 1878. For a number of years, the post office was called Associated. That name finally came into conformance with the railroad name.

The name, of course, is a reference to Shakespeare's Avon River.

AZUSA

Azusa is located in Los Angeles County. Father Juan Crespi, a missionary with the Portola Expedition, wrote about "The Azusa" in 1769. The name is Indian, derived from *suaka-gna*, the name of a Shoshonean Indian tribe. Locally, the Indians were known as the Gabrieno.

Another source suggests the name came from the Gabrielino Indian dialect, and means "skunk hill" or "skunk place," named after a nearby hill.

The land on which Azusa stands was granted by the Mexican government in 1841 to Luis Arenas. He called his new home "Rancho El Susa." Three years later, Arenas sold the land to Henry Dalton. Dalton renamed the ranch "Azusa Rancho de Dalton." The San Gabriel River, which once was a boundary for the ranch, was called the Azusa River.

The town was laid out in 1887 by J. S. Slauson and his associates. During the 1920s, land developers coined the phrase, "Everything from A to Z in the U.S.A.," to promote development in the town.

BADGER

Badger, Tulare County, was known as Camp Badger as early as 1892. Most people think the town was founded by settlers from Wisconsin, the "Badger State."

BAKER

Baker, San Bernardino County, is a favored watering and gas spot on U.S. Route 66 out of Las Vegas. It's the spot where down-on-their-luck gamblers swapped personal property for gas. One local service station owner was quoted as saying that "everybody in town at one time or another has been offered to share a wife in trade for gas or repairs."

The railroad station here was originally named Berry, for Joe Berry, an old prospector. To avoid confusion with similar names, the Tonopah & Tidewater Railroad renamed the site for its president, R. C. Baker.

A post office was established as Baker in 1933.

BAKERSFIELD

Located in Kern County, Bakersfield was named for Colonel Thomas Baker, a civil and hydraulic engineer. In 1864 the colonel built a home in the center of what is known today as Bakersfield.

The colonel enclosed his property with a fence and used it for a corral. People began to call it "Baker's field." The name became that of the county in 1868.

Baker did not know it, but a little more than 30 years later, oil was struck in the Kern River area . . . near his field.

BALBOA

Balboa, Orange County, was developed in 1905 by the Newport Bay Investment Company. The site was named by the Peruvian consul in Los Angeles, for V. N. de Balboa. He discovered the Pacific Ocean.

BALDWIN PARK

Baldwin Park, Los Angeles County, is a city that developed around the 1912 Pacific Electric station. It took the name of E. J. "Lucky" Baldwin. Lucky was one of the biggest promoters of the late 19th century, investing much of his Alaskan fortune here in California.

Baldwin Park is located on Lucky's old property, Puente de San Gabriel rancho.

BALLARET

The gold-mining town of Ballaret, Inyo County, was named in about 1890 for the gold-mining town of the same name in Australia. The post office opened under that name in 1897.

BALLARD

Ballard, Santa Barbara County, has a name with an unusual origin. The town was named in 1881 by George W. Lewis, in honor of his wife's first husband, W. N. Ballard.

For most of the 1860s, Ballard was the stage coach station agent here. At that time it was known as Alamo Pintado.

BALLENA

The name for this San Diego County town comes from the Spanish for "whale." The name was given after a whale was stranded on a local beach. Other sources suggest that the name was given because a ridge of land resembled the hump of a whale. During the Spanish settlement, sailors referred to the shape of southern California as Ballena.

BANGOR

Bangor, Butte County, was settled by the Lumbert brothers, who arrived here from Bangor, Maine in 1855. That name comes from an old psalm hymn. Other towns with the name of Bangor are more likely named for the Welsh town.

BANNING

During the 1850s, Phineas and Alexander Banning operated the first regular stage line between Los Angeles and San Pedro.

This Riverside County locale was founded in 1884, and named by Welwood Murray for Phineas.

Throughout his life, Phineas Banning was a strong proponent of improvements in transportation in southern California.

BARD

This Imperial County town's name has no connection with Shakespeare, as some might assume.

The post office in the town of Bard was established in 1910, and named for Thomas R. Bard, for his work in promoting the vast irrigation district.

BARDSDALE

Bardsdale, Ventura County, has the same roots as Bard—Thomas R. Bard. A post office was established as Bardsdale in 1892, before the name donor was elected to the U.S. Senate.

BARSTOW

Barstow, San Bernardino County, was a thriving mining center in the late 19th century. It was named in 1886 for railroad president William Barstow Strong. They were forced to use his middle name because his last name already adorned another community, Strong City.

Barstow was established in 1886 as a depot and hotel for the Atchison, Topeka & Sante Fe Railroad. Before the Sante Fe arrived, the station had been established by the Southern Pacific, and was called Waterman Junction—for the neighboring mining community where former California Governor Robert W. Waterman owned a silver mine. In the 1860s, the spot was called Fishpond.

About 10 miles northeast of Barstow is Calico Ghost Town. After more than $85 million worth of gold and silver was drawn from the "calico hills," the town declined. In 1889, "Borax" Smith revived the town with his profitable borax mining operation.

BARTLE

Located in Siskiyou County, Bartle commemorates cattlemen Abraham and Jerome Bartle. The name appeared on the McCloud River Railroad station here in 1904.

BARTLETT SPRINGS

Bartlett Springs, Lake County, bears the name of Green Bartlett, a Kentuckian who located the springs in 1870 and was "cured" by its waters. He got his money together and purchased the land, erected a hotel and started a health resort.

BASSETTS

Bassetts is a summer resort in the highlands at the headwaters of the North Fork of the Yorba River. The name commemorates an early landowner.

BASS LAKE

Bass Lake, Madera County, apparently takes its name not from the fish, but from the trees that surrounded the lake. Bass was another name for the linden tree.

BAXTER

Baxter's name, we are told, probably came from John Baxter, who raised cattle in the Owens Valley.

BEAR VALLEY

Bear Valley contains the waters of Big Bear Lake. The name for this Mariposa County site was given by Frémont in 1848.

BEAUMONT

Beaumont's name, "beautiful mountain," came after a long line of names.

BEAUMONT

In 1887, a group of developers descended on this Riverside County area and bought the townsite, giving it the French name. In earlier incarnations, the town had been known as Edgar Station, for a physician on a mid-19th century survey party. In 1875, the name was changed to Summit; nine years later, it was changed to San Gorgonio, for the mountain.

BECKWOURTH

Beckwourth was named for James Beckwourth, an early settler and explorer from Virginia. "Old Jim," as he was known, did not know how to spell and, as a result, his name can be found on various landmarks as either Beckwourth or Beckwith.

BEEGUM

The name of this town originally signified a hollow gum tree where bees lived. Later the name came to mean any bee hive. In fact, the actual reason behind the naming of this particular locality in Tehama County has nothing to do with bees or a gumtree.

It would appear that Beegum Peak was named by some Southerner who thought it looked like a beehive. The peak is composed of limestone with many holes throughout. As one might imagine, many of the holes are inhabited by bees.

BELDEN

At an earlier time, Belden was known as Belden Bar, the starting point for trips up the east branch of the North Fork of the Yorba River. Both the Western Pacific Railroad station and post office in this Plumas County location were named in 1909 for Robert Belden, a miner and property owner.

BELL

J. G. and Alphonso Bell founded this Los Angeles County community in 1898. For a brief period of time, the post office was called Obed.

BELLA VISTA

Bella Vista, Shasta County, was founded by the Shasta Lumber Company. A post office was opened here in 1898, and given the Spanish name for "beautiful view."

BELLFLOWER

In the earliest days of this Los Angeles County community, it was called Willows, then Wilderness, Firth, and Somerset. The town was founded in 1906 by F. E. Woodruff as Somerset. Three years later, however, when they applied for a post office, officials suggested that the town look for a new name; they feared confusion with Somerset, Colorado.

They selected Bellflower, for the bellflower apples grown nearby by William Gregory.

BELL GARDENS

In 1930, when the vegetable gardens planted by Japanese gardeners were subdivided into building lots, the new Los Angeles community was called Bell Gardens, after the neighboring community of Bell. The town was incorporated as Bell Gardens in 1961.

BELLOTA

In 1873, this San Joaquin County spot was called Donnel. The next year, it was Belota. The current spelling, Spanish for "acorn," was used by postal authorities when the office opened here in 1879.

BELMONT

Belmont, San Mateo County, took its name from the hotel built here in 1850 or 1851. It was named by Steinburger & Beard because of the "symmetrically rounded eminence nearby." The town which grew up around the hotel was listed as early as 1855.

The name is translated from the French, "fine mountain," and is a variation of Beaumont.

BELVEDERE

The name of Belvedere, Marin County, comes from the Italian for "beautiful sight," an apt title.

This town was founded in 1890 by the Belvedere Club of San Francisco, and built on what was known as Peninsular (or de Silva's) Island.

BENHUR

Benhur, Mariposa County, takes its name from the title character in Lew Wallace's novel. The novel was reaching its peak of popularity in about 1890, when this community selected the name.

BENICIA

Benicia, Solano County, was named for the wife of one of the town's founders, General Mariano Guadalupe Vallejo. The other founder was Robert Semple. No one knows what his wife's name was.

Benicia became California's third state capital in 1853–54, and has the oldest standing capital building.

Located here was Benicia Barracks, in active service from 1849 to 1908. It was one of the first U. S. Army military posts in California. In 1851, the army opened an ordinance supply depot, Benecia Arsenal, that was active until 1963. Military luminaries, such as George Crook, Ulysses S. Grant and William T. Sherman, served here as lieutenants. Colonel James W. Benet, father of poet Steven Vincent Benet, was the commanding officer.

The Army's "camel experiment" ended here in 1863, when the remaining camels were assembled and auctioned off. (See VALLEJO, California.)

BEN LOMOND

The town of Ben Lomond, Santa Cruz County, is supposedly named for the Scottish mountain. The Scotch use *ben* for "mountain."

A post office was established here as early as 1872.

BENTON

During the mining boom of 1865, the town of Benton, Mono County, came into being. A post office was established two years later.

Since the area was involved in silver mining, it would seem somewhat logical to name it for Senator Thomas Hart Benton, Frémont's father-in-law and a strong advocate of "hard cash" money.

BERENDA

The name of this Madera County location comes from *berrenda*, the Spanish word for "female antelope." It was given because the countryside was overrun with the animals.

BERKELEY

One authority strongly suggests that the city was named for George Berkeley, Bishop of Cloyne, Irish clergyman and philosopher, who authored that famous line, "Westward the course of empire takes its way." In 1728, the bishop came to America, specifically to Rhode Island, to establish a college in the Bermudas.

In 1853, Henry Durant opened a school in Oakland which became the College of California. When a permanent home was considered, the site of Berkeley was selected in 1858. Eight years later, at the suggestion of Frederick Billings, the trustees of the college may have named the town for the bishop.

The University of California was chartered in 1868. Berkeley likes to be known as "the Athens of the West."

BERRY CREEK

The post office at Virginia Mills was established in 1875 as Berry Creek. The name came from the waterway here in Butte County. Some think that the creek, a rich mining haven in the mid-19th century, was named for Henry Berry, a Pennsylvanian.

BETHANY

John Mohr, the landowner of Mohr Station, deeded this San Joaquin County site to the Southern Pacific Railroad. In an attempt to avoid confusion with another station, Moore's Station, the name was changed to Bethany, for the biblical place in Palestine.

BEVERLY HILLS

Beverly Hills, Los Angeles County, is one of the most elegant residential communities in southern California. It is home to many well-known stage, screen and television personalities.

The name for this community, it is said, came from a 1907 newspaper account that spoke of President William Howard Taft spending a great deal of time at a place called Beverly Farms. At first, the town was called Beverly. It became Beverly Hills in 1911.

Beverly Hills is also home to the famous Rodeo Drive, comparable to New York's Fifth Avenue and Rome's Via Condotti.

BIEBER

Nathan Bieber built the first store and house at this Lassen County locale in 1877. Two years later the post office was established in his name.

BIG BAR

Big Bar, Trinity County, took its name from the discovery of "rich and extensive bars of placer gravel." The railroad called it Pulga, Spanish for "fleas." To the north is Flea Valley.

BIG BASIN

Big Basin took its name from the geographic feature, "a natural amphitheatre." The basin is about five miles long and four miles wide, and contains a forest of primitive redwoods.

BIG BEAR LAKE

Big Bear Lake took its name from the body of water by the same name. The lake was created in 1884 with the construction of the Old Bear Valley Dam.

BIGGS

The California & Oregon Railroad named their station at this Butte County site in 1870 for Major Marion Biggs. The major was the first rancher to ship grain from here.

BIG OAK FLAT

The first name for this Tuolumne County community was Savage Diggings, for miner James Savage who set up his operation here in the mid-19th century. Two years after Savage got started, the name was changed to Big Oak Flat.

The source of the name was a gigantic oak tree—11 feet in diameter—that stood in the center of town. The tree is long gone, but pieces of it have been preserved in a monument built by high school boys.

The Big Oak Flat post office was established in 1852.

BIG PINE

Big Pine commemorates the ancient bristlecone pine, preserved in Inyo National Forest. Some of the trees are over 4,000 years old—a millenium older than the giant cedar! The town is also located at the mouth of Big Pine Creek.

BIG RIVER

Big River took its name from the waterway, and is located where the river flows into the cove. On an 1844 map, the waterway is noted as Rio Grande, Spanish for "big river."

BIG SUR

Big Sur, Monterey County, took its name from the river, which originally was called Rio Grande del Sur, the "big river of the south."

BIRDS LANDING

The birds that landed here were not of the feathered variety. John Bird moved here from New York in 1865, and proceeded to operate a grain warehouse landing on the Montezuma Slough, about a mile-and-a-half southwest of the town.

BISHOP

Bishop is located on Bishop Creek. The Inyo County town and the waterway were both named for an early cattleman, Samuel A. Bishop. He came to California from Virginia in 1849.

BLAIRSDEN

James A. Blair was a prominent leader in the financing of the Western Pacific Railway. This Plumas County town was named for Blair's country home here.

BLOCKSBURG

Located in Humboldt County, Blocksburg was named for Benjamin Blockburger, the town's founder. Blockburger arrived in the area in 1853, fought Indians, and finally opened a store here in 1872. Five years later, when a post office was established, it was named Blocksburgh in his honor. During the late 19th century purge of "burgh" towns by postal authorities, Blocksburgh became Blocksburg.

BLOOMFIELD

Bloomfield's name came from Frederick G. Blume, physician from Germany who was quite prominent in the area beginning about 1847. His name was altered to an American spelling, but the pronunciation remained the same.

Located in Sonoma County, Bloomfield was first settled in 1855. The next year, the post office was established in Dr. Blume's name.

BLOOMINGTON

The Semi-Tropic Land & Water Company developed this San Bernardino County community in 1887. They hoped it would be a "blooming town."

BLUE LAKE

Blue Lake, Humboldt County, was named for the nearby body of water.

BLYTHE

Riverside County's Blythe was named for Thomas H. Blythe. The town was established by the Palo Verde Land & Water Company in 1908. Bythe, a San Franciscan, owned the valley land in which the irrigation project was developed. He had purchased the property more than a quarter of a century earlier.

BOCA

The name of this Nevada County community came from the Spanish for "mouth." When the Central Pacific Railroad established the Truckee-Verdi section of track in 1867, they named this station Boca because it was located near the mouth of the Little Truckee River.

BODEGA (— Bay)

Bodega, Sonoma County, has a name that translates from the Spanish to mean "wine-vault." The name actually came from Juan Francisco Bodega y Quadra, a Spanish explorer and captain of the *Sonora*, who gave his name to the bay in 1775. He was a great friend, we are told, of George Vancouver.

The bay had a number of early names, including Porto y Rio del Capitan Vodega (1755) and Port Bodega (1821).

The Russians established a post here in 1809. When they used the port, they called it Romanzou (1812–41), Hafen Bodega oder Port Romanzou (1830). The modern name for the bay was established by the Coast Survey in 1850.

The town was settled in 1853 by George Robinson. Twenty years later, it was recorded as Bodega Corners.

BODFISH

A "bodfish" does not swim along the California coast. Actually, the town of Bodfish recalls Orlando Bodfish, an early settler from Massachusetts.

BODIE

Bodie, Mono County, was named for an early miner, Waterman S. Body. Even then, they had trouble spelling! Body discovered ore deposits here in 1859.

As mining yields diminished in the 1850s, prospectors began to cross the Sierra Nevada and explore the eastern slope. The first strike here (of gold placers) happened in 1859, but problems in transporting supplies and equipment over the mountains diminished the results. The mines only produced slightly more than $70 million!

Killings were an everyday occurrence in Bodie, and the phrase "bad man from Bodie" really meant just that!

BOLINAS

Bolinas, located in Marin County, took its name from the bay. The word is Spanish for "whale." Another source thinks the name came from that of an Indian tribe, the Baulenes. The current spelling of the name became official in 1863, when the first post office was established.

During Mexican occupation, Bolinas was one of California's chief ports.

BONITA

The original name for Bonita was Bonetas, a Spanish word for "bonnets." Some think the name really should have been *bonetes*, a reference to the three points on a clergyman's hat. Still others believe that Bonita is the diminutive of *buena*, "pretty."

Located in San Diego County, the Bonita Ranch was founded by Henry E. Cooper in 1884. It was part of the 1845 Rancho Nacional Mexican grant.

The post office which was later established here took on the name of the ranch.

BONSALL

James Bonsall came from Pennsylvania and set up a nursery at this San Diego County site in the 1870s. When a post office was established in 1889, townspeople selected his name as their own.

Originally known as Mount Fairview, the town's name was changed to Osgood, for the chief engineer of the Southern Railway Survey. Townspeople hoped that by currying favor in this way, the railroad would establish a station here. The railroad did not.

BOONVILLE

This Mendocino County town was founded in 1864, as Kendall's City. A short time later, W. W. Boone bought the store owned by Levi & Straus and changed the town's name to Booneville.

In the 1880s, when the post office was established, postal officials dropped the "e" for no good reason.

BORON

From 1912 through 1938, the station located here in Kern County on the Santa Fe Railroad was called Amargo. The name is the Spanish word for "bitter," an obvious reference to the taste of borax deposits found here.

After the Pacific Coast Borax Company moved their operations here from Death Valley, they changed the name of the rail station and the post office to Boron. Boron is a nonmetallic element in borax.

BORREGO SPRINGS

The Borrego Springs post office was opened here in San Diego County in 1949. The name translates from the Spanish to mean "lamb" or "sheep." Most authorities believe this is a reference to the Nelson bighorn sheep raised here.

BOULDER CREEK

A boulder or boulders that marked a crossing gave rise to the creek's name. The creek, in turn, gave its name to the community, which is located at the point where three canyons come together: the San Lorenzo, Boulder Creek and Bear Creek.

Boulder Creek became the name for the Santa Cruz County lumber camp of Lorenzo in the 1880s. The name conformed to that of the post office which had been established a decade earlier.

BOULEVARD

This San Diego County town was so named because it was located on U.S. Route 80, which the local residents called "the boulevard" to the Imperial Valley.

BOWMAN

The first commissioner of agriculture for Place County was Harry H. Bowman. A popular merchant, Bowman gave his name to this Placer County town.

BOYES HOT SPRINGS

The hot springs located here in Sonoma County were first used by the Indians for medicinal purposes. Years later, they were owned and operated by Captain H. E. Boyes. He developed them into a community.

The Boyes Hot Springs post office was established here in 1912.

BRADBURY

L. L. Bradbury owned this Los Angeles County property at the turn of the 20th century. The town was incorporated under his name in 1957.

BRADLEY

When the Southern Pacific Railroad arrived at this Monterey County place in 1886, they named the station for the landowner. Bradley V. Sargent was a state senator in the late 1880s.

BRANSCOMB

The first postmaster—and name donor—for this Mendocino County site was Benjamin Branscomb, from Ohio. The office opened in 1895.

BRAWLEY

The town of Brawley, Imperial County, was laid out by the Imperial Land Company in 1902. The property belonged to J. H. Braly, of Los Angeles.

Braly was not quite certain that the land development would succeed, and did not want his name attached. A. H. Heber, the company's general manager, compromised by naming it Brawley, after one of his friends from Chicago.

BRAY

This Siskiyou County community was named for the Bray Ranch. The post office was opened under that name in 1907.

BREA

The Spanish word for "pitch" or "tar" is used in this Los Angeles County town's name. The reference is to pools of petroleum or asphalt. References to these asphalt pits were made as early as the Portola expedition.

BRENTWOOD

The name of this Contra Costa County community comes from that of the ancestral home of John Marsh. Marsh owned Rancho Los Meganos, where the present town is located. Brentwood was laid out as a town in 1878, on land donated by Marsh's heirs.

Other sources, misinformed however, suggest that the name came from Brentwood, New Hampshire, which was originally chartered as Brintwood.

BRICELAND

Briceland, Humboldt County, was named for John C. Briceland, a Virginian who bought the ranch on which the present-day town was established. The post office carried his name as early as 1892.

BRIDGEPORT

Bridgeport does not have a port, but it does have a covered bridge.

BRIDGEVILLE

This Humboldt County location was so named because of its location at the bridge over the Van Duzen River.

BRISBANE

When this San Mateo County community was first founded in 1908, it was called Visitacion City. When a post office was established 23 years later, postal officials feared confusion with nearby Visitacion Valley. So the townspeople opted for Brisbane, to honor noted journalist Arthur Brisbane.

Another source feels the name was given by Arthur Annis, a settler from Brisbane, Australia.

BROCKWAY

There are hot mineral springs located at Brockway, Placer County. These springs drew Frank Brockway Alverson, an associate of "Lucky" Baldwin, in the waning days of the 19th century.

Alverson built a resort here on the shore of Fallen Leaf Lake. When the post office opened here in 1901, Alverson had it named for his uncle, Nathaniel Brockway.

BROOKS

At an 1884 town meeting held to decide on the name for the post office, townspeople decided that Brooks would be an appropriate name for their Yolo County community: A brook flows by their village.

BROWNS VALLEY

Browns Valley, Napa County, was a mining camp that was in operation before 1853. The name apparently came from John E. Brown. Brown had purchased a large piece of Salvador Vallego's Napa grant "for a horse and buggy."

BROWNSVILLE

Brownsville, Yuba County, was named for I. E. Brown, who built the first sawmill here in 1851.

BRYN MAWR

The post office at this San Bernardino County site was established as Bryn Mawr in about 1895. The name translates from the Welsh as "high ground." The name source is probably Bryn Mawr, Pennsylvania.

BUCKS LAKE

The community of Bucks Lake, Plumas County, takes its name from the body of water. The lake, valley, creek, mountain, and reservoir were named for Horace (Francis) Bucklin, known familiarly as "Buck." He settled in the area in 1850.

BUELLTON

William Budd, this Santa Barbara County community's first postmaster, named his office in 1916 for Rufus T. Buell. Buell, a native of Vermont, settled here in 1874.

BUENA PARK

This name is an amalgamation of the Spanish for "good" and the English "park." Located in Orange County, Buena Park was founded in 1887. The railroad station, Northam, was renamed by the Santa Fe Railroad in 1929 to conform to the town's name.

Housed in Buena Park is Knott's Berry Farm. Years ago, people would come from far and wide to a 10-acre fruit patch to taste Mrs. Knott's home cooking. Today the "farm" is a 150-acre theme park.

BUENA PARK. Here we see Mrs. Knott preparing one of her famous berry pies. The berries came from her husband's 10-acre berry patch. (Knott's Berry Farm)

BUENA PARK. Today's Knott's Berry Farm is a major theme park, complete with a trip through a logging camp of the Old West ending with a breath-taking drop down a 42-foot chute. (Knott's Berry Farm)

BUENA VISTA

Buena Vista, Spanish for "good view," takes its name from Buena Vista Lake. The name commemorates Taylor's 1847 victory over Santa Ana.

BULL CREEK

The Humboldt County community of Bull Creek took its name from the waterway.

In the early 1850s, a band of Indians stole a bull from a white settler near Briceland. They slaughtered it by the creek, which explains the name for the waterway. The settlers killed the Indians in revenge for the theft!

BURBANK

Burbank, one of the largest cities in the San Fernando Valley, is best known for its film and television studios. "Beautiful downtown Burbank" became a derogatory reference in the "Laugh-in" television show during the 1960s.

Many authorities contend that Burbank, Los Angeles County, took its name from Luther Burbank (1849–1926), the "plant wizard." Burbank, a native of Lancaster, Massachusetts, moved to Santa Rosa, California, where he bred a number of new varieties of fruits and vegetables. His credo was: "I shall be contented if, because of me, there shall be better fruits and fairer flowers." According to at least one source, the city was laid out in 1887 on the Providencia rancho. One of the landowners was a Los Angeles dentist, Dr. David Burbank.

According to the dictionary, the verb "burbank" means "to modify and improve plant life." The famed horticulturist is buried under a cedar of Lebanon which he himself planted in Burbank Memorial Park, Sonoma County.

BURLINGAME

Burlingame, San Mateo County, was named by William C. Ralston in 1868 for a friend, Anson Burlingame (1822–70). Burlingame was a career diplomat who spent more than a decade developing ties with the Chinese government.

Another source believes the name came from Burlingame, England, which is possible for the family name but not for the name of this town.

BURNEY

When R. M. Johnson established the post office at this Shasta County site in 1872, he named it Burney Valley.

With the name, he was honoring Samuel Burney, a Scottish trapper and guide who was killed by Indians in 1857.

Postal authorities reduced the name to Burney in 1894.

BURNT RANCH

This Trinity County village was named for an 1849 incident in which Canadian miners burned down an Indian ranchero. Another story has the Indians burning down a settler's ranch. This was not the case.

The Burnt Ranch post office was established as early as 1858.

BURRELL

Before the railroad arrived here in 1889, this Fresno County location was known as Elkhorn Station, for a ranch of the same name.

Elkhorn Ranch was owned by Cuthbert Burrell (Burrel), who arrived here in 1846 and became one of the pioneer cattlemen. The station was renamed in his honor, as was the post office, established in 1912.

BURSON

Burson, Calaveras County, took the name of railroader David S. Burson when the post office was established in 1884. The railroad station, on the other hand, was known as Helisma.

BUTTE CITY

Butte City, Glenn County, was named for the Sutter Buttes. Located on the east bank of the Sacramento River, the town was listed as Butte on an 1854 map, but did not develop as a population center until about 1875 with the establishment of the Marysville-Shasta stage line.

BUTTONWILLOW

Buttonwillow, Kern County, was the name given to both the railroad station and post office in 1895, when a branch line was established here from Bakersfield.

The name goes back to the days when cowboys used a single buttonwillow tree by the slough bank as a landmark. Buttonwillow is a California term for the buttonbush whose leaves resemble those of the willow.

BYRON

The first use of Byron at this Contra Costa location was for the Southern Pacific Railroad station that opened here in 1878. The name probably came from one of many Byrons "back East," as one source puts it.

Hot mineral springs are located at Byron and were called Sulphur, Salt and Hot Springs before assuming the Byron name.

C

CABAZON

Cabazon, Riverside County, was named by the Southern Pacific in the 1870s, after a nearby Indian ranchero. In 1884, a town was laid out around the railroad station and named for it. The name might have come from that of a nearby peak.

Local tradition has it the name came from the chief of the Coahuilla Indians, the "diggers." The word is Spanish for "big head." Chief Cabezon had a very large head, we are told. Others believe the word means "shirt collar" or "tax collector"—which makes no sense at all.

CADIZ

Cadiz took its name from the Spanish city, but it is also the third name in an alphabetical listing of stations. The railroad station, around which the town grew, was established by the Atlantic & Pacific in 1883.

CAHUILLA

This Riverside County locale takes its name from that of the Indian tribe. *Ka-we'-a* is supposed to mean "master" or "leader" in the native tongue.

CAJON JUNCTION

Located in San Bernardino County, this community took its name from the pass in the Sierra Madre range. In 1772, Governor Pedro Fages chased a band of deserting soldiers from San Diego into the Imperial Valley. In the course of his pursuit, he discovered Cajon Pass, the Mojave Desert and the San Joaquin Valley! *Cajon* is a Spanish word, meaning "box," which is quite descriptive.

CALABASAS (— Highlands)

Calabasas, Los Angeles County, carries the Spanish word for "pumpkins," "squash," or "gourds." The name was given because of the abundance of wild gourds or pumpkins found here at the time of settlement.

Prior to 1795, the name was applied to the rancheria at the site. Located here is a well-restored two-story adobe ranch house, built about 1844. It was once the home of Miguel Leonis, a colorful figure in Los Angeles history.

CALEXICO

This San Diego County town was so named because of its location on the California-Mexico border.

CALIENTE

Caliente, Kern County, was established in the 1870s as a trading post for Indians and cowboys. The place was named after the Spanish word for "hot" or "warm," and the name referred to the region's hot springs. When the Southern Pacific opened a camp here in 1874, they kept the name.

Previous to Caliente, the place was known as Allen's Camp, for the sheep owner who had his camp here.

CALIMESA

Calimesa, Riverside County, took its name from a combination of "Cali-," for California, and "mesa," for a "flat-topped hill."

CALIPATRIA

The Latin *patria*, "country" or "fatherland," combined with "Cali-," from California, gives us the name of this Imperial County place name. At Christmas, town fathers run colored lights up a flagpole. The top of the pole is precisely at sea level—184 feet!

CALISTOGA

Located about a mile north of Calistoga is the Old Faithful Geyser of California. It is one of the few regularly erupting geysers in the world.

Calistoga, Napa County, was founded by Samuel Brannan, a Mormon settler who purchased the land in which the hot springs were located in 1859. He had in mind the springs at Saratoga, New York. In fact, he boasted that the town would be the "Saratoga of California." The town's name is a combination of California and Saratoga.

CALLAHAN

In 1851, M. B. Callahan built himself a cabin here at the foot of Mount Bolivar. The next year, he opened a hotel. This Siskiyou County place was named for him.

CALPELLA

The name of this Mendocino County locale came from an Indian chief, and later from the members of his tribe. The chief's name was mentioned as early as 1851. The town was founded seven years later.

The name itself appears to translate from *khal* or *hal*, "mussel," and *pela* or *pelo*, "carry" or "pack." Literally, it means "mussel bearer."

CALPINE

Calpine is shortened from the name, McAlpine. One source thinks that the abundance of trees in the area and a local lumber mill might have suggested California pine.

Located in Sierra County, Calpine was developed in 1919 around the mill of the Davies-Johnson Lumber Company. At that time, it was called McAlpine.

Four years after the town was founded, postal authorities rejected McAlpine, and the new name was substituted.

CAMARILLO

Camarillo, Ventura County, came into being in the 1880s when the Southern Pacific built its Ventura line in this area. The station's name was given in honor of Juan Camarillo. He owned Rancho Calleguas from 1859 until his death in 1880.

CAMBRIA (— Pines)

Developed in 1866, Cambria comes from the Roman name for Wales. The word itself translates from the Welsh *Cymry*, "Welsh-men." The name was a decided improvement over the earlier name, Slabtown.

Because the town was built on Rancho Santa Rosa, townspeople were torn between calling it Santa Rosa or Rosaville. When no one could make a decision, one resident, a Welshman, put a sign up over his shop, "Cambria Carpenter Shop," and won the support of his fellow citizens.

CAMPBELL

William Campbell, who established a sawmill at this Santa Clara County site in 1848 and a stage coach station four years later, gave his name to the creek.

The town, founded in 1885 by his son Benjamin, carries on the family name.

CAMPO

Located in San Diego County, Campo carries the Spanish word for "camp," "field" or "plain." Early Mexican workers used the word to mean "mining camp."

CAMPTONVILLE

In Camptonville, Yuba County, Lester Allen Pelton invented an improved waterwheel that bore his name. His wheel used split buckets which produced added power.

The town began in the early 1850s, when J. M. and J. Campbell opened their hotel here, the Nevada House. By 1854, the town was named to honor its blacksmith, Robert Campbell.

CANBY

This Modoc County town was named for U. S. Army Brigadier General Edward R. S. Canby who was murdered by Indians.

Canby met with Captain Jack in 1873 under a flag of truce. The Indians were restless, and suddenly Captain Jack shot the general and "Boston Charley" slew the Reverend Eleazer Thomas, a peace commissioner. Another commissioner was saved by a squaw who shouted a false warning to the Indians.

The name is also repeated in a city in Oregon.

CANOGA PARK

An earlier name for Canoga Park, Los Angeles County, was Owensmouth. That name, in fact, was used from about 1912 to 1931.

The Canoga name first appeared on a railroad station sign when the Southern Pacific branch from Burbank arrived in the 1890s. Later, when the community developed, "Park" was added.

CANTIL

When the Nevada & California Railroad extended from Owens Lake to Mojave in the early 20th century, the new station at this Kern County site was called Cantil. The word translates from the Spanish to mean "steep rock," but the roots of the name might be deeper than that.

The engineer who did the naming had a fondness for names that began with the letter "C," such as Cambio, Ceneda, Cinco, and others.

CANYON (— County; — Dam; — Lake)

The town of Canyon, Contra Costa County, was originally known as New Redwood Canyon when the post office opened in the 1910s. A decade later, the name was changed to Sequoia but returned as simply Canyon a short while later.

The word, canyon, comes from the Spanish *canon*, and originally meant "pipe" or "cannon." Later the word came to mean the narrow watercourse among mountains.

CAPAY

Capay, Yolo County, took its name from the Capay Valley. The name is Southern Wintu Indian for "stream."

The earlier names for the community, coming from the names of early settlers, were Munchville and Lanville.

CAPISTRANO BEACH

When a post office was first established in 1925 at this Orange County location, the name was given as Capistrano Beach. Six years later, the name was changed to Doheny Park. The new name was for the California oil promoter, E. L. Doheny, who had laid out the townsite in the 1920s. The name was changed back to Capistrano Beach in 1948. The name is a modification of San Juan Capistrano.

CAPITOLA

The Spanish name for this Santa Cruz place translates as "capitol," the building where the legislature meets.

The community began its life in 1869 as Camp Capitola, a place where campers came with their own tents. It was developed as a resort in 1876 by F. A. Hihn. Hihn, who allegedly made his fortune in gold, coined the name as a publicity tool to draw people to his development.

CARDIFF BY THE SEA

Formerly known as San Elijou, this San Diego town was laid out by J. Frank Cullen in 1911, and named for the Welsh seaport.

CARIBOU

Caribou, Plumas County, took its name from the nickname for an early settler who had been involved in the 1858 gold rush in the Cariboo region of British Columbia.

Others believe the name just migrated south.

CARLOTTA

Carlotta, Humboldt County, received this name in 1903, when the Northwestern Pacific built its station here. The town was laid out by John M. Vance, who named it for his youngest daughter. The town is famous for its cherries.

CARLSBAD

Carlsbad is a resort named for the town and springs in Bohemia, now Czechoslovakia. However, the spas at this San Diego County site have long since disappeared.

John Frazier attracted people here after he discovered the springs by touting the benefits of the mineral water which bubbled from a coastal well. Two years later, in 1886, Gerhard Schutte tested the waters, and found them similar to those in Karlsbad. Translated from the German, the name reads "Karl's watering place." During World War I, patriotism shrunk the name to Carl. After the war, when things cooled down a bit, the full name returned.

CARMEL (— Highlands; — Valley)

Carmel, Monterey County, was established in 1904 as a colony for writers and artists. It gained a great deal of attention in the 1980s when movie star Clint Eastwood ran for mayor—and won.

The name first appeared on the river, which was named in 1603 by Viscaino, the Spanish explorer. The name was given because Viscaino was accompanied by three Carmelite friars: the fathers Andrés de la Asuncion, Thomàs de Aquino and Antonio de Palacios.

It was here that the most significant California mission stood. Mission San Carlos de Borromeo (more frequently called Carmel Mission) was the headquarters of the two most famous Franciscan priests, Junipero Serra and Fermin Francisco de Lasuen. Of the 21 California missions established, these two priests were responsible for 18!

Father Serra founded Carmel Mission in 1770 at the Presidio of Monterey as the second mission in California. A little more than a year later, he relocated it here. When Serra died in 1784, Father Lasuen succeeded him.

CARMICHAEL

Carmichael, Sacramento County, was named in 1910 by the landowner—for himself.

CARNELIAN BAY

The name for this Placer County community was taken from the region's carnelian, or Cambay stone, and other semi-precious stones. The bay was named by the Whitney Survey, and appeared on a map in 1874.

The Carnelian Bay post office was established in 1910.

CARPINTERIA

Carpinteria, Santa Barbara County, drew its name from the Spanish for "carpenter shop." Members of the Portola expedition of 1769 named the town in this way, because, as their leader explained, "The Indians have many canoes, and at the time were building one, for which reason the soldiers named this town La Carpinteria."

The post office, without the "La," was established in 1868.

CARRVILLE

Carrville, Trinity County, took its name from the Carr Ranch, which had been started in 1852. The ranch was owned by James E. Carr and his family.

CARSON

Frémont honored his guide, Christopher "Kit" Carson (1809–68), by having the explorer's name replace the earlier name of Pilot River. The river's name first appeared as Carson in 1848.

CARTAGO

Cartago is the Spanish version of Carthage, the ancient city in North Africa. The name was given in 1909 by the Southern Pacific for a new railroad station. Ten years later, the name also appeared on the post office.

CARUTHERS

Located in Fresno County, this place was named in the late 19th century for a local farmer, W. A. Caruthers.

CASITAS SPRINGS

Casitas Springs, Ventura County, bears the Spanish name for "cottages." A creek by the name of Arroyo de las Casitas, "the creek of the little houses," appeared on an 1864 map.

CASMALIA

No one is quite certain of what this Santa Barbara County town's name means. The best that can be said is that it is a Spanish version of an Indian word. The name first appeared in print as part of a land grant in 1837.

CASPAR

Sometime before 1860, Siegfrid Caspar settled in this Mendocino County area. The next year, two men came to the area and built a sawmill on what was then called Caspar Creek. Jacob Green bought the land in 1864, and called his new town Caspar.

CASSEL

Originally called Hat Creek, this Shasta County place had its name changed to Cassel in 1888, at the insistence of a real estate developer who just happened to have been born in Cassel, Germany.

CASTAIC

Castaic, a town in Los Angeles County, takes its name from an Indian village. The Chumas Indian word means "my eyes."

CASTELLA

The name for Castella, Shasta County, is taken from the Latin for "castles," and refers to the nearby Castle Crags.

CASTRO VALLEY

Castro Valley, Alameda County, was named for Guillermo Castro, who owned a large rancho in this area in 1841.

Others suggest General Jose Castro, a leader in Mexican independence. When the Americans took possession, Castro and the other leaders fled to Mexico. It does not seem likely that Jose (or Fidel, for that matter) was included in the thinking when this name came about.

CASTROVILLE

Castroville, Monterey County, was laid out and named in 1864 by Juan B. Castro. The town was located on land which had been granted to his father, Simeon Castro, in 1825.

CATHEDRAL CITY

Cathedral City, Riverside County, took its name from the Cathedral Canyon. Colonel Henry Washington gave the name to the canyon in 1858 because he thought it resembled the interior of a cathedral.

The city was named in 1925 because of its proximity to the canyon.

CATHEYS VALLEY

Andrew Cathey settled in the valley that now bears his name in about 1850. The post office in this Mariposa County place was established in 1879.

CAVE ROCK

This community takes its name from nearby Cave Rock. The cavern deep within the rock was once the hiding place for bandits.

CAYUCOS

Located in San Luis Obispo County, this town's name translates from the Spanish to "small fishing boats" or "dug-out canoes." It is a rendering of the word used in Alaska for the same type of craft—kayak.

The town was laid out and named in 1875.

CAZADERO

Cazadero, Sonoma County, has a Spanish name that means "place for pursuing game" or "hunting place." The name was given to a North Pacific Coast Railroad station in the late 1880s since it was located in good deer-hunting country.

CECILVILLE

Even mapmakers can make mistakes! This Siskiyou County place was named for John Baker Sissel. He arrived in the Shasta Valley sometime before 1849. His name was misspelled on an 1857 map, and again when postal authorities set up shop here in 1879.

CEDAR (— Flat; — Glen; — Grove; —pines Park; —ville)

Many of the towns bearing the name "Cedar" are named after forests of cedars or similar trees. Often, if a tree was coniferous, settlers decided it was a cedar.

That was not the case with Cedarville, Modoc County. J. H. Bonner named the town in 1867 after his Ohio hometown.

CENTRAL VALLEY

The name for Central Valley was given because of its central location to the rest of the state. It also helped that the town sprang up during the 1938 construction of Central Valley Project.

Two Shasta County towns were named after the undertaking: Central Valley and Project City.

CENTURY CITY

Century City was developed on the back lot of 20th Century Fox Film Studios.

CERES

Ceres was the Roman goddess of agriculture. The railway station that was established at this Stanislaus County location was named in 1874, by Elma Carter, a daughter of one of the first settlers. She considered the name quite apt.

CERRITOS

Cerritos, Los Angeles County, bears a name that is Spanish for "little hills."

Originally part of the Los Cerritos land grant of 1834, the town was named when a station of the Pacific Electric Railroad was built here.

CHALLENGE

Challenge, Yuba County, developed around the Challenge Lumber Mill. The town was named in about 1856.

CHAMBERS LODGE

Chambers Lodge, Placer County, was formerly known as McKinney's and Chambers. The name came from that of a nearby resort. The post office was established under the Chambers Lodge name in 1928.

CHATSWORTH

Chatsworth, Los Angeles County, was named during the building boom of 1887. The name came from Chatsworth, England.

CHERRY VALLEY

It is ironic that this valley would be called "Cherry." There are no true cherries indigenous to California. A few cherry-like berries, however, do appear throughout the state, such as the chokeberry.

CHESTER

Chester is located on the northern shore of Lake Almanor. It was named in the early 20th century by Oscar Martin. The name for this Plumas County place came from Chester, Vermont.

CHICO

Chico, Butte County, was begun in 1850 by General John Bidwell (1819–1900), after he bought the land that was then called El Rancho Chico, "The little Ranch." His home, The Esplanade, was built between 1865 and 1868, and is still standing and open to visitors. Bidwell ran unsuccessfully for governor of California three times. He was the Prohibition Party's presidential candidate in 1892.

Chico's name was borrowed from Arroyo Chico, Spanish for "little stream." Bidwell acquired Rancho Chico in 1847. Thirteen years later, he founded the town on his ranch and donated much of the land.

Colonel Mariano Chico, a Mexican congressman, served as governor of Alta California from December 1835 to July of the next year. He stirred up trouble and flaunted his mistress at public events. He was called "the most hated ruler the province ever had."

CHILCOOT

This Plumas County locale was named at the turn of the 20th century. The name came south from Chilcoot Pass, Alaska. The pass was the gateway to the gold rush in the Klondike.

CHILDS MEADOWS

This community took its name from the Children's Forest, a woodland area dedicated to the memory of young people who had died.

CHINA LAKE

China Lake, Kern County, took the name of a nearby large dry lake in 1948.

CHINESE CAMP

Chinese Camp was a settlement for Chinese workers during the gold rush.

The Toulumne County town was founded in 1849 by a group of Englishmen who were importing Chinese labor to work in the mines. Within a short period of time, Chinese Camp became the headquarters for four of the six Chinese tongs in the state. In 1856, the town was the site of a tong war between the Yanb-Wo and the Sam-Yap tongs. About two thousand workers were engaged in the battle, but there were only eight casualties.

CHINO

The name of Chino, San Bernardino County, was given during the days of Spanish control, and refers to a person of mixed extraction, not necessarily one of Chinese background. The name is derived from the land grant of Santa Ana del Chino.

Chino Rancho, located about 25 miles east of Los Angeles, was owned by Isaac Williams and was the 1848 site of the first battle of California independence.

CHINQUAPIN

Chinquapin began its life as a ranger station in Yosemite National Park. The name is that of a shrub, *Castanopsis sempervirens*, which is native to California and Oregon. The name did not appear until 1893 or 1894.

CHOLAME

Cholame, San Luis Obispo County, was named for an Indian rancheria, about 14 leagues from Mission San Miguel. It is first mentioned in 1804 as Cholan, then almost 40 years later as Cholame.

CHOWCHILLA

The name for this town came from that of an Indian tribe, a branch of the Moquelumnan family. The tribal name also appears on the Chowchilla Creek, the place from whence this town received its own.

CHUALAR

The name of this Monterey County location translates from the Indian to mean "place where the chual grows."

Chual is the common pigweed, or lamb's quarters, that the tribe used as a food.

CHULA VISTA

Chula Vista takes its name from the Spanish for "pretty view." The San Diego County town was laid out and named in 1888 by the San Diego Land & Town Company. The first post office carried the name as a single word. That was changed to the current two-word name in 1906.

CIMA

The name for Cima, San Bernardino County, comes from the Spanish for "summit," or "peak."

The San Pedro-Los Angeles-Salt Lake Railroad named the town in 1907. It is located at the top of the pass between Kelso and Ivanpah.

CISCO GROVE

Cisco Grove, Placer County, took the name of John J. Cisco, treasurer of the Central Pacific Railroad. An earlier name was Heaton Station.

CLAREMONT

When the Pacific Land & Improvement Company, a subsidiary of the Santa Fe, laid out this Los Angeles town, they asked the owner of the land, H. A. Palmer, if he would mind having the town named after him. He did, but offered them a number of Spanish names as suggestions.

The directors, not particularly happy with any of the Spanish names, asked for English equivalents. One of the directors came from Claremont, New Hampshire, and leaned on his colleagues for the name.

CLARKSBURG

Clarksburg, Yolo County, was named for Judge Clark who settled here in 1849.

CLAY

This Sacramento County place was named simply because the soil was mainly clay.

CLAYTON

Clayton, Contra Costa County, is a town that took its name from an 1857 settler by the name of Joel Clayton. The town was known one day in 1861 as Clayton's, then two days later as Claytonville. For many years, Clayton was the social center for the Mount Diablo coal mines.

CLEAR LAKE
Clear Lake took its name from that body of water. The lake is the largest body of fresh water entirely within the state of California.

CLEARLAKE (— Oaks)
(See CLEAR LAKE, California.)

CLEMENTS
It was on Thomas Clements' land that this San Joaquin County community was established in the 1870s.

CLEONE
Some think the name of Cleone, Mendocino County, came from the name of the Keliopoma, the northern branch of the Pomo Indians. Others think it is just some woman's name.

CLIO
The town of Clio has no relationship to the Greek muse of history. Rather, the name was selected in 1905 by the person who wanted to rename the post office. He noticed the tradename on a stove, and thought it was a catchy name for the place.

Before Clio arrived on the scene, the town had been known as Wash as early as the 1870s.

CLIPPER MILLS
Clipper Mills, Butte County, took its name in about 1900 from the Clipper Shingle Company. The town of Clipper in Washington has the same derivation. The post office was established here in 1861.

CLOVERDALE
Located in Sonoma County, this community's name was given because of the rich growth of clover in the valley where the town is located. Though the town had originally been called Markelville, for landowner R. B. Markle, the name was changed to Cloverdale in 1857.

CLOVIS

Clovis, Fresno County, was a lumber community. Its name came from Clovis Cole. Cole owned the ranch through which the Southern Pacific built its branch line in 1889.

COACHELLA

Coachella's name is the result of a typographical error that occurred when the name of this place was transferred from the official map.

Before the turn of the 20th century, the valley here in Riverside County was called Cahuilla and Conchilla, Spanish for "little shell." That name was given because fossil shells were found in the area.

The first post office was established as Coachella in 1901.

COALINGA

Coalinga, Fresno County, was a loading spot for the Southern Pacific Railroad when the town was founded in 1888. At that time, it was called Coaling Station A.

When the place blossomed into a permanent settlement following the discovery of oil in 1896, its name was abbreviated. At one time, it is alleged, Coalinga produced one-fifth of the world's petroleum supply.

COARSEGOLD

Coarsegold, Madera County, exploded into existence with the third California gold rush. By 1850, the town counted over ten thousand residents. Thirty years later, the gold was gone, but not the town. After the gold mining died out, the town gained new recognition as a stagecoach station.

The name was given in 1849 by miners from Texas because of the type of gold found in the local mines. The gold was granular, not dust.

COBB

The town, the valley, the creek, and even the mountain are named for John Cobb, a Kentuckian who built a combined saw-grist mill at this Lake County location in 1859.

COLEVILLE

This Mono County place was named for career-politician Cornelius Cole. He served in the House and the Senate during the 1860s and 1870s.

COLFAX

The town of Colfax was named in 1865, upon the visit of "Smilin' " Schuyler Colfax (1853–85). When he arrived at this Placer County locale, he was only Speaker of the House. Three years later, he was Grant's vice president. Colfax did not contribute much to the administration and, when Grant ran for reelection, Colfax was not included on the ticket.

A more important reason for his exclusion was his participation in the Credit Mobilier scandal and the fact that, in 1868, he accepted a sizable contribution from an envelope supplier when he was chairman of the House post offices and post roads committee.

An earlier name for the town was Illinoistown.

COLMA

Three suggestions have been advanced regarding the source of this town's name:

1) As a personal name it appears in MacPherson's *Songs of Selma*.

2) It was adopted from the name of a town in Switzerland, or Colmar in Alsace.

3) It is a shortening of the family name Coleman or Colman.

Colman was well-known for its acres of violets.

Easier to place names appeared on this San Mateo community in the past. At one time, it was simply called Station; later, School House Station, because of its location. In fact, the first post office here was established under that name in 1869. The Colma name did not appear as a post office designation until 1891.

COLOMA

In January 1848, near Captain John Sutter's sawmill on the American Creek, in Eldorado County, John Marshall, Sutter's boss carpenter, discovered gold. "My eyes," he remembered, "was caught with the glimpse of something shining in the bottom of the ditch." Sadly, Marshall never saw anything else "shining" after that.

By the summer, more than two thousand miners were sifting through the sands near Sutter's Mill, and Coloma became America's first gold rush town, and the first white settlement in the foothills of the Sierra Nevada. By December of that year, we are told, more than $6 million of gold dust had been drawn from the California placer mines. Some historians believe that the discovery of gold was one of the reasons California was granted statehood in 1850.

Coloma's name came from that of an Indian tribe. The post office was established here in 1849, but the name was spelled Culloma.

COLTON

This San Bernardino County town was named in 1875 by the Southern Pacific Railroad, for Colonel David D. Colton, an early and prominent citizen. Colton was also financial director of the Central Pacific at the time.

The town had been settled two years earlier by the Slover Mountain Colony.

COLUMBIA

Columbia, Toulumne County, was one of the largest and most important mining towns along the Mother Lode. Between 1850 and 1870, more than $90 million in gold was drawn from the local placer mines! At that point in the town's history, it was known as Hildreth's Diggings.

In 1853, Columbia was the third-largest town in the state and was known as the "Gem of the Southern Mines." Population and the output of the mines declined in about 1860 and Columbia never regained its former popularity.

The community's name was given in 1850 by Majors Farnsworth and Sullivan and Mr. D. G. Alexander.

COLUSA

The name for this Colusa County town was sometimes misspelled as Colusi. This town took its name from the county, which derived its name from the Kolu or Colusi Tribe.

The town was founded in 1850 by Charles D. Semple, who held title to the Colus ranch. He called it first Salmon Bend, then Colusi. The post office that opened the next year was also called Calusi, as was the county, formed in 1850. That name was changed to Colusa in 1854.

COMPTCHE

Some authorities believe that this name, appearing on a Mendocino County town, came from an Indian name, possibly the Pomo village of Komacho.

COMPTON

For many years, Compton was known as the "Beverly Hills of the Black Belt," a reference to the concentration of middle-class black families living here.

Located in Los Angeles County, the Los Angeles & San Pedro Railroad station of Compton was named in 1869 for Griffith D. Compton. He had founded a Methodist temperance colony and was one of the founders, in 1880, of the University of Southern California.

CONCORD

Concord, in Contra Costa County, was named for the Massachusetts town. That name was slipped in without the landowner really knowing it.

The land, part of the Monte del Diablo rancho, was developed into a town in 1860 by the owner, Salvio Pacheco. Being magnanimous, Pacheco offered free lots to anyone who wanted to build at his settlement, which he called Todos Santos.

The people who took advantage of Pacheco's largesse were from the New England area and took greater advantage by renaming his town for their old hometown.

COOL

Cool, El Dorado County, was a placer mining camp in the 1850s. Mining continued here until the end of the 19th century.

A Cool post office was established in 1885. No one knows why the name was selected, except that it was short—and unusual.

COPPEROPOLIS

Copperopolis, Calaveras County, was founded in 1861 when prospectors discovered a rich vein of copper. Between 1862 and 1865, Copperopolis was the main copper-producing area in the United States, but a drop in the world prices in 1866 brought mining to a halt. There was a brief rebirth in the 1870s, but by 1872 the mines here had been abandoned.

The name was made up to represent the extensive copper mines in the area, and the addition of the Greek *opolis*, for "city."

CORCORAN

Not far to the east of Corcoran is Tulare Lake. The lake was discovered in 1773 by Fages. While searching for deserters, his expedition came upon the body of water and called it Los Tules, because it was surrounded by marshes choked by reeds, or tules. Tulare translates to "a place of rushes."

The town, located in Kings County, was established in 1905 by H. J. Whitley. The name came from a civil engineer who worked for the Santa Fe Railroad.

CORONA

Bearing the Spanish word for "crown," this Riverside County community was laid out in 1886 by the South Riverside Land & Water Company. They called it South Riverside.

When the town was incorporated a decade later, Baron Harden-Hickey, owner of the El Cerrito orchards, suggested the present-day name. Corona was nicknamed Circle City in the teens because of the auto races held here that pitted Barney Oldfield against Eddie Rickenbacker.

CORONA DEL MAR

When George E. Hart developed this Orange County site, he named it for the Spanish words that mean "crown of the sea."

The major interests in the property were acquired in 1915 by the F. D. Cornell Company. Thinking the name needed some help in order to advertise it more effectively, they renamed the place Balboa Palisades. The public outcry quickly returned the old name.

CORONADO

This San Diego County community was named for the Spanish explorer, Francisco Vàsquez de Coronado, who attempted to locate the legendary Seven Cities of Cibola. The "seven cities" turned out to be nothing more than Indian pueblos. Or at least that is what some authorities would like us to believe.

Coronado was surveyed and named in 1887 by the Coronado Beach Company. The company was organized by Elisha Babcock and H. L. Story. They borrowed the name from the Los Coronados islands, located off the coast of Baja California.

North Island Naval Air Station was established on Coronado Island in 1911. It was the site of Charles Lindbergh's departure for his around-the-world flight.

CORTE MADERA

Corte Madera, Marin County, has a name that was shortened from the Spanish *corete de madera*, either "cut of wood" or "felled timber."

The Corte de Madera del Presidio was so named because it supplied the presidio at San Francisco with lumber. That name was applied by John Reed (or Read, or Reid) in 1834, when he built a sawmill in this Bay area.

COSTA MESA

Costa Mesa, Orange County, was named in 1915 when, as George Stewart puts it, "enthusiasm for Spanish names outran respect for grammar." As a result we end up with "coast mesa" to describe this location.

The site was originally known as Harper, but when a railroad station was scheduled to open here in 1915, they could not duplicate the Harper name. There was already a Harper on the Pacific Electric Railroad line. A contest was held and the winning name was Costa Mesa.

The post office was established here as Costa Mesa in 1921.

COTTONWOOD

Cottonwood takes its name from the Cottonwood Creek. The waterway's name was given because of the abundance of cottonwood trees along its banks.

COULTERVILLE

Coulterville, Mariposa County, was once quite proud of its Hang Tree, which stood in the public square.

The town was named for George W. Coulter, a Pennsylvanian who opened a store here in 1849. The post office, however, established in 1852, took the name of Maxwell's Creek. In 1872, the name became Coulterville.

COURTLAND

Located in Sacramento County, this community took its name from Courtland Sims. Sims was the son of the landowner on whose land a steamboat landing was constructed in the 1860s.

COVELO

Some authorities believe that this Mendocino County community name is an adopted one, perhaps from Spain. Another tradition, however, suggests it came from Covolo, in the Tirol.

Still another asserts that Charles H. Eberle gave the name in 1870 for a Swiss fortress. Sadly, there is no Covelo in Switzerland.

COVINA

Covina's name was made up and applied to a housing subdivision of La Puente Rancho in the 1880s. Tradition has it the name came from a "cove of vines."

COYOTE

Located in Santa Clara County, this town's name comes from the Mexican *coyotl*, "prairie wolf."

CRANE FLAT

Crane Flat is located in Yosemite National Park. The name came from the appearance of the Mexican or sandhill cranes who passed through on their annual excursion from the arctic cold to the tropic heat.

CRANNEL

From around the turn of the 20th century until about 1924, this Humboldt County community was known as Bullwinkel or Bulwinkle, for landowner Conrad Bulwinkel.

In 1924, the post office was named for Levi Crannell, president of the Little River Redwood Company. Need more be said?

CRESCENT CITY

Crescent City, the largest city in Del Norte County, was founded in 1853 as a gold-mining supply center. The city borders a harbor defined by a crescent-shaped beach, and that is what triggered J. F. Wendell to name it such.

CRESCENT MILLS

Crescent Mills, Plumas County, was named because of the mills located here. The area contained lime springs, but in 1870 when the post office was established, the springs were ignored in favor of the industry.

CREST (—line; —ton; —view)

"Crest" was a favorite word for namers. It was used to describe places located near or at a crest.

Crestline, San Bernardino County, had its name suggested by a Dr. Thompson when the post office was established here in 1920.

The San Luis Obispo County town of Creston was named for its location on the crest of a ridge. It was named in 1887 by J. V. Webster, part owner of the Huerheuro grant.

Crestview, Mono County, had the same nativity.

CROCKETT

Crockett, Contra Costa County, was named for Judge J. B. Crockett, a member of the California Supreme Court.

The town was laid out on the judge's property in 1881 by Thomas Edwards. The judge had received 1,800 acres as a fee for settling a land case!

CROMBERG

Until 1880, this Plumas County location was called Twenty-Mile House. It was 20 miles from Quincy, on the road to Reno.

When a post office was established here, the first postmaster, Gerhard A. Langhorst, decided to name it with an Americanized version of his mother's maiden name, Krumberg—German for "curved mountain." The name, by the way, is appropriate for this town's location.

CROSS ROADS

At one time, the road to the river crossed the highway near this spot in San Bernardino County. Since then the road was washed out by floods. The post office was named Cross Roads when it opened in 1939.

CROWS LANDING

Crows Landing, Stanislaus County, took its name from the pioneering, land-owning family of Walter Crow. He settled the area with his sons after 1849.

Another source suggests the name came from John Bradford Crow, who owned 4,000 acres of land along the San Joaquin River in 1867. Others, we have found, suggest the name is a reference to a murder of crows.

The post office was established as Crows Landing in 1870.

CULVER CITY

Culver City, Los Angeles County, was an early home to movie studios.

The name was given by Harry H. Culver. Arriving from Nebraska in 1914, he acquired and subdivided a portion of the Ballona land grant.

CUMMINGS

Cummings, Kern County, was the beginning of the Bell Springs Grade. During stage coach days, it was the only route, and a steep one it was. The road rises to an elevation of more than four thousand feet and slides down to Dyerville. At Cummings, one also begins to see the stands of redwoods.

The town of Cummings was named for the valley. George Cummings, an Austrian, arrived in California in 1849. In the 1870s, he established residence and raised cattle in the valley that bears his name.

CUPERTINO

Cupertino, Santa Clara County, was named in honor of St. Joseph of Cupertino.

When an 18th-century exploring party came upon the creek, they named it Arroyo de San Jose Cupertino. Later, it was called "Stephen's or Cupertino Creek" in 1878. By 1899, the creek's name was Stevens Creek, but the post office, established in 1882, remained Cupertino. When that post office closed in 1895, the name was transferred to the one at West Side.

CURRY VILLAGE

Curry Village, once known as Camp Curry, is located directly beneath Glacier Point. It takes its name from David Curry, "the Stentor of Yosemite," an early host. Curry, it was said, had a gigantic voice. When he shouted from the valley floor, his words could be heard on top!

CUTLER

The town of Cutler, Tulare County, was named in 1903 by representatives of the Santa Fe Railroad. The railroad station here had been built on land owned by Judge John Cutler.

Cutler allowed them to use his land but, in a 1898 proviso, insisted that the station bear his name.

CUYAMA

Cuyama came from the name of an Indian *rancheria*, or village, meaning "clams" in the Chumash tongue. It is also the name of a mountain and river.

CYPRESS

Cypress, Orange County, was named for the existence of cypress trees planted here.

DAGGETT

The name of Daggett, San Bernardino County, was brought to California from the town in Indiana. At least, that is what one expert contends. A more logical explanation for the naming of this San Bernardino County community is that when the Southern Pacific Railroad came through in 1882, they named it for California's then-Lieutenant Governor John Daggett. Daggett went on to build one of the first houses here, and laid out the town.

For many years, 20-mule teams dragged colemanite, borax ore, from Death Valley to Daggett for refining.

DALY CITY

Daly City, San Mateo County, was conceived in crisis. Refugees from the 1906 San Francisco earthquake and fire settled here. The town was incorporated in 1911 and named for the owner of a local dairy ranch, John Daly.

DANA (— Point)

Dana Point had its origins in the mid-19th century. By the end of that century, it was the only major port between Santa Barbara and San Diego. The Dana Point post office was established in 1929 and named for the point.

The town of Dana, Shasta County, was named for Loren Dana, and laid out in 1888. Dana had settled at the Big Springs in the late 1860s.

The Dana post office was established here in 1892.

DANBY

Danby was named in the same way as Amboy: Lewis Klingman, of the Atlantic & Pacific Railroad, liked to name stations in the West for things "back East." (See AMBOY, California.)

DANVILLE

Danville, Contra Costa County, is not really sure how it got its name.

One story that is told about the naming of the post office in 1867 centers around members of the Inman family, who settled here in 1858. Certain Inmans thought the town should be called Inmanville. But Daniel and Andrew Inman objected to it. Andrew's mother-in-law interjected, "Call it Danville." Daniel relates that, out of respect for her, the town was named Danville. She had been born and raised near Danville, Kentucky.

That story does not hold up—the Danville post office had already been established in 1860!

DARDENELLE

The name of the straits in Turkey, popularized in the Crimean War, was a popular one for mines during the mid-19th century. The serrated range nearby is called the Dardanelles.

DARWIN

This Inyo County community was named for English naturalist Charles Darwin (1809–82). Darwin developed a theory of evolution through natural selection in his 1859 *Origin of Species*.

A number of California mountains were named for scientists, apparently before fundamentalists got there. These include Darwin, Huxley and Spencer. Not far from Darwin Mountain is Evolution Lake!

Another source contends that the name for the town came not from the naturalist, but from Dr. E. Darwin French, who had a ranch at Fort Tejon and prospected in the area in the fall of 1850.

DAVENPORT (— Lodge)

Homer Davenport was California's greatest cartoonist, discovered by Hearst. His name, however, is not on the sign for the Santa Cruz County community of Davenport. The honor for that name goes to Captain John H. Davenport. The town was named in about 1868, for the whaling station called Davenport Landing, which the captain started in the 1850s.

DAVIS (— Creek)

Davis, Yolo County, took its name from Jerome C. Davis, a settler who arrived here in the mid-19th century. Originally called Davisville, the name was reduced to Davis when the railroad came through a decade later. The University of California at Davis, home of the agricultural school, is located here. In the early days, it was known as The Farm.

Davis Creek, Inyo County, commemorates David Davis, who arrived here in about 1866, married an Indian woman, and raised cattle and potatoes to supply the mining camps.

DAY

The post office at this Modoc County site was named in 1892. The probable name donor was Nathaniel H. Day, a pioneer.

DEATH VALLEY JUNCTION

This town's name recalls Death Valley, so named because of the hostile environment and the large number of fatalities among settlers passing through between 1848 and 1850.

Death Valley is almost 300 feet below sea level, surrounded by the Black Mountains and Funeral Range to the east and the Panamint Mountains to the west. It is about 130 miles long and from six to 14 miles wide.

DELANO

Delano, Kern County, was reached by the Southern Pacific Railroad in 1873, and named for Columbus Delano. At the time, Delano was Grant's secretary of the interior.

DELHI

Delhi, Solano County, was named for the city in India, probably because it sounded like an exotic name. It was listed as a railroad station in 1884.

DEL LOMA

The name, meaning "of the hill" or "by the hill," was given to this Trinity County town by postal authorities in 1927.

DEL MAR

Del Mar's name is Spanish for "of the sea." And it is. The community is best known for its years of battling and compromising between real estate developers and residents.

The Del Mar Thoroughbred Club, located here, was organized in the 1930s by Bing Crosby and some of his cronies, including actors Pat O'Brien, Gary Cooper, and Oliver Hardy. Crosby thought it would be fun to have a track near his Rancho Santa Fe home.

The town was founded in 1884 by Colonel Jacob S. Taylor. One of the promoter's wives, Mrs. T. M. Loop, suggested the name because the town was not too far from the setting in Bayard Taylor's poem, "The Fight of Paso del Mar."

DEL REY OAKS

This Fresno County village takes its name from the Spanish for oaks "of the king."

DELTA

Located in Shasta County, this town was named because of its wedge-shaped form at the top of a hill. In fact, the land on top of the hill and the meeting of the Sacramento and Dog Creek form a perfect Greek *delta*.

DE LUZ

This community in San Diego County possibly could have taken its name from the Spanish for "the light" or "inspiration." Another authority thinks it came from the Spanish interpretation of the English name "Luce."

At one point, we are told, an Englishman by the name of Luce kept his horses in a corral. Spanish speakers referred to his pen as Corral de Luz. When the post office was established in 1882, it became De Luz.

DENNY

The name of Denny, Trinity County, first appeared on a town sign as New River City in 1882. A few years later, postal officials rejected the name. The miners proceeded to rename the place for Denny Bar, who owned the store.

When the town was abandoned in 1920, the post office—and the name—moved to Quimby, which very quickly became Denny.

DeSABLA

DeSabla, Butte County, was named for Eugene De Sabla. He masterminded the power plant for the Pacific West & Electric Company in 1903.

DESCANSO

Originally a stage station, Descanso, San Diego County, took its name from the Spanish for "rest from labor." Some say that surveyors ate their meals here in the 1880s. But the name appeared on the post office in 1877—several years before the surveyors came for lunch.

DESERT (— Center; — Hot Springs; — Shores)

All the "desert" names reflect the fascination people have had for the foreboding arid expanses of this country.

DEVILS DEN

California has a hold on the largest number of geographic features and places that contain the word "devil." There are almost 50 different combinations with "devil." Devils Den, Kern County, is just one of them.

DEVORE

When the California Pacific Railroad came through Cajon Pass and arrived at Kenwood in 1885, the station was renamed Devore. John Devore was a principal landowner in the area. His name supplanted that of a Chicago merchant who also was a landowner, though an absentee one!

DIABLO

The town takes its name from Mount Diablo, which is Spanish for "devil's woods."

Legend has it that the Spaniards called the town El Monte del Diablo and believed the devil lived within the mountain and hurled down rockslides. The legend continues that when Spaniards were fighting Indians here in 1806, a gigantic figure, garbed in warpaint, jumped at them as if from the bowels of the mountain. With swift blows, he dispatched many; the rest fled, shouting "El Diablo! El Diablo!"

Bret Harte added to the legend when he told the story of one Padre Haro who met the devil in person on the mountain's summit. The devil told the padre that the "gringos" would take over from the Spaniards. The priest was injured in the encounter, and his companion said he met up with a bear. Disbelievers agreed he was hearing things; believers cautioned that the devil takes on many manifestations.

The Diablo post office was established in 1917.

DIAMOND (— Bar; — Spring)

When prospectors were poking around this El Dorado County area in 1849, they came across sparkling quartz crystals, and thought they were diamonds. This spawned a major rumor that a diamond mine had been found. All that remains is Diamond Spring, without a diamond.

DILLON BEACH

George Dillon, an Irishman, settled in this Marin County location before 1867. When the post office was established in 1923, it took the name of George Dillon and his descendants.

DINKEY CREEK

In 1863, a dog by the name of Dinkey engaged in a major fight with a grizzly bear along the stream and, though mortally injured, came out the winner. Hunters named the waterway (some say it was Dinkey Lake) after the pooch, and the town followed suit.

DINUBA

The railroad's to blame for this name in Tulare County. It does not mean a thing, but it was short, exotic and one of a kind. A construction engineer gave it that title when the branch line was built here between 1887 and 1888.

DIXON

This Solano County community was named in 1870 for Thomas Dickson, a pioneer settler. Dickson donated 10 acres for the townsite, and what did he get? A misspelled name!

DOBBINS

The town of Dobbins, Yuba County, was named for an early settling family—and not for their horse! The town was named for William and Mark D. Dobbins, who settled the creek that also bears their name in 1849.

DOMINIQUEZ

The Dominiquez Rancho, from which this community takes its name, was one of the earliest Spanish grants in California. It was given to Don Juan Jose Dominiquez in 1785. He was one of the leaders of the failed Dominiquez-Escalante expedition of 1776 that did not find a passage from New Mexico to Monterey.

It was here in 1846 that native Californians battled American forces, with the Americans coming up short.

At different periods of its life, Dominiquez has been called Elftman, for a landowner (before 1923) and Davidson City, for Davidson Investment Company (until 1937).

DONNER LAKE

This community takes its name from the nearby lake. The lake and the pass commemorate the disastrous Donner Party of 1846–47.

A covered-wagon train, under George Donner and his brother Jacob, later called the Donner Party, left Independence, Missouri, and, in October 1846, reached the summit to the Sierras—and the early snowstorms. The icy weather killed their cattle and demolished their foodstuffs. A few were able to cross the Sierras and reach salvation. Of the 81 who stayed there, 36 died of cold and starvation. Tales of cannibalism continue to haunt the memory of that party. A letter, allegedly from Edward M. Kern, stated: "And they lived on the dead bodies of their friends—drying the Meat when one perished."

DORRIS

The railroad station here in Siskiyou County was named by the Southern Pacific in about 1907, for local cattlemen Presley A. and Carlos J. Dorris, who began business in the 1860s. They moved from the area in 1870, and took up claims in Modoc County. There, the Dorris Reservoir also bears their name.

DOS PALOS

Located in Merced County, this community's name is Spanish for "two trees," a description of the lack of vegetation at the time of settlement.

The Southern Pacific Railroad gave the name in 1889. For many years, the post office name was spelled Dospalos. In 1905, the name was changed to its Spanish configuration. The modern town was founded in 1907 by the Pacific Improvement Company.

DOS RIOS

Dos Rios is Spanish for "two rivers," a description of the branches of the Eel River that meet here in Mendocino County.

DOUGLAS CITY

Douglas City, Trinity County, was named for Stephen Arnold Douglas (1812–61), of Illinois. Douglas, long-time public official and politician, was known as the "Little Giant." He was a strong proponent of western expansion.

Once in the U. S. Senate, Douglas became chairman of the Committee on Territories. This brought him directly into the conflict over slavery in the territories. He came up with his own notion, "popular sovereignty," in 1854. This concept, he felt, was equitable and fair because the people would be able to settle the question of slavery themselves, rather than have the politicians do it for them.

Stephen Douglas rose to national prominence and, through a series of debates with Abraham Lincoln during the 1860 presidential campaign, allowed Lincoln to rise from relative obscurity to the presidency.

DOWNEY

After two years as governor of California (1860–62), John G. Downey got back to reality. In 1865, Downey subdivided Rancho Santa Gertrudis and donated his name to this Los Angeles County town.

DOWNIEVILLE

Downieville, Sierra County, was named for a pioneer, "Major" William Downie, a Scotsman who panned gold here. The town, located at the meeting of the north and south forks of the Yuba River, was founded after gold was discovered near here in 1849. At first, the town was known as the Forks.

Within a year, the town became the center for surrounding mining camps and the name changed. Even though fires in 1852 and 1859 destroyed most of the town, the residents rebuilt. The lure of making a fortune was more powerful than personal inconvenience.

The Methodist Church located here, built in 1865, is the oldest Protestant church in continuous use in the state.

DOYLE

The Nevada-California Oregon Railway named its station here in Lassen County for John W. and Stephen A. Doyle, settlers from the 1860s.

DRAKESBAD

The 1860s landowner of the property upon which Drakesbad grew was E. R. Drake. It is located on Hot Springs Creek below Flatiron Ridge in Plumas County. While Drake operated the place, it was known as Drake's Place or Drake's Hot Springs.

Initially, when the Sifford family bought the place in 1900, they changed its name to Sifford's, but to avoid confusion, and probably to maintain a constant flow of customers, they ultimately brought back Drake's name, and added the German -*bad*, for "bath."

DRYTOWN

Drytown, Amador County, has a name tinged with irony. The town was not named for the absence or water or, heaven forbid, of liquor. (On the short main drag of Drytown, there were over 30 taverns!) Rather, it was named because the miners had a difficult time supplying enough water to wash gold.

In August 1855, a band of Mexican bandits was spotted heading toward Rancheria, not far from Drytown. A rider was dispatched to warn the settlers, but he was too late. The bandits had robbed the town, taking $10,000 from the local bank and murdering nine men and one woman, and wounding two others.

DUARTE

Duarte, Los Angeles County, bears the name of Andres Duarte. He settled this area on the Ranch Azusa grant in 1841. The grant was subdivided in 1864 and 1865, and became the center for the town almost a quarter of a century later.

DUBLIN

Sometime after 1852, James W. Dougherty bought a portion of Rancho San Ramon in Alameda County, and settled on it. When a post office was opened in the 1860s, it was known as Dougherty's Station. It seemed that Mr. Dougherty called the south side of the road Dublin because so many Irishmen lived there. The post office's name was changed to Dublin in the 1890s.

DUCOR

Because the original name of this town was too long, the railroad shortened it. The first name was Dutch Corners, because four German settlers had adjoining homesteads in this Tulare County location.

DUDLEY

Dudley, Kings County, took its name from a town in Massachusetts.

DULZURA

Dulzura, San Diego County, took its name from the nearby creek. The waterway was named about 1870 because of a new industry: the production of honey.

The Spanish word, *dulzura*, has been variously translated to mean "sweetness," "gentleness" or "forbearance." With the idea of bees and honey, the first meaning is probably on target.

John S. Harbison introduced the honey industry into the region in 1869. The name was suggested in 1887 when the first post office was established, legend has it, by a Mrs. Hegenbeck who loved wild flowers.

DUNCANS MILLS

Duncans Mills was named for S. M. and A. Duncan, who built a mill here in 1860. A post office bearing that name was established in this Sonoma County area in 1862.

DUNLAP

This Fresno County site was named in 1882, when the first post office was established. The first postmaster, by the way, was George Dunlap Moss.

DUNNIGAN

The Northern Railway Company named this Yolo County site for A. W. Dunnigan when they reached here in 1876. Dunnigan had settled here in 1853.

DUNSMUIR

Dunsmuir, Siskiyou County, bears the name of Alexander Dunsmuir, a "coal baron." Dunsmuir passed through Cedar Flat, a station on the Southern Pacific in the late 1880s, and he promised the townspeople a fountain if they would name this town after him.

The station—nothing more than a boxcar—and the new name were moved to a new site, called Pusher, in 1887. The fountain was later presented to the townspeople and erected at the railroad station.

DURHAM

Durham has a name that was borrowed from a town of the same name in Maine. That seems the easy way out.

This Butte County town was named by the railroad in the 1870s, for W. W. Durham, a millowner.

EAGLE ROCK

Eagle Rock, Los Angeles County, takes its name from a rock formation that, around noon, provides the shadow of an eagle on it.

EAGLEVILLE

Eagleville, Modoc County, bears the name of the favorite bird name in the state of California.

EARLIMART

Earlimart is the only California town founded, financed and governed by black Americans. The town was founded in the early 20th century by a Colonel Allensworth.

When the Southern Pacific arrived at this Tulare County site, the station was called Alila, simple and the same spelled backwards. The 20th century promoters coined Earlimart to indicate that crops matured faster when grown here.

EARP

Good old Wyatt Earp, pioneer, peace officer and miner from Arizona, was honored in the naming of this San Bernardino County town. At the request of residents and the Santa Fe, postal authorities allowed the name to be used on this post office in 1929. Before that, since about 1910, the town was known as Drenna.

EASTON

When it was first settled in the 1870s, this town was called Covell, for A. T. Covell. He was the resident manager of the Washington Irrigated Colony.

When a post office was established here in Fresno County in 1882, the place was renamed for O. W. Easton. Easton was the colony's land agent.

EDISON

This Kern County community was founded—and named—by the Southern California Edison Company, when it built its substation here in 1905.

EDWARDS

Earlier known as Muroc Air Field, this military installation in Kern County had its name changed to Edwards Air Base in 1950. The name was changed to honor Captain Glenn W. Edwards, a test pilot who was killed in the crash of the experimental YB-49, "Flying Wing."

The post office name was also changed to Edwards in that year.

EL CAJON

El Cajon, San Diego County, has a name that comes from the Spanish phrase for "box" or "chest." The name was applied because of the high-walled canyon.

The ranch established here was known in 1875 as El Cajun Rancho, but when the modern town was formed, the old name of El Cajon was brought back. Postal authorities, without of a sense of history, ran the two words together before 1905.

EL CAMPO

Located in Marin County, El Campo is Spanish for "the flat country."

EL CENTRO

El Centro, Imperial County, is the market center for the Imperial Valley, one of the richest farming areas in the world. It was named when the town was platted in 1905 because of its central location. For a brief period, the railroad station was called Cabarker, for C. A. Barker, a friend of the landowner.

EL CERRITO
El Cerrito takes its name from El Cerrito Creek. The town is located at the base of a hill by that name.

ELDERWOOD
Elderwood, Tulare County, takes its name from the common shrub or tree that is native to sections of California.

EL DORADO HILLS
El Dorado, Sacramento County, comes from the Spanish for "golden land." The name was originally that of the legendary Indian city. Later it became the city of gold that Spanish explorers sought. Finally, by 1827, the name became associated with any place where gold was found.

    This particular site was established in 1962 as a modern real estate development.

EL GRANADA
El Granada, San Mateo County, is located on a hillside overlooking San Francisco Bay. The post office was named in 1910, for the last Moorish stronghold in Spain.

ELK (— Creek; — Grove)
There are more than 50 geographic features in the State of California that recall this animal. Elk, Mendocino and Fresno counties, Elk Creek, Glenn County, and Elk Grove, Sacramento County, carry on that tradition.

    In the case of Elk Grove, the name is dead on target. In 1850, James Hall opened his Elk Grove House, with an elk's head painted over the door.

ELMIRA
Elmira, Solano County, took its name from Elmira, New York.

    When the California Railroad was built in 1868 from Vallejo to Sacramento, the name Vaca was given to the station—after Vacaville, west of the site.

About 1875, when the road extended to Rumsey, Vacaville became a station. So, to eliminate duplication, the railroaders changed the name of the newer town to Elmira.

EL MIRAGE

El Mirage, San Bernardino County, was named for the lake that was named for the optical illusion most frequently associated with the desert.

El Mirage was settled and had a post office by 1917.

EL MODENA

Before the post office was established, this Orange County community was content to go by the Italian name of Modena. But postal authorities feared people would confuse the name with Madera. So, in about 1890, the post office added the Spanish article El to avoid confusion. Twenty years later, they discovered you cannot use a masculine article to modify a feminine noun and changed the name to El Modeno. That did not last.

EL MONTE

El Monte, Los Angeles County, was the end of the Santa Fe Trail for westbound travelers in the mid-19th century. The name is Spanish for "the thicket," and refers to a thick stand of willows. The original post office name here was Monte, but postal authorities added the El to the name before 1880. About five years later, they contracted the two words into one. In 1905, the name was returned to El Monte.

The town was founded in 1851 by expatriate Texans. It was the first American settlement established in southern California.

EL PORTAL

The Yosemite Valley Railroad provided this Spanish name to this Mariposa County location. The word means "gateway," and the station was the entrance to the park.

EL RIO

This Ventura County town was founded by Simon Cohn in 1875, and it was called New Jerusalem. About 1895, postal authorities changed the name to Elrio, and in 1905 it became two words. The name translates from the Spanish to mean "the river."

ELSEGUNDO

Elsegundo, Los Angeles County, was given its name in 1911 by Colonel Rheem of the Standard Oil Company. This was his company's second refinery in California.

EL VERANO

El Verano, Sonoma County, has a name that is Spanish for "the summer." The name was selected by George H. Maxwell in about 1890. His family's home was nearby, and he felt that "the climate here was considered about perfect."

EMERYVILLE

At an earlier time, there was an Indian shell-mound here that produced many interesting artifacts. It has long disappeared in the face of progress.

Emeryville, Alameda County, was named for Joseph S. Emery in 1897. Emery was a landowner in the area where the town is now situated.

EMIGRANT GAP

Emigrant Gap, Placer County, was named for the pass through which the 1849 pioneers crossed a divide and descended into Bear Valley.

ENCINATAS

The name for this San Diego County town comes from the Spanish for "little oaks." It was part of the Los Encinitos grant of 1842, but the modern community was started in 1881, when Nathan Eaton built the first house. And what a house it was! Eaton, brother of Civil War General C. Eaton, built the house from used lumber and shingled the roof with flattened tin powder cans. He scrounged both items from a local construction site.

The Santa Fe Railroad station was called Encinitos in 1881, but by 1892 the name was up to its modern spelling.

Located at Encinatas is the Self Realization Fellowship, a retreat and place of worship for a Native American religious sect.

ENCINO

Encino's roots go back to the Rancho El Encino, a 4,500-acre cattle and sheep spread. It was a stage coach stop from 1845 to 1915. The Spanish word *encino* translates to mean "live oak," but Americans used the word to connote any type of oak tree.

When the Southern Pacific extended its line from Burbank in the late 19th century to this Los Angeles County site, the name was Encino. The same was true in 1938, with the establishment of the post office.

ENTERPRISE

This Butte County community's name came, we are told, from the Union Enterprise Company. They built flumes here in 1852.

ESCALON

This town was named Escalon because the town's founder, James W. Jones, liked the sound of the word. It comes from the Spanish and means "step of a stair." Perhaps Jones thought this was the first rung on the ladder of success.

Jones laid out this San Joaquin County town in 1895 or 1896.

ESCONDIDO

Escondido, San Diego County, was founded in a place where water was hard to find. The town takes its name from the nearby stream, and the word translates from the Spanish to mean "hidden."

The Alvarado family built an adobe home here in 1840. The town, however, was not laid out until 1885. In that year, a syndicate of businessmen bought the Rancho El Rincon del Diablo, Ranch of the Devil's Corner, and called it Escondido after the creek.

ESPARTO

When the Vaca Valley Railroad (later the Southern Pacific) came into this Yolo County area in 1875, officials named the station Esperanza, Spanish for "hope." In the 1880s, when the town tried to get a post office, they found there was another Esperanza, and changed their name to Esparto, Spanish for "feather grass."

ESSEX

The station of the Atlantic & Pacific Railroad at this San Bernardino County site was known as Edson in 1883. In 1906, the Santa Fe changed the name for convenience. Local tradition has it the name came from a local miner.

ESTRELLA

Estrella, San Luis Obispo County, takes its name from the Estrella River.

ETNA

Originally called Rough and Ready, this Siskiyou County site was changed by law in 1874 to the contemporary spelling of the town's mills, Aetna. (See AETNA SPRINGS, California.)

EUREKA

The name for Eureka, Humboldt County, was drawn from the Greek. The word means "I have found it!" The chief port between San Francisco Bay and the Columbia River, Eureka was named in 1850 by C. S. Ricks and J. T. Ryan. This appears to be the first use of the name in the United States.

Fort Humboldt, active from 1853 to 1867, was established on a bluff overlooking Humboldt Bay and the Pacific. Lieutenant George Crook arrived with the first detachment, and Captain Ulysses S. Grant served between 1853 and 1854. Legend has it that Grant's resignation from the Army was brought about by his heavy drinking at Ryan's Tavern here in Eureka. The drinking led to disagreements with his commanding officer, a Colonel Buchanan. A few years later, Grant commanded the entire Army! What remains of Fort Humboldt is open for tours.

Eureka is also home to a large number of Victorian masterpieces, including the Carson Mansion, built in 1885 by the Newsom brothers for timber baron William Carson. The Newsoms also built The Pink Lady, across from the Carson house.

FAIRFAX

The name of this Marin County community was drawn from Charles Snowden Fairfax, of Virginia. Locally he was known as "Lord Fairfax." "Good Time Charlie" had a reputation for being a "devil-may-care" sort of guy, and he was a most hospitable host at his home in Manor.

He settled here in 1856 on part of Rancho Canada de Herrara.

FAIRFIELD

Fairfield, Solano County, was named by Clipper Ship Captain Robert H. Waterman (1808–84) in 1859. He donated the land for the city, and he named it after his home in Fairfield, Connecticut.

FALLBROOK

The name for Fallbrook, San Diego County, has nothing to do with a waterway or falls. The town was named by its first postmaster, Charles V. Reche, in 1878.

Reche's ancestor was Vital Reche, who arrived here in 1858 from Fallbrook, Pennsylvania. The postmaster's middle name, by the way, was Vital.

FALLEN LEAF

Fallen Leaf, El Dorado County, took its name from Fallen Leaf Lake. It is said that the lake was named by a surveying team that looked at it from above. Looking down, they thought the lake resembled a fallen leaf.

FALLON

Luke Fallon settled in this Marin County area in 1854. He was followed five years later by James L. Fallon. One would suspect that, when the North Pacific Coast Railroad opened a station in these parts in the late 19th century, it just might honor one of the pioneering Fallons.

FALL RIVER MILLS

Fall River was named by Frémont because of its cascades. This Shasta County town takes its name from the mills along the banks of the Fall River. The mills were built here by W. H. Winters in 1872.

FAMOSO

When the Southern Pacific Railroad reached this Kern County location in the 1870s, they established a station and called it Poso, after the Poso Creek.

Postal officials called the post office here Spottiswood, because Poso was too close to Pozo, San Luis Obispo County. Townspeople did not like the Anglo-Saxon, and offered the Spanish word for "famous" or "celebrated," *famoso*.

FARMERSVILLE

The name of this Tulare County site is descriptive, so it was easy for the post office to take on the name in the 1870s.

FARMINGTON

Located in San Joaquin County, Farmington was different from its neighbors. To distinguish this farming community from its adjacent mining towns, W. B. Stamper convinced the town fathers to name it Farmington in 1859.

FAWNSKIN

An earlier name for this community was Grout, named after the nearby Grout Creek. In the late 19th century, travelers used to camp in a little meadow above Grout Canyon. On one of these trips, the people found a number of fawn skins stretched across the trees to dry. As time went on, people referred to the area as "Fawn Skin" Meadows. When Grout looked for a better name, they picked the name most people called the area.

The Fawnskin post office was established at this San Bernardino County site in 1918.

FEATHER FALLS

Feather Falls takes its name from the falls, located about three miles above the Fall Rivers confluence with the Middle Fork. John Augustus Sutter (1803–80) named the river before 1840 after seeing the local Indians making clothing and blankets from feathers.

It is possible that he first named it in the Spanish form: Rio de las Plumas. The Feather Falls post office was established at this Butte County site in 1921.

FELLOWS

Fellows was named in 1908 by the Sunset Western Railroad Company. The name on this Kern County spot honored Charley A. Fellows, a building contractor.

FELTON

Located in Santa Cruz County, Felton was founded in 1878 and named by the landowner, George Treat. He named it for his friend, Charles N. Felton, a career politician in California.

FENNER

This San Bernardino County town was named for a town in New York's Madison County. The New York community honors a former governor of Rhode Island.

Fenner's selection was in no way connected with either New York or the governor. Lewis Klingman (see AMBOY) named the town, and the "F" fitted into his alphabetical run.

FERNBRIDGE

(See FERNDALE, California.)

FERNDALE

Although Ferndale, Humboldt County, was settled in 1852 by Seth and Stephen Shaw, two young men from Vermont, it was Danish pioneers who later developed the town's dairy business in the 1870s. The Danish and Portuguese dairymen built homes that became known as "butterfat palaces."

The most representative of these is the Gingerbread Mansion, 400 Berding Street. Formerly a hospital, it is now a bed-and-breakfast.

The town was named for the profusion of ferns in the valley. The name "fern" attached to a place is a sure giveaway of what was there.

FERNWOOD

(See FERNDALE, California.)

FIDDLETOWN

This Amador County community was founded in 1848 by a band of miners from Missouri. In their spare time, these folks danced to the sound of the fiddle.

Thirty years later, the town's judge used his influence to change the name. The judge was embarrassed each time he had to write Fiddletown on a San Francisco hotel register. He wanted something more substantial, so he had it named Oleta in 1878, Indian for "old home spring."

Oleta did not last too long. Interested parties interceded and the name was returned to Fiddletown in 1932. Bret Harte drew attention to the town in *An Episode in Fiddletown.*

FIELDS LANDING

This Humboldt County location was listed as a site in 1890, and a year later as a station on the Eel River & Eureka Railroad. The station was named for an early settler, Waterman Field.

FILLMORE

Fillmore was an oil-producing community on the Santa Clara River, near the mouth of Sespe Canyon. Some think the name honors President Millard Fillmore, who signed into law California's entry into the Union on 9 September 1850. Others do not.

The Ventura County site was actually named by the Southern Pacific Railroad in 1887, for J. A. Fillmore, the general superintendent of the line's Pacific division.

FINLEY

John Syler was the founder of this community in Lake County in 1889. When Syler wanted to open a post office, postal authorities requested a list and accepted Finley as the name. That name was the middle name of Syler's father, Samuel Finley Syler.

FIREBAUGH

Andres J. Fierbaugh opened a trading post here and established a ferry on the San Joaquin River for the Butterfield Overland Stages in 1854. The misspelling of his name began about two years later, with Firebaugh's Ferry. About 60 years later, the town voted to incorporate, calling itself the "City of Firebaugh."

FISH CAMP

Located in Mariposa County, Fish Camp began as a camp for workers at the Sugar Pine Lumber Mill. In later years, a fish hatchery opened and suddenly people found their mail addressed to Beery's Fish Camp. The town was registered under that name, until the post office arrived. In an effort to streamline service, they cut Mr. Beery's name from the site.

FIVE POINTS

Five different roads converged at this Fresno County location when the post office was established in 1944.

FLORIN

The name of this Sacramento County site was given by E. B. Crocker, of the Central Pacific Railroad, during construction of the line in the 1860s.

Some think Crocker picked the name for the silver coin that was once used in Europe. Others believe it was because of a large number of flowers in the area when he arrived.

FLORISTON

The name of this Nevada County town is made up. The root of the word is taken from the Spanish *flor*, "flowers," and indicates "flowertown."

The railroad station that was located here in the 1870s was called Bronco, after the nearby creek. When a post office was established in 1891, the name was changed to Floriston.

FLOURNOY

The Flournoy family began farming in this Tehama County area as early as the 1870s. The post office, established in 1910, was named for the family.

FOLSOM

This Sacramento County town was once the end of the Pony Express. It was laid out in 1855 by Theodore D. Judah, as the temporary terminal for the Sacramento Valley Railroad. He named it for Captain Joseph L. Folsom who, during the mid-19th century, owned the land on which the railroad was built.

In 1849, the village was called Negro Bar because the first miners were blacks. The town is best known as the site of one of California's major prisons.

FONTANA

Fontana took the name of the company that developed it: the Fontana Development Company. The name comes from the Spanish for "fountain."

The San Bernardino County town had been laid out by the Semi-Tropic Land & Water Company in 1887, but the town did not develop. The Fontana Company bought them out before 1905 and the town took off. A. B. Miller, an official of the company, called the new town Rosena. That name was changed in a solemn 1913 ceremony to honor the company.

FORBESTOWN

Ben Forbes, an emigrant from Wisconsin, opened a store here at this Butte County site in 1850. The town name naturally honored him.

FOREST (— Falls; — Glen; —hill; — Knolls; — Ranch; —ville)

Forest, alone or in combination, is a popular American place name, and California has its share.

Foresthill, Placer County, was once spelled as two words. It is located on the Forest Hill Divide. The name is descriptive of what was there when the town was settled in the mid-19th century.

Forest Falls, on the other hand, came by its name in a different manner. This San Bernardino County community took its post office name when two other offices were discontinued: Fallsvale and Forest Home.

FORKS OF SALMON

The name of this former mining camp in Siskiyou County was taken from its geographic location: the forks of the Salmon River. The post office took on that name when it was established in 1859.

FORT BIDWELL

Fort Bidwell, located in Modoc County at the head of Upper Lake, was founded by U. S. Volunteer troops in 1865–66 to protect settlers from the Indians of northern California, southern Oregon and western Nevada. In the late 19th century, a town grew around the post. The post ceased being an active military installation in 1893. The post was taken over by the Indian Bureau, and a boarding school operated there until 1930.

The name came from General John Bidwell (1819–1900), an early California pioneer and, in 1841, a member of the first group of emigrants to make the wagon-train trek from Independence, Missouri, to California.

FORT BRAGG

The military installation of Fort Bragg was established here in 1857 on the Mendocino Indian Reservation. At the outbreak of the Civil War, California Volunteers replaced Army Regulars. The fort was abandoned in 1864 after most of the Indians had left the reservation. The post had been named by Lieutenant H. G. Gibson, for Lieutenant Colonel Braxton Bragg. Bragg had made a name of himself in the Mexican War. The name he made during the Civil War was a mite different.

The town of Fort Bragg, Mendocino County, grew following the war and the opening of western lands to settlement.

Fort Bragg is home to the Skunk Railroad, a vestige of the old logging days. The road, which extends about 40 miles from Fort Bragg to Willits, dates back to 1885.

FORT DICK

Civil War records first list Fort Dick Landing at this Del Norte location. The "fort" was a log house built for defense against Indians and bore the last name of a settler.

In 1888, the Bersch brothers opened a shake-and-shingle mill here, and called their community Newburg. That name lasted until a post office was established in 1896, when the antique name was revived.

FORT JONES

Fort Jones was a small military post in the Scott River Valley, established by companies A and E, First Dragoons, in 1852 to protect gold miners from the Indians. The fort was only in existence until 1858. Lieutenant George Crook and Captain Ulysses S. Grant both served here. The Siskiyou County town of nearby Willard decided to rename their town for the fort. In 1860, their post office, called Ottitiewa, was officially changed to Fort Jones.

FORT SEWARD

This Humboldt County site took its name from the military installation established here in 1861. It was named for Lincoln's secretary of state. The post office, under that name, was opened in 1913. (See SEWARD, Alaska.)

FORTUNA

This Humboldt County community was originally called Springville because of the abundance of springs in the area. Later the name was changed to Slide. An aggressive land owner, a minister named Gardner, did not think either name had class. So in the 1870s he had the name changed to the Spanish for "fortune."

FOSTER CITY

Foster City, San Mateo County, was established in 1965, and named for T. Jack Foster. Foster had donated a large parcel of land to the county.

FOUTS SPRINGS

The springs at this Colusa County site were discovered in 1873 by John F. Fouts.

FOWLER

In 1872, when the railroad named its switch here in Fresno County, they called it Fowler's Switch. It was located on the Fowler Ranch.

The town grew up around the ranch, and took on the name. The honoree is Thomas Fowler, the state senator from Fresno in the 1870s.

FRAZIER PARK

Frazier Park, Kern County, took its name from the mountain which was named after the Frazier Mine. The naming was accomplished by Harry McBain in 1926.

FREEDOM

One of 11 saloons in this town during the late 19th-century displayed an American flag and below it a sign that read "The Flag of Freedom." The townspeople felt that was a good name for this town in Santa Cruz County.

FREEMAN JUNCTION

The road from the San Joaquin River across Walker Pass enters the main route here.

FREESTONE

Freestone was named because of the abundance of easily worked, free sandstone in this Sonoma County area.

The Freestone post office was established in 1870.

FREMONT

Fremont, Ventura County, was created in 1956 by the incorporation of five southeastern San Francisco Bay communities.

Spanish missionaries and the Ohlones Indians established a mission in this area in 1797. Reputedly named for General John C. Frémont, local legend has him so in awe of the mission that he offered to buy adjacent land for his own home. Frémont's greatest contribution to the Golden West, some authorities contend, was not from his activities as an explorer. Rather, he contributed greatly by synthesizing the discoveries of others with his writings of impression and observation.

Frémont was quite popular following the Mexican War, but his popularity did not last. Even Fremont County became Yolo County.

By the early 19th century, the town had discovered artesian wells and Fremont became a resort area. In 1915, Charlie Chaplin filmed "The Tramp" here.

FRENCH GULCH

French Gulch, Shasta County, was once a gold-mining community. The post office was established here in 1856, and named after the gulch where French miners had prospected in 1849 and 1850.

FRESHWATER

Freshwater, Humboldt County, took its name from Freshwater Lagoon. The lagoon was once a bay of the sea but over the years it became separated by long narrow sandbars.

FRESNO

Fresno, located in Fresno County, took its name from its county, which was named for the river. *Fresno* is the Spanish word for "ash," and indicates the heavy growth of the Oregon ash along the river's banks.

Sometime before 1860, an attempt had been made to create a Fresno City—where Tranquility is today. Twelve years later, the Central Pacific Railroad reached the site of the modern town, and called it Fresno.

According to the Chamber of Commerce, Fresno produces more turkeys than anywhere else in the United States. There is also a monument in town that marks the geographic center of California. Though Fresno is centrally located, it is not at the geographic center. Now, about the turkeys. . . .

FRIANT

Charles Converse established the Converse Ferry at this Fresno site in 1852. Later, the ferry became Jones' Ferry. In 1891, when the Southern Pacific made this place the terminus of a branch, they named it Pollasky, for Marcus Pollasky, an agent for the railroad. The name was changed to Friant in the 1920s for Thomas Friant, partner in the White-Friant Lumber Company.

FRUTO

Fruto, located in Glenn County, was named because of its location in a large fruit-growing district. The name was given to the post office in about 1890.

FULLERTON

The town of Fullerton, Orange County, was founded by Edward and George Amerigue, the Wilshire brothers and the Pacific Land & Improvement Company in 1887. The president of the company— and an employee of the California Central Railroad—was George H. Fullerton. He routed the railroad through the Amerigue's property, received an interest in the townsite and got the town named for himself!

FULTON

Two brothers from Indiana, Thomas and James Fulton, founded and named this Sonoma County site in 1871.

FURNACE CREEK RANCH

Furnace Creek Ranch takes its name from the ranch, which took its name from the creek. The creek, located in Death Valley, gives the clue to the name.

The town, established in 1870, was called Greenland in the 1880s and sometimes Coleman, for the owner, William T. Coleman. The town was named by the Pacific Coast Borax Company sometime after 1889.

GALT

Galt, Sacramento County, was settled by John McFarland in 1869. McFarland named it for his former home in Ontario, Canada. That place bore the name of the Scottish novelist, John Galt.

GARBERVILLE

Garberville, located in a valley in Humboldt County, was named for Jacob C. Garber. Garber's town had a post office beginning in 1880.

GARDENA

Gardena, Los Angeles, has a popular American place name. People wanted to liken their community to the Garden of Eden.

GARDEN GROVE

Garden Grove was named by Dr. A. G. Cook when he purchased a small parcel of farming land here in 1875. Garden Grove is also home to the Crystal Cathedral of the Reformed Church in America, the bailiwick of televangelist Robert Schuller.

This Orange County community is also a great producer of both red and green chili peppers.

GARDEN VALLEY

According to local legend, Garden Valley, El Dorado County, got its name from the sense people had that it was more profitable to farm than to look for gold. Sadly, the name was on the property even while it was a rich gold camp.

The Garden Valley post office was established during the gold rush period, in 1852.

GARLOCK

Eugene Garlock opened the first stamp mill in the Randsburg Mining District in 1895 at a Kern County site called Cow Wells. The name was changed to recognize Garlock.

GASQUET

During pioneering days, Gasquet was headquarters for the stage and packtrains.

Many historians like to think the name for this Del Norte County community came from Horace Gasquet, a Frenchman who arrived here before 1860 and ranched. Howard Gasquet, on the other hand, was the first postmaster in 1883, and also ran the hotel. Take your choice.

GAVIOTA

Gaviota, Santa Barbara County, took its name from a Spanish word meaning "sea gull." In 1769, members of the Portola expedition killed a sea gull at what their officers called San Luis, after the King of France.

GAZELLE

Where some towns favored Antelope, the townspeople in this Siskiyou County community did not want to be one of the pack, so they opted for Gazelle. The name appeared on the post office in 1870.

GENESEE

Genesee, Plumas County, took its name from that of the valley. Some think the name was brought west by the New York Ingalls family. They settled in the valley in the 1860s.

GEORGETOWN

Georgetown, Eldorado County, saw great mining activity beginning in 1849. At one point, the town rivalled Placerville in growth. According to one authority, the town was named for George Washington. But he was wrong.

Georgetown was started in 1849 by George Ehrenhaft, but there is some disagreement over whether it was for him or for George Phipps that the town was named. Phipps led a group of prospectors here in 1849. Whichever the case, it had nothing to do with George Washington.

By the way, the nickname for Georgetown was Growlersburg.

GERBER

The Southern Pacific Railroad named this Tehama County community in 1916, for H. E. Gerber. Gerber sold the land to the railroad. The post office was established here in 1917.

GEYSERVILLE

Originally known as Clairville for John Clar, Geyserville was founded in 1851 by Elisha Ely. He named it thus to advertise the local geysers, the erupting hot springs.

GIANT FOREST VILLAGE

The reference in this village's name is not to a large forest, but to the size of the trees, *Sequoia gigantea.*

The name for the Giant Forest, which has the largest concentration of big trees, was given by John Muir in 1858. Some of the trees are older than the Pyramids of Egypt!

GILMAN HOT SPRINGS

The hot springs at this Riverside County location were known to the Indians long before the Branch family arrived in the 1880s to exploit them. The family called the place San Jacinto Hot Springs. The name was changed in 1913 when William E. and Josephine Gilman bought the place. A post office opened under the name of Gilman Hot Springs about 25 years later.

GILROY

Gilroy, Santa Clara County, should be called Cameron.

In 1814, a Scotsman by the name of John "Old Gilroy" Cameron jumped ship in Monterey Bay. He traveled to the Ortega Ranch, adopted his mother's maiden name and married the rancher's daughter, Maria Clara Ortega.

Another story suggests he was left ashore by the Hudson Bay ship *Isaac Todd* because he had scurvy.

He acquired some land, and a small town developed around it. By 1870, Gilroy, né Cameron, lost the ranch because of heavy gambling debts. Regardless, the town grew and thrived. Gilroy was the first non-Spanish person to settle permanently in California.

GLAMIS

Glamis, Imperial County, carries, we suspect, a literary name. The name recalls the castle—Glamis or Glammis—in Shakespeare's *Macbeth.*

The post office appeared with this name in 1887; the railroad station, by 1900.

GLEN AVON

Glen Avon, Riverside County, combines the word glen with *avon*, Celtic for "river." The name was developed by L. W. Brown in 1909.

GLENDALE

Located at the east entrance to the San Fernando Valley, Glendale, Los Angeles County, occupies historic land. It was here that the first land grant in California was given in 1784 by King Charles IV of Spain. The land was granted to José Maria Verdugo for his military service.

The town developed soon after the railroad extended from Los Angeles to San Fernando between 1873 and 1874. The first name given was Riverside, but postal authorities rejected it. The post office was then called Mason, but its name was changed to Glendale sometime after 1886. The name was descriptive of the terrain.

GLENDORA

The first part of this Los Angeles County town's name is descriptive, but the second is an abbreviation of a woman's name—Ledora. As one source puts it, she was "the charming consort of a subdivision king in the boom of the late '80s." Leodora was the wife of George Whitcomb, who named the town in 1887.

GLEN ELLEN

About a mile west of Glen Ellen, in Sonoma County, is the home and final resting place of author Jack London (1876–1916).

London, a native of San Francisco, traveled the countryside trying to find his own niche. Finally, in frustration, he joined the Klondike goldrush in mid-1897, but poor health forced him to return home. There he resumed his writing. Drawing from London's personal experience, his writing became popular. But his popularity did not alleviate his personal pain and his alcoholism. On 22 November 1916, he committed suicide at Glen Ellen.

Charles V. Stuart named the town in 1869, for his wife Ellen Mary. The post office carried her name beginning in 1871.

GLENN

Glenn carries the name of its county. Glenn County was formed in 1891, and it was named for Dr. Hugh Glenn, an early wheat baron in this area. In the 1870s, Glenn owned a ranch of more than 50,000 acres. The place was named after a branch of the Southern Pacific Railroad was built here in 1917.

GLENNVILLE

James Madison Glenn, a Tennessean, settled in Linn's Valley in 1857. When the post office was established in the 1870s, it honored him.

GOFFS

(See AMBOY, California.)

GOLD RUN

O. W. Hollenbeck, an early developer in this area, laid out this Nevada County site as a city in 1861, complete with hotel and post office. At first he called this town Dixie, and finally Gold Run, for the stream that ran nearby.

During the mid-19th century, Gold Run was the site of intense hydraulic mining activity.

GOLETA

Goleta is located in Santa Barbara County. The name is the Spanish word for "schooner," and, as tradition has it, the name was given before 1846 because of a schooner that was stranded here and was visible for a number of years.

The community grew on the La Goleta land grant, dated 1846. The town was laid out in 1875 and was named for the grant.

It is home to the University of California at Santa Barbara.

GONZALES

In 1836, Teodoro Gonzales was granted Rincon de la Punta del Monte de la Soledad. On his grant, the town of Gonzales grew. Some suspect the Monterey County town was named for one of his sons. Alfredo and Mariano were both associated with the Monterey & Salinas Railroad.

GOODYEARS BAR

There is no reference to a drinking establishment in the naming of this Sierra County locale. The town, originally Goodyear's Bar, was a thriving gold-mining camp of 1849.

The name came from a long "bar" of land, formed by the bend in the north fork of the Yuba River. Miles and Andrew Goodyear, no relation to the tire company, were early settlers, discovering gold in 1849. Two years later their name was on the town, replacing an earlier one: Slaughter's Bar.

GORDA

This Monterey County town's name is the Spanish word for "fat" or "full-fed." In reality, the town's name preserved the old name of the cape, Punta Gorda—now known as Cape San Martin.

GORMAN

H. Gorman was the first postmaster in this Los Angeles County site. The post office, first called Gorman's Station, was opened in 1877. The current name was brought forth in 1915.

GOSHEN

Goshen was named by an employee of the Southern Pacific, when the road reached this Tulare County site in 1872. The name of the Egyptian land the Pharaoh gave to Jacob is a popular place name. In this case, it probably migrated from "back East."

GRAEAGLE

Graeagle, Plumas County, took its name from the Gray Eagle Creek. Someone thought it would be cute to merge the two names.

When a post office was established here in 1919, the name was Davies Mill. Two years later it became the present one.

GRANADA HILLS

The name logically came from the Spanish city, but is more commonly believed to have come from Washington Irving's 1829 *Conquest of Granada*.

GRANITEVILLE

Graniteville, Nevada County, was either a rich gold mining area or the site of quartz mines. Pick your own authority! The town was known as Eureka as early as 1850, but when the post office opened here in 1867 the name had to be changed to avoid confusion.

GRANT GROVE (— Village)

Grant Grove took its name from the Grant Groves, a preservation of redwoods provided through the generosity of Madison and Joseph Donohoe Grant.

GRASS VALLEY

George Knight stubbed his toe in this Nevada County area in 1850. When he looked down, he noticed that the offender was a piece of quartz, laced with gold. At least that is how one story goes. History, on the other hand, tells us that prospectors discovered placer gold here a year before. By the next year, the town of Grass Valley had grown up around the mining camp.

Using advanced mining techniques, Grass Valley became the richest gold-mining town in California. Its name came from the lush grass that grew here. The soil was so moist and rich that the grass was green even in midsummer.

In the early days of settlement, the town was alternately called Grass Valley or Centerville. In fact, in 1851, when the first post office was established, it was under the name of Centerville. That changed the next year, when it became Grass Valley.

During the winter of 1852–53, Grass Valley was the scene of "the Hungry Convention." The winter had been severe and prices for supplies ran at the goldrush prices of 1849. A meeting was called to decide what measures to take. Before long, the serious discussions broke into comedy, with one committee reporting to declare war on San Francisco and get supplies "peacably if we can, forcibly if we must."

One of Grass Valley's most illustrious residents was Lola Montez (1818–61). A famous actress, known as the Mexican Spitfire, Montez made her mark as a dancer in the gold mining era. At one time, she was the mistress of Louis I of Bavaria, who made her Countess of Lansfeld. Though she died in Astoria, New York, she retired here, and her home is still standing.

GREEN (—brae; —field; — Valley; — Valley Lake; —view; —ville; —wood)

The town of Greenfield, Monterey County, was laid out sometime between 1902 and 1905 by the California Home Extension Association on the Arroyo Seco Rancho. At first it was called Clarke City, honoring one of the association's officers, John S. Clarke. Postal authorities refused Clarke's name in 1905, and accepted Greenfield from a list supplied by the townspeople.

Green Valley, Contra Costa County, took its name from the description, "Canada Verde," on the 1833 San Ramon grant.

Greenville, Alameda County, took the name of John Green, an Irishman who came to California in 1857, and operated a store and farm.

Greenwood, Eldorado County, was named for John Greenwood. The son of famed trapper and guide Caleb Greenwood, John opened a trading post here in 1850.

GRENADA

The region in which this Siskiyou County community is located was originally called Starve-Out because of the poor soil. After an irrigation project came in, things improved. Some think the town was named for Grenada, Mississippi, a place known for fertile soil.

GRIDLEY

The land on which the Southern Pacific built its station here in Butte County in 1870 was owned by George W. Gridley.

GRIMES

This Colusa County town was named in about 1865 for the man who founded it, Cleaton Grimes.

GROVELAND

The original name for this Tuolumne County town was Garrote, taking its name from a breathtaking event in its past.

The Garrote name was given in 1850 when miners hanged a thief here. A post office under that name was established in 1854, and continued until 1875. In that year, another town decided to take on the name and call itself Second Garrote. This forced the original place to call itself First Garrote. By 1879, townspeople threw up their hands and let the post office be called Groveland.

GROVER CITY

Located in San Luis Obispo County, Grover City was originally named Grover in 1892, for Henry Grover. In 1937, it was renamed Grover City.

GUADALUPE

Mariano Guadalupe Vallejo was one of the most powerful figures in California in the early 19th century. He was one of the men who supported the movement to declare "California independent in 1847–1848, as soon as a sufficient number of foreigners should arrive."

Another possibility often preferred is that this community was named for the Treaty of Guadalupe Hidalgo of 2 February 1848, which recognized the cession of California to the United States.

GUALALA

Gualala takes its name from the Gualala River. The town is located at the waterway's mouth. No one is quite certain what the name means, though they suggest "where the waters meet" or "water coming down place, river mouth."

GUASTI

Before Secondo Guasti arrived here in 1900, the San Bernardino County town was named South Cucamonga. Upon arrival, he established the largest vineyard in the world; it was known as the Italian Vineyard. The name was later changed to honor Guasti.

GUATAY

The name for this San Diego County town comes from the Diegueno Indian *kwaitai,* meaning "large rock." The nearby Guatay Mountain is indeed large!

Mexican and American pioneers settled here in the mid-19th century.

GUERNEVILLE

Guerneville, Sonoma County, was settled in 1860. When the post office was established 10 years later, the name honored George E. Guerne. He had built a saw- and planing-mill at this location in 1864.

GUERNSEY

The name of this Kings County site came from James Guernsey. He owned the land on which the Santa Fe Railroad built its station here in 1902.

GUINDA

Guinda, Yolo County, carries the Spanish word for "cherry." The name was given by the Southern Pacific because of the presence of an old cherry tree in the area.

GUSTINE

Gustine was laid out in this Merced County location by Henry Miller. He named it for his daughter Augustine, who had been killed in a horsing accident. The name first appeared on the railroad station in 1900.

HACIENDA HEIGHTS

Located in Santa Clara County, Hacienda Heights bears the Spanish word for "estate." It was selected as a modern real estate promotion.

HALF MOON BAY

The name for Half Moon Bay, San Mateo County, is descriptive. The bay has a semi-circular shape to it, from which the town took its name. The post office at Halfmoon (one word) Bay appeared in 1867. In about 1905, postal authorities allowed the name to be as it is today.

HALLORAN SPRINGS

Although the source of this San Bernardino County site's name has not been determined, the current name was in place in 1875. Probably the name relates to the person who either found—or owned—the springs located here.

HAMBURG

Hamburg, Siskiyou County, was a mining camp established in 1851. The town was named by Sigmund Simon, probably for the German seaport. At one point, the site was called Hamburg Bar. What would McDonald's say about that?

HAMILTON CITY

This settlement in Glenn County was begun in 1906 by a sugar company. The name came from J. G. Hamilton, the town's promoter.

HANFORD

Hanford was founded in 1882, but named in 1877 for James Hanford, the Southern Pacific Railroad's treasurer. Hanford was a powerful member of the community, perhaps because he paid millions of dollars of workers' wages in gold.

At one point in Hanford's history, it had one of the largest Chinese communities in California.

Hanford is the seat of Kings County. It was also the site of the bloody climax to the Mussel Slough feud. In the early 1870s, settlers moved into the area and began to carve productive land out of the soil. When the railroad forged through their lands, the ranchers questioned the railroad's rights. The spat came to a head in 1880 when on 11 May, a mass meeting of settlers erupted into violence. By the end of the day, five ranchers and two deputy sheriffs were dead. The incident was used as background for Frank Norris' novel, *The Octopus*.

HAPPY CAMP

Because a man shouted that this particular day was the happiest of his life, this town in Siskiyou County was named Happy Camp . . . or so we are told. Another story has it that the camp was mentioned in 1851, as "Mr. Roache's 'Happy Camp.'"

HARBISON CANYON

John S. Harbison arrived in this San Diego County area in 1869 and settled in the canyon that bears his name. The town located here also bears that name.

An avid beekeeper, Harbison is considered the father of the honey business in southern California.

HARBOR CITY

When W. I. Hollingsworth laid out this city in 1912, he called it Harbor Industrial City. When the connection with Los Angeles harbor did not materialize, the "Industrial" was removed from the name.

HARMONY

Harmony may have developed from a feud between two local families over trespassing. One family—both were dairy farmers— was forced to travel across the other's land. The feud escalated into a blood bath. To stop the bloodshed, the road was rerouted.

Years later, when a school was built here, the route of the road had to be changed again. This time, everyone cooperated and they called the school Harmony. The town that grew up around the school took on that name. That is one story.

Another explanation is that the name Harmony appears all over the United States, and it was especially popular during the Civil War. This particular town in San Luis Obispo County was named during that period. The post office name, adopted in 1915, was suggested by Marius G. Salmina, an official of the Harmony Valley Creamery Association.

HARRIS

Located in Humboldt County, the town of Harris was probably named for the town's postmaster and hotelkeeper, William C. Harris.

HAT CREEK

According to one authority, the name was given in 1852 to the body of water and had to do with a lost hat. A member of the Noble party lost his hat in the stream. The Indians referred to the steam as Hat'-te we'-we, which might point out an Indian root for the name. Or perhaps the Indians adapted the English name. The mountain and town took the creek's name.

The Hat Creek post office was established in 1884, but four years later it was changed to Cassel. The original name was returned in 1909.

HAVASU LAKE

Havasu Lake is an artificial body of water on the Colorado River. It was named by John C. Page. The word *havasu*, from the Mojave language, means "blue," an apt description of the water. The San Bernardino County community took its name from the lake.

HAVILAH

This Kern County community's name comes from the Bible; it means "land of gold." Gold was discovered at the site.

The place was named in 1864 by town-founder Asbury Harpending.

HAWTHORNE

Mrs. Laurine H. Woolvine, daughter of H. D. Harding, the town's founder, named this community in Los Angeles County in about 1906 for her favorite author, Nathaniel Hawthorne.

HAYFORK

The original name for this Trinity County community was Hayfields, when the Ruch family settled here in 1852. It was the major cultivated area in a mountainous region. The current name came from a branch of the Trinity River that was called Hayfork.

HAYWARD

Hayward, Alameda County, took its name from a popular hotel located here. William Hayward opened his hotel here in 1852, and the area became known as Hayward's, then Haywards.

The town was laid out by Castro in 1854, but he retained Hayward's name. The first post office was established here in 1860, under the name Haywood, even though the postmaster was William Hayward. Again, the people in Washington had difficulty with their spelling. Twenty years later, the error was fixed, and by 1911, the present spelling appeared.

HEALDSBURG

Healdsburg, Sonoma County, was named for Colonel Harmon G. Heald, an early settler, in 1857.

Founded in 1867, Healdsburg was once part of the 48,800-acre Sotoyome Rancho owned by widow Josefa Fitch and her 11 children. Earlier it had been a rancheria of the Sotoyome Indians.

While there was Indian unrest and the Mexican War, Widow Fitch took up sanctuary at Sutter's Fort. During her absence, Harmon Heald and a group of other failed miners illegally squatted on her land. Fitch won ownership, but Heald bought some of the rancho and donated land for a park, school, cemetery, and church—and named the town for himself.

Before Heald arrived in 1846, the town was known as Russian River.

HEARST

This Mendocino County site was not named for famed publisher and utterer of "Rosebud," William Randolph Hearst (1863–1951). The name was given in 1892 for George Hearst, a U.S. senator (1887–91).

HEBER

The president of the California Development Company, A. H. Heber developed this Imperial County community in 1903.

HELENDALE

Located at the Santa Fe Station, Helendale, San Bernardino County, was originally called Point of Rocks. The name was changed to Helen in 1907 for the daughter of A. C. Wells, a railroad vice president. Eleven years later, the name was again changed—to Helendale.

HELM

Helms Meadow, Helms Creek and the town of Helm in Fresno County all bear the name of William Helm. Helm, a Canadian, came to California in 1859. For years, he raised more sheep than anyone else in central California.

HELMET

No one is quite sure where this Riverside County name came from. The Helmet Dam was built between 1886 and 1890, and the post office bore that name in 1898. How it got here, no one is quite certain.

HENLEYVILLE

This Tehama County site was named for William N. Henley, an emigrant from Indiana who was listed on the voting rolls here in 1866.

HERCULES

This Contra Costa County town took the name of its major industry: the Hercules Powder Company, which established itself here in the late 19th century. The Hercules post office was in use in 1915.

HERLONG

Herlong began when the Sierra Ordnance Department was established at this Lassen County site. The War Department named it for Captain Henry W. Herlong (1911–41), the first American ordnance officer to be killed in World War II.

HERMOSA BEACH

The name for Hermosa Beach, Los Angeles County, comes from the Spanish *hermoso*, "beautiful." The use here of the feminine occurred because of the age-old association of beautiful things with the female. The name was used as a sales promotion tool by the Hermosa Beach Land & Water Company, which laid out the subdivision in 1901.

HERNDON

When the Central Pacific Railroad crossed the San Joaquin River at this Fresno County site in 1872, they decided not to establish a townsite here. Rather, they created Fresno.

The railroad station here, then called Sycamore, was renamed Herndon about 1895. The reason given is that Herndon was a relative of the promoter of a local irrigation project.

HESPERIA

The California Southern Railroad station, here in San Bernardino County, was named in 1885. Most think it was named for Hesperia, Michigan. On the other hand, Greek and Roman poets used Hesperia to mean "The Western Land."

HICKMAN

Hickman, Stanislaus County, was established as a station in 1891 by the Southern Pacific Railroad. The name came from a one-time mayor of Stockton, Louis Hickman. He also owned the land adjacent to the station.

HIGHGROVE

Located in Riverside County, this town was mapped and recorded in 1887 by A. J. Twogood and S. H. Herrick. They named it Highgrove because of the orange groves on the hillside. Prior to this, since 1882, the station of the California Southern Railroad had been East Riverside.

HIGHLAND (— Park)

Highland Park was a suburb in the late 19th century, located between Los Angeles and Pasadena. The early residents tried to maintain a decided Eastern feel to the town which can be seen in its architecture. The names are all that remain of the short-lived Highland City that was planned for the high divide between the Carson and Stanislaus rivers.

HOLLYWOOD

The irony of it all! Hollywood created as a religious village!

Hollywood was laid out in 1886 and named by Horace Wilcox. The town was incorporated in 1903 as a community with a religious orientation. Seven years later, it became part of Los Angeles. In 1911, the first motion picture studio was opened here, and the religious orientation went out the window. In an effort to justify the name, Wilcox imported two holly trees. Unfortunately, they could not survive the climate of southern California.

HOLLYWOOD. Also known as Tinsel-town, Hollywood brought entertain-ment to the world. The Keystone Kops in the silent-film days amused with-out the need for dialogue. The slap-stick antics of the Kops were part of a universal language. (The author's collection)

Although with the advent of television Hollywood has ceased to be the film capital of the world, its name is still synonymous with the industry.

A major attraction in town is the famous "Hollywood" sign on Mount Lee. The sign was erected in 1923 as a promotional device for a real estate development called "Hollywoodland." The "-land" was taken off the sign in 1949.

HOLMES

Holmes, Humboldt County, was named in 1908 for the chief boss in a logging company that operated here. At that time, the name was Holmes Camp. When a post office was established here in 1912, the "camp" was dropped.

HOLTVILLE

This Imperial County community was created and named Holton in 1903 by W. F. Holt, president of the Holton Power Company. Holt also helped organize the 1899 irrigation project in the county. At the request of postal authorities, the name was changed to Holtville.

HOLY CITY

This Santa Clara town was founded in 1920 by W. E. Riker as a "whites only" religious community. Riker named it because "of the principles revealed for an indisputable solution for the Economic, Racial and Spiritual problems of this world."

The Holy City post office was opened in 1927.

HOME (— Gardens; —land; —stead; —wood)

Homewood is located near the base of Barker Peak. Homestead Valley, Marin County, took the name of the valley. It was named in 1903 by the Tamalpais Land & Water Company for the country home of S. M. Throckmorton.

HONCUT

Theodor Cordua, owner of an 1844 land grant wrote: "The name I have given my ten-league grant because the Honcut River formed the northern boundary of my . . . holdings. . . . The names of the rancherias or Indian villages I found rather pretty, for instance . . . Honcut."

HONEYDEW

In the early days of settlement, there was an unnamed creek that flowed into the Mattole River near this Humboldt County site. One night a group of pioneers camped on the banks of this stream, under a canopy of cottonwood trees. When they awoke in the morning, they found themselves covered with a sweet, sticky goo secreted by the trees. The mess smelled and tasted like honey, so they named the stream Honeydew Creek. By the time a town was established by the creek, the name had taken hold.

HOOD

When this Sacramento County community was named in 1910, William Hood was the chief engineer for the Southern Pacific Railroad. The namer was Madison P. Barner, a railroad official.

HOOPA

Hoopa, Humboldt County, took its name from the Hoopa Indians, a tribe on the lower Trinity River.

Folklore, which is far more interesting than fact, has it that the Indians used the name after hearing the drivers shout "whoopah, whoopah," as they rounded up the mules in their pack train.

HOPLAND

The name for this Mendocino County locale came from the crop that was cultivated here: hops.

Hopland was started in 1859 when three men opened a saloon. For a time, the place was called Sanel, after the land grant. The name was changed in 1874 when Stephen Knowles' experiment in growing hops here was proved successful.

HORNBROOK

The Southern Pacific Railroad named this Siskiyou County spot in 1886. The name came from a brook that ran through David Horn's property.

HORNITOS

Hornitos, "little ovens," was founded by Mexican prospectors in the early 1850s. The miners had been driven from nearby Quartzburg (Kernville) by a group of American vigilantes.

The post office at this Mariposa County site was established as Hornitas in 1856. The current spelling was installed in 1877.

HORSE CREEK

Horse Creek, Siskiyou County, took its name from a waterway.

HUME

At the turn of the 20th century, the major industry of Hume, Fresno County, was a sawmill. It took its name from the lake that the Hume & Bennett lumber company impounded from the waters of Tenmile Creek.

HUNTINGTON (— Beach; — Harbour; — Lake; — Park)

Each September, Huntington Beach is the site of an annual surfing competition that draws surfers from all over the world.

The name, many think, comes from Collis P. Huntington who, at the urging of Theodore D. Judah, helped incorporate the Central Pacific Railroad by buying a modest share of stock. Huntington was joined by Mark Hopkins, Leland Stanford and Charles Crocker. Others think the name came from that of Collis's nephew, Henry E. Huntington. In fact, Huntington Beach, Orange County, was originally named Pacific Beach and changed in 1903.

The young Huntington was the donor of more geographic feature names than any other industrialist. Huntington Park, Los Angeles County, was laid out in 1903 and named by E. V. Baker for his friend.

Huntington Lake, Fresno County, took its name from Huntington Lake, located in the Sierra Nevada. The lake is man-made. The reservoir was named in 1912 by the Pacific Light & Power Corporation whose president was Henry E. Huntington.

The last battle of the Mexican War took place north of Huntington Park. The battle of La Mesa, fought by Commodore Stockton against the native Californians under General Flores, took place on 9 January 1847 along the dry bed of the Los Angeles River. The Americans swept the Californians back and opened the way to Los Angeles.

HURON

Huron, Fresno County, received its name in 1877 when the Southern Pacific established a station on the route between Goshen and Tres Pinos. Again, it is a case of a "back East" name.

The name came from that of four tribes of Indians, located in Ontario.

HYAMPON

Hyampon, Trinity County, has a name that comes from the Indian word *hiam-pom,* which translates as "valley of plenty," a descriptive term.

The town was settled in 1855 by Hank Young. The post office was opened in 1890.

IDYLLWILD

A description of the unspoiled resort area, the name of this Riverside County community was suggested by Mrs. Laura Rutledge. The name was accepted by postal authorities in 1899.

IGNACIO

Ignacio, Marin County, was not named for St. Ignatius. The honor belongs to Ignacio Pacheco, the 1840 grantee of the San Jose grant on which this town was built. Before the post office was established here in 1895 as Ignacio, the community's name was Pacheco.

IGO

Local legend has it that this town was named in the late 1850s by George McPherson. McPherson, superintendent of the mining operations here, had gone a bit too far. The digging had so undermined the town of Piety Hill that he decided to lay out a new town about half a mile west.

McPherson's small son, it is said, constantly pestered his father about moving plans by asking: "Daddy, I go?" Tradition has it he relished the questioning and named the new town Igo. However, in 1874, the name for the community was Piety Hill, which discounts the McPherson tale. Another source says there was a family by the name of Igo that lived in the area. Another folk tale links Igo with nearby Ono, a cute play on words that has no basis in fact.

The post office was established as Igo in 1873.

IMPERIAL (— Beach)

The earlier name for this site was Colorado Desert. The name was changed to Imperial Valley, a name that became that of the county in 1907. Later it was shortened to Imperial.

Imperial Beach, San Diego County, was given this name by E. W. Peterson of the South San Diego Development Company for advertising purposes. The Imperial Beach post office opened in 1910.

INDEPENDENCE

Independence is located about three miles south of the site of Camp Independence. Charles Putnam built the first house in this Inyo County area in 1861, and called the settlement Putnam's; later, Little Pine. A year later, a regiment of California cavalry raced through Owens Valley after they decided the land was "worth fighting for," and, on 4 July, established the camp. The name was given in patriotic fervor. The present-day townsite was laid out by Thomas Edwards in 1866.

INDIO (— Hills)

Indio, Riverside County, took its name—Spanish for "Indian"—from the nearby Indian Wells. The name was given by the Southern Pacific Railroad in 1876.

INGLEWOOD

The city of Inglewood, Los Angeles County, resides on much of the land once held by Rancho Centinela, owned by Daniel Freeman. It was founded in 1887 on part of the rancho and was allegedly named by a visitor from Inglewood, Canada.

INGOT

Ingot, Shasta County, was originally a mining town where metal ingots were cast. It has been known by that name since the turn of the 20th century.

The Ingot post office was first established in 1919.

INVERNESS

Located in Marin County, Inverness was started as a camp in 1888 or 1889 by a Scotsman named Thompson. The resort community that was later laid out here by James M. Shafter was named Inverness, supposedly after Thompson's birthplace, Inverness, Scotland.

INYOKERN

This town is located near the boundary line of Inyo and Kern counties, which explains the name. The earlier name, Magnolia, was not to the liking of postal authorities, so the residents voted in 1913 to change Magnolia to Inyokern.

IONE

Settled in 1840, this Amador County town had several previous names that did not convey the most favorable image of the community. In earlier times, Ione had been known as Dead Dog, Freeze-Out and Bedbug.

Offended by disregard for good taste, one resident might have borrowed the name Ione from his reading of *The Last Days of Pompeii*. Ione was the name of the book's heroine. Perhaps he simply liked the name and lobbied to have the town's name changed.

Another story has it that this place was situated on land owned by William Hicks, founder of Hicksville. The name, we are told, came from his habit of using the phrase "I own" in talking about his property.

Some of Ione's chief products were terra-cotta, brick and other clay items drawn from the town's extensive clay beds.

The town was originally in Calaveras County, and it was called Jone Valley when the post office was opened here in 1852. Five years later, it was Jone City, then Ione City. By 1861, it was called Ione Valley and, finally, in 1880, it became Ione. The best solution to the name source seems to be the post office mistaking the "J" for an "I." (See IONE, Oregon.)

IOWA HILL

Gold was discovered here in this Placer County area in 1853 by miners who came here from Iowa. Although the town was devastated by successive fires, it still endured.

IRVINE

Irvine, Orange County, is a planned community, built on the Irvine Ranch, a former Spanish land grant.

The Irvine ranch, founded by Irish immigrant James Irvine, was six times larger than Manhattan! Irvine purchased Rancho San Joaquin in about 1870, and established his famous orchards. When the Sante Fe arrived at Fallbrook Junction in 1888, they named the station after him. A quarter of a century later, they named a siding on a spur to Venta for Irvine's son, calling it Myford. This proved to be a problem when the post office was established in 1899. They could not honor Irvine here, because there was already a post office known as Irvine in Calaveras County. They had to wait until 1914 for that office to close so that they could honor James Irvine.

When the University of California opened a campus here in 1965, the post office became East Irvine.

IRWINDALE

Irwindale was named for a citrus grower here in Los Angeles County. The Irwindale post office was established in 1899, and the town was incorporated in 1957.

ISLAND MOUNTAIN

Island Mountain is just about an island because of the creek that almost encircles it. That is how settlers in the mid-19th century saw it and marked it on their maps. This Trinity County town was named for the mountain.

When the post office was opened here in 1905, it was simply called Island; two years later, Irma. In 1915, the full name became official.

ISLETON

Isleton is just that: a town on an island—Andrus Island, to be exact. The name was given by Josiah Pool and John Brocas when they built the town in 1874.

IVANHOE

Ivanhoe, like so many other places by that name in the United States, attests to the popularity of Sir Walter Scott's novel. The name did, however, first appear on the school district before it appeared on the town's signs.

Originally, the Tulare County community was known as Klink, for the Southern Pacific's auditor, George T. Klink. At one time, the Venice Hill Land Company attempted to have the name changed to Venice Hill, but the residents would have none of it. Ivanhoe became the name in 1924, spurred on by the Ivanhoe Farm.

IVANPAH

Ivanpah, San Bernardino County, bears a Southern Paiute name meaning "clear spring."

The first Ivanpah was established as a mining camp in the 1870s near a clear spring, but vanished. When the Santa Fe entered the Ivanpah Valley, company officials confiscated the name for their station, but that station also disappeared in 1920.

The Union Pacific picked up the name to replace that of their Leastalk station. Leastalk, by the way, is "salt lake" as a word-jumble!

J

JACKSON

Jackson, Amador County, was first settled by gold miners in 1849. At that time, the town was known as Botilleas—a reference to the hundreds of bottles found near a local spring.

Later, "Colonel" Alden M. Jackson, a New England lawyer, arrived in town and gained the miners' trust. He was able to settle their disputes without going to court. When the post office was established in 1851, it was named for him. The town was almost destroyed by an 1862 fire and a flood in 1878. The town fathers had the good sense to rebuild in brick.

The town has the dubious distinction of closing its bordellos as recently as 1956!

JACUMBA

One source feels that Jacumba's name comes from the Diegueno Indian and has something to do with "water," but that is as far as one can decipher the name.

La Rancheria llamada en su idioma Jacom, "the village called Jacom in their language," is mentioned in 1795, and other times under an assortment of spellings.

JAMESTOWN

The first gold discovery in Tuolumne County was made near this town in 1848. Earlier known as Jimtown, the town has been used as a movie set for such films as "High Noon" and "Butch Cassidy and the Sundance Kid."

The town was founded in 1848 by Colonel George F. James. He had a number of problems with Mexican settlers that finally resulted in James' departure. After he left, the name was changed to American Camp, but later it was restored to Jamestown.

JAMUL

An authority traces this name to the Diegueo Indian *ha-mul*, "foam" or "lather." Others translate the word to mean "slimy water" and "place where antelopes drink water." The name was first mentioned in 1776, but was not frequently mentioned until the 1820s. Pio Pico was given permission to occupy the place but, in 1837, the place was overrun by Indians and the caretakers were murdered. Pico received a regrant in 1845.

Jamul, San Diego County, was a rancho that was frequently raided by Mexican cattle rustlers in the "good old days."

JANESVILLE

The postmaster in this Lassen County location, L. N. Breed, named the place in 1864 for someone named Jane. The woman in question could have been Jane Bankhead. Her husband was the town's blacksmith. Or it could have been Jane Hill. She was born here in 1862. No one is quite sure which Jane was honored. One authority even thinks it could have been named for both.

JENNER

Jenner, Sonoma County, is located where the Russian River empties into the Pacific Ocean. About 12 miles north of town is a reconstruction of Fort Ross—Russia's major fur-trading post in California. The fort was originally built in 1812. When they depleted the coast of seal and otter, the Russians sold the post to John Sutter in 1841.

The town bears the name of Elijah K. Jenner, or his son Charles. Both were living hereabouts in the 1860s when the town was named.

JENNY LIND

Jenny Lind, Calaveras County, was named in the mid-19th century for the "Swedish nightingale," who toured the United States from 1850 to 1852. Her tour was promoted quite well by the legendary

Phineas T. Barnum. Contrary to many accounts, Jenny Lind never visited California.

Another account contends that the town was founded in 1849 by a John Y. Lind and was originally called Dry Diggings because of the lack of water.

JOHANNESBURG

Johannesburg, a mining community in Kern County, took the name of the city of the same name in South Africa. The town founders— Chauncey M. Depew and his associates—hoped that the same success the South African town had would radiate in California.

The first important gold strike was made in 1895. The town, founded two years later, was popularly known as Joburg.

JOHNSON (—dale; — Park; —ville)

Hiram Johnson was a governor of the state in the early 20th century.

Johnsondale, Tulare County, was named in 1938 for Walter Johnson, an official of the Mount Whitney Lumber Company. The company was active in the area.

Johnsonville, Plumas County, on the other hand, was founded in 1876 and named for William Johns. Johns was the manager of the Plumas Eureka Mine. The name was firmly ensconced when the post office opened here in 1882.

JOLON

One source thinks Jolon is Salinian Indian and means "valley of dead trees." The Monterey County community took its name from the valley. A post office by this name appeared before 1861.

JOSHUA TREE

Joshua Tree took its name from the Joshua Tree National Monument, where one can find spectacular desert plants, including cacti, Joshua trees, ocotillos, palo verdes, pinon pines, smoke trees, yuccas, and other specimens.

The tree was named by the Mormons, who likened the *Yucca brevifolia* to a symbol of Joshua leading them to the promised land. A Joshua Tree post office was established here in 1946.

JULIAN

Julian, San Diego County, was a gold-mining town beginning in 1870. The town was laid out in that year by Drew (or Drury) Bailey, and named for his cousin, Mike S. Julian. Julian had discovered gold quartz on his claim.

JUNCTION CITY

Junction City, Trinity County, received its post office in 1861, when it was transferred from Messerville. The place was called Junction because, about 11 years earlier, the mining settlement had grown where Canyon Creek met the Trinity River.

JUNIPER SPRINGS

The name of this site came from the juniper tree, *Juniperus occidentalis,* and the presence of springs.

KAWEAH

Kaweah is derived from the name of the Yokuts Indian tribe, Kawia or Ga'-wia. A river, a mountain peak, a basin, and a gap also bear this name.

The post office was called Kaweah in 1889 because it was headquarters for the Kaweah Cooperative Colony.

KEDDIE

Keddie, Plumas County, received its name from Arthur W. Keddie in 1910.

Keddie was a Scotsman who became surveyor of Plumas County, and he was the drafter of the original Western Pacific route.

KEELER

Not far from Keeler, on the slope of White Mountain, marble mines were opened in the 1880s. Also, in the mountains to the northeast of town was the famous Cerro Gordo mine, producer of silver, lead and zinc. The ore was discovered in 1865 by a trio of Mexicans, all but one of whom were killed by Indians.

Located in Inyo County, the Keeler railroad station was named in 1882 for J. M. Keeler. He was the manager of the Inyo Marble Quarry.

KEENE

The post office at this Kern County site was established in 1879 and named for a member of the Keene family.

KELSEY (—ville)

The original name of Kelsey, El Dorado County, was Kelsey's Diggings. It was a mining camp as early as 1848. James Marshall died in a hotel here in 1885. He is not buried here, however. His remains are interred in Coloma under a monument in his honor.

The name honors Andrew Kelsey, leader of the famous Stevens-Murphy Party which entered California in 1844. The party's entry marked the first time a wagon train had traveled from Missouri to California. Kelsey was killed in 1849 by Indians seeking revenge for his abuse of them.

Other sources contend that the honor should go to Kelsey's brothers, Benjamin and Samuel. They apparently opened the diggings here in 1848.

Kelseyville, Lake County, was formed in the 1860s and was named for Andrew Kelsey. The post office here was first Uncle Sam, for the mountain of the same name. About 1885, the name became Kelseyville.

KELSO

Kelso, San Bernardino County, was named in 1906 for an official of the San Pedro, Los Angeles & Salt Lake Railroad.

Another source thinks it came from the town in Scotland.

KENTFIELD

Kentfield, Marin County, bears the name of local resident Albert Emmett Kent. Kent built his home here in 1872 and called it Tamalpais. The nearby station of the North Pacific Coast Railroad also went by that name until the end of the 19th century. It was changed to Kent to avoid confusion with the new Tamalpais Scenic Railway.

When the post office was established here, the name became Kentfield.

Another source thinks the name came from William Kent, a conservationist who donated Muir Woods to the American people.

KENWOOD

Kenwood, Sonoma County, was named sometime before 1897 for a town in Illinois.

KERMAN

The railroad station at this Fresno County locale was originally called Collis, for Collis P. Huntington, when the connector from Fresno was completed in 1895.

In 1906, when S. G. Kerckhoff and Jacob Mansar settled a colony of Germans and Scandinavians from the Midwest, they decided to name both the station and the town after themselves. Kerman is made up of the first three letters in the last names of the town's promoters!

KERNVILLE

Located in Kern County, this town took its name from its county, which was named for the three Kern brothers. It is also located near the Kern River. The town's original name was Whiskey Flat until the mines became exhausted in 1879.

KETTLEMAN CITY

Kettleman City, Kings County, took the name of David Kettleman, a Forty-Niner. The city was laid out in 1929 as the first "oil town." Kettleman's name also appears on the plain and hills.

KEYES

Most authorities believe that this Stanislaus County spot was named by the Southern Pacific in about 1897 for Thomas J. Keyes. Keyes had been a state senator from this county before his death.

KING (— City; —s Beach; —sburg)

The Southern Pacific Railroad established Kingsburg in 1875. The town today reflects the influence of early Swedish immigrants.

Kings Beach, Placer County, was named by the townspeople for Joe King's gifts to the community. The Kings Beach post office was established here in 1937.

The Monterey County community of King City was named for C. H. King. He laid out the town on his Rancho San Lorenzo when the Southern Pacific reached his place in 1886.

Kingsburg, Fresno County, received its name in 1875. Originally it had been known as Kings River Switch, taking its name from the waterway.

KIRKVILLE

Kirkville, Sutter County, was originally Colegrove Point until 1974 when T. D. Kirk laid out the new town. He called it Kirksville. Postal authorities modified it slightly.

KIT CARSON
This Amador County town's name came from the pass, named by Frémont in 1833 for his famous guide, Christopher "Kit" Carson (1809–68).

KIRKWOOD
The station of the Central Pacific Railroad from Willows to Tehama was built at this Tehama County site in 1882. Railroad officials honored Samuel J. Kirkwood with the name. Kirkwood was the Secretary of the Interior at the time.

KLAMATH (— River)
Klamath took its name from the river and, ultimately, from the Indian tribe: Tlamatl. The town is located at the north end of the bridge over the Klamath River.

KNEELAND
The name of this Humboldt County town does not indicate additional room in some airline's business class section.

The name of the post office, established before 1880, was taken from Kneeland's Prairie. John A. Kneeland settled here in the mid-19th century.

KNIGHTSEN
Knightsen, Contra Costa County, was named for G. M. Knight. He had donated the land for the San Francisco-San Joaquin Railroad right-of-way in 1898. Someone suggests the name was created from Knight's name and a part of his wife's maiden name, Christen*sen*.

KNIGHTS (— Ferry; — Landing)
Knights Ferry, Stanislaus County, was named for Captain William Knight, a hunter and trapper who followed Frémont through here in 1844. He moved here five years later and opened a ferry across the Stanislaus, just as he did across the Sacramento at Knights Landing. After his death, the ferry operation was taken over by John C. and Lewis Dent, U. S. Grant's brothers-in-law, and their associate.

KNOWLES
The founder of this Madera County town was F. E. Knowles. The Southern Pacific honored him with the name in 1890.

KNOXVILLE

One of the owners of the Manhattan Quicksilver Mine, located here, was a man by the name of Knox.

The post office was opened here in 1863 when it still was part of Lake County. It is now part of Napa County.

KORBEL

This Humboldt County community was named for early settlers. The Korbel brothers moved here and built a mill in 1882.

Nine years later, when the post office was established, the Korbel name became official.

KYBURZ

The first postmaster of this El Dorado County spot in 1911 was Albert Kyburz. His father, Samuel, had arrived here from Switzerland and had been quite active at Sutter's Fort before and during the gold rush.

LA CANADA FLINTRIDGE

The Spanish word *canada*, "valley," was a popular name in California before the Americans occupied the area. Sadly, it did not survive as a place name—except in this instance.

This particular Los Angeles County town name translates to "the Flintridge Valley." At one time, the subdivision of the Rancho la Canada was known simply as Flintridge. The division came in 1920, and was named for a U.S. senator from California, Frank P. Flint.

LA COSTA

This San Diego County community, technically a part of Carlsbad, has a Spanish name which means "the coast."

Oliver H. Borden and his family were the first settlers, arriving in 1879. It is suspected locally that he built the first concrete house in the area. The La Costa post office opened in 1896.

LA CRESCENTA

From the site of his new home in Los Angeles County, Dr. Benjamin B. Briggs could see three crescent-shaped rises formed by the foothills of the San Rafael hills on the southeast, the Verdugo hills on the southwest, and the Sierra Madre range. He was so taken by the view that he named his home "La Crescenta"—using the English "crescent" with a Spanish tinge.

The community that grew up in the vicinity of his house adopted the name. The post office was established here in 1888.

LAFAYETTE

The first settler in this Contra Costa County area was Elam Brown. Brown bought the Acalanes rancho, and settled near here in 1848. Twenty-five years later, the community was named by storekeeper Benjamin Shreve for the Marquis de la Fayette, making it one of more than 50 places in the United States to honor the young Frenchman who aided Washington during the American Revolution.

When Shreve made his decision, the town's name was spelled La Fayette. In fact, that is how the post office called it when it was opened in 1857. The name has since been streamlined.

LA GRANGE

La Grange was a mining community of the mid-19th century made famous by Bret Hart's "The Four Guardians of La Grange." It took its name from Baron La Grange who operated a gold mine of the same name here. Another source ties the name to that of the Marquis de la Fayette. La Grange was the name of his country home.

Called French Bar in the mid-19th century, and then Owen's Ferry, the name was changed to La Grange in 1857 when the town was made the seat of Stanislaus County.

LAGUNA (— Beach; — Hills; — Niquel)

Laguna Beach, Orange County, has long been an artists' colony. The name was modified from the Spanish word for "lake," and it was drawn from the nearby Laguna Canyon. The canyon's name came from Canada de Las Lagunas, noted in 1841 on the Niguel grant.

LAGUNITAS

This Marin County community takes its name from the Spanish for "little lakes." There were "little lakes" north of Mount Tamalpais. They have been converted into reservoirs.

LA HABRA (— Heights)

Taken from the name of the valley in which the town is situated, the name of La Habra, Orange County, comes from the Spanish *abra*, "defile, gorge" or "pass through the mountains," an obvious geographic reference. The La Habra post office was established here in 1912.

LA HONDA

The name is not a vestige of the Japanese automobile "invasion." Rather, it is Spanish for "deep." In this case, the name refers to Arroyo Ondo, a nearby creek. When a post office was first established here in 1880, the La Honda name was applied. About 15 years later, postal officials streamlined the words into one. In 1905, however, the past was restored, and the town resumed its earlier name, La Honda.

The Younger Brothers, legendary bandits of the 1860s, helped build a store here. They also used this San Mateo area for a hideout.

LA JOLLA

The Indians called this place La Hoya, "the cave." At an earlier time there were a number of caves dotting the shore here. The Spaniards changed it to La Jolla, which translates as "the jewel." Both are pronounced the same way. Others prefer to think the name came from the Mexican name for "a hollow" in mountains or in a river bed. Still others feel the Spanish word *joya*, "jewel," was the word of choice.

La Jolla, San Diego County, was laid out in 1869 and a map, drawn a year later, shows a hollow called La Joya nearby. The first post office, established in 1888, was called La Jolla Park. The name became Lajolla 14 years later. In 1905, the original name, without the "park," was restored.

Beyond La Jolla is the Scripps Institution of Oceanography, a marine biology and meteorology research facility.

LAKE ARROWHEAD

This San Bernardino County community takes its name from the body of water. When the post office was first established at Arrowhead Lake in 1922, they juxtaposed the words to avoid confusion with other towns named Arrowhead.

LAKE CITY

Lake City is far from being a city, located near the south fork of the Yuba River, between Upper and Middle Alkali lakes. The Modoc County town received its post office in the 1870s. The lakes, by the way, are more familiarly known to residents as Surpise Valley Lakes.

LAKE ELSINORE

This community took its name from Lake Elsinore, the largest fresh water lake in southern California.

LAKEHEAD

The Southern Pacific Railroad applied this name to their station, opened in Shasta County, because it was located at the "head" of Shasta Lake.

The Lakehead post office was established in 1950, and it was named after the railroad station.

LAKE HUGHES

The post office at Lake Hughes, Los Angeles County, was named for the lake in 1925.

LAKE ISABELLA

Isabella Lake was created by the U. S. Army Corps of Engineers in 1953 when they dammed the Kern River. The town that borders the man-made lake took the name.

LAKEPORT

Lakeport, Lake County, is located on the western shore of Clear Lake, which the Pomo Tribe called Lupoyoma.

The town was settled by William Forbes in 1859, and he called it Forbestown. When his community became the county seat, its name was changed.

LAKEVIEW

The post office at Lakeview, Riverside County, was established at the end of the 19th century. It was so named because of its spectacular view of Lake Moreno.

LAKEWOOD

At one time called Lakewood Village, this Los Angeles County subdivision was laid out in 1934 on Rancho Los Cerritos. Developers from the Montana Land Company named it Lakewood Village because it was near Bouton Lake.

LA MESA

La Mesa, San Diego County, bears the Spanish name for "the plain." This was the location of the "famous" battle of La Mesa, where Juan B. Alvarado defeated elements of José Antonio Carrillo's forces. The encounter has been described as "for the most part one of tongue and pen rather than artillery and guns." An informal armistice followed the encounter.

LA MIRADA

When the Sante Fe Railroad opened a station at this Los Angeles County site in 1888, railroad officials called it La Mirada. The name is a Spanish phrase for "the transient view," "a gaze," "a glance." When the olive grove here was subdivided for housing in 1953, the resulting town took on the station's name.

LA MOINE

La Moine, Shasta County, received its name in 1898. The namers were the Coggins brothers, who owned the Lamoine Lumber & Trading Company. They named it for their former home in Maine.

LAMONT

Like La Moine, Lamont bears a "homesick" name. The MacFadden family, owners of the land in this Kern County area, named the townsite for their native home in Scotland.

LANARE

Lanare's name came from that of the man who promoted the Fresno County settlement: L. A. Nares. The name first appeared when the Laton & Western Railway was built here in 1911.

LANCASTER

The name for this Los Angeles County community migrated from the town of the same name in Pennsylvania, from where the original settlers came. The name first appeared here in 1877.

LA PORTE

La Porte is Spanish for "the postage," or French for "the gate." The previous name for La Porte was Rabbit Creek, a name it took from the nearby waterway. The town went into decline in 1883 when hydraulic mining was stopped. But is that the name's source?

Some think that La Porte, Plumas County, was named in 1857 for La Porte, Indiana. That was the former home of town banker Frank Everts.

LA PUENTE

Bearing the Spanish for "the bridge," La Puente began its existence as a post office in Los Angeles County in 1884. At that time, it was merely Puente. The "la" was added in 1955.

LA QUINTA

La Quinta, Riverside County, bears the Spanish for the "country house or estate." The name came from La Quinta Hotel, and was borrowed when the post office was established here in 1931.

LARKSPUR

Because blue larkspur grew profusely in this Marin County location, settlers decided that was the name when they founded the town in 1887.

LA SELVA BEACH

La selva is Spanish for "jungle, woods, forest."

LAS FLORES

Las Flores, San Diego County, took its name from the lake, whose name is Spanish for "the flowers."

The town is located on the Santa Margarita grant, the "last of the ranchos," that once was almost a quarter of a million acres in area!

LATON

Laton, Fresno County, is situated on the Laguna de Tache, a once great Mexican grant. The community was named for Charles A. Laton. Together with L. A. Nares, he purchased the grant in the late 19th century.

LATROBE

Latrobe, El Dorado County, does not have a name that migrated from Pennsylvania.

F. A. Bishop, chief engineer for the Placerville & Sacramento Valley Railroad, named the station here in 1864 for Benjamin H. Latrobe. Latrobe had constructed the famous Thomas Viaduct over the Patapsco River in the 1830s for the Baltimore & Ohio.

LAWNDALE

This town's name merely describes what the town namers first saw. Located in Los Angeles County, the town was named by Charles Hopper in 1905.

LAWS

The first cabin in Owens Valley was built here in 1861. More than 20 years later, when the Carson & Colorado Railroad built a narrow gauge line here in 1883, the cabin grew into a community. The railroad named its station here in Inyo County for R. J. Laws, the line's assistant superintendent.

LAYTONVILLE

Laytonville, Mendocino County, was named for Frank B. Layton. He arrived in California from Nova Scotia in 1867, and settled here eight years later.

LEBEC

About three miles north of Lebec is Fort Tejon, a restored Army Dragoon post from the 1854–64 era. Fort Tejon was the western terminus for the U. S. Camel Corps, an experiment that used 25 camels to bring supplies from San Antonio, Texas.

Lebec, Kern County, received its name from an inscription carved into a tree near the town site: "Peter Lebeck, killed by a X bear, Oct. 17, 1837." The spelling of his name was changed to Le Beck by William Blake of the Pacific Railroad Survey who just copied it wrong. Others contend that early settlers thought Peter Lebeck was actually a Frenchman, Pierre Lebeque. There is no substance to this idea.

When the post office opened here in 1895, officials continued the history of misspelling by calling it Lebec.

LEE VINING

Lee Vining, once spelled Leevining by the post office, was named for Leroy "Lee" Vining. Vining operated a sawmill here in the mid-19th century. The post office at this Mono County location was established as Leevining in 1928. In 1957, Mr. Vining was given his whole name back.

LEGGETT

For many years, this Mendocino County location was known as Leggett Valley, for an early settler. In 1949, postal officials abbreviated the name.

LE GRAND

Le Grand, Merced County, was established as a station for the San Francisco & San Joaquin Valley Railroad in 1896. The name honored William Legrand Dickinson, the owner of large areas of land here.

LEMON (— Cove; — Grove)

The "lemons" associated with these areas are of the citrus variety. Lemon Grove, San Diego County, has been accused of run-away development. At one time in the recent past, the town was allowed to cut down all its lemon trees and replace them with a gigantic concrete lemon at the town's entrance.

LEMOORE

Lemoore, Kings County, took the name of a prominent citizen of the 1870s, Dr. Lovern Lee Moore.

The town was originally settled by John Kurtz in 1859. Twelve years later, Dr. Moore arrived and called the settlement Latache. He then founded the Lower Kings River Ditch Company. As Moore was a prominent citizen, it did not seem too far-fetched for postal authorities to rename the place for him in 1875.

LENNOX

Lennox, Los Angeles County, took its name from Lenox, Massachusetts, the former home of an early settler.

In its earlier days, Lennox had been known as Inglewood Rancho, then as Jefferson. In 1921, the town fathers recognized the Lennox name by changing Olivian Avenue to Lennox Avenue, now Lennox Boulevard.

LENWOOD

Similar to Lemoore, Lenwood took its name from a person. In this case it was for Ellen Woods. Her husband founded the San Bernardino County town in the 1920s.

LEUCADIA

English settlers, enamored with things Greek, named their town for the Greek island, which means "sheltered place." The island is also known as Santa Maura.

Many of the San Diego County town's streets have Greek names. The town was founded in 1885 and received its post office three years later.

LEWISTON

Located in Trinity County, Lewiston was named for the town's first settler, B. F. Lewis. He arrived in 1853; the next year, his name was on the post office sign.

Another source believes the town was named for the city in Maine.

LIKELY

When the residents of this Modoc County town petitioned postal authorities for a post office of their own in 1876, all their choices were rejected. Finally, in 1878, one frustrated gentleman remarked that it was "not likely" they would ever get a post office. Someone picked the word "Likely" because it was unlikely that it had ever been used. There is no proof for this story, but it sounds great! It sounds so great that South Fork Mountain is now called Likely Mountain.

West of town is the Infernal Caverns battlefield. In September 1867, General George Crook defeated 120 renegades of the Shoshone, Piute and Pit tribes. During the two-day battle, Crook lost a third of his 65-member command to casualty and had to fight on the ground with a rifle, like a common soldier.

LINCOLN

Lincoln was not named for Abraham Lincoln, as many suggest. The town's title came from the middle name of the town's founder, C. Lincoln Wilson. Wilson, of the California Central Railroad, established the site in the late 1850s.

LINDA

The name of this town does not recall the wife or girlfriend of a founder. It was the name of a miniature steamboat! The town was laid out in 1850 by John Rose.

LINDEN

In 1860, this San Joaquin County site was called Linden Mills. Seven years later, postal officials shortened the name to its present length.

There are no linden trees hereabouts, so most sources think the name traveled from elsewhere.

LINDSAY

The maiden name of town founder Captain A. J. Hutchinson's wife was selected as the town's name in 1888. Lindsay is located in Tulare County.

LITCHFIELD

Litchfield was named in 1912 for the Litch family—early settlers. The Litchfield, Lassen County, post office was established three years later.

LITTLE LAKE

Little Lake, Inyo County, was named after a "little" lake.

LITTLE RIVER

This Humboldt County community took its name from the waterway.

LITTLEROCK

Littlerock, Los Angeles County, was named after a small geographic feature.

LIVE OAK

The evergreen oak was evident in the Sutter County area when the naming took place. The town was named in 1874 by H. L. Gregory.

LIVERMORE

Livermore, Alameda County, was named for Robert "Don Roberto" Livermore (1799–1858), an English sailor who owned the greater part of the valley that bears his name.

Livermore married Josefa, daughter of Jose Higuera, at Rancho Agua Caliente, Warm Springs. Together with Jose Noriega, he settled here in 1835. Rancho Las Positas was granted the two men in 1840.

The town of Livermore was first named Laddville, for Alphonso S. Ladd. He built the first building in town in about 1864. The name was changed when the post office opened five years later. Then it was called Nottingham, for Livermore's hometown. Later the same year, William H. Mendelhall platted the townsite into lots and named it Livermore.

LIVINGSTON

When the Southern Pacific Railroad's valley route reached this spot in Merced County in 1871, officials named the station Cressey, for the landowner.

The next year, Postmaster O. J. Little—he also owned land—registered his resentment at the name, and he picked the name of David Livingstone, the central African explorer best remembered for "Dr. Livingstone, I presume?" Somewhere along the line, postal officials dropped his "e."

LODI

This town in San Joaquin County was named Lodi by the railroad simply because the word was short. In other places, the name was given to commemorate Napoleon's Italian victory at Lodi, Italy, in 1796.

The original name of the Central Pacific Railroad station at this site was Mokelumne in 1896, but they changed it to Lodi for fear that people would confuse Mokelumne with other places of that name in the state. Thank goodness!

LODOGA

This Colusa County community's name was spelled Ladoga in 1902, and might have been named after the large lake between Finland and Russia, or after a place in either Wisconsin or Indiana. Another possibility is the Spanish *lodo*, "mud." Unfortunately, the only ones who spelled it with the "o" were postal officials when they established the office here in 1898.

LOLETA

Some say the name of this Humboldt County town is the Mexican colloquial for "Mary of the Sorrows." Others contend that the name is of Indian origin, and means "pleasant place."

The town's original name was Swauger, for landowner Samuel A. Swauger. That was given by the railroad in 1883. Ten years later, residents applied for a better name. Mrs. Rufus F. Herrick selected this one. Another tradition has it as an Indian word. No one really knows.

LOMA LINDA

Located in San Bernardino County, Loma Linda bears a Spanish phrase meaning "boundary hill," marking a corner in the old Spanish land grant. At least that is what some authorities think.

Others indicate that the town was named Mound Station in 1875 or 1876. After 1787, Southern Pacific Railroad maps refer to it as Mound City. At the end of the 19th century, Seventh Day Adventists built a sanatorium here. When a post office was established in 1901, the name Lomalinda, or "pretty hill," as one source puts it, was given. The name was split at a later date.

LOMA MAR

Loma Mar, San Mateo County, bears the Spanish name for "hill by the sea."

LOMITA

Lomita, Los Angeles County, carries the Spanish title for "little hill." The name probably came from Lomita del Toro, noted on a surveyor's map of the San Pedro Rancho.

LOMPOC

Though it bears an undefined Chumash Indian place name, we can be sure that Lompoc, Santa Barbara County, took its name from a rancheria, Lompoc o Lompocop, run by Mission La Purisima in 1791.

LONE PINE

About nine miles north of here are the remains of Manzanar, the internment camp where thousands of Japanese Americans were confined during World War II.

The town of Lone Pine, Inyo County, was named in 1860 by members of the Hill party who were prospecting the Iowa silver mine. The name referred to a local landmark.

LONG BARN

The barn referred to in the name of this Tuolumne County community was very long indeed. It housed 140 horses, a feed and tack room, and bunks for stable hands.

The building was the last stopping point for the logging and freighter teams who needed to rest their horses before going over the Sonora Pass into Nevada. The expression of the crews, "Let's meet at the Long Barn," became descriptive of the location.

LONG BEACH

Given in 1887, the name of this ocean-front community in Los Angeles County is descriptive. It was founded, however, as Willmore City in 1882 by William E. Willmore. Three years later, the Long Beach Land & Water Company applied the new name.

The Chautaqua Association of Southern California held a one-day assembly here in 1884. Before long, the town drew the group's summer school which began in 1895. "No saloons are tolerated," one visitor wrote, "and all objectionable elements of society are kept out."

Long Beach, the fifth-largest city in the state, is home to the *Queen Mary*. The ship, launched in 1934, was one of the most luxurious ocean liners afloat. It was purchased by the city fathers of Long Beach in 1964 and is currently used as a strong tourist attraction. Not too far from the ship is the "Spruce Goose," the largest wooden aircraft ever constructed. Created by Howard Hughes in 1942, the plane flew only once: 2 November 1947.

LONGVALE

The name of Longvale, Mendocino County, was adapted from Long Valley.

LOOKOUT

Located in Modoc County, Lookout was named in about 1860 after the hill above the town.

Local residents tell the story that Pit River Indians stood watch there to warn their villagers when the Modoc tribe came through on wife-stealing forays. Others say the name was given because of the extensive view.

LOS ALAMOS

The original grant of 50,000 acres was made in 1839 to José Antonio de la Guerra y Carrillo, who was noted for lavish entertaining. His Rancho Los Alamos was a favored stopping spot for travelers between Santa Barbara and Monterey. The name is Spanish for "the poplars."

LOS ALTOS (— Hills)

Los Altos, Santa Clara County, took its name from its location: It is "the heights." The name was chosen in 1907. The next year, postal authorities accepted it for the post office name.

LOS ANGELES

The present site of Los Angeles, Los Angeles County, was first visited by an expedition under Gaspar de Portola in 1769. They named the river located here el Rio de Nuestra Senor la Reina de Los Angeles de la Portoinola, "the River of Our Lady, Queen of the Angels of the Little Portion." The Franciscan shrine near Assisi is called the Portinola.

When it was established 12 years later by Felipe De Neve, governor of the colonial province of Alta, the town took on the name of the river: La Pueblo de Nuestra Senor la Reina de Los Angeles. Beginning in 1846, the name was shortened to Pueblo de los Angeles, then to the present bite-sized form. Following Mexican independence from Spain, Los Angeles served as capital of Alta California from time to time. It was the last place to surrender to the United States during the Mexican War in 1847.

Los Angeles became the center of the motion picture industry in the early 20th century, when East Coast filmmakers realized that the temperatures on the West Coast were constantly mild and allowed them to film almost year-round.

The La Brea Tar Pits were discovered in Los Angeles in 1769. Fossilized remains of prehistoric animals and evidence of human occupation were found here, leading scientists to estimate that humans lived here 15,000 years ago!

LOS BANOS

Located in Merced County, Los Banos took its name from the creek. The name is Spanish for "the baths." The name was quite fitting because pools in the stream afforded early settlers an opportunity to take a bath.

Gustave Kreyenhagen built a store here in about 1870, and the place became known as Kreyenhagen's. When a post office was established in Kreyenhagen's store in 1874, it was called Los Banos. In 1889, after the railroad was built here, Henry Miller, who had leased the land to Kreyenhagen, and his partners laid out the town.

LOS GATOS

Los Gatos, Santa Clara County, is guarded by two mountain ridges, El Sombroso, "the shadowing one," and El Sereno, "the night watchman." The town was founded in about 1868, on a portion of an 1840 Spanish land grant, known as La Rinconada de los Gatos, "the corner of the cats."

The reference was to the presence of mountain lions and wild cats that lived in the nearby hills. The town was laid out by J. A. Forbes in 1850. Seventeen years later, the post office opened under the same name. In 1878, railroad officials made it perfect; they, too, named their station Los Gatos.

LOS MOLINOS

Los Molinos carries the Spanish name for "the mills" or "the millstones." It took its name from the nearby stream, Mill Creek. The waterway's original name was Rios de los Molinos, "River of Millstones."

LOS OLIVOS

This Santa Barbara County community was named by the Pacific Coast Railroad in about 1890. The railroad station had received its name for the abundance of olive trees in the area. The name translates from the Spanish for "the olives."

LOST HILLS

This Kern County town was named for some mountains that are smaller than others, almost hidden from view.

LOTUS

Local tradition holds that the name was selected because the people in town were as easy-going as the lotus-eaters in Homer's *Odyssey*.

At first the El Dorado community was named Marshall for James W. Marshall who discovered the gold at Sutter's mill. After California was admitted to the Union in 1850, townspeople petitioned for—and won—Uniontown. That might have remained the name, but the people petitioned for a post office and, to avoid confusion with Union House, Sacramenton County, they gave up the name. The town's first postmaster, George E. Gallaner, suggested the new name.

LOWER LAKE

Lower Lake, Lake County, was located near the outlet of a lake. The town was established in 1860; the post office, in 1859.

LOYALTON

Loyalton, Sierra County, was known as Smith's Neck—for the Smith Mining Company—until 1864. In that year the entire town cast votes for Abraham Lincoln. When they realized they agreed on the candidate, they voted to change the name to Loyalton.

Another source contends that the name was merely given by the town's postmaster, the Reverend Adam G. Doom, for the strong Union sentiment the town felt during the Civil War.

LUCERNE (— Valley)

Lucerne took its name from the Swiss city. Located on the shore of Clear Lake in Lake County, Lucerne's location resembles that of the town on the Swiss lake. The post office was established here in 1926.

LUCIA

Lucia, Monterey County, took its name from its location at the foot of the Santa Lucia Mountains. The first post office was established here in 1900.

LUDLOW

Ludlow, San Bernardino County, was named in the 1870s by the Central Pacific Railroad for William B. Ludlow. Ludlow was a master car-repairman of the line's Western Division. However, from 1902 to 1926 the post office name was Stagg. The town was almost destroyed by fire in the early days of the 20th century.

LYNWOOD

Lynwood, Los Angeles County, was named for Lynn Wood Sessions, the wife of an early dairyman. The town was incorporated in 1921.

LYTLE CREEK

Lytle Creek, San Bernardino County, was named for Captain Andrew Lytle. He led a division of members of the Church of Jesus Christ of Latter-day Saints into the valley in 1851.

MADELINE

This Lassen County community's name honors the memory of a little girl who was killed by the Indians in the mid-19th century. The name first appeared on the pass west of Mud Lake.

A post office bearing her name appeared in the 1870s.

MADERA

After Madera County was formed from part of Fresno County, it took on the name of this town. Madera is Spanish for "lumber," a major commodity in this area at the town's founding. In fact, the town was named in 1876 by a lumber company.

MADISON

While many places bearing this name across the nation honor the memory of James Madison, fourth president of the United States, this Yolo County town does not.

In 1877, the Vaca Valley & Clear Lake Railroad extended from Winters and laid out a new town. Madison was named by Daniel Bradley Hulbert. Hulbert was a native of Madison, Wisconsin.

MAD RIVER

Mad River was named in 1849 by the first explorers. The proper name came to mind when Josiah Gregg gave vent to his violent temper. Apparently, members of his group refused to wait for him while he made scientific calculations on the exact latitude of the mouth of the river.

The town took the name of the waterway.

MADRONE

Located in Santa Clara County, Madrone took its name from a tree. The madrona is an evergreen tree of northern California.

MAGALIA

A clipping from the *Gold Nugget Gazette* of 28 December 1862 tells it all:

> Our ancient village of Dogtown is as unfortunate as a yearly widow—eternally finding it necessary or convenient to change her name. When the old Dog died, Butte Mills slid in through the post office requisition, and now, through the same channel, Butte Mills is crowded out of the kennel, and the euphonious Magalia usurps the hour. Who discovered the name? Has not the post office department mistaken the word sent on? Was it not Mahala? However, the thing is fixed now, and the Dog's dead; the post office of old Dogtown in the future is to be addressed as Magalia, and A. C. Buffum is to be the postmaster.

The town's original name, if you haven't guessed, was Dogtown. It was founded by E. B. Vinson and Charles Chamberlain. *Magalia* is a Latin word for "cottages," a decided improvement in a place name.

The post office name arrived in this Butte County town when the office at Butte Mills was moved here in 1861.

MALAGA

Malaga, Fresno County, took the name of the grapes grown here, and, indirectly, from the town in Spain. In 1852, Colonel Arpad Haraszthy imported the muscat grapes from Malaga, Spain.

The post office was established as Malaga in about 1885.

MALIBU

The name for Malibu, basically a strip of beach from the Pacific Palisades section of Los Angeles west to the Ventura County line, is of Indian origin and was used as the name of a village. The present spelling first appeared in the Topanga Malibu Sequit land grant in 1805.

MAMMOTH LAKES

Mammoth Lakes, not named because of size, carries the name of Mammoth City, a boom-town-went-bust created by the Mammoth Mining Company in 1878.

MANCHESTER

Manchester, Mendocino County, was named for another of those places "back East."

MANHATTAN BEACH

At the suggestion of Stewart Merrill, who founded this Los Angeles County town, the name of Shore Acres became Manhattan Beach. Merrill named the town for the island of Manhattan in New York City.

MANTECA

Though the name is Spanish for "lard" or "fat," when the town was named in 1905, someone felt the word was closer to "butter." This San Joaquin County town was the site of a creamery in those days.

An earlier name for this community was Cowell, for Joshua Cowell who donated the right-of-way to the Southern Pacific Railroad. The railroad, by the way, was responsible for the name change.

MANTON

J. M. Meeder named this Tehama County town in 1892. Most local people feel he named it after the town in Rhode Island.

MANZANITA LAKE

There is a Manzanita Lake located in Marin, San Diego and Tehama counties. The name was given because of the extensive growth of manzanita brush. The Spanish *manzanita*, "little apple," is the common name for the genus *Archtostaphylos*.

MARICOPA

Maricopa is the name of an Indian tribe native to Arizona. Apparently, people from that state liked the name enough to transfer it here.

In reality, the name came from the Southern Pacific Railroad when, in 1903 or 1904, it extended its spur from what is now Hazleton.

MARINA

The Spanish word for "seacoast" or "shore" appeared on the post office at this Monterey County location.

MARIN CITY

The name here goes back to 1775 when Spanish explorers named a small bay: Nuestra Senora de Rosario de Marinera.

Another source suggests the name came from an Indian chief who was given the name Marin. The name was a corruption of *El Marinero*, "the sailor." The chief gave up his warlike ways and started a ferry between San Francisco and the northern shore of the Golden Gate.

MARIPOSA

Originally called Logtown, this town in Mariposa County was named for the river. One authority thought the name came from a flower that grew in the area. But *mariposa* is Spanish for "butterfly," and there are accounts of Spanish explorers encountering swarms of butterflies in the vicinity during their 1806 expedition. Padre Munoz, who was with Gabriel Moraga on that trip, wrote, "This place is called (place) of the *Mariposas* (butterflies) because of their great multitude, especially at night and morning...."

A more interesting story about the town centers around John C. Frémont who, upon learning of the 1848 discovery of gold at Coloma, expanded his Mexican land grant, Rancho Las Mariposas, about 50 miles east to include mountain country.

The next summer, gold was discovered on his ranch at the southern end of the Mother Lode. By 1863, Frémont lost control of the Mariposa, but the town grew.

MARKLEEVILLE

Markleeville is county seat to the smallest county—by population—in California, Alpine.

Its name honors Jacob J. Marklee, who arrived here in 1861. Marklee was killed in an argument over the land on which the town was built.

The town was incorporated in 1864, and kept the name of the post office that was established in 1863.

MARSHALL

The town was originally named Marshalls, for Alexander James Marshall and his brothers—James, Hugh and Samuel. They settled in Marin County in the mid-19th century and built a hotel here in 1870.

Others think the name belongs to James Marshall—boss carpenter to John A. Sutter, and the man who triggered the California gold rush.

MARTINEZ

This Contra Costa County community was named for a prominent Spanish settler, Ignacio Martinez. Martinez was *commandante* at the Presidio of San Francisco from 1822 to 1827. The town of Martinez was laid out in 1849 by Colonel William M. Smith on Rancho El Pinole. The rancho had been granted to Martinez in 1823 for his military service.

Martinez was also home to naturalist John Muir (1838–1914) who, in 1892, founded the Sierra Club. Muir, a native of Scotland, became interested in horticulture after suffering from an injury to his eye in 1867. That same year, he walked from Indianapolis to the Gulf of Mexico. He wrote up that account, published in 1916 as *A Thousand Mile Walk to the Gulf*. In 1868, Muir went to California. Using California as a base, he traveled far and wide and studied trees, forests and glaciers. Through his efforts, Yosemite National Park came into being.

According to one source, Martinez was originally called La Hambre, "the hunger."

MARTINEZ. John Muir, the famous naturalist, was the most famous resident of Martinez. Muir was the driving force behind the first American land conservation laws, and the establishment of Yosemite National Park. (National Park Service, John Muir National Historic Site)

MARTINEZ. The house in Martinez where John Muir lived. The home is now a National Historic Site. (National Park Service, John Muir National Historic Site)

MARYSVILLE

At a public meeting held in January 1850, townspeople in this Yuba County community approved the naming of their community for Mrs. Mary Murphy Covillaud, wife of the town's principal landowner and a survivor of the Donner Party.

Charles Covillaud surveyed this river-port town in Yuba County in 1849, and it almost immediately became a thriving steamboat landing.

The town was originally called New Meckleburg by Theodore Cordua, who came from Meckleburg. "I called my whole settlement New Meckleburg," Cordua announced, "hoping that I would be able to share it with many of my own countrymen." He operated a trading post on land that he leased in 1842 from Sutter. Eight years later, he sold half of his land to Charles Covillaud, his overseer.

In 1851, Marysville was terrorized by Joaquin Murieta, a notorious bandit. He was opposed by Stephen Field, later to become Chief Justice of the U. S. Supreme Court, and attorney William Walker. Called the "gray-eyed man of destiny," Walker invaded Nicaragua and became its president from 1856 to 1857. He was executed by a firing squad in 1860 after trying to foment revolt in Honduras.

MATHER

The name of Mather recalls Stephen T. Mather, the first director of the National Park Service, who served from 1917 to 1929. The post office bearing his name was established in 1921.

MAXWELL

Maxwell, Colusa County, was founded in 1878, and named for an early resident, George Maxwell, an 1849 gold miner. Maxwell Creek, in Mariposa County, also bears his name.

MAYWOOD

The name for Maywood, Los Angeles County, was reached by public vote when the town was incorporated in 1924.

McARTHUR

McArthur, located in Shasta County, was named by the John McArthur Company for John McArthur. He settled in the Pit River Valley in 1869 and owned most of the land.

McCANN

This Humboldt County town was named for Willard O. McCann. He arrived in the county in 1869 and built a mill. The railroad station was named to honor him in 1881.

McCLOUD

McCloud took its name from the river, which was named for the leader of the trappers from the Hudson Bay Company from 1828 to 1829, Alexander R. McLeod. Apparently, they spelled his name phonetically.

The town began in the late 19th century as a company town, and it was the company town with the most longevity. In 1965, the U. S. Plywood Corporation purchased the town, lumber mill and surrounding forests, but allowed the residents to purchase their own homes.

McFARLAND

One of the founders of this Kern County community was J. B. McFarland. The town was named for him in 1908.

McKINLEYVILLE

McKinleyville, Humboldt County, was named in honor of President William McKinley, shortly after his assassination in 1901. The post office began operation two years later.

McKITTRICK

In the early 1890s, when the Southern Pacific extended its line from Bakersfield to the asphalt beds, the station was named Asphalto. After oil was discovered, the railroad again extended its line. This time, the station was named McKittrick, for Captain William H. McKittrick, son-in-law of landowner General William Shafter.

MECCA

Mecca, a town in the desert of Riverside County, was aptly named for the Arabian city. Though it was an arid area following a significant irrigation project that did not bring the cultivation of dates here, the name was more to the point than Walters, the original name.

Walters was the name of the settlement from 1896 until 1903. The new name was suggested by R. H. Myers, founder of the Mecca Land Company.

MELONES

The name for this Calaveras County location was moved here from an earlier camp nearby. The gold found there was so coarse that miners thought it resembled melon seeds.

An earlier name was Slumgullion, we are told, so they improved on their image by using the Spanish word for "melons" as their corporate title. Slumgullion, alas, only existed in Bret Harte's imagination.

Another source feels the name was a misreading of McLeans or McLanes, names to which references were made in a number of contemporary diaries.

MENDOCINO

Authorities feel that Mendocino is an adjective derived from the family name Mendoza. The name was recorded on a 1587 map that honored L. Suerez de Mendoza, a Spanish viceroy from 1550 to 1583.

Local tradition, however, believes the name was associated

with Antonio de Mendoza, the 1542 viceroy when the cape for which the town was named was allegedly discovered.

The Mendocino County town was founded and named by William Kasten in 1852, two years after the county was formed. The post office was opened as Mendocino in 1853.

Mendocino is a major attraction for tourists and artists on the north coast of California.

MENDOTA

The Southern Pacific Railroad named this Fresno County town in 1895 when it extended its line from Fresno. The name migrated, we suspect, from the Midwest and has no local reference.

MENLO PARK

D. J. Oliver and D. C. McGlynn, brothers-in-law from Menlough, County Galway, Ireland, established ranches here in 1854. They named their joint ranches after their homeland. In fact, they erected a giant gate at their joint property with the legend: "Menlo Park" and the date. When the San Francisco & San Jose Railroad reached here in 1863, it adopted the men's property name for the station. The sign, by the way, lasted until 1922, when a car struck and destroyed it.

MENTONE

The name for Mentone, San Bernardino County, was adopted for advertising purposes by the Mentone Company in 1886. The name was supposed to suggest a resemblance to the Riviera resort.

MERCED (— Falls)

Merced, Merced County, took its name from the county which acquired it from the Merced River. Merced is Spanish for "mercy," and the name is usually used with a religious reference. In this case, the river's original name was Nuestra Senora de la Merced, "Our Lady of Mercy." The title was given in 1806 by a Spanish expedition.

MERCY HOT SPRINGS

An early cattle rancher in this Fresno County area was John N. Mercy, who gave his name to the developing community. He raised stock here in the 1860s and 1870s.

MERIDIAN

Postal authorities named this Sutter County community Meridian because it was a scant quarter-mile west of the Mount Diablo meridian.

MERRIMAC

The post office was established at this Butte County location about 1885. The name, some suggest, came from the legendary Civil War battle of the *Monitor* and *Merrimac*. Others think it originated in New England.

MEYERS

Meyers, El Dorado County, was named for an early homesteader who arrived here before 1860. The Meyers post office was established in 1904.

MICHIGAN BLUFF

Michigan Bluff, Placer County, is perched on a steep mountainside. Between 1853 and 1855, when the town's location was a little lower than it is today, Leland Stanford kept a store here.

The town's name was given by a group of miners from Michigan who worked here in the mid-19th century. The town began as Michigan City a half-mile away. Because the mines threatened to weaken the entire settlement, the town was moved to the present site and called Michigan Bluff.

MIDDLETOWN

Middletown, Lake County, received its name in the 1860s. The name was selected because the town was the stage stop midway between Lower Lake and Calistoga.

MIDLAND

The name for this Riverside County community moved here from Michigan. The name was given in 1928 by O. M. Knode of the U.S. Gypsum Company.

MIDPINES

N. D. Chamberlain named this Mariposa County site in 1926 because, as he put it, it was "amidst the pines and midway between Merced and Yosemite."

MILFORD

J. C. Wemple built a gristmill at this Lassen County site in 1861. He thought the name was quite appropriate.

MILLBRAE

Millbrae, San Mateo County, took its name from the owners of a local estate, Darius Ogden Mills and his family. Mills built the family mansion on part of the Buri Buri rancho. Besides being a '49er and banker, Mills was one of the leading bankers in San Francisco.

The Millbrae name (*brae* is Scottish for "hill slope") was applied first to the railroad station and then to the post office in 1867.

Ogden Livingstone Mills, one of the better-known members, was secretary of the treasury under Hoover.

MILL CREEK

Mill Creek, Tehama County, was not named, like hundreds of other communities across the country, because a mill was operating here.

John Bidwell named the site Mill Creek in 1843 because it looked like a good place to build a mill. At first, this community was called Mill Creek Homesite. In 1937, the current name was applied to the post office.

MILL VALLEY

Mill Valley, Marin County, is a residential community at the base of Mount Tamalpais.

The valley was so named because John Reed (Reid, Read) built a sawmill here in 1834. In 1889, the Tamalpais Land & Water Company purchased the land, built a branch of the North Pacific Coast Railroad on the site and laid out the town of Mill Valley.

MILLVILE

One of the first gristmills in Shasta County was built here before 1855 by D. D. Harrill. In 1855, the place was known as Harrill's Mill; the next year, Buscombe, for Harrill's North Carolina birthplace; and finally, Millville in 1857.

MILPITAS

Milpa is Spanish for "little field." The name of this Santa Clara town is the diminutive of that word. Does that mean this is an itsy-bitsy field? The post office was established in 1856.

Some spoilsports say the word came from *milpa*, an Aztec word for "land sown with seed," but they never say how the Aztecs got here.

MILTON

Authorities are still out on the source of this Calaveras County name. Some believe the name of the 1871 station on the Stockton & Copperopolis Railroad was chosen to honor Milton Latham, governor of California for five days in 1860 and an unsuccessful railroad builder. It could also be a misspelling of the name of W. J. L. Molton, a director of the railroad.

MINERAL (— King)

Mineral, Tehama County, was established in 1894. The name came from the Morgan Mineral Springs. When the post office was moved to a new location, it kept the name.

Mineral King, Tulare County, was so named because the promoters thought it was the "king" of all mining districts. The town grew up around the mine that opened here in 1872. An earlier name was Buelah.

MINERAL. Bumpass (then spelled with only one "s") Hell leads to steam vents spewing forth boiling water and other evidence of volcanic activity. Bumpass, by the way, comes from the French for "good pass." (Lassen Volcanic National Park, National Park Service)

MINERAL. Mineral is the base for the Lassen Volcanic National Park. In this archival photograph, the viewer is at milepost 20, with Lassen Peak in the background. (Lassen Volcanic National Park, National Park Service)

MINKLER

In 1910, the Santa Fe built a spur line from Reedley to Delpiedra and named the station Minkler. Most authorities believe the donor of the name was Charles O. Minkler, a local farmer.

MIRA LOMA

Mira Loma, Riverside County, was previously named Stalder, for an early settler. The name was then changed to Wineville when the Charles Stern Winery was built here. The current name, which appeared when the post office was established in 1930, means "Behold the hill."

MIRAMAR

Miramar, San Diego County, wears the Spanish phrase for "behold the sea." The name was given by E. W. Scripps for his Linda Vista Ranch. The name appeared on the post office in 1930.

MIRAMONTE

Miramonte, Fresno County, was named for the view. The phrase is Spanish for "behold the mountain."

MISSION BEACH

Originally the bay on which Mission Beach, San Diego County, is located was called Puerto Anegado, "overflowed port." In 1782, it was noted as Puerto Falso, "the false bay." It maintained that name until 1915 when the Geographic Board decided to call it Mission Bay. The town that grew up on its shores assumed its name.

MISSION HILLS

Mission Hills takes its name from the Mission San Fernando Rey de Espana, founded in 1797.

MISSION HILLS. This photograph from the late 1890s shows the Convento at Mission San Fernando Rey de Espana in decaying form. The building was constructed in 1822 after nearly 13 years of construction. After the Secularization Act of 1833, the convento was used as a private residence. In 1847, John C. Frémont used it for his headquarters. (Chancery Archives of the Archdiocese of Los Angeles)

MISSION HILLS. After restoration, the convento, the largest adobe structure in California, holds one of the most extensive collections of Mission Era artifacts. It has been seen in many feature motion pictures and television shows. (Chancery Archives of the Archdiocese of Los Angeles)

MISSION VIEJO

Mission Viejo carries the Spanish phrase for "old mission."

MI-WUK

Mi-Wuk, Tuolumne County, took its name from the Mi-Wuk or Mi-Wok Indians who had their reservation about 10 miles from town.

The name was selected by Harry Hoeffler who developed the community in 1955 after consulting with Chief Fuller of the Miwok tribe.

MODESTO

The earliest settlements in this Stanislaus County location were nothing to brag about; they were merely thrown-together lodgings for gold miners.

In 1870, however, after the Central Pacific Railroad arrived in 1870, surveyors laid out a city along the Tuolumne River. The community wanted to name the new town in honor of W. C. Ralston, but he declined. One source believes Ralston's occupation to have been that of the town's banker. His act resulted in the townspeople selecting Modesto, the Spanish word for "modesty."

Modesto became the county seat in 1871.

MOJAVE

Mojave, Kern County, was named for the desert which bears the name of the Indian tribe. In Arizona, the name of the tribe and of a corresponding town is spelled Navaho.

The desert was discovered accidentally by Governor Pedro Fages; he was in pursuit of a band of deserters, not on an exploring expedition.

MOKELUMNE HILL

This Calaveras County name came from the Miwok Indian language and referred to the name of a small tribe or village. The town is also located near the Mokelumne River.

MONO (— Hot Springs; — Lake)

The community of Mono Lake took its name from the nearby 700,000-year old lake. Over the years the salts and minerals have become so concentrated that the fish cannot live in the lake, but the brine shrimp and flies that flock here draw migratory birds and water fowl.

Some authorities think the "mono" in this title means "pretty," "funny" or "monkey"—none of which makes any sense.

MONOLITH

This Kern County site was named by William Mulholland in 1908. Mulholland was the builder of the Los Angeles Aqueduct, but he named the town for the Monolith Portland Cement Company that operated here.

MONROVIA

Monrovia was named for Major William N. Monroe, one of the town's founders. He helped lay out this Los Angeles County town in 1886 on 60 acres of Ranchos Santa Anita and Azusa de Duarte.

Monrovia is also the name of Liberia's seaport capital. Established by the American Colonization Society in 1822 and named for President James Monroe, it was a haven for ex-slaves from the United States.

MONTAGUE

Romeo and Juliet had no part in the naming of this Siskiyou County community. The name came from S. S. Montague, chief engineer for the Central Pacific Railroad. The name came about between 1886 and 1887, when the Southern Pacific was extending its line from Dunsmuir to the state line.

MONTALVO

This Ventura County community was named for the Spanish poet, Garci Ordoñez de Montalvo. It was in his work, *Las sergas de Esplandian,* that the word "California" probably first appeared.

Another suggestion is that the name came from the estate of James Phelan, in Santa Clara County. The town's name was applied in 1887 when the Southern Pacific reached here and established a station.

MONTARA

The experts are out on this one. On one side we have those who think the name is a misspelling of the Spanish *montana*, "mountain," or some other word or words. Others think it is a family name. Whatever it is, it is also the name of a mountain.

The mountain's name first appeared as Montoro in 1867, but two years later it became Montara.

MONTEBELLO

According to the son of the founder of this Los Angeles County community, this is "another of the many instances . . . of the lack, among Californians, of proper historic respect for pioneer names."

His reference was to the 1920 changing of the name of Newmark to Montebello. Harris Newmark had settled in this area on part of the Repetto ranch in 1887, and named the town for himself. Though the town was Newmark, the settlement was called Montebello, Spanish for "beautiful mountain."

MONTECITO

Montecito, Santa Barbara County, took its name from the Spanish-American usage for "little forest."

The name was mentioned as early as 1783, as a location for a mission, and it did become the site for Mission Santa Barbara, founded in 1844. The present town is located east of the original site.

MONTEREY

Monterey, Monterey County, was named for the Conde de Monterey, viceroy of New Spain (Mexico) at the time. His name is Spanish for "mountain of the king." Another source suggested "the king's woods."

Monterey was the capital of Alta California—as opposed to Baja California—under Spanish, Mexican and American rule.

The first approach to settlement was made here in 1602 by Sebastian Viscaino, who named the bay for his sponsor. More than 150 years later, Father Junipero Serra landed at the same place and began in earnest the conversion and development of California. With the help of Governor Gaspar de Portola, he founded the presidio and mission of Monterey in 1770. It was the second in Alta California.

John Steinbeck used Monterey as the locale in *Cannery Row* and *Sweet Thursday*. In the author's day, the row was filled with sardine canneries. Today it is a tourist attraction, filled with restaurants and shops.

Also located in Monterey is California's version of Independence Hall: Colton Hall. In 1849, delegates drafted the first state constitution in the tastefully restored building.

MONTGOMERY CREEK

Montgomery Creek, Mono County, took its name from the waterway. Apparently, the creek's name was taken from that of the man who operated a mill here before 1873.

MONTROSE

The name for this Nevada County community was chosen by a contest in 1913. The name is usually thought to come from Sir Walter Scott's popular *Legend of Montrose*. The subdivision is located on a portion of La Crescenta.

MOORPARK

Moorpark, Ventura County, has nothing to do with Othello.

The town was founded at the turn of the 20th century, and it was named for an English variety of apricots. The Moorpark was popular in southern California.

The Moorpark post office opened in 1904.

MORAGA

Moraga, Contra Costa County, bears the name of the Moraga family. The first Moraga to make his mark in California was José Joaquín Moraga. He arrived in California in 1776 as lieutenant commander of the Anza expedition. The family name is Spanish for "bundle made by gleaners."

The first post office was established here in 1886, then reestablished in 1915 when the town was developed.

MORENA (— Village; — Valley)

No one is quite sure why representatives of the Santa Fe Railroad gave their station this name in San Diego County. The name is Spanish for "brown." The station was in existence before 1900.

MORGAN HILL

The Costanoan Indians, a peaceable tribe, lived here before Spanish soldiers and priests arrived in 1776. The first English-speaking community grew around a thriving estate, the Morgan Hill's Ranch, in 1845.

Morgan Hill acquired his ranch at the time of his marriage to Diana Murphy, the daughter of a rich landowner and cattleman. The town was named in about 1892 and incorporated in 1906.

MORMON BAR

Mormon Bar, Mariposa County, was named because early settlers, ca. 1847–50, were members of the Mormon Church. The name has nothing to do with the dispensing of alcohol. The "bar" is a reference to a geographic feature.

MORONGO VALLEY

Morongo Valley assumed the name of the area in which it is located. The valley takes the name of a Shoshonean village. The word *maronga* translates to "largest."

When the community went for a post office in 1947, the name selected was Morongo. Later it was expanded to Morongo Valley.

MORRO BAY

The name Morro, as found in the bay in San Luis Obispo County and the nearby town, is Spanish for "castle." The name was given because an outcropping of rock at the north of the bay resembled a castle. It juts out of the Pacific Ocean about 578 feet.

The bay was named for the rock; the San Luis Obispo County town, for the bay.

MOSS BEACH

Moss Beach, San Mateo County, was named for the appearance of a sea moss and other salt-water specimens found here.

MOSS LANDING

Unlike Moss Beach, Moss Landing was not named for a plant. It was named for Charles Moss, who built a wharf here in Monterey County in about 1865.

MOUNT BALDY

Mount Baldy, San Bernardino County, began its life as Camp Baldy. The name was changed in 1951, "upon petition of the residents."

MOUNT BULLION

An earlier name for the mining community of Mount Bullion was Princeton.

The town, located in Mariposa County, was named for the mountain on Frémont's Mariposa estate. That feature was named by the general for his father-in-law, Thomas Hart Benton (1782–1852). Benton, a strong proponent of hard-cash currency, was known as "Old Bullion."

The Mount Bullion post office opened in 1862.

MOUNT HEBRON

Mount Hebron was also named after a peak. The craggy Mount Hebron bears the name of an ancient town in Palestine.

The Siskiyou County community was settled before 1891.

MOUNT SHASTA

Mount Shasta is a small community named for a very large mountain. Not far from town is Lake Siskiyou, the only lake created by California solely for recreational purposes. It is also the place where those wonderful reflecting photographs of Mount Shasta are taken.

Mount Shasta was earlier known as Mount Shasta City and Sisson, after a pioneer storekeeper.

MOUNTAIN VIEW

Mountain View, located in the Santa Clara Valley, has a more than adequate view of the mountains.

MURPHYS

Located in Calaveras County, Murphys was founded by Daniel and John M. Murphy. They discovered placer gold on Angel's Creek in 1848.

The town that grew around the camp was originally called Murphy's Diggings, then Murphy's Camp and finally Murphys. Several of the mining era buildings, including the Murphys Hotel, still stand. The hotel, opened in 1856 as the Sperry & Perry, has a guest register that lists such notables as Horatio Alger and Ulysses S. Grant. Both men visited the area to stand in awe of the giant sequoias in nearby Calaveras Big Trees State Park.

Bret Harte wrote about Murphys, but he called it Wingdam. Joaquin Murieta began his violent career here. Before his death and decapitation, Murieta was responsible for the death of no less than three hundred people.

MURRIETA (— Hot Springs)

Murrieta, Riverside County, was named, according to one source, for the owner of the land on which the town was built, a John Murrieta. Another source suggests the name came from that of a famous bandit, Joaquin Murieta. Joaquin was a Mexican bandit of the worst possible type. Along with his lieutenant, "Three-fingered Jack," he terrorized California from 1851 to 1853. The two renegades were killed in an attack by a company of rangers, led by Captain Harry Love. Following his death, Murieta's head was cut off and exhibited through the state. It stayed on display in Doctor Jordan's Museum in San Francisco until 1906, when it was destroyed in the earthquake.

Murieta's reputation has been transmogrified by Hollywood; it made him into the image of a California version of Robin Hood.

The real name donor was the ranchowner, who was, for many years, the bookkeeper in the sheriff's office. The Murrieta post office was opened in 1885.

MYERS FLAT

Myers Flat, Humboldt County, was simply Myers when it began. Named for the Grant Myers Ranch, the community was renamed in 1949, when the post office was established. The addition of "flat" was to avoid confusion with another Myers in El Dorado County.

NAPA

Napa, Napa County, takes the name of its county which, in turn, was named for the valley. *Napa* is an Indian word meaning "city" or "house." Another source suggests the name means "fish," a reference to the inhabitants of the river. Still others come up with "grizzly bear." The final, most plausible answer comes from Mariano Vallejo's son who learned the Suisun Indian language. He said the name meant "near mother," "near home" or "motherland."

The Napa Valley, known today for its quality wine production, began in the mid-19th century during the gold rush. The original vines were grown from cuttings brought here by priests from the missions at Sonoma and San Rafael.

NATIONAL CITY

When California was still part of Mexico, the site of this town was on part of the land occupied by Rancho de la Nacion. The ranch, owned by Frank, Warren and Levi Kimball, was called National Ranch in 1868. Three years later, the community became known as National City.

Though that is what the gringos called it, the Mexican name of Nacion still appeared on the Santa Fe railroad station here in San Diego County until the late 19th century.

NAVARRO

The name for this town came from the small Navarro River. Most probably, the waterway took its name from that of an early family, though some like to suggest some connection with the Spanish province of Navarra.

The Navarro River's name appears as early as 1862. This Mendocino County town had its name changed from Wendling to Navarro in 1914, when the post office made the official change.

NEEDLES

The town of Needles, San Bernardino County, was founded in 1833 when the Atlantic & Pacific Railroad built toward the west and met the Southern Pacific coming from the east toward Los Angeles. They met at Needles, on the Arizona side of the Colorado River. Later that year, the railroad transferred the name to the California side. Another source lists settlement as late as 1882.

The town's name, originally The Needles, was drawn from the sharp mountain peaks nearby. The name was later shortened.

NEVADA CITY

The seat of Nevada County, Nevada City has been a center for gold-mining since the mid-19th century. Since its founding, the county has produced more than half of California's gold production. The town was laid out in 1849, yet a year later it was only a motley collection of tents and brush huts.

Both the county and the city took their names from the Nevada Mountains. The name is Spanish for "snowed upon, snowy." In the fall of 1849, a prospector named the place Deer Creek Dry Diggings. Later it became Caldwell's Upper Store, for Dr. A. B. Caldwell, who set up a business here in the same year. The name Nevada was suggested by O. P. Blackman in 1851 when the place was incorporated as the City of Nevada. A post office is listed under that name in the same year.

The city is one of the best preserved mining towns in Northern California. When the town was devastated by fire in 1851, it was rebuilt with brick! The Nevada Theater, Broad Street, was built in 1865. It is California's oldest theater in continuous use.

NEWARK

This Alameda County site was named by the South Pacific Coast Railroad Company in 1876 for the New Jersey home of A. E. Davis.

NEWBERRY SPRINGS

The Southern Pacific Railroad named its station in Newberry, San Bernardino County, in 1883. In 1919, the name was changed to

Water, since the natural springs hereabouts supplied all the water they needed. The name Newberry was restored in 1822. Later the "springs" was added.

NEWBURY PARK
Formerly the Conejo Postoffice, this Ventura County spot had its name changed to Newbury Park in 1875. E. S. Newbury was its postmaster.

NEWCASTLE
Newcastle is not a "coal town" as its name might suggest. It is a fruit shipping point. The Placer County community had its Central Pacific Railroad station name placed on it in 1864. The name came from an old mining community. One source thinks the name was derived from a similarly-named place in the eastern United States.

The Newcastle post office was listed in 1867.

NEWELL
During World War II, Newell, Modoc County, was a Japanese relocation center. The name honored Frederick H. Newell. Newell was the first chief engineer of the U.S. Reclamation Service.

NEW IDRIA
New Idria was named for the quicksilver center in Carniola.

NEWMAN
The dairying community of Newman in Stanislaus County was established in 1887 when the Southern Pacific reached here. The name came from Simon Newman who donated the land for the railroad's right-of-way.

NEWPORT BEACH
Newport Beach, Orange County, is made up of Balboa, Balboa Island, Lido Isle, Corona del Mar, Newport Heights, Harbor Island, Bay Shores, and Linda Isle.

Some people like to think of the area as Beverly Hills-by-the-sea because of its yacht and country clubs.

Newport Beach began in 1873 when the McFadden brothers established a lumber business here. Three years later, they named their steamer *Newport* and, in 1892, they had the community platted as a beach resort. Townlots here were not sold, only leased. Finally the land was sold to W. S. Collins and his partners. In 1904, they filed for a subdivision to be called Newport Beach.

NICASIO

According to local tradition, this town was named for an Indian chief who selected a Spanish name at the time of his baptism.

Nicasio, Marin County, was settled in 1852 by Noah Corey. The Nicasio post office was established in 1870.

NICE

Nice (pronounced NEECE) was named for the French city of Nice. That city is located in the Califonie District of France. The namers thought the Lake County town's topography resembled that of the Mediterranean.

The town's original name was Clear Lake Villas, but the residents changed the name in 1927 or 1928 for the French city.

NICOLAUS

Nicolaus, located on the lower Feather River in Sutter County, was named for Nicholaus Allgeier. A native of Germany, Allgeier came to California in 1840. Two years later, he received a tract from Sutter, where he built a hut and operated a ferry.

The early name for his settlement was Nicholaus' Ranche or Nicholas Ferry. The post office maintained the correct spelling of his name as early as 1851.

NILAND

The name for Niland, Imperial County, is a contraction of Nile Land. The name was selected in 1916 by the Imperial Farm Lands Association because the area was quite fertile.

When the Southern Pacific branched into the Imperial Valley here, the company named the station Old Beach. From 1905 to 1916, it was Imperial Junction.

NIPINNAWASEE

Nipinnawasee, Madera County, was named in about 1908. Locally the name is supposed to mean "plenty of deer."

The name came from Michigan with Edgar B. Landon. He gave the name to the settlement in 1908, and in 1915 the name was accepted by postal authorities.

NIPOMO

Nipomo, San Luis Obispo County, was laid out in 1899 on Rancho Nipomo, a 38,000-acre ranch owned by William Goodwin Dana. Dana was from Boston and a cousin of author Richard Henry Dana, Jr. The adobe ranch house, built in 1839, is still standing.

Nipomo was a major stopping spot on El Camino Real between the missions at San Luis Obispo and Santa Barbara.

The town's name was originally the name of a Chumash Indian rancheria.

NIPTON

Tradition has it that Nipton, San Bernardino County, received the name of one of the survey engineers who helped build the San Pedro, Los Angeles & Salt Lake Railroad in 1904. Sadly, a 1905 railroad map showed the station as Nippen. The present name did not surface until 1910.

NORCO

The name for this Riverside County town came from the North Corona Land Company. Rex B. Clark is credited with coining the name in 1922.

NORD

Nord, Butte County, was laid out by G. W. Colby in 1871. It was named Nord by his wife. The word is German for "north."

NORDHOFF

This Ventura County community was named for journalist Charles Nordhoff (1830–1901). He devoted a great deal of his writing to the promotion of California, many times at the request of the railroads. His grandfather, Charles B. Nordhoff, was coauthor of *Mutiny on the Bounty.*

NORTH FORK

North Fork came into existence in 1878 and was named because of its location. It is located on the North Fork of the San Joaquin River in Madera County.

The post office was established here in 1888, as a single word.

NORTH RIDGE

The Southern Pacific Railroad arrived here in 1908 when its San Fernando branch line was extended. At that time, this Los Angeles

County site was known as Zelzah. It had the biblical name because that is what it was: "a watering place in the desert."

The name was changed in 1933 to North Los Angeles. Two years later, it became Northridge. Carl S. Dentzel is credited with suggesting the name. He did not have to be too creative: The town is located near the base of the San Fernando Valley's northern ridge.

NORTH SAN JUAN

After he discovered rich gold deposits here in Nevada County in 1853, Christian Kientz named the area San Juan Hill. A veteran of the Mexican War, he thought the hill's shape was quite similar to that of San Juan de Ulloa in Mexico. The settlement that grew around it was known as San Juan.

In 1857, when the post office was established, "North" was added to the name to distinguish it from another San Juan in Benito County.

NORWALK

The original settlers to this Los Angeles County location were Atwood and Gilbert Sproul. They arrived in 1877 and called the place Corvallis, after their former home in Oregon.

Two years later, when the post office was established, the name was changed to Norwalk, after the town in Massachusetts. Some of the other settlers came from there.

NOVATO

Novato, Marin County, is located north of San Francisco. Though its name translates from the Spanish to mean "new," the town was actually named for a chief of the Coast Miwok tribe. The chief assumed a Spanish name at the time of his baptism.

The name was mentioned as early as 1828, designating the place where the cattle for Mission San Rafael grazed. The Novato name was applied to a land grant in 1836, and 20 years later to the post office.

NOYO

The name for this Mendocino County community came from that of the river. The waterway, we are told, bears the name of a Northern Pomo Indian village. That might be the easiest part of the story.

The stream was called No'-yo-bida by the Indians, but the name was appropriated by the Coast Survey, and it was moved to another river south of Fort Bragg.

NUBIEBER

Nubieber, Lassen County, is New Bieber—the railroad's phonetic spelling for the station.

Extensions of the Great Northern and Western Pacific railroads met at this location in 1931. The railroad just called it "New Town." Later, the name "Big Valley City" was suggested, but that was shot down by postal officials. L. H. Martin, from the Bieber Chamber of Commerce, suggested the name New Bieber.

NUEVO

Located in Riverside County, this town's name is Spanish for "new" or "modern." It was so named in 1916, at which time it was new.

OAKDALE

Oakdale, Stanislaus County, took its name from the live oaks nearby. The town came into existence when the Copperopolis & Visalia Railroad reached this point in 1871.

O

OAKLAND

Oakland, Alameda County, was Bret Harte's boyhood home and the hangout for Jack London. In fact, the port area is now known as Jack London Square. The Last Chance Saloon, located on Webster Street, was one of the author's favorite haunts.

At the time of settlement, the site was known as an *encinal*, "an oak grove." The town was laid out by Julius Kellersberger in 1850, for Horace W. Carpertier, Edson Adams and Andrew J. Moon. At the time of incorporation two years later, the town fathers took the description of the fine stand of oak trees and made it their own.

Gertrude Stein was raised in Oakland, but left. "The trouble with Oakland," she said, "is there is no there."

OAKLEY

Oakley, Contra Costa County, was settled in the late 19th century and named by R. C. Marsh. Marsh, who became the town's first postmaster in 1898, named it for the proliferation of native oak trees. He added the Old English suffix, *ley,* for "field."

OAKVILLE

Oakville, Napa County, was named in the 1870s, after the railroad's Napa-Calistoga branch had been completed.

OASIS

Oasis, Mono County, was a fertile area in a desert region.

The name actually came from the Oasis Ranch, settled in 1864 by N. T. and Samuel Piper. The ranch was quite productive.

O'BRIEN

This Shasta County community was named for the creek and the mountain. Both geographic features honored Con O'Brien, owner of the old Conner Hotel on the Sacramenton-Yreka road in 1873.

OCCIDENTAL

The word "Occidental" is usually used to differentiate Eastern, or "Oriental," from Western. This Sonoma County town is located not far from the Pacific Ocean . . . about as far west as you can go in the Continental United States.

The name actually came from a church, not from the town's location. A Methodist church was built here in 1876, on land donated by M. C. Meeker. He also laid out the town.

The Occidental post office was established here in the same year as the church. The name is quite unique. There is no other Occidental in the United States.

OCEAN BEACH

Ocean Beach is just that. Located in San Diego County, the town was laid out by William H. Carlson and Albert E. Higgins in 1888. They also gave it the name.

OCEANO

Oceano, San Luis Obispo County, bears a Spanish name, which was derived from the site's location near the Pacific Ocean.

OCEANSIDE

Oceanside, San Diego County, is situated at the mouth of the San Luis Rey Valley with more than 3½ miles of beach on the Pacific Ocean. The town was founded in 1883 and named by J. C. Hayes.

Near Oceanside is Camp Pendleton, the U. S. Marine Corp's amphibious training camp. About four miles east is the Mission San Luis Rey de Francia. This mission was the 18th in the chain of missions, and the largest.

Mission San Luis Rey was founded in 1798 by Father Fermin de Lasuen, and it was named for Louis IX, King of France.

OCOTILLO (— Wells)

Ocotillo, San Diego County, took the name of a desert plant, *Fouquiria splendens.* The post office was established under this name in 1957.

OJAI

Ojai, Ventura County, is located in a valley by the same name, enclosed by mountains. One authority thinks the name is Indian for "nest." Another feels it is Chumash Indian for "moon." Since Ojai was earlier the name of an Indian village, it seems logical that the first definition is more on target.

The town was laid out by R. G. Surdam in 1874. He named it for Charles Nordhoff (See NORDHOFF, California.). In 1916, the town was renamed for the valley.

Frank Capra used the Ojai Valley as the setting for his 1936 classic, *Lost Horizon.* Nearby Lake Casitas was the site of the 1984 Olympic rowing events.

OLANCHA

Olancha is located at the southern end of Owens Lake. The name came from an Indian tribe that resided on the lake's shore west of Olancha Peak.

OLD STATION

Located in Shasta County, Old Station was just that: an old station. After the Hat Creek stage station and the military post were closed down in 1858, the remaining townspeople referred to it as the "old station."

OLEMA

Olema's name came from that of the creek. The waterway took the name from an Indian tribal one. Some suspect the name is associated with the Miwok Indian word for "coyote."

The name appeared as early as 1802, as Olemos and Olemus. The Olema post office opened its doors in 1859, but the Olema station of the Wells Fargo Company was called Point Reyes.

OLIVE

Franciscan priests introduced the olive tree to California with seed from Mexico.

The olive trees on nearby Burruell Point were in abundance when this Orange County town, named Olive Heights, was laid out in 1880. Postal authorities reduced the name in 1890 when the first post office opened.

OLIVEHURST

Yuba County. (See OLIVE, California.)

OLYMPIC VALLEY

The name Olympic Valley replaced that of Squaw Village, Placer County, in 1960. The name was changed in anticipation of the Winter Olympic Games here at Squaw Valley.

O'NEALS

Located in Madera County, O'Neals was named for an early settler, Charles O'Neal. Better yet, it took the name of his hotel. The post office was established here, probably in the hotel, in 1887.

ONO

When the post office asked the townspeople of Eagle Creek, Shasta County, to change their community's name, a Baptist minister stepped forward. The Reverend William S. Kidder suggested the Biblical name of Ono. The town's name is mentioned only once (I Chron. 8:12). Ono was approved in 1882.

ONTARIO

George B. Chaffey named this San Bernardino County town Ontario in 1882, for his home province in Canada.

ONYX

This name was selected because the post office considered it short and unique . . . and absent from the Postal Guide.

Located in Kern County, the town was first known as Scodie's Store, as early as 1860. When the post office was established 30 years later, the Scodie name was rejected because it sounded too much like Scotia.

ORANGE (— Cove)

With payment in 1869 from a client of 1,300 acres in lieu of cash, two lawyers, Glasell and Chapman, planned the city of Orange. They first called it Richland, an appropriate title considering the circumstances, but that name was rejected by postal officials who cited the existence of another Richland. Orange was then agreed upon—after all, it was part of Orange County.

ORCUTT

Orcutt was laid out in Santa Barbara County by the Union Oil Company in 1803. The town was named for the company's geologist, W. W. Orcutt.

OREGON HOUSE

Oregon House, Yuba County, was named by gold-seeking miners who came here from Oregon State.

ORICK

The name of this Humboldt County town may have been transported from a village name in the Yukon territory. More likely, the name was local.

The Indians of Redwood Creek, we are told, were "termed Oruk by the Coast Indians." A Yurok Indian village, Ore-q was located near the site of the present-day town.

ORINDA (— Village)

No one is quite sure how this Contra Costa County name came to be. Some suspect the name has an *oro*, "gold," sound to it. Anything that had to do with gold was popular in California naming. Another authority, however, suggests that the name was coined in the 16th century and was quite popular in 17th century England when they called the poet Katherine Fowler Philips "the matchless Orinda." No offense to the poet, but the first explanation sounds more logical.

Theodore Wagner, the U.S. Surveyor General for California in 1880, named his estate Orinda Park. About eight years later, a post office was established there under that name. The post office name was transferred from the Wagner estate in 1895 to what became Orinda Village. By 1945, the name had moved to the "cross roads," formerly known as Bryant.

ORLAND

Some authorities feel that this Glenn County community's name migrated from Maine. Another source contends that the name is a shortening of "orange-land," since citrus is big business here.

Local tradition, however, indicates the name was pulled from a hat and just happened to be the English birthplace of an early settler.

ORLEANS

Orleans, Humboldt County, was indirectly named for New Orleans, Louisiana. It was named for the New Orleans Bar! The town was an early gold camp, settled in 1850. The name was shortened from New Orleans Bar to Orleans Bar in 1855. The present form went into effect four years later.

ORO GRANDE

The name of this San Bernardino County community is Spanish for "fine gold," though another source thinks the name means "coarse gold." Interestingly enough, it could be either.

The name goes back to a gold-mining camp of 1878. The town was established four years later, but called Halleck. In 1925, the name of both post office and town was changed to Oro Grande, after the Oro Grande mine which was still in operation.

OROSI

Orosi, Tulare County, took the first part of its name from the Spanish for "gold." The second part could be Spanish for "yes." Others think it might be the English word "see."

The town was founded in 1880 by Daniel R. Shafer and his partners. The name, they suggested, came from Neal McAllan, who saw fields of golden poppies around the townsite. The post office for Orosi opened in 1892.

OROVILLE

Cherokee Indians migrated to this Butte County location in the mid-19th century to work in the gold mines north of town. The town of Oroville, "gold town," was so named because of the nearby gold mines. The town was settled in 1849 by Colonel John Tatam and a group of miners. The town became known as Ophir City, an analogy to the gold land mentioned in the Old Testament. When the post office opened six years later, the name had to be changed and Judge J. M. Burt coined the name that is in use today.

Diamonds were discovered in the hills, and the Cherokee Diamond Mine opened in 1873. After producing about three hundred industrial-quality diamonds, the mine closed. All that is left of Cherokee is a ghost town.

OTAY

Located in San Diego County, Otay's name came from an Indian rancheria. The name translates from Diegueno Indian as "brushy." The post office at Otay was listed in 1871.

OWENYO

This Inyo County town's name is a combination of Owen and Inyo. The name was coined by some clever minion of the Carson & Colorado Railroad in 1905. When the extension to Mojave was built five years later, the station was moved here and called New Owenyo. The prefix was dropped the next year. The community is located near Owens Lake.

OXNARD (— Beach)

Oxnard, Ventura County, was named for Henry T. Oxnard by the Southern Pacific Railroad in the late 19th century. Oxnard built a beet-sugar refinery here in 1897.

PACIFICA

In 1957, the residents of the San Mateo County communities of Edgemar, Fairway Park, Linda Mar, Pacific Manor, Pedro Point, Rockaway Beach, Sharp Park, Vallemar, and Westview voted to incorporate as the city of Pacifica. The name is an obvious reference to their location by the ocean.

PACIFIC (— Beach; — Grove; — House; — Palisades)

Pacific Grove, Monterey County, originated with the Pacific Grove Retreat Association. The group incorporated in 1875 as a "Christian Seaside Resort and Camp Meeting Ground," based on the example of Ocean Grove, New Jersey. The Southern Pacific Railroad promoted the attraction by calling it "the great Family Resort of the Pacific Coast within the means of all . . . a home and a haven for the gentle, the refined, the cultured, where arousing and dissipation are unknown."

The Point Piños Lighthouse, in operation since 1855, is located at Pacific Grove. Pacific Grove was also home to John Steinbeck's grandparents. A museum in his honor is located here and open to the public.

Pacific Palisades, Los Angeles County, took its name from the steep bluffs that overlook the beaches. The town was founded in 1921 by a Methodist church group. The post office was established in 1924.

The name for this San Diego County community was selected in 1887 when the town was established by the San Diego College of Letters. The college did not last long.

PAICINES

Paicines was the name of a Costanoan Indian village. Noted desperado, Tiburci Vasquez, and his men raided this town in the 1870s in typical Wild West fashion.

The post office in this San Benito County area was established before 1880 and named for the Rancho Cienega de los Paicines, granted in 1842. The Indian village was noted as Paisi-n. The Spanish *cienega* means "marsh."

PAJARA

Pajara took its name from the river, which was drawn from an experience of the 1769 Portola Expedition. Members of that group found a dead bird that some Indian had stuffed with straw and left behind. *Pajara* is Spanish for "bird."

By 1868, Pajara was referred to as a "considerable" town.

PALA

Pala, San Diego County, took its name from the Mission San Antonio de Pala. Originally designed as a branch of the Mission San Luis Rey de Francis, its first building, constructed in 1810, was the grannary.

Mission San Antonio was projected as the second line of inland missions, but the idea was rejected. Though the name reflects St. Anthony's home, it is Spanish and, ironically, describes a wooden shovel used for shoveling grain. Another source thinks the word is Luiseno Indian and means "water."

PALERMO

Palermo's name came from the Sicilian town of the same name.

In 1887, the name was selected because the climate here in Butte County was conducive to olive growing—just like in Italy.

PALMDALE

Located in Los Angeles County, Palmdale was named for the growth of what people thought were palm trees. The tree was actually a Joshua tree, sometimes called a yucca palm.

German Lutherans settled this town in 1886 and called it Palmenthal. A post office was established under that name in 1888. Two years later the name was changed to Palmdale.

PALM SPRINGS

One of the most fashionable resorts in California, Palm Springs is located in the upper Colorado Desert at the foot of the 10,804-foot San Jacinto Peak in Riverside County. Its mineral springs have drawn visitors ever since they were discovered. Today it is one of the best examples of conspicuous consumption in the United States.

The town became Palm Springs in 1890 when the post office was opened. Formerly, it had been known as Palmetto Springs, Big Palm Spring and Agua Caliente. Except for the "hot water" name, all the former names refer to the palm trees which were the source of the current name. Palm Springs became the official name in 1890. It almost was Agua Caliente, but there already was a town by that name, so postal officials went for Palm Springs. One can only wonder if the place would have been as popular with the "hot water" name.

Entertainer Bob Hope is honorary mayor of Palm Springs, and he is only one of many celebrities who frequent the town. Stars began to arrive at Palm Springs in 1930, when Charlie Farrell and Ralph Belamy bought 200 acres—at $30 an acre! That was the beginning of the Palm Springs Raquet Club. Nearby Tahquitz Canyon was used in the original film production of *Lost Horizon* as Shangri La.

PALO ALTO

Palo Alto, Santa Clara County, took its name from a double-trunked redwood tree that was used as a landmark for travelers and explorers as early as 1769. The name translates from the Spanish for "high timber" or "tall tree."

The tree is recalled in the corporate seal of Stanford University, founded on the Stanford Farm in 1885, as the Leland Stanford Junior University. The main buildings of the university were defined by Frederick Law Olmstead.

Leland Stanford Sr. (1824–93) named the university in honor of his son, who died of typhoid fever at the age of 16. The father was the first Republican governor of California, holding office during the Civil War. He later went on to the United States Senate.

Another source suggests that a "palo alto" was a hat that was quite popular with gold rush miners.

STANFORD. A. Leland Stanford founded Stanford University in 1885 and named it for his son who had died at a young age. The elder Stanford was a multi-millionaire who financed and built the Central Pacific Railroad, served as California's governor and as a U.S. senator. (Stanford University News Service)

PALO CEDRO

The townsite at this Shasta County location was laid out in 1891. The Spanish name, meaning "cedar timber," was given because of a cedar tree on the property.

A post office was established in this name in 1893, but as a single word.

PALOMAR MOUNTAIN

The most famous resident of this San Diego County community is the Palomar Observatory, home to a 200-inch telescope. The name translates from the Spanish to mean the "place frequented by the doves."

PALO VERDES (— Estates)

Palo Verdes, a posh community in Los Angeles County, is located on the Palo Verdes Peninsula and took its name from the jutting of land. *Palo verdes* is Spanish for "green timber."

The town is situated on a Spanish land grant originally given to the Sepulveda family.

PANAMINT SPRINGS

This name was derived from an Indian tribe, a branch of the Shoshonean Indians.

PANOCHE

Panocha was a sweet delicacy made from reeds and wild fruit. Originated by the Indians, it was adopted by the Mexican-Spanish settlers. The name indicates some event that involved panocha.

PARADISE

When the first store opened here in 1873, storekeeper Bill Anderson knew the town as Paradise Prairie. Local tradition has it that this Wise County community was named for the beautiful flowers that once graced the area. As usual, the post office streamlined the name at a later date.

PARAISO SPRINGS

Paraiso Springs, Monterey County, took the Spanish form of "paradise." The name was given by missionaries who were granted 20 acres of land in 1791. They called it their "earthly paradise."

PARAMOUNT

This town was named for its main boulevard which, in turn, was named for the film company. The Los Angeles county town was formed by the 1948 merger of the cities of Hynes and Clearwater. The president of the local Kiwanis Club suggested the name.

PARKER DAM

A branch of the Santa Fe Railroad was built between 1905 and 1907. The new station in Arizona was called Parker, for Earl H. Parker, the railroad's location engineer, and also for the Indian village of Parker that was nearby.

When a dam was proposed to shift water into Arizona from this San Bernardino County area, the name was changed to Parker Dam. The post office was listed in 1936.

PARKFIELD

Townspeople at this Monterey County location wanted to name their community Russelsville, but postal authorities would have none of it. Finally, in 1883, the local postmaster selected this name because of the natural park of oak trees that surrounded the area.

PARLIER

Parlier, Fresno County, took its name in 1898 from the town's first postmaster, I. N. Parlier. He settled here in 1876.

PASADENA

Pasadena carries the Indian name for "crown of the valley." Home of the California Institute of Technology (Cal Tech), Pasadena also

PASADENA. The Elks entry of "I Love a Parade." (Pasadena Tournament of Roses)

hosts the famous Parade of the Roses each New Year's Day before the Rose Bowl Game.

The Los Angeles County community was settled in 1874 by a group that came from Indiana. At first they called their settlement Indiana Colony. The choice of a permanent name for this community—and for the post office—was, however, an involved affair.

In 1885, the townspeople were looking for an Indian name that would be suitable to the geographic location. Since no Indians were native to this particular area, Dr. T. B. Elliott requested a missionary to the Chippewas to come up with a name. The instructions were that the name should translate to "Crown of the Valley" or "Key of the Ranch."

The missionary came up with four long names, all ending in "Pa sa de na," his idea of "in the valley." Dr. Elliott accepted the last four syllables and presented Pasadena as the name. Poor Elliott! The etymology of the Chippewa word comes out to something different, such as "space formed by intersecting a range of hills or mountains." Another source says the word more likely means "valley town."

Direct train connections opened up in 1881 and so did the tourism business. Pasadena so impressed one Boston travel agent that the agency selected Pasadena, not Los Angeles, as its customers' stopping place.

PASKENTA

The name for this Tehama County village came from the Wintu Indian, *paskentic,* for "under the bank." A post office was established under that name at this location in 1872.

PASO ROBLES

The original name of this San Luis Obispo County community was El Paso de Robles, Spanish for "passage through the oaks." The city was founded as a rancho in 1886 and was incorporated three years later with the name Paso de Robles. Of course, for postal reasons, the name was reduced.

The springs here were thought to be helpful for internal and external uses.

PATRICK CREEK

Patrick Point was the first place in Humboldt County to honor Patrick Beegan. In 1851, Beegan claimed the land through which the Patrick Creek flows and where this community is located. The community grew on Patrick's Ranch.

PATTERSON

Patterson resides on a part of the old Spanish grant of Rancho del Puerto. The land was purchased by John D. Patterson in 1864. About 1910, his nephew Thomas W. Patterson, a banker from Fresno, laid out the town and honored his uncle with the name.

PAUMA VALLEY

The name of the San Diego County valley came from a Luiseno Indian village—Poteros de Paoma, mentioned in 1841. The word, according to some linguists, has something to do with water.

The land grant was issued in 1844 as Pauma or Potrero de Pauma.

PAXTON

The earlier name of Paxton, Plumas County, was Soda Bar, because of the local mineral springs.

A post office was established here in 1917 and named for the general manager of the Indian Valley Railroad and the Engel Mining Company, Elmer E. Paxton.

PAYNES CREEK

Paynes Creek, Tehama County, is another case of mistaken identity. The name of the settlement was listed in a newspaper directory in 1878, but it was apparently named after Paines Creek.

The Paynes Creek post office was established in 1879.

PEANUT

In 1898, the original postmaster of this Trinity County place presented this name. Postmaster A. L. Paulsen gave three reasons for it. First, the name was unique; second, he liked peanuts; and finally, he ate them all the time. The Peanut name was ensconced by 1900.

The townspeople had gone to him with a completely different idea. They wanted to change the name from Cuff's Store to that of Cuff's wife.

PEARBLOSSOM

In 1924, Guy C. Chase named this Los Angeles County location Pearblossom because it was a center of pear orchards. The name continued, even though blight killed the pears and were replaced with peaches.

PEBBLE BEACH

The name, Pebble Beach, was descriptive. The Pacific Improvement Company kept that name when it acquired the site in 1880. The post office also took that name in 1810.

This Monterey County town is not as well known as its golf course.

PEDLEY

The most logical choice for the name source of this Riverside County community is Francis X. Pedley. A native of England, Pedley came to California in 1882 and to Riverside County in 1894. The name arrived with the railroad station in 1905.

PEPPERWOOD

Pepperwood is the name the locals gave to the California laurel. When the post office was established at this Humboldt County site in 1900, it was named for a grove of pepperwoods.

PERRIS

Perris, Riverside County, carries the name of the chief engineer of the California Southern Railroad and a founder of the town, Fred T. Perris.

The town was laid out in 1886.

PESCADERO

Pescadero, San Mateo County, took its name from the stream of the same name. The Spanish has been translated to mean either "fishmonger," "small fish" or "fishing place." The last name seems appropriate, since the town itself was a fishing town.

In fact, in 1861, a pioneer stated that "the Pescadero draws its name from the fact of our catching salmon there" in 1814.

The town was settled in the mid-19th century by Spanish speakers.

PETALUMA

Located in Sonoma County, Petaluma took its name from the Petaluma River. The river's name was taken from an Indian word for "duck pond." Another source contends that the word is Coast Miwok Indian and means "flat back." In fact, there was an Indian village by that name east of the waterway.

The area was originally a hunter's camp on the river, but it grew quickly when frustrated gold miners/dreamers returned to reality and tried to make a living hunting and fishing here.

The headquarters of one the richest and most powerful men in California—General Mariano Guadalupe Vallejo—, Rancho Petalum is located a few miles east of town. The building was constructed by the owner's brother between 1835 and 1844. The actual town was laid out in 1851, and a post office was established by that name the next year.

The region around Petaluma was used, although disguised, by Gertrude Atherton in her novel, *Ancestors.*

PETROLIA

Petroleo is Spanish for "petroleum." Most authorities believe this name signifies "where petroleum was found." And right they are!

This Humboldt County area was the place where a U.S. Army officer discovered the first California oil deposits to be exploited commercially. Reports of the discovery appeared in 1861, and the first shipment of oil left San Francisco four years later. The first post office opened in 1865 using the name, spelled Petrolea.

PHELAN

Senator James D. Phelan used his vast influence to get a post office established at this San Bernardino County location. The result was the Phelan post office that opened in 1916.

PHILLIPSVILLE

Phillipsville, Humboldt County, was named for an early settler, George Stump Phillips. He settled here about 1865, and the community became known as Phillips Flat. The Indians, on the other hand, called it Kettintelbe.

In 1883, the name was changed for postal reasons to Phillipsville. That name was changed to the Indian name. In 1948, Phillipsville returned in triumph!

PHILO

This Mendocino County community was named by Cornelius Prather, landowner and postmaster, in about 1868. He named it for his favorite cousin, Philomena.

PICO RIVERA

In 1958, the Los Angeles County towns of Pico and Rivera incorporated under the merged name. The post offices did not. They remained separate at the time of incorporation.

PIEDMONT

This Alameda County town is situated at the foot of the Berkeley Hills. The name comes from the French *pied*, "foot," and *mont*, "mountain." It is a municipality completely surrounded by Oakland.

The residential part of Piedmont began in 1900; the post office, in 1904.

PIEDRA

Located in Fresno County, Piedra took its name from the Spanish for "stone." In America, stone meant "rock." In 1911, the Santa Fe built a spur line to carry rock from a quarry. They named the station Piedra.

PIERCY

When the name was given to this Mendocino County locale in 1920, the honor went to Sam Piercy. Piercy was the oldest white settler of the district.

PILOT HILL

Pilot Hill took its name from the elevation between the Middle and South forks of the American River. The word "pilot" was used in the navigational sense. Located in El Dorado County, the town was a mining camp as early as 1849. By 1854, it had a post office.

PINE (—crest; —dale; — Grove; — Ridge; — Valley)

The several Pine-named towns, Pinecrest, Tuolumne County, Pinedale, Fresno County, Pine Grove, Amador County, Pine Ridge, Fresno County, and Pine Valley, San Diego County, were all named after the tree. There are almost 20 different varieties of pine in California.

PINOLE

Located in Contra Costa County, Pinole's name is taken from the Mexican-Spanish for a meal ground of corn or seeds. In Spanish the word means "parched corn."

The post office was established here in the 1870s.

PIRU

The name for this Ventura County community came from the Shoshonean *pi'idhu-ku,* which was the name of a plant. A place is mentioned under the name as early as 1817. Various spellings of the name followed over the years.

By 1850, and the American years, the name was spelled Piro; Rio Peru, four years later. The town was laid out in 1888 and called Piru City, after the Piru ranch of Chicago publisher David C. Cook.

PISMO BEACH

Pismo Beach is best known for its namesake, the thick-shelled Pismo clam. Pismo originates from a local Indian word, *pismu,* meaning "tar."

The name of the San Luis Obispo County site came from the 1840 Pismo land grant on which it was built. The "beach" was added to the name after 1904.

PITTSBURG

In 1863, coal was discovered near Mount Diablo, and this new Contra Costa County settlement was named Black Diamond. The coal proved inferior, and salmon fishing became the major town occupation. The name was changed to Pittsburg, the "steel city" of the West. Unfortunately, someone beat the "h" out of the name. The Pennsylvania town's name is Pittsburgh!

PITTVILLE

This Lassen County site was established as a post office in 1878, and named after the river.

PIXLEY

The founder and editor of the San Francisco *Argonaut* was Frank Pixley. His name was given to this Tulare County community in the 1880s.

PLACENTIA

The name, we are told, was brought here from a well-known bay in Newfoundland. Some say it is ersatz Spanish for "pleasing place."

Mrs. Sarah J. McFadden named the school district in this Orange County area Placentia in 1884, after the Newfoundland town and bay. The community adopted that name as its own.

PLACERVILLE

In the mining area of Eldorado County, this town was the location where surface dirt was washed away to expose the valuable minerals. The word "placer" came from the Spanish *plaza*, which means "place." *Placer*, in Spanish, translates "to please" or "satisfaction."

The original name for the town was Old Dry Diggings, but that was a misnomer because the town became quite prosperous and quite lawless as well. Crimes took place so frequently that lawbreakers were executed singly, then in groups. The town then became known as Hangtown. In 1850, the name was finally changed to Placerville.

John M. Studebaker, known locally as "Wheelbarrow John," worked as a wheelwright at a local blacksmith shop. Along with his brothers, Clement and Henry, he acquired enough money to open his own factory and manufacture the Studebaker car. Mark Hopkins sold groceries, and another local, Philip Danforth Armour (1832–1901), the creator of Armour & Company, ran the butcher shop.

PLANADA

Planada's name came about through a lottery held in 1911. The word came from the Spanish for "plain," and it was selected as a descriptive name. The post office at this Merced County site was called Geneva, and the railroad was called Whitton.

PLANTATION

This particular town was named for a local inn or roadhouse—the Plantation House. The post office in this Sonoma County spot was established in 1900.

PLASTER CITY

The main office of the Portland Cement Company, later United States Gypsum, was located here. With the establishment of the post office in 1936, an appropriate name was given.

PLATINA

This town was named Platina because people suspected that the native alloy of platinum could be found here. Platina comes from *plata*, "silver." The post office opened under that name in 1921.

PLAYA DEL REY

Playa del Rey is Spanish for "beach (or playground) of the king."

.

This Los Angeles County site was named in 1902 for the failed Port Ballona project which touted itself as the "playground of the king."

PLEASANT GROVE

What a pretty name! It is head and shoulders above the previous name of this Sutter County site: Gouge Eye! The name was given in the 1860s with the establishment of the local post office.

PLEASANTON

This community carries the name of Alfred Pleasonton, a Civil War general. The Alameda County locale was named in 1867 by John W. Kottinger, who may have served with Pleasonton in the Mexican War.

The misspelling of the general's name was corrected with the establishment of the post office in 1867, but within a few years the townspeople went back to their old ways.

Located in the Amador Valley, Pleasanton was once the home of Mrs. Phebe Apperson Hearst. Her home was known as Hacienda del Pozo de Verona. It later became a country club.

PLYMOUTH

The Sobon Estate, located at Plymouth, was founded in 1856 by Adam Uhlinger, who dug the winery into a hill. It is one of the oldest wineries in California.

The Amador County community was developed on the site of an old gold-mining camp, called Puckerville or Pokerville. The post office, established in 1871, took on the name of the nearby Plymouth Mines which had begun 20 years earlier.

POINT ARENA

The Latin word *harena*, or "sand," and "point" give us a description of the location of this Mendocino County town. The town of Point Arena developed around a store that had been built here in 1859. When the post office was opened in 1867, the name was Punta Arenas.

Located here is the Point Arena Lighthouse. The original lighthouse was built in 1870, but it was destroyed by the San Francisco earthquake of 1906. It was rebuilt and provides a beautiful view of the sea.

POINT REYES STATION

This Marin County town was named for the point on which the lighthouse was built. The Spanish called it Punta des Reyes, "point of the kings."

Captain Francis Drake was supposed to have landed in the shelter of Point Reyes in 1579.

POMONA

This Los Angeles County city was named for the Roman goddess of fruit. The Latin *ponum* translates to "fruit." California State Polytechnic University is located here. The largest county fair in the United States, the Los Angeles County Fair, is held here annually.

Pomona was a new settlement in 1875, when the Los Angeles Immigration & Land Co-operative Association applied the name. The name had resulted from a contest that was held by the association. The winner was Solomon Gates, a nurseryman.

PONDOSA

Pondosa is the trade name for the ponderosa pine, *Pinus ponderosa.* The name was given at the time the post office opened here in 1926.

POPE VALLEY

No Vatican influence here. Pope Valley and Pope Creek, located in Napa County, bear the name of William (Julian) Pope. He was a member of the Pattie's 1828 party, and had received the Locoallomi grant in 1841.

POPLAR

This Tulare County town is one of the few places in California to bear this tree's name. Perhaps this lack is due to the fact that Californians call several species of poplars cottonwoods.

PORTA COSTA

Porta Costa was named because it was the "port" in Contra Costa County. The name was given in 1878 by the Southern Pacific Railroad. It was once a major grain shipping port.

PORTERVILLE

Royal Porter Moore—he preferred his middle name—operated a stage coach station at this Tulare County site in 1859. Then called

Porter's Station, the place's name changed when Moore opened a store as Porter's Trading Post or Porter's Store.

Business must have been good, because in 1867 he laid out the town and called it Portersville. By 1900, the "s" was lost.

PORTOLA (— Valley)

Portola was named for Gaspar de Portolà, leader of the 1769 Spanish expedition. Portolà explored the valley also, but the name was given long after his death.

Portolà has been described as having all the characteristics of a good leader.

POSEY

This Tulare County name, we are told, came from the Spanish *pozo* or *poso*, "well" or "waterhole." A post office bearing that name appeared in 1915.

POTRERO

This San Diego County community bears the Spanish word for "pasture." A very common feature in California, "potrero" never achieved the success in naming that "canyon" or "corral" did.

POTTER VALLEY

The first white settlers in the Chico region were William Potter and his brother. They moved to the Mendocino County valley that bears their name in 1853.

The Indian name for Potter Valley was Be-loh-kai, "leafy valley."

POWAY

While it is said that Poway's name came from a local Indian village, possibly meaning "end of the valley," in fact the name came from a rancho of Mission San Diego. The rancho was mentioned in 1828 as Paguay. The post office for this San Diego County location was listed in 1880.

POZO

The name of this San Luis Obispo County town came from the number of wells in the area. *Pozo* is Spanish for "wells."

PRATTVILLE

When first settled, this Plumas County community was named Big Meadows. That was before Dr. Willard Pratt established the first post office here in the 1870s.

PRINCETON

When the townspeople here in Colusa County were looking for a name for their post office in 1858, they turned to Dr. Almon Lull for advice. Dr. Lull was a graduate of Princeton University.

PROBERTA

Proberta was named in 1889 by the Southern Pacific Railroad for Robert Probert. The "a" was added for euphony.

PROJECT CITY

Project City, Shasta County, was founded in connection with the building of a dam as part of the Central Valley Project. The name was adopted in 1939.

PULGA

Pulga is Spanish for "flea." Named for an old gold-mining boom town, Pulga Bar, this town is located south of Flea Valley. The Spanish name does give some class to the name!

   The name of this Butte County community was given by the Western Pacific Railroad in 1907 when they built their line here.

PURISMA

Purisma comes from the Spanish for "most pure." The appelation is usually limited to the Immaculate Conception of Mary.

   This particular town in Santa Barbara County was so named because of a Spanish mission here dedicated to Mary. The stream on which the town is situated is also called Purisma Creek. The post office was established here in 1880.

Q QUAIL VALLEY

The quail is California's state bird, and there are more than 20 geographic features in the state that bear that avian name.

QUARTZ HILL

Quartz has always been important in California. Gold was often found in quartz deposits.

QUINCY

This Plumas County locale grew up around a hotel, built by H. J. Bradley in the mid-19th century. Bradley built the hotel on his American Ranch and, when the town became seat of the new county in 1854, he called it Quincy for his home town in Illinois. (See QUINCY, Oregon.)

RAINBOW

Rainbow takes its name from the Rainbow Mountain, so named because of the multi-colored vegetation on the rock.

R

RAISIN

When the post office opened in 1906 in this Fresno County location, it was named Raisin for the principal item produced here.

RAMONA

Ramona, San Diego County, was named in 1892 for a popular novel: *Ramona* by Helen Hunt Jackson (1830–85). The novel, set in romantic old California, caused quite a stir when it was published because it presented the American Indian in a very sympathetic role.

Though not as popular as *Ramona*, Jackson's previous book, *A Century of Dishonor,* forced the federal government to investigate the conditions of the Mission Indians.

RANCHO (— Bernardo; — California; — Cordova; — Cucamonga; — Mirage; — Palos Verdes; — Santa Fe)

"Rancho" was a designation used by Spanish-Americans to indicate a hut or a number of huts where laborers lived. In the early days, they were the farms of the missions, presidios and pueblos. A rancho of a presidio was referred to as a rancho del rey, and, in Mexican times, as a rancho nacional. In Mexico, a rancho was a small farm; in the southwestern United States, it came to mean a grazing land.

The name that followed the word "rancho" in these place names was a locator term. Not all these "rancho" places date back to the earlier days. Rancho Mirage, Riverside County, did not receive a post office designation until 1961.

Rancho Sante Fe was home to crooner Bing Crosby. The first Bing Crosby Pro-Am was held at the Rancho Sante Fe Golf Course, considered one of the finest courses in Southern California.

Rancho Sante Fe was part of the Osuna family grant from the King of Spain.

RANDSBURG
Gold was discovered in this area in 1894. This mining town was named—with very high expectations—for Witwatersrand, "The Rand," one of the richest mining districts in South Africa. This Kern County town grew in support of the Yellow Aster Mine.

Their hopes became reality and, three years later, the Sante Fe Railway built a line here. During a celebration for the arrival of the first locomotive, a dynamite explosion set several buildings on fire. A few months later, the rest of the town was destroyed. But, as local tradition has it, the miners stayed until the last scraps of gold, silver and tungsten were removed from the ground in the 1920s.

Randsburg is one of the few gold-mining towns that has not become a ghost town.

RAVENDALE
Ravendale, Lassen County, has a unique name. While there are numerous towns in the country that tie a "raven" into their names, this is the only Ravendale in the United States. A post office was listed here in 1910.

RAVENNA
This Los Angeles County community has a typical railroad name, one imported from the East.

RAYMOND
This Madera County town was named in honor of Raymond Whitcomb. He organized a tour company, Raymond-Whitcomb Yosemite Tours, which escorted tourists to Yosemite by stage coach from this point. The major industry for many years was granite mining.

RED BLUFF
One explanation is that when naming this city, the residents of this Tehama County site noted a reddish-colored high bank on the nearby Sacramento River. The Indians used the mineral, known to

them as cinnabar, to paint themselves. More likely, the name was taken from the old rancho south of town, Barranca Colorada, which translates to Red Bluff.

Located near Red Bluff is a memorial to William B. Ide, an 1850 adobe home that remembers Ide, the founder and first and only president of the California Republic.

In 1846, American settlers heard rumors that Mexican authorities were going to expel all Americans. Together with two dozen other settlers, Ide precipitated the Bear Flag Revolt. California became an independent country, with Ide as president. His term of office only lasted 26 days—until the Mexican War and occupation by American troops.

The family of famed abolitionist, John Brown, settled in Red Bluff following his execution.

REDDING

Redding, Shasta County, took its name from B. B. Redding, the land agent for the railroad when the town was laid out in 1872. According to one source, B. B. Redding was considered "one of the foremost nature-students on the Pacific coast. . . ."

The California legislature acted two years later to change the name to Reading (pronounced Redding) for Pierson B. Reading, a local pioneer. The railroad, however, did not change its name. The legislature relented in 1880 and returned the name to Redding. Redding showed his appreciation by donating a 245-pound bell to the local Presbyterian church.

Another source thinks the honor rests with a Major Redding, one of the earliest American pioneers in this area.

REDLANDS

Redlands is named for the color of its soil. Nearby is San Bernardino Asistencoa. Built as a branch of the San Gabriel Mission in 1830, it became part of a ranch a decade later. The buildings have been restored and are open to the public.

Redlands, San Bernardino County, grew after the California Southern opened a line here to connect with the Santa Fe in 1885. The town was platted two years later by E. G. Judson and Frank E. Brown.

REDONDO BEACH

Redondo Beach, located in Los Angeles County, took its name from the Rancho Sausal Redondo, Spanish for "round willow grove," even though the town is located on the lands of Ranch San Pedro!

The town was founded in 1881 and was incorporated 11 years later. The post office was established in 1889.

REDWOOD CITY

This San Mateo County community was named not so much because of the abundance of redwood trees, *Sequoia gigantea*, in the area, but more for their exploitation.

The trees from this area were felled to build the San Francisco of the early days. The first raft of redwood logs left here in 1850. The town, built almost entirely of wood, was almost demolished in a series of fires in 1850–51.

During the mid-19th century, the town's name was Mezesville, for S. M. Mezes, the landowner. The name was changed to Redwood City by 1860.

REEDLEY

When Thomas L. Reed donated land to the town in 1888, he did not want his name attached to it. After much compromise, he agreed to the addition of "-ley" to the name. The suffice is traditional English for "open country." Reed, by the way, accompanied Sherman on his march to the sea during the Civil War.

REQUA

Requa is Spanish for "request." Another source believes it to be an Indian tribal name, Re'kwoi, meaning "mouth of a creek." The Indian name for the Del Norte County town was Rech-wa, so it would appear that the current name is an adaptation of the Indian one.

RESEDA

Reseda is the botanical term for a plant of the mignonette family. The name was originally applied by the Southern Pacific Railroad to a station on the line from Burbank to Chatsworth in 1889. About 1920, the name was shunted to this place in Los Angeles County, originally a station of the Pacific Electric called Marion.

RHEEM VALLEY

Donald L. Rheem owned the property on the east slope of Mulholland Hill. He started a subdivision development in 1944.

RIALTO

According to one authority, this town's name came from Shakespeare's *The Merchant of Venice*, in which it described a place where businessmen congregate.

Rialto, San Bernardino County, was founded in 1887 by a group of Methodists from Halstead, Kansas. The name given was a contraction of Rivus Altus, the grand canal of Venice. To be accurate about the naming, no one can be quite certain whether the settlers picked a Shakespearean name or that of a Venetian canal.

Bolinas Bay and Bolinas Lagoon were listed as Rialto Cove in 1850.

RICE

Rice, San Bernardino County, was the name of the Parker branch of the Santa Fe Railroad sometime before 1919. The name was for Guy R. Rice, the chief engineer of the California Southern.

RICH BAR

At first called Rich Bar, then abbreviated to Rich and finally changed back, Rich Bar, Plumas County, was a thriving gold-mining town where gold could be "scooped up by the handful." As early as 1850, the miners were writing that one spot was "yielding not less than 50 dolls. worth pr day to each miner, and some had taken out 60 lbs. of gold in a day."

RICHGROVE

Richgrove, Tulare County, was named by S. R. Shoup and W. H. Wise of the Richgrove Development Company in 1909.

RICHMOND

The name of this Contra Costa County community migrated from Richmond, Virginia. The town actually took its name from Point Richmond which had been originally called Point Stevens in 1851. The next year, it was made into Point Richmond.

The town of Richmond began in 1897 when the Santa Fe Railroad established a station just north of the point. At first that settlement was called Santa Fe, but when the town was laid out on the Barrett ranch it was called Richmond. The post office was opened in 1900.

Richmond, as *Fortune* magazine reported in 1945, was a place where "The twelve movie houses can't keep everyone amused, even though four of them are open all night . . . There's not much they can spend their money on but booze." Times, however, have changed.

RICHVALE

Richvale, Butte County, was a subdivision developed and named in 1909 by Samuel J. Nunn. When the post office opened here three years later, Richvale was substituted for the original name, Richland. There was another Richland in the state.

RINCON SPRINGS

Located in Riverside County, Rincon Springs took part of its name from Rincon Cape, and the rest was taken from mineral springs. *Rincon* is Spanish for "corner" or "inside corner."

RIO DELL

The original name for this Humboldt County town was Eagle Prairie. When the townspeople petitioned for a post office, they suggested the name River Dell, but because it sounded too close to Riverdale, the name was rejected. The stalwart citizens then translated the first word to Spanish, and got their name: Rio Dell.

RIO LINDA

This Sacramento County community was founded and named in 1913 by an official of Sears Roebuck & Company. He picked the name because he thought it meant "pretty river."

RIO OSO

The Sacramento Northern Railroad named their station at this Sutter County location in about 1907. They picked it because of the location on the Bear River.

RIO VISTA

The name of this town means "river view." Before the Americans took control, the settlement was called Brazos del Rio, "arms of the river."

Founded in 1857, Rio Vista, Solano County, was named by its owner Colonel N. H. Davis. He called it Brazos del Rio because it was near the three arms of the Sacramento River. Three years later, the name was changed to Rio Vista. When that town was wiped out by a flood in 1862 and rebuilt, the new town was named New Rio Vista. The newness soon wore off.

RIPLEY

This Riverside County town was the end of the Santa Fe's branch line. It was named in 1921 for E. P. Ripley. Ripley had been a president of the line.

RIPON

Ripon's name was borrowed from a town in Wisconsin. Applias Crooks, the town's first postmaster, named it in 1876. He was born in Ripon, Wisconsin. That name replaced the earlier Stanislaus City.

RIVER (— Bank; —dale; — Pines; —side; —ton)

Towns with "River" in their titles received their names from their location. For example, River Bank, Stanislaus County, was named in 1911 by the Santa Fe Railroad because their station was located on a bank of the Stanislaus River.

Riverdale, Fresno County, was once known as Liberty Settlement. But, in 1875, postal officials changed the name to indicate the town's position on Kings River.

Located in Riverside County, the town of Riverside took its name from its location.

Riverside is situated on part of the old Jurupa Rancho. The ranch was granted by Governor Alvarado to Juan Bandini in 1838. It was laid out as a town in 1870 and called Jurupa. Soon afterwards the name was changed to Riverside.

Riverside is home to the agriculture arm of the University of California.

Riverton, El Dorado County, had its name changed in 1895 from Moore's Station—because postal officials feared confusion with a place of the same name in Butte County—to Riverton. The town is located at the South Fork of American River.

ROADS END

This Tulare County town was originally located at the end of the road from Kernville. Though the road was extended past this location, the name remained.

ROBBINS

"RHP" is what the military says: Rank hath privilege. That is a truism as far as this Sutter County site is concerned. Originally named Maddox, for the manager of the Sutter Basin Company, the town's name was changed in 1925 to that of George B. Robbins, the company's president.

ROCK (—lin; —port)

The name for Rocklin, Placer County, was given by the Central Pacific Railroad in the 1860s. The extensive quarries nearby suggest the name. The suffix "-lin" is Celtic for "spring" or "pool," in addition to "ravine."

Similarly, Rockport, Mendocino County, was where they built a wharf on the rocky coast in 1876. The name replaced Cotineva four years later.

RODEO

Rodeo, Contra Costa County, took its name from the Spanish for roundup, the place where cattle is exhibited for sale. This name appeared on a plat of a rancho on the Pinole Grant in 1860 as Rodeo Valley. A post office was listed under that name in 1898.

ROHNERT

Paul Golis began this Sonoma County development and incorporated it in 1962. The name came from the Waldo Rohnert Seed Company.

ROHNERVILLE

Rohnerville, Humboldt County, was named for Henry Rohner, an early settler. He opened a store here in 1859. The post office was established in the 1870s.

ROMOLAND

The original name for this Riverside County town was Ramola, a variation of the popular Ramona. When postal authorities asked the town to change its name in 1925—to avoid confusing it with Ramona—this is what they came up with.

ROSAMOND

Gold was first discovered in Tropico Hill in 1894, and the Tropico Mine and Mill still hang precariously against the hill.

The station for the Southern Pacific Railroad located at this Kern County site was named in the late 19th century for a railroad official's daughter.

ROSE (—dale; —mead; —ville)

Though the seeming reference is to that fragrant flower, these California places were so named because the names sounded nice . . . and promotable.

ROSS

James Ross gained the Rancho Punta de Quintin in 1859, and he named it Ross Landing. Later this Marin County name was shortened to fit on an envelope.

ROUGH AND READY

This Nevada County community was founded in 1849 by settlers from Wisconsin. The group was led by Captain S. A. Townsend, who had served under General Zachary Taylor during the Mexican War. Taylor was known as "Old Rough and Ready," and Townsend borrowed that name to call his settlers the Rough and Ready Company.

When the government levied taxes on the gold mines, the residents here were so incensed that they seceded from the Union, wrote their own constitution and established a new country: The Great Republic of Rough and Ready. No one took them seriously, let alone the federal government which continued to levy taxes on them.

Rough and Ready was made famous by Bret Harte and his story about "The Millionaire of Rough and Ready."

ROUND MOUNTAIN

Round Mountain, Shasta County, took the name of the mountain northwest of the town.

ROWLAND HEIGHTS

John Rowland, a merchant and trader from New Mexico, emigrated to California in 1841—to escape a threatened Indian uprising at Taos and Sante Fe. He became one of the largest landholders in southern California.

RUBIDOUX

Rubidoux, Riverside County, bears the name of Louis Rubidoux (Robidoux), a pioneer who acquired large amounts of land, including part of Rancho Jurupa.

Mount Rubidoux, which is situated on the site of the old rancho, also bears his name. A cross and a memorial tablet to Father Junipero Serra was unveiled here on the mountain's summit in 1909 by President William Howard Taft.

RUMSEY

The town of Rumsey, Yolo County, was laid out and named in 1892 for Captain D. C. Ramsey. He just happened to own the land. The post office was established in the same year.

RUTH

When the post office was established at this Trinity County site, the name came from Ruth McKnight, daughter of a pioneering family.

RUTHERFORD

Both the railroad station and the post office in this Napa County location were named in the 1880s for Thomas L. Rutherford. Rutherford was related by marriage to George C. Yount, founder of nearby Yountville.

RYAN

Formerly called Devair, the town of Ryan was named for John Ryan, manager of the Pacific Coast Borax Company.

S SACRAMENTO

In 1839, the Mexican government granted Captain John Sutter, an immigrant from Switzerland, a 50,000-acre tract at the confluence of the Sacramento and American Rivers. Sutter named his settlement "Nuevo Helvetia," New Switzerland.

The town of Sacramento was laid out on Sutter's property by his son and Sam Brannan in 1848, the same year that Sutter's carpenter, James Marshall, discovered gold near the South Fork of the American River (also on Sutter's property).

The first railroad in California connected Sacramento with Folsom in 1856. Fourteen years later the transcontinental rail system was complete. Sacramento was also the western terminus for the Pony Express from St. Joseph, Missouri.

Though devastated by two floods and two fires in the mid-19th century, Sacramento was named the state's capital in 1854.

The county and the city were named for the Sacramento River. The waterway was named in 1808 by Gabriel Moraga for some incident regarding the Eucharist, or "Holy Sacrament." The name is Spanish and translates to "sacrament."

SAINT HELENA

St. Helena, Napa County, was settled by Henry Still in 1853. Two years later he founded the town and named it "from the name given to the Division of the Sons of Temperance established there about that time . . . On account of the fine view obtained of St. Helena mountain. . . ." The post office was established under this name in 1858.

The mountain, many think, was named by Russians who had settled at Fort Ross. They named it for a favorite Russian saint or for the Empress of Russia. Sadly, the empress in 1841 was Alexandra, not Helena. Another source refers to the saint as a French favorite. Still another suggests the name came from the experience of a "niece of the Czar," Princess Helena de Gagarin. The princess, we are told, braved the elements, waved the Russian flag from this mountain top, and named it for her patron saint. Suffice it to say, St. Helen had friends.

St. Helena is also home to the Charles Krug Winery. First opened in 1861 when Count Haraszthy loaned Krug a small cider press, it is the oldest winery in the Napa Valley.

SALINAS

Salinas, Monterey County, was named for the Salinas River. The waterway was named because of the presence of salt springs or salt deposits at its mouth. It is well known as the birthplace of John Steinbeck (1902–68), winner of the 1937 New York Critics' Circle Award, a 1940 Pulitzer Prize and the 1962 Nobel and Pulitzer prizes for Literature.

Author of numerous novels and plays, Steinbeck is best re-membered for his volatile *Of Mice and Men*. That novel, later a the-atrical production and motion picture, caused as much attention, some say, as Harriet Beecher Stowe's *Uncle Tom's Cabin*. Steinbeck's birthplace has been converted into a restaurant.

The last unaltered adobe house from Mexican California in Monterey County is located in Salinas: the Jose Eusebio Boronda Adobe.

SALTON CITY

Salton City, San Diego County, is located on the Salton Sea and took its name from that body of water. In 1892, it was a dry lake bed. The "sea" was created by floodwaters from the Colorado River in 1905 and is quite shallow. The average depth is 20 feet and 265 feet below sea level.

One of the largest inland bodies of salt water, the Salton Sea was first discovered and explored by William Blake of the Pacific Railroad Survey in 1853 and 1854.

SALYER

When it came time to name the post office in this Trinity County town in 1918, the honor fell to a prominent local mining man, Charles Marshall Salyer.

SAMOA

Samoa, Humboldt County, was named for the island in 1889. At that time, the island was in the news because of a major crisis. Another source suggests the name was that of an Indian chief.

The town, originally named Brownsville for dairy rancher James D. H. Brown, was organized by the Samoa Land & Improvement Company. The developers felt that Humboldt Bay resembled the harbor at Pago Pago.

SAN ANDREAS

Townspeople in San Andreas contend that their town was the site of the short story "The Jumping Frog of Calaveras County" by Mark Twain. Notorious criminal Black Bart was also tried and convicted of highway robbery here.

The famous San Andreas Fault, known to many earthquake watchers, took its name from this location. But, if an earthquake takes place, the locals like to say, it isn't San Andreas' fault.

The town carries the Spanish version of the name of Scotland's patron: St. Andrew.

SAN ANSELMO

The name of this Marin County community first appeared as Canada de Anselmo on the 1841 Punta de Quinta land grant. The name was given to this locale in the 1890s as the title for a North Pacific Coast Railroad station.

Many believe the name came from that of a baptized Indian, and sainthood was given at a later date.

SAN ANTONIO HEIGHTS

San Antonio Heights, San Bernardino County, was named for St. Anthony of Padua. San Antonio is the third most popular "saint" place name. It appears in 337 different locations in North and South America.

The "heights" name was in use before 1888.

SAN ARDO

When originally named, this town was called San Bernardo after the San Bernardo Ranch which had been granted in 1841. But postal authorities disapproved of the name because it was too similar to San Bernardino.

The ranch owner, M. J. Brandenstein, then canonized a new saint by taking off the first four letters: St. Ardo!

SAN BERNARDINO

Though founded by Mormons in the mid-19th century, San Bernardino was named for an old Spanish mission. San Bernardino County, by the way, is the largest county in the United States.

The name was first used on the secondary settlement of the Mission San Gabriel, and commemorates St. Bernardino of Siena, the 15th-century Franciscan preacher. The name was given in 1810 by Father Francisco Dumetz, the last of Junipero Serra's companions, because his arrival was on that saint's feast day.

In 1851, Brigham Young instructed Amasa M. Lyman and C. C. Rich to lead a group of Mormons from Salt Lake City to the Cajon Pass in California and establish both an agricultural community and a Mormon inroad. The group purchased Rancho San Bernardino from the Lugo family and laid out the town.

The colony prospered but, six years later, Young ordered the group back to Salt Lake City; most complied and abandoned the settlement.

SAN BRUNO

San Bruno, San Mateo County, appears to take on the name of the nearby San Bruno Mountain. St. Bruno was the 11th-century founder of the Carthusian Order.

The town, however, grew up around the 1862 San Bruno House, operated by Richard Cunningham on the San Bruno toll road.

SAN CARLOS

San Carlos, San Mateo County, took its name from the Spanish version of St. Charles. The St. Charles in this instance was St. Charles Borromeo, the 16th-century bishop of Milan.

The name was given in 1887 by the developers who believed that Portola first saw San Francisco Bay on St. Charles' Day in 1769.

SAN CLEMENTE

San Clemente Island was named by Vizcaino in 1602 for St. Clement, the third pope.

San Clemente, Orange County, is more famous as the western White House during the late 1960s and early 1970s when President Richard M. Nixon made use of Casa Pacifica on a 25.4-acre estate.

The town was founded by Ole Hanson in 1925 and was named for the off-shore island. Just south of San Clemente is Camp Pendleton, the largest base of the U. S. Marine Corps.

SAN DIEGO

San Diego, located in the county of the same name, has a corrupted title. Though Diego is the Spanish equivalent of James, the name is usually used as Santiago. Vizcaino is supposed to have given the name on St. Didacus' day in 1682. He named it San Diego de Alcala, for St. Diego, a 15th-century Franciscan monk who lived at Alcala de Henares, New Castile. Another source contends that San Diego commemorates St. Ingo, the patron saint of Spain. This does not seem possible, especially when one realizes that Vizcaino's flagship bore the name of *San Diego*.

Discovered in 1542 by Juan Rodreguez Cabrillo—but named San Miguel—and claimed for the Spanish crown, San Diego is considered the birthplace of California. Two centuries passed, however, before actual settlement took place.

In 1769, Gaspar de Portola and a group of Spanish settlers founded a military post on what is now called Presidio Hill. With Portola was a Franciscan friar, Father Junipéro Serra. Serra founded the Mission San Diego de Alcala, the first of a chain of missions along the California coast.

Serra established 21 missions and one assistencia between 1769 and 1823. Each was a day's journey along the northern extension of El Camino Real. The Spanish crown's idea was to convert and civilize the Indian population and make it more acceptable to Spanish rule.

San Diego did not make any major growth steps until the late 19th century when San Francisco businessman Alonzo E. Horton decided to move the center of town closer to the harbor. When World War II forced the United States to relocate its Pacific Command from Honolulu, San Diego was selected. It is now home base to the 11th Naval District. San Diego County, the seventh largest in the nation, has a greater population than a dozen states!

SAN DIMAS

San Dimas is named for the "Good Thief," the man who repented on the cross next to Christ. The San Jose Land Company laid out and named the town in 1886 or 1887 at what was formerly known as Mud Springs.

SAN FELIPE

San Felipe, Santa Clara County, bears the Spanish name form of St. Philip, who was crucified for his faith in 1st century Asia Minor.

SAN FRANCISCO

Depending on who you read, San Francisco could have been named for the old Spanish mission of San Francisco de Assisi, or for the religious order to which Father Junipéro Serra, who discovered the bay, belonged. The name most likely came from the mission.

Located in San Francisco County, the city was established in 1776 when construction of the military post, or presidio, was begun

SAN FRANCISCO. Gull's eye view of San Francisco's North Beach from Fisherman's Wharf to Telegraph Hill. Basins in the foreground harbor the city's fishing fleet. The white column is Coit Tower with the Bay Bridge beyond. (San Francisco Convention & Visitors Bureau)

at the end of the peninsula. During the same year, the Mission San Francisco de Asis was built.

After the presido and the mission were completed, a rest stop grew up halfway between the two places. Called El Paraje de Yerba Buena, "the place of the good herb," this little community became the town of Yerba Buena in 1835. It would later become the city of San Francisco in 1847.

The gold rush brought population increases and a resultant financial boon. In 1906, San Francisco suffered a devastating earthquake and fire that destroyed 80 percent of the city. The earthquake destroyed the water system and made all fire-fighting equipment useless. The city rebuilt itself and today is one of the most charming cities in the United States.

Like Tony Bennett, many of us have left our hearts in San Francisco.

San Francisco is the name of 275 places in North and South America. It is the fourth most popular saint's name to appear on places.

SAN FRANCISCO. More than half-a-million people annually visit the former prison island of Alcatraz in San Francisco Bay. The prison's last inmates were removed in 1963, but the prison is still seen in big-screen and made-for-television movies, not to mention the old prison flicks of the Thirties and Forties. (National Park Service Photo by Richard Frear, San Francisco Convention & Visitors Bureau)

SAN GABRIEL

San Gabriel, Los Angeles County, is named for the Spanish Mission del Santo Arcangel San Gabriel de los Temblores, founded in 1771 by Fathers Angel Somera and Pedro Benito Cambon, as part of Father Serra's mission-chain. *Temblores*, "earthquakes," was added to the name because tremors had been felt in the area when the Portola expedition traveled through here.

The present church was built between 1791 and 1805 to replace the earlier adobe chapel that had been destroyed by floods. The mission's belltower was destroyed in an 1812 earthquake but was restored three years later. It was again damaged by an earthquake in 1987.

San Gabriel Mission was the western end of the overland trail founded by Captain Juan Bautista de Anza in 1776. The post office of San Gabriel was established here in 1854.

SANGER

Joseph Sanger, Jr., was an official of the Pacific Improvement Company in 1888, when the Southern Pacific station for the Fresno to Porterville branch was opened. The improvement company was a subsidiary of the railroad.

SAN GERONIMO

San Geronimo was not named for the chief of the Apaches. Some feel the Marin County town was named in honor of one of the several St. Jeromes. Others maintain that the name belonged to a baptized Indian. Geronimo is the Spanish version of Jerome.

The name first appeared on a North Pacific Coast Railroad station in 1875 and on the post office in 1898.

SAN GREGORIO

The name of this San Mateo County locale first appeared on the 1839 San Gregorio grant. The name honors St. Gregory the Great, a member of the Benedictine Order and a pope.

The San Gregorio post office is listed in the 1870s.

SAN JACINTO

Located in Riverside County, San Jacinto took the name of St. Hyacinth, a 13th-century member of the Dominican Order. The town is located at the foot of the mountain of the same name.

San Jacinto was developed around the 1872 store of Procco Akimo, a Russian exile.

SAN JOAQUIN

The one-time post office of San Joaquin, Fresno County, took its name from its river, which was named for St. Joachim, the father of the Virgin Mary. The river was named on or near his birthday of 20 March. The name translates from the Spanish for "whom Jehovah has appointed." San Joaquin, Contra Costa County, did not get its name the same way.

This community was named by W. H. Davis, for his mother-in-law's ranch. Davis took his father-in-law's name, Jose Joaquin Estudillo, extracted this middle name, and added the "San" for saint.

SAN JOSE. San Jose possesses one of the most beautiful, yet bizarre mansions. The Winchester Mystery House is a 160-room Victorian mansion filled with oddities, such as staircases leading nowhere, doors that open into walls and windows in the floor. (San Jose Convention & Visitors Bureau)

SAN JOSE. More than a billion dollars went into the restoration and renaissance of San Jose. The capital of the Silicon Valley, San Jose is California's third-largest city and the nation's eleventh. (San Jose Convention & Visitors Bureau)

SAN JOSE

Named for the patron saint of Mexico, St. Joseph, San Jose, Santa Clara County, was founded as Pueblo de San José de Guadalupe in 1777 by Lieutenant José Moraga with a party of 65 soldiers. It was created to raise crops and cattle to feed the presidios at San Francisco and Monterey.

In 1849, San Jose became California's first capital. It retained that honor for a decade.

The name San Jose is the most popular of all saints' names that appear on places. It appears on 429 places in North and South America.

SAN JUAN BAUTISTA

San Juan Bautista grew from the largest of Father Serra's missions, but it was founded by Father Lasuen in 1797 as Mission San Juan Bautista—named for John the Baptist. Because of its importance, the mission once had nine bells; only three remain.

The Mexican government established San Juan Bautista as a pueblo in 1835, just after it secularized the mission.

San Juan's name is the second most popular saint's place-name. It appears on 365 places in North and South America.

The post office at this San Benito County location was established in 1852 as San Juan. About 1905, the name became complete.

SAN JUAN CAPISTRANO

Father Junipéro Serra founded the Mission San Juan Capistrano in 1776. The mission was dedicated to the memory of St. John Capistran, the Franciscan hero of the 1456 siege of Vienna.

The mission is most famous today because of the swallows that return every year on 19 March, the feast of St. Joseph, and leave on 23 October, St. John's Day. These frequent flyers make their annual trek of approximately six thousand miles from Goya, Argentina, to raise their young in California. Though the swallows' story was first recorded in the mission archives in 1777, it was a regular tradition with the villagers.

SAN LEANDRO

San Leandro, located across the bay from San Francisco in Alameda County, was built on land granted to Jose J. Estudillo in 1842. The town was named for St. Leander—"Apostle of the Goths" and Archbishop of Seville—and laid out in 1855. The post office had already been in operation for two years.

SAN LORENZO

The town of San Lorenzo took its name from the 1824 Rancho de San Lorenzo, which was part of the Mission de San Jose. The name undoubtedly came from that of the river.

The San Lorenzo River was named by the 1769 Portola expedition. The name honored St. Laurence, whose feast day was closest to the date of discovery.

SAN LUCAS

This Monterey County town carries the Spanish form for St. Luke the Evangelist. The name was first applied to a land grant, dating back to 1842.

The modern-day community, however, does not date back so far. The name was applied to a Southern Pacific Railroad Station in 1886 when the line extended from King City to Paso Robles. That name came from the grant, even though the station was not within its boundaries. A post office followed in 1892.

SAN LUIS OBISPO

San Luis Obispo, located in the county of the same name, was named for Mission San Luis Obispo de Tolosa. The mission honored St. Louis, the Bishop of Toulouse and son of the King of Naples and Sicily. The mission was founded in 1772 by Fathers Serra and Cavaller. Some suggest the name was given because of a strangely-shaped rock nearby that resembles a bishop's miter.

San Luis Obispo was laid out as a town by William R. Hutton in 1850, with a post office opening the next year. It did not become a full-fledged town until 1894, when the Southern Pacific Railroad was completed and access to the area was made easier.

The Ah Louis Store, located on Palm Street, was opened in 1844 to accommodate the Chinese laborers who helped build the Pacific Coast and Southern Pacific railroads.

SAN LUIS REY

Located in San Diego County, the name for San Luis Rey was supposed to be San Juan Capistrano el Viejo, "Old Capistrano," because the name had been used for a mission elsewhere. At the request of the viceroy, the name became San Luis Rey de Francia, in honor of St. Louis (Louis IX), King of France, a member of the Franciscan Order.

SAN MARCOS

San Marcos is located in San Diego County and named for an old Spanish land grant: Los Valleoitos de San Marcos, "the little valleys of St. Mark."

SAN MARINO

At this point, we must interrupt the Litany of the Saints.

San Marino, Los Angeles County, was named in 1878 by James de Barth Shorb. Shorb built a house here on land given to him and his wife by her father, "Don Benito" Wilson. He selected the name from his birthplace in Emmitsburg, Maryland.

The property was purchased in 1903 by Henry E. Huntington, who kept the name. Huntington's estate is now home to the Huntington Library and Art Gallery.

SAN MARTIN

Martin Murphy, an Irish emigré, came to California with his family in 1844 and settled on the San Francisco de las Llagas grant. According to tradition, Martin, a good Roman Catholic, named his Santa Clara settlement for his patron saint. But we know better, don't we?

SAN MATEO

Located in San Mateo County, this community became a suburb of San Francisco. The Spanish name honors St. Matthew the Apostle.

    The city of San Mateo was laid out in 1863 by C. B. Polhemus when the San Francisco-San Jose Railroad was built here that year.

SAN MIGUEL

San Miguel, San Luis Obispo County, carries the name of Mission San Miguel Arcangel, which honored St. Michael the Archangel. The mission was founded in 1797 by Father Lasuen, assisted by Father Buenaventura Sitjar.

    The name was accepted by the Southern Pacific Railroad for its station when the line arrived in 1886. The post office followed suit the next year.

SAN ONOFRE

San Onofre, San Diego County, resides in the shadow of San Onofre Mountain. The name was drawn from the Egyptian St. Onuphrius. The name was first mentioned in regard to a rancho of San Juan Capistrano Mission in 1828.

    The name was given to the Santa Fe Railroad station here when it opened in the late 1880s.

SAN PABLO

The name of San Pablo, Contra Costa County, recalls the memory of St. Paul. Ironically, the town on the other end of San Pablo Strait is named San Pedro, so we have the combination of Saints Peter and Paul!

    The strait is mentioned in an 1811 diary and later as Rancho San Pablo. The post office was established here in 1854.

SAN PASQUAL

San Pasqual, San Diego County, was originally a small Indian village. The name first appeared on an early 19th-century map and in 1835, as a pueblo of former members of Mission San Luis Rey. The present spelling—originally Pascual—came into use after 1846.

The name commemorates St. Paschal, a 16th-century Franciscan.

SAN PEDRO

San Pedro, Los Angeles County, bears the Spanish form of the name of St. Peter the Apostle. The name was given in 1602 when one of Vizcaino's men spotted the bay on the saint's feast day.

The town was mentioned in the mid-19th century, with the establishment of the post office in 1858. (See SAN PABLO, California.)

SAN QUENTIN

San Quentin, located in Marin County, is best known for the federal prison located there. The site was named for a notorious Indian chief, known to the Spanish as Quintin. The chief had been captured here in 1824. Depending on the source, Quintin was either a daring warrior or an infamous thief.

The name first appeared on the point, then called Punta de Quintin. Later, it applied to land grants such as Punta Quintin (1834) or Punta de Quintin (1840). When the coast was charted in 1850, the name was Americanized and sainted.

SAN RAFAEL

San Rafael, seat of Marin County, grew up in the early 19th century around the Mission San Rafael Arcangel. The mission was founded in 1817 by Father Vincente Sarria.

The mission, established as an asistencia to Mission San Francisco, was razed for progress, but a replica was built in 1949 approximately where the old mission stood.

The city of San Rafael began sometime before 1841 when Timoteo Murphy was granted a lot near the mission and built his home. A post office was established here in 1851.

SAN RAMON

The name of San Ramon, Contra Costa County, was used on several land grants—the oldest dating to 1833. The name did not, contrary to popular opinion, venerate a saint.

"The name was given," we are told, "by a mayor domo (from Mission San Jose) by the name of Ramon" who tended the sheep here. The town began its existence in the mid-19th century, and a post office was listed in 1859.

SAN SIMEON

San Simeon is best known for the estate of newspaper giant William Randolph Hearst (1863–1951).

In 1919, Hearst began to build an estate on La Cuesta Encantada, "The Enchanted Hill," a 1,600-foot mountain that overlooks San Simeon. He utilized the services of architect Julia Morgan. For 28 years, Hearst continued to build, modify and rebuild. At his death in 1951, it was still not complete.

Hearst began a journalism career in 1887 when his father allowed him to take over the San Francisco Chronicle. Twelve years later, he invaded New York by purchasing the failing New York Morning-Journal and taking on the empire of Joseph Pulitzer. Hearst built a publishing empire, the remnants of which exist to this day.

For some historians, Hearst and his papers were the cause of the Spanish-American War. Orson Welles used Hearst as his inspiration of the central character in *Citizen Kane.*

San Simeon, San Luis Obispo County, was once a rancho of Mission San Miguel, mentioned in 1819. The name recalls St. Simeon. A post office was first established here in 1864, but it was not until 10 years later that Leopold Frankl opened a store here and became postmaster in 1878. We can consider that to be the start of the actual San Simeon. When Hearst began to develop his estate, Frankl sold most of his land to the media mogul.

SANTA ANA

Santa Ana, Orange County, took its name from the nearby river. The river was named in 1769 by members of the Portola Expedition. The name honors St. Anne, the mother of the Virgin Mary.

The contemporary city of Santa Ana did not come into being until 1869, when it was founded and named.

SANTA BARBARA

In 1602, Sebastian Vizcano sailed into what is now Santa Barbara Bay and named it for his favorite saint, who is also patron saint of the artillery. The day of the naming also coincided with St. Barbara's feast day. The saint was beheaded by her father because she became a Christian.

A presidio, Canon Perdido, the site of that outpost, was developed in 1782 under the direction of Governor Felipe de Neve, José Francisco Ortega and Father Serra. The mission was founded by Father Fermin Francisco de Lasuen four years later.

Mission Santa Barbara, called the "Queen of the Missions," was completed in 1820 and is considered the best preserved of all of the missions. It is still in use as a Catholic church.

The bloodless, but wordy "Battle of Santa Barbara" took place here in 1825. A quarrel developed between Colonel José María Encheandîa, the new governor, and José María Herrara, the government's chief fiscal officer in California, and it culminated in a revolt led by Joaquîn Solîs and some half-starved soldiers at Monterey. Both groups fired on each other for three days—". . . at the expiration of which General Solîs, having expended his ammunition, and consumed his provisions, was compelled to withdraw, having sustained no loss, except that of a horse!"

The modern-day Santa Barbara was incorporated as a city in 1850. To the east of the town, Charles Chaplin built the Montecito Inn to house visitors when he was making movies here before moving to Hollywood.

SANTA CLARA

Located in Santa Clara County, this community was named for Mission Santa Clara de Asis, founded in 1777 by Father Tomas de la Peña as the eighth Franciscan mission in Alta California. The present building, located on the Santa Clara University campus, is a replica of the third mission built in 1825.

The name was given by the Portolà Expedition on the feast day of St. Clare of Assisi, who founded the first Franciscan order of nuns in 1769.

SANTA CRUZ

Santa Cruz, located in the county of the same name, was another in Father Serra's mission-chain. All that remains of the original mission, built in 1791 but destroyed by the 1857 earthquake, are the ruins of the soldiers' barracks and some of the stone foundations. A replica of the mission is on the grounds of Holy Cross Church.

Villa de Branciforte was established here in 1797 at the mouth of the San Lorenzo River. It was the last of the three pueblos or villas that the Spanish created in Alta California. Branciforte absorbed the mission when it became secularized in 1834. It gave up its name when Santa Cruz annexed it into the city. Santa Cruz, Spanish for "holy cross," was established as a town in 1850 and opened its post office the same year.

SANTA FE SPRINGS

Santa Fe Springs, Los Angeles County, dates back to an 1886 citrus ranch. The town was named by its owner, the Santa Fe Railroad, for publicity purposes.

The new name replaced that of Fulton Sulphur Springs and Health Resort, a sanitarium established by J. D. Fulton in 1873.

SANTA MARGARITA

Santa Margarita, San Luis Obispo County, was established as an *asistencia*, little chapel, by the priests from Mission San Luis Obispo. The name was to honor St. Margaret of Cortona.

The modern town began in the 1870s, with a post office listed in 1880.

SANTA MARIA

Santa Maria is located in the Santa Maria Valley in Santa Barbara County. The name came from the Virgin Mary, mother of Christ. A Santa Maria Rancho was listed in an 1837 land grant. A post office was established in 1880.

SANTA MONICA

Santa Monica, Los Angeles County, was named for the nearby mountains. The mountains were named by the Portola Expedition in 1770, on the feast day of St. Monica, St. Augustine's mother.

Santa Monica was founded in 1875 by Nevada Senator John P. Jones and Colonel Robert S. Baker on Rancho San Vicente y Santa Monica. A post office was listed five years later.

For an American city, Santa Monica has a largely British population. Locals seem to think the Brits are drawn here because of the cooler, foggier climate.

SANTA PAULA

Santa Paula, Ventura County, is located where the Santa Paula Canyon opens into a widening valley.

A Santa Paula stock ranch, part of Mission San Buenaventura, was listed as early as 1834. The name, we are told, came from St. Paula, a Roman matron who became a student of St. Jerome.

The modern Santa Paula was founded on the Santa Paula y Saticoy grant in 1872, by Nathan W. Blanchard and E. L. Bradley.

SANTA RITA

This Monterey County town was laid out in 1867 on the Los Gatos or Santa Rita grant, dated 1837.

The name came from St. Rita of Cassis, an Augustinian.

SANTA ROSA

Santa Rosa, Sonoma County, is the site of Luther Burbank's home and gardens. The town was named after the creek. The waterway was named on 30 August 1769, the feast day of St. Rose of Lima. At least that's one opinion.

Another source suggests the name came from that given by a missionary priest to a young Indian girl he had captured—and baptized. The story has never been substantiated, though some even list the priest's name and the date. A post office was established here in 1852.

Burbank, an outstanding horticulturist, created more than 600 new varieties of plants and 200 varieties of fruits, vegetables, etc. When he first arrived from New England, Burbank wrote "I firmly believe . . . that (Santa Rosa) is the chosen spot of all the earth, as far as nature is concerned." (See BURBANK, California.)

SANTA SUSANA KNOLLS
Santa Susana Knolls bears the name of the third-century Roman virgin and martyr, St. Susanna.

SANTA YNEZ
This Santa Barbara County community was named for the old Spanish mission, Mission Santa Ynez, the "Mission of the Passes," which honored St. Agnes.

The site for the mission was selected by Governor Borica and established in 1804. The town of Santa Ynez was not founded until 1882, when it began as a trading center for the College Ranch.

SANTA YSABEL
Santa Ysabel, San Diego County, was founded in 1821 as an *asistencia*, and it was named for St. Isabel, daughter of the King of Aragon. The town was shown on a land map in 1879.

SANTEE
This San Diego County community was first known as Fanita, for a Mrs. Fanita McCoon, then as Cowles, finally becoming Santee in 1902 by popular vote.

The name, a family name of the first postmaster, did appear four years earlier, as the post office name. So much for the voice of the people!

SAN YSIDRO
A rancho, San Ysidro, was mentioned as an outreach of San Diego Mission in 1836, but then the name was forgotten.

Throughout the late 19th century, this San Diego town was known as Tia Juana, just like its sister-city south of the border. In 1909, however, when the Little Landers Colony was established, the name was changed. William E. Smythe, colony founder, considered the name "too sporty."

The town's name honors St. Isadore the Plowman.

SARATOGA

Saratoga, Santa Clara County, was named for the community in New York State.

Originally called McCarthysville, for miller Martin McCarthy who founded the town in 1851, the name was changed when a post office was established here in 1867. Someone thought that the nearby Pacific Congress Springs resembled those of Congress Springs at Saratoga.

SATICOY

Saticoy was the name of a Chumash Indian village. It was where tribal members gathered for annual ceremonies, which included human sacrifice.

Modern-day Saticoy, Ventura County, began in 1861, when settler J. L. Crane arrived in 1861. A post office was established about a decade later.

SATTLEY

When this Sierra County town was named in 1884, the honor went to the oldest person in town: Mrs. Harriet Sattley Church.

SAUGUS

The original name of the railroad station at this Los Angeles County community was Newhall, for Henry M. Newhall. In 1878, the station was moved—along with the name—two miles south. The old station, the one located here, was then named Saugus—for Newhall's hometown in Massachusetts.

SAUSALITO

Located in Marin County, Sausalito was originally named Saucelito, Spanish for "little willow grove."

Sausalito is linked to San Francisco by ferry, which is fine for many of the residents who are artists and like their solitude.

SAWYERS BAR

Sawyers Bar, Siskiyou County, was a mining camp in the 1850s. The town was named for Dan Sawyer who lived and mined near the site of the contemporary town.

SCOTIA

Scotia, Humboldt County, was so named because many of its settlers came from Nova Scotia. *Scotia* is the Latin form of Scotland.

The town was called Forestville in 1885 when the Pacific Lumber Company built its mill here. The name was changed for postal reasons in 1888.

SCOTT (— Bar; —s Valley)

John S. Scott discovered gold in 1850, and his name is remembered by the Siskiyou County bar and valley, both mentioned by name in 1851.

SCOTTY'S CASTLE

Walter "Death Valley" Scott was a champion roughrider with Buffalo Bill's shows. In 1923, together with A. M. Johnson, Scott bought a ranch here and began building the home—or "castle"—for the ailing Johnson.

SEAL BEACH

The name of this Orange County location was given because, at an earlier time, sea lions congregated here. Originally called Bay City, the town got its present name from Philip A. Stanton. A Seal Beach post office was in operation in 1915.

SEA RANCH

When, about 10 miles south of Gualala, five thousand acres overlooking the Pacific were developed into vacation homes for the affluent, environmentalists went wild! Developers of Sea Ranch bowed to pressure, creating paths to the beach that are accessible to the public, and building houses that fit into the native surroundings.

SEARLES

Searles, Kern County, was named for John W. Searles who, with his brother Dennis, discovered borax in the Mohave Desert in 1863. The post office, established in 1898, was called Searles.

SEARS POINT

This Sonoma County locale took its name from the Northwestern Pacific Railroad station that was in operation here before 1888. The name came from Franklin Sears, an 1845 settler.

SEASIDE

When Dr. J. L. D. Roberts founded this town in Monterey County in 1888, he named it East Monterey. A few years later, the name was unacceptable to postal authorities. So, in 1890, Roberts changed the name to Seaside.

SEBASTOPOL

Because of the Crimean War, this Sonoma County town became well known in America. In fact, during the mid-19th century it was a popular place name, based on the 1854 siege of the Russian seaport by the British and French. Of the five in California, only this one remains.

The original name, given by founder H. P. Morris in 1853, was Pine Grove, but that was changed during the Crimean War. It has been suggested that the name was selected during a fight among some of the residents. One group barricaded themselves inside the general store and the others laid siege to it, just like the original Sebastapol.

The Sebastapol post office was in operation by 1859.

SEDCO HILLS

Sedco Hills, founded in about 1915 in Riverside County, bears the name of the *South Elsinore Development Company*.

SEELEY

The overflow of New River in between 1905 and 1907 destroyed Blue Lake and the surrounding community. A new town in this Imperial County area was created a few miles to the north. The name given was that of Henry Seeley, an early pioneer in the development of Imperial Valley.

SEIAD VALLEY

The name for the valley in Siskiyou County came from either the Shasta or Yurok Indian tongue, and it may mean "far-away land." The name was originally spelled Sciad.

The town was settled in 1854 by an expatriate New York farmer who settled here. A post office was listed in 1867 with the current spelling.

SEIGLER SPRINGS

The springs were named for the man who discovered them, Thomas Sigler. The name was correctly placed on the community in the 1880s, but the misspelling won out in the end.

SELMA

Some say this Fresno County community was named after Selma, Alabama. It is not so.

The town was named by the Southern Pacific Railroad in 1880 for the daughter of Max Gruenberg at the urging of Leland Stanford. Another source believes the name came from Selma Michelson Kingsbury, wife of a Central Pacific Railroad official.

SENECA

Seneca, Plumas County, took its name from its township, which had been named in 1854. The name, one must assume, migrated from another town of the same name farther east.

SEPULVEDA

The Los Angeles County community of Sepulveda bears the name of a Spanish family. The name was first applied to the railroad station built here in 1873. They probably picked that name because Fernando Sepulveda's adobe was located not too far from the railroad outpost.

SHAFTER

This Kern County community was named after General William "Pecos Bill" Shafter. Shafter commanded U.S. forces in Cuba during the Spanish-American War. Following his retirement from the active service, the general moved to his 10,520-acre ranch near Bakersfield in 1901. Eight years after his death in 1906, his property was subdivided and the town was established.

SHANDON

Postal officials had no trouble in 1891 accepting this, at the time unique, name for the community in San Luis Obispo County. Dr. John Hughes suggested the name, supposedly after reading a story in *Harper's* magazine.

SHASTA

The name for Shasta is derived from that of the Indian tribe: Saste, or Shastika. When miners formed a new mining district at the head of the Sacramento Valley between 1850 and 1852, a trading center developed called Reading's Spring. The name was later changed to Shasta.

Shasta's prosperity died when the California & Oregon Railroad bypassed it in 1872.

SHAVER LAKE

Shaver Lake, Fresno County, was named for C. B. Shaver, an official of the Fresno Flume & Irrigation Company. Shaver's company built a reservoir and sawmill here in the late 19th century. Earlier maps show the name as Saver and Saver's Peak. It is possible, as one authority suggests, that the name was modified after Shaver arrived.

SHEEP RANCH

Though most authorities think this Calaveras County community was named because of the abundance of sheep ranches located here in the mid-19th century, more likely the animals loaned their name to the Sheep Ranch Mine, once owned by George Hearst. The mine was named because it had previously been a sheep corral.

SHELL BEACH

Shell Beach, San Luis Obispo County, was named for obvious reasons.

SHELTER COVE

Shelter Cove's name indicates it was a safe spot for a sailing vessel.

According to an 1854 hydrographic survey, the harbor offered "an anchorage from northwest winds, and may, perhaps, be regarded as a harbor of refuge for small coasters which have experienced heavy weather off Cape Mendocino, and are short of wood and water, both of which may be obtained here from one or two gulches opening upon the sea."

The Humboldt County community assumed that name.

SHERIDAN

When the Roseville-Marysville branch of the Central Pacific Railroad was completed following the Civil War, its station was named for the Union cavalry leader, Philip Sheridan.

SHERMAN OAKS

Sherman Day was a noted California politician. He served as a state center from 1855 to 1856, then as the state's surveyor-general from 1868 to 1871.

SHINGLE SPRINGS

This name was given because shingles were made here, near a spring. The first house was built in 1850 by a man named Bartlett. He created his product "from a shingle machine . . . at a cluster of springs, situated on the western extremity of the village." The Shingle Springs, El Dorado County, post office was established in 1853. By the end of the 19th century, the name had been shortened to Shingle. But, in 1955, history ruled and the original name was returned. (See SHINGLETOWN, California.)

SHINGLETOWN

On the East Coast, this place name usually indicated the presence of a single dwelling that was covered with shingles. Not so here in California.

Shingletown, Shasta County, received this name because at one time in its history there were six shingle mills in operation here at the same time.

SHOSHONE

Shoshone takes its name from that of the Indian tribe that once lived and hunted in the area. The name was given at the beginning of the 20th century when the Tonopah & Tidewater Railroad opened its station here in Inyo County. A post office was established under that name in 1915.

SIERRA CITY

Sierra City was named for its location in the northern part of the Sierra Nevada.

SIERRA MADRE

Sierra Madre took its name from the mountains, a name no longer used. The name literally means "the mother mountain range," an attempt to indicate the importance of the mountain range. Our source indicates that early settlers picked that name because it appeared that "the Sierra Nevada, the Coast Mountains, and other ranges seem to spring from it."

This Los Angeles County town was named when Nathaniel C. Carter subdivided part of Rancho Santa Anita in 1881.

SIGNAL HILL
While the Coast Survey was establishing its Los Angeles Base Line between 1889 and 1890, John Rockwell erected a signal on the hill known as Los Cerritos. The old Spanish name was retained until oil was discovered here in 1921.

SILVERADO
The name of this Orange County town is analogous to El Dorado. The idea was that the mine was full of silver instead of gold. Silver was discovered here in the 1870s, and a Silverado post office opened in 1832.

SIMI VALLEY
Surrounded by the Santa Susana Mountains, Simi Valley was once home to the Chumash Indians. The Ronald Reagan Presidential Library is located here.

The name is Chumash for "place, village."

SISQUOC
This Santa Barbara County name came from the Chumash and means "quail." The name appeared on an 1845 land grant. The name was borrowed to apply to the station of the Pacific Coast Railroad when it was built in 1887.

SITES
Sites was named for an early landholder, John H. Sites, not because it was a "site" in Colusa County.

SKYFOREST
Founded in 1928, Skyforest, San Bernardino County, is located on a wooded ridge that is over one mile high!

SLOAT
Commodore John Drake Sloat officially raised the first American flag over California soil on 7 July 1846. Commodore Thomas Ap Catesby Jones did it first, but his was "by accident" in 1842.

This Plumas County town's name first appeared on the sign over the Western Pacific Railroad station in 1910.

SLOUGHHOUSE

A slough is another word for swamp. In the case of this Sacramento County town, it received its name from a hotel, the Slough House. The hotel was built about the middle of the 19th century by Jared Sheldon.

SMARTVILLE

James Smart built a hotel here in 1856, and he called his Yuba County community Smartsville. The post office decided to drop the "s" when they opened up here in 1867.

SMITH RIVER

The Del Norte County community of Smith River is not located on the Smith River that flows nearby. It was established on the banks of Rowdy Creek. The river—and this town—carry Jedediah Strong Smith's name. Smith was a trapper who explored this area in 1828. Unfortunately, the stream he named for himself in that year is the present-day Klamath!

SNELLING

During the summer of 1851, three men erected a hotel here in Merced County. Later in the year, Charles V. Snelling and his family bought them out, and the place became known as Snelling's Ranch. The post office listing for 1867 carries that name.

SODA SPRINGS

Soda Springs, Nevada County, was so named because of the presence of carbon dioxide in the water which gave it an effervescent quality. Some residents thought that the inclusion of the water in their biscuit dough made the end product the lightest biscuits in the world.

The springs were exploited by Mark Hopkins and Leland Stanford about 1870, and the area became known as Hopkins' Springs. That was until the post office was established here in 1875—the year that Soda Springs came into being.

SOLANA BEACH

Solana Beach was named in 1923 when Colonel Ed Fletcher platted the town. The name translates from the Spanish to mean "sunny place."

One of Solana Beach's attractions is the "Pill Box," the name residents gave to Fletcher Cove because of the bunker-like lifeguard station on the cliffs above the beach.

SOLEDAD

Soledad, Monterey County, took its name from the Mission Nuestra Señora de la Soledad, the "Mission of Our Lady of Solitude," founded in 1791 by Father Lasuen. The original mission consists today of adobe ruins and a restored chapel. Father Junipéro Serra died here one Sunday morning as he walked up the steps of the altar. The post office, established in 1870, adopted the name of the mission.

Another source dredges up the story that the name came by word of mouth from the Portola expedition. A member of the group asked an Indian his name and he replied "'Soledad,' or so it sounded to them."

Soledad is remembered from more recent events. During the turbulent 1960s, a white guard killed three black convicts at the Soledad correctional training facility. The guard was acquitted, but shortly after another white guard was found beaten to death. Three black convicts were charged with murder and became known as the "Soledad Brothers." One of them, George Jackson, earned the convicts national attention through his book *Soledad Brother*.

SOLVANG

Solvang was established in 1911 by the Danish-American Corporation, a group of educators from a Danish college in Des Moines who wanted to build a Danish folk school.

The name is Danish for "sun meadow" or "valley of the sun."

SOMES BAR

Local tradition has it that this Siskiyou County spot was named for a local gold miner. The name appears on official records in 1879 as Some's Bar, and, in 1891, as Sumner's Bar. The post office, established in 1892, carries the current name.

SOMIS

The name for this Ventura County town came from that of a Chumash village. The name has appeared as Somes and Somo. The current spelling appeared on the Southern Pacific Railroad station here in 1899 or 1900 with the completion of the Ventura-Burbank extension.

SONOMA

Located in the county from which it draws its name, Sonoma was allegedly named for the chief of the tribe mentioned in 1815 baptismal records as Chucuines o Sonomas. The name translates to "nose," probably a reference to the size of the Indian's olfactory organ. The name was recorded as Sonomi in 1816.

It was at Sonoma on 14 June 1846 that California proclaimed itself a republic by raising the Bear Flag. Less than a month later, it was replaced by the Stars and Stripes.

Sonoma was founded in 1835 by then-Lieutenant Mariano Guadalupe Vallejo, under orders from Governor José Figueroa. Vallejo and his men acted as a buffer against Russian expansion until the Russians withdrew in 1841. Sonoma Pueblo was the chief military base of the Mexican government in Alta California from 1835 until the end of the Mexican period.

The Mission San Francisco Solano was also located here. The mission was founded in 1823, and it was the last of the 21 California missions—established 54 years after the first mission. It is now a museum. The Sonoma post office was established under that name in 1849.

SONORA

Mexican miners who settled here in 1848 carried with them the name of their hometown: Sonora, Mexico. It was first called Sonorian Camp, to distinguish itself from American Camp.

When named seat of Tuolumne County, the name was changed to Stewart, for Major William E. Stewart. The name returned to Sonora in 1850 because of popular opinion. Sonora was known as the "Queen of the Southern Mines." The name is Spanish for "sonorous."

Located here is St. James Episcopal Church. The church, built in 1860, is the second oldest frame church in California. Legend has it that Bret Harte taught school here in 1854.

SOQUEL

Soquel, Santa Cruz County, took its name from that of an Indian village. The place is mentioned as early as 1807, as Rio de Zoquel. Through time, the name has been spelled Soquel, Sauquil, and Shoquel until the final authority of these things made the decision. In 1857, the post office was established under the name of Soquel.

When Portola's expedition came upon this area, his scribe wrote, "Here are trees of girth so great that eight men placed side by side with extended arms are unable to embrace them."

SOULSBYVILLE

Soulsbyville dates back to 1856. In that year, the Platt brothers discovered gold in this Tuolumne County area. Two years later, Benjamin Soulsby and his sons struck even greater deposits. The town was named for them.

A post office by the current name was established here in 1877.

SOUTH GATE

The name of South Gate, Los Angeles County, came from the South Gate Gardens, located on the Cudahy Ranch. The gardens were opened to the public in 1917. Six years later, when the city was incorporated, the name was shortened. South Gate is located to the south of Los Angeles.

SPRECKELS

This Monterey County town bears the name of a famous California family. Peter Spreckels was one of the founding fathers of the California Immigrant Union, created in 1869 "for the purpose of Encouraging Immigration to the State of California."

On the other hand, Claus Spreckels established a sugar refinery at this site in 1899. It is likely that Claus had more clout in the naming than Peter.

SPRING (— Garden; —ville)

Spring Garden, Plumas County, and Springville, Tulare County, were named for the existence of natural springs near their settlement.

SQUAW VALLEY

Squaw Valley, Placer County, took its name from the valley in which it is located. The name goes back to the early mining and lumbering industries of the area and was recorded as early as 1857.

Squaw Valley became a popular winter sports center. The 1960 Winter Olympics were held here.

STANDISH

Standish took its name from Miles Standish, the Plymouth Colony pioneer. The Lassen County town was laid out in 1897, and it was named two years later by H. R. T. Coffin.

STANTON

Stanton, Orange County, was named for its founder. Philip A. Stanton was a Los Angeles politician. The Stanton post office was established in 1912.

STATELINE

Stateline, El Dorado County, is located on the Nevada border. The post office opened in the early 20th century, and officials thought the name was quite appropriate.

STEVINSON

James J. Stevinson obtained a large parcel of land in this Mercer County location in 1852. The post office bearing his name was opened in 1908.

STEWARTS POINT

In 1875, members of the Coast Survey called a secondary triangulation point Point Stewart. The name was for Corps of Engineers Lieutenant Colonel C. S. Stewart. That year, Stewart removed Noonday Rock, near the Farallones.

The town assumed the name of the geologic projection.

STINSON BEACH

Stinson Beach, Marin County, is a favorite spot for relaxing San Franciscans. It was named for Nathan H. Stinson, who acquired the land here—including the beach—in 1871.

STIRLING CITY

The name for this Butte County town came about in 1903. In that year, J. F. Nash, superintendent of the Diamond Match Company, built a sawmill here. He picked the name because he noticed "Stirling Boiler Works" on the boilers that had been ordered for the mill.

STOCKTON

Stockton, San Joaquin County, was named for Commodore Robert Field Stockton, who took possession of California in the Mexican War.

The town was established in 1847 by Captain Charles Weber, but grew during the gold rush of 1849–1850 as a river port on the lower San Joaquin River. Weber first named his settlement Tuleburg, but changed the name to honor his friend shortly after Stockton took possession of California.

Legend has it that notorious bad-guy Joaquin Murieta arrived in Stockton and found a wanted poster in his name. The reward was $5,000. He scribbled across the face of the poster, "I will give $10,000—Joaquin!"

STONYFORD

John L. Smith established the first town on this Colusa County site in 1863, and named it Smithville—for obvious reasons. In 1890, the Stony Creek Improvement Company purchased the place and moved the town one-half mile to a spot called Stony Ford.

STORRIE

In 1926, the first postmaster of this Plumas County community was R. C. Storrie. Storrie also built the Bucks Creek Power House.

STOVEPIPE WELLS

Stovepipe Wells was actually the name given to a collection of water holes north of town. The name was chosen because the location of the wells was marked with stovepipes.

STRATFORD

Though some might think this Kings County name has some relation to Shakespeare, they are wrong.

Stratford was named Stratton in 1907 on the old Empire Ranch, for William Stratton. He was the ranch manager. The post office rejected the name, so, with a little ingenuity, the name became Stratford, acceptable to Washington . . . and the manager.

STRATHMORE

Strathmore's name, often borrowed from the Scottish district, means "big valley"—an apt choice.

The Tulare County town was laid out by the Balfour Guthrie Company, from Scotland, in about 1908. The name was suggested by Mrs. Hector Burness, the wife of a company official. Before the company arrived, the town had been known as Roth Spur and Santos.

STRAWBERRY

Located in El Dorado County, this town took the name of a popular innkeeper whose name was Berry, and he went by the nickname of "Straw." The town was once an important stage station.

STUDIO CITY

The motion picture industry is the source of this town's name.

SUGARLOAF

Sugarloaf was descriptive of a cone-like hill. Into the 19th century, sugar was dispensed in standing loaves of about five inches in height. People scooped spoonfuls from the central source.

This San Bernardino County community had its name changed from Big Bear Park to Sugarloaf in 1947. Mrs. Mary E. Hebert suggested the name because the town was located on Sugarloaf Mountain.

SUISON CITY

This Solano County community took its name, which translates as "big expanse," from an Indian tribe.

SUMMERLAND

The name of this community describes its year-round temperature. Under the ocean, drilling for oil replaced the tourist trade.

The Santa Barbara County town was laid out in 1888 by H. L. Williams, who took advantage of the recently arrived San Francisco & San Joaquin Valley Railroad.

SUMMIT (— City)

Summit City, Shasta County, was founded in 1938, during the construction of Shasta Dam. The town was so named because of its location near the summit.

SUN (— City; —land; —vale)

Sun City, Riverside County, was created as a retirement community by the Del Webb Corporation in 1963.

The area around Sunnyvale, Santa Clara County, is known as Silicone Valley for the headquarters of more than 650 computer-related companies. At one time, there was a dirigible base at this location. The hangar containing the craft was almost a quarter of a mile long. Sunnyvale was named in the early 20th century by W. E. Crossman for a subdivision of a parcel of the Pastoria de las Borregas grant.

SUNOL
Sunol, Alameda County, took the name of Don Antonia Suñol who settled here in 1818. By 1839, he was part-owner of the Rancho El Valle de San Jose, upon which the contemporary town was built.

Suñol, a native of Barcelona, Spain, was a long-time member of the French Navy. Legend has it he was present at Napoleon's final surrender.

SURF
Located in Santa Barbara County, Surf was named for its location near the ocean. The post office opened under that name in 1897.

SUSANVILLE
Tradition has it that Susanville was named for the black-eyed daughter of Isaac Roop, secretary of the "Territory of Nataqua." The territory was organized in 1856, and it included part of western Nevada in addition to this part of California. Roop's Ford, a log fortification built by him in 1854, is a town landmark. Prior to becoming Susanville in 1857, the Lassen County community was called Rooptown.

SUTTER (— Creek)
Both of these locations in Sutter County were named for Colonel John Augustus Sutter. It was on his land that gold was first dis-covered in California.

SWANTON
A leader in the development of public utilities in Santa Cruz County was Fred W. Swanton. This town bears his name.

TAFT
President William Howard Taft is remembered in this town's name. The Kern County place was named in 1909, shortly after Taft was elected. The railroad branch from Pentland reached here the same year, but the station was called Moron. That name continued until 1918. Was there some irony in the comparative names?

T

TAHOE (— City; — Pines; — Valley; —Vista)

Tahoe is an Indian word meaning "big water." The name for these communities came from the lake.

Lake Tahoe was spotted by John C. Frémont and his guide, Kit Carson, in 1844. Before that, the area was the summer camping place for the Washoe Indians. Hotels and resorts popped up around the lake in the mid-19th century. Even with current development, Lake Tahoe's waters are still clear. In fact, some contend that one can see an object 75 feet below the lake's surface.

TARZANA

Everything was fine for this Los Angeles County community until residents applied for a post office in 1928. Called Runnymede III, it was part of the historic San Fernando Mission. Postal authorities informed the townspeople that there was another Runnymede and that they would have to come up with another name.

A local resident, Edgar Rice Burroughs, owned the largest parcel of land and, in 1917, called it Tarzana Ranch. He, of course, named his ranch for his breadwinner: Tarzan of the Jungle! The townspeople contacted the author and received permission to use his character's name as their town name. In 1931, that name appeared as a postmark.

TAYLORSVILLE

Taylorsville, Humboldt County, was named for a local settler. J. T. Taylor built the first barn, mill and hotel at this site in 1852.

TECATE

Tecate's name was Spanishized from that of an Indian village. It was first mentioned as a rancheria in 1830.

The name for this San Diego County town came from the mountain. The town opened its post office as Tecate in 1913.

TECOPA

Tecopa was named for a vain Paiute Indian chief, Cap Tecopa. His name translates from *tecopet*, "wildcat." The chief ruled sections of southern Nevada and southeastern California.

Chief Tecopa, according to local legend, owned a lead-silver claim in the No-pah mountains, but he would not part with it. A local entrepreneur, realizing how vain the chief was, took to wearing an embroidered jacket and a tall silk hat. The chief followed the man around day after day, trying to caress the jacket. Finally, the jacket's owner allowed the chief to try it on. He would not take it off, and he traded his claim for the hat and jacket. The claim, it is said, became one of the richest producers in the area.

Another legend suggests that the chief was a fine individual who once saved the lives of settlers in the Pahrump Valley from marauding Indians.

The most plausible story is that the town, then a mining camp, was named by J. B. Osbourne before 1892. The chief demanded $200 for the use of his name. No one knows what Osbourne did, but another settler paid the chief tribute of a plug hat each year. A photograph of the chief, complete with plug hat, was published in a local magazine in 1943.

TEHACHAPI

The history of this Kern County community began in 1854, when John Moore Brite settled in the valley that now bears his name. Brite opened his home as a general trading post for miners and ranchers.

Tehachapi, Kern County, is named from the Indian *Tah-ee-chay-pah*, the word they used to describe the creek. The name, we are told, means "frozen" in the Southern Paiute language, and it probably referred to the creek's appearance at one time.

The current town is not in the original location, nor is its name spelled the same. When the railroad moved into the area in 1875, local merchants moved their stores three miles to the west to be closer to the railroad. When a post office was first established here in 1870, its name was spelled Tehichipa. Tehachapi is considered the dividing line between northern and southern California.

TEHAMA

Located in the county of the same name, Tehama supposedly took its name from an Indian word meaning "high water," "low land" or "shallow water crossing." Some think the name was imported from Saudi Arabia, since Gibbon mentioned such a place—not far from Medina—in one of his works. Another source thinks it came from the Mexican word *tehamanil*, "shingle."

The Indians named it because the Sacramento River would overflow its banks at this point during the rainy seasons.

Tehama was laid out on R. H. Thomes' Saucos Rancho in 1850.

TEMECULA

Temecula carries the name of a Luiseno Indian village, with a Spanish adaptation. The name Temeca appeared as early as 1797 on an Indian rancheria. The current spelling was in place by 1820. No one is quite sure what the name means, but one source thinks the word has something to do with "sun."

The Temecula post office was named before 1880.

TEMPLE CITY

Temple City was named in 1923 for Walter P. Temple, founder of the town and the president of Temple Townsite Company.

Another source believes the name for this Los Angeles County community came from nearby Temple Rock. To early settlers, the crag resembled a religious edifice.

TEMPLETON

John Temple was one of the largest ranchers in southern California in the mid-19th century. But was he the man behind the name? No one is quite sure.

Some believe the name for this San Luis Obispo County site came from Templeton Crocker, a grandson of one of the founders of the Central Pacific Railroad. This idea makes sense. In fact, when the West Coast Land Company laid out the town in 1886, anticipating the coming of the railroad, they named it Crocker. A short time later, the name became Templeton.

TENNANT

The post office at this Siskiyou County town was established about 1922, and it was named for an official of the Long Bell Lumber Company.

TERMO

This Lassen County town was named by the general manager of the Nevada-California-Oregon Railroad. He liked station names that ended in "o," and connected them with "terminus" or "terminal."

TERRA BELLO

When the Southern Pacific Railroad branch from Exeter to Famoso was opened here in 1889, the station here in Tulare County was named Terra Bello. The Latin for "land" and the Spanish for "beautiful" was what they saw when they viewed the countryside.

THERMAL

The name of this Riverside County community was given first to its railroad station in 1888. The name was selected because of the intense heat in this Salton Sea area.

THE WILLOWS

At the time that this town was founded, this part of the valley was virtually treeless except for a clump of willow trees.

THORNTON

The New Hope Ranch, owned by Arthur Thornton, a Scottish emigré, was established here in San Joaquin County during the mid-19th century.

The place was known as New Hope until 1907, when the Western Pacific Railroad built across the ranch property and named the station for the landowner.

THREE RIVERS

The post office, established in 1878 at this Tulare County location, was named Three Rivers because it was located at the junction of three forks of the Kaweah River.

TIBURON

Tiburon is a very trendy island in the Gulf of California. The name is Spanish for "shark," and it was first applied to the point in San Francisco Bay after the sighting of a shark.

Tiburon's post office was established in about 1885.

TIPTON

The Southern Pacific Railroad station at this Tulare County site was named Tipton in 1872–73, when the line built its Tulare-Delane branch. The name, quite popular in the United States, migrated from the English town in Staffordshire.

TOLLHOUSE

Tollhouse, Napa County, took its name from the house that was used to collect the tolls on the stage coach roadway.

TOMALES

This is a Spanish adaptation of the name of the Tamal Tribe. The name was first applied to the bay when it was discovered by Vizcaino's expedition of 1603. The Marin County town took on that name.

TOPANGA (— Beach)

This Los Angeles County name, we are told, came from the Shoshonean Indian and indicates "place." The name was first applied to the canyon.

TOPAZ

T. B. Rickey moved into this Mono County area in pioneering days, and within a few years his little enterprise had grown to include all the amenities of a much larger community.

His wife, fascinated by the topaz coloring of the local trees, quaking aspens, cottonwoods and others, decided that "topaz" would be a good name for the village. The name became official in about 1875.

TORRANCE

Torrance, Los Angeles County, was planned as a model city by Frederick Law Olmstead, the noted landscape architect. It was named in 1911 for the owner of the property, Jared S. Torrance, a capitalist and philanthropist.

TRABUCO CANYON

The name of this Orange County town means "blunderbuss," a name given the place by members of the Portola expedition of 1769 because "at this place, where is a small arroyo, they lost a blunderbuss."

TRACY

This San Joaquin County rail center was named for Lathrop J. Tracy, an official of the Southern Pacific Railroad.

TRANQUILITY

The Southern Pacific Railroad named its station here in Fresno County when the Ingle-Hardwick branch reached here in 1912. The post office opened in the same year, adding an extra "l" to the name.

TRAVER

Traver, located in Tulare County, was founded in 1884, and it was named for Charles Traver. He had interests in the land and canal development projects in the area.

TRES PINOS

Tres Pinos, San Benito County, carries a Spanish name meaning "three pines." Three pines had nothing to do with this particular site. The name was transferred from another location.

TRIMMER

Trimmer took its name from Morris Trimmer, an early settler.

TRINIDAD

Trinidad took its name from the Bay of Trinidad, which was named by Spanish explorers, Bruno de Heceta and Juan Francisco de la Bodega y Cuadra, because they took possession on the day following the feast of the Holy Trinity on 9 June 1775.

The explorers planted a huge pine cross when they landed. That cross was replaced by a massive granite cross in 1913.

The waters around Trinidad were first visited by a Portuguese expedition in 1595.

Trinidad was a boom town during the gold rush of 1851–1852, and it was the county seat of the now-defunct Klamath County.

TRINITY CENTER

This community took its name from the Trinity River which explorers in 1845 thought emptied into the Bay of Trinidad. They were wrong. Trinity Center was settled by miners in 1850. A post office followed eight years later. (See TRINIDAD, California.)

TRONA

The official name for this small town in San Bernardino County is dihydrous sodium carbonate and bicarbonate ($Na_2CO_3.NaHCO_3.2H_2O$).

The name came from one of the salts drawn from the nearby Searles Dry Lake. Alfred de Ropp, a German engineer, made the great discovery in 1908 that he could make soda and potash from the brine of the lake. The product was then known as trona.

The name of this San Bernardino County town was applied in 1914.

TRUCKEE

The name of this community came from the river, which was named for the Indian guide of the 1844 Stevens Party. "Captain" Truckee was one of Frémont's favorite guides.

About a mile from Truckee is the Donner Memorial State Park. It was here during the winter of 1846–1847 that 89 members of the Donner Party were stranded. As members died, those remaining resorted to cannibalism to survive. Only 47 were rescued.

The town of Truckee was born in 1863 or 1864, when the Central Pacific Railroad surveyed the area. They called it Coburn Station for a local saloon keeper. The Truckee name was returned in 1868.

TUJUNGA

In 1840, Rancho de Tujunga was a separate land grant to Francisco and Pedro Lopez. Their ranch became the site of the present-day Los Angeles County community.

The name, one "authority" contends, translates to "old woman's place" if one transposes the "n" and "g" in "tujugna." In reality, the name is drawn from *Ti'anga*, "mountain range."

In 1887, the first post office to open here misspelled the name as Tuhunga.

TULARE

Located in Tulare County and taking its name from that division, the community's name is from an Indian word that translates to "place of tules (reeds)." For those unfamiliar with that name, a tule is also known as a bullrush or a cattail.

Frank Norris used Tulare as his model for the town of Benneville in *Octopus*.

TULELAKE

It can be assumed that this is a reference to the nearby Tule Lake, a lake that contained reeds. This Siskiyou County spot took the name of the lake when it opened its post office here at the turn of the 20th century. (See TULARE, California.)

TUNITAS

The first mention of this San Mateo County community appeared on the 1839 San Gregorio and Canada Verde grants.

Tunita is the Spanish diminutive for the fruit of the prickly pear cactus.

TUOLUMNE (— Meadows)

Tuolumne took its name from its county, which was taken from the river, which was named for an Indian tribe. The name is supposed to be a corruption of *talmalamne*, "group of stone huts" or "collection of wigwams."

The town was formerly known as Summerville, founded by Franklin Summers in 1854. When a post office was opened it was known as Carter, for C. H. Carter who used his general store for postal matters. When a lumber company opened its own, more convenient post office, it became Toulumne. For a long time, the town went by all three names.

TUPMAN

The people of this Kern County spot voted in 1920 to name their town for H. V. Tupman. Tupman had just sold his land to Standard Oil Company. The post office bearing his name opened in 1922.

TURLOCK

Turlock is adapted from the name of Turlough, County Mayo, Ireland. The town was the site of one of the earliest irrigation systems in California.

When the railroad reached this Stanislaus County site in 1871, they planned to name their station for John W. Mitchell. Mitchell suggested the Irish name, and it was accepted.

TUSTIN

This Orange County site was founded in 1867, and it was named by its founder, Columbus Tustin.

TUTTLE (—town)

Tuttle, Merced County, bears the name of R. H. Tuttle, the Santa Fe Railroad superintendent at Fresno. The station was named in 1900 shortly after the line was purchased.

Tuttletown, Tuolumne County, was named for Judge Anson H. Tuttle who built a log cabin here in 1848. Some called the town Tuttletown; others, Mormon Gulch, for the Mormon miners of 1848.

TWAIN (— Harte)

Twain Harte, Tuolumne County, was founded and named in 1924. It was named because it was near the Mark Twain-Bret Harte Trails.

The irony of the naming is that Twain and Harte hated each other.

Twain, Plumas County, was named in 1907. Legend has it the Western Pacific Railroad station here was named in memory of Mark Twain.

TWENTYNINE PALMS

In the 1870s, Twentynine Palms was an oasis between the Mojave and Colorado deserts, flanked by 29 Washingtonia palms. There are many more than that today.

TWIN PEAKS

The name of this San Francisco County spot might have been chosen with tongue in cheek.

The town takes its name from the descriptive name of the nearby landmark. The name of that geologic feature was known as Las Papas, "the potatoes," in 1828. Another Spanish name was one placed upon it: Los Pechos de la Chola, "the breasts of the Indian girl." Was the conversion to Twin Peaks in 1890 an attempt to avoid a sexist term?

TWO ROCK

Located in Sonoma County, this community took its name from two large rocks that were used as markers in Mexican times. In fact, they were called Dos Piedras.

John Schwobeda settled here in the mid-19th century and kept the Spanish name. But, when the post office was established here in 1857, the name was translated from the Spanish to Two Rocks. The name was turned into Two Rock by the post office in 1874. No reason was given. Maybe some clerk felt that the singular was proper.

UKIAH

Located in Mendocino County, Ukian's name is a corruption of Yokaia, an Indian tribe's name, which translates to "lower valley" or "stranger." Another source feels it comes from the Pomo Indian language and means "deep valley." Based on its location, the latter definition seems more accurate.

The first appearance of the name was recorded in 1844, but the first white settler did not arrive until 12 years later. That same year, Judge J. B. Lamar named the town. The valley was known as Parker Valley until about 1858, when it, too, became Ukiah.

UNION CITY

Union City, Alameda County, took this name in 1851, making it the oldest town of the name in the state.

UNIVERSAL CITY

Universal City, Los Angeles County, was established in 1915, and it was named after the Universal Pictures Company. The film company had been organized the same year.

UPLAND

Upland, San Bernardino County, received this name in 1902 because citizens wanted it.

Upland replaced North Ontario, a name given to distinguish it from the lower-elevation Ontario. The town began its life in 1887 when the Bedford brothers opened what they called Magnolia Villas.

UPPER LAKE

When the first post office opened here before 1867 in Lake County, authorities called the place Upper Clear Lake, for the town's location on the northern shore of Clear Lake. The name was reduced in 1880.

VACAVILLE

Because this Solano County area was once a large cattle-raising area, one authority contends that it derived its name from the Spanish for "cow" and that the name means "cow town."

Another source, a little more reliable, tells us the town was named for Juan Manuel Vaca who had a ranch here in 1845. The town was platted on his land.

VALLECITO

Vallecito, Calaveras County, was a sleepy little town after it was settled in 1850. That all changed two years later when gold was discovered here. The town became the gateway to the Moaning Cave, which had been discovered a year earlier.

When Moaning Cave was first explored in 1851, the miners did not discover the gold for which they hunted; rather, they found human remains.

The name is Spanish and means "small" or "little valley." At first, when the post office was opened here in 1854, the name was Vallicita. The original Spanish spelling was returned in 1940. Better late than never!

VALLEJO

Vallejo, Solano County, was named for General Mariano Guadalupe Vallejo, the founder of this town. The general was a citizen of California both under Mexican and American rule. He also happened to own the land on which the town was laid out in 1850. Nearby Benicia carries the name of the general's wife.

Vallejo is located at the junction of the Carquinez Straits and the Napa River. It served twice as the state capital between 1851 and 1852.

VALLEY (— Center; — Ford; — Springs; — Village; — Vista)

Valley names are quite specific terms when placed on California places. Valley Center, San Diego County, was named in the 1870s because it was located in the center of the valley.

Valley Ford, Sonoma County, was the spot on the Estero Americano that settlers forded in the 1860s. Valley Springs, Calaveras County, was originally Spring Valley because of the mineral springs located nearby.

VALYERMO

This community name was coined in the 1909 from the Spanish *val*, "valley," and *yermo*, "desert." The name was given in 1909 by W. C. Petchner. He owned the Valyermo Ranch here. The Valyermo post office was established in 1912.

VAN NUYS

Van Nuys, Los Angeles County, is located on a former barley field. It was named for Isaac N. Van Nuys, when the post office was established in 1912. Van Nuys had been involved in 1876 with his father-in-law, Isaac Lankershim, in the first successful cultivation of wheat on a large-scale in southern California.

VENICE

This Los Angeles County town was originally laid out with a number of canals. The similarity to Venice, Italy, was quite apparent.

Abbott Kinney, a wealthy businessman from Los Angeles, developed 16 miles of canals on his Ocean Park Tract in 1904, sailed gondolas down them and built scaled-down replicas of Venetian landmarks. His dream did not stand the test of time, and only three canals remain.

VENTUCOPA

Ventucopa was a made-up name in 1926. Since it was midway between Ventura and Maricopa, some sage (tradition has it the person was Dean "Dinty" Parady) decided to blend the names together.

VENTURA

Ventura is one of the oldest towns in California. Before white settlement it was a Chumash Indian village. The name for this Ventura county community does not come directly from the Spanish *ventura*, "happiness," as some sources contend.

Ventura took its name from the Mission San Buenaventura, founded in 1782 and completed in 1809. In fact, the town's corporate name is San Buenaventura.

VERNALIS

The name of this San Joaquin County community translates from the Latin to mean "spring-like." The name was given by the Southern Pacific Railroad when it opened its station here in 1887.

VERNON

Vernon's name came from that of an early settler. Captain George R. Vernon, a Civil War veteran, settled here after 1871. At first the town was known as Vernondale, but the name was shortened in 1905 when the city was incorporated.

VERONA

While many American place names bearing the Verona name are for the Italian city, this particular place is not. When it was laid out in 1849, the original name for this Sutter County community was Vernon, but since that was a duplication of another, the townspeople modified the name in 1906 to satisfy the post office.

VICTORVILLE

Victorville, located on the Mohave River, was named Victor in 1885 for J. N. Victor. He was the construction engineer for the railroad.

Postal authorities asked that the name be changed in 1901 to prevent confusion with Victor, Colorado.

Near Victorville, the Mojave River runs above ground. This is one of the few places where the river appears.

VIDAL (— Junction)

The town of Vidal, San Bernardino County, was founded in 1907 by Hansell Brownell, who named it for his son-in-law.

VILLA PARK

When this Orange County site was first established, it was called Mountain View. The name was changed to Villa Park in 1890 at the urging of postal authorities who feared confusion with a Mountain View post office in Santa Clara County.

VINA

The name for Vina comes from the Spanish *vina*, "vineyard." The town is located on the old Stanford Ranch, established by Leland Stanford. The place was listed as a post office in 1880.

VINEBURG

Vineburg's name came from this Sonoma County community's involvement in the winery business.

VINTON

Summit, the original name for this Plumas County spot, was changed in 1897 to honor Vinton Bowen, the daughter of Henry Bowen, an official of the Sierra Valley Railway.

VIOLA

B. F. Loomis named this Shasta County place for his mother. Loomis filed for a homestead here in 1888, and then he built the Viola Hotel.

VISALIA

Visalia was founded in 1852, and it is the oldest city between Stockton and Los Angeles.

Some think the name "moved" from Kentucky, where the town of the same name was founded by a settler named Vise, and that this town was founded by a member of Vise's family.

Others say the town was founded in 1852 and was named for Nat Vise, a famous bear hunter of the mid-19th century. Everybody is right. The name did migrate from Kentucky, and was, in fact, named in the mid-19th century for a relative of Nat.

When Visalia became the seat of Tulare County in 1853, the name was changed to Buena Vista. The next year, irate citizens demanded the return of the original name. They learned that you can fight city hall!

VISTA

Located in San Diego County, Vista's name is Spanish for "view."

VOLCANO (—ville)

Volcano was named by the first wagon train to come through this Amador County locale. They thought that a certain rock formation was a volcano and named the town for it. They were wrong!

Gold discovered here—the town was then known as Soldiers' Gulch—in 1848 helped spur growth. Within seven years the ore had been played out.

The town of Volcanoville, El Dorado County, was named in the same way as Volcano—mistaken identity.

VOLTA

Volta's name indirectly honors Alessandro Volta, the Italian scientist. The name was given in 1890 by the Volta Improvement Company when they laid out this Merced County town in 1890. Two years later, the post office was established under that name.

WALKER

Walker was named for Joseph Reddeford Walker, Frémont's guide on his second expedition. More directly, the name came from the Walker Pass which he discovered in 1833, named in his honor by Frémont 11 years later.

In his own right, Walker opened the Salt Lake-Humboldt trail, one of the most important emigrant trails to California, and he discovered the Yosemite Valley. Washington Irving called him "one of the bravest and most skillful of the mountain men." His remains are buried in a small cemetery in Martinez, California.

WALLACE

David S. Burson, the founder of this Calaveras County town, forgot to record for whom he named it. Regardless, the post office bore this anonymous Wallace's name in 1883.

WALNUT (— Creek; — Grove)

Walnut's original name was Lemons. In 1912, townspeople in this Los Angeles County spot changed the name to remove any derogatory reference.

Though English walnuts have been grown at Walnut Grove, Sacramento County, the name came from the settlement here of "woodchoppers" before 1850. The post office took on that name in the early 1860s.

Walnut Creek, Contra Costa County, refers to a different type of walnut tree. The name came from a translation of the Spanish *Arroyo de Los Nogales,* a reference to the creek of the nuts. When a post office was established in the 1860s, the town took on the name of the waterway.

WARNER SPRINGS

Warner Springs, San Diego County, was once known as Warner's Hot Springs.

This town in San Diego County was founded by Jonathan Trumbull Warner from Connecticut, who became a Mexican citizen in 1841 and changed his name to Juan José Warner. Between 1844 and 1846, he gained two land grants from the Mexican government and built a house at Agua Caliente, an Indian village, now the town.

Warner lost Rancho Agua Caliente in 1857 when a U. S. District Court found for an earlier claimant. By 1861, he lost the rest of his property to mortgage foreclosure to John Rains, a cattle baron.

WASCO

The Santa Fe Railroad established a station here in this Kern County location in 1898 and promptly named it Dewey. Dewey had recently received adulation for his victory at Manila Bay. Unfortunately, there was another Dewey in the state, so an old-time resident was asked to come up with a name. He selected Wasco, the name of his hometown in Oregon.

Herbert Hoover once had a farm at Wasco.

WATERFORD

When the Southern Pacific Railroad built their Stockton-Merced branch in 1890, the name of this Stanislaus County station was

Waterford. The reason for the name was that the station was close to a much-used crossing place through the Tuolumne River. Waterford is also the name of a famous old city of Ireland.

WATERLOO

Waterloo seems to be a popular name in America. It appears in several states from east to west and from north to south. The name usually commemorates the Duke of Wellington's 1815 victory over Napoleon Bonaparte at Waterloo, Belgium.

In the case of this San Joaquin County spot, the name came from an actual land title fight in the 1860s.

WATSONVILLE

Watsonville, Santa Cruz County, was named for its first settler, Colonel James Watson. Another source suggests he merely put his name on the map in 1853. A more likely choice would be Judge John H. Watson who, with D. S. Gregory, took up part of Rancho Bolsa del Pajaro in 1852.

The Watsonville post office is listed in 1854.

WAUKENA

Waukena's name comes from the proper pronunciation of the valley in which it finds itself: the San Joaquin Valley.

The town, located in Tulare county, was laid out by a development company in 1886.

WAWONA

Wawona has gone through a number of name changes, beginning in 1857 when Galen Clark built a cabin here and called it Clark's Station. Later, when he sold a half-interest in 1869 to Edwin Moore, it became Clark and Moore's.

The Washburn brothers bought out the property in 1875, and they changed the name to Wawona. According to local Indians, the name means "big tree." The word comes from *woh-woh'-nau*, an imitation of the sound of an owl lodged in the big tree.

WEAVERVILLE

Weaverville, Trinity County, was a mining community in 1849, named for John (or George) Weaver.

Weaver discovered gold on Weaver Creek in 1849. Within a year, the miners who flocked to the area had created the town. One of the remnants of the contribution of the Chinese mineworkers is the Weaverville Joss House, built in 1874 and used as a house of worship by the Oriental workers.

WEED (— Patch)

The town of Weed, Siskiyou County, was named for Abner Weed, who opened the first sawmill here in 1900. Besides being a pioneering lumberman, Weed was also a one-time state representative.

Weed Patch, Kern County, on the other hand, was named because, when settlers first came upon it, the site had produced a bumper crop of weeds. Apparently, a flow of water had helped that one spot in an otherwise barren area.

WEIMAR

While there are several locations across the nation that bear this name and honor the German city, this particular location was named for an Indian chief whose name was Weima or Weimah. The spelling was changed to conform to that of the city.

The original name of this Placer County community was New England Mills in 1886, but the post office thought the name was too long, so the townspeople honored the old chief.

WEITCHPEC

Located in Humboldt County, Weitchpec was named for an Indian town, called Weitspus, a "junction of rivers." The reference was to the Klamath and Trinity rivers.

WELDON

Weldon, Kern County, was named for William Weldon, a cattleman of the mid-19th century.

WENDEL

Thomas Moran, president of the Nevada-California-Oregon Railroad, named this Lassen County spot in 1905 for a dear friend. Unfortunately, we do not know if Wendel was his first or last name. The post office opened here in 1915.

WENGLER

The first postmaster of this Shasta County spot, established about the turn of the 20th century, was E. M. Wengler. He also was part owner of the Wengler & Buick mill.

WEOTT

Weott, Humboldt County, bears an Indian tribal name. The Humboldt Bay tribe's name was Wiyou. The post office under the current spelling was opened in 1926.

WESTEND

Hanksite was the name of this San Bernardino County spot until 1919 when F. M. "Borax" Smith changed it. He was president of the West End Consolidated Mining Company. The Westend post office was established here in 1919.

WESTLEY

This Stanislaus County community was named in 1888. Townspeople wanted to honor John Westley Van Benschoten. Van Benschoten was a butcher who came with Frémont in 1846, and settled on the San Joaquin four years later.

WESTMINSTER

The Reverend L. P. Weber founded this community in Orange County in the 1870s. Weber's colony was composed of people who followed the ideals set down by the mid-17th century Westminster Assembly of the Presbyterian Church.

WESTMORLAND

According to one authority, this Imperial County town was so named because there was "more land in the western" part of the district.

WEST POINT

In 1845, Kit Carson named this Calavaras County community; it was the westernmost point reached by his expedition. Before that, it was known as Indian Gulch. Carson might have been a great guide, but he really lacked creativity.

WESTPORT

Located in Mendocino County, Westport was named in 1877 by James T. Rodgers who came from Eastport, Maine. It appeared logical that his new location was at a western port.

WESTWOOD

Westwood, Lassen County, was a lumber town. It was founded by the Red River Lumber Company of Minnesota in 1913, and called Westwood because the company already had eastern operations.

WHEATLAND

When the railroad arrived in this Yuba County location in 1867, they decided on this particular name because the station was located in a wheat-producing district.

The Wheatland post office was established in 1867.

WHISKEYTOWN

According to local tradition, a mule train carrying kegs of whiskey ran into problems, and one of the packs broke loose and fell into the stream. The kegs floated away and into the hands further down the creek. To commemorate that event, the stream was named Whiskey Creek.

When this Shasta County town requested a post office, the prudish officials would not accept Whiskeytown, and the towns-people suffered through such names as Blair, Stella and Schilling. It was not until 1952 that the postal authorities relented and allowed the people their choice.

WHITE (— River; — Water)

White River, Tulare County, was originally named Tailholt because a miner nailed a cow's tail on his door for a handle. When the town needed a post office in the 1860s, people did not think that name quite suitable, so they adopted the name of the White River that runs by the community.

White Water, on the other hand, received its name because of the milky appearance of the river water, caused by fine sand deposits. The post office in this Riverside County spot was established in 1926.

WHITMORE

Whitmore, Shasta County, took the name of the town's blacksmith who instigated to get the post office established in 1883: Simon H. Whitmore.

WHITTIER

The name of this Los Angeles County town, home to Whittier College, was named for the Quaker poet, John Greenleaf Whittier (1807–92).

The town was founded by the Pickering Land & Water Company, members of the Society of Friends, in 1887. Former President Richard M. Nixon spent his boyhood here.

WILDOMAR

When the old Rancho Laguna in Riverside County was subdivided in 1883, this new name was suggested. It represented the names of the new owners: *Wil*liam Collier, *Do*nald and *Mar*garet Graham.

WILLITS

When the post office opened here in the late 1870s in this Mendocino County area, the name was given for Hiram Willits, an early settler.

WILLOW (— Creek; — Ranch; — Springs; —s)

Willows, Glenn County, was named for the abundance of willow trees at the time of founding. Today, the Sacramento National Wildlife Refuge acts as a wintering spot for migratory birds, especially water fowl.

Like Willows, Willow Creek, Humboldt County, Willow Ranch, Modoc County, and Willow Springs, Kern County, were named for the proliferation of willow trees.

WILMINGTON

Wilmington, Los Angeles County, was founded by General Phineas Banning in 1858. He named it for his home back in Delaware.

Located at Wilmington are the remains of Fort Drum, a camp established as a Civil War garrison and depot. What remains is the "Accompanied Officer Quarters," which is now a museum.

WINCHESTER

This Riverside County community was named for one of the landowners when the place was subdivided in 1886.

WINDSOR

What a difference a name makes! This Sonoma County spot was originally known as Poor Man's Flat. In 1855, with the establishment of the post office here, the name was given a little more nobility. It was named Windsor for England's Windsor Castle.

WINNETKA

Winnetka's name apparently came from Illinois. There, the name dates back to the mid-19th century. It was manufactured from the Algonquian *winne*, "beautiful," and the rest for euphony. It is not an Indian word. This Los Angeles County community was originally named Weeks Poultry Community. The post office was established as Winnetka in 1947.

WINTERHAVEN

Because of the pleasant climate here, the name is quite appropriate for those who live in snowy, freezing areas. This Imperial County place was named in 1916 because of the experience of a group of women. They were playing cards in a 120-degree patch of shade and felt the name was quite fitting.

WINTERS

Winters is located on Putah Creek. Half the land on which this Yolo County town is situated was donated by Theodore W. Winters. Winters developed the town in 1875, when the Southern Pacific arrived.

WINTON

It all depends on how you look at this Merced County town name. The Cooperative Land & Trust Company subdivided the old Winn (or Wynn) Ranch in 1910, and the new town was called Windfield. A year later, when the Santa Fe arrived, they named their station Winton, for Edgar Winton, one of the surveyors who laid out the town.

Now, the name could have come from him or from the original owners. The choice is up to you.

WOFFORD HEIGHTS

The post office of Wofford Heights, Kern County—established in 1953—was named for the town's founder, I. L. Wofford.

WOOD (— Acre; —fords; —lake; —land; —land Hills; —side; —ville)

The early use of the word "wood" in place names indicates what was there when settlers arrived.

WOODY

The town of Woody was founded in 1862, and it was named for ranchowner Sparrell W. Woody.

WRIGHTWOOD

When they subdivided the old Circle C Ranch here in San Bernardino County in 1924, the townspeople named it for the developer. Five years later, the post office was established under that name.

YERMO

Originally, this San Bernardino County spot was called Otis, after the station of the San Pedro, Los Angeles & Salt Lake Railroad was opened here in 1904 or 1905. The name was changed in 1908, when the post office was established. The word *yermo* is Spanish for "desert."

YETTEM

"Paradise" is what the Armenian settlers, led by the Reverend Jenanya, used to describe their settlement here in 1902.

YOLO

Yolo, Yolo County, has a Patwin Indian name, meaning "place abounding with rushes" or "possession of royal blood." Others think that the name is that of a tribe of the Patwins.

The Yolo post office was established in 1853, and it replaced the earlier name of Cacheville.

YORBA LINDA

Yorba Linda was part of the original Rancho Santa Ana, which was granted to Jose Antonio Yorba in the early 19th century.

In 1888, a town grew up not far from the present-day site. Called Carlton, it failed because of a lack of water. Learning from hard experience, the next developer sold water stock with each acre. So in 1908 Yorba Linda began.

The name is a combination of linda, "beautiful" in Spanish, and the family name. Another authority indicates that Yorba merged with the town of Olinda in about 1913, and thus the name would be a combination of two towns.

The Richard Nixon Library and Birthplace are located here.

YORKVILLE

In the 1870s, when this Mendocino County community was getting ready to have its own post office, a promise arose. Who should they honor with the name? There were two prominent families, the Hiatts and the Yorks. Since they could not settle it in any other way, they had the heads of both clans involve themselves in a contest of some sort. Richard H. York won. Elijah M. Hiatt was consoled. He was named the first postmaster in Yorkville.

YOSEMITE VILLAGE

Yosemite Village took its name from the nearby Yosemite National Park. Yosemite Park was the first "national" park, set aside by Abraham Lincoln on 30 June 1864 as a state park. Twenty-six years later it officially became a national park. The name was taken from the Yosemite River.

The Yosemite Valley was discovered by Joseph R. Walker in 1833.

YOUNTVILLE

George C. Yount arrived here in 1835 and built the first home in the Napa Valley. It was a two-story log cabin similar to what he remembered from his home in North Carolina. The Yountville name appears on an 1860 map of the Rancho Caymus grant.

YREKA

The stories behind the naming of this Siskiyou County community are filled with legend and an inability to translate the Indian tongue into some semblance of English. Some say the name was the original title for Mount Shasta. The first syllable translates from the Shasta Indian tongue to mean "north." Another opines that the word *I-e'-ka* means "white."

According to local tradition, the name was created by a drunken cowhand who shot up a local bakery. He shot the "B" out of the sign, and flipped it over so it read "YREKA." The only problem is that not only would the word be reversed, the letters would be, too.

The more logical—but less fun—suggestion was that the townspeople wanted to name the town after Mount Shasta, then known as Yreka or Ieka. Unable to figure out how to spell the name, they spelled it as it sounded.

Yreka was incorporated in 1857, six years after Abraham Thompson's mules pulled up chunks of grass with gold flecks in the roots!

YUBA CITY

The name was taken from Yuba County, which was named for the river. The original Spanish name for the river was el Rio de las Uvas, "the river of the grapes."

Yuba City was founded in 1849 as part of the gold rush. An interesting sidelight . . . Cuba City, Wisconsin was originally named Yuba to honor this city. Postal authorities rejected the name.

YUCAIPA

This San Bernardino County town was named for the Yucaipa Valley, once inhabited by the Serrano Indians. The Indians called the valley "Green Valley," but early 19th century settlers could not pronounce the guttural Indian, so they wrote it down as Ucipe or Yucaipe.

YUCCA VALLEY

Located in San Bernardino County, the valley took its name from the abundance of *Yucca brevifolia*, the Joshua tree.

ZAMORA

Until the Southern Pacific Railroad decided in 1910 to change the name of their station in Yolo County, it was called Blacks.

Zamora is the name of a Spanish city and province. The post office used that name beginning in 1916.

ZENIA

Zenia, Trinity County, was named in 1900 by the first postmaster, George Croyden, for an unidentified young woman.

Lhe first official forays into the territory that became Nevada began in 1843 and were led by Captain John C. Frémont. The first permanent settlement in this area grew up around a trading post, established by Mormons from Salt Lake City, Utah, in 1850. They called the settlement Mormon Station. Today, it is Genoa. Five years later, the Mormons set up another mission fort, which became today's beacon in the desert: Las Vegas.

Before 1850, Nevada—then part of the Utah Territory—was merely a vast desert, an obstacle that had to be crossed on the way to golden California. Nevada came into its own when gold was discovered in that year in what became known as Gold Canyon. It was not until a decade later that gold miners realized that the blue clay they had been scrapping out of their claims and throwing away was actually silver ore. The discovery of the Comstock Lode, possibly the richest finds of silver and gold in the world, gave Nevada a new, singular identity.

After Comstock, Nevada was separated from the Utah Territory and became a territory of its own. Three years later, in 1864, Nevada became a state. Many believe the reason for statehood was that two more votes were needed for the 13th amendment to abolish slavery!

Everyone seemed to gain from statehood. President Lincoln gained support for his programs and the Republican Party. Business and industry leaders in the state also gained. After all, the Comstock Lode helped finance Union operations during the War. During this boon period, a miner-turned-reporter helped create the drama and romance of the diggings. Samuel Clemens, better known as Mark Twain, made life in the gold and silver mines forever famous. But the mines could not last forever.

The "Big Bonanza" of the 1870s brought with it prosperity, but left behind depression. There was a resurrection of the old mining days in the early 20th century with gold and silver discovered at

Tonopah, in the south. That was followed by another find at Gold-field in 1902. Then copper was found at Ely.

The people of Nevada by then had learned from their past mistakes. Rather than base their total economy on the precious metals of the ground, they decided to begin a recyclable economy.

What were once desert regions became fruitful through newly-developed irrigation techniques. Shepherds found that the verdant land was also conducive to the raising of sheep. But they all paled by 1931. In that year, gambling was legalized in the state, and Las Vegas and Reno became meccas to the sporting crowd. Along with legislation that liberalized divorce and marriage regulations, Nevada grew into one of the busiest year-round resort locations in the nation.

The cities, towns and villages of Nevada reflect its past in vivid tones. The dust of gold, silver and copper can still be found in many names. So, too, can we find the thread of Nevada's history—its people, their passions and their times.

ADAVEN
On your toes: Adaven is "Nevada" spelled backwards.

ALAMO
This old Mormon settlement was named for the cottonwoods that proliferated the area. *Alamo* is Spanish for "cottonwood tree."

This town was laid out by Fred Allen, Mike Botts, Bert Riggs, and Thomas F. Stewart. Many early settlers were immigrants from Fredonia, Arizona. The Alamo post office opened here in 1905.

ALUNITE
This Clark County community was named for the Alunite Mining District.

The Alunite Mine was opened in 1908 by Robert T. Hill, a mining geologist, who mined alunite.

ARDEN
Arden, Clark County, grew up around the Arden Plaster Company's mill. The mill operated here until 1919.

An Arden post office was established in 1907, two years before the mill opened. This suggests that the name, given by the Union Pacific Railroad, indicated a more classical touch. (See ARDEN, California.)

ARTHUR

The town of Arthur, Elko County, was named for President Chester A. Arthur. The president had been elected in the same year that this community opened its first post office.

ASH SPRINGS

This Lincoln County community drew its name from the ash trees that proliferate in the area and the presence of a group of large natural springs.

ARTHUR. Chester Alan Arthur was the protégé of New York's Roscoe "Boss" Conkling, leader of one of the most notorious political machines. When President Garfield was assassinated, Vice President Arthur moved into the White House and surprised everyone by reforming the civil service, a hot-bed of the spoils system. (Print and Picture Department, Free Library of Philadelphia)

AUSTIN

According to local legend, Austin came into being in 1862, when a Pony Express horse kicked over a stone that capped the mouth of a silver-filled cave. Others suggest William Talcott discovered silver here in 1863.

The boom created many fortunes and much disappointment. The output of the mines began to peter out in 1868, and people began to move away to Eureka and Hamilton. When the Central Pacific Railroad bypassed the town, it sounded the death knell.

A relic of Austin's former affluence is Stokes' Castle, built for Anson Phelps Stokes in 1897. A businessman from the East with large mining holdings, Stokes had his home built of hand-hewn granite slabs. It is now an empty three-story replica of a Roman tower that can be seen for miles in the desert.

Austin became seat of Lander County in 1863 after wrestling power away from Jacobsville, eight miles northeast of Austin.

The source of the name is up for grabs. Depending on which source you read, Austin came from: David Buel, who laid out the townsite and named it for Alvah C. Austin, his partner; Buel, who came from Austin, Texas; a move to honor pioneer John Austin; or Leander Kelse Austin, uncle of Jumbo Mine developer George Austin.

An early name for Austin was Pony, a designation given the site by riders of the Pony Express. In 1862, when William M. Talcott, an agent for the Overland Stage, came across a silver float in Pony Canyon, he called it Pony Ledge. The first settlement was around the silver mine, and it was called Clifton. When a better site was selected up the mountain, Clifton, Austin and Upper Austin were merged into one in 1864.

BABBITT

Located in Mineral County, Babbitt was once operated by the U.S. Navy, and it was named for Captain H. S. Babbitt in 1935. At the time, the captain was Inspector of Ordnance in Charge of the Naval Ammunition Depot at Hawthorne.

BAKER

Baker, White Pine County, was established as a post office in 1895 near the ranch of George W. Baker. Baker was one of the earliest settlers to the Snake Valley.

BASALT

Basalt, Mineral County, received its first post office in 1906. Once a minor supply center for prospectors, it was named for the abundance of black basalt rock in the area.

BATTLE MOUNTAIN

This Lander County community, located where the Reese River joins the Humboldt, took its name from the nearby Battle Mountain, which was named after an 1857 Indian raid against pioneers. The Indians attacked a wagon train at Gravelly Ford and killed several people before escaping with a great deal of loot. They were pursued and hit twice, suffering so heavily that this episode ended Indian attacks along the river. No one is quite sure if the raid was on the John Kirk road-building party or on an emigrant train.

Minerals were discovered in Copper Canyon in 1866. The Little Giant mine, discovered the next year, was located at the original Battle Mountain camp, a few miles from the present site. In 1868, the town of Battle Mountain was established to supply the new mining camps. With the arrival of the railroad in 1870, it became the transfer point for mining supplies between the stage and railroad.

BEATTY

Located on the banks of the Amargosa River, Beatty was the terminus of the Tonopah & Tidewater Railroad where it was a supply base for the mining camps.

Beatty handled most of the freight for the Bullfrog Mining District, first explored in 1904. The town proudly proclaimed itself the "Chicago of Nevada."

The town's namesake was M. M. Beatty, known locally as the "Old Man" or "Jim" Beatty who owned a ranch here in Nye County. The town was platted in 1904 or 1905, and the post office was established in 1905.

BEOWAWE

Before white settlement in this Eureka County area, Beowawe was a Paiute year-round campsite because of the hot springs and geysers to the south.

The name, it is said, was drawn from the Paiute language and was intended to describe the location. The word translates as "pass" or "gateway." Others indicate the name was that of an Indian or that it means "big posterior."

Beowawe was the home of the famous Horseshoe Ranch. The railroad arrived in 1868, with a station under this name.

BLUE DIAMOND

This Clark County town grew up around the Blue Diamond Corporation, producers of lime. The California-based company's founder, J. J. Jamison, felt that the quality of his product—plaster-board—was comparable to that of the most precious of all gemstones. When the post office was opened in 1942, the people agreed that Blue Diamondville was a good name for them. By the end of the year, the "-ville" was gone. An earlier name was Cottonwood.

BOULDER CITY

Boulder City, Clark County, was constructed in 1932 by the federal government to house employees of the Bureau of Reclamation, Park Service and Bureau of Mines branches in the area during construction of Boulder Dam. Construction workers preferred living near their work, rather than commuting 30 miles to Las Vegas. The town was designed by S. R. de Boer.

When the town was under construction, the Department of Interior's Bureau of Reclamation thought of possible names, such as Adaven, Hidam, Hoover City, and Wilber. Boulder City was the final selection. In 1931, a post office opened under that name.

Because of the federal involvement and the details of the original land grant, Boulder City is the only place in Nevada without legalized gambling.

BUNKERVILLE

Bunkerville, Clark County, is an old Mormon settlement—originally called Mesquite.

The current town honors Edward Bunker, of St. George, Utah. Bunker came to Nevada in 1877 as a missionary to the Indians. He had also served as a member of the Mormon Battalion in the Mexican War.

Mesquite, about six miles north of here, was founded in the 1870s by other Utah emigrants. When a post office opened in this area in 1879, the name was changed to Bunkerville.

CACTUS SPRINGS

Located in Clark County, Cactus Springs took its name from the mining district in which it is located. That name came from the Cactus Mountain Range. As one might imagine, there are abundant collections of cacti hereabouts.

CALIENTE

Caliente, Lincoln County, was first named Dutch Flat when settled in the 1870s with the founding of the Jackman Ranch.

When the Clark Road, later the Union Pacific Railroad, extended service here and opened a station in the late 1880s, the stop was called Clover or Cloverdale Station—after the nearby stream.

In 1901, when the town was laid out, the name became Calientes, Spanish for "hot," because of the hot springs found in the area. When the post office opened later in that year, the "s" was dropped from the corporate name.

CAL NEV ARI

Cal Nev Ari is located where California, Nevada and Arizona meet.

CANDELARIA

Candelaria, Mineral County, took its name from the Mexican word for a species of branching cactus.

Silver was discovered in this area by Mexican prospectors in 1864. A year later, the largest deposit was claimed, but the owner did not take advantage of his good luck. It was not until 15 years later that the lode, called the Northern Belle, was rediscovered.

A Candelaria post office was opened here in 1876. Over the years, the name has been spelled Candalara and Candalaria. The post office was still in operation when Mineral County was formed from Esmeralda.

CARLIN

Before the arrival of the railroad in 1867, the gorge at Carlin Pass had been impassable. Emigrants camped near the site of the present-day Elko County community before detouring northwest through Emigrant Pass in the Mary Creek Mountains.

The town of Carlin was settled about then by J. A. Palmer, S. Pierce, C. Boyen and James Clark. Because of its location, the town grew. Railroad shops were built here because of a large spring of pure, cold water. The Carlin post office was established in 1868.

Railroad officials named the community for Civil War General William Passmore Carlin, who served at Camp Floyd, Utah Territory, during the 1850s.

CARP

Located in Lincoln County, Carp was first settled in 1907. At first they called the community Cliffdale, which was descriptive.

Railroad officials, on the other hand, called the station Carp, for an employee. Since the station agent was also the postmaster, the Carp name survived. The post office was officially Carp in 1925.

CARSON CITY

Carson City was named for Kit Carson when it was founded in 1858. It became the state's capital in 1864. Before it became Carson City, the town had several names.

During the winter of 1851, a group of gold-seekers found that their dream of great wealth was not to be a reality. Discovering no gold, they decided to build a log cabin and turn it into a trading post. While they were working, one of their number shot an eagle and nailed the skin to a wall. This gave the place the name of Eagle Station. Later, the name became Eagle Ranch and the area around it came to be called Eagle Valley.

Many of the people coming through Eagle Valley were Mormons and Eagle Ranch became a social center. This ended in 1857 when Brigham Young called his followers to the City of the Great Salt Lake in Utah. The Mormon settlers sold off their land to John Mankin at bargain prices—paid for in wheat! Mankin later sold the land.

A year later, Abraham V. Z. Curry had the present town laid out and surveyed. He expected the western part of Utah to be separated from the east, soon becoming a state. In his desire to get the town developed, Curry offered free land to anyone who would construct a building here.

Major William M. Ormsby took Curry up on his offer. A major promoter of the town, he named it in honor of Kit Carson. The post office at Carson City was established in 1858.

Sierra Academy was opened here in 1860 by Hannah Clapp. It was one of the first coeducational institutions in the West. Clapp, an ardent suffragette, operated the school for about 25 years before moving to Reno. There, she and the university president were the entire faculty and staff at the beginning of the University of Nevada.

When legislators laid out the Nevada territory into counties, Carson City was named seat of Ormsby County. Ormsby and Carson City were ultimately consolidated into one municipal government.

CASELTON

Caselton, Lincoln County, was created by Combined Metals Reduction Company in the 1920s. The town was named for J. A. Caselton, an official of the National Lead Company.

CENTERVILLE

Centerville, Douglas County, took its name from its location. The town is situated in the middle of the valley.

CHERRY CREEK

Cherry Creek, White Pine County, took its name from the nearby Cherry Creek. The waterway, in turn, was named for the chokeberries found there.

Between 1872 and 1883, the camp here was the center of its district. As the mining intensified, most of the buildings from the camps at Schellbourne and Egan Canyon were moved here. Ten years later, copper, lead, silver, and gold had been removed and the town's popularity declined. A post office was established here in 1873. The name has varied in spelling over the years; sometimes the name is one word, sometimes two.

COALDALE

Coaldale, Esmeralda County, was named because deposits of low-grade coal were found here.

William Groetzinger (Groezinger) discovered the bituminous deposits and mined 150 tons, which he sold to the Columbia Borax works in 1894. A post office was established here in 1904.

COLD SPRINGS

Cold Springs, Churchill County, took its name from "a small running brook of icy-cold, pure water . . . which, after running a few hundred yards, sinks. . . ."

CONTACT

Contact was a mining camp, established in 1895 in the Contact Mining District. The district was so named because it was on the "contact" of limestone and granite. A post office under the name of Contact was established in 1897.

CORDERO MINE

Cordero Mine, Humboldt County, took the name of the Cordero Mine which operated west of Quinn River. *Cordero* is Spanish for "lamb," but some sources believe the true source is a family name.

CRESCENT VALLEY

Turquoise was discovered here in 1894 by an Indian, known as Prospector Johnnie. A year after his discovery, a New York operation began work as the Toltec Gem Company.

Crescent Valley is located in Eureka County, and its name was taken from the valley along the Eureka-Lander county line. The name of the valley is descriptive of its shape.

CRYSTAL BAY

The resort community of Crystal Bay, Washoe County, is located on Crystal Bay. The body of water was so named because of its clear water. A post office was established here under that name in 1937.

CURRANT

Located at the western base of the Grant Range, Currant was also known as the Callaway Ranch. The town, in Nye County, took its name from a tributary of the Wild Cat Creek. Wild currants were found around Currant Creek when it was first named.

CURRIE

At one time a shipping point for cattle and sheep on the Nevada Northern Railroad, Currie was named for an early settler.

Joseph H. Currie, who operated a ranch here in Elko County in 1885, had his name emblazoned on the town, the railroad station and the post office, which was established in 1906.

DAYTON

The first quartz mill in Nevada was built here on the banks of the Carson River to treat ore from the Comstock Lode.

The earlier name for Dayton, Lyon County, was Ponderer's Rest, because California-bound settlers would often stop here and decide whether to proceed westward or turn south to settle along the rivers. Later, in about 1853, Spafford Hall created a permanent station and called it Hall's Station. After he sold it to James McMarlin the next year, it became known as McMarlin's Station.

By 1855, gold fever had taken over and work began at Gold Canyon Flat Diggings. The next year, because of the dominance of Oriental workers, the townsite was called Chinatown. This offended the sensibilities of some, who proceeded to call the village either Mineral Rapids or Nevada City. Another source even suggests the town was once called Clinton!

Finally, in 1866, the townspeople voted and named the town Dayton. The honoree was John Day, a surveyor who was passing through town and agreed to plat the site only if the people named the town after him. Two years later, Day was elected Surveyor General of Nevada. The first post office was established here in 1868.

DEETH

Deeth was, at one time, a shipping point for ranchers on the Mary's River. The town, located in Elko County, was established in 1868, with the building of the Central Pacific. Railroad officials named the station and ultimately the town for the first settler. The post office was established in 1875.

DENIO (— Junction)

Denio, Humboldt County, was a lonely outpost in the desert, almost on the Oregon state line. The town was named for Aaron Denio, a pioneer who moved to the Winnemucca area from Illinois in the 1860s. The first Denio post office was established here, on the Oregon side of the line, in the latter part of the 19th century. The post office at the Nevada site was established in 1951.

DIXIE VALLEY

One source thinks the word "Dixie" came from a Creole pronunciation of Jeremiah Dixon who, with Charles Mason, surveyed the boundaries between Pennsylvania and Maryland. Their boundary line became known as the Mason-Dixon Line.

Dixie Valley, Churchill County, took its name from the valley of the same name. The valley was originally known as Osobb. A post office was opened at Dixie Valley in 1918.

DRESSLERVILLE

In 1917, William F. Dressler gave 40 acres in Douglas County to the Washo Indians "in trust" as long as the tribe lived there.

DUCKWATER

At one point in its history, in the early 20th century, Duckwater was nothing more than a ranch house that sometimes was used as a base for hunters.

The town, in Nye County, is located in and named for Duckwater Valley, which is watered by Duckwater Creek. The nearby marshes act as natural feeding grounds for water fowl all winter.

The post office was first established here in 1873.

DUNPHY

Dunphy, Eureka County, was headquarters to the Dunphy Ranch, one of the largest cattle ranches in the state. The name-source, of course, is the family.

DYER

This Esmeralda County community, near the California state line, was named in 1889 by Alex P. Dyer, the town's first postmaster.

EASTGATE

Until 1876, Eastgate had been a stage station for years, located at the mouth of a narrow canyon. It was considered the "eastern" entrance to the canyon. In 1876, George B. Williams assumed ownership and began the Williams Ranch.

Three years later, Williams had a little house built of tufa-block construction. Tufa is lighter than sandstone and is considered ideal for building construction. A second tufa building was erected in 1908.

Eastgate was a popular stopping-off spot for new settlers. The locals would stage mock murders, hangings and all the other "fun" things that happen in theme parks today.

ECHO BAY

Echo Bay was named for a canyon in Clark County, the Echo Wash. The name came from the sound wagons and horses made when they ran on the main road from old Saint Thomas to Callville.

ELGIN

This Lincoln County community was named at the time of settlement, around 1882, about a mile north of where it is today. The name came from Elgin, Illinois, the town in Scotland, or the Earl of Elgin.

It is most likely the name came from Illinois since it was a railroad practice—and the Union Pacific named the station—to migrate names from the East. The Elgin post office was established in 1913.

ELKO

Elko, Elko County, began as a freight point for local mining camps. Even before the Central Pacific Railroad built a construction camp here in 1868, there were people in town who could arrange for trail bosses, riders, real estate, or whatever. In fact, the first settler was George F. Pattleford. The post office was established here in 1869.

In the late 19th century, Elko was the "reluctant" site of an execution—the only woman ever hanged in Nevada.

It seems that this woman had married a second husband while on vacation in California. The only problem was that she never divorced her first husband. When #2 followed her back to Elko County, she murdered him and hid the body under her house. She and #1 husband left, but the body was quickly discovered. She was apprehended, tried and convicted.

The town's name came from the Shoshone Indian, meaning "white woman." Elko was the first town that interrupted the line of railroad town names, given by the Central Pacific's Charles Crocker, that bore Civil War veteran's names. Tradition has it that Crocker, regardless of the Indian derivation, took the word "elk," and added the "o" for euphony.

Another story is that a pioneering party found a starving Indian boy near the site of present-day Elko. The people cared for him—along with another ailing child, a white boy. They learned the Indian child was the son of a chief. When the young white child died, the Indians chanted death songs, and the chief cried "Elko" again and again. When the white child's father returned to the site, he found a gravestone over his son's grave. It was marked "Elko," and he learned the word meant "beautiful." It is a charming story, but quite fictional.

ELY

Ely, White Pine County, was founded in 1868 as a silver-mining camp by George Lamb. At first, the village was called Murry Creek Station. The town blossomed when the Nevada Northern Railway arrived in 1906.

A. J. Underhill named the town either for Smith Ely or for John H. Ely of Pioche. Smith Ely was an absentee mine owner. Underhill had borrowed $5,000 from him to purchase and lay out the townsite. Ely was a typical mining man. He made and lost millions of dollars, over and over again.

A post office opened under the name of Ely in 1878. In 1887, it became the county seat.

EMPIRE

Empire, Washoe County, was created by the Pacific Portland Cement Company in 1922. The company operated a gypsum plant here, and "Empire" was the brand-name for some gypsum products.

The Empire post office was established here in 1951.

EUREKA

"Eureka" was the phrase an early miner allegedly shouted when a rich vein of ore was discovered. The expression comes from a legend about Archimedes. The Greek mathematician and inventor was supposed to have shouted that phrase when he discovered a way to determine the purity of the gold in King Hiero's crown.

A group of prospectors from Austin, W. O. Arnold, W. R. Tannehill, G. T. Tannehill, J. W. Stotts and Moses Wilson, discovered the first significant silver-lead deposit in the United States in 1864.

Because no one knew how to smelt the ore, there was no great influx of miners. The surge did not occur until 1869, when Major W. W. McCoy employed R. P. Jones and John Williams, two experienced Welsh smeltermen who devised a small smelter that would process the ore. The town of Eureka was then founded by the miners. By 1890 or 1891, the miners had exhausted the supply and moved off for new digs. (See EUREKA, California.)

FALLON

Fallon, the seat of Churchill County, came into being as a result of reclamation and irrigation activities following the completion of the Lahontan Dam in 1914.

When the post office was opened on Mike Fallon's Ranch in 1896, the name became that of the rancher.

FRENCHMAN

Frenchman is the official name for this Churchill County community. Previously, it had been called Bermond, Frenchman Station or Frenchman's Station.

GABBS

This Nye County community took its name from Gabbs Valley. A creek by the name of Gabbs also flows through the valley. When a post office was established here in 1942, it was called Toiyake. The next year, it was changed to Gabbs. The name commemorates E. S. Gabbs, an engineer.

GARDNERVILLE

In 1879, Lawrence Gilman bought a piece of the homestead owned by John M. Gardner and his wife Mary. Gilman moved a hotel that was known as Kent Hotel to the site, and renamed it the Gardnerville Hotel, in honor of John and Mary.

The post office was established at this Douglas County site—in the hotel—in 1881.

GENOA

Genoa was founded in 1849 by H. S. Beattie, one of the traders sent out by Mormon leader Brigham Young. It is the oldest permanent settlement in the state, begun while Nevada was still part of western Utah. Its original name was Mormon Station.

In 1851, the site was selected by Colonel John Reese and Jacob A. Dinsey (or Kinsey) for a trading post. Four years later, after the town was surveyed, Judge Orson Hyde, one of the 12 apostles of the Mormon Church, renamed it Genoa. The judge had visited Italy and was struck with the similarity between the cove in the "mountain" and Columbus' birthplace. The first post office of Genoa was opened in 1852 as Carson Valley—in Utah Territory. It was transferred to Nevada Territory in 1861.

In 1859, the first territorial legislature met here to discuss separation from the Utah Territory. Congress, realizing the importance of the Comstock Lode in financing Union efforts during the Civil War, established the Territory of Nevada in 1861. Genoa was named seat of Douglas County in that year.

Genoa was the site of the demise of "Fighting" Sam Brown, a man from Virginia City who boasted he had filled a cemetery. Brown came to Genoa to attend the murder trial of one of his cronies and to intimidate the judge. He failed in his attempt: District Attorney Bill Stewart took his testimony while holding a revolver to Brown's head.

Brown was a mite angry when he left Genoa and fired off some random shots at a quiet resident of the town, a Dutchman by the name of Henry Van Sickle. Van Sickle snapped. He took his shotgun, trailed Brown, and killed him in a fair fight. The jury's verdict read that Brown had "come to his end from a just dispensation of an all-wise Providence."

GERLACH

Frémont's expedition camped in this Washoe County during the winter of 1843. The town, however, was settled in 1906 and named for the Gerlach Land & Cattle Company, located on the nearby Gerlach and Waltz Ranch.

Located in Washoe County, Gerlach's post office was established in 1909.

GLENBROOK

Glenbrook, Douglas County, is a resort on Lake Tahoe. In 1861, Glenbrook became a lumbering town after a sawmill was erected here. In fact, the mill was the first sawmill erected on the Nevada side of the lake.

The name for the community came from the old Glenbrook House, a hotel that was named for its location in a glen, by a brook.

GLENDALE

When Mormon settlers established a station here in Washoe County in 1852, they called it Jamison's Station. For several years, it was the only station on the Truckee River. Five years later, the post office was opened here under the name of Stone and Gates' Crossing, for store-owners John F. Stone and Charles C. Gates.

Sometime before 1866, John Larcombe, of Weymouth, England, arrived and opened a combination store-post office. Larcombe suggested that the name become Glendale. The Glendale post office began operation a year later.

GOLCONDA

Golconda took its name from the city in India. Golconda, India, was the capital of the Kutb Shahai dynasty, and it was famous for its diamonds.

The Humboldt County town has been inhabited since 1861 and was once a shipping spot for cattlemen. Located here are the Golconda Hot Springs, long valued for their therapeutic value.

The settlement was built in 1868, and it was first known as Greggsville. W. C. Gregg was the discoverer and owner of the Golconda Mining District.

The Golconda post office was established in 1869.

GOLDFIELD

Goldfield was the offspring of Tonopah. A few miles from the silver mines at Tonopah, Tom Fisherman, a Shoshone, found a gold nugget. Fisherman showed off his find, and Tom Kendall, owner of the Tonopah Club, provided the money for Billy Marsh and Harry Stimler to look for the spot where Fisherman found the gold.

They staked their first claim in 1902, even though the ore found there was of low yield. Marsh and Stimler lost some of their claims, but pointed out "good" spots to newcomers. One of these "good" spots turned into the Jumbo Mine. It earned Charles Taylor $1.25 million. It had been the location of Marsh and Stimler's first stake! After this discovery, Goldfield blossomed. Metallurgic experts assayed the land and found gold running for miles in all directions, and the ore was high-grade. Production reached its peak in 1910.

Part of Goldfield's success came from the entrepreneur's leasing system that not only developed the area but also publicized its existence.

This Esmeralda County community took its name from Goldfield, Colorado, even though the donor had suggested Goldfields (in the plural) as the name. The Goldfield post office was established here in 1903.

GOLD POINT

This Esmeralda County site was first settled as a town in 1872. A post office was opened here under the name of Gold Point in 1932, replacing the earlier name of Hornsilver. The current name came from the Gold Point Mining District.

GOODSPRINGS

Goodsprings, Clark County, took its name from the source of the water found here. The town began as a mining camp for silver, gold, platinum and vanadium.

The springs commemorate Joseph Good, who settled here in 1868. During the next decade, Good built a small hand smelter to test ores. The town was organized around Good's settlement in about 1885. The Goodsprings post office was established in 1899.

Many motion pictures have been filmed in the vicinity of the town, since it appears almost as a stereotypical view of the "Old West," complete with cactus and Joshua trees.

HALLECK

Located on the north bank of the Humboldt River in Elko County, Halleck was established to serve Camp—then Fort—Halleck. The original name was Halleck Station.

Camp Halleck was established in 1867 and closed 20 years later. The troops here were never engaged in battle, but their presence aided in encouraging immigration by protecting the Central Pacific Railroad and stage routes. Captain S. P. Smith, Company H, 8th U. S. Cavalry, established the post under orders from Major General Henry W. Halleck (1815–72), for whom the installation was named. In 1879, Camp Halleck became Fort Halleck.

The fort site is identified to today's visiters by a stone marker in a privately-owned meadow.

HAWTHORNE

Hawthorne, seat of Mineral County, was settled in about 1939 by prospectors and miners who made some interesting discoveries. At one point, there was a naval ammunition depot located here.

Hawthorne came into being in the early 1880s with the construction of the Carson & Colorado Railroad. The post office was established at this site, then in Esmeralda County, in 1881.

The town name came from William Hawthorn, a cattleman and early justice of the peace. His name appeared without the "e" prior to 1883, at which time his name appeared in the *Walker Lake Bulletin* with the "e" added. At one time, the community had been known as Hawthorne City.

HAZEN

Hazen, Churchill County, was once the trading center for ranchers. It was located at a junction of the Southern Pacific Railroad with the Tonopah & Goldfield.

The town was first settled in 1869, and it was named for William Babcock Hazen. Hazen was an Army officer who served as an aide to William Tecumseh Sherman.

The Hazen post office opened its doors in 1904.

HENDERSON

Henderson, Clark County, was established during World War II as housing for employees at a local magnesium plant.

Basic Magnesium, a subsidiary of Basic Refractories, of Ohio, entered into a contract with the Defense Plant Corporation in 1941. With power available from Boulder Dam, the company promised to deliver 112 million pounds of magnesium a year. Political leaders recognized the future potential of the plant following the war and successfully lobbied to have the plant remain in operation.

Laid out in 1942, Henderson was known for a while as Basic, for the company. The Henderson name honors State Senator A. S. Henderson. The post office opened under his name in 1944.

HIKO

Hiko, Lincoln County, was founded with high expectations in 1866, but little ore was found here. The first name for the community was Paah Ranagat. In fact, a post office was opened under that name in March of 1867. By June of the same year, the post office name was Hiko.

Some feel the word comes from the Shoshone and means "white man" or "white man's city."

HUMBOLDT

Humboldt took its name from the river, which was named by Frémont for Alexander von Humboldt, the German explorer. As early as 1827, the river was known as the Unknown River. Later it became Mary's River, for the Indian wife of Peter Skene Ogden, a Hudson Bay Company explorer; Ogden's River; and Paul's, for one of Ogden's men, who was killed on the bank of the stream.

The town's origins go back to a trading post, operated in 1860 by Louis Barbeau and A. Gintz. The two Frenchmen reported a mineral bonanza which attracted so much attention that the city was created.

IMLAY

Imlay in Pershing County honors a civil engineer named Imlay who surveyed the town in 1908. A post office by that name was established the same year.

INCLINE VILLAGE

Incline Village, located on Incline Creek, was founded in 1882. Located in Washoe County, the town took the name of the waterway. The name came from the sixteen-hundred-foot incline up which lumber was hauled before it was sent to the mines.

INDIAN SPRINGS

At one time, Indian Springs, Clark County, was a stop on the stage coach, a veritable desert oasis, located near warm springs. A post office opened here under the Indian Springs name in 1917.

JACK CREEK

This Elko County site is located at the confluence of Harrington and Jack creeks. The town took the name from the latter waterway.

Both names recall Jack Harrington, an early rancher. The creek's name appears on early maps as Harrington Creek.

JACKPOT

This name was given because the major business of this village on the Idaho border was—and still is—gambling.

Originally named Unincorporated Town No. 1, this Elko County spot became Jackpot in 1959.

JARBIDGE

The name Jarbidge was presumably applied to this area because of the rugged terrain and the presence of hot springs. The name may have come from the Shoshone Indian *ja-ha-bich*, the "devil." Another suggestion is that the word came from *Tswhawbitts*, the name of a mythical giant who preyed on Indians.

The town grew up around gold and silver mines, which were exploited beginning in 1910. Considered the most isolated mining camp in the state, Jarbridge had its postal link with the outside world established in 1910.

JEAN

Jean took the name of the wife of George Fayle who lived in this Clark County area. A post office, established in 1905, carried her name.

JIGGS

The name of Jiggs came as a result of a dispute among town residents over a permanent name for the community. Originally it was called Mound Valley, Skelton and Hilton. The name came from a comic strip, "Maggie & Jiggs," by George McManus. Some federal official remembered the strip for Jiggs' ongoing feuds with his wife Maggie.

Zane Grey used this site in some of his fiction as the headquarters of King Fisher. The post office at Jiggs opened its doors in 1918.

LAMOILLE

Lamoille, founded in the mid-19th century, took its name from the nearby Lamoille Canyon and stream. The name came from a French trapper who, tradition tells us, built a cabin here.

Lamoille Canyon was reportedly named in 1865 by Thomas Waterman for his Vermont home. The name has been spelled a num-

L

aber of ways, such as Lemoille, La Moile and La Moille. In 1868, the settlement begun by John P. Walker was called The Crossroads.

LAS VEGAS

Las Vegas was once an oasis for pioneers enroute to California. It began as a Mormon settlement in 1855 and grew during the silver boom.

The Mormons were successful in their reclamation efforts and were able to grow crops in the desert. They did have some trouble with their mining efforts. The bullets they made, it was found, were "very hard to smelt." They never realized that the lead they used to cast bullets contained galena ore which carried silver.

The town officially began in 1855, when William Bringhust and a band of 30 were dispatched by Brigham Young from the City of the Great Salt Lake "to go to Las Vegas, build a fort there to protect immigrants and the United States mail from the Indians, and to teach the latter how to raise corn, wheat, potatoes, squash, and melons." One year later, a post office was established here and called Bringhurst. This was one of the few instances where Mormons were involved in mining.

The mines closed in 1857 when the Mormons abandoned the site. When O. D. Glass acquired the land and water rights, the town and ranch were in the Territory of Arizona. He sat on the territorial legislature. During the Civil War, three companies of cavalry and one of infantry were stationed here to protect travellers on their way to California. The post was known as Fort Baker. Mining was revived and the Eldorado Canyon became an important gold and silver producer. But, as in other areas, the ore supply petered out.

Ranching brought life back to Las Vegas in the late 19th century. In 1903, W. A. Clark, a former senator from Montana, acting for the San Pedro, Los Angeles & Salt Lake City Railroad, acquired the old Glass ranch, and established a townsite. Before he could get things moving, J. T. McWilliams acquired land beside it and called it McWilliamstown. It was quickly flooded with settlers, and it is now part of "Old Town" Las Vegas.

Las Vegas began a new age in 1904, with the arrival of the Union Pacific Railroad. In 1911, the Nevada legislature created the City of Las Vegas. In 1931, as construction work began on Hoover Dam, Las Vegas enjoyed a windfall: legalized gambling. Casinos sprang up to cater to the hundreds of men who flocked into Las Vegas and Boulder City to find work on the dam. After World War II came the big hotels, the big casinos, the world's greatest singers, dancers and comedians.

Las Vegas is flash and glitz, but it is an American institution. Its name comes from the Spanish for "meadow." In early days, the grassy meadows made fine camping places.

LAUGLIN

In 1970, we are told, Lauglin was nothing more than an unnamed bait shop on the Colorado River. With the advent of gambling, it was turned into a gambling mecca. It is located near the southern tip of Nevada on the California border and across the Colorado River from Arizona.

LEE (— Canyon)

Lee, Clark County, was settled in 1863, but it was named at a later date by J. L. Martin, for Lee Creek. The waterway was named in 1869 for Confederate General Robert E. Lee.

The post office here was established in 1882.

LIDA

Lida, Esmeralda County, is located in the Lida Valley Mining District from whence it took its name. The district was discovered in 1869 by William Scott. A post office under the Lida name was transferred here from California in 1873.

The name itself is a shortening of Alida, the wife of David Buel, of Austin.

LOGANDALE

Logandale, Clark County, was first settled by Mormons in 1864, and called Saint Joseph. The name was changed—again by Mormons—in 1881 to Logan "after the principal settlers of the new migration." Robert Logan was a prominent member of the sect and a settler in the Moapa Valley.

A Logan post office was established in 1895, but it was then changed to Logandale in 1917 to avoid any confusion with Logan, Utah.

LOVELOCK

At an early stage in its life, this Pershing County area was the site of a gigantic camping ground used by emigrants. It was called Big Meadows. The first settlers on the meadows were James Blake and his family. In addition to having a large spread of land, Blake ran the stage station.

In the early 1860s, George Lovelock purchased Blake's property and built a small stage coach station. When the Central Pacific Railroad was being constructed, Lovelock made some concessions to the company and had the station located here, even though the railroad had originally decided on Oreana. The name they picked was Lovelock's, and the post office, established in 1875, was the same—without the apostrophe. Later, in 1922, the "s" was removed entirely.

LUND

Lund was a Mormon settlement located in Mineral County. The town was settled in 1898 and named for Anthony G. Lund, one of the leaders of the Church of Jesus Christ of Latter-Day Saints. The Lund post office opened under that name in 1898.

LUNING

In 1879, silver, lead and copper mines were located here. During World War I, this Mineral County town was an active producer of copper.

At an earlier time, the stage station here was known as Deep Wells. The current town was founded late in 1881, when the Carson & Colorado Railroad reached here. The name was changed at that point to honor Nicholas B. Luning, a Californian who held a great quantity of bonds in the railroad. The Carson & Colorado was later bought out by the Southern Pacific.

MANHATTAN

This Nye County place had first begun settlement during the 1860s, but when it seemed the gold was gone by 1871, the mines were abandoned. In 1905, John Humphrey stumbled over gold at the foot of April Fool Mountain. His discovery triggered a new gold rush, and drew prospectors and miners from far and wide.

Placer mines existed here between 1907 and 1915, and rich gold ore was discovered in the lower levels of the White Caps Mine which spawned yet another rush.

The town was named for the Manhattan Mines, located southwest of Belmont. The Manhattan post office was established in 1905.

MASON

Mason, Lyon County, carries the name of Henry A. "Hock" Mason. Mason settled the ranch that bore his name in 1859. At that time, the Mason Ranch formed part of the boundary of Douglas County.

The town was surveyed and built in 1909, becoming home to the Nevada Copper Belt Railroad, also known as the Mason Valley Line. The Mason post office opened in 1908.

An earlier settlement existed here, we are told, under the name of Mason Valley (1881), and Greenfield (1871).

McDERMITT

McDermitt took its name from old Fort McDermit. The fort, and now the town, honor Lieutenant Colonel Charles McDermit, commander of the Nevada Military District, 1864–65.

McDermit was killed by an Indian ambush near the creek that now bears his name. In 1865, the name of the Quinn River Camp No. 33 was changed to Camp McDermit in the colonel's memory. In 1879, the camp became a fort.

A Camp McDermitt post office—the second "T" is a post office addition—was established in 1866. The name was changed to Fort McDermitt in 1879; then, to McDermitt in 1891.

McGILL

The Nevada Consolidated Copper Company created this White Pine County town. The name came from the Adams McGill Ranch, located several miles northeast of the town, which supplied water for the smelter and the town.

The town is located on land that used to be the McGill Ranch, owned by William McGill. The first post office, established here in 1907, was called Smelter. Postal authorities changed the name in 1908.

MERCURY

In the 1950s, the Atomic Energy Commission established the Frenchmen's Flats area in southern Nevada as the Nevada Proving Grounds. The center within the testing site became the town of Mercury. A post office was established here in 1964.

The name, we are told, was taken from the Mercury Mine, located a few miles north of here. The Mercury post office was established at this site in 1952.

MESQUITE

Mesquite was settled on the banks of the Virgin River in 1880 by Mormons from St. George, Utah. They later abandoned the settlement, resettling it in the late 1890s.

The name of this Clark County community came from the mesquite in the area. The pods of the plant were stored by the Indians for use during the winter.

The first post office, opened in 1880, was called Mesquit. The name was changed to the current spelling 17 years later.

MIDAS

Midas, Elko County, was—of all things—a gold mining camp!

The town came into existence when Paul Ehlers located his Elko Prince Mine here in 1907. The same year, a post office was established as Midas.

The name, quite obviously, came from the legendary Phrygian king who, with the help of the god Dionysus, was able to turn all that he touched into gold. It might have worked in the legend, but it did not work here in Nevada.

MILL CITY

In 1862, J. Gianacca dreamed of a canal along the Humboldt River. In his mind, he could see the canal transporting ore to central smelters and providing the water to run the mills. Three years later, Gianacca built 30 miles of canal, but, with the arrival of the railroad along the same route, he had a difficult time getting investors. He also found that the soil was not fit for a canal; it was too porous.

Ten years later, he constructed 60 miles of canal and established a 10-stamp mill at this site, calling it Mill City. A Mill City post office was opened in 1864.

MINA

Mina is Spanish for "mine." The town is located in a Mineral County region devoted to mining. A post office bearing that name was established here in 1905.

MINDEN

A German immigrant, Henry Fred Dangberg, arrived in this Douglas County locale in 1855. He ignored the get-rich-quick philosophy, and he established a ranch here. Learning irrigation techniques from the Mormons, he ditched his fields and raised hay. During the rush for Washoe, he was able to get $300 a ton for the hay. He later grew alfalfa, the first in the state.

Dangberg married Margaret Ferris in 1864. His brother-in-law was the man who built the Ferris wheel that appeared at the first Chicago Fair.

Two years before he died in 1904, Dangberg created H. F. Dangberg Land & Livestock Company and the Virginia & Truckee Railroad. The land company established Minden in 1905, which then became the county seat. Dangberg was born in Halle, a village near Minden, Westphalia. A Minden post office was opened here in 1906.

MOAPA

Moapa, Clark County, took its name from the Moapa—or Muddy—Valley.

The valley, settled in 1865, was farmed by Mormons from Utah who planted trees and established the towns of Saint Joseph, Saint Thomas, Overton and West Point.

The name is derived from the Indian tribe, the Moapas. Their name comes from *Moapariats,* the "mosquito creek people." Another suggestion is that their name comes from *Mo-a-pats,* "the people who live on the Muddy (River)." The Moapa post office was established in 1889.

MONTELLO

Montello is the railroad's abbreviation of Montebello. At least, that is what one authority contends.

This Elko County site was named by agents for the Southern Pacific Railroad. The name was given in 1869, probably for an older station in the East.

The Montello post office opened here in 1912. At that point, the name of the office was changed from Bauvard.

MOUNTAIN CITY

Mountain City, Elko County, has an elevation of 5,641 feet, and it was settled in 1869. The town's name, of course, is descriptive of its location. A post office was established here in 1870.

Prior to 1881, Mountain City's silver mines produced more than a million dollars. The silver petered out and was replaced by the Rio Tinto copper deposits.

NELSON

Nelson has sometimes been called Eldorado. Spaniards, it is said, had discovered valuable ore in the Eldorado Canyon as early as 1775, but more than a hundred years passed before the mineral finds were exploited.

Nelson began when a mining camp was platted here in Clark County in 1905. The name remembers Charles Nelson, a miner who was murdered in his mine by an Indian in 1897. A Nelson post office was opened in 1905.

NIXON

George S. Nixon, a native Californian, made his mark in Nevada. Nixon, along with George Wingfield, consolidated the numerous claims at Goldfield and gained control in 1906. He later went on to represent Nevada in the United States Senate. His house is located in Reno.

Both the town and the post office of Nixon were established in 1912. The town was built on an old Indian village that was described by Frémont as "a collection of straw huts" when he camped here in 1844.

NYALA

The name of Nyala appears to be a modification of the name of its county, Nye. At an earlier time, the settlement was known as Mormon Well.

The Nyla post office was established here in 1914.

OASIS

Oasis, Elko County, was just that, in its early days. In the 1930s, the town was a Red Cross station. The town took its name from the Oasis Ranch, started by E. C. Hardy in the late 1880s.

OREANA

Located in Pershing County, Oreana bears the Latin name for "town of gold." But that is only one side of the story . . .

Others see "ore" and the Greek *ana*, "greatly" or "excessively," which gives us a great amount of ore. Still others see a corruption of the Spanish *orejano*, "unbranded," for cattle. In cattle country, the word *oreano* was used to note a young, unbranded calf.

In 1867, this was the site of the Montezuma Smelting Works that treated ore from the Arabia and Trinity mining districts. It was supposed to be the first smelter in the United States to ship lead to a commercial market. The town's location has been shifted. At one point, the Southern Pacific Railroad moved the town from its original site on the highway to its present location.

The Oreana post office was opened here in 1867.

OROVADA

Orovada, Humboldt County, has a name that combines the Spanish word for "gold" and the state's name: Nevada. A post office was established here in 1920.

OVERTON (— Beach)

Overton, Clark County, was founded by Mormons. The town is located just south of the 2,000-year-old Lost City of the Pueblo

Indians. Lost City stretched for 30 miles along the Muddy River. Its residents were farmers who built above-ground housing. The Lost City is really "lost" today. It is now located under Lake Mead. The current Overton was relocated here after 1880. The suggestion is that the name came from "Over-Town," a reference to the moving of the settlement "over the river."

Overton was once part of the Patterson Ranch. The ranch had been purchased around 1881 by a woman from Utah. The first post office at this site was established in 1870, but in Pah Ute County, Arizona. The office transferred from there to Nevada and finally to Clark County when it was formed in 1909.

OWYHEE

Owyhee, Elko County, took its name from the river of the same name. The waterway was originally known as Sandwich Island River. When the Sandwich Islands became Hawaii, the river's name was changed.

The Owyhee post office was established in 1889.

PAHRUMP

This Nye County name came from the town's location in the Pahrump Valley. That name seems to have come from the Southern Paiute *pa*, "water," and *timpi*, "stone." The last word, we are told, was modified to *rumpi* or *rimpi*. The name translates to a spring in a rock.

Local tradition gives the meaning of the name great latitude, with translations including "great spring," "water mouth," "big flow of water," "big orifice," or "cave from which water flows."

The Pahrump post office was first established in 1891.

PALISADE

Palisade, situated by the Humboldt, took its name from the sheer walls east of the town site. In 1833, Zenas Leonard described them as a "cluster of hills or mounds, which presented the appearance, from a distance, of a number of beautiful cities built up together."

This Eureka County location was once the northern terminus of the Eureka-Palisade Railroad that brought lead and silver from the mines at Eureka.

The post office at Palisade was established in 1870.

PANACA

Panaca was founded in 1864 by Mormons led by Francis Lee. According to one tradition, the name came from the Packacker

Ledge, a mining claim. The name is of Indian origin and refers to ore. *Pa-na-ka* is Southern Pauite for "metal." The Utes called "metal, money, wealth" *Pan-nuk kir.*

One source wonders whether the Indian who found the ore gave his name to the town, or whether he received the name because he found the ore. It seems highly likely that the Indian was named for his find. The discovery of ore here did lead to Mormon-Gentile strife.

The Panaca post office was established in 1867.

PARADISE VALLEY

The community of Paradise Valley took its name from the area. The Paradise Valley was settled before 1865, but named—for a brief time—Paradise City. The name was given by early settlers, and it is quite appropriate. The Paradise Valley post office, located in Humboldt County, was opened in 1871.

Camp Winfield Scott was located about five miles east of town and was founded in 1866 to protect settlers from the Paiutes.

PIOCHE

Pioche, Lincoln County, was a tough mining camp-town. By the time its first resident died of natural causes, there were already 75 graves in Boot Hill!

The inscription on one tombstone indicates that arbitration or mediation was unknown: "Fanny Peterson, July 12, 1872. They loved til death did them part. He killed her."

The town is also well-known for its "Million Dollar Courthouse." The construction bid for the building was only $30,000, but, by the time it was completed in the late 19th century, the price approached a million! The courthouse was condemned in 1933. The building and the four town lots on which it stood were sold 25 years later—for $150. The courthouse has been restored and is now open to the public, but tourist literature cautions that it "may be closed during bad weather."

William Hamblin, a Mormon missionary, was permitted into the area by Paiutes in 1863. Though Hamblin's discovery of the Panacker Ledge spawned a boom, there was no real development until F. L. A. Pioche, a French banker from San Francisco, began to speculate in 1864. The town was laid out by P. McCannon, L. Lacour and A. M. Bush, and named Pioche—"at the suggestion of Mrs. Carmichael Williamson."

A post office was established in 1870 and carried the Frenchman's name. An earlier name was Ely, for John H. Ely, who arrived shortly before Pioche.

PRESTON

Preston, White Pine County, was founded by Mormons from Moroni, Utah, in 1897. They named their town for their presiding bishop, William B. Preston.

The Preston post office was established in 1899.

RENO

R

Reno has been an important place in northern Nevada since 1859, when C. W. Fuller opened an inn on the south side of the Truckee River, built a crude bridge across the stream and called the site Fuller's Crossing.

Four years later, Fuller sold his inn and toll bridge to Myron C. Lake who changed the name to Lake's Crossing. For five years, Lake had no competition and the mines made him rich with the constant flow of food and materials to the Comstock. But his monopoly soon ended.

The Central Santa Fe (later the Central Pacific) Railroad came across the Sierra Madre Mountains in 1868 and set up shop. Lake cut a deal with Charles Crocker, superintendent of the railroad, to donate land north of the river to the railroad if they would build a station here. Five days after the railroad arrived, a land auction was held. Within a month, more than a hundred homes were erected.

The name for this Washoe County metropolis was given by Crocker who wanted to honor Union Army General Jesse Lee Reno, a Union officer killed at South Mountain in 1862. The town followed suit a few years later. The Reno post office was opened in 1868.

Before the introduction of no-fault divorces, Reno had the reputation for quick divorces, a process used to great advantage by movie stars and dilletantes. Reno is also a popular word on crossword puzzles. Remember it is a town on the Truckee!

RIVERSIDE

Riverside is located just north of the Virgin River in Clark County. It took its name from its location.

ROUND MOUNTAIN

Ore was discovered here in 1907 by Louis D. Gordon. Other sources suggest Slim Morgan. Either way, the town took its name from nearby Round Mountain, a rock formation "of porphyry and rhyolite."

The Round Mountain post office was established in 1907.

RUBY VALLEY

This Elko County town is in the valley formed by the Ruby Mountains. The name, we gather, was given by a pioneering party of the 1840–50 period. Captain James H. Simpson wrote in 1859 that the valley took its name from "rubies having been picked up in it. . . ." The reference is to the red garnet stones found there. The stones were called ruby garnets.

The Ruby Valley post office was opened first in Utah Territory in 1862. That site was probably Camp Ruby or Fort Ruby, a military installation set to guard the mail route.

RUTH

The center of Ruth once was the Copper Pit, a hole more than a mile in diameter, from which the town's riches were mined.

In 1900, Edward F. Gray and David P. Bartley came to Ely, an 1868 gold-mining camp that was all but forgotten, to try their luck. They established two claims, the Ruth and the Kearsage. The Ruth claim was named by D. C. McDonald for his daughter.

The partners discovered copper and, by 1902, were able to form the White Pine Copper Company. The company created the Nevada Northern Railroad by 1908. In the 10-year period ending in 1917, the Ruth Mine enabled the company to pay dividends in the amount of $75.8 million!

Gray and Bartley's operation became the Kennecott Copper Corporation. The Ruth post office was established in 1904.

SANDY VALLEY

Sandy Valley, located in the southeast section of the Mesquite Valley in Clark County, took its name from a former settlement and post office: Sandy. Sandy was the site of the Keystone Mine and was originally called Taylor's Well.

SCHURZ

Schurz, Mineral County, was the headquarters for the Walker Lake Indian Reservation.

A post office and Southern Pacific Railroad station were established here in 1891. Both were named for Carl Schurz, American statesman and author. Schurz was born near Cologne, Germany.

SCOTTY'S JUNCTION

Scotty's Junction, Nye County, is located at the junction of U.S. 95 and Nevada Route 72. Route 72 leads to Scotty's Castle in California.

The castle was built by Walter "Death Valley" Scott. He had been a champion roughrider in Buffalo Bill's show. (See SCOTTY'S CASTLE, California.)

SEARCHLIGHT

Legend has it that this Clark County town was named after a box of matches!

As the story goes, two brothers camped here in 1898 and found inspiration from the striking of a match.

At one time, a claim here that later produced more than a million dollars was sold for "$1,500, a team of mules, a buckboard, and a double-barreled shotgun." Another, which produced $150,000, was traded for a pint of whiskey.

A more logical explanation is that the name donor was Floyd Searchlight, who developed a number of mining claims here in about 1897.

SILVER CITY

Silver City was named for the precious metal it began producing in 1850. Located in Lyon County, it was in the early days the third most important mining camp after Virginia City and Gold Hill.

The Silver City post office went back to territorial days, when it was established in Carson City, Utah, in 1860.

SILVERPEAK

Silverpeak, Esmeralda County, is located on the western edge of the Silver Peak Marsh in the foothills of the Silver Peak Range. Three guesses on the source of the name? The post office was established as Silver Peak in 1866, then as a single word in 1916.

SLOAN

This Clark County community was named for the limestone-dolomite-carnotite district. The area was first settled in about 1912 and received its first post office in 1919, under the name of Ehret, for members of the Ehret family. The name was changed to Sloan three years later.

SMITH

Smith, Lyon County, received its name from a group of herdsmen who settled near the West Walker River in 1859. The name was selected "on account of the predominance of 'Smith' in the party." Members included Timothy B., R. B., and Cyrus "Adobe" Smith.

The Smith post office was opened in 1892.

SPARKS

Sparks, Washoe County, was established in 1903 when the Southern Pacific Railroad moved some of its railroad buildings to the eastern edge of Reno. When a post office was opened here in 1903, it bore the name Harriman, for the railroad's president, Edward H. Harriman. Harriman asked that the name be changed, and East Reno and Glendale were suggested. Finally, in 1904, with the creation of the town's post office, the name became Sparks.

The town was named for the state's governor, John Sparks. Sparks, a Mississippi-born Texan, was credited with driving in a herd of longhorns in 1868.

SPRING CREEK

The Spring Creek in Elko County gave rise to the town of the same name.

STATELINE

This Esmeralda County site took its name from its location near the California line.

STEWART

Stewart, Carson City County, took its name from the Stewart Institute, a school for Indians operated by the federal government. The institute was founded in 1890 through the efforts of Senator William M. Stewart. A popular man, Stewart served in the Senate for 28 years following his election on the first ballot in 1864.

Bill Stewart was a lawyer from Yale. He was prosecuting a case against a man for murder. Into the courtroom walked Sam Brown, a notorious killer, who had advised the townspeople that this trial against his friend offended him.

Stewart reached in his pockets and pulled out a pair of derringers. Aiming them at Brown's heart, Stewart took the killer's testimony, forcing him to say that the defendant had a bad reputation.

On cross-examination, Brown said he came to town to hire Stewart as his attorney, since he was under indictment in California for an assault charge. He handed Stewart $500, and he bought drinks for everyone at the bar. Later that day, Brown got into a shoot-out with tavern-keeper Henry Van Sickles and died, as Stewart said, "from a just disposition of an all-wise Providence."

Before a post office was established here in 1905 as Stewart, the location was known as Carson Indian School.

STILLWATER

In about 1880, a temperance group appeared in Stillwater, a town of 44. They offered sinners three pledges: Abstain from tobacco; abstain from alcohol; abstain from both. The group didn't last long. But that has nothing to do with the naming of this Churchill County community.

Stillwater took its name from the Stillwater Slough, a waterway that was named for the sluggishness of its flow. The Stillwater post office was established in 1865.

SUN VALLEY

This Washoe County town took its name from the valley in which it is located.

SUTCLIFFE

Sutcliffe, Washoe County, was named after James Sutcliffe, a local ranch owner. The post office under the Sutcliffe name was established in 1929.

THORNE

This Mineral County site established its first post office in 1912. The name was adapted from that of Hawthorne, the town south of here.

THOUSAND SPRINGS

Thousand Springs, Elko County, took its name from the valley in which it resides. The name for the valley was drawn from the countless hot, cold and mineral springs in the area.

TIPPETT

Located in White Pine County, Tippett was named for a wealthy sheepman from the locale. The Tippett post office was established in 1896.

TONOPAH

During a thunderstorm in 1900, James Butler, a rancher from Belmont, took cover under a ledge. While he was there, he idly chipped away at the stone to kill time. Suddenly, he noticed that the stone in

T

his hand was actually silver ore. Not too long afterward, Walter Gayhart, of Austin, laid out the town in this Nye County locality.

Thirteen years later, area silver production netted $9.5 million! The name came from the Shoshone or Northern Paiute Indian and means "little water" or "greasewood spring."

The Tonopah post office was established in 1905, changed from Butler, an earlier name.

TUSCARORA

In the late 19th century, the mines at Tuscarora produced $25–40 million. At the time, it was considered to be a very rough place. In fact, one story has it that a man by the name of Rockafellow was cursing a blue streak at Major John Dennis. The cursing was so great that the sheriff arrested him.

Dennis bailed him out . . . for one purpose: to beat the living daylights out of him!

Tuscarora was originally settled by the John and Steve Beard. Though they discovered a placer mine in 1867, it was not until W. O. Weed discovered a silver lode in 1871 that the town began to prosper. The town was touted as "another Comstock," but it never lived up to its publicity.

The name of this Elko County community is drawn from the Turcaroro Mountains. The name was offered by John Beard in 1871. Beard came from North Carolina, where the Tuscaroro "hemp gatherers" lived.

UNIONVILLE

Unionville, Pershing County, was one of the oldest mining camps in Nevada. Located along the Buena Vista Canyon, the town site—then called Buena Vista, for its location—was first visited by Hugo Pfersdorff and J. C. Hannan in 1861, but it was William Whitney who claimed a homesite at the head of the canyon.

As time progressed, Whitney's site, Upper Town, was added to Lower Town, also known as Dixie, and Centerville. When the three sections merged, the town became known as Unionville. Some think that the name was changed because of pro-Union sentiments at the start of the Civil War, since the name was changed in 1861. In that same year, Unionville was named seat of Humboldt County.

URSINE

The namers of this town decided not to call it Bear, but to use the Latin form.

Ursine, Lincoln County, was settled in 1863 by a small colony of Mormons. Their settlement in Ursine Valley—known locally as

Eagle Valley—was supposed to be called Eagle Valley, but the post office interfered. Eliminating fear of confusion over the Eagle names, this town became Ursine in 1895 with the establishment of a post office.

VALMY

The Southern Pacific Railroad named this Humboldt County community Valmy after the French village, famous for the 1796 battle.

The older name for the site was Stone House, but the Valmy name went up on the post office in 1915.

VERDI

Verdi, Washoe County, was once a lumber camp that grew up around O'Neil's Crossing—an earlier name for the site. O'Neil was the man who built a bridge here in 1860.

With the arrival of the Central Pacific Railroad, officials of the company leaned toward Verdi, for Giuseppe Verdi, the great Italian composer. The Verdi post office was established in 1869, with a name change from Crystal Peak.

Verdi was also the site of the 1870 train robbery of the Central Pacific's Train No. 1. Seven robbers hit the train here and ran off with the payroll of the Yellow Jacket Mine on the Comstock. Sheriff Jim Kinkead recovered the loot.

VIRGINIA CITY

The name for this Storey County city was given in 1859 by an old prospector, James Fennimore, who called himself "Old Virginny." He was supposed to have found the largest gold nugget in America. He gave the name to get some use out of the liquor he had spilled on her soil. When he accidently broke the bottle, he sprinkled the remainder on the ground, saying, "I battize this spot Virginia Town."

When counties were laid out in 1861, Virginia City was named seat of its county.

During the 1870s, Virginia City was a virtual gold mine. John W. Mackay and James G. Fair struck the "Heart of the Comstock" in 1873. The Comstock Lode, an underground vein about 400 feet deep and 150–320 feet wide, gave the town unrivaled prosperity. Ore extracted from the Consolidated Virginia Mine has been estimated at $234 million—as a minimum!

Mark Twain and Bret Harte both worked here as reporters on the *Territorial Enterprise*, Nevada's first newspaper . . . and one suspected of making up the news from time to time.

VISTA

This Washoe County site was named primarily for its "pleasant prospect."

WABUSKA

Wabuska, Lyon County, we are told, has a name that comes from the Northern Paiute Indian. No one is certain what it means. One possibility is that the word has roots in *washo*, "white grass" or "vegetation."

The Wabuska post office was established here in 1874.

WADSWORTH

Prior to the arrival of Frémont in 1844, the Paiutes used this Washoe County location as a seasonal village. Later, a trading post was established, but not until the arrival of the Central Pacific Railroad in 1869 did the town come alive.

An earlier name for the town was Drytown, then Lower Emigrant Crossing. It was finally named Wadsworth by representatives of the Central Pacific Railroad in 1868. The name was given to commemorate Civil War General James Samuel Wadsworth. Wadsworth was killed in 1864 in the Battle of the Wilderness.

The Wadsworth post office was established in 1868.

WARM SPRINGS

Warm Springs, Nye County, took its name from the tepid natural springs in the area. The Warm Springs post office was established under that name here in 1924.

WEED HEIGHTS

Weed Heights, situated in Lyon County, was a company town, founded by the Anaconda Copper Company in 1952. The Weed Heights post office opened the next year. The name has nothing to do with the growth of the non-grass elements in a lawn.

The town was named by company officials for Clyde E. Weed, the vice president in charge of all Anaconda operations.

WELLINGTON

Wellington began as a stage stop owned by Jack Wright and Len Hamilton. The name came from Daniel Wellington. He purchased the station from Wright and Hamilton in 1863 and called it Wellington's Station.

The Wellington post office was established in 1865, replacing the postal name, Mammoth Ledge.

WELLS

Wells received its name from the Humboldt Wells because of the springs scattered over the meadows here in Elko County. The settlers called the springs wells because they thought they were bottomless. One observer wrote: "You look on a still surface of water, perhaps six or seven feet across, and nearly round. No current disturbs it; it resembles a well more than a natural spring."

Though Wells grew up when the Central Pacific Railroad was built, the area just northwest of town was one of the principal camping spots along the California Trail.

The Wells post office was established in 1869.

WHITE ROCK

Elko County's White Rock, earlier known as White Rock City, took its name from the nearby White Rock Creek. The White Rock post office opened in 1871.

WINNEMUCCA

Winnemucca, Humboldt County, came into being during the 1849 gold rush. It was the only place for miles around where wagons could ford the Humboldt River. The first settler was a Frenchman who opened a trading post here in 1850.

An Army survey team that mapped the northern Nevada area is credited with selecting the name. As tradition has it, the lieutenant in charge was hard-pressed for names and could not figure out why this spot was called French's Ford. He was unaware of the Frenchman and his trading post, so he decided to name it for the local chief.

By the mid-19th century, old Chief Winnemucca was a white man in disguise. He loved to drink and gamble. On special occasions, he even wore an Army general's uniform! His name was descriptive and given to him as a child. He had a great deal of trouble keeping moccasins on both feet. The town took his name in 1868. Winnemucca is Piute for "one mocassin."

A local legend speaks of small children tossing pebbles into the blue buckets hanging from wagons passing through here. On closer examination, it was found that these "pebbles" were actually gold nuggets. Though efforts were made to locate the "Blue Bucket Mine," it was never found.

Before the Winnemucca post office was established here in this Humboldt County area in 1866, the camp was known as French

Ford or French Bridge—for the span built here by the Lay brothers and Frenchman Frank Band in 1850. Later, we find it called Centerville: a center for northbound settlers.

At another time, the community went by the consolidated name of Winnemucca of French Ford.

YERINGTON

Yerington, Lyon County, was established along the banks of the Walker River in the 1860s, and the town was named for Henry Marvin Yerington, superintendent of the former Virginia & Truckee Railroad.

Previously, the town had been known as Poison or Pizen Switch (before 1860) and Greenfield (in 1861). The name "pizen," we are told, was given because of the quality of liquor served by Mr. Downey, the owner of a local saloon. "Switch" came from the name of a small saloon made from willow wood, called Willow Switch. Another story has it that the name came from the large number of "buckaroos" who ended up in the town.

The Yerington post office was established in 1894.

ZEPHYR COVE

This Douglas County town was so named to indicate a "pleasant breeze" (a zephyr) that blew through the cove.

Mark Twain made jest of the Washoe Zephyr, a local term for a strong westerly gale in Nevada. Twain wrote about feeling one coming on: "A soaring dust-drift about the size of the United States set up edgewise came with it, and the capital of Nevada Territory disappeared from view."

The Zephyr Cove post office was opened in 1930 on the east shore of Lake Tahoe.

Alaska was the first territory admitted to the United States that was not contiguous to the rest of the states. That is not the only difference.

Alaska is America's largest state. In fact, some Alaskans think that they should split their state in half and reduce Texas to the third largest state!

According to some scientists, the first people on the Alaskan territory arrived about 12–14,000 years ago. They arrived, it is surmised, by walking across the Bering Sea on a strip of land that connected the North American continent to Siberia. These travelers lived in peace for centuries . . . until 1741. That was the year the Russians discovered Alaska, even though the history books tell us that Vitus Bering, a Danish navigator in Russian service, spied it in 1728. For more than a century and a half, Alaska was Russian America and, during that time, the Russians gathered up the furs of sea otters and seals and shipped them back to Mother Russia.

The early residents fought back. At times they were successful. The Tlingits massacred the Russians at Sitka and Yakutat, but in the long run it was a losing battle. The native Alaskans were no match for their enemies. They were crushed, worn down and nearly destroyed.

The Russians were fervent in their desire to rid themselves of this territory. Throughout their history, they had limited success with colonies not connected to them by land. But the United States was not willing to acquire the land. In 1867, the United States had just completed the Civil War and was in the throes of impeaching President Andrew Johnson. Yet it was almost predestined that the United States would one day possess Alaska.

Through the efforts of Edouard de Stoeckl, a parvenu with a made-up royal title who represented Russia, interest was kept alive in both Moscow and Washington. Secretary of State William Seward saw Alaska as the Arctic bastion of his nation, but his was not the final word—even though the land deal was nicknamed "Seward's Icebox," "Seward's Folly," "Walrussia," and others not suitable for print. When it came time for a vote, the U.S. Senate begrudgingly agreed—by one vote! The House of Representatives, on the other hand, held back the money needed to complete the deal for several months. "If we were so eager to show Russia our appreciation for the help she gave us during the Civil War," one congressman wrote, "why didn't we give her the seven million and tell her to keep her damned colony? It'll never be of any use to us." Little did he—or anyone else—realize what the future would hold for United States' interests in Alaska.

The Russians sold off their interests in Alaska to the United States for $7.2 million. The price came out to about two cents an acre! Ironically, the first shipment of crude oil sent from Alaska after the completion of the trans-Alaska pipeline was valued at the same amount. The natives who had fought so bitterly to retain their God-given land were labeled "uncivilized tribes" in the Treaty of Cession.

Following the years after American acquisition, Alaska lived an almost idyllic existence. After all, at the time of purchase, only its fringe had been explored by Europeans. It was the perfect place for people to view the raw natural beauty that was Alaska, and to hunt and fish. Then gold was discovered in 1880, and Alaska changed, never to return to that Eden-like past.

The federal government in Washington had avoided Alaska for many years, letting it live without interference. But the discovery of gold gave rise to a need for law and order. With this, came civil, criminal and homesteading laws. Finally, in 1906, Alaska was empowered to send a non-voting delegate to Congress. The Territory of Alaska was created in 1912, which resulted in the presidential appointment of a territorial government. Four years later, Alaska attempted to join the Union as a state. But as World War I intervened and gold deposits diminished, Alaska was virtually ignored. That all changed with the outbreak of World War II.

Because of its location, Alaska was the closest American possession to Japan. In 1942, Japanese bombers attacked the U.S. Navy base at Dutch Harbor in the Aleutians. A few days after the attack, Japanese soldiers occupied the Aleutian Islands of Attu and Kiska. The next year, American forces fought to regain Attu. They succeeded, but the toll was great. The percentage of American casualties during that battle was second only to the fight for Iwo Jima. This threat of attack on the American mainland caused the hasty construction of the Alaskan Highway.

Following the war, GIs stayed, raised families and fought for statehood for their adopted land. In 1959, Alaska became the 49th state of the Union. Some feel that Alaska might not have become a state if it had not been for the yet-undiscovered oil deposits that helped fuel Americans fascination with automobiles.

The places of Alaska bear the ethnic tones of the people who originally lived here as well as those who attempted to erase these qualities from the lands. We find remnants of the dominant Indian cultures, the Tlingits, Haidas, Athapaskans and Tsimshians. We find their names in more or less original form, and some in translation through the Russian to English. We discover others that relate to Captain Cook's voyages up the Pacific from the Sandwich Islands—with native Hawaiian names on the Pacific Northwest coast. What we detect is a unique blend that is neither totally Indian, nor Russian, nor English nor American. Alaska's place names are, in a word, Alaskan.

AKHIOK

The native name for this village was first reported in the 1880 census. It may have appeared earlier, in 1814, as Oohaiack. In a change of direction, the bay was named for the village, not the other way around.

Other spellings include Alitak. In fact, a post office was established under that name in 1933.

AKIACHAK

The original name of this Eskimo village was Akiatshàgamut, meaning "Akiakchak people." In 1889, it was listed as Akiakchagamiut. The post office was opened here in 1934 under its current name.

AKIAK

The point for crossing to the Yukon during the winter, Akiak probably got its name from the Eskimo for "crossing over." A post office was established here in 1916.

Alternate spellings of the name include Ackiagmute, Akiagamuit, Akiagamute, Akiagmut, Akkiagamute, and Akkiagmute.

AKUTAN

There was a time when the village of Akutan could be smelled before it was seen. It was the home of an American Pacific Whaling Company station. A post office was opened here in 1914.

The name was taken from the island, and it was purportedly drawn from the Aleut expression *ha-kuta*, "I made a mistake." The Russians apparently misapplied the name.

ALAKANUK

The post office was established here in 1946, though the Eskimo village is much older. The name, it is suggested, means "wrong way" or "mistakes." The reason seems to be that the Alakanuk Pass, a waterway between channels at the mouth of the Yukon River, is mazelike and causes confusion.

ALEKNAGIK

Aleknagik is located on the shore of the lake of the same name. At one time, we are told, there were two villages named after the lake. The other has disappeared.

The lake's name is Eskimo and was recorded in 1826 as Alyaknagik. By 1852, the name was reduced by the Russians to the current spelling. The word *alaknakik* translates to "well studded with beautiful pine-covered islands." A trader recorded the name as Agoulouikatuk, which means "testicle." The first definition seems to be more descriptive of the lake.

ALEXANDER

Alexander, located near the mouth of Alexander Creek, was named in 1867 by the U.S. Coast & Geodetic Survey for the reigning czar, Alexander II (1818–81), "the Liberator." His nickname came from his emancipation of the serfs in 1861.

Alexander was also the Russian leader who decided that his nation should sell Alaska to the United States.

Alexander Glacier, on the other hand, was named in 1905, and it honored Beno Alexander, a porter who accompanied the Duke of Abruzzi when he climbed Mount Saint Elias in 1897. Lake Alexander was named for Annie M. Alexander in 1907. She founded the University of California's Alexander Alaska Expedition. Point Alexander was named by Vancouver in 1793 for Daniel Asher Alexander, a British architect.

ALLAKAKET

The name of this village came from the Athapascan Indian tongue and means "river mouth." The town is located on the banks of the Koyukuk River at the mouth of the Alatna.

In 1906, Hudson Stuck, an Episopal archdeacon, established a mission here where two native villages were situated. One, Allakeket, on the south bank, was for Indians; the other, Alatna, on the other bank, was for Eskimos.

A post office was opened here in 1925 as Alatna. The name was changed to Allakaket in 1938.

AMBLER

Ambler is an Eskimo village, founded in the late 1950s and located on the Ambler River.

The river honors the memory of Dr. James M. Ambler, of the U.S. Navy. Ambler died of starvation in 1881, after the U.S.S. *Jeannette*, commanded by Lieutenant Commander George Washington DeLong, was trapped in an Arctic ice pack. A post office was opened here in 1963.

ANAKTUVUK PASS

At one time the caribou migrated through this area in mass. The village name came from the Eskimo *anaq* for the pass and means "dung everywhere," a logical name for the remains of the annual migration.

The first white men to travel through here on their way to the North Slope were spotted by Eskimos in 1901. The Anaktuvuk Pass post office was established in 1951.

ANCHORAGE

Anchorage is Alaska's largest and most sophisticated city. It is home to more than half of the state's population.

It began as a construction camp for the federally-built Alaska Railroad in 1913. The next year, town lots were sold. In the earliest days, water sold for a nickel a pail and garbage was dumped into the outgoing tide on a daily basis. Bohunk Village was the name applied to the area where the single workmen from Southern Europe lived. Another section, reserved for prostitutes, was called South Anchorage.

The original name for Anchorage was Knik Anchorage. The prefix was dropped in 1914 when the first post office was opened. Other names attributed to Anchorage include Alaska City, Brownville, Ship Creek, Port Woodrow, and Woodrow.

In 1964, a three-minute earthquake nearly destroyed Anchorage, along with Valdez and Kodiak. The shock was followed by a tidal wave that swept away the town of Valdez. Though traces remain, Anchorage began rebuilding immediately.

ANCHOR POINT

The village of Anchor Point on Kenai Peninsula took its name from the nearby point of land. Captain James Cook lost an anchor there in 1778.

The Anchor Point name was given in 1894 by the U.S. Bureau of Fisheries. A post office was established in 1949.

ANDERSON

P. H. Anderson was a missionary at Cheenik who helped organize the mining districts on the Seward Peninsula in 1898. He had arrived in Alaska only the year before.

But the real donor of the name for this village was Arthur Anderson who "subdivided his homestead into quarter-acre lots and was elected one of the first councilmen."

ANGOON

In the late 19th century, a "bomb lance" on a whaling boat exploded, killing a native worker. His tribe demanded 200 blankets from the company, as the Indian custom demanded. Being refused, the Indians kidnapped two white men who had no affiliation with the company and held them at Angoon. This was also a custom of the tribe—if they did not get their blankets.

The *Corwin*, a revenue cutter, was dispatched to retrieve the men. When the ship arrived, the Indians let the men go. But the captain wanted an explanation, and what the tribesmen told him was insufficient. What happened, he told them, "was an accident. You get no pay for that. But I want you to pay four hundred blankets for capturing and holding these two miners." He gave them two hours to deliver, "or I'll shell your village."

The tribe could only find 50 blankets, which the captain threw overboard. He ordered the tribe to vacate immediately. Then he destroyed the entire village of Angoon. In 1889, the federal government reimbursed the tribe for property destroyed, giving them $6,000 worth of cloth, tobacco and other items. In 1974, the Indians were given $90,000 by the federal government to settle the lawsuit.

In 1880, this Tlingit Indian village was known as Augoon, but no one has translated it. When the post office was established in that same year, the name was spelled in its current form.

ANIAK

Simensen Lukeen, a Russian trader, discovered gold near the mouth of the Aniak River. He built a fort there, which he called the Yellow River.

The village, taking its name from the adjacent river, was founded about 1910. The post office was opened four years later.

ANVIK

When Andrei Glazunof arrived here in 1834, Anvik was a fairly large village of the Inkalik tribe, located at the mouth of the river of the same name. The tribe's name is supposed to mean "lousy," because tribe members never washed their hair. The village was known as the "place of the louse eggs." To get rid of the lice, the Indians had daily sweat baths and urine rinses. Another source suggests the name means "going-out-place."

Missionaries of the Episcopal Church founded a mission here in 1886.

Over the years, the village has been known as American Station, Anvic, Anvig and Anwig. The first post office was opened here in 1897 under the name of Anvick.

ARCTIC VILLAGE

This Indian village was known as Arctic in 1909 when the first post office was opened. The descriptive name was changed to the present one in 1959.

ATKA

The Korovin Volcano is located on the east coast of Atka Island. It is one of the Aleutian Islands. The Aleutians were named in about 1780 by the Russians, who modified the Chukchi word *aliuit*, "beyond the shores." The Russians also built a church here as early as 1829.

Graphite was a major find on Atka Island, which gave its name to the village. Atka's name translates to "island in the Aleutians."

ATTU

"The loneliest spot this side of hell," as they once called this Aleutian Island, is the westernmost spot of the United States in the North American continent. In the month of June, the sun sets at Attu at the precise moment that it rises in Maine!

The Imperial Japanese Navy took control of Attu in the early days of World War II. American bombers softened the island during the winter of 1942 and into 1943. Finally, on 11 May 1943, the beach at Attu was hit by American forces. The entire Japanese garrison was wiped out by fighting that lasted more than a month, and ranged from rock to rock. This was the only ground battle of World War II to take place on North American soil. Most of the village was destroyed during those operations. At that time, the U. S. military called the village Chicagof.

The island, for which the village was named, was originally named Saint Theodore by Captain Alexei Ilich Chirikov in 1742.

BARANOF

Baranof took its name from the island on which it resides. The island was named for Alexander Andreievich Baranof (Baranov), the first governor of the Russian-American Company, then called the Shelikov Company. This company was given exclusive rights in 1799 to the fur trade in Russian America.

In that same year, Baranof founded Novo Arkhangelsk, the capital of Russian America. His first choice of a name, however, was Slavorossiia, "The Glory of Russia."

A post office, named Baranoff, was opened here in 1907. The final "f" was dropped in 1930.

BARROW

Barrow is the northernmost settlement in Alaska. It is 340 miles north of the Arctic Circle on the edge of the Arctic icepack. Barrow is one of the world's largest Eskimo settlements, and its name was taken from nearby Point Barrow.

Originally called Nuwuk, "the point," by native Alaskans, the town was renamed in 1826 by Captain Frederick W. Beechey, of the *H.M.S. Blossom*, to honor Sir John Barrow (1764–1848), an English geographer. Sir John had been greatly involved in encouraging polar expeditions. He also was a founder of the Royal Geographic Society in 1830.

English-speaking settlers found the Eskimo name, Utkiakvik, "high place for viewing," difficult to pronounce. The village of Barrow had its post office opened under that name in 1901.

BEAVER

Beaver is located on the northern bank of the Yukon River, near the mouth of the Beaver Creek. It was established about 1906 as a river landing. There are more than 80 spots in Alaska that recognize the beaver.

A town site was platted in about 1911. A post office was opened here in 1913.

BEECHEY POINT

In 1826, Captain Frederick William Beechey charted the southern coast of the Seward Peninsula to Cape Prince of Wales. This locale was named for the nearby point of land. The land mass was named in 1826 by Sir John Franklin for "my friend Capt. Beechey. . . . "

BELKOFSKI

The name for the Aleut village of Belkofski was given by the Russians before 1835. Its name, from the Russian *belka*, translates to "squirrel."

A post office was opened under the name Belkofski in 1888.

BETHEL

Bethel, located near the mouth of the Kuskokwim River, was founded in 1885 by William H. Weinland and John H. Kilbrick as a Moravian mission. The Moravian influence remains: Bethel is a "dry" community. The name, of course, has Biblical reference: "And God said unto Jacob, Arise, and go up to Bethel, and dwell there; and make there an altar unto God" (Gen. 35:1). Bethel translates from the Hebrew to mean "house of God."

The village was originally an Eskimo village and trading post of the Alaska Commercial Company, known as Mumtrekhlogamute. That name translates to "smokehouse people." A Bethel post office was established in 1905.

BETTLES

Bettles, named for Gordon C. Bettles, printer for the Fort Adams Press in 1893, was developed around the trading post Bettles opened in 1899. A post office under this name first opened in 1901.

BIG DELTA

The village of Big Delta was established in 1904 by the U. S. Army Signal Corps as the McCarthy (McCarty) Telegraph Station. A post office was opened here in 1905 as Washburn. The post office became Big Delta in 1925.

The village is located at the junction of the Delta and Tanana rivers.

BIG LAKE

Big Lake took its name from the body of water next to which it was established in the late 1950s.

BILL MOORES

Bill Moores is situated on the left bank of Apoon Pass. Originally it was a river landing and woodyard known as Bill Moore's Slough. In 1899, R. L. Faris noted the village as Konogkelyokamiut, suggesting the existence of an Eskimo village.

BIRCH CREEK

The community of Birch Creek is located on the right bank of Lower Mouth Birch Creek.

BOUNDARY

A placer mining camp was established here in 1940, complete with a post office. The town was so named because it is only three miles from the Alaska-Canada boundary.

BREVIG MISSION

Sheldon Jackson, a Presbyterian missionary, established a community here in 1892 as Teller Reindeer Station. He applied the name to honor Henry Moore Teller (1830–1914). Teller had served as a U. S. senator and secretary of the Department of the Interior.

The station was operated by the federal government from 1892 to 1900. In September of 1900, a Norwegian Evangelical Lutheran mission was started here. Six years later, the government role decreased and the religious mission prospered. The Brevig Mission post office was opened here in 1963 in honor of the Reverend T. L. Brevig. The superintendent of the Teller Mission, Brevig had served as Jackson's assistant, then returned as a Lutheran minister.

BUCKLAND

Buckland is located on the Buckland River, from which it took its name. A Buckland post office was established here in 1935.

The river was named in 1826 by Captain Frederick W. Beechey "in compliment to Dr. Buckland, the Professor of Geology at Oxford. . . ." The Indians called the river Kanyk.

C

CAMPBELL

This community took its name from the Hudson Bay Company's Robert Campbell, the discoverer of the Pelly (Yukon) River in 1840. Campbell also founded Fort Selkirk in 1848.

CANDLE

Candle is located in the middle of what was the Candle Creek placer gold district. The name was given because of a local scrubby brush or shrub, similar to "candlewood" or "greasewood," that would burn easily when lit. The Eskimos used the plant to light their homes.

CANTWELL

Cantwell is named for the Cantwell (River) Creek, the old name for the Nenana River. Some sources believe the name donor was

494

Lieutenant John C. Cantwell, who explored the Kobuk River area from 1884 to 1886. He was a major contributor to our knowledge of the Alaskan territory.

CAPE FANSHAW

This community was named for the Cape Fanshaw, three miles southwest of the town. A post office under that name was established in 1902.

CAPE POLE

This logging community is located at Cape Pole on the coast of Kosciusko Island. The point of land was named in 1793 by Vancouver for a fellow officer, Captain Morice Pole. The island was named almost a century later to honor the Polish-born hero of the American Revolution.

A post office was established here in 1949.

CAPE YAKATAGA

Cape Yakataga is located on Cape Yakataga. *Yakataga* is an Indian word, we are told, that translates as "canoe road." The reference is that two reefs provide canoe passage to the village. A post office opened here in 1935.

CARO

Caro was established as a mining camp in about 1906. A post office was established under that name in 1907. The name was given to honor Caro Kingland Clum, daughter of the Fairbanks postmaster in that year.

CENTRAL

The Central House was a roadhouse on the way to the Circle. When a post office was opened here in 1925, the "house" was dropped.

CHALKYITSIK

Chalkyitsik took its name from the Tranjik-kutchin Indian word for "to fish with a hook, at the mouth of the creek." At times, the village was known as Fishhook, Fishhook Town and Fishhook Village.

CHANDALAR

Chandalar took its name from the Chandalar Lake on whose banks it resides. The settlement began as a mining camp in 1906 or 1907, and a post office opened under that name in 1908.

Sources disagree on the name source. Some contend that Chandalar came from John Chandalar of the Hudson Bay Company.

Others suggest the name was given by French-Canadian members of the Hudson Bay Company in the early 19th century. The name might have been used to describe the local Indians, coming from the French *gens de large*, "nomadic people." Converting it to English, we get the current spelling.

CHATANIKA

Chatanika, like Chandalar, took its name from a nearby waterway which bears a Tanana Indian name. The Chatanika River is formed by three creeks: Faith, Hope and Charity—all named by prospectors.

The settlement began about 1904 as a mining village. The Tanana Valley Railroad arrived three years later. In 1908, the post office opened under this name.

CHATHAM

Chatham is located on Chatham Strait and took its name from that feature. A post office bearing this name opened in 1906.

The strait was named by George Vancouver in 1794, in honor of "the Great Commoner," William Pitt, the first Earl of Chatham (1708–78). The earl's name is remembered all over the United States in places that begin with Pitt and those called Chatham. But we must also remember that one of Vancouver's ships was the H.M.S. *Chatham*.

CHEFORNAK

Chefornak is an Eskimo village located at the confluence of the Keguk and Kinia rivers.

CHENA HOT SPRINGS

Chena Hot Springs is located on Monument Creek, a tributary of the Chena River from which the town derives its name. The composition of the springs found at the river's headwaters were similar to those found at Karlsbad, Bohemia.

The closest one can come to a derivation of the name is that *-na* in the Athspascan language means "river."

CHENEGA

Located on the southern end of Chenega Island, this Indian village had its post office established in 1946.

CHEVAK

This Eskimo village is the "new" Chevak. The "old" village was abandoned and relocated here. A post office was opened at the new site in 1951. The name, however, is a reference to the old town site. The name means "a connecting slough" on which the former Chevak was situated.

CHICHAGOF

Chichagof Island carries the name of Russian Admiral Vasilii Yakov Chichagof, an Arctic explorer. The island was named in 1805 by Captain U. F. Lisianski. The town, established in 1905 when gold was discovered on Klag Bay, took its name from the island.

A post office under this name was opened in 1909.

CHICAKALOON

The village of Chicakaloon took its name from the river. The term, *chic cloon*, came from the Athapascan language.

The town was established in 1916 as the terminus for the Matanuska Branch of the Alaska Railroad. The Chicakaloon post office opened in 1918.

CHICKEN

There are no less than three stories about the naming of Chicken. One has it that the name was given about 1895 for the nearby Chicken Creek. The stream was named for the small amount of gold found there.

The second refers to the size of the gold kernels, sometimes likened to the size of cracked corn or chicken feed.

The final story suggests the name came from the many wild birds that once populated the area, such as grouse, which are known as "Chicken of the Flats."

The Chicken post office opened here in 1903, the same year as the mining camp.

CHIGNIK (— Lagoon)

Chignik's name appears to be of Aleut origin, but was translated by the Russians in 1847. The village is located at the head of Anchorage Bay. A post office was opened under this name in 1901.

Besides this community, the name also appears on Chignik Lagoon and Chignik Lake.

CHISANA

Chisana is located on the Chisna River. *Chistna* is Tanana Indian for "red river."

A post office was opened here in 1901 as Chisna, but the name was changed seven years later to Dempsey. The town kept its earlier name.

CHISTOCHINA

Sources suggest Chistochina's name came from the Athapascan Indian *che-les'-chi-tna*, "marmot-river."

The village began under that name as a U. S. Army Signal Corps telegraph station in 1903. During the construction of the Glenn Highway, the name was applied to a roadhouse. The name did appear earlier on the Chistochina River (1887) and the Chistochina Glacier (1900).

CHITINA

Chitina's name is a compound Indian word: *chiti*, "copper," and *na*, "river." This community took its name from the waterway that flows into the Copper River.

The village was established in 1908, near an Indian village, as the northern terminus for the Copper River & Northwestern Railroad.

CHRISTIAN

Christian is a Kutcha-kutchin Indian village which was named for the Christian Creek. Most sources contend that the waterway's name belonged to a prospector.

CIRCLE CITY

Circle City is an Eskimo village located on the banks of the Yukon River. Its name is a mistake. Prospectors thought the village was located on the Arctic Circle. It is about 50 miles south of it.

Circle, as it was then called, was established in 1887 as a mining supply town. L. N. McQuestern opened a trading post here in that year.

In 1893, a New Hampshire prospector found gold here near Birch Creek. Four years later, a post office was established.

CIRCLE HOT SPRINGS

Prospector George Growe was trailing a moose across an unusually warm creek in the fall of 1897. He followed it to hot springs which ran about 139 degrees Fahrenheit at their source. As a result of this discovery, Circle Hot Springs became a year-round resort. But not for Growe.

The next spring, Growe found some attractive plants. He cooked and ate the plants that turned out to be wild parsnips. He was not aware—until too late—that the roots were poisonous.

Another source suggests that the springs were discovered by William Greats in 1893. The town was homesteaded in 1905 by Franklin Leach who converted the place into a resort. The Circle Hot Springs post office was opened in 1924.

CLAM GULCH

Clam Gulch took its name from the nearby Clam Gulch ravine. A post office was established here in 1950. At one time, the community was known as Clam Gulch Store. The name, of course, is descriptive of what could be found there.

CLARKS POINT

John W. Clark, a trader who accompanied A. B. Schanz, named Lake Clark in 1891.

Clarks Point, however, took its name from the nearby point of land by the same name. That land mass was named in 1890 by the U. S. Bureau of Fisheries supposedly for Samuel Fessenden Clark of Williams College.

COAL CREEK

Coal Creek, taking its name from the waterway on which it resides, was originally a mining camp. A post office was opened under this name in 1936.

The stream was so named because, as a contemporary wrote, "coal seams occur along the course of the stream."

COFFMAN COVE

Coffman Cove took its name from the cove on the northeast coast of Prince of Wales Island. It was named in 1886 by Lieutenant Commander A. S. Show, in honor of Lieutenant Dewitt Coffman, a member of his crew.

COHOE

The word Cohoe is a modification of "coho," a kind of salmon. This was an agricultural community that opened its first post office in 1950.

COLD BAY

Cold Bay took its name from the body of water on which it is located. The bay's name was a translation of the Russian Zaliv Morozovskii.

The village is situated near the site of Fort Randall. A post office opened here in 1954.

COLDFOOT

Coldfoot, an early mining camp located at the mouth of Slate Creek, went by the name of the waterway as early as 1899. The next summer, green stampeders got as far up the Koyukuk as this point, then got cold feet, turned around and departed. After that event, the town's name changed. A post office opened under the name of Coldfoot in 1902.

COLLEGE

College was created as the home of the Alaska Agricultural College and School of Mines, now the University of Alaska, in 1915. The university is the northernmost institution of higher learning in the United States.

COOPER LANDING

This village was named for the nearby Lake Cooper. No one is sure for whom the lake was named. Cooper Gulch was named for Joe Cooper, a prospector; Cooper Island, on the Beaufort Sea, for an officer on the H.M.S. *Plover*; and Cooper Islands, in the Bering Sea, by Lieutenant William Gibson for the schooner *James Fenimore Cooper*.

COPPER CENTER

Copper Center is located at the junction of the Klutina and Cooper rivers. A trading post was established here in about 1896. The village grew around the post as miners wintered here in 1898–99.

Copper Center is considered by many to be the first "town" in the interior of Alaska. The U. S. Army Signal Corps opened a telegraph station in 1901, and a post office opened in the same year.

CORDOVA

Cordova, located on Cordova Bay, was once the shipping center for copper from the Kennecott Mines. It was the port city for the Copper River & Northwestern Railroad. A post office opened here in 1906. The mines and the railroad shut down operations in 1983, and access to Cordova is now limited to arrival by plane or ferry.

Puerto Cordoba y Cordoba was first named in 1792 by Spanish explorers for their naval commander, Luis de Cordoba y Cordoba. The name was recorded by Vancouver in 1798.

COUNCIL

In its youth, Council had 14 major saloons with connected gambling dens and houses of ill repute.

Located at the junction of Melsing Creek and Niukluk River, Council was named by members of a San Franciso group, Daniel B. Libby, A. P. Mordaunt, L. F. Melsing, and H. L. Blake, who arrived here in 1897, found gold and made it their camp. They also named the creek.

The Council post office was established in 1900.

CRAIG

Craig is located on Prince of Wales Island. Originally named Fish Egg, for nearby Fish Egg Island, the community changed to Craig Millar for the local cannery owner. The "Millar" was dropped in 1912 when the post office was established.

CROOKED CREEK

The village of Crooked Creek is located on the Kuskokwim River, east of the junction of Crook Creek, from which it takes its name.

The community was established about 1909 near a small Indian village. In 1910, it was known as Portage Village because it was at the south end of a portage route. Eight years later, with the opening of the Parent Trading Post, the town changed its name again. Finally, in 1927, when the post office was established, the name became Crooked Creek.

DAWSON CITY

For a brief period of time at the turn of the 20th century, Dawson City was the "most refined city" north of San Francisco and west of Winnipeg.

Located at the confluence of the Yukon and Klondike rivers, the town honors George M. Dawson, a geologist for the Canadian government who did extensive exploration of the Yukon. The town was platted and named in 1896 by Joseph Ladue, a trading post operator.

DEADHORSE

Deadhorse remembers Dead Horse Gulch, where overloaded pack animals fell from the cliffs into the canyon below. U.S. Army exploration teams gave the life expectancy of a pack horse as a few days to a few weeks.

In 1916, the mining camp here was known as Dead Horse. Eight years later, with the opening of a station, the Alaska Railroad named it Curry, for Charles Forrest Curry (1858–1935), a member of Congress from California.

DEERING

Deering is located on a southern bay of the Kotzebue Sound. The sound was named for its discoverer, Otto von Kotzebue (1787–1846), a German explorer. Between 1815 and 1818, he tried to locate a passage across the Arctic Ocean, and discovered the sound near the Bering Strait.

In 1901, the village was established and a post office was opened. The name, it has been suggested, came from the schooner *Abbie M. Deering* that sailed the waters here at the turn of the 20th century.

DELTA JUNCTION

Delta Junction is located (surprise, surprise) by the Delta River.

The village, established about 1919 as a camp for road construction workers on the Richardson Road, from Valdez to Fairbanks, was called Buffalo Center. It was the center of the Alaska Bison Range, a government reserve for herds of buffalo shipped north from the continguous United States.

DENALI

Indians knew Mount McKinley as Denali, the "High One." The name has also been translated as "home of the sun." Denali National Park was created in 1917 to preserve 37 species of mammals, including grizzlies, caribou, Dall sheep, and wolves. By 1980, the park had grown in size to six million acres.

Situated near the mouth of Valdez Creek, the town was also called Valdez Creek when it began as a mining camp in about 1907.

DENALI. The earliest residents of Alaska knew Mount McKinley as Denali, the "High One." The name has been translated to mean "home of the sun," an appropriate name for a peak so large. (National Park Service photography by P. Steuck)

A post office here, called McKinley, began operation in 1908 or in 1909. By 1922, a new post office was opened under the name of Denali.

DILLINGHAM

Dillingham was named in 1904 in honor of William Paul Dillingham (1843–1923). Dillingham, a former governor of Vermont, was a U. S. senator who led an extensive tour through Alaska. For years, Dillingham was one of the senate's experts on Alaska.

When it was still an Eskimo village, the town was known as Ah-lek-nug-uk, then as Kanakanak and Chogium. When the post office was established in 1904, the name became Dillingham.

DOT LAKE

The settlement here was established in 1954. It is located on the Alaska Highway at Dot Lake. The body of water, one would think, was so called because of its size.

DUTCH HARBOR

The village of Dutch Harbor is located on the harbor of the same name. Tradition has it that the name came about because the first ship to enter the harbor flew a Dutch flag. The native name for the harbor was Udakta.

Dutch Harbor was the site of a major naval installation. That site was attacked by the Japanese on 3 June 1942.

EAGLE (— River, — Village)

Eagle is located on the left bank of the Yukon River, about 10 miles from the international boundary.

It was the first settlement to be reached on the Yukon in American Alaska. When Moses Mercier established a log trading station here in 1874, he called it Belle Island. With the establishment of a mining camp in 1898, the land was platted into townsites and named Eagle City for the American eagles that roosted atop nearby Eagle Bluff. The Eagle post office was opened in 1898.

Eagle was the center of government for Alaska's Interior until Fairbanks began to grow. An Army post, Fort Egvert, operated here until 1911.

Eagle River took its name from the waterway on which it is located. The post office was established here in 1961.

Eagle Village's early name was Johnnys for the Indian chief who lived there.

EDNA BAY

The major industry of this village was lumbering. In 1943, a post office was established here. The name was drawn from the bay of the same name, which, as E. F. Dickins wrote in the early 20th century, was "named by our party, has no local name."

EEK

Eek was named for the river on which it is located. The waterway's name was originally recorded as Ik in 1826. Since 1880, the name has been written as Eek. A post office was established under that name in 1949.

It has been said that the name was drawn from the Eskimo *eet*, "the two eyes."

EGEGIK

Egegik is located at the mouth of the Egegik River. The name translates from the Aleut and means "swift." The Eskimos called the settlement Igagik.

EKLUTNA

In the late 19th century, Russian missionaries came to this town to convert the Athabascan tribe of Indians. They constructed the St. Nicholas Russian Orthodox Church. That log structure still stands.

The Alaska Railroad opened a station here in 1918, and a post office opened in 1926. The settlement took its name from the river on whose banks it resides.

EKUK
Explorers located an Eskimo village here in 1828, which was known as Ekouk and Ikuk. It took its name from the Ekuk Spit.

EKWOK
Originally known as Billy Hurleys for the white trader who operated here, Ekwok bears a native name. The name, in this spelling, first appeared in 1910.

ELFIN COVE
The post office at Elfin Cove began operations in 1935. The name was drawn from the nearby cove. That name was probably given because of the size of the cove.

Originally, fishermen called it Gunk Hole, an East Coast term for a safe harbor with a narrow inlet. About 1928, Ernest O. Swanson built a salmon salting operation here, and when the post office was opened, the "gunky" name was dropped.

ELIM
Elim was established in 1915 as an Eskimo village. The post office, under that name, opened in 1943. It has also been known as Elim Mission Roadhouse.

ENGLISH BAY
English Bay took its name from the nearby bay. Earlier, the village was a Russian settlement known as Alexandrovsk, then as Odinochka, "a person living in solitude."

The bay was named "English" either because Captain Cook had surveyed the area, and the Russians called it Angliiskii, or because the area was charted by an Englishman, Captain Nathaniel Portlock.

ESTER
Ester, a mining camp in operation before 1905, took its name from the nearby Ester Creek. When a post office was opened here, the name was Berry. In 1965, the name was changed to Ester.

At one time, the waterway was called Esther, named by prospectors probably for a wife or girlfriend. Over the years, the town has been known as Ester, Ester City and Berry—for miners Clarence and Frank Berry. Clarence made a fortune during the Klondike Gold Rush.

EUREKA

A camp was established here in 1899. When a telegraph station opened five years later, the name was Glen. In 1909, the post office opened and authorities dubbed it Eureka—the name that stuck. (See EUREKA, California.)

EVANSVILLE

An Indian village began in 1945 when Bettles Field was developed as part of the exploration of Naval Petroleum Reserve No. 4. A post office was established here as Bettles Field in 1950.

F

FAIRBANKS

A trading post was established here in 1901 by Captain E. T. Barnette. He opened shop here because a riverboat captain refused to take him any further on the Chena River. He called his settlement Barnettes Cache.

Gold was discovered a year later, and Barnette's settlement grew. The prospector who struck it rich was Felix Pedro. He left his name on Pedro Creek. The town was renamed in 1902 for Charles W. Fairbanks (1852–1918) of Indiana. Fairbanks had been vice president under Theodore Roosevelt and a former member of the U. S. Senate. The post office at Fairbanks was opened in 1903.

Half a century later, oil was discovered 390 miles north at Prudhoe Bay. This sparked a second wave of development.

FALSE PASS

False Pass is so named because at first glance it seems to be the passageway between the Pacific Ocean and the Bering Sea for ocean vessels.

False Pass was the English name for the Isantoski Strait, on which the town is located. The post office was established here in 1921.

FLAT

Flat took its name not from a description of its land but from the nearby Flat Creek. A post office opened here in 1912.

FORTUNA LEDGE (Marshall)

Gold was discovered here on the Wilson Creek in 1913 by E. L. Mack and Joe Mills. Three years later, the townspeople voted to call the town Marshall, in honor of Thomas Riley Marshall (1854–1925), vice president under Woodrow Wilson. Marshall is best-remembered for his comment, "What this country needs is a good five-cent cigar."

The post office which opened in 1915, however, listed it as Fortuna Ledge.

FORT YUKON

Fort Yukon, just north of the Arctic Circle, was established by the Hudson Bay Company as a trading post in 1847. Located at the confluence of the Porcupine and Yukon Rivers, the fort was built by Alexander Hunter Murray.

When the United States purchased Alaska from Russia in 1867, the English company was asked to leave. They moved their post, but found it was within American territory. Finally, they moved it 20 miles up the Porcupine. Shortly, it was replaced by the more powerful Alaska Commercial Company.

The post office at Fort Yukon was opened in 1898.

Fort Yukon is now an Athabascan Indian village. Grave markers in the local cemetery date back to the year after the United States purchased Alaska from Russia.

FORTUNA LEDGE (MARSHALL). Thomas Riley Marshall, Woodrow Wilson's vice president, had to dig into his own pocket to pay for presidential entertaining expenses while Wilson was incapacitated. To earn the money, Marshall took to the road, giving speeches for pay. (National Archives)

FOX

Located on the Fox Creek, this settlement was a former mining camp instituted before 1905. The post office was established here in 1908.

The creek was named because of its proximity to the Fox River. There are 26 creeks and 39 other geographic features in the State of Alaska that honor the fox.

FUNTER

One of the earliest canneries in Alaska was opened here. The community is located on the bay of the same name. A post office under that name was opened here in 1902.

The bay was named in 1883 by W. H. Dall in honor of Captain Robert Funter, an English explorer who charted parts of the northwest coast of North America in 1788.

GAKONA

The name for Gakona was taken from the Gakona River. The waterway's name is from the Athapascan Indian *gakatna*, "rabbit river."

In 1905, a post office and trading post were established here.

G

GALENA

On Bishop's Rock, near Galena, there is a marker where Bishop John Charles Sehgers was murdered by his lay worker, Francis Fuller, in 1886. Fuller "aroused the bishop from a sound sleep," the story goes, "and after a few insane ejaculations, shot him dead."

The community was established about 1919 as a supply point for galena (lead) mining south of the Yukon River.

The post office at Galena was opened in 1932. Galena is also the site of an earlier Indian village, known as Natulaten or Notaglita.

GAMBELL

This village at the northwest tip of St. Lawrence Island was named in 1898 by William F. Doty. Doty suggested the name "in honor of the noble missionaries" Mr. and Mrs. Vene C. Gambell, Presbyterian missionaries and teachers who worked here from 1894 to 1898.

Returning from a much-deserved vacation, they were drowned when the schooner *Jane Grey* sank in 1898.

GEORGETOWN

Georgetown was originally the name of a trading post, established here in about 1910 by George Fredericks. A post office, again run by Fredericks, was opened in 1912.

GIRDWOOD

While some other towns across the United States bearing this name refer to a method of making a clearing, this village on the northeast shore of Turnagain Arm does not.

Girdwood was named for James E. Girdwood, a miner who arrived here in 1896. A post office bearing his name opened in 1907.

GLENNALLEN

U. S. Army Captain Edwin Forbes Glenn and Lieutenant Henry Tureman Allen were early explorers of the Copper River area. When it came time to name this village, the decision was made to merge their two names.

Along with Walter C. Mendenhall, Glenn and Allen mapped the area from Cook Inlet to the Tanana River in 1898.

GODDARD

Goddard is named for Dr. F. L. Goddard. Goddard established a hotel at the site of the five natural hot springs on Baranof Island.

A community began here about the turn of the 19th century by Russians who called it Teplyya Tseplitel Yuchya Klyuchi, "sheltered curative hot springs." A Russian hospital operated here in 1841.

When a post office was opened in 1908, the community was called Sanitorium. The name was changed to honor Goddard in 1924.

GOLOVNIN

Golovnin is located on Golovnin Bay, from which it took its name. The bay was named by Adolph Karlovich Etolin and Michael Vasilief in 1822, when they explored Norton Sound. The name came from Captain Vasili M. Golovnin (Golofnin) of the Russian Navy. Golovnin explored the area in 1810 and 1818.

Before the Russians arrived, there was an Eskimo village here called Ikalikhvig-myut. In about 1890, John Dexter, a miner from the nearby Omalik mines, married an Eskimo woman and opened a trading post. When gold was discovered in 1891, Golovnin became a supply center for the Council gold mines. When the first post office was opened here in 1899, the town was called Chennik. In that same year, a Golovnin post office was established south of this location, probably at Golovnin Mission. Dexter was postmaster of both offices. Finally, a new Golovnin post office was merged here in 1906.

GOODNEWS BAY

Goodnews Bay took its name from the bay, which was named by the 1818–19 Vstiugof and Korsakof expedition. The name, it is presumed, is a direct translation from the Russian: Port Dobrykh Vestet.

Lütke suggested, "it might better be called the 'Bay of False Reports.'"

GORDON

The Gordon community was named for Thomas Gordon, a Scotsman who arrived in this area in 1888 and opened a trading post.

GRAYLING

Grayling was named after the creek. The waterway was so named in 1925 because a fishing party caught the first grayling (a game fish similar to the trout) of the season here.

GULKANA (— Junction)

Gulkana is located on the Gulkana River. The name is probably Athapascan Indian because of the *-ana*, which means "river." The rest is uncertain.

The village was established in about 1903 as a U. S. Army Signal Corps telegraph station named Kulkana. This, some authorities believe, was the original name of the river. The spelling was changed by Army Captain W. R. Abercrombie. A Gulkana post office opened here in 1909.

GUSTAVUS

Gustavus took its name from Point Gustavus. Because of the connection—Glacier Bay—between Point Gustavus and Point Adolphus, it would seem that the name donor was King Gustavus Adolphus (1594–1632) of Sweden. The point was named in 1879 by W. H. Dall.

King Gustavus Adolphus was killed on the field at Lützen, near Leipzig. His heart was removed from his body and transported back to Stockholm in his bloodied silk shirt. His death left Sweden the strongest power in Europe.

A more likely choice, though it does not go back to the king, is the British trader Gustavus, who visited this site about three years before Vancouver did in 1794. The name for this village was authorized in 1948. Previously, it had been called Strawberry Point.

HAINES

Haines, located near the head of Chilkat Peninsula, was originally a trading post for Chilkat and Interior Indians. Settled by the Tlingit Indians, the town was called Dtehshuh, "end of the trail."

George Dickinson, the Northwest Trading Company agent, was the first white man to establish himself here, arriving in 1878. The next year, Presbyterian missionary S. Hall Young, and naturalist John Muir decided this would be a perfect spot for a place to bring Christianity and education to the Indians. Two years later, Young founded the Willard Mission. In 1884, a post office was established in the name of Haines, even though the village's name was Chilkat or Chilcoot. The name honors Mrs. Francina Electra Haines, of the Presbyterian Board of Home Missions.

The nearby Chilkat Bald Eagle Preserve contains the largest concentrations of bald eagles in the world.

An Army post, Fort William H. Seward, was established here in 1903. During World War I, the fort was used as an induction center for Alaskan recruits. The name was changed to Chilkoot Barracks in 1923, and for almost two decades it was the only Army post in Alaska. Following World War II, the "Barracks" were sold to a group of veterans who considered developing the area as a recreational center. In 1970, Port Chilkoot (the name they gave the old military post) merged with adjacent communities and became the City of Haines.

HAMILTON

Charles H. Hamilton was the assistant manager of the North American Trading Company when they opened a supply post and riverboat landing here in 1897. Prior to that—at least before 1844—there was an Eskimo village near here known as Aunguamut.

HAWK INLET

Hawk Inlet is located on northern part of Admiralty Island. The community's name comes from the inlet on which it resides.

HAYCOCK

Haycock is located on Dime Creek, north of Norton Bay. A mining camp was established here about 1914, and so named because of a nearby mound that looked like a haycock.

HEALY

Captain M. A. Healy, with Lieutenant George M. Stoney, identified the Kobuk River.

The village began as a mining camp, established about 1905. A post office called Healy Fork was opened in 1921. The town is located on the Nenana River, near the mouth of Healy River. At different times in its existence, Healy has been known as Dry Creek and Healy Fork.

HOGATZA

About 1940, a mining camp was established here and named after the river.

HOLLIS

Hollis had its start as a mining community about the turn of the 20th century. A post office under that name was opened in 1901. The name is a personal one.

HOLY CROSS

Holy Cross was established in 1886 or 1887 as a mission operated by Jesuit priests. At this location, Father Jules Jetté made his studies of the dialects of the Yukon Indians. It was here that Father Robaut printed in 1899 the first school primer written in the Eskimo language.

Before the arrival of the white man, there was an Indian village here, called Anilukhatpak, and Anilukhtak-kak before 1842. A post office opened here in 1899. It took the name of Koserefski, the Russian name for the village across the Walker Slough. The name was changed in 1912 in honor of the mission.

HOMER

When the schooner *Excelsior* landed a party of gold and coal prospectors here in 1895, the group was led by Homer Pennock. They never found gold!

The Homer post office opened in 1896.

HOONAH

Hoonah, located on Chichagof Island, bears the name of a local tribe. Their name, *hooniah*, translates to "cold lake." A post office under this name was opened in 1901.

HOOPER BAY

The Eskimos referred to the Hooper Bay as Napareyaramiut, "stake village people." This village took its name from the bay. The village's Eskimo name was Askinuk, Askeenac or Askinaghamiut. In 1934, postal authorities made things a little easier by naming the post office Hooper Bay. The name came from Captain Calvin L. Hooper of the U.S. Revenue Cutter Service.

HOPE

In the summer of 1895, prospectors found strong gold deposits on Cook Inlet. By the spring of the next year, the area was swarming with hopeful gold-rushers. They named their community Hope City, symbolic of their feelings. It might also have been helped along by the fact that the village is located near the mouth of Resurrection Creek.

Very few claims produced much and by the fall of 1896, most of the prospectors had returned home. A post office opened as Hope in 1897.

HORNER

Originally known as Horner Hot Springs, this community was unknown until 1913, when Indians introduced F. G. Horner to the springs.

HOUSTON

Houston began as a station on the Alaska Railroad before 1917. The town took the name of Representative William Cannon Houston, chairman of the Committee on Territories that entered the Alaska Railroad bill into Congress.

HUGHES

Hughes was founded in 1910 as a riverboat landing and supply center for the Indian River digs, and it was named in honor of Charles Evans Hughes (1862–1848). Hughes was then governor of New York. Later, the town evolved into a Koyukan Indian village.

A post office was opened here in 1914.

HUSLIA

The Koyukan Indians moved their village of Cutoff or Cutoff Trading Post to a new location on the left bank of the Koyukuk River. They named it Huslia, after the nearby stream. A post office, under the name of Cutoff, was opened in 1947. When the post office moved to higher ground, the name was changed to Huslia.

HYDABURG

Hydaburg's name appears to have been drawn from the Haida tribe of British Columbian Indians. That island, along with Kasaan, was the tribe's home.

Hydaburg was founded in 1911, and a post office was established the next year.

HYDER

Hyder was created in 1907 as a mining community, under the name of Portland City. The name was given because it was the easternmost village in Alaska. When a post office was created in 1915, the Portland City name was denied.

Frederick Hyder, a Canadian mining engineer, visited the site in 1914 and examined some claims. One of the claims, the Big Missouri Mine, owned by Daniel Lindeborg, was so favorable that the owner proposed Hyder's name for the post office.

IDITAROD

Iditarod took its name from the waterway on which it was founded: the Iditarod River.

The river was discovered in 1841 by Simensen Lukee, a Russian trader. He called it Yellow River.

The community of Iditarod was founded in 1910, and shortly after it became the center for the Innoko-Iditarod placer mine district. A post office was opened in 1912.

IGIUGIG

Igiugig was a fishing village here when the post office opened in 1934. The name came from the Aleut *kigusig*, "volcano."

ILIAMNA

Authorities believe the name of this village is Eskimo. The name is supposed to be that of a mythical blackfish that bites holes in natives' boats. The name was first employed in naming the lake.

Before 1935, this name was given to another village at another site. After the move, the old village became known as Old Iliamna. Old Iliamna received its first post office in 1901, then moved here and kept the name.

IVANOF BAY

The community of Ivanof Bay is located at the northern end of the bay of the same name. An Ivanof post office was opened here in 1952.

J

JUNEAU

Joe Juneau and Richard Harris discovered gold along the banks of the Gastineau Channel here in 1880, and this started the first Alaskan gold rush. They were led to the golden riches by a Tlingit chief named Kowee. He did not get his name on the town, even though for a time it was known as Harrisburg.

At one time, the Alaska-Juneau and Treadwell mines were producing an average of 20,000 tons of ore daily. When the price of gold fell and the cost of extraction rose in 1944, mining operations ended.

Joe Juneau sold off his holdings because he was afraid he would not live long enough to spend his money. Fortunately, Juneau lived long enough to spend that fortune and several others. Unfortunately, he died penniless. His uncle Solomon, by the way, helped found Milwaukee, Wisconsin.

Juneau is Alaska's capital city. The territorial capital was moved here in 1906 from Sitka. The Juneau post office was established in 1882.

KACHEMAK

Kachemak took its name from the bay, which uses an Eskimo word to denote "big water cliff." Another source thinks the word came from the Aleut dialect for "smoky bay," since coal seams once smoldered in the nearby clay banks.

The town of Kachemak was incorporated in 1961.

KAGUYAK

Kaguyak is located at the head of Kaguyak Bay, and took its name from the bay. In 1880, the community's name was listed as Kaguiak. One authority thinks this village might be Aleutsk Selen Kaniyagmyut, reported by the Russian-American Company in 1849.

KAKE

This name was taken from the Tlingit Indian tribe of the same name. The original name of the tribal village was S'ikanakhse'ni, "from a black bear town." Another source thinks it was Klu-ou-klukwan, "the ancient village that never sleeps." Isn't that the nickname Frank Sinatra popularized for New York City?

The Kake post office opened in 1904.

KAKHONAK

Kakhonak was an Eskimo village that gave its name to the bay at the other end of Iliamna Lake.

KAKTOVIK

Kaktovik, located on the north coast of Barter Island, carries the Eskimo name for that island. One source suggests the name translates to the "seining place."

KALSKAG

In 1880, this village was called Kaltkhagamut; nine years later, it was Kal-tchagamut.

KALTAG

Kaltag's name is of Eskimo origin, but interpreted by the Russians. One source suggests the name refers to a particular species of salmon. Another feels the name came from the Eskimo *kaltkhagamute.* All they can say is that *-mute* means "people."

KANAKANAK

Kanakanak is an Eskimo village that absorbed the former sites of Dillingham and Kanakanak. A post office was established here in 1929.

KANTISHNA

The name of Kantishna was drawn from the river. The village was begun in 1905 as a gold-mining camp. It was also called Eureka in an earlier time; again, named for the waterway. The river, over the years, has been known as Contaythno, Kantishana, Tutlut and Toclat. The last name, we are told, translates as "dish water."

KARLUK

When Captain Lisianski reported the name of this village in 1805, he called it Carlook and Karloock. Twenty-four years later, the Russian-American Company referred to it as Kunakakhvak.

A post office was opened here in 1892 under the name Karluk.

An interesting sidelight is the naming of Karluk Island. Some sources contend that the island was named for the whaler *Karluk*, commanded by Captain Steven Cottle in 1909.

KASAAN

This village is located on Kasaan Bay, from which it derived its name. The village began in the 1890s when a salmon-packing plant was built here. Haida Indians from Kasaan, now Old Kasaan, moved here and, when the post office opened in 1900, it was named for the old place.

The name is supposed to mean "pretty village."

KASHEGA

This community is located at the head of Kashega Bay.

The bay was named in honor of Yefim Koshigin. Koshigin spent the winter of 1763 at Unalaska. Another source suggests the name came from the Greenlandic language for "men's clubhouses."

KASHEGELOK

This village's name is Eskimo for "little meeting house." Originally, the name of the village was Kasheg-e-loge-mute.

KASILOF

In 1786, the Russians built two log houses here surrounded by a stockade and called it St. George. That was the beginning of Kasilof . . . or was it?

In 1937, surveyors uncovered a partially buried village near here. The cabin walls were constructed of bricks, logs, sod, and beach sand. Interestingly, the town is several miles from the coast! It was estimated at the time that the ruins were at least 300 years old.

KATALLA

Katalla, Indian for "bay," is located on Katalla River which took its name from Katalla Bay. The post office was opened here in 1904.

For years the ribs of an infamous ship, the steamer *Portland,* lay on the beach here. The *Portland* was the ship that steamed into Seattle with "a ton of gold" in 1897, and the event spawned the Alaskan gold rush of the next year.

Originally named *Haytian Republic* in 1885, the ship had been confiscated for smuggling ammunition to Haitian rebels during the Hippolyte rebellion. Four years later, she turned up in the Pacific as a cannery boat and passenger steamer. The ship was seized by the government when it was found that she was being used to smuggle illegal Chinese immigrants and opium into this country.

In 1910, the ship was wrecked on the beach here and ripped apart for the brass she contained.

KENAI

Russian fur traders under the command of Grigor Konovalov, commander of the *St. George,* established Redut Svataya Nikolaya, "Fort Saint Nicholas," at this location in 1791. It is one of the oldest permanent Alaskan settlements. The Russians also called the village Pavlovskaya, "Paul's Fort." In 1869, the U. S. Army called the area Fort Kenai for the Indians living nearby.

The Kenai post office was established in 1899.

The name for the town came from that of the river, which was originally written in the Athapascan as Kakny. Some think the name is a Russian adaptation of Knaiakhotana or Kenaiohkotna, "non-Eskimo people."

The oil strike here on 19 January 1957 has been called "perhaps the most important date in all of Alaska's colorful history."

KENNICOTT

Kennicott was named by the Kennecott Mines Company. The company opened a camp here in 1906, and its name was taken from the Kennicott Glacier. Unfortunately, the company misspelled the name. The glacier took its name from Robert Kennicott (1835–66), a pioneer explorer of Alaska.

Robert Kennicott was a delicate child, unable to attend school with other children his own age. This did not stop him, however, from making a natural history survey of southern Illinois for the Illinois Central Railroad by the age of 20. Four years later, he went to Alaska and explored for three years, finally reaching Fort Yukon.

The year before he died, he was put in charge of the Western Union Telegraph Company's exploration team.

The post office, with the misspelled name, was opened in 1908. Later, the spelling was modified to honor the explorer.

KETCHIKAN

According to local residents, Ketchikan is "Five miles long, four blocks wide and two blocks up Deer Mountain." The same residents call their hometown the salmon capital of the world.

Ketchikan is located on the south coast of Revillagigedo Island. The island was named in 1793 by Vancouver for the Viceroy of Mexico, Revilla Gigedo. Vancouver had a habit of naming things after his crew and friends. The Ketchikan site was the summer fishing home of the Tlingit Indians. White fishermen and hunters did not begin settlement until 1885. Two years later, a cannery was built and growth skyrocketed.

The name of this city came from the Tlingit Indian tongue and means "wing-like," a reference to a rock in the middle of a waterfall that makes it look split. Another source thinks that the town looks like a spread eagle when viewed from above. The town has been known as Kach Khanna, Kitsan, Kitchikan, and Kichikan.

"The First City" is what Alaskans call Ketchikan. They do not do so because it was founded first or because it is the largest. The name was given because, before air travel, Ketchikan was the first port of call for northbound passengers. A post office was established here in 1892.

KIANA

Kiana became known to prospectors in the late 19th century, and there was a mild gold rush in 1910. Originally an Eskimo village, the town became a supply center for the Squirrel River placer mines. A post office opened here in 1915.

KING COVE

A fishing village, King Cove was named for its founder, Al King, head of the King Cove Cannery. The King Cove post office opened in 1914.

KING SALMON

A King Salmon post office was opened at the King Salmon Air Force Base in 1949. The name apparently was derived from the King Salmon River.

KIPNUK

Kipnuk was an Eskimo name for this village as early as 1922.

KIVALINA

Kivalina is located at the mouth of the river of the same name. The village was originally located at the northern end of the lagoon. In 1847, its name was written as Kivualinagmut.

A post office was established here in 1940.

KIWALIK

Kiwalik, like Kivalina, is located at the mouth of a river of the same name. The Russians reported the river's name as Kualiug-muit in 1850.

Towards the end of the 19th century, the village became a supply post for mining operations in the Candle area.

A post office opened here in 1902, but under the name of Keewalik.

KLAWOCK

The first salmon canned in Alaska was processed here. The town's name came from that of a Tlingit Indian chief. An Indian village was reported by the Russians in 1853. It was called Thlewhakh.

A cannery was built here in 1878; a post office, four years later.

KLUKWAN

Klukwan was earlier known as Chilcat of Klukquan because of its location on the Chilkat River. The name, from the Tlingit Indian *klukquan*, means "always town," literally the old town.

KNIK

Knik took its name from the Tanaina village located on the Knik River that preceded the town. The Eskimo word *ignik* means "fire." More probably, the name came from that of the tribe.

The present village began around Palmer's Store, a 1903 trading post. A year later, the post office was established as Knik.

KOBUK

Kobuk took its name from the Kobuk River, surveyed by Lieutenant John C. Cantwell in 1884. At one time it was the name of the post office for Shungnak, a native word for "jade." The Shungnak post office was opened in 1903. Twenty-five years later, the name was changed to Kobuk.

Kobuk, we are told, means "big river." Perhaps the river's name is a redundancy.

KODIAK

Alexander Baranov, a Russian explorer/trader, moved his original 1784 headquarters at Three Saints Bay to this location in 1792. He named it Pavlovsk Gavan, "Paul's Harbor," and it served as Alaska's first capital until 1804.

With the Russians came their priests. Baptisms of the Aleuts took place for the personal gain of their godfathers rather than for any Christian belief. New Christians were "devoted" to their godfathers and "gave pelts to them exclusively."

The oldest European structure in Alaska, the Baranof House, still stands by the ferry dock here. The house was built in 1793 as a Russian commissary.

Kodiak is Inuit for "island," and Kodiak is the largest island in the area. The first time the name Kodiak was published was in 1869 when the post office was established.

During World War II, Kodiak was an important naval station in America's North Pacific defense.

KOKRINES

Kokrines is located between the mouths of the Ranana and Koyukuk rivers. The village was named for a Russian trader.

KOLIGANEK

The original Eskimo village bearing this name was four miles upstream of this location. The earlier village was known as Kalignak in 1880 and Kah-lig-y-nak in 1910.

KONGIGANAK

Kongiganak was the name of an Indian village which, in 1878, was reported as Kongiganagamiut, "Kongiganak people," which suggests the name is that of a sub-tribe.

KOTLIK

Kotlik, located on an island in the Yukon delta, is at the mouth of the Kotlik River—from which it takes its name. Some sources suggest the name came from "an incident that occurred a hundred years ago (mid-19th century), when a Russian was killed here." Others think the name is Eskimo for "breeches."

KOTZEBUE

Kotzebue took its name from the sound, named in 1816 by Russian navy Captain Otto von Kotzebue—for himself.

Locals like to say that Kotzebue has four seasons: June, July, August, and winter! They also call their community "The Polar Bear Capital of the World."

When a reindeer station was located here in about 1897, the village of Kotzebue was established as a permanent Eskimo village. Prior to that it was a summer fishing camp, known as Kikikhtagyut. The post office, named Kotzebue, opened in 1899. (See DEERING, Alaska.)

KOYUK

Koyuk, located on the banks of the Koyuk River, was an Eskimo village from 1842 to 1844, known as Kvynkhak-miut, "Kvynkhak people." About 1900, a trading post was opened and called Norton Bay Station.

KOYUKUK

The name for this village reflects Eskimo influence and bears the name of its river. The suffix "-kuk" is Eskimo for "river."

A post office was opened here in 1898.

KUPREANOF

Kupreanof bears the name of the island, named for Captain Ivan Andreevich Kupreanov, successor to Baron Ferdinand P. von Wrangell as governor of Russian America in 1836. He retired four years later.

KWIGILLINGOK

Located on Kuskokwim Bay, Kwigillingok originally bore the name of Quillingok. Only part of the name is decipherable: *Kwiga* means "river."

L

LAKE MINCHUMINA

This village took its name from the body of water. The name means "clear lake."

The post office opened here in 1930.

LARSEN BAY

Larsen Bay took its name from the bay. The native name for the settlement was Uyak. The bay was named for Peter Larson, a professional hunter, trapper and guide from Unga Island.

LATOUCHE

Latouche is located on the island that bears its name. It was named in 1794 by Vancouver in honor of the French naval commander LaTouche-Tréville, though Portlock had named it Foot Island in 1787 because it resembled a human foot.

A post office was opened here in 1905.

LEVELOCK

The original Eskimo name for this village was Kvichak, after the river on which it resides. Other names include Old Kvickhak and Livelock.

When a post office was established in 1939, the name became Levelock, allegedly the name of a pioneering family.

LIME VILLAGE

Originally called Hungry Village, the town now has a name that refers to the nearby Lime Hills. The hills were named in 1914 for their limestone composition.

LIVENGOOD

Livengood took its name from the Livengood Creek, a tributary of the Tolovana River. The creek was a great source of gold. The ore was discovered in 1914 by N. R. Hudson and Jay Livengood.

During that winter, a village was established when hordes of people converged on the gold site. A post office was opened in 1915.

LONG

The village of Long is located on the left bank of Long Creek. A 1911 mining camp was the embryo of the contemporary settlement. A post office, under the name of Long, opened the next year. The name for the waterway, it has been suggested, was the surname of a prospector.

LOWER TONSINA

Lower Tonsina took its name from its location on the Tonsina River. The waterway's name translates as "cottonwood."

MAKUSHIN

Makushin was named for the bay on which it rests. The bay was named in reference to the volcanic Mount Makushin.

The current location of Makushin is a few miles from where it originally was located.

MANLEY HOT SPRINGS

Manley began its existence as a trading post for placer miners. It came alive in 1902 when the U. S. Army Signal Corps opened a telegraph station. The village that grew up first became known as Baker Creek, after the nearby creek. Later, it became known as Baker Hot Springs.

In 1907, Frank Manley built a four-story Hot Springs Resort Hotel here. A post office was established in that year as Hot Springs, but changed half a century later to Manley Hot Springs.

MANOKOTAK

Manokotak was first reported as an Eskimo village in 1948. The name is native and, at present, undefinable.

MARYS IGLOO

Marys Igloo honors the memory of an Eskimo woman named Mary. According to tradition, she "held open house there for visiting miners, trappers and other travelers, who never arrived too late or too early for snacks and coffee at Mary's house or 'igloo,' the Eskimo word for 'shelter.'"

The post office, noted as Igloo, opened in 1901.

MATANUSKA

Matanuska was named for the Matanuska River. The name is a corruption of *mednorechka*, Russian for "copper." Copper ore was found in the stream. The name was also applied by the Russians to the Indians in the area. The word was transmogrified into its present form, passing through the Indian tongues to the Americans.

The Matanuska Valley was selected in 1935 by Harry Hopkins, Federal Relief Administrator, as the site for a New Deal experiment in town planning. The project called for the settlers to pay off 40-acre tracts with modern houses over a 30-year period. The group was called the Matanuska Valley Far Cooperative. The valley itself was originally occupied by the Knik Indians.

The village was established in 1914 as a railroad station. The town was laid out two years later.

MAY CREEK

This community is located on Dan Creek Road at May Creek crossing. It took its name from the waterway. According to some authorities, the name commemorates an early prospector. Others believe the creek was discovered during the month of May.

McCARTHY

At one time, McCarthy was called Shushanna Junction. The mining camp settlement was established about 1908, and it was named for the nearby stream.

The creek honors the memory of James McCarthy, a miner who drowned there in 1910. The post office was opened in 1912.

McCORD

McCord is located on the McCord Bay. The name came from that of a local miner. The McCord post office opened in 1929.

McGRATH

McGrath, located at the confluence of the Kuskokwim and Takotna rivers, was settled by Abe Appel, who opened a trading post in 1905. The name came from nearby Mount McGrath.

J. E. McGrath led the American party that surveyed the Yukon River in 1887. The town's name, however, was used to honor U. S. Deputy Marshall Peter McGrath who established his headquarters here in 1907. A post office bearing his name opened in 1913.

McKINLEY PARK

McKinley Park is the entrance to the Mount McKinley National Park. The park was established by an act of Congress in 1917.

Most authorities believe the mountain was first sighted by Cook and Vancouver in the late 18th century. The natives called the peak Bulshaia, a modification of the Russian word *bolshoi*, and Traleika. Both words translate to "great."

W. A. Dickey led a group of prospectors through the Susitna Valley in 1896, and named it Denali, "home of the sun." When Dickey returned and learned of William McKinley's (1843–1901) election to the presidency, he renamed the mountain.

This community began its life as Riley Creek, but in a slightly different location. The Riley post office was established in 1922 and the name was changed later in that year.

MEADE RIVER (ATKUSUK)

The Eskimo name for this village is Atkusuk, but when the post office established in 1951, it adopted the name Meade River, because of the village's location on the banks of the river. Another name was listed for the village in 1951: Tikiluk.

The river was named by Captain P. H. Ray in 1883 to honor U. S. Navy Admiral Richard Worsam Meade, who had surveyed southwest Alaska.

MEDFRA

Medfra began as a trading post and landing on the Kuskokwim River in the early 20th century under the name of Berrys Landing. When a post office was established in 1922, the name became Medfra; no one knows why.

MEKORYUK

Mekoryuk is a village at the mouth of Shoal Bay. It was first reported in 1937 as an Eskimo village. It took its name from the Mekoryuk River which flows into the bay at this settlement.

MENTASTA LAKE

The name of the lake is Athapascan and came from *mantasna*. As far as authorities go, they can decipher the "-na" for river.

The village drew its name from the body of water, but it seems that the village was located at several spots around the lake. One settlement, spotted in 1898, was an Indian's house, called John's House or John's Village.

The U. S. Army Signal Corps opened a telegraph station here in 1902. A post office, however, was not opened until 1947.

METLAKATLA

Located on Annette Island, Metlakatla began as a cooperative Indian village in 1887. Before then, the Indians who made up the original settlers were located at Metlakatla, British Columbia.

The British Columbian settlement was the result of the efforts of the Reverend William Duncan, a Scottish missionary of the Church of England. Duncan arrived in British Columbia in 1857, learned the language of the Tsimshian Indians and began to preach in their own tongue.

For a long time, Duncan and his settlement lived in peace. Trouble, however, arose between Duncan and the Established Church. He was replaced by Bishop Ridley. It was not too long afterwards that the bishop had to call for a man-of-war to protect him from his flock.

Duncan, on the other hand, moved with about 400 members of his congregation and had the federal government set aside Annette Island as a reservation for the tribe. This was done by an act of 4 March 1891. As with his experiment up north, Duncan's project was a success. He died in 1915.

A post office opened in 1888, closed, and reopened in 1892 as New Metlakahtla. The spelling was altered to Metlakahtla three years later. The current spelling was returned in 1904. The name means "a passage joining two bodies of water."

MEYERS CHUCK

Meyers Chuck began as a fishing village. The name, we are told, came from "a prospector named Meyer who found his food in the woods." That is only half the story. The other half is that, in Chinook jargon, *chuck* means "water."

A post office opened here as Meyers Chuck in 1922.

MILLER HOUSE

Miller House took its name from that of a roadhouse. Before Fritz Miller took over the place in 1896, it was known as Mammoth House. Mammoth House came from the Mammoth Creek, where searchers have uncovered tusks and bones of preglacial lions, mammoths and mastodons.

MINTO

Minto took its name from the Minto Lakes. The name is Tanana Indian and only part of it has been translated: *Min* means "lake." Another source believes the name was given to honor Gilbert John Elliot-Murray-Kynynmont, the fourth earl of Minto. Our hyphenated noble was governor-general of Canada from 1898 to 1904.

In 1909, the place was known as Minto Telegraph Station because of the installation built there by the U. S. Army Signal Corps.

MOOSE PASS

According to local legend, in the early 20th century a group of Eskimo hunters were camped near the current townsite. When they awoke in the morning and noticed moose spoor, one said, "Moose pass by in night time." Believe it or not!

Another source contends that the name came about in 1903, when a "mail carrier driving a team of dogs had considerable trouble gaining the right-of-way from a giant moose." More reliable sources indicate that moose frequent the area. A post office was established as Moose Pass in 1928.

MOSES POINT

Moses Point, named for the Moses Roadhouse once located here, gave its name to the point of land on Norton Bay.

MOUNTAIN VILLAGE

The name of Mountain Village was given because "it is located at the foot of the first mountain met with going up the Yukon."

NABESNA

Nabesna took its name from the river, whose name came from the Athapascan Indian language. It was their name for the upper Tanana River.

The village began as a Nabesna Mining Company camp. The first post office was established in 1909.

NAKNEK

Naknek, located in Kvichak Bay, took its name from the Naknek River that drains Naknek Lake.

The Russians were the first to report an Eskimo village here in 1821. They spelled the name Naugeik. Later, the name was spelled Naugvik and Naknek. The Russians built a fort here, and called it Fort Suvarov. By 1880, the name was listed as Kinghiak. In 1907, when the post office was established, the name was firmed up as Naknek.

NAPAKIAK

This Eskimo settlement was first recorded as Napahaiagamute.

NAPASKIAK

An Eskimo village appeared at this site in 1867, by the name of Napasiak. Later spellings included Napaskiagamute and Napasheagamiut. The current spelling was used by J. H. Kilbuck, a Moravian missionary, in 1898.

The name, it seems, is adapted from Napaskiagmute. *Napa* means "wood," and *mute* means "people."

NELSON LAGOON

Nelson Lagoon took its name from the lagoon of the same name. The body of water was named in 1882 by W. H. Dall, in honor of Edward William Nelson. Nelson, a member of the U. S. Signal Service, explored the Yukon Delta between 1877 and 1881.

NENANA

Nenana is located at the confluence of the Tanana with the Nenana River, and its name was taken from that body of water. An Indian village in 1902, the town was reconstructed in 1916 as a camp for the Alaska Railroad.

The Nenana post office was established here in 1908. The site was well known as the home of the Marks Indian Mission; then, in 1923, President Warren G. Harding drove the golden spike, completing the railroad.

NEWHALEN

Newhalen was named for the Newhalen River. It is located on the shore of Iliamna Lake, near the mouth of the river.

The name of the Eskimo village located here was Noghelingamute, "people of the Noghelin," in 1890. The current spelling is an English pronunciation of the Eskimo word.

NEW STUYAHOK

New Stuyahok is located on the site of an Eskimo village, called Stuyahok. The "new" name first appeared in 1950. A post office was opened here in 1961.

NIGHTMUTE

Nightmute is another Eskimo work that defies translation. All we can say with any certainty is that *mute* means "people."

NIKOLAI

Nikolai was the head chief of the Copper-Chitina River Indians. Explorer Henry Allen had his life saved by the chief in 1885.

This Ingalik Indian village, established in 1925, was located a few miles up the South Fork. There appears to be strong Russian influence in this area, so the name may have been given to honor Tsar Nikolas.

NIKOLSKI

Nikolski is located on Nikolski Bay. The bay obtained its name from this village in 1939.

The village's name, in 1834, was Recheshnoe. Almost 50 years later, the name became Nikolski.

NINILCHIK

A group of "colonial citizens," or senior citizens as we would call them, of the Russian American Company were ordered to settle here in about 1830.

Originally a fur-farming and fishing village, Ninilchik became an agricultural community. The name has been determined to be of native origin, without a plausible translation. A post office was opened during the 1940s.

NOATAK

Noatak is located at the lower end of the Noatak River. The waterway's name is Eskimo for "inland river."

In 1880, the village was listed as Noatagamute, "Noaktak (River) people." A Noatak post office was established in 1940.

NOME

When gold was found on the beaches at this location by the "Lucky Swedes," thousands of fortune hunters flocked to the remote shores in 1898. At the height of the gold rush, more than 30,000 people lived in a 15-mile tent city here. The good mining ended in 1963.

The name is supposed to be a combination of "No Name." A more reliable source suggests the name came about from a draftsman's error. When the chart of the area was being drawn, someone pointed out that this point had no name, so they listed it as "? name." When the map was inked in, the draftsman read the "? name" as a "C. Nome," and named it "Cape Nome." The name has remained. An earlier—but short-lived—name was Anvil City, for the Anvil Creek. A post office was opened under the Nome name in 1899.

Nome is hometown to World War II hero, General James Doolittle. Doolittle piloted the 1942 air raid to Tokyo.

NONDALTON

Nondalton is located on Clark Lake, at the source of the Newhalen River. The name is listed as being of Tanaina Indian origin, its meaning unknown. The post office was established here in 1938.

NOORVIK

Noorvik is where Rockwell Kent discovered "the only professional artist of the Far North": Twok. Twok, whose Christian name was George Allen Ahgupuk, was crippled from a childhood injury. Unable to pursue the usual employments, he turned to art.

The Eskimo village was listed in 1908 as Oksik. The Noorvik post office was established here in 1937.

NORTH POLE

The name for this community was given at the time of incorporation in 1953. The idea was to trade on the commercial possibilities of having children write to Santa Claus, c/o The North Pole!

NORTHWAY (— Junction)

Northway was built during World War II as a link in the Northwest Staging Route. The name honors James A. Northway, a steamboat captain, stagecoach driver and operator of a trading post.

NULATO

Nulato began in 1838 when the "Russian Creole," Malakhov (Nalakov), built a blockhouse and stockade on the site. It was burned to the ground the next year during his absence, and it was rebuilt in 1842 by Russian Navy Lieutenant Zagoskin. His successor, Vasili Derzhavin (Derabin), perpetrated acts of cruelty toward the natives. In 1851, the Koyukuk Indians massacred the garrison, killing Derzhavin and a Lieutenant Barnard, from the H.M.S. *Enterprise.*

Nulato has been called "Stop-a-bit" by the natives. The actual translation of the name works out to the "place where the dog salmon come." A post office was opened here in 1897.

NUNACHUAK

Nunachuak is located on the banks of the Nunachuak River, and took its name from that of the waterway. The name is of Eskimo origin.

NYAC

A mining camp in 1915 was the start of the village of Nyac. The name was drawn from the New York Alaska (Gold Dredging) Corporation.

A post office, under the name of Nyac, was established in 1926.

OHOGAMUT

Ohogamut's name came from the Eskimo Okhnagamiut, "village on the other side (of the river)." The name appeared as Ohogamut in 1916.

O

OLD HARBOR

Old Harbor is on the southeast shore of Kodiak Island.

In the 1890 Census, the name is listed as "Old Harbor, named Staruigavan by the Russians and Nunamiut by the natives. . . ." At one point, this was an important site for the Russian Fur Company.

The Old Harbor post office was established in 1931. The name was drawn from the cove of the same name which was called Star(y) Gava, "old harbor," by Captain Tebenkov in 1852.

OLD RAMPART

Though located on the Porcupine Creek, this village took its name from the Rampart Creek. The stream's name was given because of the "rampart-like mountains" which are drained by the creek.

OLNES

This village began as a mining supply center and railroad station on the Tanana Valley Railroad. When the post office was established here in 1908, the name was Olness. In 1922, the name assumed its current spelling.

According to one source, the town was named for a miner who spelled his name Olnes.

OPHIR

The name of this town was borrowed from that of the creek. The waterway, named by the same group that christened Council and Melsing Creek in the late 19th century, honors the region that supplied gold for King Solomon's temple. One of the namers, H. L. Blake, found gold in the creek.

Another source suggests the name was borrowed from a local prospector. The Ophir post office opened in 1909.

OSCARVILLE

Oscar Samuelson settled at Napaiskak for a few years during the early 20th century. He moved across the Kuskokwim River, where he operated the Oscarville store until his death in 1953.

OUZINKIE

Located on Spruce Island, above Kodiak, Ouzinkie was settled by the Russians. The village took its name from the Russian *uzen'kii*, "very narrow." That was the name given to what is now called Narrow Strait.

The Ouzinkie post office was established in 1927.

OWENS

This community was named for Johnny Owens. Owens operated the trading post at Togiak Station.

P

PAIMIUTE

Paimiute's name came from the Eskimo for "people at the river's mouth." The village was originally located across the Yukon River, but moved in 1915 to higher ground.

PALMER

Though Palmer was established as a station on the Alaska Railroad about 1916, its growth is the result of a social experiment.

In 1935, people from the relief rolls of northern Minnesota, Wisconsin and Michigan arrived to settle the land. Lots were distributed and the settlers were subsidized until they became self-supporting.

The experiment had its successes and its failures. The press attacked the program because of the cries of the failed persons who alerted the media. Some of the complaints were justified: Eighteen tractors, supplied by the federal government, could not plow 200 farms at once, nor could one sawmill produce enough boards for the demand. But Palmer succeeded in his goals.

The town is named for George Palmer, a late 19th century trader in the Knik Arm area. A Palmer post office was established here in 1917.

PARADISE

Paradise is the site of an old native village, in existence before 1902. Riverboat pilots used the names Paradise and Bonasila for the site from 1898 until 1910. Bonasila came from the name of the river.

PARKS

The first postmaster of this locale on the bank of the Kuskokwim River was Eugene W. Parks. Parks operated the office from 1909 to 1910.

PAXSON

Paxson was named for the operator of a roadhouse situated here. The town's earlier name was Paxson's Road House. Paxson Lake is named for the same individual.

PEDRO BAY

Felix Pedro struck gold near Fairbanks in 1902. His name is recalled in this village, Pedro Bay, Pedro Camp, Pedro Creek, Pedro Dome, Pedro Glacier, Pedro Gulch, and Pedro Mountain.

A post office was opened at Pedro Bay in 1936.

PELICAN

The village of Pelican was named by the town's founder, Charles Raatikainen, for his fishing boat, *The Pelican*. A post office was first opened here in 1939.

PERRYVILLE

After the Indian village of Katmai was destroyed by the eruption of Mount Katmai in 1912, Lieutenant Commander K. W. Perry of the USRCS *Manning* transported the residents of that village to this spot and helped them to settle. The town was named in his honor.

At first the village was called Perry, but the name was changed to Perryville in 1930 when the post office was established under that name.

PETERSBURG

In 1897, Peter Buschmann decided to build a cannery on Mitkof Island. First, he learned, he had to build a sawmill. He opened his cannery in 1897. The town bears his name, not that of St. Petersburg in Russia.

Because many of the settlers are of Norwegian extraction, the town has been called "Little Norway." In fact, the town annually celebrates Norwegian Independence Day!

PETERS CREEK

The village of Peters Creek bears the name of a nearby waterway. The creek was named for a local prospector.

PILE BAY

This village took its name from the estuary, Pile Bay. The original name of that body of water was Spiles Bay, but it was shortened by local usage.

PILOT POINT

Pilot Point, located on the eastern shore of Ugashik Bay, was originally called Pilot Station about 1900 for the river pilots who were stationed there. The name was changed to Pilot Point in 1933 when a post office was established in that name.

PILOT STATION

The origin of Pilot Station is similar to that of Pilot Point. The name, given by riverboat pilots, first appeared in 1916. Prior to this village, there was a native village located nearby by the name of Potiliuk.

PITKAS POINT

Pitkas Point was named for a trader "named Pitka whose store was a branch of the Northern Commercial Company's station at Andreafski."

PLATINUM

In 1927, Johnnie Kilbuck, an Eskimo prospector, discovered "white gold" in Fox Gulch. The first production of platinum from the Goodnews Bay area for that year totaled 17½ ounces.

Eleven years later, reporters picked up the story of three Alaskan miners who uncovered a heavy layer of platinum and caused a stampede into the area.

A post office was established here in 1935. Adjoining Platinum was an Eskimo village, Agvik, whose name translates as "small stone to sharpen knives."

POINT BAKER

Point Baker is located on an island off the tip of Prince of Wales Island. The name was in place when the post office opened in 1942.

The tip of the island was named in 1793 by Vancouver . . . for Lieutenant Joseph Baker of H.M.S. *Discovery*. The small point in Kasan Bay was named in 1885 for another Baker—Marcus Baker, a government cartographer.

POINT HOPE

Point Hope was named in 1826 by Captain Beechey. The name honors Sir William Johnstone Hope, a member of a noted English naval family.

At one time, the post office was listed as Tiekaga, Eskimo for "forefinger." The town is the most northwestern point of the United States. The name, we are told, was given because the point jutting out into the Chukchi Sea drew the whales close to shore.

POINT LAY

The Eskimo word for this village's name was *Kali*, "mound." This is a reference to the elevated ground on which the village sits.

POORMAN

The town of Poorman came into being with the discovery of gold on the Poorman Creek. Poorman is located on the creek's banks. The name of the creek was that of a prospector.

PORTAGE

Portage is located at the head of Turnagain Arm of Cook Inlet. Captain Cook entered the inlet in 1778, searching for the northwest passage. Forced to return to the head of the inlet, he named it Turnagain River, and he named the inlet for himself.

The name was given when pioneers had to carry their canoes across land to reach the next body of water. In 1919, the village was only a flag stop on the railroad; by 1966, it was a major station.

PORTAGE CREEK

(See PORTAGE, Alaska.)

PORT ALEXANDER

This fishing village was named for the estuary on which it is located. The Port Alexander post office was opened in 1926.

The name came from Alexander Andreevich Baranov, the general manager of the Russian-American Company and, simultaneously, the governor of Russian America from 1799 to 1818.

PORT ALSWORTH

The post office at Port Alsworth was established in 1950. Previously known as Tanalian and Tanalian Point, the town received its current name when the post office opened. Townspeople honored Babe Alsworth, an old-time bush pilot who operated the trading post and post office.

PORT ASHTON

The post office at Port Ashton was established in 1952 and was named for Captain Ashton Brooks, who opened a fish-processing plant here in 1918. Previously, Port Ashton had been known as Sawmill Bay.

PORT GRAHAM

Port Graham is located on the south shore of Port Graham. Its post office opened in 1938. Port Graham came from Graham's Harbour. That was the name Captain Nathaniel Portlock gave it in 1786.

PORT HEIDEN

Located on the north shore of Port Heiden, this village was originally an Eskimo village, called Mishik. The Port Heiden post office began operations in 1912. The Russian name, given by Captain Feodor Petrovich Lutke in 1828, was Baie Compte Heyden, for some "Count Heiden."

PORT LIONS

Port Lions was created in 1964 by the Lions Club International. The port was named for the 49th District Club which had built the place in order to house the people displaced from Afognak. That village had been destroyed by a 1964 earthquake, followed by a tidal wave.

PORTLOCK

Portlock was named in 1888 for Captain Nathaniel Portlock, an English fur trader and commander of the English *King George* who first discovered, in 1786, deposits of coal here. Located on the south shore of Port Chatham, Portlock received its first post office in 1921.

Portlock had been master's mate on Captain Cook's 1779 voyage to Alaska.

PORT MOLLER

Port Moller took its name from the bay. Before a cannery opened in 1916, this was a native village called Mashikh. The Port Moller post office was established in 1916.

PRUDHOE BAY

This community took its name from the bay on which it is located. The bay was named by Sir John Franklin (1786–1847) in 1826.

Sir John honored a fellow naval officer, Algernon Percy, fourth duke of Northumberland and first Baron Prudhoe.

QUINHAGAK

This Eskimo village was reported as Koingak in 1826 by the Russians. The name went through several transmutations, including Quinhagamut, "newly formed river." The name suggests reality: The channel of the nearby Kanektok River was constantly changing. A post office was established as Quinhagak in 1905.

RAMPART

Early prospectors named this town Rampart City in 1896 when placer gold was discovered in the nearby creeks on the Yukon River. The sheer bluffs on the river, the "Ramparts of the Yukon," some reaching 300 feet, resembled ramparts to the traveler. A post office called Rampart City was opened in 1898.

Rex Beach lived here and used the area as the background for his book *The Barrier*.

RED DEVIL

This town took the name of the nearby Red Devil Mercury Mine. A post office was established here in 1957.

RICHARDSON

Richardson was named for U. S. Army General Wilds P. Richardson, the first president of the Alaska Railroad. The general "established a sled road between Valdez on the coast, and Fairbanks, the largest settlement in the interior, a distance of 370 miles." Richardson Mountains, on the other hand, were named for Sir John Richardson, a surgeon on the Franklin expeditions of 1819 to 1822 and 1825 to 1827. The post office opened in 1906.

The nearby Gasoline Creek was so named because cars from Fairbanks once stopped here to refuel.

RUBY

Ruby was once a gold-rush town, and took its name from the Ruby Creek. Gold was discovered near here in 1907, but the town did not materialize until four years later.

A post office, named Ruby, opened in 1912. The creek was named by prospectors for the ruby-red colored stones found in the stream's bed.

RUSSIAN MISSION

Russian Mission was once the mother mission of all Russian churches in Russian America. The Russian-American Company opened its first fur trading post here on the Yukon River in 1837.

The Eskimo name for this settlement, as reported by the Russians in 1842, was Ikogmyut, "people of the point." In 1851, the Russian Orthodox Church began a mission here, called Pokrovskaya Mission. The church was built by Jacob Netzvetov, a Creole priest. Creole, in this context, indicated a combination of Russian and Aleut.

At the turn of the 20th century, the name Russian Mission replaced the Eskimo title.

SAINT MARYS

Saint Marys was the name the post office gave to this community in 1955 to honor the Roman Catholic mission located here. Before that, the name was Andreafsky.

Andreafsky was formed in 1898 or 1899 as a supply depot for the Northern Commercial Company's river fleet. That name may have come from the Andreafsky River, which was once called Clear River. One source contends that the village and river were named from members of the Andrea family who helped build the Russian church here.

SAINT MICHAEL

A port on St. Michael Island, Saint Michael was a fortified trading post called Michaelovski or "Redoubt St. Michael" in 1833. The name came from Captain Michael Dmitrievich Tebenkov. Tebenkov was a governor of the Russian-American Company who charted the area in 1831.

Following the gold strike in the Klondike in 1897, a Saint Michael post office and a military post called Fort Saint Michael was established here. During the Klondike Gold Rush, Saint Michael acted as the deepwater port where ocean-going vessels transferred their goods to shallow-water vessels for transfer up the Yukon.

SAND POINT

Sand Point took its name from the flat, sandy spit of land on the west coast of Popof Island. The spit was named in 1872 by Captain

William Healey Dall. The first post office at Sand Point was opened in 1891.

SAVOONGA

This Eskimo village was named for the point of land, Savoonga Point, which is located west of the community. The post office was established here in 1934.

SAXMAN

Saxman is located on the northeast shore of Tongass Narrows. Established in 1894, the Tlingit Indian village was named for Samuel Saxman, a local school teacher. The post office opened here in 1897.

SCAMMON BAY

This Eskimo village, known to the natives as Mariak, was named for the nearby bay. The bay was named in 1870 by William Healy Dall (1865–99) for Captain Charles M. Scammon. Scammon was "Chief of Marine of the Western Union Telegraph Expedition."

The post office, established in 1951, standardized the name, supplanting the native one.

SCOW BAY

Scow Bay took its name from the bay, which was named in 1925 for "charting purposes." The community is considered a suburb of Petersburg.

SELAWICK

Selawick took its name from the Selawick River, a body of water on which the town is located. The river was first explored by Hudson Bay Company surgeon Thomas Simpson in the mid-19th century. The name refers to either an Eskimo tribe or a species of fish.

Selawick's post office opened in 1930.

SELDOVIA

Located on Kachemak (Seldovia) Bay, Seldovia took its name from the Russian *sel'devoi*, "herring bay." Some feel the name means "herring bay." Herring-curing was a major industry here.

A post office opened under the name of Seldovia in 1898.

SEWARD

Seward, an ice-free port located on Resurrection Bay, was named for William H. Seward (1801–72) who, as secretary of state, negotiated the purchase of Alaska from Russia for $7.2 million. It was then known as "Seward's Folly."

Along with Russian Ambassador Edouard de Stoeckl, Seward was able to wrestle through the language of a treaty the night before Congress was to adjourn. The Russian flag was lowered for the last time in Alaska in 1867.

Seward was actually founded in 1902 or 1903 when surveyors arrived to plan for the railroad to the Interior. Prior to the arrival of the railroad, the community was called Seward, with its first post office opening in 1895.

SHAGELUK

Shageluk was an Ingalik Indian village as early as 1850 when the Russians mapped it as Tlégoshitno. By 1880, the U. S. Census called the collection of camps or villages here "Chageluk settlements." The name, we are told, is Ingalik for "village of the dog people."

A post office, using "s" instead of "c," opened in 1924.

SHAKTOLIK

Located at the river's mouth, Shaktolik took its name from the Shaktolik River.

SHELDONS POINT

This Eskimo village was named for the point of land on which it resides. The Eskimo name for the land projection was Nunamekrot, "long land."

The point of land was named for "a man named Sheldon, who had a saltry on the point."

SHISHMAREF

Shishmaref took its name from the nearby inlet. Shishmaref Inlet was named for Captain Lieutenant Glieb Shishmaref, second in command to Count Otto von Kotzebue who explored this area in 1816.

The Shishmaref post office was established in 1901.

SHUNGNAK

Shungnak's name, we are told, was taken from that of the river. The name is derived from *shung-nack*, a native word for jade, an element found in the vicinity of this village.

Shungnak is located about 10 miles from where it originally stood.

SINUK

Sinuk's name came from the waterway of the same name. The name translates from the Eskimo to mean "stream mouth."

SITKA

Sitka was founded in 1799 by members of the Russian-American Company, led by Territorial Governor Alexander Baranov (Baranof). The group built a fort, but their local neighbors, the Tingit Indians, took offense at the trespassers. By 1802, tribal members had burned down the Russian encampment.

A group of Russians established a more permanent settlement here in 1804, which became the capital of Russian American. They called the settlement New Archangel (Novo-Arkhangelsk) for the Russian city. Castle Hill, the site of Baranov's headquarters, marks the 1867 transfer of Alaska to the United States. Every year on 18 October, that transfer is reenacted in Sitka.

The first foreigners to sail into Sitka's harbors were sailors under the command of Captain Alexei Chirikof in 1741. The Russians were followed in 1775 by the Spanish and in 1787 by the British, though Captain Cook had visited nine years earlier. The Sitka post office was established in 1867.

No one is certain what the name means, but when it is used elsewhere, like in Sitka, Kansas, it describes very, very cold weather, a reference to this spot. One source, however, suggests the name came from the Tlingit language and means "in this place," "this is the place," "the best place" or "by the sea."

SKAGWAY

Skagway was the jumping off spot to the Klondike for men caught up in the gold lust of 1897–98. Within three months of the first gold strike, the town grew from one cabin to a thriving metropolis of 20,000! During the summer of 1898, Skagway was the largest town in Alaska. The Skagway post office was established in 1897.

Skagway was home to a legendary character, Jefferson R. Smith. Smith arrived in Skagway in the fall of 1897, looking for his fortune. Once in town, he established a gang to run shell games, conduct robberies and worse. But he made sure he did not offend the "proper" people. He organized a troop of men called the "First Regiment, Alaska Militia," and offered them to President McKinley for the Spanish-American War. McKinley, of course, declined the offer.

Smith is still in Skagway. When his reign of terror was too much for the populace, a citizens' meeting was called. Smith rushed there, a little inebriated and armed with a rifle. He picked a fight with Frank Reid, the man who was guarding the door, and both fell from the exchange of shots. They are buried near one another in Gold Rush Cemetary. Townspeople remember Reid as the man "who gave his life for the honor of Skagway," which is etched on his tombstone. Smith, however, just has a simple wooden plank for a headstone.

The town's name, we are told, came from that of the Skagway River. The waterway's name came from *schkagué*, the Tlingit Indian for "home of the north wind." Another source contends that the name came from the Tlingit *sch-kawai*, "end of the salt water." The name was first recorded in 1883.

SKWENTNA

This village took its name from the Skwentna River, on whose bank it resides. The Tanaina Indian name for the river was Skwent River. Again, the *-na* in the name indicates "river," but that is all we know.

The Skwentna post office opened in 1937.

SLANA

The Indian village of Slana is located on the Slana River. The river's name was first recorded in 1885. No one is quite sure of what the name means.

SLEETMUTE

Sleetmute, also known as Sleitmut, is located on the Yellow River. It was mentioned as an Eskimo village called Sikmiut as early as 1907. The word *sleitmut* is supposed to mean "stones people" or "whetstone people."

SOLDOTNA

The first homesteaders to this area were World War II veterans who, arriving here in 1947, were given a 90-day option to pick out and file for land. The community's name was drawn from the local stream. The Soldotna post office was established in 1949.

The waterway's name was derived, we are told, from the Russian for "soldier." Others think the name is native in origin and means "stream fork" or else it was derived from *tseldatna*, "a kind of herb."

SOLOMON

Solomon took its name from the river on which it is located. The village began as a mining camp during the summer of 1900. At that time, the name was listed as Erok. A post office opened here in 1900.

The river's name, it has been suggested, refers to an early prospector.

SOUTH NAKNEK

South Naknek is located on the south bank of the Naknek River. The waterway's name is Eskimo in origin. The South Naknek post office opened in 1937.

SQUAW HARBOR

In 1911, the name of this village was reported as "Baralof or Squaw Harbor." The name, we must assume, was adapted from the East Coast Algonquian *eshqua*, "female deer."

STEBBINS

This village on the northwest coast of St. Michael Island was first reported in 1898, with the name published two years later. The Eskimo name is Atroik. Stebbins is apparently the way early Eskimos referred to Stephens Pass, on which Stebbins is located.

STERLING (— Landing)

Sterling's name was formalized when the post office was established in 1954.

Sterling Landing was a riverboat landing in 1932. It is possible both names came from the cannery ship *Sterling* that sank at Sterling Shoal. All the Sterling references go back to Hawley Sterling, an engineer for the Alaska Road Commission.

STEVENS VILLAGE

According to local tradition, this Indian village was founded by three brothers from Kokrines. The brothers, Old Jacob, Gochonayeeya and Old Steven, named their settlement Denyeet, "canyon." When Old Steven was elected tribal chief in 1902, the village assumed his name.

STONY RIVER

Stony River is a village on an island in the Kuskokwim River, at the mouth of Stony River. The original settlement here was a trading post and riverboat landing called Moose Village because it was then located near the mouth of Moose Creek. Since then, the village has moved to a new location—with a new name.

The Stony River post office was established in 1935. The waterway's name is descriptive, given by prospectors at about the turn of the 20th century.

SUSITNA

Susitna, like Stony River, took its name from the local body of water. Originally spelled Sushitna, the word means "sandy river." The spelling was changed to protect those of prurient interests.

The Susitna post office opened in 1906.

SUTTON

Sutton was founded in 1918 as a station on the Alaska Railroad. A post office was started 30 years later. No one is sure where the name came from.

T

TAKOTNA

Takotna is located on the Takotna River, established as a riverboat landing by the name of Takotna Station in 1910.

When the post office was established in 1914, the name was spelled Tokotna. The name assumed the present form in 1926. The waterway's name is of Ingalik Indian origin.

TALKEETNA

Talkeetna is located at the point where the Talkeeta, Susitna and Chulitna rivers meet. The name of this village is supposed to come from the Tanaina tongue, and means "river of plenty," indicating an abundance of fish and game.

The Talkeetna post office was established in 1916.

TANACROSS

Tanacross is located on the Tanana River. This is where the original telegraph line crossed the river. The village was then called Tanana Crossing.

The name was contracted to Tanacross in 1932. The post office established here in 1920 was called Saint Timothys, but it was changed to Tanacross in 1934.

TANANA

Located at the mouth of the Tanana River, this village was first visited by white men in 1860. Russian traders visited the mouth of the stream and called the waterway the "River of the Mountain Men." The Athapascan *tananatana* translates to "mountain people river." Another source believes the name came from *tananah*, "river trail."

Prior to the arrival of the white man, there was a strong Indian trading post, called Nuklukayet. Captain C. W. Raymond called the site "Fort Adams (American Station)" on his 1869 map. Arthur Harper opened his Alaska Commercial Company trading post here, called Nuklukyet, in 1880. Others referred to it as Harpers Station.

TATITLEK

When Ivan Petroff referred to this village in 1880, he called it Tatikhlek. The present spelling was adopted in 1910. The original site of this village was at the head of Gladhaugh Bay, but it later moved to its present site.

The Tatitlek post office was established here in 1946.

TAYLOR

Taylor was once the seat of Kongarok placer mining. A mining camp was founded here in 1906. In that same year, the post office opened.

The town is named for David Taylor, a Hudson Bay Company employee who arrived here around 1912.

TELIDA

Telida was a native village, established about 1916. The current location is a distance from the "old" location—nearer to Lake Minchumina.

TELLER

Teller is a port on the Bering Sea. The town was founded in 1892 as a reindeer station by Sheldon Jackson, and it was named for Henry Moore Teller, Colorado's first senator. At the time, Teller was secretary of the interior.

Captain Beechey first spotted the village, "called Nooke by the natives," in 1827. Captain Daniel B. Libby used the site during the winter of 1866–67 as camp for the Western Union Telegraph Expedition. It was known then as Libbysville or Libby Station.

In 1867, it was referred to as "Nook, the spot which divided Grantley Harbor from Port Clarence."

Teller's post office was established in 1900.

TENAKEE SPRINGS

Tenakee Springs took its name from a cannery that was located about four miles east of this settlement. The warm springs located here helped make it a health resort.

When the post office started in 1903, the name was Tenakee. Twenty-five years later, "Springs" was added. In 1891, Lieutenant Commander H. E. Nichols called it Hoonah Hot Springs.

TETLIN (— Junction)

This name came from the Tetlin River, a tributary of the Tanana River. The waterway honored Chief Tetling (or Tetlin). His village was in this locale in 1885.

Up until 1942, the village was called Tetling, but the spelling was altered to agree with the name of the river.

THORNE BAY (— Arm)

This logging settlement was reported as late as 1960. It is located on Thorne Bay, which was named in 1891 for Frank Manley Thorn, superintendent of the U. S. Coast & Geodetic Survey from 1885 to 1889. The "e" is an apparent typographical error.

On the other hand, Thorne Arm on Tevillagigedo Island is spelled correctly. It honors Charles Thorne, captain of the steamer *California* which regularly traveled between Portland, Oregon, and southeastern Alaska.

TIN CITY

The name of this former mining camp was derived from the ore which was excavated on Cape Mountain. Tin ore was discovered in 1902 but, five years later, only "a few widely scattered houses" made up Tin City.

The Tin City post office was established in 1904.

TOFTY

Tofty was a mining camp, established about 1908 as a supply point for the Sullivan Creek digs. A post office was opened the same year.

The name came from A. F. Tofty, a miner who discovered gold nearby. Reports have it he took out 376 ounces in six weeks!

TOGIAK

Togiak is located on Togiak Bay. As early as 1826, Lieutenant Gavrila Andreevich Sarichev reported an Eskimo village, called Tugiak Village, located here.

By 1880, Petroff listed two villages, Togiagamute and Togiak Station. Togiak Station had been called Owens, for trader Johnny Owens.

TOK

Depending on whom you believe, Tok could be a native word meaning "peace," "tree," or a World War II-era abbreviation of Tokyo.

Tok took its name from the Tok River, originally the Tokai River. It is located at the junction of the Glenn Highway with the Alaska Highway.

TOKSOOK BAY

Toksook Bay was named for the Toksook River. The river bears an Eskimo name.

TRAPPER CREEK

Trapper Creek took its name from the waterway of the same name. The source of the name is obvious.

TULUKSAK

Tuluksak, located on the southern bank of the Tuluksak River, took its name from its waterway. The river's name is Eskimo and means "raven." Originally the name was published as Tul'yagmyut about 1842.

TUNTUTULIAK

The Eskimo village of Tuntutuliak was listed in the 1950 census. The name means "many caribou."

TWIN HILLS

Twin Hills took its name from the mountains of the same name. The term is descriptive.

TYEE

Tyee is located near the southern point of Admiralty Island. Its name was drawn from that of Tyee Mountain, and it means "anyone of superior status," "chief" or "head man." The Tyee post office was established in 1907.

TYONEK

Tyonek is located on the eastern shore of Cook Inlet. In 1880, Ivan Petroff reported the village to be composed of Tanaina Indians. If one uses the Indian language to translate the name, it means "little chief." On the other hand, the name—coming from the Eskimo *Tu-i-u'nuk*—means "marsh people."

The town's first post office was called Tyoonok in 1896. The spelling was changed to Tyonok in 1905, Beluga in 1909, Moquawkie in 1915, and the current form in 1933.

UGANIK

Uganik is located on the Northeast Arm of Uganik Bay. An Eskimo village, it was reported as Oohanick in 1805. By 1890, the name became Uganak. Uganik was the correct spelling, however.

UGASHIK

Ugashik, located on the banks of the Ugashik River, took its name from that waterway. It was listed by Petroff in 1880 as Oogashik. An Ugashik post office was established in 1932.

UMIAT

Umiat bears an Eskimo name that describes the large, walrus-skinned boats used by the Eskimos. The name was given because river boats were hidden here. During World War II, the name was borrowed for an emergency airfield. By the end of the war, Umiat became a supply base of the oil exploration in Naval Petroleum Reserve No. 4.

UNALAKLEET

Unalakleet is located on the Unalakleet River, and its name was taken from that stream. In an 1850 map, Russian Navy Lieutenant L. A. Zagoskin spelled it Ounalaklik. The name, we are told, was derived from a native term meaning "the southernmost one."

Unalakleet's post office was established in 1901.

UNALASKA

Unalaska was founded between 1760 and 1770 as a fur-trading station by Solovief. Its original name was Iliuliuk. Some say the word *ilulaq* translates to "harmony," "good understanding" or "dwelling together harmonious." Others contend that the meaning is simpler: "curving beach."

Unalaska's name developed from the same Aleut root as that of the state *alashka*—and means "great land" or "mainland." The addition of the "un" is used as a differentiator. A post office, under the name of Ounalaska, was opened in 1888. The name was changed to the current spelling 10 years later.

During World War II, the carrier-based planes of the Japanese Imperial Navy attacked Dutch Harbor and, for two days, wreaked great damage. They were routed by Army Air Corps planes based at Umnak.

UNGALIK
Russian Navy Lieutenant L. A. Zagoskin reported the village to be Eskimo and called Ounag-touli and Unagtuligmut between 1842 and 1844. Almost 40 years later, Petroff listed it as Oonaktolik. The name is Eskimo.

VALDEZ

Valdez was established in late 19th century as an outfitting point for miners headed over Valdez Glazier to the goldfields of the north. It is Alaska's northernmost ice-free port. It is located on Prince William Sound.

The port was named in 1790 by Spanish explorers for the famous Spanish naval officer, Antonio Valdés y Basan.

Valdez presently resides four miles west of where it once was located. The Good Friday 1964 earthquake forced the town to move to Port Valdez. The town, the Southern terminus of the Alaska Pipeline, made the news in 1989 when the *Exxon Valdez* caused the world's largest oil spill.

Originally called Copper City, the town changed its name to Valdez in 1899 when the first post office opened. The port, the glacier and the water passage all commemorate the Spanish naval officer.

VENETIE (— Lodge)
Venetie took the name of an Indian tribe. A post office was established here in 1938. No one even hints at the source of the name.

WAINWRIGHT

Wainwright Lagoon (Inlet) was named in 1826 by Captain Beechey for Lieutenant John Wainwright, an astronomer in his party. The Eskimo name for the bay, reported in 1853, was Olrona. In 1861, however, the Russians noted it as Tutagvak, "bit labret."

The village took its name from the inlet, and it is the most recent settlement here. Over the centuries, the area has had many settlements in the vincinity. The Wainwright post office opened in 1916.

WALES

Wales is located on the coast of Cape Prince of Wales, and its name was taken from the cape. Captain James Cook named the cape in 1778 for the king's oldest son, Prince George Augustus Frederick (1762–1830). The Prince of Wales ruled as King George IV.

In 1827, Captain Beechey noted a village here, called Eidannoo, and another inland, King-a-ghe. By 1880, the village was reported as Kingigamute.

Ten years later, the American Missionary Association of the Congregational Church established a mission here. In 1894, the U. S. government opened a reindeer station. The Wales post office started in 1902.

WARD COVE

Located on the shore of Ward Cove, this village took its name from that geographic feature.

The cove's name came from that of an officer from the U.S.S. *Patterson.* It was the first Coast Survey ship to enter Alaskan waters in 1884.

The village of Ward Cove began in 1883–84, when W. W. Waud established his saltery. In 1920, when the first post office opened, with Eugene Wacker as postmaster, the town's name was Wacker City, then merely Wacker. The current name replaced Wacker in 1954.

WASILLA

Wasilla was founded in 1916 as a station on the Alaska Railroad. The post office opened a year later. Wasilla's Frontier Village preserves its past with the town's first school, two log cabins, a smithy and the first public bath.

The village was named for the creek, which was named for a chief of the Knik Indians. Some think the name is a corruption of the Russian name Vasiliev, "Basil."

WHITE MOUNTAIN

White Mountain is a village located on the Fish River. The name came from the mountain to the north of town. The White Mountains are named because they are composed of white limestone.

White Mountain was created in 1899. C. D. Lane erected a large warehouse here to house the supplies he expected to sell to the gold claims in the area. The White Mountain post office was established in 1932.

WHITSHED

Whitshed took the name of nearby Point Whitshed.

The point of land was named after 1794 by Vancouver. Though Point Whitshed had been "discovered" by James Johnstone, the donor of the name was Captain Whitshed of the Royal Navy. Don Ignacio Arteaga called it Punta de Treville in 1779, for French Admiral Louis René Madelaine le Vasson de Latouche Treville, who died in 1804.

WHITTIER

Whittier, a small community on Passage Canal, can only be reached by train or ferry. It is not connected to the state's highway system. The town came into being during World War II when the Army established it as a major supply port, and its name was taken from the Whittier Glacier.

Whittier Glacier was named in 1915 to honor American poet John Greenleaf Whittier (1807–92).

WILLOW (— Creek)

The village of Willow began as a stop on the Alaska Railroad when gold was discovered in the area about 1897. The Willow post office was opened in 1948.

Willow Creek was a mining camp, begun in 1908. The name came from the village's location—at the junction of Willow Creek and Iditarod River. The creek's name, of course, came from the abundance of willow trees along its shores.

WISEMAN

The village of Wiseman is located at the junction of Wiseman Creek and the Middle Fork of the Koyukuk River.

In about 1911, a new town developed near the roadhouse of B. E. Wright, at the mouth of Wiseman Creek. The first settlement was known as Wrights. Later, the name became Nolan for the nearby creek where gold was found.

The first post office to open in 1909 was called Nolad, but the name was changed to Wiseman in 1923. That name remembers Peter Wiseman, a prospector who struck gold in the vicinity of Nolan and Wiseman creeks.

WOODCHOPPER CREEK

Woodchopper Creek is located on—guess what?—Woodchopper Creek. Early explorers and prospectors found mastodon bones here, but the town only goes back to the 1940s.

The stream's name came from the steamboat crews' habit of chopping wood along the creek for fuel.

WOOD RIVER

Army Lieutenant C. E. S. Wood allegedly discovered Glacier Bay. Purists dismiss his claim because he did not believe in 1877 that he had made an important discovery. Besides, he published his findings in a popular magazine, not in an academic journal. Shame on him! More people probably read of his findings there.

This village, however, is located at the confluence of the Wood and Nushagak Rivers, on the site of an Eskimo village called Ah-lek-nugh-uk.

Some sources say the name of the waterway came from the fact that a riverboat woodyard was established near the river's mouth.

WRANGELL

A stockade established by the Russians in 1834, Wrangell served the gold rushes of 1861, 1872 and 1898. The town is located on Wrangell Harbor. The Russians called it Redoubt Saint Dionysius. The British changed the name to Fort Stikine. When the Americans took over in 1867, the military post was called Fort Wrangell.

The name, given by an American whaler, came from Baron Ferdinand Petrovitch von Wrangell (1794–1870), vice-admiral of the Imperial Russian Navy and director of the Russian-American Company from 1830 to 1835. The island, reached by the baron in 1821, was sighted by Sir Henry Kellet 28 years later.

Over the course of its history, Wrangell has existed under three flags—Russian, British and American.

YAKUTAT

Yakutat is a Tlingit Indian village on Yakutat Bay. It is the principal winter village for the Yakutats, a subtribe of the Tlingits.

The first post office opened here in 1892, called Yakitat. The name was changed to the present spelling in 1901.

It was at this location that Vitus Jonassen Bering (1681–1741) first caught sight of Alaska on St. Elias Day, 1741. He gave the name of that saint to the mountains (Mount St. Elias) he saw in the distance.

Polynesians from South Pacific Islands, such as the Marquesans and Tahitians, arrived in what is now the Hawaiian Islands between the sixth and 10th centuries. They brought with them in their outrigger canoes their families, their goods, their livestock, a variety of plantlife, and their gods.

We find in the modern-day State of Hawaii remnants of all, especially traces of their religion. Though they worshipped nature, they did stand in awe of several god-like manifestations, such as Ku, the war god; Kaneloa, who ruled the land of the dead; Lono, the harvest god; and Pele, the fire goddess. Of all, perhaps Pele was the most respected and feared. It was she who ruled the volcanoes that erupted in rage on these islands, destroying people and their property. Throughout the eight islands, (Hawaii, Kahoolawe, Kauai, Lanai, Maui, Molokai, Niihau, and Oahu) one can find reminders of that early religion in the ruins of stone temples, or *heiaus*.

For more than 10 centuries, the people of the islands lived in peace, isolated from any outside influences. Each island was self-governed, with its own chief, or *alii nui*, and its own privileged classes. That tranquility ended in 1778 when Captain James Cook arrived with two ships at Waimea, on Kauai. Cook spent two weeks exploring Kauai and Niihau, then named the islands the Sandwich Islands. After all, he was sailing under the auspices of the Earl of Sandwich. Cook returned slightly more than a year later and explored the Island of Hawaii, the Big Island. After he was satisfied with his forays into the countryside and had fully provisioned his ships, Cook set sail. Unfortunately, bad weather damaged one of his ships and he had to return to the islands for repair. While the ship was being repaired, the islanders—fascinated with iron nails—stole several iron tools and burned a small boat in order to make nails. Cook could not countenance this action. With a band of sailors he strode across the beach and attempted to take the chief and his family hostage. In the fight that followed, Cook was wounded.

Previously, the islanders had considered him a god, but gods were impervious to injury. They set upon the wounded navigator and stabbed him to death. Cook's men buried his remains in the bay, and no one returned for almost seven years.

When Cook had arrived in Hawaii, he was unaware of the political struggle that was all but complete. In the mid-18th century, a great and powerful monarch, Kamehameha I, was born. He and his descendants created a monarchy that, though it led to vast bloodshed, united the islands and brought their people into almost a century of peace and prosperity. But the comings and goings of the British and American missionaries, traders and whalers infected and affected the islanders and their future.

Within a century after Cook's arrival, about 80 percent of the native population had been wiped out by diseases of Western civilization. On a more positive side, these visitors also brought with them farming techniques, new crops, and the means to sell these products to the outside world. By 1819, the islands were again in turmoil. Kamehameha's son, Liholiho, had abolished the time-honored *kapu*, or taboo system. This allowed outside religions to convert the people to their Western religions. The Reverend Hiram Bingham, a Protestant clergyman from Boston, came in 1820, and set up churches and schools. He is also credited with clothing the unrestrained island women in the now-traditional *muumuus*, the loose, long dresses that cover a multitude of sins—and blessings. The United States recognized Hawaii as an independent nation in 1842.

The Protestant missionaries were followed by the Catholics, and later by the Mormons. Each brought Christian teachings, large-scale conversions and a firm refusal to live under the dictates of the Hawaiian monarchy.

The Christian teachings caused the ruling class to reevaluate the basic rights of man. This, along with the separateness of the visitors, caused a major change in the way Hawaii was governed. Though Kamehameha V tried to restore absolute authority to the throne, he died in the late 1860s without naming a successor. This brought about the election of kings. As usual, there were fights over who should rule, and those fights led to bloodshed. That all ended in 1893 when Sanford B. Dole became head of a provisional government. Ties between the islands and the United States became stronger.

The Hawaiian Legislature declared itself a republic in 1894, and six years later Hawaii became a Territory of the United States. As a territory, Hawaii became a magnet for immigrants who arrived here from everywhere to work the sugar plantations and, later, the pineapple industry. With an influx of people from Japan, China, the Philippines, Spain, Russia, Korea, Portugal, and the European nations, the pure-blood Hawaiians became a minority in their own land.

Once Hawaii became a territory, it became America's chief defense base in the Pacific. Then, on 7 December 1941, "a day that will live in infamy," planes of the Imperial Japanese bombed Oahu and brought the United States into World War II. "Remember Pearl Harbor" became the battlecry of Americans throughout that period and beyond.

Following the war and numerous attempts to gain equality in the nation of states, Hawaii was admitted to the Union in 1959 as the 50th of the United States.

There is no comparison between the place names of the Hawaiian Islands and those of the other 49 states. The ties to religion, the land, the sea, and the people echo throughout these names in a language that is beautiful to the ear but almost impossible to the pen.

AHUIMANU

The name of this village on Oahu translates as "bird cluster." Some say the name came from the habit the natives had of tying together the birds caught here.

In 1845, Kamehameha III granted a tract of land to the Catholic mission for the establishment of the first Catholic church in the Hawaiian Islands.

Each street name in the housing subdivision here combines *Hui*, "flock," with the name of a bird.

AIEA (— Heights)

During Kamehameha's drive to unite the islands, a strategic battle took place near Aiea, Oahu. The battle took place between Kalauao and Aiea—inside the eastern arm of what is now Pearl Harbor—on 12 December 1794.

AIKAHI

Like many of the names in Hawaii, the name for Aikahi, Oahu, is a description of what happened here. The name literally translates as "eat scrape." The allusion is that, at one time, people gathered here to scrape the sides of a poi bowl; in other words, to eat everything. Street names in this subdivision all begin with Ai.

AINA HAINA

Aina Haina, Oahu, was developed after World War II. The name came from Aina, "the land of," and the Hawaiianized name of Robert Hind, who started the Hind-Clarke Dairy here in 1924.

ANAEHOOMALU

Archeologists from the Bishop Museum announced in 1971 that many of the petroglyphs found on this Island of Hawaii site were from A.D. 1500, even though they suspect the village was in use in 800.

The name translates to "restricted mullet," an apparent reference to limitations placed on the fishing here.

B

BARBERS POINT HOUSING

Oahu's Barbers Point Housing, formerly called Kalaeloa, was named for Captain Henry Barber. Barber's ship was wrecked here on a coral shoal in 1796.

C

CAPTAIN COOK

This Hawaii town was named for Captain James Cook, who was killed at Kealakekua Bay in 1779.

E

ELEELE

Port Allen was called Eleele Landing until 1909. In that year, it was renamed to honor Samuel Cresson Allen, a Honolulu merchant. This Kauai Island name translates as "black."

ENCHANTED LAKES

Enchanted Lakes was formerly called Kaelepulu Pond. The name is descriptive.

EWA (— Beach)

Legend has it that the gods Kane and Kanaloa threw a stone to determine land boundaries. The stone was lost, but was later found at Piliokahe.

About 1832, William French asked the chiefs here on Oahu if he could rent land for agricultural purposes. He and his partner wanted to raise cotton and cattle. Their request was denied. Eight years later, the Reverend Artemas Bishop had a mill running here by water power, and he made several tons of sugar and molasses for himself and the natives.

FERNANDEZ VILLAGE

Fernandez Village, Oahu, was named for Abraham Fernandez, a full-blooded Hawaiian. Born in 1857 to Kalama Mahoe, he was adopted by her second husband, Peter Fernandez.

FOSTER VILLAGE

Foster Village, Oahu, was developed in 1957 by T. Jack Foster, Sr.

GLENWOOD

Glenwood was built in 1901 as the terminal for the Hilo Railroad. No one is quite sure how the name came about, but since it was named by the railroad, one can only assume the name was transported to the Island of Hawaii from the mainland.

HAENA

The native word for Haena, Hawaii, translates to "red hot" or "heat of the sun." The name is quite descriptive.

HAIKU

An American farmer had more than 50 acres planted here on Maui in 1838. The name translates as "speak abruptly" or "sharp break," and was probably given because of the terseness of speech of an early resident.

HAKALUA

Hakalua, located on the "Big Island," Hawaii, has a name that translates as "many perches." The name might describe a place where people or birds "perched."

HALAWA

Halawa, Molokai, bears a descriptive name. The word means "curve."

HALE O LONO

Hale O Lono, Molokai, bears a name that denotes ownership: "house of Lono." *Hale* is the Hawaiian word for "house" and is seen on many different places.

Legend has it that the rains were so torrential here that all vegetation was swept away. The irate people caught some rain and put it in an oven, watching it escape as a cloud.

HALEIWA

Haleiwa, Oahu, was the "house of the frigate (iwa) bird." The iwa birds were admired for their beauty.

The first missionary church on Oahu's north coast was built here. Haleiwa was also the favored vacation home for Queen Liliuokalani. The first resort hotel was built here in 1899.

HALEKOU

Located on Oahu, Halekou's name means "kou-wood house." It describes the type of homes that were built here.

HALENA

The cream-colored beach rock found here at Halena, Molokai, is valuable for flagstones. The word itself translates to "yellowish."

HALIIMAILE

The name for Haliimaile, Maui, is descriptive. The word means "maile vines strewn." Haliimaile is the former name of the palace grounds and the home of Boki and Liliha.

In 1849, Stephen Reynolds, a former trader, bought part ownership in Haliimaile Plantation and produced sugar. A few years later, he assumed full control. After investing considerable money in the plantation, Reynolds went mad in 1855 and left the islands. The next year, Charles Brewer II and Captain James Makee bought up Reynolds' property and called the place the Brewer Plantation.

HAMAKUAPOKO

Hamakuapoko, Maui, bears a name descriptive of its location: The word means "short Hamakua (corner)."

HAMOA

One authority believes this name is an abbreviation of Haamoa, an old name for Samoa. Another source maintains that the name of this settlement on Maui translates to "chicken trough." Based on the Hawaiian use of descriptive terms in the naming of their places, it seems likely the name had something to do with the raising and feeding of chickens.

HANA

The town of Hana, Maui, is steeped in tradition. It was here that ancient chieftains from the island of Hawaii fought for control of Maui, and where Kamahameha fought one of his battles that resulted in his reign as king.

Here too, Queen Kaahumanu, Kamahameha's wife, was born, and Chief Helio, who in the 19th century converted more than 4,000 people to Catholicism, is buried. The name, however, translates as "rest from hard breathing."

HANALEI

At least one source believes this name on Kauaia translates to "crescent bay." Another, however, suggests it means "lei making."

Hanalei was first seen by Polynesians in about the year 800. They called the valley Hanohano, "most beautiful."

In 1816–17, Kaumualii gave the valley and other tracts of land to Georg Anton Scheffer, a surgeon for the Russian-American Company. Scheffer acted as emissary for the company to regain the cargo of the *Bering*, a ship that had run aground at Waimea.

Scheffer built a fort at the site and raised the Russian flag. He was high-handed in his dealings with everyone and by 1818 had left the islands.

HANAMALU

Apparently this location at Kauai was not a nudist beach—even in the earliest days. The name translates as "loincloth bay."

HANAPEPE

This Kauai name translates as "crushed bay" or "to crush." It is an obvious reference to the landslides that occurred here.

HAUULA

Hauula, Oahu, bears a name that means "red hau tree." The designation was like a signpost for early residents.

In November 1854, Moses Kuaea, one of the first Hawaiians ordained in a Christian church, took charge of the church here.

HAWAII KAI

Hawaii Kai, Oahu, was developed by industrialist Henry J. Kaiser. The name was drawn from his name.

HAWI

Hawi is the northernmost community on the island of Hawaii. King Kamehameha the Great was born in this area. In 1880, a statue of the king was lost as it was being shipped from Italy to Honolulu. With the insurance money, the government was able to obtain a replica which can be seen in front of the Judiciary Building in the state capital.

Not long after the replica was in place, the original was found in a junkyard at Port Stanley in the Falkland Islands. It was brought back to Hawaii and it now sits on a pedestal in Kapaau, four miles east of here.

HEEIA

According to one legend, during a battle with people from Leeward Oahu, a tidal wave washed (*he'e'ia*) the natives out to sea. When they returned, they were victorious and fulfilled a prophecy.

Another legend tells us that souls were judged here, with the white (pure) souls going to He'eia-kea, the black (sinners), to He'eia-uli.

He'eia was also the name given by the goddess Haumea to her foster child. Heeia is located on Oahu.

HILEA

Someone slipped here and from then on the place on Hawaii was known as "careless."

HILO

Hilo, located on Hilo Bay, is the Big Island's capital. The city has strong Japanese roots, as migrant workers settled here at the turn of the 20th century. A local newspaper still publishes in Japanese.

Hilo's harbor was once circled by businesses. In 1946, a *tsunami* (tidal wave) destroyed great stretches of land. Another tsunami in 1960 continued the devastation.

The name, which translates as "twisted," is apparently given for a kind of crab grass.

HOEA CAMP

Hoea Camp, Hawaii, bears a name which means "to arrive at camp" or the "arrival camp."

HOLUALOA

Holualoa, Hawaii, is known as the "long sled course." The name is descriptive of an activity that would take place here.

HONAUNAU. The Painted Church.

HONAUNAU

The remains of the Hawaiian kings were kept in the Hale-o-Keawe mausoleum, at Honaunau, Hawaii.

HONOHINA

Honohina, Hawaii, has a name that refers to a "gray bay," "Hina's bay" or simply the personal name Hina.

HONOIPU LANDING

Honoipu Landing, Hawaii, was an ancient surfing area. The name describes what was found there: "gourd bay."

HONOKAHAU

The name of this place on Maui is quite descriptive of the moisture in the air as the sea rolls in: "bay tossing dew."

HONOKOWAI

The name of Honokowai, Maui, is similar to that of Honokahau. It means "bay drawing water" and is descriptive.

HONOLULU

Honolulu, Oahu, has been the capital of the Hawaiian Islands since 1843, when King Kamehameha III made it his permanent residence. When Hawaii became America's 50th state in 1959, Honolulu was the obvious choice for the state capital.

The name came from *hono*, a valley with a bay in front of it, and *lulu*, "sheltered." Combining the two we have various meanings, such as "fair haven," "quiet harbor," or "sheltered harbor."

Honolulu was not discovered until 1794. A year later, Kamehameha landed at Maunalua Bay, between Diamond and Koko Heads, and fought his final battle for island unification. Kamehameha and his men forced the Oahu forces to the top of Nuuanu Pali where, tradition has it, many leaped to their deaths rather than face capture. Following unification, the chief of all the islands resided here from 1803 to 1811.

The principal beach in Honolulu is Waikiki: *Wai* means "water," and *kiki* means "to spurt or spurting."

HONOMAKUAU

Apparently, Hawaiians feared this location on the Big Island, calling it the "harbor of fear."

HONOMU

To distinguish it from places with a roaring surf, Hawaiians called this Big Island location Honomu—"silent bay."

HONOULIULI

Honouliuli, Oahu, bears a name that means "dark bay."

HONUAPO

Honuapo, Hawaii, was probably a great place for catching turtles. The name means "caught turtle."

HOOKENA

To indicate that one could find potable water here, Hawaiians called the place "to satisfy thirst."

HOOLEHUA

Hoolehua, Molokai, is said to be name of a chief. That is quite possible since the name means "acting the expert."

HOOPULOA

Legendary god Omoka's and Okoe, his wife, lived here. When travelers visited, the gods put them in an oven where they "stayed for a long time." Finally, Omoka's and Okoe were pushed into a net by Ka-miki and his brother. They were released only after they promised not to do it again.

The name, adopted from Big Island folklore, means "put in together for a long time."

HUEHUE RANCH

The name of Huehue Ranch on the Big Island is quite descriptive. It means "overflowing."

When Hualalia erupted in 1801, people felt that Pele started it because she wanted things from different areas, and she was jealous of Ka-mehameha's wealth. Ka-mehameha offered a sacrifice and the volcano ceased its eruption.

KAALUALU

As seen from the sea, the rock fissures resemble wrinkles, which explains the translation of Kaaluala, Hawaii, "the wrinkles."

KAANAPALI

The name of this Maui location means "Ka'ana cliff." In 1850, Samuel Kauwealoha was ordained and installed as pastor here.

KAELEKU

The name of Kaeleku, Maui, refers to its base substance: "basaltic rock."

KAHALUU

In the early days, fishermen used to dive here for fish. Kahaluu, Oahu, has a name that refers to that practice; it means "diving place."

KAHANA

In Hawaiian, *kahana* means "cutting." The name of Kahana, Oahu, describes what took place here.

KAHUA

Another Hawaiian legend is commemorated at Kahua, Hawaii. Its name means "the jealousy."

KAHUKA (— Ranch)

The name for Kahuka, Hawaii, means "hooked post." At one time, a post was used as a directional marker.

KAHUKU

Legend has it that Oahu was once two islands, ruled by a brother and sister. At a pool called Polou, the siblings linked fingers and pulled the two islands together. Hawaiians refer to Kahuku as "the projection."

In 1849, James Kekela was formally ordained into the priesthood here, becoming the first native Hawaiian to receive ordination and be installed at an independent church.

KAHULUI

Kahului's beaches contain "Maui Diamonds," small pieces of white quartz that once fooled early explorers. Its name means "the winning," and refers to an early competition.

KAILUA

Kailua's name translates to "two seas" or "two ocean currents." Kailua, Maui, is the second largest city on the Hawaiian Islands.

KAILUA-KONA

Kailua-Kona is the Big Island's oldest and most developed resort area. It was a favorite spot for Hawaiian royalty. Kamehameha I spent a great deal of time here. To the south is Kamehameha III's early home.

The Big Island's coffee industry had its beginnings here. Though there are no large coffee plantations in operation today, the Superior Tea & Coffee Company arranges the cultivation of 47,000 acres of privately-owned plots.

Because water approaches it from two sides, the name means "two seas."

KAINALIU

The name of this Big Island settlement translates as "billowy sea"—a descriptive term. Bernice Pau-aki Bishop was born here.

KALAE

The people here are noted for their failure to observe the taboos of others. The name of this Molokai settlement might be indicative of their feeling about themselves. *Kalae* means "the clearness."

KALAHEO

Hawaiians named Kalaheo, Oahu, "the proud day," to commemorate an important time in their existence.

KALAOA

Kalaoa, Hawaii is said to be named for Kalaoa Pu'uomi, sister of Ka-palaoa, the mother of the riddling expert, Kala-pana.

Kalaoa is also a stick for catching eel, called "the choker."

KALAUPAPA

It was to the village of Kalaupapa, the "flat plain," now known as Ka-laupapa National Historical Park, that a young Belgian priest, Joseph de Veuster (1840–89), came in 1863 to replace his ailing brother.

Father Damien, as he became known after ordination, stayed his entire life ministering to the victims of Hanson's Disease, leprosy. Beginning in about 1866, victims of this dread disease were left at the remote Kalawao Cove in an effort to reduce the contagion. Father Damien brought order to the colony and helped minister to the sick. He died of the disease himself in 1889. Medical research has since arrested the disease, and there have been no new admissions to Kalaupapa since 1969.

KALAWAO

Kalawao was the original site of the Molokai leper colony. Its name means "announce mountain area," and indicates its location.

KALUAAHA

To early Hawaiians, Kaluaaha was "the gathering pit." The first Christian mission on the island of Molokai was established by the Reverend H. R. Hitchcock in 1832. Father Damien also built Our Lady of Sorrows Church here in 1874.

The Reverend and Mrs. Elias Bond established two select boarding schools here in 1842.

KALUAIHAKOKO

Kaluaihakoko, Maui, is supposed to be the name of a chief, but other authorities believe the name translates as the "pit for wrestling."

KAMAILI

The name of Kamaili, Hawaii, means "the pebbles," a description of what could be found here.

KAMALO

Originally known as Kamaloo, "the dry place," Kamalo's name seems to be a reduction of the original.

Not far from this village, Kamehameha the Great fought one of his many battles for unification of the islands. In 1876, Father Damien, the "Martyr of Molokai," built the little frame chapel of St. Joseph.

KAMAOLE

Kamaole, Maui, describes someone who once lived here without children. The name means "childless."

KANAIO

Kanaio, Maui, bears a name that means "the bastard sandalwood tree." One can only assume what that means.

KANIAHIKU VILLAGE

Kaniahiku means "call of Hiku." The village is located on the Big Island.

KAPAA

The name of Kapaa, Kauai, means "the solid" or "the closing."

KAPAAU

Kapaau, Hawaii, is supposed to mean "elevated portion of *heiau*." A *heiau* is a "temple."

KAPAIA

"The walls" or "bowers" is the literal translation of this Kauai location's name.

KAPALAOA

According to legend, Kane and Kanaloa sent a whale here to pick up Makua-kau-mana, their worshipper, and take him to the legendary land of Kane-huna-moku, where he would live in the "deathless land of beautiful people." The name of Kapaloaoa, Hawaii, means "the whale" or "the whale tooth."

KAPALUA

The name of Kapalua, Maui, means "two borders."

KAPEHU

Kapehu, Hawaii, bears the name of a stream. The stream's name means "the swelling," an apparent reference to a subterranean spring.

KAPOHO

Early Hawaiians obtained salt here by evaporating water. The settlement on the Big Island bears a name that means "the depression." This would refer to the way they decanted the water to gain the sale.

KAPULENA

Kapulena, Hawaii, was named for the king shark of Hamakua. *Kapu* means "taboo, forbidden, keep out."

KAPUNA

Kapuna is Hawaiian for "the spring."

KAUMAKANI

Early visitors in this Kauai location referred to it by this name, which means "place in wind."

KAUMALAPAU

Kaumalapau was the place on Lanai where residents took the ashes from their fires and used them as fertilizer. The name means "soot placed (in) gardens."

KAUNAKAKAI

The former name for this village was Kauna-kahakai, "beach landing." The current name seems to be a condensation of the original. Kaunakakai is the principal town on the Island of Molokai. Kamehameha V, who reigned from 1863 to 1872, once made his summer home here.

KAUPAKULUA

Kaupakulua, Maui, bears a roadsign name: "two ridgepoles."

KAUPO

Kaupo, Maui, was the place where people in outrigger canoes could land with ease at night. The name means "landing [of canoes] at night."

KAUPULEHU

One legend has it the name of this Big Island village is a contraction of Ka-imu-pulehu-a-ke-aku, "the roasting oven of the god." Another authority suggests the name refers to an island delicacy, "roasted breadfruit."

KAWAIHAE

Kawaihae, Hawaii, is a busy commercial port, but its name means "the water of wrath." The port carries cattle from the Parker Ranch to feed-lots on Oahu. Legend has it people once fought for water from a pool in this dry area.

KAWAILOA (— Beach, — Camp)

The name Kawailoa, appearing in Kawailoa Beach and Camp on the Island of Oahu, means "the long water."

KAWAINUI

Kawainui, a name that appears on the Big Island, means "the big water."

KAWELA

This Oahu village carries a name that refers to the local temperature. *Kawela* means "the heat."

KEALAKEKUA

This is the bay where Captain Cook was killed. Legend has it that the gods often slid down a cliff here, leaving an impression. The idea was they wanted to cross the bay quickly. The name of this community on the Island of Hawaii translates as "pathway of the god."

KEALIA

The name of Kealia, Hawaii, translates as "the salt incrustation."

One legend has it that the name came not from salt but from a local incident. Once, a chief became too absorbed in the day's activities to leave when his wife wanted him to. He turned to her and said, "Alia no, a napo'o ka la," "Just wait until the sun sets." The phrase is used with anyone who stays late.

KEAMUKU

Legend has it that women, children and the aged hid in caves here on the Big Island during wartime. They had to put out any burning fires if an enemy approached. The name, however, translates to "cut-off lava."

KEANAE

It was here that Kane, accompanied by Kanaloa, was supposed to have thrust his kauila staff into rock, drawing water. The name of this Maui site, however, refers to "the mullet," a fish.

KEAUKAHA

Keaukaha, Hawaii, has a name that means "the passing current."

KEAWAIKI

"The small passage" is what Keawaiki, Hawaii, means.

KEAWAKAPU

Keawakapu, Maui, was known to early Hawaiians by this name, which means "the sacred (or forbidden) harbor."

KEHENA

The name of Kehena, Hawaii, sounds romantic. That is true of most Hawaiian names. Sadly, this one translates to mean "place for refuse."

It was the birthplace of the Reverend J. W. Kanoa, the first Hawaiian missionary on the Gilbert Islands.

KEKAHA

The name of this Kauai site, which translates as "the place," is also the name of a native Hawaiian who, in 1856, exhibited the best example of wheat at the annual meeting of the Royal Hawaiian Agricultural Society.

KEOKEA

The name of this Big Island site means "the white sand," or perhaps "the sound of white caps."

KIHEI

Kihei, Maui, is where the only Canadian-style totem pole exists in the state. It is a monument to George Vancouver, who was supposed to have landed here in the early 19th century.

Kihei means either "cape" or "cloak."

KIHEI. The outrigger canoe shares an identity with the Hawaiian Islands. These canoes belong to the Kihei Canoe Club on the island of Maui. (Hawaii Visitors Bureau, photograph by Peter French)

KIHOLO

The name of Kiholo, Hawaii, means "fishhook." It is also the name of a fish pond supposedly built by Ka-mr-ehamrha I. It was destroyed by an 1859 volcano eruption. The lava flow, legend tells us, was provoked by Pele, who hungered for the ewa and mullet here.

KILAUEA

The name of Kilauea, Kauai, is descriptive of its location. The name means "spewing," "much spreading" or "rising smoke clouds," all of which refer to volcanic eruptions. The name came from a nearly continuously active volcano on the flank of Mauna Loa.

KIPAHULU

Kipahulu, Maui, was the home of Laka, a god for canoe makers. The name means "fetch from (exhausted) gardens," and probably refers to a farming site that had not had its crops rotated and had been depleted of its nutrients.

KIPU

The name of Kipu, Kauai, means "hold back." It was a site visited by Kamapuaa.

KOAE

Some think the name of this Big Island settlement came from Puna-aikoae, a supernatural being in the form of a tropical bird. Some say he still can be seen flying over Kilauea Crater. *Koae* means "tropic bird."

KOELE

Koele, Lanai, bears a name that reflects what was harvested here: "dark sugar cane."

KOKEE

Apparently, the sugar cane that grew up here on Kauai was imperfect, and led Hawaiians to use this name, which means "to bend," "to wind" or "crooked cane."

KOKOKAHI

Kokokahi, Oahu, was found in 1935 by the Reverend Theodore Richards. He also gave the name. The old one was Ke-ana. The new name means "one blood," signifying that all men are created equal.

KOKOMO

The original name of this Maui village was Koa-Komo, which meant "koa tree entering." There was a koa tree at the entrance to the village. It has no relationship to the other Kokomo.

KOLO

In Hawaiian *kolo* means to "crawl" or "pull." Kolo is located on the Island of Molokai.

KOLOA

The first sugar mill on the Island of Kauai was built here in 1835 by Ladd & Company. It became part of Grove Farm in 1948. Legend has it the village was named for a steep rock called Pali-o-ko-loa.

KUALAPU'U

Kaulapu'u, Molokai, was established as a Del Monte pineapple cannery village. Its name means "hill overturned."

KUAU

Kuau is Hawaiian for "handle." The village of Kuau is located on Maui.

KUHIO VILLAGE

Kuhio Village, Hawaii, was named for Prince Jonah Ku-hio Ka-lani-ana-'ole (1871–1922), delegate to Congress and father of the Hawaiian Homes Commission Act.

KUKAIAU

Apparently, it was near this village on the Big Island that the people could see the breakers come in from the sea. The name means "current appearing."

KUKUI
The name of Kukui, Hawaii, means "candlenut lamp," and refers to light of any kind.

KUKUIHAELE
Night marchers were once seen here, and Hawaiians began to call the place Kukuihaele, "traveling light." A healing god, legend has it, once lived here.

KUKUIULA
We will not venture to guess on this Kauai village name. The name translates as "red light."

KULIOUOU
The name of Kuliouou, Oahu, means "sounding knee." It refers to a *puniu*, a drum attached to the knee.

The first Carbon-14 dating (A.D. 1000 +/− 180) in Hawaii was based on carbon taken from a cave here in 1950.

KUMUKUMU
Kumukumu, Kauai, bears a name that means "stubs" in Hawaiian. One suggestion is that the reference was to cut-down crops.

KUNIA CAMP
Kunia is Hawaiian for "burned." Kunia Camp, located on Oahu, probably got its name from the way the fields were prepared for the next planting.

KURTISTOWN
Kurtistown, Hawaii, was named for A. G. Curtis, a pioneer at Ola'a in 1902 when the Ola'a Sugar Company opened.

LAHAINA
Once known as the whaling capital of the mid-Pacific, Lahaina, Maui, lost out to Honolulu.

King Kamehameha established his capital here after he conquered the islands (1820–45). Lahaina, whose name means "cruel sun," a reference to early droughts, remained the seat of government until 1843.

L

LAIE

Laie, located on Oahu, refers to the "ie-leaf." Tradition has it Laie was the birthplace of the sacred princess, Laieikawai. She was taken to the mythical paradise of Pali-uli, "green cliff," on Hawaii.

Since 1864, Laie has been the Hawaiian center for the Church of Jesus Christ of Latter-day Saints.

LANAI CITY

According to one source, the name of Lanai City means "day (of) conquest." Another source, on the other hand, suggests it came from *lanai*, which every crossword puzzler knows is Hawaiian for "porch." All the roads on this island radiate from Lanai City.

LANIKAI

The original name of this Oahu community was Kaohao. When development began in 1924, the name was changed to Lanikai, in the belief that the new name meant "heavenly sea." Another source translates the word to mean "sea (or marine) heaven."

LAUNIUPOKO

In the Hawaiian lexicon, Launiupoko means "short coconut leaf." The village of Lauiupoko is located on Maui.

LAUPAHOEHOE

Laupahoehoe's name translates as "leaf of lava" or "smooth lava flat." It is a leaf-shaped peninsula of black lava, located on the Big Island.

According to legend, a man who lived here turned into a pau-o fish and his sister turned into an a'awa fish. Fishermen who tried to catch them were startled when they returned to human form.

Kamehameha once lived here following a retreat from his enemies in the late 18th century.

LEHUA LANDING

The name of this Nihau Island community refers to the "lehua flower." Nihau is the westernmost island of the main Hawaiian chain.

LIHUE

Lihue is the county seat of Kauai. Its name means "cold chill." In 1849, Henry A. Peirce revisited the islands and conceived the idea of establishing a sugar plantation near Nawiliwili Bay. He organized H. A. Peirce & Company, with the help of Judge W. L. Lee and Charles R. Bishop. This was the beginning of the Lihue Plantation, a model plantation.

MAALAEA

The name of this Maui village is perhaps a contraction of Maka-alaea, "ocherous earth beginning."

MAHAIULA

According to a legend, fishermen brought gifts to Pohaku-o-Lama, a stone fish goddess at this Big Island location. They brought presents every month except May, June and July. During those months, the sea turned yellowish and the people thought the goddess was menstruating. The name is a literal translation of that phenomenon.

MAHINUI

Mahinui, Oahu, bears a name that means "great champion." Legend tells us that a hero who was defeated by Olo-mana had his body thrown from Mount Olo-mana to the present location of the mountain.

MAHUKONA

A 600-year-old Hawaiian village has been uncovered at nearby Lapakahi State Historical Park. Visible after all these years are the remains of houses, canoe sheds and a curbed trail that led to the villagers' mountain farms. The name of Mahukona, Hawaii, means "leeward stream."

MAKAKILO CITY

The people who previously lived at this Oahu city site were busybodies. The name translates as "observing eyes."

MAKALAWENA

The legendary hero, Ka-miki, destroyed some ghosts who were fishing here. The ghosts made the mullet and goatfish taste bitter. The name of Makalawena, Hawaii, means "release (of) glow."

MAKAPALA

Though the name of Makapala, Hawaii, means "sore beginning to heal," there is no data to tell us about the injury.

MAKAWAO

In 1845, the government attempted to provide the people with their own land. A new land law was passed in that year, which, in effect, would convey land to the people for purchase or gift. When the king visited here the next year, he announced that the entire district, except for McLane's plantation, was to go to the people for "fee simple."

The name of Makawao, Maui, means "beginning of the forest," a description of the location.

MAKENA

Makena in Hawaiian means "abundance." Makena is located on the island of Maui.

MAKUA (Site)

The traditional haunt of expert lua fighters, Makua, Oahu, bears a name that means "parents."

MALA

In Hawaiian, *mala* means "garden." Mala is located on the island of Maui.

MALAE

Malae, in Hawaiian, means "clear." Malae, Oahu, bears that name, a reference to the clarity of the water.

MANA

Home of the owners of the Parker Ranch, Mana, Hawaii, bears a name that means "arid."

MANA

The settlement at the dry western end of the island of Kauai also bears the "arid" name.

MAUNA LOA

Mauna Loa, the largest settlement on the western end of Molokai, was a Dole company town until 1975. In that year, the company began to shut down its operation. Old plantation buildings have been converted into shops for local artisans.

The name came from the active volcano—the world's most active present day volcano, the second-highest mountain in Hawaii. The area was famous for adze quarries, holua sliding and the trees from which kalai-pahoa sorcery images were made. The name means "long mountain," and Mauna Loa is every inch of that. It is probably the largest single mountain mass on earth.

MAUNAWIL

The Hawaiian word for this Oahu community means "twisted mountain."

MILOLII

According to one story, this village on the Island of Hawaii was named for an expert sennit twister who lived here. The name has also been interpreted as "small swirling." As the village was noted for its fine sennit cord, the other translation of "fine twist" might be more appropriate.

MOKAPU

Mokapu, Oahu, was originally named Moku-kapu, "sacred district," because Kamehameha I met his chiefs here. The word has lately been translated to mean "taboo district."

MOKULAU

There are numerous rock islets in the sea here, which explains the Hawaiian name of this Maui locale: *Mokulau* means "many islets."

MOKULEIA

The Hawaiian historian Kamakau was born in this community on Oahu. The name means "isle (of) abundance."

MOPUA

Though this Maui village has a name that means "melodious," some suggest the name came from that of some legendary character.

MOUNTAIN VIEW

This island of Hawaii location was named for the Mountain View House. The house was built in 1891 as the half-way stop on the way to the volcano from Hilo.

NAALEHU

The name of this island of Hawaii village means "the volcanic ashes."

NAHIKU

The name of Nahiku, Maui, meaning "the sevens," refers to the number of districts in the area.

NANAKULI

One legend has it this Oahu village was named for the tattooed knee of the priest Ka-opulupulu, whose chief turned a deaf ear to his advice. The name means "look at knee" in Hawaiian.

Another translation of the name comes out to "look deaf." This was a practice of the people here when they were asked to share food with passerbys. They did not have enough for themselves, so they acted like they were deaf.

NAPILI BAY

Napilia Bay, whose name is Hawaiian for "the joinings" or "pili grass," is located on the island of Maui.

NAPOOPOO

The first sustained Western contact with the Hawaiian Islands took place here at Napoopoo with the presence of Captain James Cook. In fact, the first Christian funeral on the island was presided over by Cook at this site.

This Big Island village's name translates as "the holes." During an early time, people in canoes in the bay looked ashore and could see the villagers peeking out through holes (doors) in their grass houses.

NAWILIWILI

Nawiliwili, Kauai, was named for the "the wiliwili trees."

NINOLE

A cannibalistic hag, or so the legend goes, lived here and her pretty granddaughter lured travelers to her cave where the old woman ate them! The name of this Big Island site has nothing to do with the legend. The name means "bending."

NIU VALLEY

Niu is Hawaiian for "coconut," so the name of this locale on Oahu would mean "valley of the coconuts."

NIULII

While *niu* is "coconut," *niulii* is used to describe a "small coconut."

NIUMALU

The use of coconuts in place names on the Hawaiian Islands extend to this Kauai Island location, whose name means "shade (of) coconuts."

NONOPAPA

While sheep were sheared in shacks here rather than in the out-doors, the name of Nonopapa, Nihau, has nothing to do with that practice. The name means "invalid," and it probably refers to an early resident.

NU VILLAGE

Nu is a descriptive term used by Hawaiians. It means "to ride," as the wind.

OHIA MILL

This Big Island location was named for the "ohia tree."

O

OLINDA

Olinda was the name of Samuel T. Alexander's home here. One source suggests he took the name from a place in Spain; another, from a city in Brazil. Alexander is also reputed to have carried the name of his Maui location with him to Shasta County, California in the early 1860s.

OLOMANA

Olomana, Oahu, "forked hill" in Hawaiian, was named for the 1,643-foot peak which, legend has it, was named for the giant who leaped from Kauai to this mountain.

OLOWALU

Hundreds of Hawaiians were treacherously murdered and hundreds more were wounded here in 1790 on the orders of Captain Simon Metcalfe.

The name of the town on Maui is descriptive and means "many hills."

ONEAWA

This section of Oahu was famous for great amounts of oio and awa fish. The name reinforces that notion.

ONEULA BEACH

The name of Oneula Beach, Oahu, is descriptive of the color of the beach sand. *Oneula* means "red sand."

OOKALA

The name of this Big Island site means "sharp digging stick" and probably refers to a method of farming.

OPAEULA CAMP

To a native Hawaiian, *opaeula* means "red shrimp."

OPIHIKAO

Because of robbers, the villagers were afraid to harvest limpets alone, so they did it in groups. The name of this island of Hawaii village means "crowd [gathering] limpets."

PAHALA

Pahala is a sugar mill community located on the Island of Hawaii. To the east lies the Ka'u Desert, a wasteland of lava and pumice reaching from the sea to the rim of Kilauea Crater.

The name of Pahala translates to mean "cultivation by burning mulch." That must be a technique similar to burning a field before planting to rid the soil of weeds and insects.

PAHOA

Pahoa, Hawaii, experienced a volcanic eruption in 1955 that devasted the area, destroying one village and several miles of sugarcane farms and orchards. The name refers to the burning. Five years later, the town of Kapoho was demolished by a similar eruption.

PAIA

Located on Maui, Paia bears a name that means "noisy." With so much at stake in tourist dollars, we assure you the reference was to the sound of the sea.

PAKALA VILLAGE

Pakala in Hawaiian means "the light shines." Pakala Village is located on Kauai.

PAPA

For people on the mainland, the word "Papa" is considered an affectionate name for a father. Not so in the islands. On Hawaii, the name means "forbidden."

PAPAALOA

Though one source believes Papaaloa, Hawaii, bears a name that means "much burned," we wonder. Could it have something to do with forbidden burning or sacrifice?

PAPAIKOU

Again, we run into the problem of translation. Does Papaikou, located on the Big Island, mean "a chief had a hut here" or does it have something to do with *papa*, or "forbidden"?

PAUKUKALO

The name for Paukukalo, Maui, means "taro piece." The taro root is the basic ingredient in a Hawaiian Islands staple: poi.

PEARL CITY

Pearl City, Oahu, is the town that surrounds Pearl Harbor.

Pearl Harbor has been etched in the American mind ever since the Japanese attack here on 7 December 1941 forced the United

PEARL HARBOR. The stack of the U.S.S. *Arizona* pokes through the water at Pearl Harbor. The ship is the final resting place for the hundreds of sailors who were killed during the surprise attack on the American military installations at Hawaii in 1941. More than half a century after the attack, oil can still be seen rising to the surface from the ship's tanks. (Photograph by the author)

States into World War II. No stopover on this island would be complete without a trip to pay homage to the 1,770 men who died during that attack.

Any visit to the U.S.S. *Arizona* Monument is a moving experience. After all these years, oil still bubbles to the surface of the harbor from the ship's fuel tanks.

The value of the harbor was first realized by Lieutenant Charles Wilkes in 1840. Dredging an outlying reef, he reasoned, would facilitate access to the harbor. About 30 years later, Army Colonel John M. Schofield recommended the government secure harbor rights. This was accomplished in 1873, but work did not begin until a quarter of a century later.

The city took its name from the harbor, named for the pearl oysters found here. The Hawaiian name is Puuloa, "long hill."

PEPEEKEO (— Mill)

The name of this island of Hawaii village goes back to warring days on the island. It means "food crushed," as if by warriors in battle.

PIIHONUA

Piihonua, Hawaii, has a name that is descriptive. It means "land incline."

POHAKUPU

Apparently, at some time in its history, people believed that there was such a thing as a "growing rock." That is what the name for this Oahu village means.

POHOIKI

Pele was supposed to have dug a crater here. The name of Pohoiki, Hawaii, reinforces the legend, because it means "small depression."

POIPU

The name of this spot on Kauai means "completely overcast" or "crashing," as in waves.

PORT ALLEN

Originally named Eleele Landing, the port of the island of Kauai was renamed in 1909 for Samuel Cresson Allen, a Honolulu merchant.

PRINCEVILLE

At one time a sugar plantation owned by Robert Crichton Wyllie, this Kauai Island site was given its name to commemorate an 1860 visit by Kamehameha IV, Queen Emma and their son, Prince Ka Haku o Hawaii. The plantation later became a cattle ranch and, in 1968, it was opened to development.

PUAKEA

Puakea, located on the Big Island, means "white blossom." The name could refer to any number of blossoms found on the island.

PUAKO

Puako, also on the Big Island, is more specific. Its name refers to the "sugarcane blossom."

PUKO'O

On the mountainside above Puko'o is Iliiliopae Hejau, "the heiau of the shrimp." According to island tradition, this heiau was used for human sacrifice, and its name came from the fact that, in the 13th century, workmen were paid one shrimp for transporting the building stones from across the island.

Again, legend has nothing to do with the name. *Puko'o* means "support hill."

PULEHU

Perhaps the people of this Maui village cooked their food differently from other islanders. *Pulehu* means "broiled."

PUNALUU

A cannibalistic hag lived here on the island of Hawaii, or so we are told. She was killed by Laka and his helpers. *Puna*, however, refers to "lime" or "coral."

PUNALUU

This village on Oahu was apparently the place where divers looked for coral. The name means "coral dived for."

PUPUKEA

Though some authorities believe that the name for this town on Oahu means "white shell," others remind us that *pupu* translates to "crazy."

PUU O HOKU RANCH

The name of Puu O Hoku Ranch means "hill of Hoku," or, in more comprehensive terms, "night of the full moon."

PUU WAAWAA RANCH

This ranch's name means "furrowed hill."

PUUANAHULU

Sometimes the legends get too far-fetched to go along with the name. In the case of this village on the Big Island, the name translates to mean "ten-day hill." Some authorities say it was named for a supernatural dog of that name.

PUUIKI

Puuiki, located on Maui, refers to a "small hill."

PUUKOLII

While Puuiki is non-specific, Puukolii, also on Maui, refers to a particular place: "kolii shrub hill."

PUUNENE

Puunene, Maui, was where a goose was spotted. The name means "goose hill."

PUUOHALA VILLAGE

The name for this Maui village refers to a "hill of pandanus."

SCHOFIELD BARRACKS

Schofield Barracks, Oahu, was named for Lieutenant-General John M. Schofield (1831–1906), who recommended that the United States obtain harbor rights to Pearl Harbor. Schofield served as Secretary of War for Andrew Johnson.

Construction on the military installation began in 1909. (See PEARL CITY, Hawaii.)

SPRECKELSVILLE

Claus Spreckels was a sugar industrialist who gave his family name to this Maui location while he reaped the good fortunes of its soil.

SUNSET BEACH

Originally known as Paumalu, this Oahu location had its name changed to help promote tourism.

UALAPUE

The name of this village on Molokai means "hilled sweet potatoes." The reference is to a manner of growing the potatoes.

ULUPALAKUA RANCH

This ranch on Maui has a name that means "breadfruit ripening (on) back (of carriers)."

The Tedeschi Winery is located on the Ulupalakua Ranch. It is a producer of pineapple wine, which can be tasted—how apropos—in an 1856 jailhouse.

WAHIAWA

Rough seas can be heard here, and the name reinforces that notion. Wahiawa, Oahu, carries a name that means "place of noise" or "landing place."

WAHILAUHUE

A well here once gave drinkable water, and the method of getting the water was apparently by way of a gourd leaf. The name of this village on Molokai means "wrap gourd leaf."

WAIAHOLE

The name of this village on Oahu describes what could be found here. It means "mature ahole water." Ahole is a kind of fish.

WAIAKA

Waiaka, located on the Big Island, has a name that means "laughing water," an obvious reference to the sound made by the sea.

WAIAKEA

A legendary individual, Ulu, lived here. He died of starvation and was buried next to a running spring. The next morning, a breadfruit tree was found there, filled with fruit, and the famine ended. His name means breadfruit, which does not explain the name of this Big Island locale.

The name Waiakea means "broad waters."

WAIAKOA

With the change of a single letter (in this case, the "e" in Waiakea to an "o") the entire sense of a name changes. This village, located on Maui, has a name that means "water (used) by warriors."

WAIANAE

A lizard goddess once lived here and stole another woman's husband, but the wind god Makani-ke-oe returned the husband to his wife. We are sure that is not the reason the village, located on Oahu, was named "mullet water."

WAIEHU

Waiehu is what you get when you stand on the shore. The name of this Maui location means "water spray."

WAIHEE

A mute, according to tradition, was told that his speech would be restored if he went to Kahiki to be married. Along the way, he was attacked by a giant squid. He killed it and threw it to Kaha-lu'u. Slime flowed over the land. The romantic name of this Maui site means "squid liquid." That sounds so much better than slime.

WAIKALUA

Depending on which source one believes, the name for this Oahu location means "water (of) the lua fighter" or "water of the pit."

WAIKANE

The original name of this Oahu village was Wai-a-Kane, and means "Kane's water." The name was collapsed into its present form.

WAIKAPU

A conch shell that was kept in a cave here could be heard everywhere in the Hawaiian Islands until it was stolen by a supernatural dog. At least that is what the local legend says. The name of this Maui town means "water (of) the conch."

WAIKAPUNA

In one story, a shark god married a local girl and she gave birth to a kindly green shark. Another story has a "skin-scratching stone" in the sea here. A boy or girl could take a sweetheart here, scratch his or her skin, and everyone would know that the person was taken. The name of Waikapuna, Hawaii, means "water (of) the spring."

WAIKII

A god is reputed to have carried water from another spring in a calabash. The name of Waikii, Hawaii, reinforces that by meaning "fetched water."

WAIKIKI

Diamond Head, a 760-foot extinct volcano crater, is, perhaps, Oahu's most famous landmark. Diamond Head received its name from 19th-century sailors who mistook the volcanic crystals for diamonds.

Waikiki's name means "spouting—or spurting—water."

OAHU. Looking at Diamond Head from Ala Moana State Park. Diamond Head has become a symbol of Hawaii from its constant appearance in "B-Roll" films shot for movies and television. (Photograph by the author)

WAIKOLOA

The authorities are out on this Big Island name. Some think it means "duck water." Others think it could be the name of the wind.

WAILEA

Wailea, Hawaii, carries a name that means "water of Lea." Lea was the goddess of the canoe makers. To avoid sentimentality, we might note that it is also the name of a fish god.

WAILUA

Wailua, Kauai, is located at the mouth of the Wailua River. Its name translates to "twin waters," an obvious reference to the double cascade of Wailua Falls.

WAILUKU

A Chinese man by the name of Hungtai built the first sugar mill here in 1824, nine years before the first white missionaries arrived. Hungtai's industry caught on, to say the least.

In the mid-20th century, the Hawaii Commercial and Sugar Company bought town lots in nearby Kahului and sold homes to its workers. Because the boundary lines between the two towns are virtually indistinguishable, they are sometimes referred to as the "twin cities" of Maui.

The name of the community translates to "water (of) destruction—or slaughter."

WAIMANALO (— Beach)

The name of these locations on Oahu mean "potable water." Another source, however, thinks the name describes "brackish water." One must admit there is a big difference between the two. The village was the site of the home of Chief Kakuhihewa.

WAIMEA

Waimea, Hawaii, is also called Kamuela to distinguish it from Waimea on Kauia. The area is primarily ranching country.

About 1809, John Palmer Parker left his ship and was employed by Kamehameha to hunt wild cattle. He married a Hawaiian woman and purchased land to build his own ranch. Today, the Parker Ranch spans 250,000 acres! It is the largest ranch in the Hawaiian Islands and in the United States.

The name means "reddish water."

WAIMEA

Just like its same-named cousin on Hawaii, Waimea, Kauai, has a name that means "reddish water."

Waimea was where Captain Cook first landed in the Hawaiian Islands in 1778. An early major whaling port, it was once the Polynesian capital of Kauai. Just south of town are the remains of a Russian fort built in 1817.

WAINAKU

The name of Wainaku, Hawaii, means "pushing water."

WAINEE

Wainee, Maui, has a name that translates as "moving water."

WAINIHA

While Wainaku and Wainee have more-or-less friendly names, Wainiha, Kauai, does not. Its name means "unfriendly water," a reference to either navigation or drinking.

WAIOHINU

The sun glistening off the ocean near Waiohinu, Hawaii, must have led villagers to call it by that name. It means "shiny water."

WAIOHULI

This Maui village is known as "water of change." The name relates to the way the surf hits the beach.

WAIPAHU

The water at this Oahu location comes from underground. This led early villagers to call the place Waipahu, "bursting water." Legend has it that the shark goddess lived here.

WAIPIO

The earth in the upper valley is red because Kanaloa bashed Maui against the rocks and his blood stained the earth.

It was in the Waipio Valley that Kalaniopuu convened a council of chiefs in 1780. The purpose was to pass the mantle of power to his son, Kiwalao, as king. At the same time, he gave custody of the war god of the Hawaiian kings, Kaukailimoku, to Kamehameha.

The name of Waipio, Hawaii, means "curved water."

WAIPOULI

The name of this Kauai village means "dark water," usually a reference to deep water.

WELOKA

One can only imagine how the name of Weloka, Hawaii, came about. The name in translation means "hit float."

Bibliography

Alaska and Its History. Morgan B. Sherwood, ed. Seattle: University of Washington Press, 1967.

Allen, Barbara. *Homesteading the High Desert.* Salt Lake City: University of Utah Press, 1987.

Allen, Thomas B. "Pearl Harbor: A Return to the Day of Infamy." *National Geographic* 180 (December 1991) 6:50–77.

Alotta, Robert I. *#2: A Look at the Vice Presidency.* New York: Julian Messner, 1981.

_____. *Old Names and New Places.* Philadelphia: The Westminster Press, 1979.

_____. *Signposts and Settlers: The History of the Place Names in the Middle Atlantic States.* Chicago: Bonus Books, 1992.

Avery, Mary W. Washington. *A History of the Evergreen State.* Seattle: University of Washington Press, 1965.

Ayto, John. *Dictionary of Word Origins.* New York: Arcade/Little, Brown & Co., 1990.

Balch, Thomas Willing. *The Alaska Frontier.* Philadelphia: Allen, Lane & Scott, 1903.

Bartlett, John. *Familiar Quotations.* Christopher Morely and Louella D. Everett, eds. Boston: Little, Brown & Company, 1938.

Battles and Leaders of the Civil War. Robert Underwood and Clarence Clough Buel, eds. New York: The Century Company, 1888.

Beach, Rex. *Personal Exposures.* New York: Harper, 1940.

Beckey, Fred. *Cascade Alpine Guide: Climbing and High Routes, Columbia River to Stevens Pass.* Seattle: The Mountaineers, 1973.

Belt, Don. "Baja California: Mexico's Land Apart." *National Geographic* 176 (December 1989) 6:714–47.

Benét's Reader's Encyclopedia of American Literature. George Perkins, Barbara Perkins and Phillip Leininger, eds. New York: HarperCollins, 1991.

Bernier, Nichole. "Monterey, Step By Step." *Meeting News,* October 1992, pp. 24–26.

Berton, Pierre. *The Klondike Fever: The Life and Death of the Last Great Gold Rush.* New York: Alfred A. Knopf, 1958.

Blow, Michael. *A Ship to Remember; The Maine and the Spanish-American War.* New York: William Morrow and Company, Inc., 1992.

Boatner, Mark M. III. *The Civil War Dictionary.* New York: David McKay Company, 1959.

———. *Encyclopedia of the American Revolution.* New York: David McKay Company, 1966.

Bunker, Stevens Dana. *Alaska, Land of Many Dreams.* New York: Crescent Books, 1985.

Cambridge Biographical Dictionary. Magnus Magnusson, ed. Cambridge: Cambridge University Press, 1990.

Cantwell, Robert. *The Hidden Northwest.* Philadelphia: J. B. Lippincott Company, 1972.

Carlson, Helen S. *Nevada Place Names, A Geographical Dictionary.* Reno: University of Nevada Press, 1974.

Carrier, Jim. "Water and the West: The Colorado River." *National Geographic* 179 (June 1991) 6:4–69.

Casey, Powell A. *Encyclopedia of Forts, Posts, Named Camps, and Other Military Installations, 1700–1981.* Baton Rouge: Claitor's Publishing Division, 1983.

Center of Military History, Norman Miller Cary, comp. *Guide to U. S. Army Museums and Historical Sites.* Washington, D.C.: U.S. Government Printing Office, 1975.

Chadwick, Douglas H. "Denali: Alaska's Wild Heart." *National Geographic* 182 (August 1992) 2:63–87.

Clark, Henry W. *History of Alaska.* New York: Macmillan, 1930.

Cleland, Robert Glass. *From Wilderness to Empire: A History of California, 1542–1900.* New York: Alfred A. Knopf, 1944.

Colby, Merle (Federal Writers' Project). *A Guide to Alaska; Last American Frontier.* New York: The Macmillan Company, 1940.

Cox, Sarah. "Catch of the Northwest: Newport, Oregon." *Richmond Times-Dispatch,* 1 November 1992, pp. H1, H5.

Delgado, James P. *To California by Sea: A Maritime History of the California Gold Rush.* Columbia, South Carolina: University of South Carolina Press, 1990.

Dictionary of Oregon History. Howard McK. Corning, ed. Portland: Binfords & Mort, 1956.

Dick, Everett. *Vanguards of the Frontier—A Social History of the Northern Plains and Rocky Mountains from the Fur Traders to the Sod Busters.* New York: D. Appleton-Century, 1941.

Dictionary of American Biography. 20 vols., index, and 4 supp. vols. New York: Charles Scribner's Sons, 1928–1974.

Dictionary of Spoken Spanish Words, Phrases, and Sentences. New York: Doubleday, 1960.

Drury, Aubrey. *California: An Intimate Guide.* New York: Harper & Brothers, 1939.

Ellis, William, "California's Harvest of Change," *National Geographic* 179 (February 1991) 2:48–73.

Elliott, Russell R., and William D. Rowley. *History of Nevada.* 2nd ed., rev. Lincoln: University of Nebraska Press, 1987.

Encyclopedia of American History. Richard B. Morris, ed. New York: Harper & Row, 1976.

Explorers and Settlers: Historic Places Commemorating the Early Exploration and Settlement of the United States. Vol. V. Robert G. Ferris, series editor. Washington: U.S. Government Printing Office, 1968.

Flexner, Stuart Berg. *I Hear America Talking*. New York: Touchstone/Simon & Schuster, 1976.

_____. *Listening to America*. New York: Simon & Schuster, 1982.

Fodor's Alaska. Andrew E. Beresky and Alison Hoffman, eds. New York: Fodor's Travel Publications, Inc., 1991.

Fodor's California, including the Wine Country and the National Parks. Kathleen McHugh and Larry Peterson, eds. New York: Fodor's Travel Publications, Inc., 1991.

Fodor's Pacific North Coast; Southeast Alaska, Washington, Oregon, British Columbia. Andrew E. Beresky, ed. New York: Fodor's Travel Publications, Inc., 1990.

Frazer, Robert W. *Forts of the West: Military Forts and Presidios and Posts Commonly Called Forts West of the Mississippi River to 1898*. Norman: University of Oklahoma Press, 1965.

Fuller, George W. *A History of the Pacific Northwest*. New York: Alfred A. Knopf, 1958.

Gannett, Henry. *The Origin of Certain Place Names in the United States*. Detroit: Gale Research Company, 1971.

Greever, William S. *The Bonanza West—The Story of the Western Mining Rushes, 1848–1900*. Norman: University of Oklahoma Press, 1963.

Gruening, Ernest. *The State of Alaska*. New York: Random House, 1954.

Gudde, Elisabeth K. *California Gold Camps; a Geographical and Historical Dictionary of Camps, Towns, and Localities Where Gold was Found and Mined; Wayside Stations and Trading Centers*. Berkeley: University of California Press, 1969.

Hammond United States Atlas. Maplewood, New Jersey: Hammond, Inc., 1989.

Heitman, Francis Bernard. *Historical Register and Dictionary of the United States Army, From Its Organization, Sept. 29, 1789, to March 2, 1903*. 2 vols. Reprint. Urbana: University of Illinois, 1965.

Hendrickson, Robert. *The Facts of File Encyclopedia of Word and Phrase Origins*. New York: Facts of File Publications, 1987.

Information Please Almanac 1992. Otto Johnson, exec. ed. Boston: Houghton Mifflin Company, 1991.

Katz, Ephraim. *The Film Encyclopedia*. New York: G. P. Putnam's Sons, 1979.

Kuykendall, Ralph S. *The Hawaiian Kingdom, 1778–1854, Foundation and Transformation*. Vol. 1. Honolulu: University of Hawaii Press, 1968.

Landelius, Otto Robert. *Swedish Place-Names in North America*. Carbondale: Southern Illinois University Press, 1985.

Lechie, William H. *The Military Conquest of the Southern Plains*. Norman: University of Oklahoma Press, 1963.

Lien, Carsten. *Olympic Battleground: The Power Politics of Timber Preservation*. San Francisco: Sierra Club Books, 1991.

Bibliography

MacInnis, Jeff. "Braving the Northwest Passage." *National Geographic* 175 (May 1989) 5:584–636.

Meany, Edmond S. *Origin of Washington Geographic Names*. Detroit: Gale Research Company, 1968.

Meinig, D. W. *The Great Columbian Plain: A Historical Geography, 1805–1910*. Seattle: University of Washington Press, 1968.

Middleton, Lynn. *Place Names of the Pacific Northwest Coast; Origins, Histories and Anecdotes in Bibliographic Form About the Coast of British Columbia, Washington and Oregon*. Seattle: Superior Publishing Company, 1969.

Morgan, Dale L. *The Humboldt: Highroad of the West*. New York: Farrar & Rinehart, 1943.

National Archives. *RG 28: Record of Appointment of Postmasters 1832– September 1971*.

The National Gazetteer. Washington, D.C.: Geographic Names Information System (GNIS), 1990, 1991 (microfiche).

Nevada: A Guide to the Silver State. Compiled by Workers of the Writers' Program of the Work Projects Administration in the State of Nevada. Portland: Binfords & Mort, 1940.

Oliver, Peter. "A Piece of 'The Rock.'" *Meeting News*, October 1992, pp. 16–17.

Olsenius, Richard. "Alaska Highway." *National Geographic* 180 (November 1991) 5:68–100.

Oregon: End of the Trail. Compiled by Workers of the Writers' Program of the Work Projects Administration in the State of Oregon. Portland: Binford & Mort, 1940.

Orth, Donald J. *Dictionary of Alaska Place Names*. Washington, D.C.: U. S. Government Printing Office, 1967.

Panati, Charles. *Panati's Extraordinary Endings of Practically Everything and Everybody*. New York: Harper & Row, 1989.

Partridge, Eric. *A Dictionary of Slang and Unconventional English*. 6th ed. New York: The Macmillan Company, 1967.

Paul, Rodman W. *Mining Frontiers of the Far West, 1848–1880*. New York: Holt, Rinehart and Winston, 1963.

Peirce, Neal R. *The Pacific States of America*. New York: W. W. Norton & Company, Inc., 1972.

Phillips, James W. *Alaska-Yukon Place Names*. Seattle: University of Washington Press, 1973.

_____. *Washington State Place Names*. Seattle: University of Washington Press, 1971.

Pomeroy, Earl. *The Pacific Slope: A History of California, Oregon, Washington, Idaho, Utah, and Nevada*. New York: Alfred A. Knopf, 1965.

Prospector, Cowhand, and Sodbuster: Historic Places Associated With the Mining, Ranching, and Farming Frontiers in the Trans-Mississippi West. Vol. XI. Robert G. Ferris, series editor. Washington: U. S. Government Printing Office, 1967.

Prucha, Francis P. *A Guide to the Military Posts of the United States, 1789–1895*. Madison: State Historical Society of Wisconsin, 1964.

Pukui, Mary Kawena, Samuel H. Elbert, and Esther T. Mookini. *Place Names of Hawaii.* 2nd ed. Honolulu: University of Hawaii Press, 1974.

Quimby, Myron J. *Scratch Ankle, U.S.A.* New York: A. S. Barnes and Company, 1969.

Rawson, Hugh. *Wicked Words.* New York: Crown Publishers, 1989.

Rearden, Jim. *Cracking the Zero Mystery: How the U. S. Learned to Beat Japan's Vaunted World War II Fighter Plane.* Harrisburg, Pennsylvania: Stackpole Books, 1990.

Records and Policies of the Post Office Department Relating to Place-names. Arthur Hecht and William J. Heynen, comp. Washington: National Archives and Records Service, General Services Administration, 1975.

Richman, Irving Berndine. *California Under Spain and Mexico, 1535–1847.* New York: Cooper Square Publishers, Inc., 1965.

Ronda, James P. *Astoria & Empire.* Lincoln: University of Nebraska Press, 1990.

Ross, Alexander. *The Fur Hunters of the Far West.* Kenneth A. Spaulding, ed. Norman: University of Oklahoma Press, 1956.

Russia's American Colony. S. Frederick Starr, ed. Durham: Duke University Press, 1987.

Sherwood, Morgan R. *Exploration of Alaska, 1865–1900.* New Haven: Yale University Press, 1965.

Shinn, Charles Howard. *Mining Camps: A Study in American Frontier Government.* New York: Alfred A. Knopf, 1948.

Soldier and Brave: Historic Places Associated with Indian Affairs and the Indian Wars in the Trans-Mississippi West. Vol. XII. Robert G. Ferris, series editor. Washington: U. S. Government Printing Office, 1971.

Stein, Lou. *San Diego County Place-names; Yesterday's People, Today's Geography.* San Diego, California: Tofua Press, 1975.

Stewart, George R. *American Place Names.* New York: Oxford University Press, 1970.

———. *Names on the Land: A Historical Account of Place-Naming in the United States.* New York: Random House, 1945.

Terling, E. M. *Trips and Trails, 2: Family Camps, Short Hikes and View Roads in the Olympics, Mt. Rainier and South Cascades.* Vancouver, B.C.: Mountain Craft, 1977.

TourBook: California, Nevada, including Baja California, Mexico. Heathrow, Florida: American Automobile Association, 1992.

TourBook: Hawaii. Heathrow, Florida: American Automobile Association, 1991.

TourBook: Oregon, Washington. Heathrow, Florida: American Automobile Association, 1992.

TourBook: Western Canada and Alaska. Heathrow, Florida: American Automobile Association, 1992.

Underwood, John J. *Alaska: An Empire in the Making.* rev. ed. New York: Dodd, Mead and Company, 1928.

Urdang, Laurence. *Names & Nicknames of Places & Things.* New York: New American Library, 1987.

Vote, Robert. "When Balloons Bombed Us," *VFW Magazine,* October 1980, pp. 42–43, 66.

Bibliography

Wallechinsky, David, and Irving Wallace. *The People's Almanac*. New York: Doubleday & Company, 1975.

———. *The People's Almanac #2*. New York: Bantam Books, 1978.

Webster's American Biographies. Charles Van Doren, ed. Springfield, Massachusetts: G. & C. Merriam Company, 1975.

The World Almanac Book of Who. Hana Umlauf Lane, ed. New York: World Almanac Publications, 1980.